Impulsivity

Impulsivity

The Behavioral and Neurological Science of Discounting

Edited by
Gregory J. Madden and Warren K. Bickel

American Psychological Association • *Washington, DC*

Published by
American Psychological Association
750 First Street, NE
Washington, DC 20002
www.apa.org

To order
APA Order Department
P.O. Box 92984
Washington, DC 20090-2984
Tel: (800) 374-2721; Direct: (202) 336-5510
Fax: (202) 336-5502; TDD/TTY: (202) 336-6123
Online: www.apa.org/books/
E-mail: order@apa.org

In the U.K., Europe, Africa, and the Middle East, copies may be ordered from
American Psychological Association
3 Henrietta Street
Covent Garden, London
WC2E 8LU England

Typeset in Goudy by Circle Graphics, Inc., Columbia, MD

Printer: United Book Press, Baltimore, MD
Cover Designer: Naylor Design, Washington, DC
Technical/Production Editor: Harriet Kaplan

The opinions and statements published are the responsibility of the authors, and such opinions and statements do not necessarily represent the policies of the American Psychological Association.

Library of Congress Cataloging-in-Publication Data

Impulsivity : the behavioral and neurological science of discounting / edited by Gregory J. Madden and Warren K. Bickel. — 1st ed.
    p. cm.
  Includes bibliographical references and index.
  ISBN-13: 978-1-4338-0477-9
  ISBN-10: 1-4338-0477-8
  1. Impulse. 2. Decision making—Psychological aspects. I. Madden, Gregory J. (Gregory Jude) II. Bickel, Warren K.

  BF575.I46I47 2010
  153.8—dc22

                          2009012095

British Library Cataloguing-in-Publication Data

A CIP record is available from the British Library.

Printed in the United States of America
First Edition

CONTENTS

CONTRIBUTORS

George Ainslie, Veterans Affairs Medical Center, Coatesville, PA

Justin J. Anker, University of Minnesota, Minneapolis

Ana A. L. Baumann, Utah State University, Logan

Warren K. Bickel, University of Arkansas, Little Rock

Marilyn E. Carroll, University of Minnesota, Minneapolis

Harriet de Wit, University of Chicago, Chicago, IL

Leonard Green, Washington University, St Louis, Missouri

Benjamin Y. Hayden, Duke University Medical School, Durham, NC

Sarah R. Heilbronner, Duke University Medical School, Durham, NC

Patrick S. Johnson, University of Kansas, Lawrence

Bryan A. Jones, Stony Brook University, Stony Brook, NY

Yulia A. Khodneva, University of Alabama at Birmingham

Zeb Kurth-Nelson, University of Minnesota, Minneapolis

George Loewenstein, Carnegie Mellon University, Pittsburgh, PA

Jami L. Mach, University of Minnesota, Minneapolis

Gregory J. Madden, University of Kansas, Lawrence

Suzanne H. Mitchell, Oregon Health & Science University, Portland

Joel Myerson, Washington University, St Louis, MO

Jennifer L. Newman, Harvard Medical School, Cambridge, MA

Amy L. Odum, Utah State University, Logan

Jennifer L. Perry, Minneapolis Medical Research Foundation, Minneapolis, MN

Nancy M. Petry, University of Connecticut Health Center, Farmington

Michael L. Platt, Duke University Medical School, Durham, NC

Howard Rachlin, Stony Brook University, Stony Brook, NY

A. David Redish, University of Minnesota, Minneapolis

Cathy A. Simpson, University of Alabama at Birmingham

David W. Stephens, University of Minnesota, St. Paul

Jeffrey R. Stevens, Max Planck Institute for Human Development, Berlin, Germany

Jalie A. Tucker, University of Alabama at Birmingham

Jonathan Williams, King's College, London

Catharine A. Winstanley, University of British Columbia, Vancouver, Canada

Richard Yi, University of Arkansas for Medical Sciences, Little Rock

FOREWORD

GEORGE LOEWENSTEIN

> Scientific research is one of the most exciting and rewarding of occupations. It is like a voyage of discovery into unknown lands, seeking not for new territory but for new knowledge. It should appeal to those with a good sense of adventure.
> —Frederick Sanger, Nobel Prize Ceremony, December 1980

Narratives of the scientific process often invoke the metaphor of geographic exploration. We speak of scientific exploration, voyages of discovery, and the frontiers of science. *Impulsivity: The Behavioral and Neurological Science of Discounting* is a book written by and for serious explorers of the intellectual variety. As the title suggests, and the first chapter elegantly narrates, it is about impulsivity and delay discounting—about how people (and other animals) make trade-offs between costs and benefits occurring at different points in time.

Delay discounting is a timely topic, perhaps nowhere more so than in the United States. Many of the most pressing problems facing the United States have their roots in impulsivity. The average family in the United States has a savings rate of −1% (they are "dissaving") and credit card debt of $9,000.

Obesity rates have risen dramatically over time, with diverse negative effects that are beginning to undermine what had been a long trend toward improving public health. It has been estimated that as much as 40% of all premature mortality in the United States is the result of unhealthy behaviors, which represent decisions favoring immediate benefits at the expense of delayed costs, and only 10% is the result of deficits in the quality of health care delivery.[1] Even global warming is centrally connected to delay discounting because it is a consequence of consumption and production decisions that provide short-term benefits but jeopardize the well-being of future generations.[2]

In the classic tale of both physical and intellectual exploration, a traveler sets out to discover X but instead discovers Y and Z. Columbus, as every schoolchild knows, set out to discover a shortcut to India but instead discovered the New World. Ernest Shackleton never achieved his goal of crossing the Antarctic continent but returned with a tale of heroism and endurance. In science, penicillin was the result of a brilliant but sloppy laboratory scientist who, on returning from a long holiday, noticed that many of his culture dishes were contaminated with a fungus. Microwave heating was discovered by a radar researcher who, standing in front of a magnetron, noticed that a chocolate bar in his pocket had melted (an experiment that he had the misfortune to follow up with an egg).

Impulsivity presents a classic tale of unscripted, often serendipitous exploration or, more accurately, a series of such classic tales. In its chapters one gleans an impression of researchers whose work took them in directions that they did not always anticipate at the outset. For example, many of the authors spent their earlier careers searching for the discount function that could make sense of intertemporal choice in animals and humans. None claim to have found it, but all have made important discoveries along the way.

In chapter 3, for example, Green and Myerson report on their search for a common process underlying discounting of time and probability. They end up concluding not only that the connection is weak but also that each form of discounting involves multiple processes, traits, and abilities. As they express it, "Not only is discounting just one part of what is meant by impulsivity, but discounting itself is not all of a piece" (p. 85). Similarly, in their discussion of neural models of delay discounting in chapter 5, Redish and Kurth-Nelson conclude by questioning the existence of a unitary mechanism: "It is unclear at this point whether these various paradigms access the same systems and mechanisms or whether there are systems and mechanisms specifically aligned to specific time courses or specific rewards" (p. 130).

---

[1]Schroeder, S. A. (2007). We can do better—Improving the health of the American people. *New England Journal of Medicine, 357,* 1221–1228.

[2]Nordhaus, W. D. (1991). A sketch of the economics of the greenhouse effect. *American Economic Review, 81,* 146–150.

The same general theme is echoed by Winstanley in chapter 4 on the neural and neurochemical basis of delay discounting and by Heilbronner, Hayden, and Platt in chapter 6 on the neural basis of risky decision making. Winstanley ultimately rejects a unitary system account of delay discounting and concludes instead that "competing circuits exist in the brain, one encouraging self-control, the other impulsive choice" (p. 115). Heilbronner et al. end up concluding that discounting of probabilities is much more complex than is typically assumed. Finally, Williams, in chapter 12 on the connection between delay discounting and attention-deficit/hyperactivity disorder, concludes that the disorder does not result from any single major endophenotype but rather from "the interacting effects of small or rare ('minor') aberrations in multiple traits and states" (p. 323).

Whether discounting results from a unitary system or from a complex interaction of different mechanisms is likely to be important for a second cross-cutting theme that is woven throughout the book: the relative importance of person versus situation in discounting. To the degree that discounting invokes diverse systems, it is likely that different systems will come into play in different situations, resulting in major cross-situational variability in discounting. The relative importance of person versus situation is the central focus of Odum and Baumann's chapter 2, "Delay Discounting: State and Trait Variable." The authors provide a balanced treatment of the relative importance of state and trait variables but focus especially on situational factors. Their chapter includes an extensive list of situational factors that have been shown to systematically influence temporal discounting.

Several of the other chapters, in contrast, focus more closely on the trait dimension. In chapter 7, for example, Yi, Mitchell, and Bickel review a large body of evidence showing strong correlations between individual differences in measured delay discounting and different types of substance abuse. In chapter 10, Petry and Madden address connections between trait impulsivity and pathological gambling. They provide a theoretical account of why such a link should exist and review relevant findings. Although they generally conclude that research supports the existence of a strong connection between delay discounting and pathological gambling, they also draw attention to, and attempt to make sense of, inconsistencies between different researchers' findings.

Yet a third cross-cutting theme is the relevance of animal findings to humans, and again one gains the impression of researchers whose journeys took unexpected directions. Several authors seemed to have begun with, but ultimately moved away from, a strong belief in the relevance of animal findings to humans. In chapter 8, for example, on drug effects on delay discounting, de Wit and Mitchell open by arguing that "studies using animal models are uniquely able to assess the effects of drugs of abuse because the drug-naive state of subjects can be assured at the outset of the study" (p. 214). However, they end up questioning the facile extrapolation of data from one subject group to the other, noting that drugs affecting discounting in laboratory animals have thus far produced little or no effect in humans. This leads them to question "whether the delay-discounting procedures in nonhumans measure the same underlying processes as delay-discounting procedures in humans" (p. 236). Odum and Baumann, in their review of situational factors that influence delay discounting, also note that some situational factors, such as reward magnitude, affect discounting in humans but not in other animals, again suggesting a discontinuity between species.

The same issue is even more prominent in chapter 9 by Carroll, Anker, Mach, Newman, and Perry on delay discounting as a predictor of drug abuse, although they reach a quite different conclusion. The authors note that most of the evidence they review comes from studies of nonhuman animals because "it is difficult to prospectively study the etiology of drug abuse in humans" (p. 245). However, the parallels they identify between findings from the many studies of nonhuman animals and those from the few studies of humans are striking and do support the idea that animal models are predictive of humans. This is especially surprising given the many differences between humans and other animals on dimensions that might be expected to play a role in drug-related behavior, such as language, consciousness, and the ability to deliberate explicitly about the long-term consequences of behavior.

Finally, in chapter 13, Stevens and Stephens review theory and evidence relating to the evolution of delay discounting and focus almost exclusively on the evolution of delay discounting in nonhuman animals. Like Carroll et al., they take a fairly strong stand in favor of continuity and, in fact, explicitly attack some of my own work in which I argue that the discontinuity in rates of delay discounting between humans and animals suggests that there are qualitative differences between human and other animals' mechanisms of delay discounting. The discontinuity, they argue, is illusory and stems from differences in the methods used to measure delay discounting in humans versus other animals. The foreword of a book is, however, probably not the best place for a rejoinder!

Addiction, a topic that occupies fully three of the book's chapters, provides an especially interesting window into the phenomenon of delay discounting and also helps to show why the research matters. One of the most successful treatment programs for addiction plays on the temporal myopia that, all three chapters suggest, both stems from and contributes to drug use. This program involves giving drug addicts vouchers, contingent on abstinence, that they can spend on small consumer goods. The success of this treatment is remarkable. Addicts often suffer disastrous consequences as a result of their habit; they lose family and friends, employment, and even, sometimes, their freedom. They would seem to have about as powerful a motivation for quitting as one could imagine, but most find it difficult if not impossible to do so. Why would such an enormous incentive to quit fail to change behavior, when a patently trivial one succeeds? Certainly, one important element of the explanation lies in delay discounting: The vouchers represent immediate, certain, and tangible rewards, whereas the rewards for kicking one's addiction are delayed, uncertain, and intangible, and the research reviewed in chapter 7 showing high discount rates by drug users helps to explain why such programs, which provide immediate rewards for abstinence, are likely to be especially effective for addicts.

The same logic can be applied to other types of behaviors and in fact is applied to health decision making by Tucker, Simpson, and Khodneva in chapter 11. They review evidence of an association between impulsivity and poor health behavior and then argue that this link can and should be taken into account in medical care by minimizing the short-term costs of accessing preventive services and by providing immediate positive contingencies, such as vouchers, for the use of preventive programs like prenatal screenings, vaccinations, and HIV testing. As in the case of drug abstinence, these short-term rewards will be especially motivating to those who need them most: people who put disproportionate weight on present rewards.

Not all of the chapters follow the paradigm of diverted exploration. Two in particular follow the also-classic paradigm of Julius Caesar: "I came, I saw, I conquered." Rachlin and Jones, in chapter 15 on the extended self, extend Rachlin's seminal work on the relationship of delay discounting to probability discounting to yet a new domain: social discounting. They point out striking parallels between the hyperbolic pattern of discounting, not only of time and probability, but also in altruism toward other people. If other authors are foxes who, as the 7th-century BCE philosopher Archilochus stated, know many things, Rachlin is the quintessential hedgehog who knows one big thing.

Ainslie is another hedgehog who knows one big thing, and it happens to be the same thing that Rachlin knows: that people discount hyperbolically, a discovery that he played a key role in making. However, whereas Rachlin looks outward and sees hyperbolic delay discounting in diverse domains of human behavior, Ainslie, in chapter 14, peers inward and sees the workings of hyperbolic delay discounting in the most basic mechanisms of the human brain. According to Ainslie, for example, appetites, which most people take as biological primitives, can instead be interpreted as processes that result from a hyperbolic weighting of reward within the brain.

As anyone who has engaged in either geographic or scientific exploration can report, progress toward the goal is seldom smooth; in fact, even when making objective progress one can experience subjective setbacks. After a prolonged and arduous ascent, for example, and believing one is on the verge of the summit, one ascends over the final bulge only to sight the true peak, high above one's current elevation and still far in the distance. Similarly, after making real scientific progress and feeling on the verge of closing in on the answer to one's central question, the very process of discovery provides an often abrupt increase in one's appreciation of the complexities of the topic. The knowledge gap between what one knows and what one wants to know widens abruptly.

Although subjective setbacks may be frustrating in both domains of exploration, they are in fact the hallmark of genuine discovery. Mountain summits and scientific questions that present obvious, easily accessible goals are not worth the trouble. In scientific as in geographic exploration, the best expeditions are as likely to reveal the broad outlines of what has yet to be discovered as to chart out known terrain. In the best of traditions, *Impulsivity* not only refines our understanding of the known world but also gives us a glimpse of what remains to be discovered.

Impulsivity

INTRODUCTION

GREGORY J. MADDEN AND WARREN K. BICKEL

Every day we are bombarded by choices that, when taken together, have important implications for who we are, how we feel, and what we can accomplish. In many of these choices we feel of two minds: the impulsive mind that lives for the moment and the self-controlled mind that considers the long-term consequences of our decisions. These minds conflict when at first we commit to a course of self-control (e.g., resolving to quit smoking) but later change our mind as an impulsive choice is made (e.g., relapse). Although the conflict of these minds was recognized by Plato, Freud, and countless other philosophers and theorists, only recently have the behavioral and neurological processes underlying these mental struggles been systematically studied. Prominent among these is the delay-discounting process, which is the subject of intensive research in psychology, economics, behavioral science, and neuroscience. As illustrated in Figure 1, the past decade has seen a seemingly exponential increase in the number of scientific articles published each year in the area of delay discounting.

Delay discounting is the process by which future events are subjectively devalued by the decision maker, and this process is thought to underlie some forms of impulsive decision making. Consider the classic research conducted by Walter Mischel and his colleagues at the Bing Nursery School at Stanford

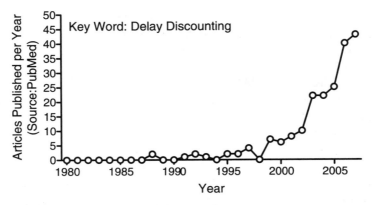

Figure 1. Published articles and book chapters listed each year in the PubMed database under the keyword *delay discounting*. Search conducted in May 2008.

University. Preschoolers were given a choice between receiving a large reward (e.g., two marshmallows) on the return of the experimenter or, at any time during the delay, forgoing the larger reward by accepting a smaller but immediately available reward (e.g., one marshmallow). In a longitudinal follow-up, preschoolers' duration of waiting before selecting the smaller–sooner reward was predictive of academic and social competence in adolescence (Mischel, Shoda, & Peake, 1988). Preschoolers who waited longer were more likely than their more impulsive peers to become adolescents who more successfully coped with stress and frustration, demonstrated better abilities to concentrate and maintain attention, better responded to reason, and scored higher on the SAT. The social significance of these findings are obvious, as are findings that individuals diagnosed with a range of impulse control and addictive disorders more strongly discount the value of delayed monetary rewards (and a host of other outcomes) than do matched controls (see chapters 2, 7, and 10, this volume).

Economists have long recognized the discounting of delayed outcomes as an important barrier to humans' ability to maximize their resources (e.g., Jevons, 1871/1911; Mill, 1848/1909). However, the origins of the experimental analysis of impulsivity and delay discounting are to be found in the animal laboratories of behaviorists studying patterns of choice in operant conditioning chambers (e.g., Davenport, 1962; Logan, 1960; Skinner, 1950). Logan (1965), for example, first used animal-choice procedures to quantitatively describe how reinforcer value declines with increasing delays (see also Chung, 1965). Soon thereafter, Chung and Herrnstein (1967) offered empirical evidence that the shape of this discounting curve might be a hyperbola, a shape anticipated by the economist Strotz (1956). In independent articles, Ainslie (1974, 1975) and Rachlin (1974) described how hyperbolic delay discounting could quantitatively predict the sorts of irrational decisions that economists, sociologists, and psychologists were tasked to explain, choices that animal behaviorists had recently demonstrated to characterize pigeons' choices under controlled laboratory conditions (e.g., Rachlin & Green, 1972). Specifically, Ainslie and Rachlin showed that if a delayed rewarding outcome loses its value according to a hyperbolic decay function, we should favor long-run maximization at all times except as smaller rewards become more immediately available (and the large, more desirable reward is still delayed). Those of us who have resolved to eat healthy foods only to fall off the wagon on finding a box of doughnuts in the break room can relate.

Predictions of these irrational defections from a committed course of self-control are not easily made by other quantitative accounts of delay discounting, and this made the findings of Mazur (1987) and Rachlin, Raineri, and Cross (1991) all the more important because their data strongly supported a hyperbolic discounting equation over other formulations in animals and humans, respectively. Because these findings have been replicated in a variety of species (e.g., Woolverton, Myerson, & Green, 2007) and specific populations of humans (e.g., Vuchinich & Simpson, 1998), a number of researchers have speculated that hyperbolic delay discounting underlies several socially important human behaviors such as drug addiction, obesity, and unsafe sex (e.g., Bickel & Marsch, 2001). The neurological processes underlying delay discounting and shifts between impulsivity and self-control are only beginning to be studied, but, as illustrated in this volume, important discoveries have already been made.

For this volume, we assembled a group of scientists who have helped to establish these across-species similarities, across-population differences, and breakthroughs in the neuroscience of decision making. The book was designed to be appropriate for basic and applied researchers, clinicians interested in impulsivity, and graduate seminars in psychology, behavioral economics, and neuroscience. Part I begins with a primer on delay discounting: what it is, why it is important, and procedural details on its quantification. The next two chapters describe the major findings in the laboratory study of delay and probability discounting. In chapter 2, Odum and Baumann discuss the evidence for delay discounting–associated impulsivity as a relatively stable trait and as a state amenable to change by experimental manipulations. In chapter 3, Green and Myerson address the hypothesis that impulsivity is a unidimensional trait by examining correlations between delay and probability discounting and between discounting of delayed rewards and losses.

Part II contains three chapters providing an overview of the neuro-science of delay discounting and risk taking. In chapter 4, Winstanley summarizes the effects of lesions to components of the limbic corticostriatal loop (including the prefrontal cortex) and the evidence for serotonin and dopamine receptor system interactions on delay discounting and other forms of impulsive behavior. In chapter 5, Redish and Kurth-Nelson bring together diverse findings in their consideration of four computational neural models of delay discounting. The chapter provides a deep understanding of the role of computation in exploring neurobehavioral phenomena. In chapter 6, Heilbronner, Hayden, and Platt explore the status of risk-sensitive decision making from the unique perspective of neuroeconomics. Accordingly, they review traditional economic and behavioral economic accounts of risk-sensitive decision making, explore the neural signatures of economic risk, and describe experiments that briefly alter brain function to demonstrate the role of specific brain regions in risk preferences.

Part III considers the relation between delay discounting and two addictive disorders. In chapter 7, Yi, Mitchell, and Bickel review the evidence that substance abuse is correlated with extreme discounting of future events. They summarize new findings suggesting that discounting rate is positively correlated with frequency of drug use and may be predictive of successful drug abstinence. In chapter 8, de Wit and Mitchell provide a comprehensive review of the effects of acute and chronic drug exposure and drug withdrawal on the rate at which delayed outcomes are discounted in value. A complementary review of the evidence that delay discounting may be predictive of drug taking in nonhuman subjects is provided in chapter 9 by Carroll, Anker, Mach, Newman, and Perry. Finally, in chapter 10, Petry and Madden summarize the evidence that pathological gambling is correlated with high rates of delay discounting and disordered decision making on the Iowa Gambling Task. These authors summarize two theories that may help in understanding the relation between discounting and gambling.

Part IV includes two chapters that consider the role of delay discounting in nonaddictive human affairs. In chapter 11, Tucker, Simpson, and Khodneva argue that future personal health, like other delayed commodities, is discounted according to a hyperbolic function. They provide an insightful discussion of how the discounting process may affect our own health and the health of future members of our society. In chapter 12, Williams reviews the evidence that delay discounting may contribute to the behavioral sequelae of attention-deficit/hyperactivity disorder (ADHD). Williams argues that ADHD is not a monolithic construct so easily accounted for. Instead, it falls on a continuum of behavioral outputs affected by multiple genetic (trait) and environmental (state) determinants affecting impulsive behavior and the behavioral cluster described as ADHD.

Part V addresses empirical and theoretical extensions. In chapter 13, Stevens and Stephens explore ecologically rational decision rules that may have been naturally selected for because they helped foraging organisms maximize income in their natural environments. Like many naturally selected traits, when the habitat-specific rule is expressed in a changed environment (specifically, the choice situations common in the study of delay discounting), the decision rule fails in the sense that suboptimal impulsivity ensues.

Stevens and Stephens present across-species comparison evidence for this theory. By contrast, in chapter 14, Ainslie critiques what he characterizes as top-down rational choice theories of self-control and impulsivity. Ainslie offers a bottom-up account based in hyperbolic temporal discounting, an account that produces temporally inconsistent choices in nonhuman animals but, in the hands of verbally capable humans, Ainslie argues, yields apparent acts of commitment or "will." That pigeons are capable of the same under manmade contingencies offers hope that environmental engineering may prove useful in increasing human maximization of long-term outcomes. With impulsive choices weighing heavily on our society and planet (e.g., the expedient decision to burn fossil fuels with the long-term outcome of global warming), Rachlin and Jones's extension of discounting to human altruism in chapter 15 is particularly important. Their findings suggest that the probability of altruistic acts declines according to a hyperbolic function as the recipient of altruism is more socially distant and therefore less likely to reciprocate. Overcoming this tendency would appear to be of great importance to the well-being of our, and other, species.

Choices between an immediate and a deferred option are among the most important decisions that shape our lives, our culture, and our world. To understand this behavior is to understand what is best and most challenging about our species. When deferred ends control our choices, we are self-controlled, altruistic, and less pathological. When controlled by the immediate option, we may make impulsive, selfish, and pathological choices. Understanding the determinants of this behavior and how it may be modified is critical. Indeed, promoting control by deferred consequences may be the real quest of modernity. We hope that this book furthers that quest.

REFERENCES

Ainslie, G. (1974). Impulse control in pigeons. *Journal of the Experimental Analysis of Behavior, 21*, 485–489.

Ainslie, G. (1975). Specious reward: A behavioral theory of impulsiveness and impulse control. *Psychological Bulletin, 82*, 463–496.

Bickel, W. K., & Marsch, L. A. (2001). Toward a behavioral economic understanding of drug dependence: Delay discounting processes. *Addiction, 96*, 73–86.

Chung, S. H. (1965). Effects of delayed reinforcement in a concurrent choice situation. *Journal of the Experimental Analysis of Behavior, 8*, 439–444.

Chung, S. H., & Herrnstein, R. J. (1967). Choice and delay of reinforcement. *Journal of the Experimental Analysis of Behavior, 10*, 67–74.

Davenport, J. W. (1962). The interaction of magnitude and delay of reinforcement in spatial discrimination. *Journal of Comparative and Physiological Psychology, 55*, 267–273.

Jevons, W. S. (1911). *The theory of political economy*, London: Macmillan. (Original work published 1871)

Logan, F. A. (1960). *Incentive*. New Haven, CT: Yale University Press.

Logan, F. A. (1965). Decision making by rats: Delay versus amount of reward. *Journal of Comparative and Physiological Psychology, 59*, 1–12.

Mazur, J. E. (1987). An adjusting procedure for studying delayed reinforcement. In M. L. Commons, J. E. Mazur, J. A. Nevin, & H. Rachlin (Eds.), *Quantitative analysis of behavior: Vol. 5. The effect of delay and of intervening events on reinforcement value* (pp. 55–73). Hillsdale, NJ: Erlbaum.

Mill, J. S. (1909). *Principles of political economy*. London: Longmans Green. (Original work published 1848)

Mischel, W., Shoda, Y., & Peake, P. K. (1988). The nature of adolescent competencies predicted by preschool delay of gratification. *Journal of Personality and Social Psychology, 54*, 687–696.

Rachlin, H. (1974). Self-control. *Behaviorism, 2*, 94–107.

Rachlin, H., & Green, L. (1972). Commitment, choice and self-control. *Journal of the Experimental Analysis of Behavior, 17*, 15–22.

Rachlin, H., Raineri, A., & Cross, D. (1991). Subjective probability and delay. *Journal of the Experimental Analysis of Behavior, 55*, 233–244.

Skinner, B. F. (1950). Are theories of learning necessary? *Psychological Review, 57*, 193–216.

Strotz, R. H. (1956). Myopia and inconsistency in dynamic utility maximization. *Review of Economic Studies, 23*, 165–180.

Vuchinich, R. E., & Simpson, C. A. (1998). Hyperbolic temporal discounting in social drinkers and problem drinkers. *Experimental and Clinical Psychopharmacology, 6*, 292–305.

Woolverton, W. L., Myerson, J., & Green, L. (2007). Delay discounting of cocaine by rhesus monkeys. *Experimental and Clinical Psychopharmacology, 15*, 238–233.

I

METHODS, MODELS, AND FINDINGS

1

A DELAY-DISCOUNTING PRIMER

GREGORY J. MADDEN AND PATRICK S. JOHNSON

Impulsivity is a colloquial term with which nearly everyone has some commerce. Although the term is sometimes used to describe socially appropriate actions (e.g., "She possessed an impulsive force to succeed in her job"), it more often refers to problematic behavior. For example, children are described as impulsive when they take a toy from a peer without considering the likely consequences of doing so (e.g., the peer crying and a reprimand from a caretaker). College students are said to be impulsive when they choose to attend a party with friends rather than study for an exam scheduled for the next day. And middle-aged adults might be similarly described if they repeatedly buy things on impulse without considering that payments (with interest) will come due at the end of the month. In this more frequent usage, *impulsivity* describes a tendency to act on a whim and, in so doing, disregard a more rational long-term strategy for success.

Psychologists have long measured impulsivity as an aspect of personality using self-report measures such as the Barratt Impulsivity Scale (Patton, Stanford, & Barratt, 1995) or the Eysenck Personality Questionnaire (Eysenck & Eysenck, 1978). Such measures quantify impulsivity as it occurs

Preparation of this chapter was supported by National Institutes of Health Grant DA023564.

in natural human environments by asking individuals to report on their tendencies to act on impulse, spend more than they earn, or plan tasks carefully. Psychologists and psychiatrists have also classified a number of disorders as failures of impulse control. These include attention-deficit/hyperactivity disorder, substance abuse, kleptomania, pathological gambling, eating disorders, and trichotillomania (e.g., American Psychiatric Association, 2000; Barkley, 1997). Each of these disorders is characterized by a failure of attention, a failure to inhibit a response, a failure to consider the probable negative long-term outcomes of the behavior, or all three.

The past several decades have seen experimental psychologists studying similar categories of impulsive behavior. Failure of attention (e.g., Robbins, 2002), inability to inhibit prepotent responses (e.g., Winstanley, Baunez, Theobald, & Robbins, 2005), and the failure of delayed events to control current choices (e.g., Ainslie, 1975) have all received considerable attention. With recent findings that the second of these precedes and predicts some aspects of drug taking in rodents (Dalley et al., 2007; Diergaarde et al., 2008), we anticipate much continued interest in the response inhibition form of impulsivity. Other fascinating findings speak to the importance of studying the third form of impulsivity—the failure of delayed outcomes to affect choice. For example, a number of studies have established that individuals addicted to a variety of drugs have a strong tendency to devalue delayed gains and losses (see the review in chap. 7, this volume). The rate at which delayed outcomes are devalued appears to be a predictor of success in drug treatment (Yoon et al., 2007) and appears to predict drug self-administration in rats (see review in chap. 9, this volume). Outside, although relevant to the study of addictions, Wilson and Daly (1997) hypothesized that the rate at which delayed outcomes are devalued may be affected by economic conditions, life expectancy, or the reliability of the local environment (see also chap. 13, this volume). Under these conditions, individuals may learn that living for the moment and distrusting the future is a maximizing strategy. Consistent with this hypothesis, behavioral researchers have provided limited demonstrations of reinforcement contingencies that may teach a form of delay tolerance, or an ability to wait to get what you want (e.g., Mazur & Logue, 1978; Schweitzer & Sulzer-Azaroff, 1988). These findings illustrate the potential benefits of a more thorough understanding of the factors affecting the devaluation of delayed outcomes.

Given the importance of these findings and the potential of further research to aid in the prediction and control of this third type of impulsivity, the primary focus of this chapter (and this book) is on choice and the failure of future events to affect current decisions. In this primer chapter, we consider two types of this form of impulsive choice: (a) preferring a smaller–sooner reward while forgoing a larger–later one and (b) preferring a larger–later aversive outcome over a smaller–sooner one. The first of these is exemplified by the toy-pilfering child with whom we opened this chapter. Taking the toy is immediately rewarded, but it is a short-lived reward because the caretaker soon returns the toy to the victimized peer. Undoubtedly, the child would prefer to play with the toy for a longer period of time, but waiting until the toy is dropped by the peer seems a weak reinforcer when compared with brief access now. To put an economic term on this phenomenon, the child appears to have discounted the value of the delayed but otherwise preferred reward. *Delay discounting* describes the process of devaluing behavioral outcomes, be they rewarding or aversive events, that happen in the future (and perhaps the past; see chap. 7, this volume).

This chapter provides a primer in delay discounting; it is intended for readers who have only a limited background in the procedures, measures, and outcomes of studies examining this form of impulsive choice. Following an overview of the delay-discounting process, its quantification, and its implications for the human condition, emphasis is placed on procedures (and critiques of these procedures). The remainder of the book is concerned with experimental findings, and for the most part, we do not review these here.

DELAY DISCOUNTING

As noted earlier, one investigative approach to impulsivity has been to study preference between smaller–sooner and larger–later consequences. When these consequences are positive reinforcers, such as food for a hungry pigeon, choosing the smaller–sooner reinforcer is regarded as impulsive because of the long-term detrimental outcome of the choice (less food). This paradigm has also been used to study choices between smaller–sooner and larger–later aversive events (Hineline, 1977; Mischel, Grusec, & Masters, 1969). As before, the impulsive choice results in an immediate benefit (e.g., a shock-free period) but a delayed detrimental outcome (a more intense shock). This general paradigm has also been extensively used in studying impulsive decisions in humans choosing between smaller–sooner and larger–later gains and losses. Together, the nonhuman and human literatures have yielded a systematic set of findings that have proven amenable to quantification and replication. These findings and their apparent relevance to socially important patterns of behavior have generated substantial interest in studying delay discounting and its causes.

Exponential Discounting

Assuming that natural selection favors organisms that choose the better of two behavioral outcomes, delay discounting appears counterintuitive because preferring a smaller–sooner over a larger–later reward fails to maximize income. Likewise, preferring a larger–later over a smaller–sooner aversive event is seemingly irrational because it fails to minimize an event that may endanger the organism. From an evolutionary perspective, what would be the advantage of discounting the value of temporally delayed events? As eloquently and more comprehensively outlined by Stevens and Stephens in chapter 13, an organism that forgoes an inferior but immediate food item, mate, or hiding place in favor of a superior but delayed alternative may find the superior food was consumed by a conspecific during the delay, that the genetically more fit mate was not receptive to one's advances, or worst of all that the better hiding place could not be reached before the pursuing predator captured its "self-controlled" prey. In other words, in the lawless (red in tooth and claw) world of our evolutionary ancestors, a bird in the hand was better than two in the bush if there was a good chance that the bush would be empty on arrival, if one arrived at all.

In modern human affairs, ample reasons persist for discounting the future (Wilson & Daly, 1997). Your brother-in-law may promise to pay you the money he owes (with interest) in a year, but in the interim period he may fall on hard times and not be able to keep his promise. Although you plan to live to enjoy the benefits of your retirement account, you may be hit by a bus tomorrow, and if you were alive to feel so, would regret the immediate pleasures forgone in favor of investing in the future. Ultimately, the only certain feature of an environment is its uncertainty, or as Heraclitus (535 BCE–475 BCE) put it, "Nothing endures but change." In turn, our species and others appear to be as acutely sensitive to differences in reward probability as we are to disparities in delay (Patak & Reynolds, 2007). Indeed, some researchers have suggested that probability and delay have related effects on the subjective valuation of outcomes (e.g., Rachlin, Logue, Gibbon, & Frankel, 1986), a topic considered in greater depth by Green and Myerson in chapter 3 of this volume.

Economists have tackled the discounting of delayed outcomes for some time and have proposed that just as the value of money in a savings account compounds with interest over time, so too should the value of future goods be discounted in a compounding fashion as the delay to their delivery increases (e.g., Samuelson, 1937). Such compounded discounting would be expected if organisms evolved in environments in which the probability of receiving the larger–later outcome decreased in a compounding fashion with each additional unit of delay. One might expect species differences in the rate at which delayed outcomes are discounted if a species evolved in a niche in which delayed outcomes were more or less likely to be received, but the form of the discounting function should be the same—an exponential decay function reflecting a compounding decline in value as delays increase:

$$V_d = Ae^{-kd}. \tag{1}$$

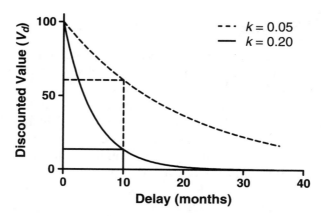

Figure 1.1. Value discounted exponentially at high (solid line) and modest (dashed line) rates. The *y*-axis values of the horizontal lines intersecting with the discounting functions indicate the present (discounted) value of the reward when delayed by 10 months.

In Equation 1, V_d is the discounted value of the future reward, A is the reward amount, d is the delay until reward delivery, and k is the discounting rate (e is the base of the natural logarithm, 2.718).

Figure 1.1 illustrates two instructional exponential discounting curves, each obtained by setting amount (A) to 100 units, delay (d) to the continuum of values along the *x*-axis, and discounting rate (k) to the different values shown in the legend. For the upper curve, $k = 0.05$, a modest rate of discounting. At a delay of 10 months, the delayed reward has lost 40% of its subjective value. If our hypothetical discounter with $k = 0.05$ is asked to choose between 60 units of the good now and 100 units after a 10-month delay, then she or he is indifferent between the two.[1] As shown by the horizontal dashed line in Figure 1.1, the discounted value of the delayed reward is equal to that of the immediate one (both equal to 0 units), hence indifference. Given the same choice between these immediate and delayed outcomes, another consumer discounting at a rate of $k = 0.20$ strongly prefers the smaller–sooner outcome. The 60 units available now far exceed the discounted value of 100 units later (now worth only 13 units). Thus, k in Equation 1 may be interpreted as the rate of delay discounting.

---

[1] An unfortunate linguistic convention is to attribute causation to patterns of behavior such as the pattern quantified by a discounting rate (k). However, we should not reify delay-discounting rate as a causal object when it is simply a quantitative description of a pattern of choices. Thus, a high discounting rate does not cause impulsive choice but is rather derived from impulsive choices. Causes of discounting rates are to be found in genetic, experiential, and neurochemical variables.

Where Do Discounting Curves Come From?

To obtain a delay-discounting curve, we need to describe how the value of an event (be it a reward or an aversive event) declines as the delay to its delivery increases. To illustrate, imagine winning a lawsuit and after paying your lawyer, receiving a guaranteed annuity worth $100,000. One of the terms of the settlement is that the annuity cannot be cashed for 10 months. Not to worry, there are many companies in the delay-discounting business who will purchase your annuity by giving you less than $100,000 in cash. The fact that these companies pay less than the face value of the annuity illustrates the basic point that delayed rewards are discounted in value; however, generating a discounting curve requires more specificity. Imagine that one of these companies offers to give you $70,000 for your annuity, and you take it. If you make this choice, then the annuity has lost more than 30% of its value because of the 10-month delay. If you discounted the delayed annuity by only 20%, it would be subjectively worth $80,000, and you would have refused the offer to purchase your annuity ($70,000 cash < $80,000 subjective value → refuse offer). If you discount the annuity by exactly 30%, then you would have viewed the company's offer ($70,000 in cash) as equal to the subjective value of the annuity ($70,000), and you would have found it difficult to choose between accepting the offer or waiting 10 months to obtain the full $100,000 settlement. However, you accepted the offer, so we know that you are discounting the delayed reward by more than 30%. To determine exactly how much more, we will gradually reduce the settlement offer until you are indifferent between accepting it and waiting to receive the entire annuity. The amount of the offer at the indifference point is the discounted value of the delayed annuity. Any smaller settlement offer would be rejected, and any larger offer would be accepted. For our purposes, we assume that an indifference point was reached when the offer was $60,000. We can now return to Figure 1.1 to illustrate how the value of the delayed reward at this indifference point can be used to determine the discounting curve. If we think of the y-axis values as percentages of $100,000, then at a 10-month delay the discounted value of the delayed annuity is worth 60% of its full value. Thus, the indifference point tells us the discounted value of the delayed reward. Because the indifference point is expressed in terms of money available now, the indifference point is often referred to as the *present value* of the delayed reward or, as in Figure 1.1, the *discounted value* of the delayed reward.

Our economic thought experiment has given us only one present value along the discounting curve. To obtain more values, we would repeat the experiment using delays spanning the range shown along the x-axis of Figure 1.1. With indifference points plotted at seven or eight different delays, we would simply use nonlinear regression techniques (available in most commercially available spreadsheet and graphics software) to fit these data points using Equation 1, the exponential discounting equation.

Hyperbolic Discounting

Despite its rationality, systematic deviations from the discounting predicted by Equation 1 have been documented in human participants (e.g., Green, Fry, & Myerson, 1994; Kirby, 1997; Ohmura, Takahashi, Kitamura, & Wehr, 2006; Rachlin, Raineri, & Cross, 1991; Simpson & Vuchinich, 2000), including individuals addicted to drugs (e.g., Bickel, Odum, & Madden, 1999; Madden, Bickel, & Jacobs, 1999; Odum, Madden, & Bickel, 2002), regardless of whether the outcomes were real or hypothetical (e.g., Johnson & Bickel, 2002; Madden, Begotka, Raiff, & Kastern, 2003) or whether delayed gains or losses were considered (e.g., Murphy, Vuchinich, & Simpson, 2001; Odum et al., 2002). Systematic deviations from exponential discounting have also been documented extensively in animal laboratory experiments in which rats and pigeons choose between immediate and delayed food rewards (for reviews, see Logue, 1988, and Mazur, 1997). Instead, studies of human and nonhuman choice have generally supported the following hyperbolic discounting equation (Ainslie, 1975; Mazur, 1987):

$$V_d = \frac{A}{1 + kd}, \tag{2}$$

where the parameters are the same as in Equation 1.

To illustrate differences between the exponential and the hyperbolic discounting functions, in Figure 1.2 we compare how well Equations 1 and 2 are able to describe data obtained in an experiment conducted by Madden, Petry, Badger, and Bickel (1997). In this study, 39 nonsmoking, non-drug-using humans made choices between immediate and delayed hypothetical monetary outcomes. Each data point in Figure 1.2 represents the discounted value of the reward when delayed by the amount shown on the x-axis. Within the range of more-brief delays (1 day to 52 weeks), which are expanded in the inset graph, the exponential discounting function overestimates the discounted values of the delayed rewards, whereas in the upper range of delays (5–25 years), the curve tends to underestimate the discounted values of the rewards. By comparison, the hyperbolic discounting function more closely fits the obtained data, and as noted earlier, this outcome is far from unique to this study.

Other discounting equations have also been suggested. For example, Green and Myerson (2004) demonstrated that significantly better fits of human discounting data are provided by adding an exponent to the denominator of Equation 2 (Green & Myerson referred to this as a *hyperbola-like*

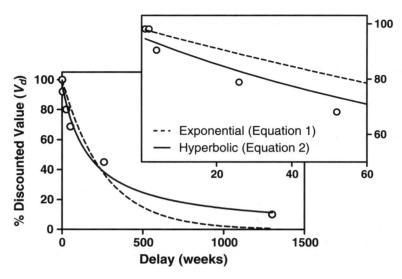

Figure 1.2. Exponential and hyperbolic discounting curves fit to average indifference points of 38 non-drug-using control participants in the study conducted by Madden et al. (1997). The inset panel expands the 1-day to 52-week range of delays so that the fits provided by the two equations can be more easily compared.

equation). As noted by these authors, better fits are not surprising when one adds a free parameter to any equation; however, they argued that the addition is required when it is important to describe precisely the shape of the delay-discounting function or to quantify precisely the rate of delay discounting in individual or groups of human participants. The latter raises a problem with the hyperbola-like equation (a problem recognized by Green & Myerson): When the value of the exponent is not equal to 1.0, the discounting parameter (k) cannot be interpreted as a simple quantitative measure of delay discounting. A second problem with the hyperbola-like equation is that several experiments involving rats and pigeons have found that adding the exponent either to the entire denominator (e.g., Green, Myerson, Shah, Estle, & Holt, 2007; Mazur, 2000; Richards, Mitchell, de Wit, & Seiden, 1997) or to just the delay (Mazur, 1986, 2007; Rodriguez & Logue, 1988) does not appear to improve the fits provided by Equation 2. Whether this human–nonhuman difference is because of obvious differences in species or to procedural differences is currently unknown. Procedural differences are certainly worth exploring because, as compared with nonhumans, human participants are given far less, or no, exposure to the outcomes of their choices and almost never experience the delays to the rewards before making their choices (see Lagorio & Madden, 2005).

Given the debate surrounding the different discounting equations, we offer the following advice. If researchers are primarily concerned with determining the shape of the delay-discounting function, then this is an empirical question and they should use more than one equation. By comparing the relative fits provided by different equations, they can obtain the best description of their data.[2] However, if the goal is to quantify sensitivity to delay (e.g., to compare delay discounting across populations or different inbred strains of mice), then all of these equations should be avoided. Instead, researchers should plot the discounted values of the delayed rewards as in Figure 1.2 and then calculate the area under these data points. This technique was suggested by Myerson, Green, and Warusawitharana (2001), and interested readers will find excellent instructions for calculating area under the curve in that article. Because area under the curve is calculated using every indifference point, the measure of sensitivity to delay is affected by obtained data rather than estimated from a free parameter of an equation that, in some cases, may not provide a good fit of the data. An additional benefit is that frequency distributions of area-under-the-curve values taken from a sample of subjects are usually normally distributed, making this measure amenable to parametric inferential statistical analyses.

Preference Reversals

As summarized earlier, one piece of evidence against simple exponential delay discounting is that Equation 1 provides poorer fits of obtained data than does Equation 2. A second piece of evidence arguing against exponential discounting is that it predicts that we will all make rational choices that are simply not observed either in our everyday lives or in the laboratory. By *rational*, we mean that all else being equal, preference should remain constant over time. However, such preference consistencies would mean that when a person chooses to join a health club, he or she would not subsequently change his or her mind and stop working out (even though he or she continues to pay for the privilege of doing so). Similarly, millions of people each year commit to a diet by purchasing several months of low-calorie mail-order meals but later decide that a hamburger today is more worthwhile than the slow weight loss that would be obtained if only the diet were followed. Such preference reversals are common. We know we should put more money into our retirement account but fail to do so. We know that our long-term family relationships benefit from daily nurturing, but we continue to watch television. We promised marital fidelity, but our divorce rates suggest that we often change our minds when faced with immediate temptations.

---

[2]Future comparisons of the hyperbolic and hyperbola-like equations might usefully be informed by the use of an information criterion such as the Akaike or Bayesian criteria (see Burnham & Anderson, 1998). These criteria are useful when determining the merits of additional free parameters in mathematical models of behavior.

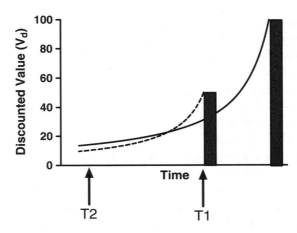

Figure 1.3. Hyperbolic discount functions fit to smaller–sooner and larger–later rewards, the latter represented by the small and larger vertical bars, respectively. The same rate of delay discounting (*k*) was used to fit both curves. At Time 1 (T1), the smaller–sooner outcome is available immediately, and the larger–later reward is not. Moving from T1 to Time 2 (T2; both rewards delayed), the discounting functions cross yielding a reversal in preference.

According to the *Diagnostic and Statistical Manual of Mental Disorders* (4th ed., text revision; American Psychiatric Association, 2000), a number of addictive disorders are likewise characterized by a persistent desire for self-control (i.e., abstinence from drug use, gambling) but repeated failures to achieve it. Thus, the treatment-seeking addict, like the rest of us, prefers the long-term benefits of foregoing an immediate pleasure at all times except when the temptation becomes immediately available. At that moment, the addict seems to lose his or her willpower, behaves impulsively, and subsequently lives with regret. As Ainslie (1992) has put it, we seem to be of two selves: the *you* of the moment who behaves impulsively and the *you* of all other times—the *you* who lives with self-disappointment.

Because nearly everyone can relate to examples of preference reversals, they have, not surprisingly, frequently been documented in the human delay-discounting literature (for a review, see Green & Myerson, 2004). It is interesting that the deeply bowed shape of the hyperbolic discounting curve (Equation 2) predicts preference reversals.[3] Figure 1.3 depicts two such curves. Represented by the vertical bars are two rewards, the objective amounts of which correspond to the height of the bars. Along the *x*-axis of Figure 1.3, we have plotted time to the delivery of the two rewards. At Time 1 (T1),

---

[3]In this instance, we use the term *predicts* because the hyperbolic shape of the discounting function has been observed so many times and in so many species that this form, and the preference reversals that are implicated by it, can be predicted.

the larger reward is delayed by an amount of time corresponding to the distance along the x-axis between T1 and the larger vertical bar. Because there is no distance between T1 and the smaller vertical bar, the smaller reward is immediately available. Thus, at T1 the choice is between a small–immediate versus a large–delayed reward. Another choice scenario is played out at Time 2 (T2), where both rewards are delayed, although the smaller reward would be available sooner (if selected) than would the larger reward.

Which will the individual choose? The answer is given by the relative discounted values of the two rewards. Assuming individuals prefer the reward that has retained more of its value at the moment of choice, then at T2 we would expect the individual to select the larger–later reward because the discounted value of the larger–later reward (solid discounting function) exceeds the discounted value of the smaller–sooner reward (dashed discounting function). From this temporal vantage point of T2, removed from the temptations of an immediate reward, one can clearly see the advantages of pursuing a course of self-control. This is the time at which those expensive mail-order diet meals are purchased. However, at T1 the smaller–sooner reward (e.g., an unexpected box of doughnuts in the break room) is immediately available, whereas the larger–later reward (improved health, physique, etc.) is not. The value of the immediate reward now exceeds the discounted value of the delayed reward, and preference reverses. This simple shift in time from T2 to T1, with no other changes, yields the preference reversal—a "change of mind," a decision that yields later regret.

Because preference reversals are predicted by the shape of hyperbolic delay-discounting functions, they should be observed in any species that discounts delayed rewards according to Equation 2. Tests with humans (Green & Myerson, 2004), pigeons (e.g., Ainslie & Herrnstein, 1981; Green, Fisher, Perlow, & Sherman, 1981), and rats (Green & Estle, 2003) have supported this prediction, but thus far no other nonhuman species has been tested. It is important to note that exponential discounting can predict preference reversals if the rate of discounting is allowed to vary with reward amount or intensity of the aversive stimulus. Although such amount-dependent discounting rates have been observed with humans (e.g., Green et al., 1994), this has not, thus far, been the case with nonhumans. For example, Kirby (1997) reported that humans discounted delayed $20 rewards significantly less than delayed $10 rewards, but this finding has not been replicated in rats when the difference in reward amount across conditions was either twofold (Richards et al., 1997) or sixfold (Green, Myerson, Holt, Slevin, & Estle, 2004). That moving from T1 to T2 in Figure 1.3 produces preference reversals in animals despite no evidence for amount-dependent discounting is a challenge to an exponential discounting equation.

A particularly interesting demonstration of the preference reversal phenomenon was presented by Deluty (1978, Experiment 3). In one condition of this study, rats chose between a 1-second shock delivered 2 seconds into a postchoice feeding period or a 2-second shock delivered 12 seconds into this feeding period. This choice is depicted at T1 in Figure 1.4. As in Figure 1.3, the consequent events are represented by vertical bars. Because the 2-second shock is objectively twice as long as the 1-s shock, it is twice as far below the x-axis. At T1, both of these shocks are delayed, and their aversive values are discounted in accord with the hyperbolic functions shown. Because the smaller–sooner shock retains more of its aversive value than the larger–later shock (i.e., the open data point at T1 is further below the x-axis than the solid data point), Deluty's rats preferred the larger–later shock (an impulsive choice). At T2, however, notice that the two discounting functions have crossed and the larger–later shock is now subjectively more aversive than the smaller–sooner shock. The choices of Deluty's rats were in accordance with these predictions of hyperbolic discounting: The rats' choices shifted in favor of the smaller–sooner shock as the rats moved from T1 to T2. Although the shape of the discounting function describing choices involving losses has been shown to be hyperbolic (Equation 2), whether the two discounting processes are affected in the same way by a common set of experimental variables is currently unknown (see chap. 3, this volume, for evidence that the two may be different processes).

Figure 1.4 provides a reasonable description of several forms of procrastination. Consider procrastinating on the task of signing up for paycheck withdrawals that will be placed in a college savings account for your children. If you start the account now, the amount of money that you will have to put away each month (analogous to the 1-second shock experienced by Deluty's [1978] rats) will be small relative to that which will have to be

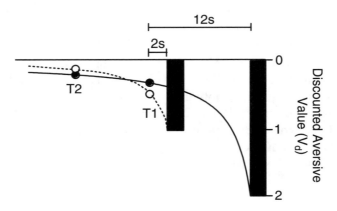

Figure 1.4. Discounting of delayed aversive consequences; modeled after the choice alternatives arranged by Deluty (1978, Experiment 3). See text for details. s = second; T1 = Time 1; T2 = Time 2.

saved each month if you continue to procrastinate (2-second shock). However, at T1 decreasing your salary by the amount saved is subjectively worse than the discounted aversive value of having to save/spend more money in the future. Recently, financial advisors have taken a page from the behavioral–economic delay-discounting literature (Thaler & Benartzi, 2004) and have asked employees to make choices about their savings at T2. That is, the advisors do not ask employees to start their savings (and experience a loss of money) now at T1, they ask them to commit to putting a percentage of their next pay raise (a delayed event) into the savings program. From the temporal vantage point of T2, employees can see that having to save more money in the distant future is worse (solid data point at T2) than having to save less money a bit sooner. This Save More Tomorrow program has significantly increased the number of employees saving for their future and the amount they have saved. As this example illustrates, delay discounting is an important behavioral process, as are the variables that can affect it. Much of the rest of this volume is concerned with these variables, be they genetic, neurochemical, or related to the environmental contingencies of reinforcement and punishment under which the organism's choices are made. To prepare the reader to tackle these chapters, in the next section we provide an overview of the most commonly used procedures for quantifying delay discounting in animal and human subjects.

PROCEDURES FOR ASSESSING DELAY DISCOUNTING

Several procedures have been used to systematically investigate impulsive decision making in human and nonhuman subjects. Borrowing from psychophysical research, most use some form of adjusting or titrating procedure to determine indifference points between smaller–sooner and larger–later rewards. Recall that at the indifference point, the value of the two rewards is equivalent, thereby providing a measure of the discounted value of the delayed reward. Because the pioneering work in assessing delay discounting was conducted with nonhuman subjects and because many of the procedures used with humans are derivative of those used with animals, we begin by examining the most commonly used procedures in the nonhuman delay-discounting literature.

Procedures Used With Nonhuman Subjects

Most of the research on delay discounting in nonhumans has been conducted with rats pressing levers or pigeons pecking keys in operant chambers to obtain immediate or delayed food or liquid reinforcers. The advantages of this general procedure are enormous: automated presentation of stimuli and rewards, automated and temporally precise data collection, and sessions conducted in an environment free of demand characteristics.

General Procedures

Several procedures are common to nearly all of the specific procedures discussed later. The first of these occurs at the beginning of a choice trial when the animal is required to press a lever, peck a key, or engage in some other response that places the animal equidistant from the two choice alternatives. The importance of the centering response is obvious: If the animal selects the alternative on the right simply because it happens to be standing on the right side of the chamber when the trial begins, then the choice tells us nothing about delay discounting.

A second general procedure is the use of forced-choice trials. On these trials, after the centering response is emitted, only one alternative is available and the trial does not end until the animal selects it and experiences the consequences of doing so. Forced-choice trials are designed to expose the animal to both sets of consequences before the free-choice trials in which they are free to select either outcome. To our knowledge, no systematic study has been made of the effects of the ratio of forced- to free-choice trials on choice or the number of sessions required until choice stabilizes.

Most procedures require a single response to register a choice (or a forced choice) and initiate the reinforcer sequence. Requiring additional responses would add effort and time to the delivery of either reinforcer and might be conceptualized as moving in the direction from T1 to T2 in Figure 1.3. Finally, an intertrial interval (ITI) follows reinforcer delivery. It holds the time between choice opportunities constant regardless of which alternative is selected. Consider an experiment in which the larger–later food reward is delayed by 10 seconds. If the animal chooses the smaller–sooner alternative, the sequence of responses and reinforcer may be over in just a few seconds. If the next trial is started immediately (no ITI), the animal would do well to repeatedly choose the smaller–sooner reinforcer because it would increase the local reinforcement rate relative to the time required to obtain a delayed reinforcer, hardly an appropriate model of impulsivity. With an ITI, selecting the smaller–sooner reinforcer yields a lower local and overall rate of reinforcement than that which could be obtained by selecting the larger–later alternative.

Adjusting-Delay Procedure

One of the first procedures used to assess rates of delay discounting was pioneered by Mazur (1987). In this procedure, the subject chooses between a large food reward delivered after an adjusting delay versus a smaller amount of food delivered after a fixed delay. The procedure is designed to identify the delay at which the subject is indifferent between the two rewards. Recall that the indifference point provides the measure of the degree of delay discounting. In the adjusting-delay procedure, that measure is the delay to the larger–later alternative, which might be thought of as the longest delay the subject will tolerate before preference shifts toward the smaller–sooner reward. Thus, if the adjusted delay is brief when stable indifference is achieved, this is indicative of more extreme delay discounting.

In a typical adjusting-delay procedure, subjects complete two forced-choice trials (exposure to both consequences) followed by two free-choice trials. If the smaller–sooner reward is selected on both free-choice trials, indifference has not been obtained so the nonpreferred outcome is made more enticing by decreasing the delay to the larger–later reward (usually by 1 s) in the next block of forced- and free-choice trials. Likewise, if the subject consistently chooses the larger–later reward on the free-choice trials, the delay to the larger–later reward is increased in the next trial block.

In the abstract, this procedure would result in an adjusted delay to the larger–later reward at which the subject was consistently indifferent. In reality, the delays are widely adjusted (by the subject's choices) up and down at first because the subjects are relatively insensitive to the changing delays. With continued experience, however, the range across which delays are adjusted is constrained, and a quantitative stability criterion may be met (see Mazur, 1987). Once stability is achieved, the mean adjusted delay obtained over the stable sessions serves as the indifference point. When this process is repeated across several fixed delay values, mean adjusted delays are plotted as a function of the fixed delay to the smaller–sooner reward. Because Equations 1 and 2 make different predictions about the characteristics of this function, deviations from these predictions can be used to support one or the other equation. Mazur (1987) found that the hyperbolic discounting function (Equation 2) provided the most accurate description of his pigeons' choices, and as noted above, this finding has frequently been replicated.

Concerns about the adjusting-delay procedure were raised by Cardinal, Daw, Robbins, and Everitt (2002), who reported that despite completing thousands of forced- and free-choice trials, most of their rats failed to reach a constrained range of adjusted delays from which indifference points could be derived. Unfortunately, studies designed to identify procedural variables responsible for the discrepancy between the Cardinal et al. findings and those from several other laboratories have not been conducted. One difference that might warrant investigation is the rate at which delays are adjusted across laboratories. Cardinal et al. adjusted by 20%–30% (range = 0.4 seconds–9.0 seconds), whereas other laboratories have adjusted in 1-second increments. Adjusting more rapidly may yield unstable indifference points if the rat's behavior requires more exposure than a single block of trials to be affected by the change in delay.

Adjusting-Amount Procedure

The adjusting-amount procedure pioneered by Richards et al. (1997) is similar to the adjusting-delay procedure. Both use the subject's choices to titrate a characteristic of one of the reinforcers (in this case, the amount of the smaller–sooner reinforcer) until a stable indifference point is attained. In the experiments conducted by Richards et al., water-deprived rats chose between a small amount of water (10 μl) delivered after a fixed delay and an even smaller amount of water delivered immediately. If the fixed alternative was selected, then the smaller–sooner amount was increased by some percentage (typically a 10%–15% increase). The opposite adjustment was made if the subject chose the adjustment-amount alternative. If the subject chose the same alternative on two consecutive trials, then it was required to complete a forced-choice trial on the other alternative. This ensured that the subject was periodically exposed to the consequences of selecting both alternatives.

Some researchers have used the adjusting-amount procedure to assess indifference points at several different delays to the larger–later reinforcer. In the original Richards et al. (1997) study, for example, five different delays were assessed in 5-day blocks, for a period of 75 days (15 days per delay). The resulting indifference points may be plotted against the fixed delays as in Figure 1.2. These indifference points may then be fit with one of the nonlinear discounting equations discussed above, using standard regression techniques.

Green et al. (2007) evaluated whether the adjusting-delay and adjusting-amount procedures yield the same discounting rates (k in Equation 2). In two experiments, they demonstrated convincingly that these procedures yield the same estimates of discounting, and they extended the use of the adjusting-amount procedure to a new species (pigeons) and a new reinforcer type (food pellets). They also reported that the number of sessions required to obtain stable indifference points was approximately the same across the adjusting-amount (22 sessions) and adjusting-delay (24 sessions) procedures.

Some researchers have adapted the adjusting-amount procedure for the purposes of studying the effects of pharmacological manipulations or neurological lesions on delay discounting (e.g., Acheson et al., 2006). In these studies, amounts are adjusted as described earlier, but the delay to the larger–later reinforcer remains unchanged across sessions until the indifference point stabilizes. This provides a baseline against which the effects of these acute or chronic manipulations may be judged.

Evenden and Ryan (1996) Procedure

Perhaps the most widely used procedure to quantify impulsive choice in nonhumans is the one developed by Evenden and Ryan (1996). This procedure is frequently used because it provides measures of sensitivity to reinforcer amount and reinforcer delay in each session, and when these measures stabilize across days, the procedure yields an ideal baseline from which to evaluate the effects of acute and chronic manipulations (e.g., drug injections or neurological lesions) on sensitivity to amount and sensitivity to a range of delays.

Under the Evenden and Ryan (1996) procedure, each session is composed of five eight-trial blocks. Within each block, the first two trials are forced-choice trials (one on each alternative), and the remaining six are free-choice trials. At each free-choice trial, the subject chooses between a smaller–sooner reward (e.g., one pellet now) and a larger–later reward (e.g., three pellets in 10 seconds). Across the five eight-trial blocks, the delay to the larger reward is systematically increased, typically from 0 seconds in the first block up to 60 seconds in the last block. Thus, the first trial block provides at least a gross measure of sensitivity to differences in reward amount (percentage choice of the larger reward), and the subsequent trial blocks provide a measure of sensitivity to progressively increasing delays (percentage choice of the larger–later reward in each block).

Although there are several advantages to the Evenden and Ryan (1996) procedure, it is not without its drawbacks. First, stable choice between two nonidentical nonadjusting outcomes arranged in a discrete trial format, like that used within each block trial of the Evenden and Ryan procedure, should result in exclusive preference for the higher valued alternative (e.g., Herrnstein, 1981); however, exclusive choice is not typically reported outside the first (no-delay) trial block. This may be because of across-subject averaging of exclusive preferences, although the few studies that have provided individual subject data (e.g., Evenden & Ryan, 1999) and our own experiences with this procedure suggest this is not the case. Another possibility is that choice in each trial block is affected by carryover effects from prior sessions or prior trial blocks within the same session. Evidence suggesting a carryover effect was reported by Fox, Hand, and Reilly (2008), who found that stable choice percentages were influenced by delays arranged in preceding sessions. When the delay to the larger–later reinforcer started at zero and increased between sessions, percentage choice of the larger–later reward was significantly higher than in a separate condition in which this delay decreased across sessions. These carryover effects are particularly problematic if one is interested in measuring steady-state impulsive choice, as was the case in the Fox et al. study designed to explore impulsivity differences across strains of rats.

A second, related drawback is that choice of the larger reinforcer in the no-delay trial block (typically the first trial block) is often not exclusively for the larger reward (e.g., Cardinal, Pennicott, Sugathapala, Robbins, & Everitt, 2001; Cardinal, Robbins, & Everitt, 2000). This suggests that under the Evenden and Ryan (1996) procedure, avoidance of the delayed reward lever during the latter portions of the preceding session carries over into the no-delay trial block of the present session. This is problematic because choice in the no-delay trial block is a putative measure of sensitivity to reinforcer amount.

A third drawback is specific to studies examining effects of drugs or neurological lesions on impulsive choice. A not uncommon outcome of these manipulations is that the entire choice function shifts upward (e.g., van Gaalen, van Koten, Schoffelmeer, & Vanderschuren, 2006), downward (e.g., Evenden & Ryan, 1999), or toward indifference (e.g., Uslaner & Robinson, 2006), which makes interpretation of the effect difficult. Evenden and Ryan (1999), for example, reported that 1.0 g/kg ethanol shifted the entire choice function downward in all trial blocks. Because preference for the larger reinforcer in the no-delay trial block declined, ethanol would appear to decrease sensitivity to reinforcer amount, but another possibility is that the enhanced sensitivity to reinforcer delay observed in the other trial blocks carried over into the no-delay trial block.

Procedural improvements would appear to be warranted. One potential improvement was actually used by Evenden and Ryan (1996) but has appeared infrequently in the literature since. In addition to the usual procedures, control sessions are periodically conducted in which no delay is arranged to the larger reinforcer in any trial block. Such control sessions may enhance sensitivity to changing delays when they are scheduled. Another potential improvement is to increase the number of forced-choice trials within each trial block. This might be accomplished by dropping the trial block in which a 60-second delay to reinforcement is typically scheduled (steady-state assessments of impulsivity reveal that most rats will not tolerate delay of more than 30 seconds). More generally, any procedural modification designed to increase the salience of the particular delay in operation within a trial block should yield a better measure of sensitivity to that delay. Given how frequently the Evenden and Ryan procedure has been used, systematic investigation of these or other procedural improvements is warranted.

Other Procedures

Two other procedures are worth a brief mention. The first is the T-maze procedure, in which a rat is released from a start box and runs to the end of one of two goal arms, one baited with food available on arrival, the other associated with a larger food reward delivered after a delay (e.g., Thiébot, Le Bihan, Soubrié, & Simon, 1985). The increased labor to the experimenter, relative to the automated operant chamber, may be responsible for the infrequent use of this procedure, but another problem is that the procedure confounds delay with the effort required to run to the goal box, thereby making it difficult to determine whether one is measuring delay or effort discounting (or both).

The second infrequently used procedure is to give monkeys a choice between two visually available rewards, the larger of the two delivered after a delay (e.g., Rosati, Stevens, Hare, & Hauser, 2007). Although rich in face validity, interpreting the results of these studies is difficult. Monkeys rarely choose a visually smaller reward even when selecting it results in a larger reward than would have been obtained had they chosen the visually larger one (e.g., Boysen & Berntson, 1995). A superior practice is to have the monkey select a choice lever with no rewards visually associated with either one (e.g., Woolverton, Myerson, & Green, 2007).

Procedures Used With Humans

The reliable finding of hyperbolic delay discounting in nonhuman animals provided a quantitative comparison for the discounting functions obtained in human studies of discounting. Had the exponential discounting equation better described human choices, then we would have been in a position to argue that humans are more economically rational than nonhumans. Alas, as outlined below, the variety of procedures used with humans support a between-species concordance in the hyperbolic delay discounting process (for evidence that human discounting may be hyperbola-like rather than strictly hyperbolic, see Green & Myerson, 2004).

Hypothetical Outcomes

The most widely used procedures for assessing degree of delay discounting in humans are derived from those pioneered by Rachlin et al. (1991). In this study, participants were asked to choose between $1,000 now and $1,000 given after delays ranging from 1 month to 50 years; all rewards were hypothetical. When the reward amounts were equal but one was delayed, participants generally preferred to receive $1,000 now. At each delay, Rachlin et al. used an adjusting-amount procedure whereby they gradually decreased the amount of money available now (e.g., $990 now vs. $1,000 in 1 month) until participants were choosing between $1 now and $1,000 after the delay. The procedure was repeated in reverse order at each delay, and the indifference point was given by the average amount of the immediate reward at the point at which the participant no longer preferred the immediate reward (amounts adjusted downward) and no longer preferred the delayed reward (adjusted upward). All told, the delay-discounting assessment yielded seven indifference points that could be plotted as in Figure 1.2.

The Rachlin et al. (1991) data were compelling not only because they quickly yielded orderly estimates of delay discounting but also because their human participants' discounting function was well described by the hyperbolic discounting equation (Equation 2) that had proven most successful in describing nonhuman choice (e.g., Mazur, 1987). Subsequent experiments using hypothetical outcomes and different reward amounts replicated this finding at the level of both group averages and individual participants (e.g., Green, Myerson, & McFadden, 1997; Kirby & Marakovic, 1995; Myerson & Green, 1995). Although these findings provided evidence for interspecies continuity of the process by which delayed outcomes were discounted, concerns about the hypothetical nature of the rewards were frequently raised (e.g., Bickel & Marsch, 2001; Kirby & Marakovic, 1995).

Real Outcomes

Concerns about using purely hypothetical rewards led some researchers to instruct their participants that there was a chance that one of their choices would have real outcomes at the end of the session. In theory, this should increase the probability that participants would make all choices as though the outcomes were real. Comparisons between this procedure and one in which all rewards were purely hypothetical revealed no differences in rate of delay discounting (Johnson & Bickel, 2002; Madden et al., 2003). Subsequent studies that further increased the proportion of real rewards also failed to show a difference in degree of delay discounting between real and hypothetical rewards (Lagorio & Madden, 2005; Madden et al., 2004). In addition, these studies showed that whether rewards were real, potentially real, or hypothetical, the form of the discounting curve was hyperbolic (Equation 2).

Nonetheless, a problem remained. Experiments designed to detect the effects of acute doses of drugs of abuse on delay discounting were failing to reveal expected effects when hypothetical or potentially real rewards were arranged (e.g., Richards, Zhang, Mitchell, & de Wit, 1999). These findings likely played a role in the development of the experiential discounting task (EDT; Reynolds & Shiffbauer, 2004). In the EDT, participants choose between a delayed, probabilistic monetary reward (e.g., a 35% chance of receiving $0.30) and an immediate, assured reward (e.g., 100% chance of obtaining $0.15). If the smaller–sooner sure thing is selected, the amount of that reward is decreased on subsequent trials, and this process is repeated until an indifference point is reached. An apparent benefit of the EDT has been that state manipulations such as sleep deprivation (Reynolds & Shiffbauer, 2004) and alcohol consumption (Reynolds, Richards, & de Wit, 2006) have been shown to increase impulsive decision making.

Unfortunately, procedural problems with the EDT make it difficult to interpret why these manipulations have increased impulsivity. First, the procedure confounds delay and probability because the larger–later reward is delivered probabilistically. Although EDT analyses of delay discounting normalize indifference points as a percentage of the discounted value of the large–immediate–probabilistic reward, little is known about the interaction between probability and delay because one or the other is manipulated (although see Yi, de la Piedad, & Bickel, 2006). A second, more serious problem with the EDT is that participants often forgo the larger–later reward at very short delays (e.g., 1 min or less), whereas previous research with humans has suggested participants should strongly prefer the larger–later reward even at much longer delays (e.g., Logue, Peña-Correal, Rodriguez, & Kabela, 1986). Some of this difference may result from the probabilistic nature of the delayed reward, but another factor appears to be that the EDT does not include a postconsequence ITI that holds constant the time between choice opportunities regardless of the alternative selected. Thus, choosing the smaller–sooner outcome increases local rate of reinforcement in the EDT and more quickly ends the portion of the experiment in which participants are required to pay attention, two outcomes that might better be described as maximizing than as impulsivity (Logue et al., 1986), particularly for sleep-deprived or alcohol-intoxicated participants. Scheres et al. (2006) demonstrated the importance of an ITI to choices made in a modified EDT (delayed rewards were not probabilistic). They reported that participants made significantly fewer impulsive choices when an ITI was included than when it was not (see also Flora, 1995). Such findings raise questions about the EDT in studying the effects of pharmacological manipulations on impulsivity or delay discounting.

Other Procedures

Two variations on the procedures just outlined are used commonly, yield indifference points rapidly, and broadly concord with those widely reported in the literature. The first is a class of titrating procedures that use a participant's prior choices to exclude from subsequent presentation any choice alternatives falling outside the range in which the participant's indifference point might fall (e.g., Johnson & Bickel, 2002; Richards et al., 1999). For example, if the participant has twice indicated that she or he would prefer $500 now over $1,000 in 5 years, then one may assume that the participant would also prefer more than $500 now over $1,000 in 5 years, and there is no utility in asking these questions. Randomizing the choice alternatives presented rather than homing in linearly on the indifference point yields hyperbolic discounting functions in approximately 15 minutes. A second, even more rapid procedure has participants make a handful of choices from which an estimate of the discounting rate may be interpolated from the pattern of choices. This procedure has proven useful in examining population differences in delay discounting (e.g., Kirby, Petry, & Bickel, 1999). Caution is warranted when comparing discounting rates across studies using different assessment procedures. Although all of the procedures outlined above appear equally capable of differentiating populations such as drug-dependent participants versus controls, several studies have shown that different procedures yield systematic and statistically significant differences in estimates of discounting rate (e.g., Epstein et al., 2003).

SUMMARY AND FUTURE DIRECTIONS

Discounting the future is a behavioral process common to every species that has been tested thus far. The procedures used across species and laboratories have varied considerably, but they have all suggested that as delays increase, the value of an outcome decays according to a hyperbolic function. New discounting equations informed by computational modeling and neuroscience findings have recently been formulated, and these will no doubt lead to productive research lines (e.g., chap. 5, this volume). New equations or old, they have in common a deeply bowed discounting function that deviates systematically from the exponential function predicted by normative economic theory. This deviation is "irrational" in the sense that we change our minds from choosing what is best for us in the long run to choosing what is best for us now. We all succumb to this temptation. We all behave irrationally, but some behave more irrationally than others.

Perhaps owing to the latter difference in the degree to which the future is discounted by different populations of humans (e.g., individuals diagnosed with addictive disorders), the past 10 years have seen a proliferation of empirical articles published on the topic of delay discounting. As illustrated in the remainder of this book, this research has yielded important findings that provide hints about the likely areas of fruitful research over the next 10 years. Future progress in the study of delay discounting will depend, we believe, on procedural improvements in both the human and the animal laboratories. In the animal laboratory, new techniques for simultaneously assessing sensitivity to amount and delay within a single session are needed for purposes of detecting effects of acute experimental manipulations (e.g., Ho, Al-Zahrani, Al-Ruwaitea, Bradshaw, & Szabadi, 1998). In the human laboratory, existing procedures have proven adequate for discriminating between populations but inadequate for detecting effects of some experimental manipulations. Improvements on the EDT such as using real delays to real consumable nonprobabilistic rewards may hold the key. Ironically, time will tell.

REFERENCES

Acheson, A., Farrar, A. M., Patak, M., Hausknecht, K. A., Kieres, A. K., Seulgi, C., et al. (2006). Nucleus accumbens lesions decrease sensitivity to rapid changes in the delay to reinforcement. *Behavioural Brain Research, 173*, 217–228.

Ainslie, G. (1975). Specious reward: A behavioral theory of impulsiveness and impulse control. *Psychological Bulletin, 82*, 463–496.

Ainslie, G. (1992). *Picoeconomics: The strategic interaction of successive motivational states within the person.* New York: Cambridge University Press.

Ainslie, G., & Herrnstein, R. J. (1981). Preference reversals and delayed reinforcement. *Animal Learning & Behavior, 9*, 476–482.

American Psychiatric Association. (2000). *Diagnostic and statistical manual of mental disorders* (4th ed., text revision). Washington, DC: Author.

Barkley, R. A. (1997). Behavioral inhibition, sustained attention, and executive functions: Constructing a unifying theory of ADHD. *Psychological Bulletin, 121*, 65–94.

Bickel, W. K., & Marsch, L. A. (2001). Toward a behavioral economic understanding of drug dependence: Delay discounting processes. *Addiction, 96*, 73–86.

Bickel, W. K., Odum, A. L., & Madden, G. J. (1999). Impulsivity and cigarette smoking: Delay discounting in current, never, and ex-smokers. *Psychopharmacology (Berlin), 146*, 447–454.

Boysen, S. T., & Berntson, G. G. (1995). Responses to quantity: Perceptual versus cognitive mechanisms in chimpanzees (*Pan troglodytes*). *Journal of Experimental Psychology: Animal Behavior Processes, 21*, 82–86.

Burnham, K. P., & Anderson, D. R. (1998). *Model selection and multimodel inference: A practical information theoretical approach* (2nd ed.). New York: Springer-Verlag.

Cardinal, R. N., Daw, N., Robbins, T. W., & Everitt, B. J. (2002). Local analysis of behaviour in the adjusting-delay task for assessing choice of delayed reinforcement. *Neural Networks, 15*, 617–634.

Cardinal, R. N., Pennicott, D. R., Sugathapala, C. L., Robbins, T. W., & Everitt, B. J. (2001, June 29). Impulsive choice induced in rats by lesions of the nucleus accumbens core. *Science, 292*, 2499–2501.

Cardinal, R. N., Robbins, T. W., & Everitt, B. J. (2000). The effects of d-amphetamine, chlordiazepoxide, alpha-flupenthixol and behavioural manipulations on choice of signaled and unsignaled delayed reinforcement in rats. *Psychopharmacology (Berlin), 152*, 362–375.

Dalley, J. W., Fryer, T. D., Brichard, L., Robinson, E. S. J., Theobald, D. E., Laane, K., et al. (2007, March 2). Nucleus accumbens D2/3 receptors predict trait impulsivity and cocaine reinforcement. *Science, 315*, 1267–1270.

Deluty, M. Z. (1978). Self-control and impulsiveness involving aversive events. *Journal of Experimental Psychology: Animal Behavior Processes, 4*, 250–266.

Diergaarde, L., Pattij, T., Poortvliet, I., Hogenboom, F., de Vries, W., Schoffelmeer, A. N. M., & De Vries, T. J. (2008). Impulsive choice and impulsive action predict vulnerability to distinct stages of nicotine seeking in rats. *Biological Psychiatry, 63*, 301–308.

Epstein, L. H., Richards, J. B., Saad, F. G., Paluch, R. A., Roemmich, J. N., & Lerman, C. (2003). Comparison between two measures of delay discounting in smokers. *Experimental and Clinical Psychopharmacology, 11*, 131–138.

Evenden, J. L., & Ryan, C. N. (1996). The pharmacology of impulsive behaviour in rats: The effects of drugs on response choice with varying delays of reinforcement. *Psychopharmacology (Berlin), 128*, 161–170.

Evenden, J. L., & Ryan, C. N. (1999). The pharmacology of impulsive behaviour in rats VI: The effects of ethanol and selective serotonergic drugs on response choice with varying delays of reinforcement. *Psychopharmacology (Berlin), 146*, 413–421.

Eysenck, S. B. B., & Eysenck, H. J. (1978). Impulsiveness and venturesomeness: Their position in a dimensional system of personality description. *Psychological Reports, 43*, 1247–1255.

Flora, S. R. (1995). Molar and molecular contingencies and effects of punishment in a human self-control paradigm. *Psychological Record, 45*, 261–281.

Fox, A. T., Hand, D. J., & Reilly, M. P. (2008). Impulsive choice in a rodent model of attention-deficit/hyperactivity disorder. *Behavioural Brain Research, 187*, 146–152.

Green, L., & Estle, S. J. (2003). Preference reversals with food and water reinforcers in rats. *Journal of the Experimental Analysis of Behavior, 79*, 233–242.

Green, L., Fisher, E. B., Perlow, S., & Sherman, L. (1981). Preference reversal and self-control: Choice as a function of reward amount and delay. *Behaviour Analysis Letters, 1*, 43–51.

Green, L., Fry, A. F., & Myerson, J. (1994). Discounting of delayed rewards: A life-span comparison. *Psychological Science, 5*, 33–36.

Green, L., & Myerson, J. (2004). A discounting framework for choice with delayed and probabilistic rewards. *Psychological Review, 130*, 769–792.

Green, L., Myerson, J., Holt, D. D., Slevin, J. R., & Estle, S. J. (2004). Discounting of delayed food rewards in pigeons and rats: Is there a magnitude effect? *Journal of the Experimental Analysis of Behavior, 81*, 39–50.

Green, L., Myerson, J., & McFadden, E. (1997). Rate of temporal discounting decreases with amount of reward. *Memory & Cognition, 25*, 715–723.

Green, L., Myerson, J., Shah, A. K., Estle, S. J., & Holt, D. D. (2007). Do adjusting-amount and adjusting-delay procedures produce equivalent estimates of subjective value in pigeons? *Journal of the Experimental Analysis of Behavior, 87*, 337–347.

Herrnstein, R. J. (1981). Self-control as response strength. In C. M. Bradshaw, E. Szabadi, & C. F. Lowe (Eds.), *Quantification of steady-state operant behaviour* (pp. 3–20). Amsterdam: Elsevier/North Holland.

Hineline, P. N. (1977). Negative reinforcement and avoidance. In W. K. Honig & J. E. R. Staddon (Eds.), *Handbook of operant behavior* (pp. 364–414). Englewood Cliffs, NJ: Prentice-Hall.

Ho, M. Y., Al-Zahrani, S. S. A., Al-Ruwaitea, A. S. A., Bradshaw, C. M., & Szabadi, E. (1998). 5-hydroxytryptamine and impulse control: Prospects for a behavioural analysis. *Journal of Psychopharmacology, 12,* 68–78.

Johnson, M. W., & Bickel, W. K. (2002). Within-subject comparison of real and hypothetical rewards in delay discounting. *Journal of the Experimental Analysis of Behavior, 77,* 129–146.

Kirby, K. N. (1997). Bidding on the future: Evidence against normative discounting of delayed rewards. *Journal of Experimental Psychology: General, 126,* 54–70.

Kirby, K. N., & Maraković, N. N. (1995). Modeling myopic decisions: Evidence for hyperbolic delay-discounting within subjects and amounts. *Organizational Behavior and Human Decision Processes, 64,* 22–30.

Kirby, K. N., Petry, N. M., & Bickel, W. K. (1999). Heroin addicts have higher discounting rates for delayed rewards than non-drug-using controls. *Journal of Experimental Psychology: General, 128,* 78–87.

Lagorio, C. H., & Madden, G. J. (2005). Delay discounting of real and hypothetical rewards III: Steady-state assessments, forced-choice trials, and all real rewards. *Behavioral Processes, 69,* 173–187.

Logue, A. W. (1988). Research on self-control: An integrating framework. *Behavioral and Brain Sciences, 11,* 665–709.

Logue, A. W., Peña-Correal, M. L., Rodriguez, M. L., & Kabela, E. (1986). Self-control in adult humans: Variation in positive reinforcer amount and delay. *Journal of the Experimental Analysis of Behavior, 46,* 159–173.

Madden, G. J., Begotka, A. M., Raiff, B. R., & Kastern, L. L. (2003). Delay discounting of real and hypothetical rewards. *Experimental and Clinical Psychopharmacology, 11,* 139–145.

Madden, G. J., Bickel, W. K., & Jacobs, E. A. (1999). Discounting of delayed rewards in opioid-dependent outpatients: Exponential or hyperbolic discounting functions? *Experimental and Clinical Psychopharmacology, 7,* 284–293.

Madden, G. J., Petry, N. M., Badger, G., & Bickel, W. K. (1997). Impulsive and self-control choices in opioid-dependent subjects and non-drug using controls: Drug and monetary rewards. *Experimental and Clinical Psychopharmacology, 5,* 256–262.

Madden, G. J., Raiff, B. R., Lagorio, C. H., Begotka, A. M., Mueller, A. M., Hehli, D. J., & Wegener, A. (2004). Delay discounting of potentially real and hypothetical rewards II: Between- and within-subjects comparisons. *Experimental and Clinical Psychopharmacology, 12,* 251–261.

Mazur, J. E. (1986). Choice between single and multiple delayed reinforcers. *Journal of the Experimental Analysis of Behavior, 46,* 67–77.

Mazur, J. E. (1987). An adjusting procedure for studying delayed reinforcement. In M. L. Commons, J. E. Mazur, J. A. Nevin, & H. Rachlin (Eds.), *Quantitative analysis of behavior: Vol. 5. The effect of delay and of intervening events on reinforcement value* (pp. 55–73). Hillsdale, NJ: Erlbaum.

Mazur, J. E. (1997). Choice, delay, probability, and conditioned reinforcement. *Animal Learning & Behavior, 25,* 131–147.

Mazur, J. E. (2000). Tradeoffs among delay, rate, and amount of reinforcement. *Behavioral Processes, 49,* 1–10.

Mazur, J. E. (2007). Rat's choices between one and two delayed reinforcers. *Learning and Behavior, 35,* 169–176.

Mazur, J. E., & Logue, A. W. (1978). Choice in a "self-control" paradigm: Effects of a fading procedure. *Journal of the Experimental Analysis of Behavior, 30,* 11–17.

Mischel, W., Grusec, J., & Masters, J. C. (1969). Effects of expected delay time on the subjective value of rewards and punishments. *Journal of Personality and Social Psychology, 11,* 363–373.

Murphy, J. G., Vuchinich, R. E., & Simpson, C. A. (2001). Delayed reward and cost discounting. *Psychological Record, 51,* 571–588.

Myerson, J., & Green, L. (1995). Discounting of delayed rewards: Models of individual choice. *Journal of the Experimental Analysis of Behavior, 64,* 263–276.

Myerson, J., Green, L., & Warusawitharana, M. (2001). Area under the curve as a measure of discounting. *Journal of the Experimental Analysis of Behavior, 76,* 235–243.

Odum, A. L., Madden, G. J., & Bickel, W. K. (2002). Discounting of delayed health gains and losses in current, never-, and ex-smokers of cigarettes. *Nicotine and Tobacco Research, 4,* 295–303.

Ohmura, Y., Takahashi, T., Kitamura, N., & Wehr, P. (2006). Three month stability of delay and probability discounting measures. *Experimental and Clinical Psychopharmacology, 14,* 3198–329.

Patak, M., & Reynolds, B. (2007). Question-based assessments of delay discounting: Do respondents spontaneously incorporate uncertainty into their valuations for delayed rewards? *Addictive Behaviors, 32,* 351–357.

Patton, J. H., Stanford, M. S., & Barratt, E. S. (1995). Factor structure of the Barratt Impulsiveness Scale. *Journal of Clinical Psychology, 51,* 768–774.

Rachlin, H., Logue, A. W., Gibbon, J., & Frankel, M. (1986). Cognition and behavior in studies of choice. *Psychological Review, 93,* 33–45.

Rachlin, H., Raineri, A., & Cross, D. (1991). Subjective probability and delay. *Journal of the Experimental Analysis of Behavior, 55,* 233–244.

Reynolds, B., Richards, J. B., & de Wit, H. (2006). Acute-alcohol effects on the Experiential Discounting Task (EDT) and a question-based measure of delay discounting. *Pharmacology Biochemistry and Behavior, 83,* 194–202.

Reynolds, B., & Schiffbauer, R. (2004). Measuring state changes in human delay discounting: An experiential discounting task. *Behavioural Processes, 67,* 343–356.

Richards, J. B., Mitchell, S. H., de Wit, H., & Seiden, L. S. (1997). Determination of discount functions in rats with an adjusting-amount procedure. *Journal of the Experimental Analysis of Behavior, 67,* 353–366.

Richards, J. B., Zhang, L., Mitchell, S. H., & de Wit, H. (1999). Delay or probability discounting in a model of impulsive behavior: Effects of alcohol. *Journal of the Experimental Analysis of Behavior, 71,* 121–143.

Robbins, T. W. (2002). The 5-choice serial reaction time task: Behavioural pharmacology and functional neurochemistry. *Psychopharmacology (Berlin)*, *163*, 362–380.

Rodriguez, M. L., & Logue, A. W. (1988). Adjusting delay to reinforcement: Comparing choice in pigeons and humans. *Journal of Experimental Psychology: Animal Behavior Processes*, *14*, 105–117.

Rosati, A. G., Stevens, J. R., Hare, B., & Hauser, M. D. (2007). The evolutionary origins of human patience: Temporal preferences in chimpanzees, bonobos, and adult humans. *Current Biology*, *17*, 1663–1668.

Samuelson, P. A. (1937). A note on measurement of utility. *Review of Economic Studies*, *23*, 155–161.

Scheres, A., Dijkstra, M., Ainslie, E., Balkan, J., Reynolds, B., Sonuga-Barke, E., & Castellanos, F. X. (2006). Temporal and probability discounting of reward in children and adolescents: Effects of age and ADHD symptoms. *Neuropsychologia*, *44*, 2006–2103.

Schweitzer, J. B., & Sulzer-Azaroff, B. (1988). Self-control: Teaching tolerance for delay in impulsive children. *Journal of the Experimental Analysis of Behavior*, *50*, 173–186.

Simpson, C. A., & Vuchinich, R. E. (2000). Reliability of a measure of temporal discounting. *Psychological Record*, *62*, 43–55.

Thaler, R. H., & Benartzi, S. (2004). Save More Tomorrow™: Using behavioral economics to increase employee saving. *Journal of Political Economy*, *112*, 164–188.

Thiébot, M. H., Le Bihan, C., Soubrié, P., & Simon, P. (1985). Benzodiazepines reduce the tolerance to reward delay in rats. *Psychopharmacology (Berlin)*, *86*, 147–152.

Uslaner, J. M., & Robinson, T. E. (2006). Subthalamic nucleus lesions increase impulsive action and decrease impulsive choice—Mediation by enhanced incentive motivation? *European Journal of Neuroscience*, *24*, 2345–2354.

van Gaalen, M. M., van Koten, R., Schoffelmeer, A. N. M. & Vanderschuren, L. J. M. J. (2006). Critical involvement of dopaminergic neurotransmission in impulsive decision making. *Biological Psychiatry*, *60*, 66–73.

Wilson, M., & Daly, M. (1997). Life expectancy, economic inequality, homicide, and reproductive timing in Chicago neighborhoods. *British Medical Journal*, *314*, 1271–1278.

Winstanley, C. A., Baunez, C., Theobald, D. E., & Robbins, T. W. (2005). Lesions to the subthalamic nucleus decrease impulsive choice but impair autoshaping in rats: The importance of the basal ganglia in Pavlovian conditioning and impulse control. *European Journal of Neuroscience*, *21*, 3107–3116.

Woolverton, W. L., Myerson, J., & Green, L. (2007). Delay discounting of cocaine by rhesus monkeys. *Experimental and Clinical Psychopharmacology*, *15*, 238–233.

Yi, R., de la Piedad, X., & Bickel, W. K. (2006). The combined effects of delay and probability in discounting. *Behavioural Processes*, *73*, 149–155.

Yoon, J. H., Higgins, S. T., Heil, S. H., Sugarbaker, R. J., Thomas, C. S., & Badger, G. J. (2007). Delay discounting predicts postpartum relapse to cigarette smoking among pregnant women. *Experimental and Clinical Psychopharmacology*, *15*, 176–186.

2

DELAY DISCOUNTING: STATE AND TRAIT VARIABLE

AMY L. ODUM AND ANA A. L. BAUMANN

Psychology is concerned with the factors that determine behavior. From the beginning of the field, two broad influences on behavior have been seen as important: factors resulting in within-person variability (state variables) and factors resulting in between-person variability (trait variables), also known as *organismic* and *environmental* influences, respectively. In this chapter, we first offer definitions of state and trait variables and give some indication of their historical and modern position. We then review state and trait influences on delay discounting. We conclude with implications for applied and clinical interventions.

STATE AND TRAIT VARIABLES

State variables are generally regarded as important contributors to behavior. The status of trait variables, however, has been debated throughout the history of psychology.

Preparation of this chapter was supported by a grant from the Ronald E. McNair Foundation. We thank Scott Bates and Tim Shahan for interesting discussion on these topics.

State Variables

Experimental psychology, in which a condition is systematically changed to examine its influence on behavior, investigates the effects of state variables. Experimental psychologists are interested in the variability that they create via their manipulations. Specifically, they ask, "How can one study the impact of experimental manipulations on specific responses made in particular situations, thereby discovering the psychological processes underlying the occurrence of the behavior?" (Buss, 1989, p. 1378). Differences between people are not typically considered by experimental psychologists and contribute only to measurement error (e.g., Buss, 1989; Cronbach, 1957).

A variety of different manipulations may produce changes in states, which change across time. States have traditionally included psychological states (e.g., anxiety), physiological states (e.g., whether a drug is present), and situational variables (e.g., task features; see Hamaker, Nesselroade, & Molenaar, 2007; Nezlek, 2007). For our purposes, we define a *state variable* as an environmental manipulation affecting behavior over a relatively short time frame.

Trait Variables

Personality psychology, in which interest focuses on already existing differences between individuals, investigates the effects of trait variables. Specifically, a personality psychologist may ask, "How can one discover the consistencies in behavior that would allow one to infer traits, what is the relationship among those traits, what are their origins, and what are the consequences of these personality dispositions for behavior?" (Buss, 1989, p. 1379). The goal is to discover sources of variance in behavior resulting from personal characteristics. Situational influences (state variables) contribute only to measurement error in this case (Hamaker et al., 2007).

In contrast to states, traits are relatively constant across time. Traits are considered interindividual differences in proneness, tendency, style, or disposition to behave in different manners (e.g., Hamaker et al., 2007). The "Big Five" personality traits are neuroticism, extraversion, openness, agreeableness, and conscientiousness (e.g., McCrae & Costa, 1999). More broadly, variables such as intellectual ability, sex, race, psychiatric symptomatology, and biologically and culturally based measures may be included as traits because they can be modeled in the same way as more conventional traits (e.g., McCrae & Costa, 1995; Nezlek, 2007). For our purposes, we define a *trait variable* as a relatively stable preexisting individual characteristic that affects behavior.

Status of States and Traits

Historically, there seems to have been no debate about the influence of state variables in general. Although some manipulations may have no effect, experimental manipulations that do have an effect make clear the contribution of environmental influences on behavior. The status of traits, in contrast, has been questioned along at least three lines.

First, traits have been criticized within personality psychology as unimportant or weak contributors to behavior (e.g., Mischel, 1968; Pervin, 1994; see also Buss, 1989; Hamaker et al., 2007; Mischel & Shoda, 1995; Nezlek, 2007). This is an empirical criticism, and some adherents of trait theories have maintained that through improvements in theory, data collection, instrumentation, and analytic techniques, it has been addressed (e.g., Buss, 1989; McCrae & Costa, 1995). That is, they have maintained that traits have been shown to be important and strong contributors to behavior. For example, Roberts, Kuncel, Shiner, Caspi, and Goldberg (2007) recently analyzed the results of a number of prospective longitudinal studies to see the predictive utility of personality traits for important life outcomes (which arguably result at least in part from relatively long-term behavior patterns). Personality traits explained as much variance in mortality, divorce, and occupational attainment as did socioeconomic status and cognitive ability. Other psychologists have explicitly recognized that regardless of personality features, behavior varies across situations. They have proposed theoretical frameworks that maintain that in addition to the main effects of states and traits, behavior is influenced by the interaction between these (e.g., Endler, 1976; Steyer, Schmitt, & Eid, 1999).

Stability over time is inherent in the definition of a trait. Measures of personality may change over time, however, sometimes substantially (see Pervin, 1994). For example, Fleeson (2001) found that the level of intraindividual variability in a 2-week period was similar to the level of interindividual variability in the same time frame. In answer to the criticism that measures of personality are not stable, some authors have argued that strong test–retest correlations over time using a variety of measurements show remarkable consistency (e.g., McCrae et al., 2000). These correlations show that people tend to retain their rank order over time (Buss, 1989), even as their level of a trait changes as part of cross-cultural maturational processes. For example, from young adulthood to middle age, people tend to become less open to experience, yet more agreeable (Costa & McCrae, 2002; McCrae et al., 2000). Women tend to become more self-controlled and responsible with motherhood (Helson, Mitchell, & Moane, 1984). People also tend to have not only a stable rank order score on a given measure over time, but also a stable level of variability in their score (e.g., Fournier, Moskowitz, & Zuroff, 2008). Whether change or stability is found also depends on the measures used. Costa and McCrae (1994) argued that basic tendencies (the Big Five traits) may change less than how these tendencies are expressed in a person's current environment. Clearly, personality is variable across time, owing in part to maturational and situational influences. Individuals tend to maintain their rank order on trait measures over time, however, and to maintain stable levels of variability in the measures.

Finally, what is the causal status of traits? Are they merely behavior patterns, or are they something more? In other words, are traits descriptive concepts, or are they explanatory concepts (Pervin, 1994)? Skinner (e.g., 1953, 1974) maintained that personality is a repertoire of behavior developed in response to a particular set of environmental contingencies. In this view, traits do not cause behavior, they *are* behavior. This and similar views can be found within personality psychology (e.g., Buss, 1989; Buss & Craik, 1983; Pervin, 1994). For example, Buss and Craik (1983) maintained, "The statement 'Mary is arrogant' means that, over a period of observation, she has displayed a high frequency of arrogant acts, relative to a norm for that category of acts" (p. 106).

Many personality psychologists have assumed, however, that traits are not reducible to behavior. Instead, traits are seen as underlying tendencies that cause and explain consistent behavior patterns (e.g., McCrae & Costa, 1995). Indeed, some have suggested that current research methods allow for investigating the causal relation between behavior and traits (e.g., Nezlek, 2007). The broader issue will not be settled here. Our goal is instead to summarize the evidence for trait and state roles in delay discounting.

DELAY DISCOUNTING

Delay discounting refers to the decrease in the present value of consequences by delay to their receipt (e.g., Mazur, 1987; see Critchfield & Kollins, 2001, for review). Here we briefly mention procedures and analyses used in the study of delay discounting. The interested reader may refer to the first chapter of this volume for a more comprehensive coverage.

Procedures

Measuring delay discounting involves titrating one outcome in some way to gauge its value against another outcome. For example, in many studies of delay discounting with people, the value of a smaller but more immediate outcome is systematically increased and/or decreased as the value of a larger but more delayed outcome is held constant (e.g., Rachlin, Raineri, & Cross, 1991). The indifference point is the point at which a person switches from preferring the smaller–sooner to the larger–later outcome (when the value of the two outcomes is about equal). This point may also be thought of as the present value of the delayed outcome and in essence indicates how much the delayed option is worth now. Finding indifference points at a variety of delays allows determination of a discount function, showing how delay affects the present value of an outcome. There are a number of other ways to evaluate delay discounting and find indifference points with humans (see, e.g., Du, Green, & Myerson, 2002; Kirby & Marakovic, 1996; Reynolds & Schiffbauer, 2004; Richards, Zhang, Mitchell, & de Wit, 1999) and nonhumans (e.g., Mazur, 1987; Richards, Mitchell, de Wit, & Seiden, 1997).

Fortunately, research to date has indicated that different methods of determining the degree of delay discounting tend to yield similar estimates. A number of studies have informed this issue (e.g., Epstein et al., 2003; Green, Myerson, Shah, Estle, & Holt, 2007; Jaroni, Wright, Lerman, & Epstein, 2004; Johnson & Bickel, 2002; Kowal, Yi, Erisman, & Bickel, 2007; Lagorio & Madden, 2005; Lane, Cherek, Pietras, & Techeremissine, 2003; Madden, Begotka, Raiff, & Kastern, 2003; Madden et al., 2004; Robles & Vargas, 2007) with the general conclusion that differences in discounting resulting from procedural variants is small. What differences do exist between indifference points obtained with the various procedures would most likely affect attempts to estimate the magnitude of an effect across studies using different methodologies. Findings from a particular study are unlikely to be affected in most cases (but see Reynolds, Richards, & de Wit, 2006). Given these similarities, in the next section we describe results from studies using a variety of methods of determining the degree of delay discounting. First, however, we briefly outline the methods used to analyze data from experiments investigating delay discounting. For more detail, the interested reader may consult chapter 1 of this volume and reviews such as Critchfield and Kollins (2001) and Reynolds (2006b).

Analysis

Data from delay-discounting procedures can easily be summarized using the area-under-the-curve measure (Myerson, Green, & Warusawitharana, 2001). Another method of analyzing indifference points is to fit a particular model to the data using nonlinear regression (see, e.g., Mazur, 1987; Myerson & Green, 1995). The interested reader may refer to chapter 1 of this volume for details.

Regardless of how the indifference points are analyzed, their theoretical import is clear. Steeper discounting is interpreted as indicating more impulsivity, defined in the behavioral literature as choosing smaller–sooner over larger–later outcomes (e.g., Ainslie, 1974). People who show steep discounting are by implication more likely to make impulsive choices, choices that may be satisfying now but potentially detrimental in the long run.

Now that we have defined states, traits, and measurement and interpretation of delay discounting, we turn to findings in the literature relating the effects of state variables on delay discounting.

STATES AND DELAY DISCOUNTING

Researchers have examined the effects of a variety of environmental manipulations that produce relatively short-term changes in the degree of discounting for an outcome. Factors that have been investigated include the amount, type, and sign of an outcome as well as the context of the choice, concurrent demands on attention, drug administration, and deprivation.

Amount of Outcome

One of the well-investigated state effects on delay discounting is the amount of an outcome. Green, Myerson, and McFadden (1997), for example, examined discounting of delayed hypothetical outcomes of $100, $2,000, $25,000, and $100,000. The degree of discounting was inversely related to the magnitude of the outcome up to $25,000. After $25,000, the degree of discounting did not change. Other studies investigating monetary and non-monetary outcomes have corroborated this finding that smaller amounts are discounted more steeply than larger amounts (e.g., Estle, Green, Myerson, & Holt, 2006; Giordano et al., 2002; Kirby, 1997; Kirby & Maraković, 1996; Petry, 2001a; Raineri & Rachlin, 1993). This effect, however, has not been replicated with nonhumans despite several attempts (Grace, 1999; Green, Myerson, Holt, Slevin, & Estle, 2004; Ong & White, 2004; Richards et al., 1997). The role of procedural and other differences separating human and nonhuman studies of amount-dependent discounting has yet to be resolved.

Type of Outcome

The nature of the outcome is a robust contributor to the degree of delay discounting in humans. Early studies focused on discounting of drugs of abuse versus money. Madden, Petry, Badger, and Bickel (1997), for example, found that opioid-dependent outpatients discounted a delayed $1,000 worth of heroin to a greater extent than they did $1,000 in cash (both outcomes were hypothetical). Bickel, Odum, and Madden (1999) found a similar effect in cigarette smokers' discounting of delayed cigarettes and money. Other studies have replicated this finding with other drugs of abuse, including alcohol (Petry, 2001a) and cocaine (Coffey, Gudleski, Saladin, & Brady, 2003).

It is interesting that edible outcomes are also discounted more steeply than money (Charlton & Fantino, 2008; Estle, Green, Myerson, & Holt, 2007; Odum, Baumann, & Rimington, 2006; Odum & Rainaud, 2003). For example, Odum and Rainaud (2003) compared discounting of a hypothetical $100, $100 worth of food, and $100 worth of alcohol in a community sample of people without gambling, alcohol, or eating disorders. Food and alcohol were discounted more steeply than money, but no differently from each other. Similarly, Estle et al. (2007) found that hypothetical money was discounted less steeply than beer, soda, and candy. Odum et al. (2006) showed that the effect was found with small amounts of food ($10 worth) that could be consumed in one sitting, demonstrating it was not peculiar to relatively large amounts as tested previously.

These findings raise the possibility that drugs of abuse are more steeply discounted because they are consumable, like food, rather than because of some unique relation between the commodity and the participant's addiction. Recent findings reported by Odum and Baumann (2007a, 2007b), however, have shown that cigarette smokers discount hypothetical cigarettes more steeply than food, which they discount more steeply than money. This result suggests differences in the degree to which drugs of abuse are discounted over and above their status as consumable outcomes. More research is needed to determine why consumable outcomes are discounted so steeply and the contribution of addiction to this process for drugs of abuse.

Sign of Outcome

Whether a delayed outcome is gained or lost is another state variable affecting how steeply that outcome is discounted. For example, in separate conditions, Murphy, Vuchinich, and Simpson (2001) asked participants about gaining or losing $500 in the future; all outcomes were hypothetical. Discounting was steeper for gains versus losses, an effect commonly termed *gain–loss asymmetry*, or the *sign effect*. Other studies have reported similar results with humans (e.g., Baker, Johnson, & Bickel, 2003; Estle et al., 2006). This effect has yet to be studied with nonhumans, however.

Context of Choice

The context in which the delay-discounting assessment is conducted has also been shown to affect the degree of delay discounting. Dixon, Jacobs, and Sanders (2006) assessed discounting of hypothetical money in pathological gamblers in two settings: one associated with gambling (an off-track betting facility) and the other not associated with gambling (e.g., a coffee shop). Money was discounted more steeply in the gambling context than in the nongambling context. The same commodity (money) may also be discounted differently depending on the inflation rate (Kawashima, 2006; Ostaszewski, Green, & Myerson, 1998). It would be interesting to extend the analysis of contextual effects to other settings, populations, and outcomes.

Working Memory

The degree to which people are required to engage in multiple tasks may decrease the extent to which they can think about any one task (i.e., working memory available). Hinson, Jameson, and Whitney (2003) examined the effect of decreases in working memory on the degree of discounting for hypothetical money. College undergraduates engaged in a delay-discounting task while performing another concurrent task showed steeper discounting than in a control condition (for an alternative interpretation of these results, see Franco-Watkins, Pashler, & Rickard, 2006). Further empirical work will be necessary to fully understand the effects of working memory load on delay discounting. The implications are quite interesting, though, for modern, multitasking life: The busier people are, the more likely they may be to behave impulsively. Additionally, if working memory availability affects delay discounting, then people with memory impairments, such as from methamphetamine abuse (e.g., Hoffman et al., 2006), may be more likely to behave impulsively.

Drug Administration

Considerable attention has focused on the acute effects of drugs of abuse on the degree of delay discounting with sometimes contradictory and puzzling results (see chap. 8, this volume). For example, alcohol has been reported to increase, decrease, and have no effect on discounting (see, e.g., Ortner, MacDonald, & Olmstead, 2003; Poulos, Parker, & Lě, 1998; Reynolds et al., 2006; Richards, Zhang, et al., 1999). The acute effects of amphetamines on delay discounting vary across studies as well. Amphetamine has been reported to produce both a decrease (de Wit, Enggasser, & Richards, 2002; Helms, Reeves, & Mitchell, 2006; Winstanley, Dalley, Theobald, & Robbins, 2003) and an increase (e.g., Evenden & Ryan, 1996) in the degree of discounting. Cardinal, Robbins, and Everitt (2000) found both an increase and a decrease in choice of the immediate outcome with rats depending on the stimulus conditions during the delay. Clearly, more work is needed to fully understand these results.

A few studies have also examined the effects of acute administration of other drugs on delay discounting. The anxiolytic diazepam (Valium; e.g., Acheson, Reynolds, Richards, & de Wit, 2006) and Δ^9-tetrahydrocannabinol, the active component in marijuana (McDonald, Schleifer, Richards, & de Wit, 2003), have been found to have no effect on delay discounting for money in humans, but diazepam has increased discounting of delayed food in rats (e.g., Evenden & Ryan, 1996). Both acute morphine (Kieres et al., 2004) and nicotine (Dallery & Locey, 2005) appear to increase delay discounting in rats, but these findings have yet to be replicated. In summary, the acute effects of drugs on delay discounting have varied across studies, and more work is necessary to identify all of the controlling variables (procedure, species, etc.).

Deprivation

What would happen to delay discounting for a particular reinforcer if an organism were deprived of that reinforcer? Intuitively, perhaps, the degree of discounting should increase, but that result has not always been found. For example, Richards et al. (1997) found no effect of water deprivation on discounting by rats choosing between smaller–sooner and larger–later water reinforcers. With static choices between a smaller immediate edible outcome and a larger delayed edible outcome, deprivation has increased, decreased, and had no effect on impulsivity with humans and nonhumans (e.g., Bradshaw & Szabadi, 1992; Eisenberger & Masterson, 1987; Kirk & Logue, 1997; Logue, Chavarro, Rachlin, & Reeder, 1988; Logue & King, 1991; Snyderman, 1987).

Few studies have examined the effects of deprivation of a drug of abuse (withdrawal) on delay discounting, but the results are interesting. Giordano et al. (2002) found that opioid-dependent outpatients showed steeper discounting of hypothetical monetary and heroin outcomes when mildly opioid deprived (before their usual dose of buprenorphine) than when relatively opioid satiated (2 hours after their usual dose). With cigarette smokers, Field, Santarcangelo, Sumnall, Goudie, and Cole (2006) found that discounting for hypothetical cigarettes and for money was increased when participants had not smoked for at least 13 hours compared with when they had smoked just before the session (but see S. H. Mitchell, 2004a). These effects could be related to an aversive state produced by withdrawal; exposure to aversive stimuli can increase impulsivity (e.g., Flora, Wilkerson, & Flora, 2003). This will be an interesting area of investigation for future research.

TRAITS AND DELAY DISCOUNTING

Researchers have examined a variety of individual differences in the degree of discounting for an outcome. Factors that have been investigated include traditional personality traits; personal aspects like age, gender, and IQ; and the presence of psychiatric disorders and substance abuse.

Personality Measures

Relatively few studies to date have examined delay discounting in relation to traditional personality trait measures. Plunkett and Buehner (2007) determined the relation between delay discounting and economic locus of control, which measures the tendency for individuals to see financial outcomes as resulting from their own actions (internal economic locus of control) or from chance or the actions of powerful others (external economic locus of control). People with an internal economic locus of control discounted personal and business monetary outcomes less steeply than did people with an external economic locus of control. Ostaszewski (1996, 1997; see Ostaszewski & Green, 1995) has examined the effects of several other personality characteristics on delay discounting of monetary outcomes. People who are more extraverted tend to show steeper discounting of monetary outcomes than people who are more introverted. Unexpectedly, though, high sensation seeking is not related to steeper discounting.

A number of studies have examined the relation between delay discounting and impulsivity as measured by self-report personality questionnaires. In a recent review of this literature, de Wit, Flory, Acheson, McCloskey, and Manuck (2007) reported that scores on personality (self-report) measures of impulsivity are sometimes positively correlated with the degree of delay discounting, but sometimes no relation is found. They noted that previous attempts to find a relation between personality measures of impulsivity and discounting have used relatively small, homogeneous samples, which could underlie the inconsistent relations. In their larger, more heterogeneous sample, scores on the Nonplanning Impulsiveness and Cognitive Impulsiveness subscales of the Barratt Impulsiveness Scale (Barratt, 1985) were positively correlated with the degree of delay discounting for monetary outcomes. In other cases, authors have noted that impulsivity is a multidimensional construct, and as such, different measures of impulsivity may not necessarily be related (e.g., Acheson et al., 2006; Winstanley, Eagle, & Robbins, 2006).

Personal Characteristics: Age, Gender, IQ, and Race–Culture

A few studies have also investigated the relation between personal characteristics such as age, gender, IQ, race, and culture and delay discounting. Age is generally inversely related to delay discounting: Younger participants show steeper discounting of monetary outcomes than older ones (but see Reynolds, 2004). For example, Green, Fry, and Myerson (1994) found that children discounted delayed hypothetical monetary outcomes most steeply, followed by young adults and then older adults. Similarly, younger adolescents discounted money more steeply than older adolescents (Olson, Hooper, Collins, & Luciana, 2007). This basic pattern has also held in other studies (e.g., Green, Myerson, Lichtman, Rosen, & Fry, 1996; Scheres et al., 2006; Yoon, Higgins, Sugarbaker, Thomas, & Badger, 2007).

Gender is not consistently related to the degree of delay discounting. Although some studies have found that men tend to discount hypothetical money more steeply than do women (e.g., Petry, Kirby, & Kranzler, 2002), most studies have found no relation between sex and discounting (e.g., J. M. Mitchell, Fields, D'Esposito, & Boettiger, 2005). These include a study with a large community sample of adult humans (de Wit et al., 2007) as well as a study with male and female rats (Perry, Nelson, Anderson, Morgan, &

Carroll, 2007). Thus, overall, sex is not a powerful contributor to the degree of delay discounting.

Scores on IQ tests are related to delay discounting. A study by de Wit et al. (2007) found that IQ, as measured by the Wechsler Abbreviated Scale of Intelligence (Wechsler, 1999), was inversely related to delay discounting of monetary outcomes. That is, higher intelligence was associated with less discounting, even when statistically controlling for other factors that were related to the degree of discounting. Olson et al. (2007) also found in an adolescent sample that Wechsler Abbreviated Scale of Intelligence scores were inversely related to the steepness of discounting. In a recent meta-analysis of more than 20 studies, Shamosh and Gray (2008) confirmed that IQ and delay discounting were negatively correlated.

Race and cultural background may also be considered traits because these are largely stable personal characteristics. Two studies have reported differences in delay discounting as a function of these variables. Du et al. (2002) examined delay discounting for money among Japanese, Chinese, and American graduate students at an American university and found that the American and Chinese students discounted money to a similar degree and more steeply than did the Japanese students. In the other study, de Wit et al. (2007) reported that adult Caucasians from a community sample discounted money less steeply than did African Americans.

Socioeconomic Characteristics: Income and Education

Income and educational level are also related to delay discounting. Green et al. (1996) found that higher income individuals (who earned more than about $40,000 per year) discounted money less steeply than did participants with lower incomes (less than about $10,000 per year). In addition, de Wit et al. (2007) found that delay discounting was inversely related to income in a large community sample.

Delay discounting is also related to educational level and academic achievement (but see Alessi & Petry, 2003). In a large community sample of middle-aged adults, the degree of discounting was negatively correlated with years of education (de Wit et al., 2007). The results of other studies are similar (e.g., Jaroni et al., 2004; Yoon et al., 2007). Academic performance in college, as measured by overall grade point average (Kirby, Winston, & Santiesteban, 2005) as well as grades in a specific course (Silva & Gross, 2004), is also negatively correlated with the degree of discounting for money.

One important implication of differences in discounting as a function of age, income, and educational level is that for participants who differ along these dimensions, the effects of any other variable of interest must be viewed cautiously (see also Bickel & Yi, 2006). Such is the case with differences in discounting as a function of IQ and race, for example, which may frequently be related to income and educational level. Correlations in any of these cases cannot be interpreted as causal relations.

Psychiatric Disorders

People have also been found to differ in the degree to which they discount delayed outcomes on the basis of psychiatric conditions such as personality and mood disorders and attention-deficit/hyperactivity disorder (ADHD). For example, Crean, de Wit, and Richards (2000) classified psychiatric outpatients as having either a high-risk impulse control disorder (substance abuse, borderline personality disorder, bipolar disorder) or low-risk impulse control disorder (mood disorders, anxiety). High-risk patients discounted monetary outcomes more steeply than did low-risk patients. Steeper discounting has also been found with people with antisocial personality disorder (Petry, 2002), schizophrenia (Heerey, Robinson, McMahon, & Gold, 2007), and a history of depressive symptomatology (Yoon et al., 2007) as compared with participants without these problems.

The relation between delay discounting and ADHD is more complex (see chap. 12, this volume, and Winstanley et al., 2006, for reviews). In choices between a smaller–sooner and a larger–later outcome, children with ADHD prefer the immediate option more than do children without ADHD (e.g., Schweitzer & Sulzer-Azaroff, 1995; Sonuga-Barke, Taylor, Sembi, & Smith, 1992). Some authors, however, have suggested that the primary controlling variable is delay aversion rather than impulsivity per se (e.g., Sonuga-Barke, Houlberg, & Hall, 1994). With delay discounting, some studies have reported that people with ADHD discount money more steeply (Barkley, Edwards, Laneri, Fletcher, & Metevia, 2001), but others have found no difference (Scheres et al., 2006). More research is needed to fully understand the processes involved here.

Pornography Consumption

Recently, Lawyer (2008) examined discounting for delayed hypothetical money in people who report viewing sexually explicit videos (pornography consumers) and people who do not. Pornography consumers discounted money more steeply than did nonconsumers. This finding is the first of its kind and so must be viewed with caution, but it could prove to be another possible trait variable (affinity for pornography) related to discounting.

Pathological Gambling

Steep discounting is also related to pathological gambling (see chap. 10, this volume). People with problems with gambling show steeper discounting of hypothetical money than do people without gambling problems (e.g., Dixon, Marley, & Jacobs, 2003; Petry, 2001b; Petry & Casarella, 1999). Furthermore, the degree of discounting is related to gambling severity (Alessi & Petry, 2003). Certainly, steep discounting is consistent with the pattern of behavior shown by people with problematic gambling.

Drug Addiction

The most widely investigated trait variable studied to date in the delay-discounting literature is drug abuse status. The classification here of addiction as a trait, as opposed to a state, variable is not without controversy (e.g., Bickel & Yi, 2006; Petry, 2006). Drug abuse tends to be an enduring behavior pattern (see, e.g., Kalivas & Volkow, 2005), so it may be considered a trait according to the definition we have given. We do not mean to suggest that we know the direction of causality between addiction and discounting—indeed, that question has yet to be answered, and the answer will be complex when it is found (see, e.g., S. H. Mitchell, 2004b, and chaps. 7 and 9 of this volume).

Across a variety of drug classes, though, people with drug addiction discount money more steeply than do people who are not addicted. For example, Madden et al. (1997) compared discounting of hypothetical monetary outcomes in people with opioid dependence and in matched control participants. The opioid-dependent outpatients discounted more steeply than the control participants. Further studies have confirmed that opioid-dependent people show steeper discounting of money than people without this addiction (e.g., Kirby & Petry, 2004). Madden et al.'s finding showing that delayed outcomes may have little value for people with drug abuse problems opened an entire area of investigation into drug addiction and delay discounting. The 10 years since the publication of this article have seen a large increase in the number of articles devoted to the topic.

Cigarette smokers also show sharp discounting of monetary outcomes (e.g., Bickel et al., 1999; S. H. Mitchell, 1999). Bickel et al. (1999) showed that adult cigarette smokers discounted hypothetical money more steeply than did matched nonsmokers. A variety of studies have investigated delay discounting in smokers and nonsmokers and confirmed this finding (e.g., Johnson, Bickel, & Baker, 2007; Ohmura, Takahashi, & Kitamura, 2005; Reynolds, 2006a; Reynolds et al., 2007).

Steep discounting of monetary outcomes by people with drug addiction has also been found for other classes of drugs. People with alcohol addiction show greater loss in value of money with delay than do people without alcohol addiction (e.g., Bjork, Hommer, Grant, & Danube, 2004; J. M. Mitchell et al., 2005; Petry, 2001a). For example, Petry (2001a) found that active alcoholics discounted hypothetical money more steeply than did abstinent alcoholics, who discounted money more steeply than did control participants with similar demographic characteristics but no drug addiction. Heavy drinkers also discount money more steeply than lighter drinkers (e.g., Field, Christiansen, Cole, & Goudie, 2007; Vuchinich & Simpson, 1998).

Although relatively fewer data exist regarding discounting by people with psychomotor stimulant addiction, delayed outcomes also appear to have little value for people with this problem. For example, Coffey et al. (2003) compared discounting of hypothetical monetary outcomes in people dependent on crack cocaine and control participants who were matched in terms of gender, age, IQ, and income. Crack-dependent participants discounted the money more steeply than did control participants. Other studies have found similar results (Heil, Johnson, Higgins, & Bickel, 2006; Kirby & Petry, 2004). Individuals with problems with methamphetamine abuse also discount money more steeply than do control participants (Hoffman et al., 2006; Monterosso, Ainslie, Cordova, Domier, & London, 2007).

Differences may be found in the degree of delay discounting between different subgroups of people with drug addiction as well. In one such study, Odum, Madden, Badger, and Bickel (2000) asked opioid-dependent outpatients whether they would share a needle with a friend to inject heroin. Needle sharing transmits blood-borne diseases, including HIV, the virus that causes AIDS. Participants who agreed to share a needle with a friend in the scenario discounted money more steeply than those who did not. Differences exist between discounting among users of different drug classes as well. People whose primary drug of abuse was crack cocaine showed sharper discounting of hypothetical monetary outcomes than did people whose primary drug of abuse was heroin (Bornovalova, Daughters, Hernandez, Richards, & Lejuez, 2005).

Does drug abuse cause steep discounting of delayed outcomes, or does steep discounting of delayed outcomes render people vulnerable to drug addiction? Alternatively, does some third factor cause steep discounting and drug abuse? These questions have yet to be answered. A few studies have informed the issue, however (see chaps. 7 and 9 of this volume and S. H. Mitchell, 2004b, for a review with cigarette smoking). Bickel et al. (1999) showed that ex-smokers of cigarettes discounted money no differently than did non-smokers. They suggested that this finding indicated that either the degree of discounting goes down after abstinence is achieved or people who are more likely to achieve abstinence discount less steeply. The distribution of the measure of discounting (see Mazur, 1987, and chap. 1 of this volume) for smokers showed the latter may be more likely: There was a cluster of smokers with a very high degree of discounting who may be those who are unlikely to be able to quit. Yoon et al. (2007) found that in women who had quit smoking during pregnancy, those with a higher degree of discounting were more likely to have relapsed to smoking by 6 months postpartum. Furthermore,

Dallery and Raiff (2007) found that smokers who were unable to maintain abstinence during a laboratory session in which they could earn money for abstinence discounted money more steeply than did smokers who were able to maintain abstinence. Finally, Audrain-McGovern et al. (2004) followed high school students from 9th to 12th grade and found that a higher degree of delay discounting was related to smoking progression (e.g., from sampling cigarettes to regular smoking). Together, these data suggest that people who discount more sharply may be more likely to initiate smoking and subsequently be unable to quit smoking.

There are limited data for other drugs of abuse on the causal relation between addiction and discounting. Perry, Larson, German, Madden, and Carroll (2005) found that rats classified as highly impulsive for food acquired intravenous cocaine self-administration at a faster rate and to a greater extent than did rats classified as less impulsive, showing that steeper discounting is related to greater propensity to take cocaine. Similarly, J. M. Mitchell, Reeves, Li, and Phillips (2006) found that mice that showed steeper discounting for delayed sucrose solution were more likely to show increased behavioral stimulation (locomotor activity) in response to ethanol, an effect that is predictive of alcohol intake.

Other data have suggested, however, that ingestion of drugs of abuse may cause steep discounting. In a cross-sectional study, Reynolds (2004) found that adolescent cigarette smokers discounted money less steeply than did young adult smokers. Given that discounting in nonsmokers generally decreases rather than increases with age (Green et al., 1994), this finding suggests that discounting may increase with cigarette exposure. Alternatively, adolescents who do not discount steeply may quit smoking by the time they are young adults. With rats, Dallery and Locey (2005) found that acute and chronic nicotine administration resulted in greater discounting for food pellets. The increase in discounting gradually diminished when chronic nicotine was discontinued. Similarly, acute morphine administration increases the degree of discounting for water in rats (Kieres et al., 2004). Both prior cocaine (Simon, Mendez, & Setlow, 2007) and methamphetamine (Richards, Sabol, & de Wit, 1999) exposure increase the degree of discounting in rats. These studies have shown that in some cases, acute and repeated exposure to a variety of drugs may increase discounting by delay.

Neural Correlates

Recent research has focused on neural correlates of delay discounting with orderly and intriguing results. In McClure, Laibson, Loewenstein, and Cohen (2004), people made choices between smaller–sooner and larger–later amounts of money while their brains were scanned using functional MRI. Areas in the limbic region of the brain (the ventral striatum, medial orbitofrontal cortex, and medial prefrontal cortex) were most active when a smaller–sooner amount was chosen. This finding has been extended to primary reinforcers (fruit juice and water; McClure, Ericson, Laibson, Loewenstein, & Cohen, 2007). Furthermore, the magnitude of activity in the ventral striatum is positively correlated with degree of discounting (Hariri et al., 2006). People with addiction are known to have exaggerated activity in the regions activated by immediate outcomes (see, e.g., Kalivas & Volkow, 2005), so these findings dovetail with the data on drug abuse and will surely be developed further.

Genetic Correlates

One of the newer areas of research concerns the relation between genetics and the degree of discounting by delay. For example, Isles, Humby, Walters, and Wilkinson (2004) examined discounting of delayed sweetened condensed milk in inbred mice. Individual mice in the different strains are isogenic, so variability within a strain represents environmental contributions, and variability across strains represents genetic contributions. There were significant differences across strains, leading to an estimate of the heritability of delay discounting of about 16%. Differences in choice of delayed reinforcers have also been found across rat strains (Anderson & Woolverton, 2005; Madden, Smith, Brewer, Pinkston, & Johnson, 2008). Eisenberg et al. (2007) examined the relation between dopaminergic genetic polymorphisms and discounting of delayed hypothetical money. For the *DRD2 TaqI* A locus, for example, people were classified as having at least one copy of the A1 allele (A1+) or not (A1–). People with the allele (A1+) discounted more steeply than those without (A1–). There was also an interaction with this genetic polymorphism and another. More data regarding the role of genetics on discounting are needed to fully understand these results, but there is sure to be an increasing number of studies devoted to this topic.

CONCLUSIONS AND IMPLICATIONS

Delay discounting is a burgeoning area of research, with orderly effects of many different state and trait variables. The amount of an outcome, the type of an outcome, the context in which it is evaluated, and how many other things a person is doing at the time of the evaluation are a few of the factors that may affect how rapidly the outcome loses value with delay. Personal factors such as age, race, IQ, socioeconomic status, and drug addiction may also contribute. Finally, the degree of discounting is related to activation in the limbic region of the brain and appears to be heritable.

The findings summarized in this chapter have important implications in applied and clinical situations. For example, if some outcomes are discounted more steeply than others (e.g., Odum & Rainaud, 2003), then some reinforcers may generate more impulsivity than others. In other words, people may be able to wait more successfully for some types of outcomes, and these therefore would be more useful in promoting self-control where it would be beneficial. Furthermore, data showing that people differ in their degree of discounting (e.g., Madden et al., 1997) point to the importance of making treatment immediately available when sought, as well as providing relatively immediate consequences for target behaviors when such behavior occurs. People who need treatment for drug abuse, for example, are not likely to be able to wait for delayed benefits that result from drug abstinence and may need immediate outcomes to bridge the delay. The success of contingency management treatment for drug abuse (see, e.g., Stitzer & Vandrey, 2008) may result in part from the focus on frequent reinforcers for drug abstinence.

Finally, discounting may prove to be a useful diagnostic tool and treatment target itself. People may respond better to therapies that are in tune with their degree of sensitivity to delayed consequences. For a person whose behavior is sensitive to delayed consequences, a therapeutic strategy focusing on immediate gains may be off-putting. For someone whose behavior is not sensitive to delayed outcomes, however, a strategy focusing on immediate gains may be critical for success. Discounting may also prove a useful target for therapy. A few studies have shown that with gradual changes in delays to larger–later outcomes, both humans and nonhumans may come to choose the delayed outcome more frequently (e.g., Mazur & Logue, 1978; Schweitzer & Sulzer-Azaroff, 1988). If people are taught to value delayed consequences in a therapeutic setting, this learning could potentially generalize to the many real-world situations involving choices between smaller, more immediate gains and larger, yet more delayed ones.

REFERENCES

Acheson, A., Reynolds, B., Richards, J. B., & de Wit, H. (2006). Diazepam impairs behavioral inhibition but not delay discounting or risk taking in healthy adults. *Experimental and Clinical Psychopharmacology, 14*, 190–198.

Ainslie, G. (1974). Impulse control in pigeons. *Journal of the Experimental Analysis of Behavior, 21*, 485–489.

Alessi, S. M., & Petry, N. N. (2003). Pathological gambling severity is associated with impulsivity in a delay discounting procedure. *Behavioural Processes, 64*, 345–354.

Anderson, K. G., & Woolverton, W. L. (2005). Effects of clomipramine on self-control choice in Lewis and Fischer 344 rats. *Pharmacology Biochemistry and Behavior, 80*, 387–393.

Audrain-McGovern, J., Rodriguez, D., Tercyak, K. P., Epstein, L. H., Goldman, P., & Wileyto, E. P. (2004). Applying a behavioral economic framework to understanding adolescent smoking. *Psychology of Addictive Behaviors, 18,* 64–73.

Baker, F., Johnson, M. W., & Bickel, W. K. (2003). Delay discounting in current and never-before cigarette smokers: Similarities and differences across commodity, sign, and magnitude. *Journal of Abnormal Psychology, 112,* 382–392.

Barkley, R. A., Edwards, G., Laneri, M., Fletcher, K., & Metevia, L. (2001). Executive functioning, temporal discounting, and sense of time in adolescents with attention deficit hyperactivity disorder (ADHD) and oppositional defiant disorder (ODD). *Journal of Abnormal Child Psychology, 29,* 541–556.

Barratt, E. S. (1985). Impulsiveness subtraits: Arousal and information processing. In J. T. Spence & C. E. Izard (Eds.), *Motivation, emotion and personality* (pp. 137–146). Amsterdam: Elsevier.

Bickel, W. K., Odum, A. L., & Madden, G. J. (1999). Impulsivity and cigarette smoking: Delay discounting in current, never, and ex-smokers. *Psychopharmacology (Berlin), 146,* 447–454.

Bickel, W. K., & Yi, R. (2006). What came first? Comment on Dom et al. (2006). *Addiction, 101,* 291–292.

Bjork, J. M., Hommer, D. W., Grant, S. J., & Danube, C. (2004). Impulsivity in abstinent alcohol-dependent patients: Relation to control subjects and type 1-/type 2-like traits. *Alcohol, 34,* 133–150.

Bornovalova, M. A., Daughters, S. B., Hernandez, G. D., Richards, J. B., & Lejuez, C. W. (2005). Differences in impulsivity and risk-taking propensity between primary users of crack cocaine and primary users of heroin in a residential substance-use program. *Experimental and Clinical Psychopharmacology, 13,* 311–318.

Bradshaw, C. M., & Szabadi, E. (1992). Choice between delayed reinforcers in a discrete-trials schedule: The effect of deprivation level. *Quarterly Journal of Experimental Psychology: Journal of Comparative and Physiological Psychology, 44*(B), 1–16.

Buss, A. H. (1989). Personality as traits. *American Psychologist, 44,* 1378–1388.

Buss, D. M., & Craik, K. H. (1983). The act frequency approach to personality. *Psychological Review, 90,* 105–126.

Cardinal, R. N., Robbins, T. W., & Everitt, B. J. (2000). The effects of d-amphetamine, chlordiazepoxide, α-flupenthixol and behavioural manipulations on choice of signaled and unsignalled delayed reinforcement in rats. *Psychopharmacology (Berlin), 152,* 362–375.

Charlton, S. R., & Fantino, E. (2008). Commodity specific rates of temporal discounting: Does metabolic function underlie differences in rates of discounting? *Behavioural Processes, 77,* 334–342.

Coffey, S. F., Gudleski, G. D., Saladin, M. E., & Brady, K. T. (2003). Impulsivity and rapid discounting of delayed hypothetical rewards in cocaine-dependent individuals. *Experimental and Clinical Psychopharmacology, 11,* 18–25.

Costa, P. T., Jr., & McCrae, R. R. (1994). Set like plaster? Evidence for the stability of adult personality. In T. F. Heatherton & J. L. Weinberger (Eds.), *Can personality change?* (pp. 21–40). Washington, DC: American Psychological Association.

Costa, P. T., Jr., & McCrae, R. R. (2002). Looking backward: Changes in the mean levels of personality traits from 80 to 12. In D. Cervone & W. Mischel (Eds.), *Advances in personality science* (pp. 219–240). New York: Guilford Press.

Crean, J., de Wit, H., & Richards, J. B. (2000). Reward discounting as a measure of impulsive behavior in a psychiatric outpatient population. *Experimental and Clinical Psychopharmacology, 8,* 155–162.

Critchfield, T. S. & Kollins, S. H. (2001). Temporal discounting: Basic research and the analysis of socially important behavior. *Journal of Applied Behavior Analysis, 34,* 101–122.

Cronbach, L. J. (1957). The two disciplines of scientific psychology. *American Psychologist, 12,* 671–684.

Dallery, J., & Locey, M. L. (2005). Effects of acute and chronic nicotine on impulsive choice in rats. *Behavioural Pharmacology, 16,* 15–23.

Dallery, J., & Raiff, B. R. (2007). Delay discounting predicts cigarette smoking in a laboratory model of abstinence reinforcement. *Psychopharmacology (Berlin), 190,* 485–496.

de Wit, H., Enggasser, J. L., & Richards, J. B. (2002). Acute administration of *d*-amphetamine decreases impulsivity in healthy volunteers. *Neuropsychopharmacology, 27,* 813–825.

de Wit, H., Flory, J. D., Acheson, A., McCloskey, M., & Manuck, S. B. (2007). IQ and nonplanning impulsivity are independently associated with delay discounting in middle-aged adults. *Personality and Individual Differences, 42,* 111–121.

Dixon, M. R., Jacobs, E. A., & Sanders, S. (2006). Contextual control of delayed discounting by pathological gamblers. *Journal of Applied Behavior Analysis, 39,* 413–422.

Dixon, M. R., Marley, J., & Jacobs, E. A. (2003). Delay discounting by pathological gamblers. *Journal of Applied Behavior Analysis, 36,* 449–458.

Du, W., Green, L., & Myerson, J. (2002). Cross-cultural comparisons of discounting delayed and probabilistic rewards. *Psychological Record, 54,* 479–492.

Eisenberg, D. T. A., MacKillop, J., Modi, M., Beauchemin, J., Dang, D., Lisman, S. A., et al. (2007). Examining impulsivity as an endophenotype using a behavioral approach: A *DRD2 TaqI A* and *DRD4 48-bp VNTR* association study. *Behavioral and Brain Functions, 3,* 2.

Eisenberger, R., & Masterson, F. A. (1987). Effects of prior learning and current motivation on self-control. In M. L. Commons, J. E. Mazur, J. A. Nevin, & H. Rachlin (Eds.), *Quantitative analyses of behavior: Volume 5. The effect of delay and of intervening events on reinforcement value* (pp. 267–282). Hillsdale, NJ: Erlbaum.

Endler, N. S. (1976). The case for person-situation interactions. In N. S. Endler & D. Magnusson (Eds.), *Interactional psychology and personality* (pp. 58–70). New York: Wiley.

Epstein, L. H., Richards, J. B., Saad, F. G., Paluch, R. A., Roemmich, J. N., & Lerman, C. (2003). Comparison between two measures of delay discounting in smokers. *Experimental and Clinical Psychopharmacology, 11*,131–138.

Estle, S. J., Green, L., Myerson, J., & Holt, D. D. (2006). Differential effects of amount on temporal and probability discounting of gains and losses. *Memory & Cognition, 34*, 914–928.

Estle, S. J., Green, L., Myerson, J., & Holt, D. D. (2007). Discounting of monetary and directly consumable rewards. *Psychological Science, 18*, 58–63.

Evenden, J. L., & Ryan, C. N. (1996). The pharmacology of impulsive behavior in rats: The effects of drugs on response choice with varying delays of reinforcement. *Psychopharmacology (Berlin), 128*, 161–170.

Field, M., Christiansen, P., Cole, J., & Goudie, A. (2007). Delay discounting and the alcohol Stroop in heavy drinking adolescents. *Addiction, 102*, 579–586.

Field, M., Santarcangelo, M., Sumnall, H., Goudie, A., & Cole, J. (2006). Delay discounting and the behavioural economics of cigarette purchases in smokers: The effects of nicotine deprivation. *Psychopharmacology (Berlin), 186*, 255–263.

Fleeson, W. (2001). Towards a structure- and process-integrated view of personality: Traits as density distributions of states. *Journal of Personality and Social Psychology, 80*, 1011–1027.

Flora, S. R., Wilkerson, L. R., & Flora, D. B. (2003). Effects of cold pressor pain on human self-control for positive reinforcement. *Psychological Record, 53*, 243–252.

Fournier, M. A., Moskowitz, D. S., & Zuroff, D. C. (2008). Integrating dispositions, signatures, and the interpersonal domain. *Journal of Personality and Social Psychology, 94*, 531–545.

Franco-Watkins, A., Pashler, H., & Rickard, T. C. (2006). Does working memory load lead to greater impulsivity? Commentary on Hinson, Jameson, and Whitney (2003). *Journal of Experimental Psychology: Learning, Memory, and Cognition, 32*, 443–447.

Giordano, L. A., Bickel, W. K., Loewenstein, G., Jacobs, E. A., Marsch, L., & Badger, G. J. (2002). Mild opioid deprivation increases the degree that opioid-dependent outpatients discount delayed heroin and money. *Psychopharmacology (Berlin), 163*, 174–182.

Grace, R. C. (1999). The matching law and amount-dependent exponential discounting as accounts of self-control choice. *Journal of the Experimental Analysis of Behavior, 71*, 27–44.

Green, L., Fry, A. F., & Myerson, J. (1994). Discounting of delayed rewards: A life-span comparison. *Psychological Science, 5*, 33–36.

Green, L., Myerson, J., Holt, D. D., Slevin, J. R., & Estle, S. (2004). Discounting of delayed food rewards in pigeons and rats: Is there a magnitude effect? *Journal of Experimental Analysis of Behavior, 81*, 39–50.

Green, L., Myerson, J., Lichtman, D., Rosen, S., & Fry, A. (1996). Temporal discounting in choice between delayed rewards: The role of age and income. *Psychology and Aging, 11*, 79–84.

Green, L., Myerson, J., & McFadden, E. (1997). Rate of temporal discounting decreases with amount of reward. *Memory & Cognition, 25,* 715–723.

Green, L., Myerson, J., Shah, A. K., Estle, S. J. & Holt, D. D. (2007). Do adjusting-amount and adjusting-delay procedures produce equivalent estimates of subjective value in pigeons? *Journal of the Experimental Analysis of Behavior, 87,* 337–347.

Hamaker, E. L., Nesselroade, J. R., & Molenaar, P. C. M. (2007). The integrated state-trait model. *Journal of Research in Personality, 41,* 295–315.

Hariri, A. R., Brown, S. M., Williamson, D. E., Flory, J. D., de Wit, H., & Manuck, S. B. (2006). Preference for immediate over delayed reward is associated with magnitude of ventral striatal activity. *Journal of Neuroscience, 26,* 13213–13217.

Heerey, E. A., Robinson, B. M., McMahon, R. P., & Gold, J. M. (2007). Delay discounting in schizophrenia. *Cognitive Neuropsychiatry, 12,* 213–221.

Heil, S. H., Johnson, M. W., Higgins, S. T., & Bickel, W. K. (2006). Delay discounting in currently using and currently abstinent cocaine-dependent outpatient and non-drug-using matched controls. *Addictive Behaviors, 31,* 1290–1294.

Helms, C. M., Reeves, J. M., & Mitchell, S. H. (2006). Impact of strain and d-amphetamine on impulsivity (delay discounting) in inbred mice. *Psychopharmacology (Berlin), 188,* 144–151.

Helson, R., Mitchell, V., & Moane, G. (1984). Personality and patterns of adherence and nonadherence to the social clock. *Journal of Personality and Social Psychology, 46,* 1079–1096.

Hinson, J. M., Jameson, T. L., & Whitney, P. (2003). Impulsive decision making and working memory. *Journal of Experimental Psychology: Learning, Memory, and Cognition, 29,* 298–306.

Hoffman, W. F., Moore, M., Templin, R., McFarland, B., Hitzemann, R. J., & Mitchell, S. H. (2006). Neuropsychological function and delay discounting in methamphetamine-dependent individuals. *Psychopharmacology (Berlin), 188,* 162–170.

Isles, A. R., Humby, T., Walters, E., & Wilkinson, L. S. (2004). Common genetic effects on variation in impulsivity and activity in mice. *Journal of Neuroscience, 24,* 6733–6740.

Jaroni, J. L., Wright, S. M., Lerman, C., & Epstein, L. H. (2004). Relationship between education and delay discounting in smokers. *Addictive Behaviors, 29,* 1171–1175.

Johnson, M. W., & Bickel, W. K. (2002). Within-subject comparison of real and hypothetical money rewards in delay discounting. *Journal of the Experimental Analysis of Behavior, 77,* 129–146.

Johnson, M. W., Bickel, W. K., & Baker, F. (2007). Moderate use and delay discounting: A comparison of heavy, light, and never smokers. *Experimental and Clinical Psychopharmacology (Berlin), 15,* 187–194.

Kalivas, P. W., & Volkow, N. D. (2005). The neural basis of addiction: A pathology of motivation and choice. *American Journal of Psychiatry, 162,* 1403–1413.

Kawashima, K. (2006). The effects of inflation and interest rates on delay discounting in human behavior. *Psychological Record, 56*, 551–569.

Kieres, A. K., Hausknecht, K. A., Farrar, A. M., Acheson, A., de Wit, H., & Richards, J. B. (2004). Effects of morphine and naltrexone on impulsive decision making in rats. *Psychopharmacology (Berlin), 173*, 167–174.

Kirby, K. N. (1997). Bidding on the future: Evidence against normative discounting of delayed rewards. *Journal of Experimental Psychology: General, 126*, 54–70.

Kirby, K. N., & Maraković, N. N. (1996). Delay-discounting probabilistic rewards: Rates decrease as amounts increase. *Psychonomic Bulletin & Review, 3*, 100–104.

Kirby, K. N., & Petry, N. M. (2004). Heroin and cocaine abusers have higher discount rates for delayed rewards than alcoholics or non-drug-using controls. *Addiction, 99*, 461–471.

Kirby, K. N., Winston, G. C., & Santiesteban, M. (2005). Impatience and grades: Delay-discount rates correlate negatively with college GPA. *Learning and Individual Differences, 15*, 213–222.

Kirk, J. M., & Logue, A. W. (1997). Effects of deprivation level on humans' self-control for food reinforcers. *Appetite, 28*, 215–226.

Kowal, B. P., Yi, R., Erisman, A. C., & Bickel, W. K. (2007). A comparison of two algorithms in computerized temporal discounting procedures. *Behavioural Processes, 75*, 231–236.

Lagorio, C. H., & Madden, G. J. (2005). Delay discounting of real and hypothetical rewards III: Steady-state assessments, forced-choice trials, and all real rewards. *Behavioural Processes, 69*, 173–187.

Lane, S., Cherek, D. R., Pietras, C. J., & Techeremissine, O. V. (2003). Measurement of delay discounting using trial-by-trial consequences. *Behavioural Processes, 64*, 287–303.

Lawyer, S. R. (2008). Probability and delay discounting of erotic stimuli. *Behavioural Processes, 79*, 36–42.

Logue, A. W., Chavarro, A., Rachlin, H., & Reeder, R. W. (1988). Impulsiveness in pigeons living in the experimental chamber. *Learning & Behavior, 16*, 31–39.

Logue, A. W., & King, G. R. (1991). Self-control and impulsiveness in adult humans when food is the reinforcer. *Appetite, 17*, 105–120.

Madden, G. J., Begotka, A. M., Raiff, B. R., & Kastern, L. L. (2003). Delay discounting of real and hypothetical rewards. *Experimental and Clinical Psychopharmacology, 11*, 139–145.

Madden, G. J., Petry, N. M., Badger, G. J., & Bickel, W. K. (1997). Impulsive and self-control choices in opioid-dependent patients and non-drug-using control participants: Drug and monetary rewards. *Experimental and Clinical Psychopharmacology, 5*, 256–262.

Madden, G. J., Raiff, B. R., Lagorio, C. H., Begotka, A. M., Mueller, A. M., Hehli, D. J., et al. (2004). Delay discounting of potentially real and hypothetical rewards: II. Between- and within-subject comparisons. *Experimental and Clinical Psychopharmacology, 12*, 251–261.

Madden, G. J., Smith, N. G., Brewer, A. T., Pinkston, J. W., & Johnson, P. S. (2008). Steady-state assessment of impulsive choice in Lewis and Fischer 344 rats: Between-session delay manipulations. *Journal of the Experimental Analysis of Behavior, 90,* 333–344.

Mazur, J. E. (1987). An adjusting procedure for studying delayed reinforcement. In M. L. Commons, J. E. Mazur, J. A. Nevin, & H. Rachlin (Eds.), *Quantitative analysis of behavior: Vol. 5. The effect of delay and of intervening events of reinforcement value* (pp. 55–73). Hillsdale, NJ: Erlbaum.

Mazur, J. E., & Logue, A. W. (1978). Choice in a "self-control" paradigm: Effects of a fading procedure. *Journal of the Experimental Analysis of Behavior, 30,* 11–17.

McClure, S. M., Ericson, K. M., Laibson, D. I., Loewenstein, G., & Cohen, J. D. (2007). Time discounting for primary rewards. *Journal of Neuroscience, 27,* 5796–5804.

McClure, S. M., Laibson, D. I., Loewenstein, G., & Cohen, J. D. (2004, October 15). Separate neural systems value immediate and delayed monetary rewards. *Science, 306,* 503–507.

McCrae, R. R., & Costa, P. T., Jr. (1995). Trait explanations in personality psychology. *European Journal of Personality, 9,* 231–252.

McCrae, R. R., & Costa, P. T., Jr. (1999). A five-factor theory of personality. In L. A. Pervin & O. P. John (Eds.), *Handbook of personality: Theory and research* (2nd ed., pp. 139–153). New York: Guilford Press.

McCrae, R. R., Costa, P. T., Jr., Ostendorf, F., Angleitner, A., Hrebícková, M., Avia, M. D., et al. (2000). Nature over nurture: Temperament, personality, and life span development. *Journal of Personality and Social Psychology, 78,* 173–186.

McDonald, J., Schleifer, L., Richards, J. B., & de Wit, H. (2003). Effects of THC on behavioral measures of impulsivity in humans. *Neuropsychopharmacology, 28,* 1356–1365.

Mischel, W. (1968). *Personality and assessment.* New York: Wiley.

Mischel, W., & Shoda, Y. (1995). A cognitive-affective system theory of personality: Reconceptualizing situations, dispositions, dynamics, and invariance in personality structure. *Psychological Review, 102,* 246–268.

Mitchell, J. M., Fields, H., D'Esposito, M., & Boettiger, C. A. (2005). Neurobiological, behavioral, and environmental relations to drinking. *Alcoholism: Clinical and Experimental Research, 29,* 2158–2169.

Mitchell, J. M., Reeves, J. M., Li, N., & Phillips, T. J. (2006). Delay discounting predicts behavioral sensitization to ethanol in outbred WSC mice. *Alcoholism: Clinical and Experimental Research, 30,* 429–437.

Mitchell, S. H. (1999). Measures of impulsivity in cigarette smokers and non-smokers. *Psychopharmacology (Berlin), 146,* 455–464.

Mitchell, S. H. (2004a). Effects of short-term nicotine deprivation on decision-making: Delay, uncertainty, and effort discounting. *Nicotine & Tobacco Research, 6,* 819–828.

Mitchell, S. H. (2004b). Measuring impulsivity and modeling its association with cigarette smoking. *Behavioral and Cognitive Neuroscience Reviews, 3,* 261–275.

Monterosso, J. R., Ainslie, G., Cordova, X., Domier, C. P., & London, E. D. (2007). Frontoparietal cortical activity of methamphetamine-dependent and comparison subjects performing a delay discounting task. *Human Brain Mapping, 28,* 383–393.

Murphy, J. G., Vuchinich, R. E., & Simpson, C. A. (2001). Delayed rewards and cost discounting. *Psychological Record, 51,* 571–588.

Myerson, J., & Green, L. (1995). Discounting of delayed rewards: Models of individual choice. *Journal of the Experimental Analysis of Behavior, 64,* 263–276.

Myerson, J., Green, L., & Warusawitharana, M. (2001). Area under the curve as a measure of discounting. *Journal of the Experimental Analysis of Behavior, 76,* 235–243.

Nezlek, J. B. (2007). A multilevel framework for understanding relationships among traits, states, situations and behaviours. *European Journal of Personality, 21,* 789–810.

Odum, A. L., & Baumann, A. A. L. (2007a). Cigarette smokers show steeper discounting of both food and cigarettes than money. *Drug and Alcohol Dependence, 91,* 293–296.

Odum, A. L., & Baumann, A. A. L. (2007b). Corrigendum to "Cigarette smokers show steeper discounting of both food and cigarettes than money" [Drug Alcohol Depend. 91 (2/3) (2007) 293–296]. *Drug and Alcohol Dependence, 94,* 292–293.

Odum, A. L., Baumann, A. A. L., & Rimington, D. D. (2006). Discounting of delayed hypothetical money and food: Effects of amount. *Behavioural Processes, 73,* 278–284.

Odum, A. L., Madden, G. J., Badger, G. J., & Bickel, W. K. (2000). Needle sharing in opioid-dependent outpatients: Psychological processes underlying risk. *Drug and Alcohol Dependence, 60,* 259–266.

Odum, A. L., & Rainaud, C. P. (2003). Discounting of delayed hypothetical money, alcohol, and food. *Behavioural Processes, 64,* 305–313.

Ohmura, Y., Takahashi, T., & Kitamura, N. (2005). Discounting delayed and probabilistic monetary gains and losses by smokers of cigarettes. *Psychopharmacology (Berlin), 182,* 508–515.

Olson, E. A., Hooper, C. J., Collins, P., & Luciana, M. (2007). Adolescents' performance on delay and probability discounting tasks: Contributions of age, intelligence, executive functioning, and self-reported externalizing behavior. *Personality and Individual Differences, 43,* 1886–1897.

Ong, E. L., & White, K. G. (2004). Amount-dependent temporal discounting? *Behavioural Processes, 66,* 201–212.

Ortner, C. N. M., MacDonald, T. K., & Olmstead, M. C. (2003). Alcohol intoxication reduces impulsivity in the delay-discounting paradigm. *Alcohol and Alcoholism, 38,* 151–156.

Ostaszewski, P. (1996). The relation between temperament and rate of temporal discounting. *European Journal of Personality, 10,* 161–172.

Ostaszewski, P. (1997). Temperament and the discounting of delayed and probabilistic rewards: Conjoining European and American psychological traditions. *European Psychologist, 2*, 35–43.

Ostaszewski, P., & Green, L. (1995). Self control and discounting of delayed rewards from an individual differences and comparative perspective. *Polish Psychological Bulletin, 26*, 231–238.

Ostaszewski, P., Green, L., & Myerson, J. (1998). Effects of inflation on the subjective value of delayed and probabilistic rewards. *Psychonomic Bulletin & Review, 5*, 324–333.

Perry, J. L., Larson, E. B., German, J. P., Madden, G. J., & Carroll, M. E. (2005). Impulsivity (delay discounting) as a predictor of acquisition of IV cocaine self-administration in female rats. *Psychopharmacology (Berlin), 178*, 193–201.

Perry, J. L., Nelson, S. E., Anderson, M. M., Morgan, A. D., & Carroll, M. E. (2007). Impulsivity (delay discounting) for food and cocaine in male and female rats selectively bred for high and low saccharin intake. *Pharmacology Biochemistry and Behavior, 86*, 822–837.

Pervin, L. A. (1994). A critical analysis of current trait theory. *Psychological Inquiry, 5*, 103–113.

Petry, N. M. (2001a). Delay discounting of money and alcohol in actively using alcoholics, currently abstinent alcoholics, and controls. *Psychopharmacology (Berlin), 154*, 243–250.

Petry, N. M. (2001b). Pathological gamblers, with and without substance use disorders, discount delayed rewards at high rates. *Journal of Abnormal Psychology, 110*, 482–487.

Petry, N. M. (2002). Discounting of delayed rewards in substance abusers: Relationship to antisocial personality disorder. *Psychopharmacology (Berlin), 162*, 425–432.

Petry, N. M. (2006). Early-onset alcoholism: A separate or unique predictor of delay discounting? Comment on Dom et al. (2006). *Addiction, 101*, 292.

Petry, N. M., & Casarella, T. (1999). Excessive discounting of delayed rewards in substance abusers with gambling problems. *Drug and Alcohol Dependence, 56*, 25–32.

Petry, N. M., Kirby, K. N., & Kranzler, H. R. (2002). Effects of gender and family history of alcohol dependence on a behavioural task of impulsivity in healthy subjects. *Journal of Studies on Alcohol, 63*, 83–90.

Plunkett, H. R., & Buehner, M. J. (2007). The relation of general and specific locus of control to intertemporal monetary choice. *Personality and Individual Differences, 42*, 1233–1242.

Poulos, C. X., Parker, J. L., & Lě, D. Z. (1998). Increased impulsivity after injected alcohol predicts later alcohol consumption in rats: Evidence for loss-of-control drinking and marked individual differences. *Behavioral Neuroscience, 112*, 1247–1257.

Rachlin, H., Raineri, A., & Cross, D. (1991). Subjective probability and delay. *Journal of the Experimental Analysis of Behavior, 55*, 233–244.

Ranieri, A., & Rachlin, H. (1993). The effect of temporal constraints on the value of money and other commodities. *Journal of Behavioural Decision Making, 6,* 77–94.

Reynolds, B. (2004). Do high rates of cigarette consumption increase delay discounting? A cross-sectional comparison of adolescent smokers and young-adult smokers and nonsmokers. *Behavioural Processes, 67,* 545–549.

Reynolds, B. (2006a). The experiential discounting task is sensitive to cigarette-smoking status and correlates with a measure of delay discounting. *Behavioural Pharmacology, 17,* 133–142.

Reynolds, B. (2006b). A review of delay-discounting research with humans: Relations to drug use and gambling. *Behavioural Pharmacology, 17,* 651–667.

Reynolds, B., Patak, M., Shroff, P., Penfold, R. B., Melanko, S., & Duhig, A. M. (2007). Laboratory and self-report assessments of impulsive behavior in adolescent daily smokers and nonsmokers. *Experimental and Clinical Psychopharmacology, 15,* 264–271.

Reynolds, B., Richards, J. B., & de Wit, H. (2006). Acute-alcohol effects on the experiential discounting task (EDT) and a question-based measure of delay discounting. *Pharmacology Biochemistry and Behavior, 83,* 194–202.

Reynolds, B., & Schiffbauer, R. (2004). Measuring state changes in human delay discounting: An experiential discounting task. *Behavioural Processes, 67,* 343–356.

Richards, J. B., Mitchell, S. H., de Wit, H., & Seiden, L. S. (1997). Determination of discount functions in rats with an adjusting-amount procedure. *Journal of the Experimental Analysis of Behavior, 67,* 353–366.

Richards, J. B., Sabol, K. E., & de Wit, H. (1999). Effects of methamphetamine on the adjusting amount procedure, a model of impulsive behavior in rats. *Psychopharmacology (Berlin), 146,* 432–439.

Richards, J. B., Zhang, L., Mitchell, S. H., & de Wit, H. (1999). Delay or probability discounting in a model of impulsive behavior: Effect of alcohol. *Journal of the Experimental Analysis of Behavior, 71,* 121–143.

Roberts, B. W., Kuncel, N. R., Shiner, R., Caspi, A., & Goldberg, L. R. (2007). The power of personality: The comparative validity of personality traits, socio-economic status, and cognitive ability for predicting important life outcomes. *Perspectives on Psychological Science, 2,* 313–345.

Robles, E., & Vargas, P. A. (2007). Parameters of delay discounting assessment tasks: Order of presentation. *Behavioural Processes, 75,* 237–241.

Scheres, A., Dijkstra, M., Ainslie, E., Balkan, J., Reynolds, B., Sonuga-Barke, E., et al. (2006). Temporal and probabilistic discounting of rewards in children and adolescents: Effect of age and ADHD symptoms. *Neuropsychologia, 44,* 2092–2103.

Schweitzer, J. B., & Sulzer-Azaroff, B. (1988). Self-control: Teaching tolerance for delay in impulsive children. *Journal of the Experimental Analysis of Behavior, 50,* 173–186.

Schweitzer, J. B., & Sulzer-Azaroff, B. (1995). Self-control in boys with attention deficit hyperactivity disorder: Effects of added stimulation and time. *Journal of Child Psychology and Psychiatry, 36,* 671–686.

Shamosh, N. A., & Gray, J. R. (2008). Delay discounting and intelligence: A meta-analysis. *Intelligence, 36*, 289–305.

Silva, F. J., & Gross, T. F. (2004). The rich get richer: Students' discounting of hypothetical delayed rewards and real effortful extra credit. *Psychonomic Bulletin & Review, 11*, 1124–1128.

Simon, N. W., Mendez, I. A., & Setlow, B. (2007). Cocaine exposure causes long-term increases in impulsive choice. *Behavioral Neuroscience, 121*, 543–549.

Skinner, B. (1953). *Science and human behavior*. Oxford, England: Macmillan.

Skinner, B. (1974). *About behaviorism*. Oxford, England: Alfred A. Knopf.

Snyderman, M. (1987). Prey selection and self-control. In M. L. Commons, J. E. Mazur, J. A. Nevin, & H. Rahlin (Eds.), *Quantitative analysis of behavior: Vol. 5. The effect of delay and intervening events on reinforcement value* (pp. 283–308). Hillsdale, NJ: Erlbaum.

Sonuga-Barke, E. J. S., Houlberg, K., & Hall, M. (1994). When is impulsiveness not impulsiveness? The case of children's cognitive style. *Journal of Child Psychology and Psychiatry, 35*, 1247–1253.

Sonuga-Barke, E. J. S., Taylor, E., Sembi, S., & Smith, J. (1992). Hyperactivity and delay aversion—I. The effect of delay on choice. *Journal of Child Psychology and Psychiatry, 33*, 387–398.

Steyer, R., Schmitt, M., & Eid, M. (1999). Latent state-trait theory and research in personality and individual differences. *European Journal of Personality, 13*, 389–408.

Stitzer, M. L., & Vandrey, R. (2008). Contingency management: Utility in the treatment of drug abuse disorders. *Clinical Pharmacology and Therapeutics, 83*, 644–647.

Vuchinich, R. E., & Simpson, C. A. (1998). Hyperbolic temporal discounting in social drinkers and problem drinkers. *Experimental and Clinical Psychopharmacology, 6*, 292–305.

Wechsler, D. (1999). *Wechsler abbreviated scale of intelligence manual*. San Antonio, TX: Harcourt Assessment.

Winstanley, C. A., Dalley, J. W., Theobald, D. E., & Robbins, T. W. (2003). Global 5-HT depletion attenuates the ability of amphetamine to decrease impulsive choice on a delay-discounting task in rats. *Psychopharmacology (Berlin), 170*, 320–331.

Winstanley, C. A., Eagle, D. M., & Robbins, T. W. (2006). Behavioral models of impulsivity in relation to ADHD: Translation between clinical and preclinical studies. *Clinical Psychology Review, 26*, 379–395.

Yoon, J. H., Higgins, S. T., Sugarbaker, R. J., Thomas, C. S., & Badger, G. J. (2007). Delay discounting predicts postpartum relapse to cigarette smoking among pregnant women. *Experimental and Clinical Psychopharmacology, 15*, 176–186.

3

EXPERIMENTAL AND CORRELATIONAL ANALYSES OF DELAY AND PROBABILITY DISCOUNTING

LEONARD GREEN AND JOEL MYERSON

Impulsivity is emerging as a key theoretical construct in a number of research areas, including behavioral economics, neuroeconomics, psychopathology, and psychometrics, and many researchers believe that a tendency toward impulsivity is reflected in the degree to which people discount delayed and probabilistic rewards. Delay and probability discounting are relatively straightforward concepts. As discussed in chapter 1 of this volume, *delay discounting of rewards* refers to the decrease in their subjective value as a function of the time until their receipt. That is, the present value of a reward to be received after a long delay is less than that of the same reward to be received after a short delay. Similarly, delayed aversive events are discounted in that their subjective value becomes less negative as a function of the time until their occurrence. Probability discounting is similar to delay discounting except that it refers to changes in the subjective value of choice alternatives as a function of the likelihood of their occurrence. A decrease in an event's likelihood decreases its subjective value when the option is a reward and makes its subjective value less negative when the event is aversive.

Preparation of this chapter was supported by National Institutes of Health Grant MH055308.

Compared with defining *discounting*, defining *impulsivity* is not so straightforward. Indeed, different researchers have defined it in different ways (Evenden, 1999). Despite differences in their conception of impulsivity, many researchers believe that it is a trait—a persistent tendency to behave in an impulsive manner. Three questions immediately arise. First, is impulsivity really a trait, in the sense of a relatively permanent tendency that persists across quite different situations? Second, is discounting a trait—that is, do people show a consistent tendency to be steep or shallow discounters across different situations? Third, what is the exact nature of the relation between impulsivity and discounting—are they isomorphic, so that impulsivity may be operationally defined as steep discounting, as some researchers have suggested, or are they merely correlated? For example, even if we are talking about traits, discounting could be just one aspect of impulsivity, so that steep discounting is a diagnostic symptom but does not define the condition. Alternatively, discounting and impulsivity could be independent aspects of behavior. This last alternative is particularly likely to be the case, at least in part, if discounting and impulsivity themselves prove to be multifaceted: Some aspects of discounting may prove to be independent of other aspects of discounting, as well as independent of some aspects of impulsivity.

DEFINING IMPULSIVE BEHAVIOR

To address these questions, we need a clear working definition (or definitions) of impulsivity. This is only the beginning, of course. Psychology is full of concepts that even when clearly defined, do not prove to be unitary constructs. For example, it is still an open question whether inhibition and executive function, both of which are sometimes discussed in relation to impulsivity, are unitary constructs (Rabbitt, 1997). With respect to impulsivity and delay discounting, it may be tempting to define impulsivity as impatience or an inability to delay gratification. Even if there are individuals who steeply discount certain delayed outcomes, however, that would not be sufficient to prove that impatience/impulsivity is a trait. If impatience is a trait, such individuals would be expected to consistently discount delayed outcomes more than do other individuals, regardless of what the outcome is, and the broad tendency to discount steeply or more shallowly would have to be a relatively permanent aspect of behavior. Similar issues arise with respect to impulsivity and probability discounting.

Let us begin, then, not by defining impulsivity, with its implications of transsituationality and relative permanence, but instead by defining what is meant by impulsive behavior. For many psychologists, impulsive choices are those that in the long run fail to maximize gains and minimize losses. With respect to delayed outcomes, impulsive behavior is choosing smaller, more immediate gains over larger, more delayed gains or choosing larger, more delayed losses over smaller, more immediate losses. With respect to probabilistic outcomes, impulsive choices diverge from those that maximize expected value and instead involve choosing potentially larger less likely gains over smaller, surer gains or, in the case of losses, choosing the chance of either a large loss or no loss rather than choosing a small but certain loss. For many psychologists, such impulsive choices result from a lack of what it takes to control one's own behavior so as to maximize gains and minimize losses. What, then, do some psychologists believe is lacking that causes individuals to make suboptimal choices?

One of the oldest ideas is that suboptimal choices result from a failure to inhibit responses to attractive but suboptimal alternatives. One current instantiation of this idea can be found in Barkley (1997), for whom impulsivity was one important result of a lack of inhibitory control, which is also associated with deficits in other executive functions putatively mediated by the frontal lobes. Baumeister took a broader view of the causes of lack of self-control, but inability to inhibit immediate desires is a prominent feature of their limited-strength model (e.g., Baumeister, 2002; Muraven & Baumeister, 2000). Other researchers have suggested that it is not a failure to inhibit but a lack of forethought or a failure to adequately consider long-term consequences that leads to impulsive (suboptimal) choices (Patton, Stanford, & Barratt, 1995). The notion that impulsive behavior reflects some kind of deficit is also implicit in characterizations that highlight a lack of patience or caution, but it is often unclear whether such terms are meant as descriptions of impulsive behavior or as explanations for it.

Deficits of some sort are not the only potential explanations for impulsive behavior. When impulsive behavior occurs, there is also a nonimpulsive alternative available, and the question that arises is why people choose the impulsive option. Is it because of a lack of whatever it is that enables one to resist such attraction, or is it because of the attraction of the impulsive option itself (Hoch & Loewenstein, 1991; Zuckerman, 1994)? Is impulsive behavior more likely in certain situations because they are associated with increased desire or because they lead to decreased resistance? Are certain desires stronger in some individuals, or is their ability to resist (or strategies for promoting resistance) weaker than in other people? Psychologists come down on both sides of this question, but the issue may be addressed by examining discounting.

Consider the discounting of delayed rewards and payments. If discounting delayed rewards depends on the ability to resist the attraction of immediately available rewards, then it should be qualitatively different from the discounting of delayed payments. In the latter case, neither option is attractive—no one likes to pay either a small amount immediately or a large amount later. Thus, the processes underlying impulsive choice in a situation involving payments would presumably differ from those underlying impulsive choice in a situation involving rewards. So, too, if discounting delayed rewards results from a failure to consider the long-term consequences of one's behavior, then such discounting should be qualitatively different from discounting of probabilistic rewards, in which consequences are often immediate. As instantiated in the typical probability-discounting task, to choose the larger, probabilistic reward over the smaller, certain reward means that one would get a reward either immediately or not at all.

Unlike failures to inhibit or carefully consider consequences, which might be reflected in both delay and probability discounting, lack of patience would be reflected only in choices involving delayed rewards. If the issue is impatience (or inability to delay gratification), then impulsive behavior should be specific to situations involving delayed rewards because this issue does not arise when outcomes are probabilistic. Alternatively, if the issue is lack of caution, then impulsive behavior should be specific to situations involving probabilistic outcomes.

Regardless of which conceptualization of impulsivity proves correct or whether a new conceptualization is required, the time seems ripe to review what is known about discounting and the way individual behavior varies across different types of discounting tasks. Accordingly, in this chapter, we discuss the experimental literature on delay and probability discounting as well as correlational analyses of individual behavior on discounting tasks. More specifically, we begin by briefly considering some issues related to the measurement of discounting. Next, we discuss the similarities and differences between delay and probability discounting of both gains and losses, highlighting the differential effects that the magnitude of the delayed or probabilistic outcomes has in these various cases and pointing out their theoretical implications. We go on to consider the results of correlational studies and the issues they raise regarding the relations between decision-making processes and personality traits. Finally, we consider findings from research with nonhuman animals and argue for their importance in understanding discounting by humans. The literature on delay and probability discounting reviewed here is of considerable interest not only in regard to the question of the nature of impulsivity but also because of its implications for our understanding of choice and decision making in general.

MEASURING DISCOUNTING

Until recently, nearly all studies of impulsivity used a psychometric approach in which participants took personality tests and correlational and factor analyses were used in an effort to reveal the dimensions of the impulsivity construct. The general conclusion from such studies is that impulsivity is multifactorial, hence the large number of alternative definitions emphasizing different putative components of impulsivity. More recently, there has been increasing focus on experimental approaches to impulsivity, with researchers devising laboratory tasks to assess performance in situations that may reveal tendencies toward impulsive behavior.

Most experimental studies of discounting in humans have used an adjusting-amount procedure, in which participants choose between a small amount of an outcome available immediately and a larger amount available after a delay (e.g., $150 now vs. $1,000 in 6 months). If the delayed outcome is chosen, the amount of the immediate outcome is increased (e.g., $200 now), whereas if the immediate outcome is chosen, its amount is decreased. Then participants are asked to choose again between the delayed outcome and the new amount of the immediate outcome. This psychophysical-like procedure adjusts the amount of the immediate outcome until participants are equally as likely to choose the immediate or the delayed outcome, at which point the amount of the immediate outcome is taken as an estimate of the subjective (i.e., present) value of the delayed outcome. A similar adjusting-amount procedure can be used to study probability discounting, with participants choosing between a small certain outcome and a larger probabilistic outcome.

With both delayed and probabilistic outcomes, one may map out a discounting function by repeating the procedure, varying the delay until, or the probability of, the occurrence of the larger outcome. Figure 3.1 shows examples of delay (left panel) and probability (right panel) discounting functions obtained using choices between hypothetical amounts of monetary reward. For

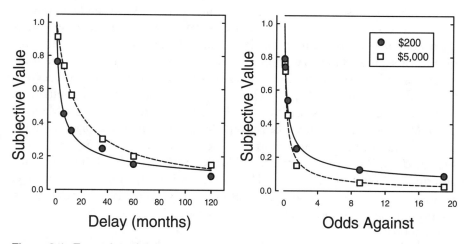

Figure 3.1. Examples of delay discounting (left panel) and probability discounting (right panel). The curves represent the hyperboloid discounting function (Equation 1). Data are from Experiment 2 of "Amount of Reward Has Opposite Effects on the Discounting of Delayed and Probabilistic Outcomes," by L. Green, J. Myerson, and P. Ostaszewski, *Journal of Experimental Psychology: Learning, Memory, and Cognition, 25,* p. 422. Copyright 1999 by the American Psychological Association.

delay-discounting data, the discounting function describes the relation between the subjective value of a delayed reward and the time until its occurrence. For probability-discounting data, the discounting function describes the relation between the subjective value of a probabilistic reward and the odds against its occurrence. Although the subjective value of a probabilistic outcome typically increases as a function of its probability, its subjective value decreases as a function of the odds against its occurrence. As Rachlin, Raineri, and Cross (1991) noted, plotting subjective value as a function of odds against reveals the similarity of probability and delay discounting.

A hyperboloid discounting function describes the relation between the subjective value of an outcome and the delay until it occurs (e.g., Ainslie, 1992; Green, Fry, & Myerson, 1994; Kirby, 1997; Laibson, 1997; Mazur, 1987; Rachlin et al., 1991; for a review, see Green & Myerson, 2004). For delayed rewards, the hyperboloid discounting function is given by

$$V = A/(1 + kD)^s, \tag{1}$$

where V represents the subjective value of an outcome, A represents its magnitude, k is a parameter governing the rate of discounting, D is the delay, and s is a parameter that represents the nonlinear scaling of amount and/or time. When $s = 1.0$, the discounting function is a simple hyperbola. When $s < 1.0$, as is often the case, the discounting curve decreases less sharply at higher delay values than does a simple hyperbola with the same discounting rate parameter, k.

For probabilistic rewards, a similar equation holds in which D is replaced with θ, the odds against receiving the reward (e.g., Green, Myerson, & Ostaszewski, 1999; Rachlin et al., 1991), and the parameter s represents the nonlinear scaling of amount and/or the odds against an outcome. Equation 1 describes both delay and probability discounting in humans, including people from different cultures (Du, Green, & Myerson, 2002) and subpopulations such as smokers, drinkers, and heroin addicts (e.g., Bickel, Odum, & Madden, 1999; Madden, Petry, Badger, & Bickel, 1997; Vuchinich & Simpson, 1998), as well as nonhuman animals (Green, Myerson, Holt, Slevin, & Estle, 2004; Mazur, 2000; Richards, Mitchell, de Wit, & Seiden, 1997). Equation 1 also describes discounting of different kinds of rewards (Estle, Green, Myerson, & Holt, 2007; Odum & Rainaud, 2003; Raineri & Rachlin, 1993) as well as discounting of aversive outcomes such as payments (Estle, Green, Myerson, & Holt, 2006).

Although Equation 1 provides a very good description of discounting data, the distributions of both the rate and the scaling parameters tend to be quite skewed, and the two parameters pose a problem when a single index is needed to characterize individuals' impulsivity. To deal with these concerns, Myerson, Green, and Warusawitharana (2001) proposed an area-under-the-curve measure of discounting. The area is calculated on the basis of proportions: Observed subjective values are normalized as proportions of an outcome's nominal value, and delays or odds against are normalized as a proportion of the longest delay or the greatest odds studied in the experiment. An area of 1.0 indicates no discounting, and an area of 0.0 indicates the steepest possible discounting. Thus, area is inversely related to the degree of discounting. Because area is calculated on the basis of observed values rather than estimates based on some mathematical function, it provides a theoretically neutral measure of discounting. Area under the curve is useful for measuring individual and group differences when a single discounting index is desired, but it is not a substitute for theoretically based discounting functions.

EMPIRICAL APPROACHES

Studies that compare discounting of delayed and probabilistic outcomes, or the discounting of gains and losses, address fundamental issues concerning the nature of impulsivity. With respect to the processes underlying impulsive discounting, the question is whether an experimental manipulation has the same effect on the discounting of different kinds of outcomes. If it does, this would be consistent with the view that the same processes are involved; if the effect of the manipulation is different for different outcomes, this would suggest that different processes are involved, at least to some extent. With respect to the traits underlying individual differences in discounting, the question is whether the degree to which individuals discount one kind of outcome is predictable from the degree to which they discount another kind of outcome. If it is, this would be consistent with the view that the same traits are involved in both cases; if one is not predictable from the other, this would suggest that different traits are involved.

Experimental Analyses

As just noted, if a given manipulation differentially affects different kinds of discounting, this strongly implies that at least some different processes must be involved, even if some other processes are shared. Next we consider the effects of such manipulations (e.g., differences in amount) on the discounting of delayed and probabilistic outcomes as well as on the discounting of gains and losses.

Delay and Probability Discounting

One of the most robust findings with respect to delay discounting is that larger rewards are discounted less steeply than smaller rewards (Green &

Myerson, 2004). This finding, termed the *magnitude effect*, is observed not only with monetary rewards but also with commodities as diverse as medical treatments (Chapman, 1996), vacation time (Raineri & Rachlin, 1993), and directly consumable rewards such as food and beer (Estle et al., 2007). A magnitude effect is also observed with probabilistic rewards but in the opposite direction: Larger probabilistic rewards are discounted more steeply than smaller rewards. This can be seen in Figure 3.1: Relative to the smaller reward, the larger delayed reward loses proportionately less of its subjective value as delay increases (left panel), whereas the larger probabilistic reward loses proportionately more of its subjective value as the odds against its receipt increase (right panel).

The opposite effects of reward amount on delay and probability discounting strongly suggest that they involve different decision-making processes. Supporting evidence for this conclusion is provided by other examples of differential effects, one of which is the finding that inflation affects the rate of delay discounting in the inflated currency while leaving the rate of probability discounting unaffected. This was shown by Ostaszewski, Green, and Myerson (1998), who took advantage of the fact that Poland was experiencing extremely high rates of inflation in the early 1990s and that to combat this, the government planned to introduce a new zloty (the Polish unit of currency). Ostaszewski et al. assessed delay and probability discounting both before and after the change in currency, using rewards specified in both zlotys and U.S. dollars (with which the people of Poland were very familiar). Before the currency change, delayed rewards specified in zlotys were discounted much more steeply than equivalent dollar rewards, whereas probabilistic rewards were discounted at the same rate regardless of currency. After the currency change, which was associated with markedly reduced inflation, delayed rewards in the two currencies, like probabilistic rewards, were discounted at the same rate.

Further evidence that delay and probability discounting involve at least some distinctly different processes comes from a recent study by Estle et al. (2007), which compared the discounting rates for delayed and probabilistic rewards when the rewards were either monetary or directly consumable in nature (e.g., food, beer). Previously, Odum and Rainaud (2003) had reported that delayed monetary rewards were discounted much less steeply than directly consumable rewards of equivalent monetary value. Estle et al. replicated this finding but discovered that it did not generalize to probability discounting. As shown in Figure 3.2, delayed monetary rewards were discounted less steeply than directly consumable rewards of approximately equivalent monetary value (left panel), but there was little difference in rates of probability discounting (right panel). Again, an experimental manipulation (varying the type of reward) produced different effects on delay discounting and probability discounting, providing even more evidence that different processes are involved in the two types of discounting.

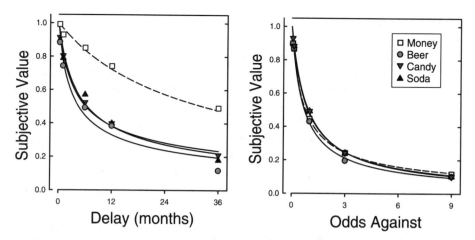

Figure 3.2. Delay discounting (left panel) and probability discounting (right panel) of monetary and directly consumable rewards. The curves represent the hyperboloid discounting function (Equation 1). Data are from the small amount condition of "Discounting of Monetary and Directly Consumable Rewards," by S. J. Estle, L. Green, J. Myerson, and D. D. Holt, *Psychological Science, 18,* p. 60. Copyright 2007 by Blackwell Publishers, Ltd. Reprinted with permission.

Discounting Gains and Losses

Another important example of the dissociation of the behavioral processes involved in choice emerges from the experimental literature on preference reversals. A person's tendency to choose a smaller–sooner reward over a larger–later reward is often taken as evidence of impulsivity. The finding of preference reversals in choice between delayed outcomes, however, demonstrates that this tendency is situation specific. People who prefer larger–later gains over smaller–sooner gains when considering outcomes far in the future often reverse their preference as the alternatives become closer in time. This phenomenon was captured experimentally by Green, Fisher, Perlow, and Sherman (1981), who showed that pigeons also experience such reversals in preference (see also Ainslie & Herrnstein, 1981), as do rats (Green & Estle, 2003). Given a choice between a small food reward available after 28 seconds or a larger food reward available after 32 seconds, all the birds preferred the larger–later reward. When the choice was between the same small reward available in 2 seconds or the larger reward available after 6 seconds, all the birds preferred the smaller–sooner reward. Moving to the second condition, the one with the shorter delays, is analogous to having time pass: The birds choose between the same outcomes as in the first condition, but it is as if they are being asked the same question again but 26 seconds later. People experience the same sort of preference reversals, expressing preference for a larger–later reward when considering outcomes well in the future, yet often reversing their preference and opting for the smaller–sooner reward as time passes and the delays to both reward alternatives decrease.

To capture the preference reversal phenomenon in humans, researchers (Ainslie & Haendel, 1983; Green, Fristoe, & Myerson, 1994) have used a procedure analogous to that used with pigeons. Green, Fristoe, and Myerson (1994) found that people overwhelmingly chose the larger amount when given a choice between $20 available in 1 year and $50 available in 2 years. When the delays to both rewards were reduced by 6 months, simulating the passage of time, the majority chose the $20 reward over the $50 reward. More important, when the rewards were increased to $500 and $1,250, maintaining the same ratio of smaller to larger, the point at which a switch was observed from the majority preferring the larger–later to the majority preferring the smaller–sooner occurred earlier than with $20 and $50 rewards, as would be predicted from steeper discounting of smaller delayed rewards (i.e., the magnitude effect).

Recently, we revisited the preference reversal phenomenon using delayed losses instead of gains (Holt, Green, Myerson, & Estle, 2008). It should be noted that when the decision is whether to make a smaller–sooner payment or a larger–later one, it is the larger–later payment that is thought of as the impulsive choice. When the payments are both far in the future, one tends to prefer paying the smaller amount even though it has to be paid sooner. As time passes, however, preference reverses, and one tends to prefer making the later payment, even though it is for the larger amount. This shown in Figure 3.3, which depicts the effect of the time until a smaller–sooner payment on choice between making either that payment or a larger payment that would have to be made either 1 year (top panel) or 5 years (bottom panel) later. Notice that when the time to the sooner payment is long (e.g., 120 months), it was preferred by nearly all of the participants in the study, but when the time to the sooner payment was relatively brief (e.g., less than 12 months), the majority now preferred the larger–later payment. More important, no magnitude effect was seen with delayed losses, as evidenced by the fact that the data points from all of the amount conditions fall along the same curve (e.g., compare the circles, indicating choices between $80 and $120 payments, and the inverted triangles, indicating choices between $12,000 and $18,000 payments).

For present purposes, these results have two important implications. First, as with gains, the tendency to make an impulsive choice (in this case, selecting the larger–later payment over the smaller–sooner one) depends on the situation: People are less likely to make the impulsive choice when both outcomes are farther in the future than when they are nearer in time. Second, unlike gains, when the ratio of the amounts of the sooner and later payments is held constant, the tendency to make an impulsive choice is not affected by the absolute magnitude of the outcomes. Taken together, these findings suggest conclusions similar to those arising from our comparison of delay and

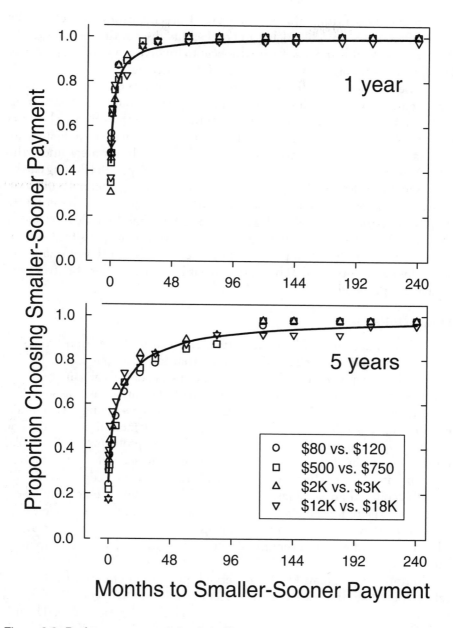

Figure 3.3. Preference reversals in choice between smaller–sooner and larger–later payments. In the top panel, the difference between the delay to the larger–later payment and the delay to the smaller–sooner payment was held constant at 1 year; in the bottom panel, it was held constant at 5 years. The curves represent the group preferences function, based on the assumption of hyperboloid discounting. Data are from "Preference Reversals With Losses," by D. D. Holt, L. Green, J. Myerson, and S. J. Estle, *Psychonomic Bulletin & Review, 15,* p. 92. Copyright 2008 by the Psychonomic Society, Inc. Reprinted with permission.

probability discounting—that is, there are clear similarities and yet equally clear differences. Thus, like delay and probability discounting of gains, delay discounting of gains and losses would appear to involve some shared processes but also processes unique to the valence of the outcome.

These conclusions are consistent with the results of a recent study by Estle et al. (2006) involving delay and probability discounting of both gains and losses. The delay-discounting data (presented in the top panel of Figure 3.4) show a robust magnitude effect for gains (larger delayed gains are associated with shallower discounting and thus with larger areas under the curve) but relatively little effect of amount for losses. A parallel finding can be seen in the probability-discounting data (see the bottom panel of Figure 3.4). Probabilistic gains show a robust magnitude effect, albeit in the opposite direction of that with delayed gains, whereas probabilistic losses do not show an effect of amount. Thus, whatever processes are responsible for magnitude effects, they are apparently not operative, or only minimally so, when losses are involved. This is true regardless of whether the losses are delayed or probabilistic.

Magnitude Effects

Several accounts of how magnitude effects arise have been proposed. Loewenstein and Thaler (1989) proposed that larger amounts may be discounted less steeply than smaller amounts because people treat gains of different magnitude differently; when gains are small, they are treated as spending money, whereas when they are large, they are treated as savings, with different discounting rates associated with the different mental accounts. The apparent lack of a magnitude effect with losses poses problems for this explanation. Just as small and large gains go into separate accounts with different discount rates, one might expect that small payments would come out of a different account than large payments. Even if these separate accounts were restricted to gains for some reason, the number of accounts that people would have to keep would appear to be implausibly large, given that the rate at which a delayed gain is discounted increases continuously as its amount is increased up to at least $10,000 (Green, Myerson, & McFadden, 1997). Furthermore, Chapman (1996) observed magnitude effects with health-related outcomes that varied with respect to the duration of good health, and the notion of separate accounts for shorter and longer duration of good health seems implausible.

Regardless of the correct explanation, however, the fact that magnitude differentially affects the discounting of gains and losses has important implications for our understanding of other aspects of decision making. For example, one of the most robust findings regarding decision making is loss aversion (Kahneman & Tversky, 1984): When asked whether they would gamble

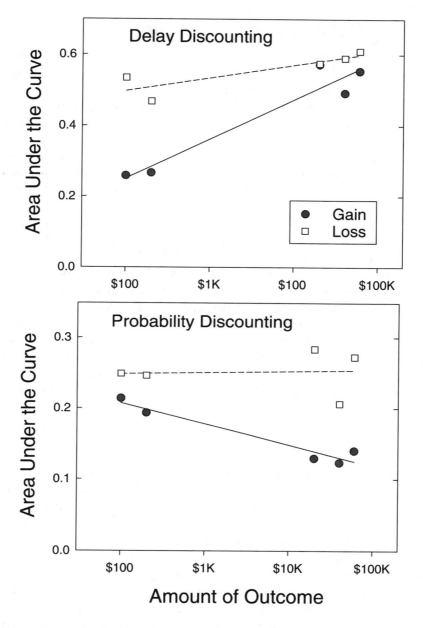

Figure 3.4. Effects of amount on delay and probability discounting of gains and losses. Smaller areas under the curve indicate steeper discounting. Data are from Experiments 1, 2, 3, and 4 of "Differential Effects of Amount on Temporal and Probability Discounting of Gains and Losses," by S. J. Estle, L. Green, J. Myerson, and D. D. Holt, *Memory & Cognition, 34,* p. 926. Copyright 2006 by the Psychonomic Society, Inc. Reprinted with permission.

money on the flip of a coin, people generally say no unless they can potentially win more money than they would lose (e.g., they are willing to gamble if the potential loss is $100 but the win would be $200, but not if the win and loss are both $100). A recent study (Harinck, Van Dijk, Van Beest, & Mersmann, 2007), however, showed that this finding does not hold for gambles involving smaller amounts of money. In fact, the opposite finding was observed: People would gamble on the flip of a coin for small amounts even when the potential loss was larger than the win. The authors suggested that this finding reflects the fact that small losses are discounted to a greater extent than are large losses. The Estle et al. (2006) findings, however, suggest that the observed result is not due to the effect of amount on how people discount losses. In fact, amount has relatively little effect on the discounting of losses, but it does affect the discounting of gains.

The more we know about the effects of outcome magnitude (e.g., its opposite effects on delay and probability discounting of gains; its relative lack of effect on discounting of losses, both delayed and probabilistic), the harder it appears to be to come up with an explanation. What these findings may be telling us is that there is more than one mechanism underlying magnitude effects (Green, Myerson, & Schneider, 2003) and that the search for a grand unified theory is misguided. If researchers were to come up with an explanation that works for all these cases, however, we would have more confidence that it is correct because of all the constraints that had to be satisfied. As noted earlier, however, the basic findings themselves, regardless of their ultimate explanation, have important implications right now for how one should parse decision-making phenomena.

Correlational Analyses

In a famous article titled "Individual Differences as a Crucible in Theory Construction," Underwood (1975) argued that nomothetic theories, even though their goal may be to understand general principles, should make predictions regarding individual differences. Differences between individuals may be thought of as natural experiments whose results can help establish the validity of theoretical constructs and models. This is particularly true for theories and constructs involving intervening variables, and discounting is such an intervening variable. The term *discounting* may be used purely descriptively to describe the fact that the value of an outcome changes as a function of its probability and the time until its occurrence. However, the term is often used to refer to an intervening evaluative process that may underlie such changes. According to Underwood, moreover, the interaction between individual differences and nomothetic theories is a two-way street. Not only do individual differences provide potential tests of nomothetic theories, but ideographic theories (i.e., theories of individual differences) may be best understood in terms of the processes described by nomothetic theories.

As Underwood (1975) noted,

> The whole idea behind behavioral theory is to reduce the number of independent processes to a minimum; to find that performance on two apparently diverse tasks is mediated at least in part by a single, more elementary, process is a step towards this long-range goal. (p. 133)

Research on individual differences provides a way of evaluating theoretical claims regarding such elementary processes. For example, if the degree to which individuals discount delayed rewards is predictable from the degree to which they discount probabilistic rewards, such a finding would be consistent with the view that the same elementary discounting process is involved in both cases. If the one is not predictable from the other, however, then either the two do not share a common process or, at the very least, differences in other processes exist and are more powerful determinants than the shared process.

The same kinds of correlational analyses that address the issue of shared versus unique processes also address the issue of common versus different traits. In fact, when it is hypothesized that two kinds of discounting reflect a common trait, it follows that these two kinds of discounting will be correlated. The discounting of delayed and probabilistic rewards constitutes a relevant example. If both kinds of discounting reflect impulsivity, as defined by an inability to delay gratification and a tendency toward risk taking, then delay and probability discounting should be negatively correlated. Those who cannot wait for rewards will steeply discount delayed rewards, and because they do not take into account the risk involved, they should also show shallow discounting of probabilistic rewards.

In our studies, however, we have yet to observe the negative correlation between delay and probability discounting predicted by such a definition of impulsivity. For example, in a study involving two large samples of more than 100 participants each, the correlations between delay and probability discounting of monetary rewards were actually positive (Myerson, Green, Hanson, Holt, & Estle, 2003). In a study that involved the discounting of both monetary and directly consumable rewards (Estle et al., 2007), delay and probability discounting were again positively correlated. Moreover, a factor analysis revealed that delay and probability discounting loaded on separate factors: The probability-discounting measures for all four commodities (money, beer, soda, candy) had loadings greater than .75 on one factor and less than .35 on the other factor, whereas the reverse was true for the delay-discounting measures.

These results, taken together with the opposite magnitude effects and other findings discussed earlier, strongly suggest that delay and probability discounting involve different processes and represent different traits. Notably, these results are contrary to predictions from any conceptualization of impulsivity that links impatience with risk taking. An inhibition hypothesis, for example, implies that "good" decision making involves the inhibition of the impulse to choose an immediate, albeit smaller reward when a larger alternative reward is delayed and also involves inhibition of the impulse to choose a larger, albeit riskier reward when one could have a certain, albeit smaller alternative. Similarly, a hypothesis that highlights lack of forethought as the essence of impulsivity implies that if one more carefully considered one's options, one would realize that there is more to be gained by waiting and more to be lost by gambling. Such hypotheses are inconsistent with the observation that the tendency to steeply discount delayed rewards is relatively independent of (or possibly even positively associated with) the tendency to steeply discount probabilistic rewards.

Even if different traits and different processes underlie the discounting of delayed and probabilistic outcomes, there will still be individuals who show a tendency to make impulsive choices in both domains. Indeed, it may be precisely these individuals who are at greater risk for numerous problems in real life (e.g., substance abusers) because they are both willing to take risks and relatively unwilling to wait. If this is so, then comparisons of extreme groups (e.g., substance abusers vs. controls) may sometimes present a misleading picture of the relations between behavioral tendencies in the wider population. It is for this reason that group studies, although necessary to characterize the specific groups under investigation, cannot substitute for correlational studies with respect to the broader issues concerning behavioral traits.

Another important issue is whether the extent to which individuals discount gains is predictable from the degree to which they discount losses. A significant correlation between the discounting of gains and losses would be consistent with the view that the same traits are involved in both cases. There does appear to be a positive correlation between discounting of monetary gains and losses, but not between health gains and losses (Chapman, 1996). Thus, whether such a correlation exists may depend on the nature of what is being discounted. Studies examining the correlation between gains and losses of other commodities are clearly needed.

Research With Nonhuman Animals

Like humans, other animals also discount delayed rewards, and their choices between immediate and delayed rewards are described by the same hyperboloid mathematical function that describes discounting in humans (Green et al., 2004; Mazur, 2000; Richards et al., 1997). Moreover, like humans, animals show preference reversals as the time until two delayed rewards is varied (Ainslie & Herrnstein, 1981; Green et al., 1981; Green & Estle, 2003).

Despite these important similarities between the ways in which humans and animals discount delayed rewards, there are several differences, although the basis for these differences is not yet clearly understood. First, there is the matter of the time scale. Animals discount delayed rewards much more steeply than do humans, although it should be noted that animals in choice experiments are typically food or water deprived and working for relatively small, directly consumable rewards, whereas humans are typically choosing between relatively large, hypothetical monetary rewards. As noted previously, humans have recently been studied with directly consumable, albeit hypothetical rewards, and under such conditions they show much more rapid discounting than with monetary rewards (Estle et al., 2007; Odum & Rainaud, 2003). Moreover, when real juice and water were used as delayed rewards for humans (McClure, Ericson, Laibson, Loewenstein, & Cohen, 2007), they showed steeper discounting than in studies using real money, although the rate of discounting was still less than that observed with animals. Thus, type of reward matters, but this does not completely explain the fact that animals discount delayed rewards more steeply than do humans.

The delayed rewards used in animal studies are arguably of greater value to the deprived subjects than are the rewards used in human studies. Nevertheless, the magnitude effect typically observed with humans does not explain the observed difference in discounting rates. That is, humans discount larger, more highly valued rewards less steeply; thus, if animals were to show similar magnitude effects, they might be expected to discount less steeply than humans. However, this brings up another major difference between discounting by humans and by animals. Animals appear to discount delayed rewards at approximately the same rate regardless of amount. Indeed, the lack of a magnitude effect has been reported in studies with rats and pigeons working for food and water rewards (Green et al., 2004; Richards et al., 1997).

Animal behavior is of interest in and of itself, of course, and in this context discounting has important implications for understanding foraging behavior (Green & Myerson, 1996; Kacelnik, 2003). For many researchers, however, animal studies of discounting are of interest for what they can tell us about human behavior. Despite the differences between discounting by humans and by animals, animal models still have the potential to shed light on discounting in humans so long as one remembers that animal models are always specific in their application. Researchers use a particular species to study a specific phenomenon because that species shows the phenomenon of interest. Biomedical researchers, for example, have used zebra fish to study the early stages of neural development because of the transparency of the zebra fish embryo, but they have used macaques to study development of the neocortex because of the similarities of human and monkey brains. Thus, the fact that discounting in animals is not perfectly analogous to human discounting does not preclude the use of animal models; it just means that research using an animal model should be focused on those aspects of discounting that the species under consideration has in common with humans. There are experiments that one can conduct with animals that would be difficult if not impossible to conduct with people (e.g., studies of drug self-administration), and this is obviously one of the major advantages of animal models. Knowing that the analogy between humans and any nonhuman species is limited, however, one must verify that results obtained with a particular species do, in fact, generalize to humans.

Although few animal studies use enough participants to look at individual differences in the same way as in human studies, one could think of animal studies investigating strain differences as being like extreme groups approaches to individual differences in humans. An extreme groups design can often be more efficient than a correlational approach in terms of the number of participants needed or the total testing time required, as when one compares people who gamble a little or not at all with those who gamble a lot (e.g., Holt, Green, & Myerson, 2003). For example, one could administer a gambling questionnaire to a large group to identify the relatively small numbers of individuals making up the extreme groups, or one could advertise for volunteers having the characteristics of the needed groups. In principle, one could test many rats or monkeys to determine their tendencies to self-administer drugs, but this would be costly and time consuming. A more efficient way would be to select animals on the basis of their discounting rates and then see whether the more impulsive are more likely to self-administer a specific drug. This latter procedure was used by Perry, Larson, German, Madden, and Carroll (2005), who divided rats into high- and low-impulsive groups on the basis of their discounting of delayed food rewards and found that the steeper discounters were more likely to self-administer cocaine.

Alternatively, one could select strains of inbred animals known for their drug self-administration tendencies and compare their tendencies to discount delayed food rewards. For example, Helms, Reeves, and Mitchell (2006) compared mice from two strains known to differ in their self-administration of both ethanol and cocaine. Contrary to expectation, the mice from the strain with a greater tendency to self-administer drugs showed less steep discounting of delayed sucrose rewards. Despite the apparent conflict with respect to the relation between discounting and drug self-administration, we would argue that the Perry et al. (2005) and Helms et al. (2006) studies may both be thought of as "proof-of-principle" demonstrations. That is, they have both demonstrated that there are efficient ways to study the relation between the discounting of delayed rewards and the self-administration of drugs in animals. Such efficiency is particularly important when one moves to study drug self-administration in nonhuman primates.

The recent finding that macaque monkeys discount delayed drug (cocaine) rewards in a hyperboloid fashion (Woolverton, Myerson, & Green, 2007) opens the door to primate research on the role of discounting in substance abuse. Previous work has shown that delay affects monkeys' choices involving drug rewards and also that monkeys responding for delayed drug rewards show preference reversals (Anderson & Woolverton, 2003), but the Woolverton et al. (2007) study is the first to show the form of the discounting function in monkeys. Moreover, in collaboration with Kevin Freeman and William Woolverton, we recently found that monkeys also hyperbolically discount delayed nondrug (saccharin) rewards. We are now in a position to ask what happens when the choice is between drug and nondrug rewards. In particular, we can ask whether monkeys will impulsively choose immediate drug reinforcement over delayed nondrug rewards, as would be predicted by impulsivity theories of substance abuse. If they do, then we will have an animal model with which to study the variables that control the likelihood of such behavior.

Finally, when studying the relation between drug self-administration and discounting in nonhuman animals (or in humans), the choice of measures can be critical. For example, although rats of the Lewis strain are more likely to acquire cocaine self-administration than are Fisher 344 rats, the Fisher rats tend to self-administer more cocaine than the Lewis rats (Kosten et al., 1997; Kosten, Zhang, & Haile, 2007). With respect to choice of an animal model of substance abuse, of course, both measures are important. We need to know what predicts whether people will try a drug or not and what predicts whether they will go on to abuse that drug, as well as the extent of such abuse. Fortunately, we may now be in a position to address these questions using animal models of discounting.

CONCLUSION

How does what we currently know about discounting inform our understanding of impulsivity? The literature on discounting, like the psychometric research on impulsivity, comes down on the side of a multifactorial conception of impulsivity (e.g., Evenden, 1999; Whiteside & Lynam, 2001). Not only is discounting just one part of what is meant by impulsivity, but discounting itself is not all of a piece.

Why do we think that discounting involves multiple processes and traits or abilities? As already discussed, the basic logic underlying this conclusion is twofold. First, if the same processes are involved in two types of discounting task, then a given experimental manipulation should have similar effects on performance of both tasks. This is similar to the logic underlying the classification of learning and memory systems as well as that for distinguishing neural systems based on functional dissociations after brain lesions (Teuber, 1955; Tulving, 1985). Second, if the same trait or ability is tapped by two tasks, then those who perform at a particular level on one task (relative to their peers) should perform at a similar level on the other task, and performance on the two tasks should be correlated. This, of course, is the basic logic underlying the study of all psychological traits (McCrae & Costa, 1995) and abilities (Carroll, 1993).

From this perspective, delay and probability discounting appear to involve at least some different processes because the two types of discounting can be experimentally dissociated (e.g., manipulating amount of reward produces opposite effects on delay and probability discounting). Delay and probability discounting also appear to reflect different traits as evidenced by the fact that the correlation between delay and probability discounting is weak at best. Moreover, when measures of the delay and probability discounting of different types of rewards are analyzed together, delay- and probability-discounting measures load on separate factors, suggesting the existence of separate delay- and probability-discounting traits.

Like delay and probability discounting, the discounting of gains and losses also appears to involve at least some different processes, as evidenced by the fact that the robust magnitude effects observed with gains are weak or absent when the outcomes being discounted are losses. There are currently limited data on whether the discounting of gains and the discounting of losses reflect different traits. Understanding the relation between the discounting of gains and losses is particularly important because of the real-world consequences of discounting losses, and indeed, discounting possible harm to oneself or to others may be the essence of risky behavior.

Because most studies of discounting have focused on monetary rewards, another issue on which we have less information than we might like concerns possible differences in the discounting of different kinds of outcomes. The same hyperboloid function describes the data in all cases, but delayed monetary rewards are discounted less steeply than nonmonetary rewards of comparable monetary value. The picture is further complicated by the finding that probabilistic monetary rewards appear to be discounted at rates similar to nonmonetary rewards of comparable monetary value. Taken together, these results suggest that the special status of delayed monetary rewards may be due to their fungibility. That is, it is possible that delayed money retains its value better than other types of delayed rewards because its value is less dependent on current needs and desires that, experience teaches us, may change over time. In fact, when inflation is high and monetary rewards do not hold their value over time, they are discounted more steeply than when inflation is low.

As is the case with delayed gains, different kinds of delayed loss may not be discounted equivalently. There has been even less research on this issue than on the discounting of different kinds of delayed gains, but it does appear that delayed health losses are discounted at different rates than comparable monetary losses. Because the delay and probability discounting of health losses are fundamental to choices involving health maintenance, this is an issue of great practical significance and clearly deserving of further investigation (see chap. 11, this volume).

A factor analysis of the Estle et al. (2007) data revealed that measures of the discounting of different types of rewards loaded on two separate factors: a delay-discounting factor and a probability-discounting factor. The finding that measures of the delay discounting of several different types of rewards, both monetary and directly consumable, all load on a single delay-discounting factor indicates that those individuals who most steeply discount one type of delayed reward also tend to steeply discount other types of delayed rewards. Moreover, individuals who steeply discount one type of probabilistic reward tend to steeply discount other types of probabilistic rewards as well. Consistent with these findings, risk tolerance with respect to gambles involving changes in income has been reported to predict behavior involving health risks such as alcohol consumption (Barsky, Juster, Kimball, & Shapiro, 1997). In contrast, the delay discounting of health and monetary outcomes appear to be independent traits (Chapman, 1996). Thus, the trait picture is complex in that not only are there separate factors for delay and probability discounting, but also the probability-discounting factor appears to include health outcomes, whereas the delay-discounting factor may not.

Moreover, the world in which people make their choices is much more complex than the experimental situations that have been studied to date. It makes sense, of course, that experimentalists simplify the choice situations they study to isolate the variables that influence discounting and analyze the processes involved in making decisions. This research strategy has revealed fundamental regularities underlying people's choices involving delayed and probabilistic outcomes, including the consistently hyperboloid form of the discounting function and the robust magnitude effects observed in every choice situation studied with humans to date. We believe that building on this foundation and progressively complicating the experimental choice situation can yield further insights precisely because one can compare observed behavior with what would be predicted from a simple additive combination of the elements making up the more complex situation.

For example, research on delay discounting has tended to focus on the simplest situation, choice between an immediate and a delayed reward, assuming that the results generalize to more complicated situations like choice between two delayed rewards. However, a study from our lab (Green, Myerson, & Macaux, 2005) has shown that prediction from the simple situation to the more complicated one is not always straightforward. Regardless of whether one or both rewards were delayed, behavior was described by the same hyperboloid discounting function. When both rewards were delayed, however, the subjective value of the later reward was less than that predicted on the basis of the assumption that people simply compare the subjective value of the two delayed rewards. Rather, people appeared to give less than full weight to the common aspect of the two delays, a phenomenon we termed *common-aspect attenuation*.

That is, given a choice between a reward available in 2 years and another available in 5 years, choice of either outcome would involve a delay of 2 years (plus an additional 3 years in the case of the later reward). Given such a choice, participants in the Green et al. (2005) study behaved as if they gave approximately half the weight to the delay common to both rewards (2 years) that they give to the delay unique to the later reward (3 years). In other words, they behaved as if they were comparing the subjective values of a reward available in approximately 1 year and a later reward available after approximately 4 years. The important point here is not the details, but the fact that we were able to interpret behavior in the complicated situation on the basis of observed deviations from what might have been expected on the basis of the simple situation.

As research proceeds to the next level in which delayed and probabilistic outcomes, both gains and losses, are studied in various combinations, an understanding of how the elements of such combinations affect behavior individually puts us in a strong position to analyze behavior in such complex, and thus often more realistic, situations. That is, just as knowledge of how individuals choose between an immediate and a delayed reward informed our understanding of choice between two delayed rewards, so, too, may knowledge of how individuals discount gains and how they discount losses provide the necessary context for understanding discounting when outcomes involve both gains and losses. In our laboratory, we have recently begun to study delay discounting in situations involving both gains and losses, as have other researchers (e.g., Ostaszewski, 2007), and comparable studies of probability discounting are likely to follow. Similarly, studies that combine delayed and probabilistic outcomes can build on both our understanding of how individuals discount delayed outcomes and our understanding of how they discount probabilistic outcomes.

Even in the relatively simple situations studied so far, however, what is abundantly clear is that discounting is not all of a piece. Clear functional distinctions are apparent between choice behavior when the outcomes are delayed versus when the outcomes are probabilistic, and comparisons of the discounting of different commodities suggest further functional distinctions, with money showing relatively unique properties, particularly when it is delayed. Understanding such distinctions will be critical as we strive to understand how discounting relates to impulsive behavior. We are well on our way to clarifying these distinctions and to figuring out how many more distinctions are necessary. That is to say, current research is laying the foundation for a taxonomy of discounting, although researchers might not describe their efforts in this way. Nevertheless, developing such a taxonomy may prove to be of fundamental importance, in part because knowing what the "natural kinds" of discounting are may ultimately redefine the concept of impulsivity.

REFERENCES

Ainslie, G. (1992). *Picoeconomics: The strategic interaction of successive motivational states within the person*. Cambridge, England: Cambridge University Press.

Ainslie, G., & Haendel, V. (1983). The motives of the will. In E. Gottheil, K. A. Druley, T. E. Skoloda, & H. M. Waxman (Eds.), *Etiologic aspects of alcohol and drug abuse* (pp. 119–140). Springfield, IL: Charles C Thomas.

Ainslie, G., & Herrnstein, R. J. (1981). Preference reversal and delayed reinforcement. *Animal Learning & Behavior, 9,* 476–482.

Anderson, K. G., & Woolverton, W. L. (2003). Effects of dose and infusion delay on cocaine self-administration choice in rhesus monkeys. *Psychopharmacology (Berlin), 167,* 424–430.

Barkley, R. A. (1997). Behavioral inhibition, sustained attention, and executive functions: Constructing a unifying theory of ADHD. *Psychological Bulletin, 121,* 65–94.

Barsky, R. B., Juster, F. T., Kimball, M. S., & Shapiro, M. D. (1997). Preference parameters and behavioral heterogeneity: An experimental approach in the health and retirement study. *Quarterly Journal of Economics, 112,* 537–579.

Baumeister, R. F. (2002). Yielding to temptation: Self-control failure, impulsive purchasing, and consumer behavior. *Journal of Consumer Research, 28,* 670–676.

Bickel, W. K., Odum, A. L., & Madden, G. J. (1999). Impulsivity and cigarette smoking: Delay discounting in current, never, and ex-smokers. *Psychopharmacology (Berlin), 146,* 447–454.

Carroll, J. B. (1993). *Human cognitive abilities: A survey of factor-analytic studies*. Cambridge, England: University Press.

Chapman, G. B. (1996). Temporal discounting and utility for health and money. *Journal of Experimental Psychology: Learning, Memory, and Cognition, 22,* 771–791.

Du, W., Green, L., & Myerson, J. (2002). Cross-cultural comparisons of discounting delayed and probabilistic rewards. *Psychological Record, 52,* 479–492.

Estle, S. J., Green, L., Myerson, J., & Holt, D. D. (2006). Differential effects of amount on temporal and probability discounting of gains and losses. *Memory & Cognition, 34,* 914–928.

Estle, S. J., Green, L., Myerson, J., & Holt, D. D. (2007). Discounting of monetary and directly consumable rewards. *Psychological Science, 18,* 58–63.

Evenden, J. L. (1999). Varieties of impulsivity. *Psychopharmacology (Berlin), 146,* 348–361.

Green, L., & Estle, S. J. (2003). Preference reversals with food and water reinforcers in rats. *Journal of the Experimental Analysis of Behavior, 79,* 233–242.

Green, L., Fisher, E. B., Jr., Perlow, S., & Sherman, L. (1981). Preference reversal and self-control: Choice as a function of reward amount and delay. *Behaviour Analysis Letters, 1,* 43–51.

Green, L., Fristoe, N., & Myerson, J. (1994). Temporal discounting and preference reversals in choice between delayed outcomes. *Psychonomic Bulletin & Review, 1,* 383–389.

Green, L., Fry, A. F., & Myerson, J. (1994). Discounting of delayed rewards: A life-span comparison. *Psychological Science, 5*, 33–36.

Green, L., & Myerson, J. (1996). Exponential versus hyperbolic discounting of delayed outcomes: Risk and waiting time. *American Zoologist, 36*, 496–505.

Green, L., & Myerson, J. (2004). A discounting framework for choice with delayed and probabilistic rewards. *Psychological Bulletin, 130*, 769–792.

Green, L., Myerson, J., Holt, D. D., Slevin, J. R., & Estle, S. J. (2004). Discounting of delayed food rewards in pigeons and rats: Is there a magnitude effect? *Journal of the Experimental Analysis of Behavior, 81*, 39–50

Green, L., Myerson, J., & Macaux, E. W. (2005). Temporal discounting when the choice is between two delayed rewards. *Journal of Experimental Psychology: Learning, Memory, and Cognition, 31*, 1121–1133.

Green, L., Myerson, J., & McFadden, E. (1997). Rate of temporal discounting decreases with amount of reward. *Memory & Cognition, 25*, 715–723.

Green, L., Myerson, J., & Ostaszewski, P. (1999). Amount of reward has opposite effects on the discounting of delayed and probabilistic outcomes. *Journal of Experimental Psychology: Learning, Memory, and Cognition, 25*, 418–427.

Green, L., Myerson, J., & Schneider, R. (2003). Is there a magnitude effect in tipping? *Psychonomic Bulletin & Review, 10*, 381–386.

Harinck, F., Van Dijk, E., Van Beest, I., & Mersmann, P. (2007). When gains loom larger than losses: Reversed loss aversion for small amounts of money. *Psychological Science, 18*, 1099–1105.

Helms, C. M., Reeves, J. M., & Mitchell, S. H. (2006). Impact of strain and d-amphetamine on impulsivity (delay discounting) in inbred mice. *Psychopharmacology (Berlin), 188*, 144–151.

Hoch, S. J., & Loewenstein, G. F. (1991). Time-inconsistent preferences and consumer self-control. *Journal of Consumer Research, 17*, 492–507.

Holt, D. D., Green, L., & Myerson, J. (2003). Is discounting impulsive? Evidence from temporal and probability discounting in gambling and non-gambling college students. *Behavioural Processes, 64*, 355–367.

Holt, D. D., Green, L., Myerson, J., & Estle, S. J. (2008). Preference reversals with losses. *Psychonomic Bulletin & Review, 15*, 89–95.

Kacelnik, A. (2003). The evolution of patience. In G. Loewenstein, D. Read, & R. F. Baumeister (Eds.), *Time and decision: Economic and psychological perspectives on intertemporal choice* (pp. 115–138). New York: Russell Sage Foundation.

Kahneman, D., & Tversky, A. (1984). Choice, values, and frames. *American Psychologist, 39*, 341–350.

Kirby, K. N. (1997). Bidding on the future: Evidence against normative discounting of delayed rewards. *Journal of Experimental Psychology: General, 126*, 54–70.

Kosten, T. A., Miserendino, M. J. D., Haile, C. N., DeCaprio, J. L., Jatlow, P. I., & Nestler, E. J. (1997). Acquisition and maintenance of intravenous cocaine self-administration in Lewis and Fischer inbred rat strains. *Brain Research, 778*, 418–429.

Kosten, T. A., Zhang, X. Y., & Haile, C. N. (2007). Strain differences in maintenance of cocaine self-administration and their relationship to novelty activity responses. *Behavioral Neuroscience, 121*, 380–388.

Laibson, D. (1997). Golden eggs and hyperbolic discounting. *Quarterly Journal of Economics, 62*, 443–477.

Loewenstein, G., & Thaler, R. H. (1989). Anomalies: Intertemporal choice. *Journal of Economic Perspectives, 3*, 181–193.

Madden, G. J., Petry, N. M., Badger, G. J., & Bickel, W. K. (1997). Impulsive and self-control choices in opioid-dependent patients and non-drug-using control participants: Drug and monetary rewards. *Experimental and Clinical Psychopharmacology, 5*, 256–262.

Mazur, J. E. (1987). An adjusting procedure for studying delayed reinforcement. In M. L. Commons, J. E. Mazur, J. A. Nevin, & H. Rachlin (Eds.), *Quantitative analyses of behavior: Vol. 5. The effect of delay and of intervening events on reinforcement value* (pp. 55–73). Hillsdale, NJ: Erlbaum.

Mazur, J. E. (2000). Tradeoffs among delay, rate, and amount of reinforcement. *Behavioural Processes, 49*, 1–10.

McClure, S. M., Ericson, K. M., Laibson, D. I., Loewenstein, G., & Cohen, J. D. (2007). Time discounting for primary rewards. *Journal of Neuroscience, 27*, 5796–5804.

McCrae, R. R., & Costa, P. T. (1995). Trait explanations in personality psychology. *European Journal of Personality, 9*, 231–252.

Muraven, M., & Baumeister, R. F. (2000). Self-regulation and depletion of limited resources: Does self-control resemble a muscle? *Psychological Bulletin, 126*, 247–259.

Myerson, J., Green, L., Hanson, J. S., Holt, D. D., & Estle, S. J. (2003). Discounting delayed and probabilistic rewards: Processes and traits. *Journal of Economic Psychology, 24*, 619–635.

Myerson, J., Green, L., & Warusawitharana, M. (2001). Area under the curve as a measure of discounting. *Journal of the Experimental Analysis of Behavior, 76*, 235–243.

Odum, A. L., & Rainaud, C. P. (2003). Discounting of delayed hypothetical money, alcohol, and food. *Behavioural Processes, 64*, 305–313.

Ostaszewski, P. (2007). Temporal discounting in "gain now-lose later" and "lose now-gain later" conditions. *Psychological Reports, 100*, 653–660.

Ostaszewski, P., Green, L., & Myerson, J. (1998). Effects of inflation on the subjective value of delayed and probabilistic rewards. *Psychonomic Bulletin & Review, 5*, 324–333.

Patton, J. H., Stanford, M. S., & Barratt, E. S. (1995). Factor structure of the Barratt impulsiveness scale. *Journal of Clinical Psychology, 51*, 768–774.

Perry, J. L., Larson, E. B., German, J. P., Madden, G. J., & Carroll, M. E. (2005). Impulsivity (delay discounting) as a predictor of acquisition of IV cocaine self-administration in female rats. *Psychopharmacology (Berlin), 178*, 193–201.

Rabbitt, P. (Ed.). (1997). *Methodology of frontal and executive function.* New York: Psychology Press.

Rachlin, H., Raineri, A., & Cross, D. (1991). Subjective probability and delay. *Journal of the Experimental Analysis of Behavior*, *55*, 233–244.

Raineri, A., & Rachlin, H. (1993). The effect of temporal constraints on the value of money and other commodities. *Journal of Behavioral Decision Making*, *6*, 77–94.

Richards, J. B., Mitchell, S. H., de Wit, H., & Seiden, L. S. (1997). Determination of discount functions in rats with an adjusting-amount procedure. *Journal of the Experimental Analysis of Behavior*, *67*, 353–366.

Teuber, H. L. (1955). Physiological psychology. *Annual Review of Psychology*, *6*, 267–296.

Tulving, E. (1985). How many memory systems are there? *American Psychologist*, *40*, 385–398.

Underwood, B. J. (1975). Individual differences as a crucible in theory construction. *American Psychologist*, *30*, 128–134.

Vuchinich, R. E., & Simpson, C. A. (1998). Hyperbolic temporal discounting in social drinkers and problem drinkers. *Experimental and Clinical Psychopharmacology*, *6*, 292–305.

Whiteside, S. P., & Lynam, D. R. (2001). The five factor model and impulsivity: Using a structural model of personality to understand impulsivity. *Personality and Individual Differences*, *30*, 669–689.

Woolverton, W. L., Myerson, J., & Green, L. (2007). Delay discounting of cocaine by rhesus monkeys. *Experimental and Clinical Psychopharmacology*, *15*, 238–244.

Zuckerman, M. (1994). *Behavioral expressions and biosocial bases of sensation seeking*. Cambridge, England: Cambridge University Press.

II

NEUROSCIENCE OF DISCOUNTING AND RISK TAKING

4

THE NEURAL AND NEUROCHEMICAL BASIS OF DELAY DISCOUNTING

CATHARINE A. WINSTANLEY

Modeling delay-discounting behavior has proved to be one of the most successful approaches in the study of impulsive decision making in laboratory animals, and in this chapter I focus on data obtained using laboratory rodents (see, e.g., chaps. 7, 10, and 12, this volume, for discussions of delay discounting in clinical research). Although the methodology adopted has been diverse, such research has yielded important data regarding the neural and neurochemical basis of the delay-discounting process. Work has focused on subregions of the frontal cortex and striatum, as well as on nuclei within the amygdala and basal ganglia implicated in reward-related learning. By determining the effects of damage to certain structures on this form of impulsive choice and considering these findings in the context of what else is known about the functions of such regions, it is possible to improve our understanding of the processes involved in making delay-discounting judgments. Likewise, by exploring the regional effects of neurotransmitters such as serotonin

Catharine A. Winstanley's lab is currently supported by grants from the Canadian National Sciences and Engineering Research Council, the Canadian Institutes for Health Research, the Michael Smith Foundation for Health Research, and the Institute for Research into Pathological Gambling and Related Disorders. She is a Michael Smith Foundation Early Career Scholar.

and dopamine, we can begin to develop hypotheses regarding the mechanism by which drugs that target these monoaminergic systems can regulate impulsive decision making.

MEASURING DELAY DISCOUNTING AS PART OF THE IMPULSIVITY CONSTRUCT

Impulsivity is not a unitary construct but rather encompasses a range of behaviors including aspects of hyperexcitability, behavioral disinhibition, and higher order decision making (Evenden, 1999; Moeller, Barratt, Dougherty, Schmitz, & Swann, 2001; Winstanley, Theobald, Dalley, & Robbins, 2004). These issues are dealt with in detail elsewhere in this volume, but it is important to note that the direction that much of the work investigating the neural and neurochemical basis of discounting has taken was influenced by previous investigations into other aspects of impulsivity. As our knowledge of the different brain regions influencing these distinct yet convergent behavioral processes improves, it is possible to compare and contrast the biological basis of different aspects of impulsivity and to obtain a deeper understanding of impulsive behavior as a result. Much of the data discussed in this chapter come from experiments in which delay discounting and other aspects of impulsivity have been modeled in laboratory animals, namely, rats.

Rats can perform many behavioral tests that incorporate aspects of behavioral disinhibition or *impulsive action*. One of the most successfully validated and widely used tasks is the five-choice serial reaction time task (5CSRT; Carli, Robbins, Evenden, & Everitt, 1983). This test is based on the Continuous Performance Test of sustained and divided attention used clinically (Rosvold, Mirsky, Sarason, Bransome, & Beck, 1956). During the 5CSRT, the animal is required to poke its nose (a *nosepoke response*) into one of five apertures (*holes*) on brief illumination of a stimulus light located in the rear of the aperture. Subsequent to beginning a trial and before illumination of a stimulus light, there is a 5-second intertrial interval during which the animal must withhold from responding at the five-hole array. Any responses made during this time are described as premature responses and are punished with a 5-second timeout during which the animal cannot initiate more trials or earn more reward. These premature responses provide an index of motoric impulsivity and are potentially analogous to "false-alarm" errors made in the Continuous Performance Test. When considering the differences between impulsive action and impulsive choice as exemplified by delay-discounting performance, I largely restrict the discussion to results obtained using the 5CSRT. The task has been extensively characterized in terms of the neural circuitry and neurotransmitter systems involved and as such provides a good starting point for comparison. Furthermore, many of the same manipulations have been conducted in both the

5CSRT and delay-discounting paradigms. Needless to say, this discussion is far from exhaustive, but it will, I hope, illustrate the key differences and similarities that become apparent when considering delay discounting as part of the broader family of impulsivity behaviors.

Modeling Delay Discounting in Rats

The central principle underlying all the delay-discounting paradigms currently in use is that subjects are trained to choose between a small reward delivered immediately (or sometimes after a short delay) versus a larger reward delivered after a longer delay. As with humans, impulsive choice is defined as the selection of the smaller–sooner over the larger–later reward. Although the concept seems relatively simple, numerous different paradigms have been developed that use different testing equipment, time scales, statistical analyses, and reward magnitudes. Such methodological divergence has, perhaps unsurprisingly, led to discrepant results concerning the effects of particular lesions or pharmacological manipulations. In most cases, such conflicts have stimulated further experimentation that has improved our understanding of the factors that influence delay-discounting behavior. However, when comparing delay-discounting data, it is important to consider the methodology used because different tasks may vary in the extent to which different areas or neurotransmitter systems are recruited.

T-Maze

One of the simplest versions of the delay-discounting paradigm is that involving a T-maze. The animal learns that one arm is baited with a larger reward, the other with a smaller reward. The rewards are typically located behind two gates that are raised to allow the rat access to the food. However, if the rat chooses the large-reward arm, as it proceeds down the arm it becomes trapped within the arm by the closing of a second gate. After a certain delay, the gate in front of the food is raised and the animal has access to its reward. As with all maze-based tasks, testing is labor intensive, and the animal can only complete a small number of trials per day (normally 10–20). The delay to the large reward is also kept constant during every daily set of trials, or session. Typically, once the animal has learned to choose the arm associated with the larger reward, it will next learn to discriminate between an immediate reward in one arm versus a larger reward for which it must endure a relatively short delay, for example, 5 to 10 seconds (Bizot, Le Bihan, Puech, Hamon, & Thiebot, 1999; Rudebeck, Walton, Smyth, Bannerman, & Rushworth, 2006). Once stable choice patterns are observed between sessions, the delay can then be lengthened and any change in an animal's choice behavior observed. This task has the advantage of simplicity. However, the structure of the training schedule may affect choice behavior because the animal learns about the different delays across sequential sessions. The choice of a large reward delayed by 15 seconds could therefore be influenced by the animal's experience with a 5-second delay. Furthermore, although there are no explicit cues such as a light or a tone to signal choice of the delayed reward, the lowering of the second gate to trap the animal in the high-reward arm likely acts as a significant cue to the animal that it could use to solve the discrimination task. Such a cue, in addition to the contextual cues associated with the high-reward arm, could act as a conditioned reinforcer (CR) as it becomes associated with access to the large reward. The ability of CRs to facilitate choice behavior is well known. Such factors could explain why choice of the large reward using maze-based paradigms is often higher than when using operant chambers, particularly because signaling the duration of the delay to the large reward in a two-lever operant task (see the next section) increases choice of the large reward and decreases the time taken to obtain stable baseline choice behavior (Cardinal, Robbins, & Everitt, 2000).

Within-Session Delay Manipulation Procedures

The task used by Cardinal et al. (2000), based on a task first published by Evenden and Ryan (1996), is now one of the most widely used delay-discounting paradigms. As shown in Figure 4.1, animals choose to respond on two levers, one of which provides a small reward of one pellet, the other a large reward of four pellets. Each session is divided into blocks of 12 trials, the first 2 of which are forced choice. In each successive block, the delay to the large reward increases from 0 seconds in the first block to 60 seconds in the last block. To ensure that choice of the large-reward option always maximizes the amount of reward earned, the length of each trial is kept constant so that the animal cannot accrue more pellets or increase the rate of reinforcement by repeatedly choosing the small reward. Animals typically show a strong preference for the larger reward early in the session when the delay to its delivery is short or absent, but shift their preference to the smaller reward as delay to the larger reward increases. Hence, a within-session delay-discounting curve can be obtained using this paradigm, which is of great value when determining the effects of drug challenges because the effects of one dose of compound on numerous delays can be obtained within the same session and the same rat. The fact that the rats are exposed to all the delays within the same session may reduce the effect of prior experience with shorter delays on choice between an immediate reward and a longer delay. However, the block design is not without its problems. Because the order of the delays are constant in each session and invariably increase in duration with each successive block, extraneous temporal factors related to how much time has elapsed since the start of the session can influence the animals' choice. Furthermore, choice of the large reward at the start of the session when its delivery is immediate is often reported as

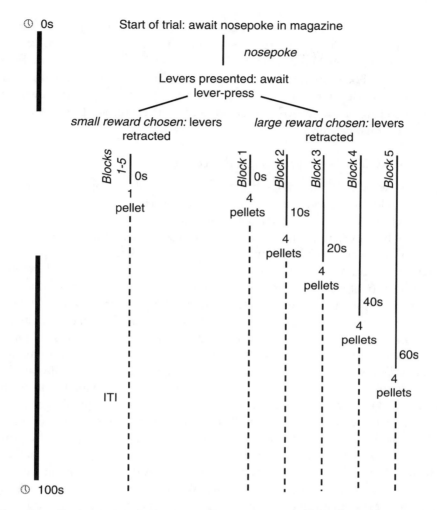

Figure 4.1. Task schematic of a delay-discounting task incorporating a within-session shift in delay to the large reward. This task is based on that originally published by Evenden and Ryan (1996) and adapted by Cardinal et al. (2000). s = seconds; ITI = intertrial interval. From "Contrasting Roles for Basolateral Amygdala and Orbitofrontal Cortex in Impulsive Choice," by C. A. Winstanley, D. E. Theobald, R. N. Cardinal, and T. W. Robbins, 2004, *Journal of Neuroscience, 24*, p. 4719. Copyright 2004 by the *Journal of Neuroscience.* Reprinted with permission.

between 80% and 90%, yet theoretically this should be close to 100% because rats are simply choosing between a small reward and a large reward. The natural tendency of rats to switch between response alternatives is unlikely to account for a 20% difference. It is more likely that the aversive quality of the delay that is associated with responding on the large-reward lever later in the session generalizes to affect all responses on that lever. Although seemingly trivial, such factors should be borne in mind when evaluating the effects of manipulations to the central nervous system. For example, this may contribute to the effects of anxiogenic compounds on impulsive choice (see "Neurochemical Systems: Focus on Serotonin–Dopamine Interactions" section). Rats may also simply perseverate on the lever that initially provides the most reward at the beginning of the session, which would bias their responding toward the choice of the large-reward lever.

Between-Session Delay Manipulation Procedures

A two-choice lever-based task design was also adopted by Mobini, Chiang, Ho, Bradshaw, and Szabadi (2000), only a much higher proportion of forced-choice trials is included per session (more than 80%) and, similar to the T-maze–based version of the task, used a between- rather than within-session shift in the delay to the large reward. Such a strategy was necessary to acquire a reasonable number of free-choice trials per delay. This group also developed a mathematical model to distinguish between the different factors that may affect delay-discounting behavior (Ho, Mobini, Chiang, Bradshaw, & Szabadi, 1999). Factors considered include not only the absolute length of delay to the large and small rewards, but the relative difference in these numbers. Likewise, the relative difference between the size of the two rewards also influences choice. To assess the effects of a particular manipulation on delay-discounting behavior using this approach, multiple comparisons must be made within the same animal over many test sessions. It is therefore always possible that the prior experience of the animal will influence its subsequent decisions, and clearly such an approach is not ideal in determining the impact of certain pharmacological challenges in which repeated dosing alters the drug's effects. However, such thorough and exacting methodology can make significant contributions to understanding why damage to a certain brain region or neurotransmitter system produces a particular pattern of choice behavior, as is seen in the discussion of the orbitofrontal cortex (OFC).

Adjusting Parameter Procedures

All the tasks considered so far can be described as *systematic* tasks, in which the experimenter varies the delay to different-sized reinforcers and then measures the choice made. *Adjusting* tasks have also been developed in which the behavior of the subject determines the delays sampled. In the adjusting-delay procedure developed by Mazur (1987), choice of the large reward leads to an increase in the delay to the large reward, whereas choice of the small reward leads to a decrease in the delay to the large reward. The adjusting-amount procedure developed by Richards, Mitchell, de Wit, and Seiden (1997) has a similar theoretical basis, but the delays stay constant within a session, whereas the size of the delayed reinforcer varies depending on the choice on the previous trial. Eventually, an indifference point is reached at which the animal chooses the large reward 50% of the time. This point is used as a measure of impulsivity. Although such adjusting tasks have made a valuable contribution to the literature, recent mathematical modeling of this behavior reveals that factors other than the delay can affect the choice pattern generated and that seemingly delay-dependent changes in choice strategy, which fulfill the criteria for reliable acquisition and performance of the task, can be obtained through random sampling (Cardinal, Daw, Robbins, & Everitt, 2002). Nevertheless, some similarities have been observed between the effects of lesions and drug challenges on both systematic and adjusting tasks, and allowing the individual subject to influence the delays it experiences is certainly a meritorious strategy despite the apparent disadvantages.

In summary, it is clear that the simple notion of choosing between a smaller–sooner and a larger–later reward can be measured in a variety of ways that vary in their complexity and sophistication. Maintaining an awareness of both the merits and the pitfalls of some of these approaches will prove invaluable when considering the exciting body of data generated in relation to the neurobiological basis of delay discounting.

NEURAL SYSTEMS: FOCUS ON THE LIMBIC CORTICOSTRIATAL LOOP

As stated earlier, much of the work investigating delay-discounting performance has been influenced by previous work on other aspects of impulsivity. Work has focused on the limbic corticostriatal loop, in part because damage to certain regions in this circuit has been shown to increase risky decision making in humans and also because of the extensive clinical and preclinical literature highlighting the importance of some of these regions in behavioral inhibition and cognitive control as well as in reward-related learning.

Nucleus Accumbens

The *nucleus accumbens* (NAC) is a key node in the limbic corticostriatal loop and is clearly involved in reward-related behavior. The NAC can be divided into two anatomically distinct parts: the core and the shell (Voorn, Gerfen, & Groenewegen, 1989; Zaborsky et al., 1985). The NAC core (NACc) in particular has a crucial role to play in allowing CRs to guide and invigorate behavior. For example, excitotoxic lesions of the NACc in rats block the acquisition and performance of autoshaped responses (Cardinal, Parkinson, et al., 2002; Parkinson, Olmstead, Burns, Robbins, & Everitt, 1999) and impair *Pavlovian–instrumental transfer* (facilitation of an instrumental response by presentation of a Pavlovian conditioned stimulus; Hall, Parkinson, Connor, Dickinson, & Everitt, 2001).

A dramatic increase in choice of the smaller–sooner over the larger–later reward is observed in rats after excitotoxic lesions to the NACc, as determined on a delay-discounting task similar to that developed by Evenden and Ryan (1996; i.e., within-session shifts in the delay to the large reward [Cardinal, Pennicott, Sugathapala, Robbins, & Everitt, 2001]). Interestingly, damage to the same region makes animals risk averse on a probability-discounting task in which animals choose between a small, certain reward or increasingly uncertain delivery of a large reward (Cardinal & Howes, 2005), indicating that damage to the NACc does not make animals universally impulsive. NACc lesions also increase the number of premature responses animals make on the 5CSRT, but this effect depends on whether the response made on the previous trial resulted in punishment or reward (Christakou, Robbins, & Everitt, 2004). Recall that the 5CSRT is a test of visual attention as well as impulsivity because rats are responding to visual stimuli presented in one of five holes. If they respond correctly in the hole that was briefly illuminated, they receive food reward. However, if they respond incorrectly (i.e., in a nonilluminated hole), they are punished by a time-out period. Damage to the NAC selectively increases impulsive responding on the trials that follow an incorrect response. Loss of accumbal processing may therefore render animals oversensitive to signals associated with the absence of an anticipated reward, or the perception of such a situation that arises when rewards are delayed in time. Activity in this region is thought to significantly contribute to learning which cues are predictive of reward (Day, Roitman, Wightman, & Carelli, 2007; Schultz, Dayan, & Montague, 1997), and recent imaging data have indicated reward-prediction error activity in the ventral striatum, an area that encompasses the NAC, during classical conditioning (Bray & O'Doherty, 2007).

However, Acheson et al. (2006) have reported that lesions to the NAC have very different effects on delay discounting as assessed using an adjusting-amount method. In this task, the size and delay of the larger–later reward were held constant during each session, and the amount of the smaller–sooner reward was adjusted on the basis of the previous response until the rat was indifferent as to which outcome it received. Both lesioned and sham-treated rats reached similar indifference points, indicating that they were discounting to the same degree. However, when the delay to the large reward was systematically varied between days to get a delay-discounting curve, NAC-lesioned rats were less sensitive to delay increases. That is, the value of the larger–later reward retained more of its value for the lesioned rats than for the sham-treated rats. The authors of this study suggested that lesions to the NAC decrease sensitivity to changes in the delay to reinforcement, and this processing deficit could give rise to behavior that appears more or less impulsive depending on the way the delay-discounting task is structured. In the adjusting-amount task used by

Acheson et al., the additional sessions used to generate the delay-discounting curve required the use of three delays that were shorter than the original training delay and only one delay that was longer. Rats with NAC lesions could therefore have biased responding toward the large-reward lever because overall it appeared to be a better option. In contrast, in the Cardinal et al. (2001) study, the large-reward lever was associated with longer delays as the session progressed, which may have biased rats away from responding on this lever.

Although this is an interesting hypothesis, it is also worth noting that both the NAC core and the shell were damaged in the Acheson et al. (2006) study, whereas just the core was targeted by Cardinal et al. (2001). It is increasingly recognized that these areas have very distinct functions in mediating reward-related learning, and damage to both regions may well result in a different pattern of behavior than damage to one or the other in isolation. The effects of selective lesions to the NAC shell on delay-discounting performance may help resolve these issues. The considerable difference in the methodology used by both research groups clearly warrants careful consideration, but experiments triggered by such controversy could ultimately deepen our understanding of exactly how the NAC contributes to the choice of delayed reinforcers.

Prefrontal Cortex

The *prefrontal cortex* (PFC) is involved in many higher order cognitive functions, including monitoring of internal resources, strategy development, and the detection of causal contingencies between events. It is perhaps unsurprising therefore to find that various areas of the frontal cortex are involved in mediating delay-discounting judgments. I focus on two areas that have been found to play important roles in goal-directed behavioral processes, namely the medial PFC (mPFC) as exemplified by the prelimbic and anterior cingulate regions and the ventral PFC encompassing the OFC and agranular insular.

Anterior Cingulate Cortex

The *anterior cingulate cortex* (ACC) was thought to be a likely candidate to play a role in delay-discounting judgments for a number of reasons. First, damage to this area increases the number of premature or impulsive responses made on the 5CSRT (Muir, Everitt, & Robbins, 1996) and has also been shown to increase other forms of behavioral disinhibition. For example, in an autoshaping paradigm, animals with ACC lesions increased the number of responses made to the unrewarded stimulus (Bussey, Everitt, & Robbins, 1997), and such lesions impaired extinction learning in a conditional visual discrimination task in that animals continued to respond on a lever even though it no longer led to delivery of reward (Bussey, Muir, Everitt, & Robbins, 1996). The ACC is also thought to play a critical role in conflict resolution, as exemplified by performance of the Stroop task (Barch et al., 2001). Patients with ACC lesions are often impaired on this test, and it has been reported that damage to the ACC impairs the sensation of exerting mental effort to resolve the conflict inherent within the task (Naccache et al., 2005). In rodents, it has repeatedly been demonstrated that ACC lesions decrease the amount of physical effort that rats are willing to expend to earn a larger number of food pellets; they instead opt for the less demanding option associated with a smaller reward (Walton, Bannerman, Alterescu, & Rushworth, 2003; Walton, Bannerman, & Rushworth, 2002). The ACC therefore appears to play an important role in determining the value of the outcome of a certain action, particularly in relation to the effort taken to obtain it. However, patients with ACC damage also choose riskier options on the Iowa Gambling Task (IGT), suggesting that information processed within the ACC is important for aspects of impulsive decision making (Manes et al., 2002; Naccache et al., 2005), and certainly there are temptations and conflicts inherent in tests of impulsive choice that one would expect to tap into processes involving the ACC.

However, lesions to the ACC do not alter delay-discounting judgments in the rat (Cardinal et al., 2001; Rudebeck et al., 2006). In delay-discounting paradigms, there is no difference in the amount of effort that must be exerted to obtain the larger reward, but the same argument can be made for the IGT, which is sensitive to ACC damage. Another interpretation of this data set is that delay-discounting judgments do not involve the same amount of conflict resolution or mental effort as more complex tests. However, it is hard to conclude that deciding how long to wait for a larger reward is somehow easier than deciding how much energy it is worth expending to obtain it.

Alternatively, the ACC may be recruited during delay-discounting judgments, but it does not play a central role under most circumstances. Using electroencephalography, it can be demonstrated that engagement in different tests of executive function such as the IGT, delay discounting, and Stroop tasks activates a pattern of activity associated with cognitive control believed to arise within the cingulate cortex (the frontal N2 waveform; Lamm, Zelazo, & Lewis, 2006). It is well established that cognitive control improves with age (Zelazo & Muller, 2002). In the Lamm et al. (2006) study, younger children generated larger N2 waveforms than adolescents when performing these executive function tasks, and the magnitude of N2 correlated negatively with performance on the IGT and Stroop tests. These findings indicate that those performing better on these tests did not need to strongly activate cognitive control generators, presumably because such inhibitory systems were better developed. Interestingly, delay-discounting performance was not correlated with N2 magnitude. It would therefore appear that the activation of the ACC during delay-discounting performance is not the critical factor governing this form of impulsive decision making, even though this area is recruited during task performance. Exactly why delay discounting differs from other tests of executive function in this regard remains to be thoroughly investigated, but it could provide valuable insight into the nature of the cognitive processing involved and adds further weight to the argument that different aspects of impulsivity are underpinned by independent biological mechanisms.

Medial Prefrontal Cortex

Although selective damage to the ACC did not alter delay-discounting performance, larger lesions to the medial wall of the rat PFC, incorporating both the prelimbic and the infralimbic cortices (PrLC and ILC, respectively), did alter choice behavior (Cardinal et al., 2001). The paradigm used a within-session shift in delay. Damage to the medial wall of the frontal cortex caused rats to choose the large reward relatively less at the beginning of the session when the delay was short, but relatively more at the end of the session when the delay was long. Although it is hard to conclude that the rats were any more or less impulsive in their decision making, it is clear that some factor determining their choice behavior had been affected by this frontal damage. One suggestion is that the rats were less able to detect changes in the reward contingencies that occurred during the session and therefore averaged their choice of the large reward across the session. The PrLC in particular has a pronounced role to play in the detection of instrumental contingencies (Balleine & Dickinson, 1998). Delay to reinforcement certainly impairs the detection of a causal contingency between response and reward delivery (Lattal & Gleeson, 1990), but theoretically such signals would be more important during acquisition than during performance of the task. Nevertheless, it is possible that input from the PrLC is needed to enable rats to adjust their choice behavior as the contingencies change.

Alternatively, the frontal lesion could have impaired temporal judgment, such that the rats were impaired at judging how much time had elapsed since the start of the session and therefore which contingency was in play. Although forced-choice trials are included in the experiment to "remind" the rat as to which delay is currently in force, internally driven temporal judgments may also play a role. In support of this suggestion, damage to the PrLC does impair aspects of temporal judgment (Dietrich & Allen, 1998). In terms of other aspects of impulsivity, lesions to the ILC but not to the PrLC increase premature responding on the 5CSRT (Chudasama et al., 2003; Muir et al., 1996), so there is a precedent for the involvement of this area in impulsive behavior. However, clearly impulsive choice and impulsive action are not always mediated by identical neural circuits.

Orbitofrontal Cortex

Human patients with damage to *ventromedial frontal cortex*, incorporating the OFC, exhibit maladaptive decision making and aberrant social behavior that is often described as impulsive. These patients persist in making risky choices on the IGT (Bechara, Damasio, Damasio, & Anderson, 1994; Bechara, Damasio, Damasio, & Lee, 1999) and make riskier bets in the presence of normal probability judgments (Manes et al., 2002). Furthermore, data from patients with unilateral lesions suggest that damage to the right ventromedial PFC is sufficient to increase impulsivity on the IGT (Tranel, Bechara, & Denburg, 2002). However, unilateral damage to the right ventromedial frontal cortex alone does not produce such dramatic impairments on other gambling tasks, and a region-of-interest analysis indicated that the deficit observed on the IGT in these patients is correlated with damage outside of the ventromedial frontal cortex (Clark, Manes, Antoun, Sahakian, & Robbins, 2003). Nevertheless, there has been intensive interest in determining whether damage to the OFC increases impulsive responding in animal models to better understand the contribution made by this structure in mediating goal-directed behavior.

Although damage to the OFC leads to a transient increase in premature responding on the 5CSRT (Chudasama et al., 2003), lesions to the OFC have resulted in both increases and decreases in impulsive choice depending on the delay-discounting paradigm used. An increase in impulsive choice was observed in a two-lever choice task using a between-session shift in delay after lesions to the OFC (Mobini et al., 2002). However, the opposite effect was reported when a within-session shift in delay was used, with animals showing a marked preference for the larger delayed reward (Winstanley, Theobald, Cardinal, & Robbins, 2004). One difference between the two experiments was that in the former, the lesions were made before animals had acquired the task, whereas in the latter, lesions were made subsequent to acquisition of stable baseline behavior. Recent data, however, have suggested that this difference is not sufficient to produce these discrepant results. Rudebeck et al. (2006) observed that damage to the OFC made subsequent to task acquisition significantly but temporarily increased choice of the smaller–sooner reward. This effect was reversed by further training. This experiment used a maze-based test in which the length of the delay to the large reward was shifted between sessions, and choice of the larger–later reward was very high (about 85%). Could the effect of OFC lesions be determined by whether animals have to shift their preference within or between sessions, or are other factors at play? As discussed earlier, there may be cues present in the maze-based task that could signal choice of the delayed reward that are not so apparent in the version run in the operant chambers. Also, the baseline level of impulsive choice may influence the effects of OFC damage.

Preliminary findings have indicated that whether inactivating the OFC through local infusions of GABA agonists increases or decreases impulsive choice can indeed be affected by whether the delay is cued and the baseline level of impulsivity shown by individual rats (Zeeb, Floresco, & Winstanley,

106   CATHARINE A. WINSTANLEY

2007). These experiments used a within-session shift in delay, as per the original Evenden and Ryan (1996) task. For one set of rats, the delay to the large reward was signaled by illumination of a cue light located above the large-reward lever (Cardinal et al., 2000). Inhibiting activity in the OFC significantly decreased impulsive choice if the delay was not cued, reproducing previous findings when using this task; however, it increased impulsive choice if the delay was cued, but only in animals that showed a low level of impulsive choice at baseline, mimicking many aspects of Rudebeck et al. (2006).

The extent to which the delay to the large reward is cued clearly has marked effects on the contribution of the OFC to this form of decision making. Given the widespread use of cues in gambling, this issue warrants further investigation. When the delay is uncued, the finding that increased choice of the large reward can be induced by damage or inactivation of the OFC also requires explanation. Although seemingly paradoxical, this persistent choice of the large reward despite its associated aversive consequences (i.e., the delay) could reflect a "myopia for the future" comparable to that reported in human patients with OFC damage on laboratory-based gambling tasks (Bechara et al., 1994, p. 18). As such, damage to the OFC may prevent the adequate integration of information about the consequences of responding for a reward with the subjective value of that rewarding outcome (Schoenbaum, Chiba, & Gallagher, 1999), such that delay fails to sufficiently devalue the larger reward. The OFC has a well-established role in updating the internal representation of value of a reward when that value changes, a process that is taxed more heavily in delay-discounting paradigms incorporating a within-session shift in delay. Alternatively, the increased choice of the large reward could reflect perseverative behavior that has repeatedly been associated with OFC lesions (Chudasama et al., 2003; Chudasama & Robbins, 2003; Schoenbaum, Nugent, Saddoris, & Setlow, 2002). Further work is needed to distinguish among these myriad possibilities.

Basolateral Amygdala

The *basolateral amygdala* (BLA) shares many reciprocal connections with the OFC, and a functional connection between these two regions has been shown to be important for aspects of goal-directed behavior (Baxter, Parker, Lindner, Izquierdo, & Murray, 2000). However, in contrast to the decrease in impulsive choice seen using a noncued delay-discounting task, lesions to the BLA increased choice of the smaller–sooner reward in the same task (Winstanley, Theobald, Cardinal, & Robbins, 2004). The increase in impulsive choice seen after BLA lesions may relate to the known role of the BLA in mediating conditioned reinforcement; although there were no explicit CRs present in the task, responding on the lever leading to delivery of the large reward, or the postresponse delay itself, may function as implicit CRs, thus helping to maintain responding despite the delay to gratification (Garrud, Goodall, & Mackintosh, 1981). An inability to use these implicit CRs to guide behavior would theoretically increase impulsive choice because the value of the larger–later reward would be represented more weakly in the absence of the BLA.

Electrophysiological data have suggested that the OFC and BLA work together to encode the value of different stimuli in an odor-based go/no-go task and to track the change in their predictive value when the contingencies are reversed (i.e., if Odor A initially predicted delivery of sucrose but subsequently predicted delivery of quinine; Schoenbaum et al., 1999). Damage to the OFC affects the ability of the BLA to accurately encode aspects of stimulus value and vice versa. Interestingly, it has recently been shown that lesions to the BLA can actually ameliorate deficits in reversal learning caused by OFC lesions, indicating that the BLA loses its ability to flexibly encode changes in stimulus value without the OFC and that this rigidity significantly contributes to the impairment in reversal learning caused by OFC lesions (Stalnaker, Franz, Singh, & Schoenbaum, 2007). Whether a similar relationship between loss of flexibility of neuronal encoding in the BLA and decreased impulsive choice after silencing of the OFC exists in the delay-discounting task remains to be investigated.

Subthalamic Nucleus

The *subthalamic nucleus* (STN) is part of the basal ganglia and as such is heavily involved in regulating motor function. However, recent data have indicated that corticosubthalamic connections are involved in more cognitive processes such as attention and behavioral inhibition. Selective damage to the STN in rats has been shown to decrease impulsive choice (i.e., promote choice of the larger–later reward in delay-discounting paradigms using within-session shifts in delay; Uslaner & Robinson, 2006; Winstanley, Baunez, Theobald, & Robbins, 2005). Given that damage to this region increases premature responding on the 5CSRT (Baunez et al., 2001) and can induce perseverative responding on other tasks, it has been suggested that impairing function within the STN may increase incentive motivation for reward (Baunez, Amalric, & Robbins, 2002; Uslaner & Robinson, 2006). The relationship between the subjective valuation of reward and impulsivity clearly merits further investigation, and some effort has already been made to incorporate this factor into delay-discounting models (Ho et al., 1999).

Summary

It is clear that the way in which delay-discounting tasks are structured can have dramatic effects on the behavioral outcome of discrete brain lesions.

Whether the delay is changed between or within sessions, and the degree to which the delay to the large reward is cued, may influence the effects of damage to the NAC and OFC. Given the profound role for conditioned stimuli and CRS in guiding our behavior, some of these effects may not be surprising. Certainly, such variation in the data has prompted valuable discussions about the processes involved in delay discounting. Nevertheless, the apparently substantial influence exerted by these variations in delay-discounting methodology makes it difficult to directly compare results from different behavioral tasks. Considering just the data obtained using tasks similar to Evenden and Ryan's (1996) two-lever paradigm, incorporating a within-session shift in delay to the large reward, we can see that damage to some structures, namely the BLA and NACC, increases impulsive choice, whereas damage to other structures, such as the OFC and STN, decreases this form of impulsive decision making. Whether these findings can be taken as evidence for two competing circuits, one promoting choice of smaller–sooner rewards and the other encouraging self-control to earn larger–later rewards, is an intriguing hypothesis that remains to be tested. For clarity, I restrict discussion of the neurochemistry of delay discounting to data obtained from similar within-session delay-discounting tasks, although I should note that as with the lesion studies, different tasks have yielded discrepant findings. As noted earlier, the fact that choice behavior at different delays can be obtained within a single session is an advantage when investigating the effects of drug challenges.

NEUROCHEMICAL SYSTEMS: FOCUS ON SEROTONIN–DOPAMINE INTERACTIONS

The hypothesis that decreases in serotonergic function are associated with increases in impulsivity has proved to be of great heuristic value (Linnoila et al., 1983; Soubrie, 1986). However, of perhaps equal importance has been the emergence of the suggestion that impulsivity is not a unitary construct and that different types of impulsive behavior may be underpinned by different biological and neurochemical mechanisms (e.g., Evenden 1999). Preclinical experiments have supported the view echoed in the human literature (Crean, Richards, & de Wit, 2002) that global decreases in 5-hydroxytryptamine (5-HT) do not necessarily increase impulsive decision making, at least as measured by delay-discounting paradigms (Winstanley, Theobald, Dalley, & Robbins, 2003, 2004), although decreasing 5-HT does increase measures of behavioral disinhibition, including premature responding on the 5CSRT (Harrison, Everitt, & Robbins, 1997). However, universally increasing or decreasing 5-HT release ignores the multiple mechanisms by which the serotonergic system modulates brain function through the plethora of different 5-HT receptor subtypes found within the central nervous system. A mixed

5-HT$_{2A/2C}$ receptor antagonist had no effect in the delay-discounting paradigm (Talpos, Wilkinson, & Robbins, 2006), but this may not be surprising given that the two subtypes may act in opposition to one another (Winstanley, Theobald, Dalley, Glennon, & Robbins, 2004) and the effects of selective 5-HT$_{2A}$ and 5-HT$_{2C}$ compounds have yet to be tested. However, systemic administration of the 5-HT$_{1A}$ receptor agonist 8-OH-DPAT dramatically increased choice of the smaller–sooner reward (Winstanley, Theobald, Dalley, & Robbins, 2005). High doses of this drug are anxiogenic; therefore, it is possible that this bias away from the larger–later reward may reflect anxiety-like behavior related to the aversive nature of the delay and its association with the large-reward lever. Regardless, this effect was still present in animals after intracerebroventricular administration of 5,7-DHT, which causes widespread selective destruction of serotonergic neurons, thus indicating that 8-OH-DPAT is increasing impulsive choice through its actions at postsynaptic 5-HT$_{1A}$ receptors. The absence of this proimpulsivity effect of 8-OH-DPAT in animals with 6-OHDA lesions of the NAC suggests that interactions between the 5-HT and either dopamine (DA) or norepinephrine (NE) systems within this region may be implicated in the drug's effect.

Evidence of 5-HT–DA interactions in controlling impulsive choice is also observed when considering the effects of the psychostimulant amphetamine. This drug remains one of the most efficacious treatments for attention-deficit/hyperactivity disorder (see chaps. 8 and 12, this volume), and its effects have been largely attributed to its ability to potentiate the actions of the dopaminergic system. In a delay-discounting task, acute amphetamine administration increases choice of the larger–later alternative (e.g., van Gaalen, van Koten, Schoffelmeer, & Vanderschuren, 2006; Winstanley et al., 2003). Although administration of the DA D$_2$ receptor antagonist eticlopride attenuates the effects of amphetamine on delay discounting, both intracerebroventricular 5,7-DHT lesions and a low dose of 8-OH-DPAT have the same effect (Winstanley et al., 2003; Winstanley, Theobald, et al., 2005). It therefore appears that there may be some redundancy in the contributions made by 5-HT and DA in terms of regulating impulsivity, such that one system can compensate for the other. The most significant drug effects appear to be obtained using compounds that affect both systems, although given that 5-HT receptors are expressed on dopaminergic neurons (Doherty & Pickel, 2000, 2001), it could be argued that manipulations that globally affect serotonin levels will also lead to changes in dopaminergic neurotransmission. Clearly, more work is needed to resolve exactly how 5-HT and DA interact to control delay-discounting performance. For example, it would be interesting to explore the effects of compounds that antagonize both 5-HT and DA transmission through specific receptor subtypes. Data from in vivo microdialysis studies may also shed some light on this issue.

In Vivo Microdialysis in Awake, Behaving Rats

One way to explore the contribution of different neurotransmitters to the control of impulsivity is through the application of in vivo microdialysis techniques to behaving animals. This technique has been successfully applied to the 5CSRT and has proved instrumental in determining and dissociating the roles of various monoaminergic neurotransmitters in regulating different aspects of task performance (Dalley, Cardinal, & Robbins, 2004). As discussed earlier, the OFC appears to play an important, if contentious, role in delay-discounting performance. Although few experiments have performed in vivo microdialysis in this region, data have been obtained from both the OFC and mPFC using this technique in rats performing the delay-discounting paradigm (Winstanley, Theobald, Dalley, Cardinal, & Robbins, 2006). To control for changes in neurotransmitter efflux caused by the earning or delivery of reward, two control groups were incorporated into the experimental design. Each animal in both control groups was yoked to a particular animal in the "master" group (i.e., the group that performed the delay-discounting paradigm while being dialysed). The "forced-choice" yoked control group learned to press two levers to obtain reward, one of which provided a smaller–sooner reward, the other a larger and progressively delayed reward just as in the delay-discounting task. However, they were never allowed to choose between the levers; whether the smaller–sooner or larger–later reward lever was presented on each trial was determined by the choice the master animal made in the delay-discounting paradigm. Animals in the "free-pellets" yoked control group did not learn to press levers to obtain food reward but simply received the same amount of food reward at the same time as animals in the master group. By comparing samples taken from the master and yoked groups, it is therefore possible to parse out changes in neurotransmitter levels specific to the performance of delay-discounting judgments from those associated with receiving or responding for reward on a particular schedule.

As shown in Figure 4.2, a dissociation was observed between 5-HT efflux within the OFC and mPFC. Although no change in the 5-HT metabolite 5-hydroxyindoleacetic acid was observed in either region, a significant increase in 5-HT efflux was observed within the mPFC but only in animals performing the delay-discounting task. No significant change was observed in either of the two yoked groups. In contrast, 5-HT levels did not alter within the OFC in any group. This suggests that serotonergic modulation of the mPFC is somehow related to performance of the delay-discounting task. Given the effects of lesions to the mPFC outlined earlier, this 5-HT signal could relate to judging how much time has elapsed during the session or contribute to detection of the different reward contingencies in play. As shown in Figure 4.3, in the mPFC, levels of DA and its metabolite, 3,4-dihydroxy-phenylacetic acid (DOPAC), increase in both the master and the yoked groups. Increased

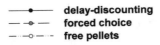

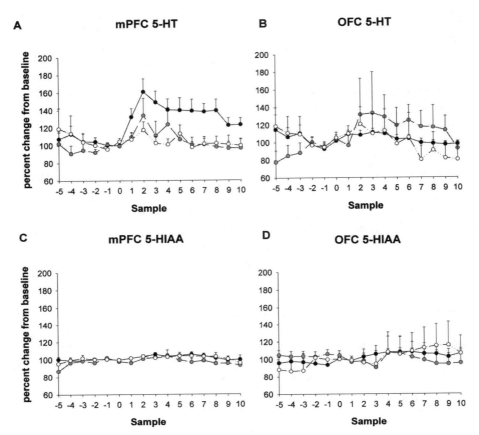

Figure 4.2. Levels of 5-hydroxytryptamine (5-HT) and 5-hydroxyindoleacetic acid (5-HIAA) in the medial prefrontal cortex (mPFC) and orbitofrontal cortex (OFC) of subjects either performing delay-discounting judgments or in the two yoked groups. Data are expressed as the percentage of change from baseline levels plus or minus the standard error of the mean. Sample 1 was the first sample to be taken during performance of the behavioral task. Samples 1 and 2 were collected when the delay to the large reward was 0 seconds, Samples 3 and 4 when the delay to the large reward was 10 seconds, Samples 5 and 6 when the delay to the large reward was 20 seconds, Samples 7 and 8 when the delay to the large reward was 40 seconds, and Samples 9 and 10 when the delay to the large reward was 60 seconds. From "Double Dissociation Between Serotonergic and Dopaminergic Modulation of Medial Prefrontal and Orbitofrontal Cortex During a Test of Impulsive Choice," by C. A. Winstanley, D. E. Theobald, J. W. Dalley, R. N. Cardinal, and T. W. Robbins, 2006, *Cerebral Cortex, 16,* p. 110. Copyright 2006 by *Cerebral Cortex.* Reprinted with permission.

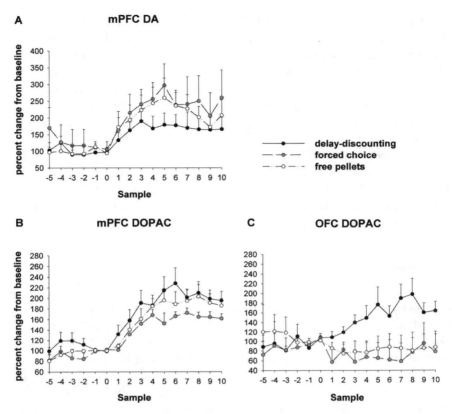

Figure 4.3. Levels of dopamine (DA) and DOPAC in the medial prefrontal cortex (mPFC) and DOPAC in the orbitofrontal cortex (OFC) of subjects either performing delay-discounting judgments or in the two yoked groups. Data are expressed as the percentage of change from baseline levels plus or minus the standard error of the mean. Sample 1 was the first sample to be taken during performance of the behavioral task. Samples 1 and 2 were collected when the delay to the large reward was 0 seconds, Samples 3 and 4 when the delay to the large reward was 10 seconds, Samples 5 and 6 when the delay to the large reward was 20 seconds, Samples 7 and 8 when the delay to the large reward was 40 seconds, and Samples 9 and 10 when the delay to the large reward was 60 seconds. From "Double Dissociation Between Serotonergic and Dopaminergic Modulation of Medial Prefrontal and Orbitofrontal Cortex During a Test of Impulsive Choice," by C. A. Winstanley, D. E. Theobald, J. W. Dalley, R. N. Cardinal, and T. W. Robbins, 2006, *Cerebral Cortex, 16,* p. 111. Copyright 2006 by *Cerebral Cortex.* Reprinted with permission.

activity of the DA system in this region may therefore signal the presence of reward or the expectation of reward delivery within this context. Looking at the OFC, it did not prove possible to accurately measure DA in this region. This was probably because levels of DA are generally lower in this region as compared with the mPFC, combined with the fact that a shorter length of dialysis membrane was used in the OFC. However, it was certainly possible to detect DOPAC. In parallel to 5-HT efflux in the mPFC, levels of DOPAC only increased within the OFC in animals engaged in the delay-discounting task, whereas no change was observed in the yoked control groups. This indicates that DA may play a specific role within the OFC in mediating delay-discounting judgments. Such a conclusion is supported by findings that 6-OHDA lesions of the OFC, which locally deplete levels of NE and DA, increase choice of the large reward when delays are increased within session, in parallel to lesions of the OFC (Kheramin et al., 2004). It would therefore appear that dopaminergic innervation of this structure is critically involved in mediating impulsive choice. Systemic administration of the DA D_1 receptor antagonist SCH-23390 has also been shown to increase choice of the small immediate reward (van Gaalen et al., 2006), although the neural locus of this effect has yet to be determined.

Norepinephrine

Although the majority of work exploring the neurochemical basis of impulsivity has focused on 5-HT and DA, it has increasingly been recognized that NE also plays an important role. The recent use of the selective NE reuptake inhibitor atomoxetine to successfully treat attention-deficit/hyperactivity disorder, particularly among adults, has further emphasized the need to understand more about NE's contributions to impulse control. In parallel with amphetamine, atomoxetine decreases impulsive choice on the delay-discounting paradigm and also decreases premature responding on the 5CSRT (Robinson et al., 2007). The contribution of different regions and receptor subtypes remains to be determined, but such work could stimulate the development of novel therapeutics for attention-deficit/hyperactivity disorder and related disorders.

Summary

This relatively brief look at the role of 5-HT and DA in delay-discounting behavior indicates that there is clearly more work to be done to resolve how and where these neurotransmitter systems interact to control impulsive choice, but that their effects may be region specific. Thus, 5-HT in the mPFC and DA in the OFC may both make important contributions to regulating delay discounting, but exactly what these neurotransmitters are signaling remains to be elucidated. It is also possible that NE may be important in the OFC, as DOPAC is formed during the metabolism of both DA and NE. If the roles of these monoamines can be understood at the level of receptor subtypes, it may be possible to design drugs to magnify or inhibit some of these effects.

CONCLUSION

Comparing delay-discounting data with those from the 5CSRT and other tests of impulsive action, it would appear that motor disinhibition and impulsive choice are underpinned by slightly different neuronal circuits that converge at key nodes such as the NAC and OFC. The fact that reducing activity in regions such as the NAC increases both response-inhibition impulsivity and delay discounting may reflect its role in cognitive processes common to both psychological constructs, such as the response to punishment or frustration. Other regions, such as the STN, appear to have opposing effects on these forms of impulsivity, which may be attributable to increased incentive motivation for reward. The fact that damage to some regions increases delay discounting whereas damage to others causes the opposite pattern of behavior leads to the idea that competing circuits exist in the brain, one encouraging self-control, the other impulsive choice. The fact that damage to different regions of the brain leads to either increases or decreases in delay discounting also reflects differences in their neurochemical regulation. For example, determining what sort of computational processes dopaminergic and serotonergic signaling influence within frontal regions may help us understand how drugs like amphetamine affect behavior. Dysfunction within the monoaminergic systems has been implicated in impulse control disorders (Faraone & Biederman, 1998), but exactly how such changes in monoamine levels give rise to impulsive symptoms is unclear. Preclinical research may be able to provide the answers to such questions by determining how changing levels of DA, 5-HT, and NE, both globally and within discrete brain regions, affect impulsive decision making. Through the continuing investigation of such issues, a more complete picture of the neural and neurochemical basis of delay discounting will, it is hoped, unfold, which could contribute to the treatment of impulse control disorders.

REFERENCES

Acheson, A., Farrar, A. M., Patak, M., Hausknecht, K. A., Kieres, A. K., Choi, S., et al. (2006). Nucleus accumbens lesions decrease sensitivity to rapid changes in the delay to reinforcement. *Behavioural Brain Research, 173*, 217–228.

Balleine, B. W., & Dickinson, A. (1998). Goal-directed instrumental action: Contingency and incentive learning and their cortical substrates. *Neuropharmacology, 37*, 407–419.

Barch, D. M., Braver, T. S., Akbudak, E., Conturo, T., Ollinger, J., & Snyder, A. (2001). Anterior cingulate cortex and response conflict: Effects of response modality and processing domain. *Cerebral Cortex, 11*, 837–848.

Baunez, C., Amalric, M., & Robbins, T. W. (2002). Enhanced food-related motivation after bilateral lesions of the subthalamic nucleus. *Journal of Neuroscience, 22*, 562–568.

Baunez, C., Humby, T., Eagle, D. M., Ryan, L. J., Dunnett, S. B., & Robbins, T. W. (2001). Effects of STN lesions on simple vs. choice reaction time tasks in the rat: preserved motor readiness, but impaired response selection. *European Journal of Neuroscience, 13,* 1609–1616.

Baxter, M. G., Parker, A., Lindner, C. C., Izquierdo, A. D., & Murray, E. A. (2000). Control of response selection by reinforcer value requires interaction of amygdala and orbital prefrontal cortex. *Journal of Neuroscience, 20,* 4311–4319.

Bechara, A., Damasio, A. R., Damasio, H., & Anderson, S. W. (1994). Insensitivity to future consequences following damage to human prefrontal cortex. *Cognition, 50,* 7–15.

Bechara, A., Damasio, H., Damasio, A. R., & Lee, G. P. (1999). Different contributions of the human amygdala and ventromedial prefrontal cortex to decision-making. *Journal of Neuroscience, 19,* 5473–5481.

Bizot, J. C., Le Bihan, C., Puech, A. J., Hamon, M., & Thiebot, M. H. (1999). Serotonin and tolerance to delay of reward in rats. *Psychopharmacology (Berlin), 146,* 400–412.

Bray, S., & O'Doherty, J. (2007). Neural coding of reward-prediction error signals during classical conditioning with attractive faces. *Journal of Neurophysiology, 97,* 3036–3045.

Bussey, T. J., Everitt, B. J., & Robbins, T. W. (1997). Dissociable effects of cingulate and medial frontal cortex lesions on stimulus-reward learning using a novel Pavlovian autoshaping procedure for the rat: Implications for the neurobiology of emotion. *Behavioural Neuroscience, 111,* 908–919.

Bussey, T. J., Muir, J. L., Everitt, B. J., & Robbins, T. W. (1996). Dissociable effects of anterior and posterior cingulate cortex lesions on the acquisition of a conditional visual discrimination: Facilitation of early learning vs. impairment of late learning. *Behavioural Brain Research, 82,* 45–56.

Cardinal, R. N., Daw, N., Robbins, T. W., & Everitt, B. J. (2002). Local analysis of behaviour in the adjusting-delay task for assessing choice of delayed reinforcement. *Neural Networks, 15,* 617–634.

Cardinal, R. N., & Howes, N. J. (2005). Effects of lesions of the nucleus accumbens core on choice between small certain rewards and large uncertain rewards in rats. *BMC Neuroscience, 6,* 37.

Cardinal, R. N., Parkinson, J. A., Lachenal, G., Halkerston, K. M., Rudarakanchana, N., Hall, J., et al. (2002). Effects of selective excitotoxic lesions of the nucleus accumbens core, anterior cingulate cortex, and central nucleus of the amygdala on autoshaping performance in rats. *Behavioral Neuroscience, 116,* 533–567.

Cardinal, R. N., Pennicott, D. R., Sugathapala, C. L., Robbins, T. W., & Everitt, B. J. (2001, June 29). Impulsive choice induced in rats by lesions of the nucleus accumbens core. *Science, 292,* 2499–2501.

Cardinal, R. N., Robbins, T. W., & Everitt, B. J. (2000). The effects of d-amphetamine, chlordiazepoxide, alpha-flupenthixol and behavioural manipulations on choice of signalled and unsignalled delayed reinforcement in rats. *Psychopharmacology (Berlin)*, *152*, 362–375.

Carli, M., Robbins, T. W., Evenden, J. L., & Everitt, B. J. (1983). Effects of lesions to ascending noradrenergic neurons on performance of a 5-choice serial reaction time task in rats—Implications for theories of dorsal noradrenergic bundle function based on selective attention and arousal. *Behavioural Brain Research*, *9*, 361–380.

Christakou, A., Robbins, T. W., & Everitt, B. J. (2004). Prefrontal-ventral striatal systems involved in affective modulation of attentional performance: Implications for corticostriatal circuitry function. *Journal of Neuroscience*, *24*, 773–780.

Chudasama, Y., Passetti, F., Rhodes, S. E. V., Lopian, D., Desai, A., & Robbins, T. W. (2003). Dissociable aspects of performance on the 5 choice serial reaction time task following lesions of the dorsal anterior cingulate, infralimbic and orbitofrontal cortex in the rat: Differential effects on selectivity, impulsivity and compulsivity. *Behavioural Brain Research*, *146*, 105–119.

Chudasama, Y., & Robbins, T. W. (2003). Dissociable contributions of the orbitofrontal and infralimbic cortex to Pavlovian autoshaping and discrimination reversal learning: Further evidence for the functional heterogeneity of the rodent frontal cortex. *Journal of Neuroscience*, *23*, 8771–8780.

Clark, L., Manes, F., Antoun, N., Sahakian, B. J., & Robbins, T. W. (2003). The contributions of lesion laterality and lesion volume to decision-making impairment following frontal lobe damage. *Neuropsychologia*, *41*, 1474–1483.

Crean, J., Richards, J. B. &, de Wit, H. (2002). Effect of tryptophan depletion on impulsive behavior in men with or without a family history of alcoholism. *Behavioural Brain Research*, *136*, 349–357.

Dalley, J. W., Cardinal, R. N., & Robbins, T. W. (2004). Prefrontal executive and cognitive function in rodents: Neural and neurochemical substrates. *Neuroscience and Biobehavioral Reviews*, *28*, 771–784.

Day, J. J., Roitman, M. F., Wightman, R. M., & Carelli, R. M. (2007). Associative learning mediates dynamic shifts in dopamine signaling in the nucleus accumbens. *Nature Neuroscience*, *10*, 1020–1028.

Dietrich, A., & Allen, J. D. (1998). Functional dissociation of the prefrontal cortex and the hippocampus in timing behavior. *Behavioral Neuroscience*, *112*, 1043–1047.

Doherty, M. D., & Pickel, V. M. (2000). Ultrastructural localization of the serotonin 2A receptor in dopaminergic neurons in the ventral tegmental area. *Brain Research*, *864*, 176–185.

Doherty, M. D., & Pickel, V. M. (2001). Targeting of serotonin 1A receptors to dopaminergic neuron within the parabrachial subdivision of the ventral tegmental area. *Journal of Comparative Neurology*, *433*, 390–400.

Evenden, J. L. (1999). Varieties of impulsivity. *Psychopharmacology (Berlin)*, *146*, 348–361.

Evenden, J. L., & Ryan, C. N. (1996). The pharmacology of impulsive behaviour in rats: The effects of drugs on response choice with varying delays of reinforcement. *Psychopharmacology (Berlin)*, *128*, 161–170.

Faraone, S. V., & Biederman, J. (1998). Neurobiology of attention-deficit hyperactivity disorder. *Biological Psychiatry, 44*, 951–958.

Garrud, P., Goodall, G., & Mackintosh, N. J. (1981). Overshadowing of a stimulus-reinforcer association by an instrumental response. *Quarterly Journal of Experimental Psychology: Journal of Comparative and Physiological Psychology, 33*(B), 123–135.

Hall, J., Parkinson, J. A., Connor, T. M., Dickinson, A., & Everitt, B. J. (2001). Involvement of the central nucleus of the amygdala and nucleus accumbens core in mediating Pavlovian influences on instrumental behaviour. *European Journal of Neuroscience, 13*, 1984–1992.

Harrison, A. A., Everitt, B. J., & Robbins, T. W. (1997). Central 5-HT depletion enhances impulsive responding without affecting the accuracy of attentional performance: Interactions with dopaminergic mechanisms. *Psychopharmacology (Berlin), 133*, 329–342.

Ho, M. Y., Mobini, S., Chiang, T. J., Bradshaw, C. M., & Szabadi, E. (1999). Theory and method in the quantitative analysis of "impulsive choice" behaviour: Implications for psychopharmacology. *Psychopharmacology (Berlin), 146*, 362–372.

Kheramin, S., Body, S., Ho, M. Y., Velazquez-Martinez, D. N., Bradshaw, C. M., Szabadi, E., et al. (2004). Effects of orbital prefrontal cortex dopamine depletion on inter-temporal choice: A quantitative analysis. *Psychopharmacology (Berlin), 175*, 206–214.

Lamm, C., Zelazo, P. D., & Lewis, M. D. (2006). Neural correlates of cognitive control in childhood and adolescence: Disentangling the contributions of age and executive function. *Neuropsychologia, 44*, 2139–2148.

Lattal, K. A., & Gleeson, S. (1990). Response acquisition with delayed reinforcement. *Journal of Experimental Psychology: Animal Behavior Processes, 16*, 27–39.

Linnoila, M., Virkkunen, M., Scheinin, M., Nuutila, A., Rimon, R., & Goodwin, F. K. (1983). Low cerebrospinal-fluid 5-Hydroxyindoleacetic acid concentration differentiates impulsive from nonimpulsive violent behavior. *Life Sciences, 33*, 2609–2614.

Manes, F., Sahakian, B. J., Clark, L., Rogers, R. D., Antoun, N., Aitken, M., et al. (2002). Decision-making processes following damage to prefrontal cortex. *Brain, 125*, 624–639.

Mazur, J. (1987). An adjusting procedure for studying delayed reinforcement. In M. L. Commons, J. A. Nevin, & H. C. Rachlin (Eds.), *Quantitative analyses of behaviour: The effect of delay and intervening events on reinforcement value* (Vol. 5, pp. 55–73). Hillsdale, NJ: Erlbaum.

Mobini, S., Body, S., Ho, M. Y., Bradshaw, C. M., Szabadi, E., Deakin, J. F. W., et al. (2002). Effects of lesions of the orbitofrontal cortex on sensitivity to delayed and probabilistic reinforcement. *Psychopharmacology (Berlin), 160*, 290–298.

Mobini, S., Chiang, T. J., Ho, M. Y., Bradshaw, C. M., & Szabadi, E. (2000). Effects of central 5-hydroxytryptamine depletion on sensitivity to delayed and probabilistic reinforcement. *Psychopharmacology (Berlin), 152*, 390–397.

Moeller, F. G., Barratt, E. S., Dougherty, D. M., Schmitz, J. M., & Swann, A. C. (2001). Psychiatric aspects of impulsivity. *American Journal of Psychiatry, 158,* 1783–1793.

Muir, J. L., Everitt, B. J., & Robbins, T. W. (1996). The cerebral cortex of the rat and visual attentional function: Dissociable effects of mediofrontal, cingulate, anterior dorsolateral, and parietal cortex lesions on a five-choice serial reaction time task. *Cerebral Cortex, 6,* 470–481.

Naccache, L., Dehaene, S., Cohen, L., Habert, M. O., Guichart-Gomez, E., Galanaud, D., et al. (2005). Effortless control: Executive attention and conscious feeling of mental effort are dissociable. *Neuropsychologia, 43,* 1318–1328.

Parkinson, J. A., Olmstead, M. C., Burns, L. H., Robbins, T. W., & Everitt, B. J. (1999). Dissociation in effects of lesions of the nucleus accumbens core and shell on appetitive Pavlovian approach behavior and the potentiation of conditioned reinforcement and locomotor activity by d-amphetamine. *Journal of Neuroscience, 19,* 2401–2411.

Richards, J. B., Mitchell, S. H., de Wit, H., & Seiden, L. S. (1997). Determination of discount functions in rats with an adjusting-amount procedure. *Journal of the Experimental Analysis of Behavior, 67,* 353–366.

Robinson, E. S., Eagle, D. M., Mar, A. C., Bari, A., Banerjee, G., Jiang, X., et al. (2007). Similar effects of the selective noradrenaline reuptake inhibitor atomoxetine on three distinct forms of impulsivity in the rat. *Neuropsychopharmacology, 33,* 1028–1037.

Rosvold, H. E., Mirsky, A. F., Sarason, I., Bransome, E. D., & Beck, L. H. (1956). A continuous performance test of brain damage. *Journal of Consulting Psychology, 20,* 343–350.

Rudebeck, P. H., Walton, M. E., Smyth, A. N., Bannerman, D. M., & Rushworth, M. F. (2006). Separate neural pathways process different decision costs. *Nature Neuroscience, 9,* 1161–1168.

Schoenbaum, G., Chiba, A. A., & Gallagher, M. (1999). Neural encoding in orbitofrontal cortex and basolateral amygdala during olfactory discrimination learning. *Journal of Neuroscience, 19,* 1876–1884.

Schoenbaum, G., Nugent, S., Saddoris, M. P., & Setlow, B. (2002). Orbitofrontal lesions in rats impair reversal but not acquisition of a go, no-go odor discriminations. *NeuroReport, 13,* 885–890.

Schultz, W., Dayan, P., & Montague, P. R. (1997, March 14). A neural substrate of prediction and reward. *Science, 275,* 1593–1599.

Soubrie, P. (1986). Reconciling the role of central serotonin neurons in human and animal behavior. *Behavioral and Brain Sciences, 9,* 319–364.

Stalnaker, T. A., Franz, T. M., Singh, T., & Schoenbaum, G. (2007). Basolateral amygdala lesions abolish orbitofrontal-dependent reversal impairments. *Neuron, 54,* 51–58.

Talpos, J. C., Wilkinson, L. S., & Robbins, T. W. (2006). A comparison of multiple 5-HT receptors in two tasks measuring impulsivity. *Journal of Psychopharmacology, 20,* 47–58.

Tranel, D., Bechara, A., & Denburg, N. L. (2002). Asymmetric functional roles of right and left ventromedial prefrontal cortices in social conduct, decision-making, and emotional processing. *Cortex, 38,* 589–612.

Uslaner, J. M., & Robinson, T. E. (2006). Subthalamic nucleus lesions increase impulsive action and decrease impulsive choice—Mediation by enhanced incentive motivation? *European Journal of Neuroscience, 24,* 2345–2354.

van Gaalen, M. M., van Koten, R., Schoffelmeer, A. N., & Vanderschuren, L. J. (2006). Critical involvement of dopaminergic neurotransmission in impulsive decision making. *Biological Psychiatry, 60,* 66–73.

Voorn, P., Gerfen, C. R., & Groenewegen, H. J. (1989). Compartmental organisation of the ventral striatum of the rat: Immunohistochemical distribution of enkephalin, substance-p, dopamine and calcium-binding protein. *Journal of Comparative Neurology, 289,* 189–201.

Walton, M. E., Bannerman, D. M., Alterescu, K., & Rushworth, M. F. (2003). Functional specialization within medial frontal cortex of the anterior cingulate for evaluating effort-related decisions. *Journal of Neuroscience, 23,* 6475–6479.

Walton, M. E., Bannerman, D. M., & Rushworth, M. F. (2002). The role of rat medial frontal cortex in effort-based decision making. *Journal of Neuroscience, 22,* 10996–11003.

Winstanley, C. A., Baunez, C., Theobald, D. E., & Robbins, T. W. (2005). Lesions to the subthalamic nucleus decrease impulsive choice but impair autoshaping in rats: The importance of the basal ganglia in Pavlovian conditioning and impulse control. *European Journal of Neuroscience, 21,* 3107–3116.

Winstanley, C. A., Theobald, D. E., Cardinal, R. N., & Robbins, T. W. (2004). Contrasting roles for basolateral amygdala and orbitofrontal cortex in impulsive choice. *Journal of Neuroscience, 24,* 4718–4722.

Winstanley, C. A., Theobald, D. E., Dalley, J. W., Cardinal, R. N., & Robbins, T. W. (2006). Double dissociation between serotonergic and dopaminergic modulation of medial prefrontal and orbitofrontal cortex during a test of impulsive choice. *Cerebral Cortex, 16,* 106–114.

Winstanley, C. A., Theobald, D. E., Dalley, J. W., Glennon, J. C., & Robbins, T. W. (2004). 5-HT2A and 5-HT2C receptor antagonists have opposing effects on a measure of impulsivity: Interactions with global 5-HT depletion. *Psychopharmacology (Berlin), 176,* 376–385.

Winstanley, C. A., Theobald, D. E., Dalley, J. W., & Robbins, T. W. (2003). Global 5-HT depletion attenuates the ability of amphetamine to decrease impulsive choice in rats. *Psychopharmacology (Berlin), 170,* 320–331.

Winstanley, C. A., Theobald, D. E., Dalley, J. W., & Robbins, T. W. (2004). Fractionating impulsivity: Contrasting effects of central 5-HT depletion on different measures of impulsive behavior. *Neuropsychopharmacology, 29,* 1331–1343.

Winstanley, C. A., Theobald, D. E., Dalley, J. W., & Robbins, T. W. (2005). Interactions between serotonin and dopamine in the control of impulsive choice in rats:

Therapeutic implications for impulse control disorders. *Neuropsychopharmacology*, *30*, 669–682.

Zaborsky, L., Alheid, G. F., Beinfield, M. C., Eiden, L. E., Heimer, L., & Palkovits, M. (1985). Cholecystokinin innervation of the ventral striatum: A morphological and radioimmunological study. *Neuroscience, 14*, 427–453.

Zeeb, F. D., Floresco, S. B., & Winstanley, C. A. (2007, November). *What makes it worth the wait? Investigating the effects of orbitofrontal cortex inactivation on impulsive choice*. Paper presented at the 37th Annual Meeting of the Society for Neuroscience, San Diego, CA.

Zelazo, P. D., & Muller, U. (2002). Executive function in typical and atypical development. In U. Goswani (Ed.), *Handbook of childhood cognitive development* (pp. 445–469). Oxford, England: Blackwell.

5

NEURAL MODELS OF DELAY DISCOUNTING

A. DAVID REDISH AND ZEB KURTH-NELSON

In this chapter, we address the question of delay discounting from the perspective of computational neuroscience. We first review why agents must discount future rewards in order to make reasoned decisions and then discuss the role of delay discounting in the context of the temporal-difference reinforcement learning family of decision-making algorithms. These algorithms require exponential discounting functions to achieve mathematical stability, but as noted in the other chapters in this volume, humans and other animals show hyperbolic discounting functions. In the second half of the chapter, we review four theories for this discrepancy: (a) competition between two decision-making systems, (b) interactions between multiple exponential discounting functions, (c) normalization by estimates of average reward, and (d) effects of errors in temporal perception. All four theories are likely to contribute to the effect of hyperbolic discounting.

We thank Nathanial Daw, John Ferguson, Adam Johnson, Steve Jensen, and Matthijs van der Meer as well as Warren Bickel, Reid Landes, and Jim Kakalios for helpful discussions. We thank Adam Johnson and Steve Jensen for comments on a draft of the manuscript. This work was supported by National Institutes of Health Grant R01 DA024080.

123

INTRODUCTION

The necessity of discounting arises from the recognition of uncertainty and risk—something may happen that precludes receiving the prima facie value of a delayed reward. Technically, the value of each choice is the expected reward integrated over all future possibilities. Thus, if the expected reward achieved from a decision is not going to be delivered for 24 hours, one has to integrate over all the possible events that could happen within that 24 hours, including starving to death, being hit by a bus, global thermonuclear war, money raining down from space, and all the other possibilities. Although many of these possibilities are so rare as to be ignorable in the first approximation, any agent[1] attempting to actually calculate this would face an inordinate calculation with nearly infinite unknown variables. Additionally, integrating over future possibilities must include all the consequences of selecting an option, carried out for the infinite future. In the artificial intelligence and robotics literatures, this problem is known as the *infinite horizon problem* (Sutton & Barto, 1998). In practice, the calculation would be extremely computationally expensive. Additionally, the calculation would require estimates of a large number of unknown variables (such as the actual probability of thermonuclear war happening in the next 24 hours). A much simpler process is to approximate the uncertainty and risk in a discounting function that reduces the value of delayed rewards. Similarly, immediately delivered rewards are more valuable than they appear on the surface because one can invest those rewards (whether in terms of monetary investments [Frederick, Loewenstein, & O'Donoghue, 2002] or in terms of energy resources for increasing offspring and improving evolutionary success [Rogers, 1997; Stephens & Krebs, 1987]). As noted earlier, this could be calculated explicitly by integrating over all possible futures following the choice. Again, this is a computationally expensive calculation with many unknown variables. A much simpler process is to approximate the lost investment of waiting by a discounting function that reduces the value of delayed rewards.

Technically, any function that monotonically decreases with time (Equation 1) will meet the primary criteria laid out earlier (accommodate uncertainty, risk, and lost investments):

$$V_d(r) = f(r,d)$$
$$f(r,d_1) < f(r,d_2) \text{ if and only if } d_1 > d_2, \tag{1}$$

---

[1]For simplicity, we use the term *agent* to refer to any decision-making system (including humans and other animals as well as simulations). *Agency* is used without any prejudice or presumption regarding free will.

where $V_d(r)$ is the estimated value of receiving expected reward r after expected delay d. However, for many reasons, an exponential discounting function (Equation 2) is a logically sound choice (Samuelson, 1937).

$$V_d(r) = r \cdot \gamma^{d/\tau} = r \cdot e^{-kd/\tau},\qquad(2)$$

where r is the expected reward and d is the expected delay before receiving the reward; τ is a constant that defines the time scale of the delay. The rate of exponential discounting can be expressed either in terms of a temporal constant $k > 0$ (usually used in the animal and human discounting literature; e.g., Ainslie, 1992, 2001; Bickel & Marsch, 2001; Mazur, 1997, 2001; Madden, Petry, Badger, & Bickel, 1997; Myerson and Green, 1995) or in terms of a γ discounting factor ($0 < \gamma < 1$, usually used in the artificial intelligence and robotics literatures; e.g., Daw, 2003; Sutton & Barto, 1998). Under simple assumptions of compound interest with no uncertainty, exponential discounting is the most logical choice for a discounting function because the discounting rate is a constant over time (Frederick et al., 2002; Samuelson, 1937); however, as noted later, there is an ongoing debate as to whether exponential discounting remains a logical choice under more realistic conditions of uncertainty and measurement error (Frederick et al., 2002; Gallistel & Gibbon, 2000; Sozou, 1998). Nevertheless, because of its underlying regularity, exponential discounting allows a simple iterative calculation of value through experience, which simplifies the learning algorithms (Bellman, 1958; Daw, 2003; Sutton & Barto, 1998).

The Bellman Equation

First discovered by Bellman in 1958, the Bellman equation provides an algorithm to learn the value of states (or situations[2]) within the environment. Once one can predict the value of situations, then one can make decisions on which actions to take on the basis of the predicted consequences of those actions. The Bellman equation, however, depends on exponential discounting (Daw, 2003). It is most easily seen in the discrete formulation (Sutton & Barto, 1998), but it is easily translatable into a temporally continuous formulation (Daw, 2003; Daw, Courville, & Touretzky, 2006; Doya, 2000b). Starting from an exponentially discounted value function

$$V(t_0) = \sum_{t = t_0}^{\infty} \gamma^{t-t_0} E[r(t)],\qquad(3)$$

---

[2]The term *situation* refers to the agent's classification of the state of the world (including the agent) from which the agent can reason about decisions. We prefer *situation* over the psychology term *stimulus* so as to include context, cue, and interactions between cues, all of which are critical for appropriate behavior. Similarly, we prefer *situation* over the robotics term *state* to prevent confusion with internal parameters of the agent (e.g., motivation states). See Redish, Jensen, Johnson, and Kurth-Nelson (2007) and Zilli and Hasselmo (2008) for further discussion of these issues.

where $V(t_0)$ is the value at time t_0 (i.e., the total integrated expected reward over the future from t_0). Because $V(t_0)$ can be written as

$$V(t_0) = r_0 + \gamma(r_1 + \gamma^1 r_2 + \gamma^2 r_3 + \cdots), \qquad (4)$$

and because value at one time step later, $t_1 = t_0 + 1$, is also

$$V(t_1) = r_1 + \gamma^1 r_2 + \gamma^2 r_3 + \cdots, \qquad (5)$$

we can thus rewrite value at time t_0 as a function of value at time $t_1 = t_0 + 1$:

$$V(t_0) = r_0 + \gamma V(t_1). \qquad (6)$$

If one stores estimates of the value of a given situation $\hat{V}(s)$, then Equation 6 provides a mechanism with which one can select actions within a given situation by estimating the value of taking an action within a given situation

$$\hat{V}(s,a) = E(r) + \gamma \hat{V}(s'), \qquad (7)$$

where $E(r)$ is the estimated reward to be received immediately on taking action a in situation s, and s' is the estimated new situation one expects to be in (at time $t + 1$). $\hat{V}(s')$ is the estimated value of being in situation s'.

Even more important, this equation provides a way of updating one's estimate of value on taking an action by calculating the value prediction error δ as the difference between the expected value estimate $\hat{V}(s,a)$ and observed values (based on the actually received observed reward and the actually identified new situation). Obviously, if one can improve the estimation of the value of the situation, then one will make better decisions the next time one encounters that situation:

$$\delta(s,a) = V(s,a) - \hat{V}(s,a)$$
$$= \left[r(t) + \gamma \hat{V}(s') \right] - \hat{V}(s,a), \qquad (8)$$

where s' is now the actual new situation one has achieved. The value estimate $\hat{V}(s,a)$ can be easily updated from this δ term:

$$\hat{V}(s,a) \leftarrow \hat{V}(s,a) + \eta\delta, \qquad (9)$$

where η is a constant that controls the learning rate.

Equations 8 and 9 can easily be extended to the continuous formulation by moving from a discrete-time state space to a continuous-time state space (Daw, 2003; Daw, Courville, & Touretzky, 2006; Doya, 2000b; Redish, 2004). In both the discrete and continuous models, all information about the agent's history is assumed to be contained in the discrete state *s* that describes the agent's understanding of the world. In the discrete-time models, the agent is assumed to take an action *a* (potentially the null action) after each discrete time step Δt, taking the agent from state $s(t)$ to state $s(t + \Delta t)$. In the continuous-time model, the agent is assumed to remain in state $s(t)$ for a given amount of time *d*. When the agent's hypothesis of the world changes (either through action taken by the agent or through events in the world), the state changes to a new state *s'*. Value of a given state is identified with entry into that state (Daw, 2003), and thus the value update must take into account the time *d* that the agent spent in state *s* before transitioning to *s'*. Thus in the continuous-time model, Equation 8 becomes

$$\delta(s,a) = \gamma^d \left[r(t) + \hat{V}(s') \right] - \hat{V}(s,a), \tag{10}$$

where *d* is the time spent in situation *s* before taking action *a* to get to situation *s'*. Because the reward was also delayed by time *d*, it must also be discounted when calculating δ.

Under specific conditions of stationarity, observability, and sufficient exploration, the exponential update equations of the Bellman equation can be proven to converge on the actual value of taking an action *a* in situation *s*: $V(s,a)$ (Daw, 2003; Sutton & Barto, 1998).[3]

Nonexponential Discounting Functions

As appealing as the exponential discounting model is, extensive evidence has shown that neither humans facing monetary decisions nor animals (including humans) facing more direct reward (e.g., food, water) decisions discount future choices with a constant discounting rate (Ainslie, 1992, 2001; Frederick et al., 2002; Green & Myerson, 2004; Mazur, 1985, 1997; Strotz, 1955). Qualitatively, experimental data show choice reversal, and quantitatively, the data are better fit by regression to nonexponential functions. Three methods have been used to measure discounting functions: questionnaires (Bickel & Marsch, 2001; Bickel et al., 2007; Myerson & Green, 1995), titrated

---

[3]New models have begun to explore the limitations of these assumptions, including relaxing assumptions of stationarity (e.g., Courville, Daw, & Touretzky, 2006; Redish et al., 2007), assumptions of observability (e.g., Daw, Courville, & Touretzeky, 2002b, 2006; Yu & Dayan, 2005), and assumptions of exploration (e.g., Daw, O'Doherty, Dayan, Seymour, & Dolan, 2006; Kakade & Dayan, 2002). Others have begun incorporating the potential effects of working and episodic memory (Zilli & Hasselmo, 2008). However, these issues are not immediately relevant to this review and are not pursued further here.

delivery of real rewards after a delay (the adjusting-delay assay; Mazur, 1985, 1997, 2001; Richards, Mitchell, de Wit, & Seiden, 1997), and correlations with decisions as they were made (Sugrue, Corrado, & Newsome, 2004; Tanaka et al., 2004, 2007).

In questionnaire assays, humans are given a set of choices between receiving a set amount r_1 at a given time t_1 (often "now") with a set amount r_2 at a later time t_2 ($t_2 > t_1, r_2 > r_1$). From the set of choices made for a given delay $t_2 - t_1$ at a given time t_1, it is possible to derive an indifference point, defined as the time t_2 at which $V_{t_1}(r_1) = V_{t_2}(r_2)$. From the set of indifference points, one can calculate the expected value of a given reward r after a given delay d (Ainslie, 1992; Bickel et al., 2007; Myerson & Green, 1995). Although there have been concerns about potential confounds of real versus hypothetical choices (Kacelnik, 1997; Kirby, 1997), experiments have found qualitatively similar results under both conditions (Johnson & Bickel, 2002; Kirby, 1997). Usually, questionnaires are given in a random order and analyses are done postexperiment, but some recent experiments have used a titration method in which intervals are narrowed until the indifference point is found (Wittmann, Leland, & Paulus, 2007). This allows questionnaire techniques to achieve a block design capable of being used with functional magnetic resonance imaging (fMRI). Although it is obviously impossible to have animals complete questionnaires about hypothetical choices, it is possible to signal the values and delays of available choices before an animal acts, providing it with a questionnaire-like behavior (Sohn & Lee, 2007).

In the adjusting-delay assay, agents are given two choices a_1 and a_2, leading to two rewards r_1 and r_2, delivered after two delays d_1 and d_2. Action a_1 brings reward r_1 after delay d_1; action a_2 brings reward r_2 after delay d_2. For a given experiment, both reward (r_1, r_2) and the first delay (d_1) variables are held fixed, and delay d_2 is titrated until the probability of choosing each action is equal: If the agent chooses action a_1, the delay d_2 is reduced on the next trial, whereas if the agent chooses action a_2, the delay d_2 is increased on the next trial. At the point at which the two actions are chosen with equal probability, we can say that the agent's estimate of the values of the two choices are equal, $V_{d_1}(r_1) = V(a_1) = V(a_2) = V_{d_2}(r_2)$. The slope of the curve of titrated d_2 delays as a function of fixed d_1 delays indicates the discounting function used by the agent (Mazur, 1997). In the case of exponential discounting (Equation 2), the slope will be 1, regardless of r_1 or r_2. In the case of hyperbolic discounting, the slope will reflect the ratio of rewards r_2/r_1 (Mazur, 1997). Experiments have consistently shown slopes significantly different from 1 and generally consistent with the ratio of rewards r_2/r_1 and with hyperbolic discounting (Mazur, 1985, 1997). A similar process can hold the delays fixed while adjusting the amount r_2. This procedure also produces slopes more consistent with hyperbolic discounting than with exponential discounting (Richards et al., 1997). Because these experiments require actual choices, actual rewards, and actual delays, these experiments are limited to fast time courses (seconds). Because these experiments are based on repeated trials, one may need to take into account the actual reward sequence achieved (or potentially available) to the animal (Daw, 2003), including the inherent variability of that sequence (Kacelnik & Bateson, 1996). Such procedures can be used in both animal (Mazur, 1997) and human (McClure, Ericson, Laibson, Loewenstein, & Cohen, 2007) experiments.

The third option is to calculate the expected value from an agent given a sequence of decision choices with a complex reward structure (e.g., Sugrue et al., 2004; Tanaka et al., 2004, 2007). These reward sequences imply changes in the value delivered to the agent. For example, Tanaka et al. (2004) tested participants in an experiment in which they had to continuously alternate between a task in which the optimal solution was to select immediate rewards (short condition) and a task in which the optimal solution was to select delayed rewards (long condition). From each participant's actual selections, Tanaka et al. calculated the estimated value (based on an exponential discounting function) at each moment in time. This function is, of course, dependent on the discounting factor γ. This calculation gave Tanaka et al. two time series: one of the value at time t that was a function of the discounting factor used and the other the fMRI blood oxygen level dependent (BOLD) signal. They then correlated the two signals to determine whether there were any significant relationships between value estimates and the BOLD signal. Similar procedures have been used in animal decision-making tasks (Bayer & Glimcher, 2005; Bayer, Lau, & Glimcher, 2007; Sugrue et al., 2004).

These experiments measure discounting functions at different time scales (questionnaires: days to weeks to years; titrated delay: seconds; decision choices: seconds to minutes) and with different substances (money, food, drugs). Although analogous procedures can be used on both humans and animals, for obvious reasons questionnaires tend to be used with humans and titrated delay experiments tend to be used with animals. Thus, some of the differences in time scales may be due to differences in subjects rather than the procedures themselves.

Discounting rates in humans have been found to change both with size of reward offered (e.g., $1,000 vs. $10,000; Green, Myerson, & McFadden, 1997; Kirby, 1997; Myerson & Green, 1995) and with substance (e.g., food vs. money; Estle, Green, Myerson, & Holt, 2007; Odum & Rainaud, 2003). Titration experiments in animals (rats, pigeons) have not found a similar effect of size of reward on discounting rate (Grace, 1999; Green, Myerson, Holt, Slevin, & Estle, 2004; Ong & White, 2004). Recent evidence, in fact, has found that reward size and delay to reward receipt are encoded in different populations of neurons within the rodent orbitofrontal cortex (Roesch, Taylor, & Schoenbaum, 2006). Although experiments comparing valuation of different substances have been done in several animal species (Kelley & Berridge, 2002; Padoa-Schioppa & Assad, 2006, 2008; Tremblay & Schultz,

1999), these experiments have not directly examined the dependence of delay on valuation. However, lexigraphic experiments in multiple species have consistently found differences in ability to inhibit responding and ability to wait (related to discounting rate) between lexigraphic rewards (in which rewards are indicated by symbols) and directly given rewards (in which the rewards are directly visible; Boysen & Berntson, 1995; Evans & Beran, 2007; Metcalfe & Mischel, 1999; Mischel & Underwood, 1974), which may indicate the importance of linguistic abilities for long delays (Beran, Savage-Rumbaugh, Pate, & Rumbaugh, 1999; Metcalfe & Mischel, 1999).

It is unclear at this point whether these various paradigms access the same systems and mechanisms or whether there are systems and mechanisms specifically aligned to specific time courses or specific rewards. However, all of the available neural models are based on the concept that all three experimental paradigms are measuring the same phenomena. Data, such as fMRI data from McClure, Berns, and Montague (2003; McClure, Laibson, Loewenstein, & Cohen, 2004; McClure et al., 2007) and Tanaka et al. (2004, 2007), have suggested that the same neural structures are involved in the discounting seen by all three methods. However, fMRI data from humans in a titrated questionnaire paradigm have suggested that there may be different structures involved with medium time scale (less than 1 year) and very long time scale (more than 1 year) discounting functions (Wittmann et al., 2007).

These experiments imply that the change in discounting produced by a set increase in the delay is not a constant (as would be true for exponential discounting). The changing discount rate is usually modeled by a hyperbolic discounting function, as suggested by Ainslie (1975, 1992, 2001) and Mazur (1985, 1997):

$$V_d(r) = \frac{r}{1 + kd}, \tag{11}$$

where r is the expected reward and d is the expected delay before receiving the reward.[4] This function fits the animal experimental data at fast time scales (seconds) significantly better than do exponential functions (Mazur, 1985, 1997) and has been found to explain a large percentage of the variance as evidenced from questionnaires (addressing long time scales [days to weeks to years]; Bickel et al., 2007; Madden et al., 1997; Myerson & Green, 1995; Reynolds, 2006). However, there is some deviation of the animal experimental data from Equation 11. Similarly, indifference points measured by questionnaires show consistent deviations from Equation 11, particularly at longer time scales (Bickel et al., 2007; Madden, Bickel, & Jacobs, 1999; Mitchell, 1999; Myerson & Green, 1995; Reynolds, 2006).

Although the issue of whether a hyperbolic discounting function is a more valid normative accounting of decision making than an exponential function

---

[4]In other chapters in this book, the term A is used for *amount of reward*. We use the term r for *reward* to avoid confusion with action a.

is still being debated (Ainslie, 1992, 2001; Frederick et al., 2002; Kacelnik, 1997; Rogers, 1997; Sozou, 1998), there is little doubt that it is a more valid descriptive account than an exponential function (Bickel et al., 2007; Mazur, 1997; Myerson & Green, 1995). Although there are still some researchers who argue that hyperbolic discounting is a consequence of the specific research methods designed to study the question (e.g., Rubenstein, 2003), if animals (including humans) did, in fact, use an exponential discounting function to discount future choices, one would still require an explanation for choice reversal. Any nonexponential discounting function must produce changing choices with changing delays—a decision that prefers Option B delayed by 2 weeks over Option A delayed by 1 week can switch when Option A is offered immediately and Option B is offered in 1 week (Ainslie, 1992, 2001; Ainslie & Monterosso, 2004; Frederick et al., 2002; Strotz, 1955). Because the discount rate for exponential discounting does not change with time, choice reversal cannot occur. However, delay-dependent choice reversal is well established at all time scales (Ainslie, 1992, 2001; Bickel et al., 2007; Mazur, 1997).

A number of other functions have also been proposed (see Rodriguez & Logue, 1988, for review), most notably the "extended hyperbolic" equation

$$V_d(r) = \frac{r}{(1 + kd)^b},$$ (12)

where b is an additional constant, which Myerson and Green (1995; Green & Myerson, 2004; Green, Myerson, & Macaux, 2005) have reported provides a better fit to the data than does Equation 11. Including the b term generalizes the standard hyperbolic discounting function to a more general power law. Whether another function can better describe the data remains an open question.

Unfortunately, hyperbolic discounting has several computational difficulties. First, because the discounting rate changes with each time step, there is no analytical solution to Equation 11, nor can the calculation be performed incrementally analogous to the Bellman equation (Daw, 2003). One can substitute the hyperbolic discounting function into the Bellman equation anyway,

$$\delta(s,a) = \frac{\left[r(t) + \hat{V}(s') \right]}{1 + kd} - \hat{V}(s,a),$$ (13)

where k is the discounting factor and d is the time spent in situation s before taking action a. This equation is equivalent to that used in the addiction simulations of Redish (2004; see also Kurth-Nelson & Redish, 2004a). A similar proposal has been made recently by Kalenscher and Pennartz (2008). Action selection based on this equation leads to generally reasonable behavior (Kurth-Nelson and Redish, 2004b), but this equation is intrinsically inconsistent because the discounting rate depends on the number of subparts identified within a task. A situation identified as a single part (situation s_0 proceeds to situation s') that lasts for a given time before an action is taken is discounted hyperbolically, but if the same situation is identified by a set of subparts (situation s_0 leads to situation s_1 leading to situation s_2 . . . eventually leading to situation s'), then the discounting function deviates from the predicted hyperbolic function dramatically.

For example, take a Pavlovian experiment, in which a cue is followed some set number of seconds later by a reward. At the appearance of the cue, the animal can predict the subsequent reward. The expected value of the cue should take into account the delay before the reward. If the neural representation encodes this as two situations (an interstimulus interval [ISI] lasting for the set number of seconds followed by reward; Daw, 2003; Daw, Courville, & Touretzky, 2006; Redish, 2004), Equation 13 only performs a single step of hyperbolic discounting. In contrast, if the neural representation encodes each second as a different situation (ISI_1, ISI_2, ISI_3, etc.; Daw, 2003; Niv, Duff, & Dayan, 2005), then Equation 13 runs through 10 steps. Because a composition of hyperbolic terms is not hyperbolic, the discounted value of the cue is no longer hyperbolic. Whether dopamine signals in the primate brain imply that time intervals are encoded by time within a single situation or by a chain of intervening states or situations is still controversial (Fiorillo, Tobler, & Schultz, 2005; Niv et al., 2005; Wörgötter & Porr, 2005).

Simulations demonstrating this effect are shown in Figure 5.1, which compares a simulated agent that remains in the ISI situation through the entire delay before transitioning to a reward-delivery situation (Panels A and B), and another in which the ISI is represented by multiple 1-second subsituations (Panels C and D). If the temporal difference reinforcement learning algorithm is implemented directly with Equation 13, then the agent shows hyperbolic discounting across the first state space but not the second. The multiple-exponentials model (see Multiple Exponential Discounting Systems section) shows hyperbolic discounting across both by maintaining multiple independent exponential discounting "microagents" (µAgent). Each µAgent applies a complete temporal-difference reinforcement learning agent (Daw, 2003; Sutton & Barto, 1998), with independent situation s_i, value estimation[5] $\hat{V}_i(s,a)$, value prediction error (δ_i), and action selection components (Kurth-Nelson & Redish, 2004a; Redish, 2004).

This analysis shows that the one-step hyperbolic equation (Equation 13) is internally inconsistent. Different conceptual representations of the time during an ISI produce different discounting functions. This means that if temporal difference reinforcement learning algorithms are implemented with a

[5]This model maintains independent value estimations across all the µAgents. If the µAgents instead maintain a shared value estimation, the model reverts to be equivalent to the direct implementation of hyperbolic discounting (Equation 13), showing hyperbolic discounting across only a single state transition.

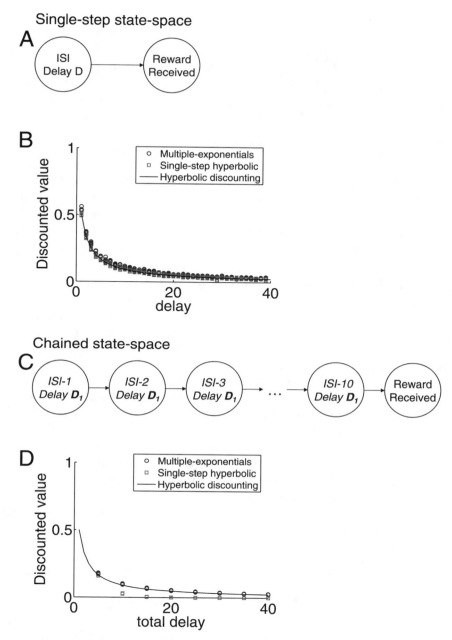

Figure 5.1. Discounting across state chains. A: Single-step state space. B: Discounting over a single-step state space as a function of the delay *D* in state S_0. Both value functions derived from Equation 13 and a sum of exponentials model (Multiple Exponential Discounting Systems section) show hyperbolic discounting. C: Chained state space. D: Discounting over a chained state as a function of total delay from state S_0 to reward state. The single-step hyperbolic model (Equation 13) no longer shows hyperbolic discounting, whereas the multiple exponentials model continues to do so. ISI = interstimulus interval.

one-step hyperbolic equation (Equation 13), it may be possible to change the discounting function by providing more or less information during ISI delays (which may drive a subject to represent the intervening interval by a different number of subintervals). Whether real discounting functions used by real animals are actually subadditive remains a point of debate (Read, 2001).

NEURAL MODELS

Because hyperbolic discounting functions are computationally difficult to work with, several neural models have been proposed that use computationally tractable mathematics internally but show behavioral discounting rates that change with time. We review four of these models and the data supporting each in turn.

Normalization by Estimates of Average Reward

Following the rate conditioning literature (see Gallistel, 1990, for review) and the observation by Kacelnik (1997) that applying discounting factors in the titrated delay task (e.g., Mazur, 1997) ignores the effects of rewards expected in future trials, Daw (2003; see also Daw, Courville, & Touretzky, 2006, and Daw & Touretzky, 2000) has suggested an alternative to the discounting concept based on the concept of average reward. This model assumes that agents have evolved to optimize the total expected reward, integrated over many multiple trials (Kacelnik, 1997; Stephens & Krebs, 1987). Kacelnik (1997) noted that Mazur's titration experiments are, in fact, repeated trials and that humans answering questionnaires (e.g., Bickel & Marsch, 2001; Bickel et al., 2007; Myerson & Green, 1995) may be treating the choices as elements of a system considering time in terms of repeated trials (but see Mazur, 2001, 2006). In this model, decisions are assumed to be made on the basis of the rate of reward rather than as a single decision between two immediate values (Daw & Touretzky, 2000; Gallistel, 1990; Kacelnik, 1997). In this model (see Daw, 2003), value estimates are updated by

$$\delta = r(t) - \rho(t) + \hat{V}\big[s(t+1)\big] - \hat{V}\big[s(t)\big], \tag{14}$$

which trains the function

$$V(t_0) = \sum_{t=t_0}^{\infty} \big[r(t) - \rho(t)\big], \tag{15}$$

where $\rho(t)$ is the estimate of the average reward available to the animal over long timescales.

The problem with these models is that titration experiments have shown that when the intertrial interval is increased after the small reward (thus matching the total time between small rewards and between large rewards), animals can still show impulsive choices (Mazur, 2001, 2006). One possible explanation for this is that animals ignore the intertrial interval and only make decisions based on the time between the cueing stimulus and the reward (Daw, 2003; Gallistel & Gibbon, 2000; Stephens & Krebs, 1987). Daw and Touretzky (2000) have shown that an average decay model that takes into account only the time between the cuing stimulus and the reward can show hyperbolic-like behavior (Figure 5.2).

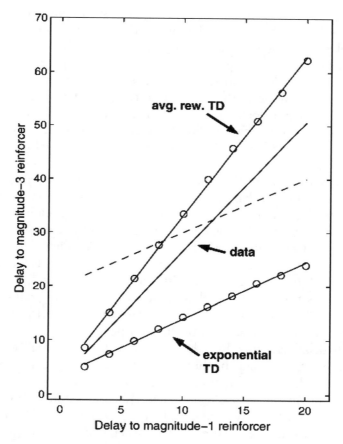

Figure 5.2. Calculation of indifference points as a function of delay in the indifference task. The indifference points are predicted by the average reward (avg. rwd.) model. Indifference points are shown as dots, and the line of best fit is also shown. From "Behavioral Considerations Suggest an Average Reward TD Model of the Dopamine System," by N. D. Daw and D. S. Touretzky, 2000, *Neurocomputing, 32,* p. 681. Copyright 2000 by Elsevier. Reprinted with permission. TD = temporal discounting.

Temporal Perception

Daw (2003, p. 98) noted that there is a strong relationship between an exponential discounting factor γ and the agent's perception of the delay d. Staddon and Cerutti (2003) made a similar proposal (see also Kalenscher & Pennartz, 2008) that hyperbolic-like discounting can arise from timing errors due to Weber's law applied to timing.

Because the discounting applied to a given delay depends not on the actual delay but rather on the perceived delay, variability in delay perception combined with a set exponential discounting function would be mathematically equivalent to a distribution of exponentials (Daw, 2003; Staddon & Cerutti, 2003), which would lead to an approximation of hyperbolic discounting (Kacelnik, 1997; Sozou, 1998), or at least to a power law (Staddon, Chelaru, & Higa, 2002). A number of researchers have noted that the perceived delay $\hat{d}$ of an actual delay d follows a Gaussian distribution with mean d and standard deviation proportional to d (Gallistel & Gibbon, 2000; Gibbon, Church, Fairhurst, & Kacelnik, 1988; Staddon & Cerutti, 2003). This is, of course, the expectation of the distribution that would arise if delay perception were driven by a clock firing with Poisson statistics (Gallistel & Gibbon, 2000).[6] Daw (2003) has shown that this simple assumption about perceived delays leads to indifference functions compatible with those found by Mazur (1997, 2001). See Figure 5.3.

As noted by Daw (2003), there is a duality between the exponential discounting rate γ and the delay to reward receipt d (see Equation 2). A uniform distribution of discounting rates $\gamma \in (0,1)$ (which produces a hyperbolic discounting function when summed) can be rewritten as an (admittedly complex) distribution of delays. However, even within this model, slight differences from hyperbolic discounting are seen at very small and very large delays (Daw, 2003; see Figure 5.3). It is not yet known whether those differences occur in actual subjects. Nor is it yet known whether the actual errors in delay estimation (producing a distribution of delays over trials) are compatible with the complex functions needed to produce realistic discounting functions.

If this delay perception hypothesis were true, then one would expect to see hyperbolic functions arising in other delay tasks, such as in memory recall tasks. Hyperbolically decreasing functions are better fits to memory recall probabilities than are exponentially decreasing functions (Rubin, Hinton, & Wenzel, 1999; Rubin & Wenzel, 1996; Wixted & Ebbesen, 1997); power laws and sums of exponentials provide even better fits than hyperbolic functions (Rubin et al., 1999; Wixted & Ebbesen, 1997). The possibility that the power laws that fit the memory recall data may arise from different forgetting factors (mathematically equivalent to discounting factors) in different subjects has been addressed

---

[6]This timing model is still controversial (Kalenscher & Pennartz, 2008; Staddon & Higa, 1999).

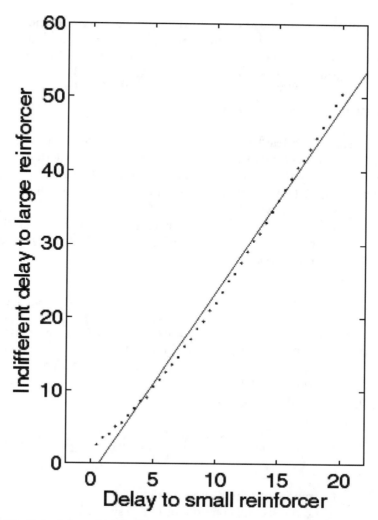

Figure 5.3. Calculation of indifference points using an exponential decay model with Poisson-like time estimation (variance of estimated delay proportional to actual delay). From *Reinforcement Learning Models of the Dopamine System and Their Behavioral Implications,* by N. D. Daw, 2003, p. 101. Copyright 2003 by N. D. Daw. Reprinted with permission.

(Anderson & Tweney, 1997). Even when looking at individuals, power laws are better fits to the memory recall data than are exponential functions (Wixted & Ebbesen, 1997). Staddon and Higa (1999) explicitly proposed a theory in which interval timing arises from multiple components, which when added together produce nonexponential timing (and thus discounting) functions.

An interesting prediction of the temporal-perception hypothesis would be that agents with faster discounting functions (such as addicts) should also show a similar overemphasis on local time-perception preferences. When asked to speculate about their future, normal participants included details ranging up to 4.5 years in the future. In contrast, addicts only included details about the next several days (Petry, Bickel, & Arnett, 1998).

Competition Between Two Systems

Even some of the early economics literature suggested that the observed changing discounting rate with time may be the result of interactions between two systems, each with different discount preferences. Generally, these proposals have entailed an impulsive subsystem preferring immediate rewards and a second subsystem willing to delay gratification.

Mathematically, this has primarily been studied from the perspective of the $\beta\delta$ hypothesis (Laibson, 1996; McClure et al., 2004, 2007) in which discounting is assumed to be

$$V_d(r) = r\beta\delta^d, \tag{16}$$

where r is the expected reward and d is the expected delay before receiving the reward. β encodes the willingness to wait for later rewards (i.e., $1/\beta$ encodes the impulsivity), and δ is an exponential discounting component (equivalent to γ; Equation 2, earlier). McClure et al. (2007) noted that Equation 16 can be decomposed into two components:

$$V_d(r) \text{ evaluated at time } t_0 \text{ is } V(t_0) = \left(\frac{1}{\beta} - 1\right)r(t_0) + \sum_{t=t_0}^{\infty} \delta^t r(t_0 + t). \tag{17}$$

The first component (the β system, impulsive) emphasizes immediate rewards ($r[t_0]$), and the second component (the δ system) shows exponential discounting (cf. Equation 2, substituting γ for δ). This model essentially entails an exponential discounting function with an added (impulsive) preference for immediate rewards. This would predict that an agent that could ignore or inactivate the impulsive system would show exponential discounting.

Although many questionnaire experiments are based on a choice of immediate rewards versus delayed rewards, Wittmann et al. (2007) used a task in which both options entailed reward receipt after delays and found equivalent hyperbolic discounting functions. Green et al. (2005) found that their more general hyperbolic equation (Equation 12) fits both situations in which an immediate reward is contrasted with a delayed reward and situations in which one delayed reward is contrasted with a later, more delayed reward. Although many animal delayed-reward experiments are based on the choice between immediate and delayed rewards (e.g., Cardinal, Pennicott, Sugathapala,

Robbins, & Everitt, 2001), the classic titrated experiments of Mazur (1985, 1997) are based on situations in which both rewards are delayed. The βδ equation cannot accommodate the nonexponential discounting seen in these paired delay experiments.

However, the fundamental hypothesis that changing discount rates are the result of competing neural systems is more general than Equation 16. All that is required is that discounting can be written as the sum of two functions:

$$V_d(r) = \alpha f_0(r,d) + (1 - \alpha)f_1(r,d), \qquad (18)$$

where f_0 has a fast (impulsive) decay function and f_1 is slower (more willing to wait); α controls the balance between the two. The underlying neural hypothesis is that these two discounting functions arise from different neural structures competing for behavioral control.

fMRI data have found positive correlations between hemodynamic activity (the BOLD signal) in specific structures (including ventral striatum, medial orbitofrontal cortex, medial prefrontal cortex, and posterior cingulate cortex) and the availability of imminent rewards (McClure et al., 2004). Direct correlations between other structures and longer delays were not found; however, McClure et al. (2004, 2007) suggested that the δ system may be engaged in all conditions, whereas the impulsive system is only engaged when immediate rewards are selected. Supporting this, they found that decisions were related to the ratio of hemodynamic activity in other structures (such as lateral prefrontal cortex) and the impulsive-related structures listed earlier (McClure et al., 2004). Whether this is because of lack of activity in "impulsive" structures or increased activity in delay-preferring structures is unknown, but it does suggest a competition between the two systems. McClure et al. (2007) recently extended these results to direct (e.g., juice) rewards with actual delays on the order of minutes rather than hypothetical delays on the order of days and found similar structures involved in the impulsive (β) component (anterior cingulate cortex, nucleus accumbens [ventral striatum], medial orbitofrontal cortex). Different structures were found to be involved in delayed rewards, including lateral frontal cortical structures and posterior parietal structures. These results imply a competition between neural subsystems, one of which drives a preference for immediate, impulsive choices and one of which drives a willingness to wait for delayed rewards (see Figure 5.4).

Lesion data have also provided support for a competition between systems hypotheses, but, again, which structures are involved in which systems is still unclear. For example, lesions of the ventral prefrontal cortex are correlated with an increase in impulsive decisions, particularly in cases of reversals and developing negative consequences (Bechara, 2005; Bechara & van der Linden, 2005; Grant, Contoreggi, & London, 2000; Torregrossa, Quinn, &

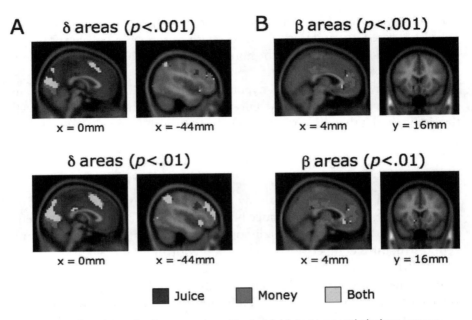

A   δ areas (*p*<.001)

x = 0mm   x = -44mm

δ areas (*p*<.01)

x = 0mm   x = -44mm

B   β areas (*p*<.001)

x = 4mm   y = 16mm

β areas (*p*<.01)

x = 4mm   y = 16mm

Juice   Money   Both

Figure 5.4. Consistent brain areas are activated for intertemporal choices across reward modality. Using a model-based correlation between theoretical constructs in the βδ hypothesis (see text), different brain areas are activated for β-related (impulsive) and for δ-related (more general decision-related) areas. From "Time Discounting for Primary Rewards," by S. M. McClure, K. M. Ericson, D. I. Laibson, G. Loewenstein, and J. D. Cohen, 2007, *Journal of Neuroscience, 27,* p. 5801. Copyright 2007 by the Society for Neuroscience. Reprinted with permission. Original figure in color.

Taylor, 2008; however, see also Clark, Manes, Antoun, Sahakian, & Robbins, 2003). The lack of consensus on definitions of substructure within the ventral prefrontal cortex has made the comparison of studies difficult (Barbas, 2007; Murray, O'Doherty, & Schoenbaum, 2007; Price, 2007). Lesions of the ventral striatum have been found to make animals more impulsive and less capable of delaying responses to receive rewards (Cardinal et al., 2001); however, other studies have found contrasting results in slightly different paradigms (Acheson et al., 2006; Cardinal & Howes, 2005). It is likely that the complexity of ventral striatal anatomy (Pennartz, Groenewegen, & Lopes da Silva, 1994; Zahm & Brog, 1992) makes interpreting the lesions difficult.

It is interesting that there are very few data on which lesions drive animals to be less impulsive. What few data there are suggest a role of orbitofrontal cortex in reevaluating the discounted delayed rewards (Winstanley, Theobald, Cardinal, & Robbins, 2004), particularly the likelihood of its delivery (Mobini et al., 2002), which may suggest a role for orbitofrontal cortex in task changes and reversals (Murray et al., 2007; Schoenbaum & Shaham, 2008; Torregrossa et al., 2008; Winstanley et al., 2004). Neural recordings from orbitofrontal cortex have suggested that some orbitofrontal cortex neurons signal the discounted value of rewards (Roesch, Calu, Burke, & Schoenbaum, 2007) and anticipate future rewards (Ramus, Davis, Donahue, Discenza, & Waite, 2007). These neurons can change their responses under changing reward conditions (Padoa-Schioppa & Assad, 2008; Schoenbaum, Setlow, Saddoris, & Gallagher, 2006; Tremblay & Schultz, 1999).

Many neuroscientists have suggested that these two systems may reflect two more general decision-making systems, one of which (often referred to as the *impulsive system*) reacts quickly to specific stimuli and the other of which is capable of considering longer term possibilities (for reviews, see Cardinal, 2006; Metcalfe & Mischel, 1999; O'Keefe & Nadel, 1978; Poldrack & Packard, 2003; Redish, 1999; Redish, Jensen, & Johnson, 2008; Redish & Johnson, 2007; Squire, 1987). Bernheim and Rangel (2004) explicitly suggested that agents switch between two modes ("hot" and "cold"), in which agents react to the highest-value, most immediately available reward when under the influence of the hot system but consider consequences (under appropriate slow discounting functions) when under the influence of the cold system (see also Metcalfe & Mischel, 1999). In Bernheim and Rangel's model, the presence of drug-related cues forces an agent into the hot mode. Many experiments have shown that when faced with drug-related cues, addicts become highly impulsive and unable to inhibit drug-related responses (Lubman, Yücel, & Pantelis, 2004; Noël et al., 2007; Tiffany, 1990).

One of the few articles to build a working model of the two systems is that of Daw, Niv, and Dayan (2005), in which the impulsive system is assumed to be a slowly learned "habit" system in which values are stored and only changed with experience, and the other (cognitive) system is a flexible "planning" system in which values are calculated on the fly from expectations. Daw et al. suggested that which system controls behavior is dependent on underlying uncertainty—the more uncertain a situation is, the more the agent should rely on the flexible, cognitive system. Although not phrased in terms of impulsivity (the cached-value system Daw et al., 2005, model also incorporates a slow discounting factor), the two systems in this model react very differently to changes in reward delivery probabilities—the cached-value system can only react slowly (if at all), whereas the planning system is more flexible. However, neither Bernheim and Rangel (2004) nor Daw et al. (2005) considered whether the average behavior of such an agent would match the discounting functions seen in the human or animal literatures.

This literature is related to the literature on impulsivity (Evenden, 1999; Glimcher, Kable, & Louie, 2007; Torregrossa et al., 2008; Zermatten, Van der Linden, d'Acremont, Jermann, & Bechara, 2005) and behavioral response inhibition (Gray, 1982a, 1982b; Gray & McNaughton, 2000). In response inhibition experiments, a participant is faced with one stimulus (S1), after which taking an action (go) leads to reward, and a second, similar stimulus (S2), after which not taking that action (no-go) leads to reward. Because S1 is shown much more often than S2, the participant expects S1 and prepares for S1. To get reward after S2, the participant has to inhibit the prepared response. Response inhibition is now known to require the anterior cingulate cortex (Botvinick, Nystrom, Fissell, Carter, & Cohen, 1999; Braver, Barch, Gray, Molfese, & Snyder, 2001; Rushworth, Buckley, Behrens, Walton, & Bannerman, 2007; Walton, Rudebeck, Bannerman, & Rushworth, 2007) and other aspects of frontal cortices (such as the supplementary motor area [Isoda & Hikosaka, 2007] and the dorsomedial prefrontal cortex [Brass & Haggard, 2007]). Anterior cingulate cortex is currently thought to monitor conflict (Amiez, Joseph, & Procyk, 2005) or to integrate historical trends (Kennerley, Walton, Behrens, Buckley, & Rushworth, 2006; Rushworth et al., 2004; Walton et al., 2007), and supplementary motor, dorsomedial prefrontal, and ventral frontal cortices to override prepotent actions stored in direct sensorimotor connections (Bechara, 2005; Bechara & van der Linden, 2005; Brass & Haggard, 2007; Chamberlain & Sahakian, 2007; Crutcher & Alexander, 1990; Isoda & Hikosaka, 2007; Okano & Tanji, 1987; Rushworth, Walton, Kennerley, & Bannerman, 2004; Tanji, 2001). Response inhibition can be envisioned as a flexible system overriding an impulsive, more habitual system (Daw et al., 2005; Gray & McNaughton, 2000; Redish et al., 2008).

Although there is strong evidence for a competition between systems, it is not completely clear which structures are involved in which systems. This may be in part because of limitations in the available resolution in fMRI, lesion, and recording experiments.

Multiple Exponential Discounting Systems

Although the sum of two exponential discounting functions leads to changing discount rates with delay and thus to preference reversals (Laibson, 1996; McClure et al., 2004, 2007), it does not closely approximate the hyperbolic discounting function (Equation 11) reported in much of the literature (e.g., Ainslie, 1992; Mazur, 1985, 1997; Vuchinich & Simpson, 1998). A larger, uniform distribution of exponential discounting functions would, however, match the hyperbolic discounting seen experimentally (Daw, 2003; Kacelnik, 1997; Kurth-Nelson & Redish, 2004a; Redish, 2004; Sozou, 1998). We (Kurth-Nelson & Redish, 2004a; see also Redish, 2004) suggested a model in which multiple microagents (μAgents) compete to make decisions. Each of these μAgents instantiates a hypothesis about the state of the world (the current situation s_i and the time t_i spent within that situation), maintains a value estimate of that state $\hat{V}_i(s,a)$, and independently carries out an individual temporal difference reinforcement learning algorithm (thus requiring an individual value-prediction error term δ_i; Bertin, Schweighofer, & Doya, 2007; Sutton & Barto, 1998) with exponential discounting $0 < \gamma_i < 1$ drawn from a uniform random distribution. The hypothesized state, $s_i(t)$, and dwell time, $t_i(t)$, of each μAgent instantiate a hypothesis of the actual state of the world, $s_W(t)$, and the actual dwell time, $t_W(t)$, of the world within that state. Even if the μAgent knows the initial state correctly, that hypothesis could diverge from actuality. To maintain an accurate belief distribution, μAgents at each time step compute the probability $P(s_i [t]|O[t])$, where $O(t)$ is the observation provided by the world at time t, and $s_i(t)$ is μAgent i's state at time t. μAgents with low $P(s_i [t]|O[t])$ update the belief to a random hypothesis consistent with the current observation by setting s_i to a random state $s*$ selected with probability $P (s*[t]|O[t])$, and setting t_i to 0. If the ∝Agent makes a transition that entails a change in estimated value, it delivers a value prediction error signal (δ_i). Actions are selected on the basis of the normalized, expected total value of the predicted state that would occur should an action be selected $Q(a)$, determined from the probability distribution over predicted states:

$$Q(a_j) = \frac{1}{n_\mu} \sum_i \left(\text{is\_possible}[a_j | s_i] \cdot \left\{ E[r(s_i')] + E[V(s_i')] \right\} \right), \quad (19)$$

where s_i is the state hypothesis of μAgent i, s_i' the state that would be achieved by taking action a_j from state s_i, $E[r(s_i')]$ the expected reward in state s_i', $E[V(s_i')]$ the expected value of state s_i', and is_possible $(a_j|s_i)$ a binary variable indicating whether action a_j is available from state s_i.

To determine the discounting function produced by our model, we modified the adjusting-delay assay of Mazur (1997; see earlier). We used a five-state state-space to provide the macroagent a choice between two actions, each of which led to a reward after a given delay. We ran the experiment for five agents (each of which consisted of 1,000 μAgents) in this state space for reward ratios of 2:1, 1:1, 3:2, and 3:1. As can be seen in Figure 5.5, the slopes of the indifference lines approximate the reward ratios, with a nonzero intercept. As reviewed earlier, this implies a hyperbolic discounting function like Equation 11 (Mazur, 1997). Thus, if each μAgent has a specific, different exponential discounting function γ_i and maintains an independent estimate of the value of taking specific actions in a given situation, then the overall, behaviorally observable macroagent will show hyperbolic discounting.

Working from anatomical studies, a number of researchers have hypothesized that the striatum consists of multiple separable pathways (Alexander & Crutcher, 1990; Alexander, DeLong, & Strick, 1986; Graybiel, Flaherty, & Gimenez-Amaya, 1991; Strick, Dum, & Picard, 1995). This suggests a possible anatomical spectrum of discounting factors that would be produced by a population of μAgents operating in parallel. Many researchers have reported that dopamine signals are not unitary (see Daw, 2003, for review). Nonunitary dopamine signals could arise from different dopamine populations contributing

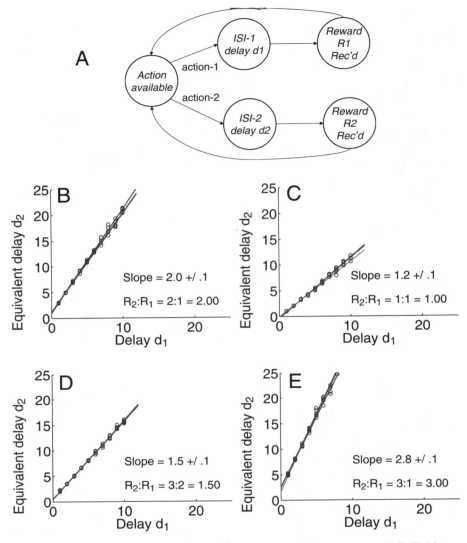

Figure 5.5. Discounting with multiple exponentials. A: State space used. B–E: Mazur plots. These plots show the delay d_2 needed to make an agent choose actions a_1 and a_2 equally for a given delay d_1. The ratio of actions $a_1{:}a_2$ is an observable measure of the relative values of the two choices. For hyperbolic discounting, the slope of the line will match the ratio r_2/r_1, with a nonzero y-intercept. A sum-of-exponentials model approximates hyperbolic discounting. ISI = interstimulus interval.

to different µAgents. Haber, Fudge, and McFarland (2000) reported that the interaction between dopamine and striatal neural populations shows a regular anatomy, in a spiral progressing from ventral to dorsal striatum. Recently, Tanaka et al. (2004) explicitly found a gradient of discounting factors across the striata of human participants (see Figure 5.6).

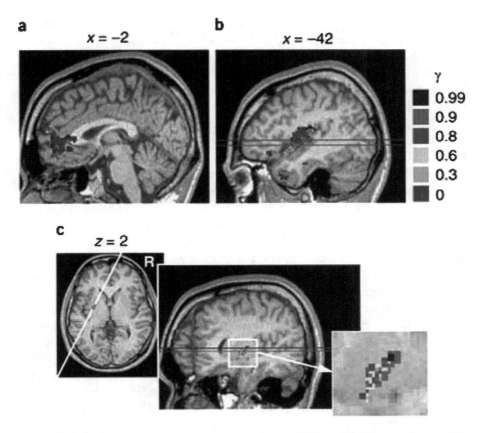

Figure 5.6. Correlations between reward prediction $V^\gamma(t)$ and BOLD signal are most correlated to different discounting factors γ. From "Prediction of Immediate and Future Rewards Differentially Recruits Cortico-Basal Ganglia Loops," by S. C. Tanaka, K. Doya, G. Okada, K. Ueda, Y. Okamoto, and S. Yamawaki, 2004, *Nature Neuroscience, 7,* p. 890. Copyright 2004 by Macmillan Publishers Ltd.: Nature Neuroscience. Reprinted with permission. Original figure in color.

In their recent fMRI experiment, Tanaka et al. (2004) found strong correlations between BOLD signals in striatum and different γ discounting factors (Equation 2). For each time step in the task, for a given sequence of choices, for a given hypothesized γ, the value at that moment could be calculated from the rewards delivered over the subsequent timesteps. This produced a family of functions $V^\gamma(t)$, which could then be correlated with the BOLD signals measured in the participants. Fast discounting factors γ → 0 were more strongly correlated with BOLD signals in ventral-anterior aspects of striatum; slower discounting factors γ → 1 were more strongly correlated with BOLD signals in dorsal–posterior aspects of striatum. Tanaka et al. found a continuous distribution of best-correlated γ factors along the ventral–anterior to dorsal–posterior axis. Because BOLD activity is more highly correlated with local field potentials (Logothetis, 2002) and local field potentials are more closely related to synaptic activity than local neural firing (Buzsáki, 2006), it is likely that the functional slices observed by Tanaka et al. (2004) reflect differential inputs rather than direct changes in striatal activity. Nevertheless, the possibility remains that Tanaka et al.'s slices may correspond to Haber et al.'s (2000) spiral loops and that both of these may correspond to μAgents.

Reinforcement learning with multiple models (sometimes called multiple experts) has a long history (Bertin et al., 2007; Doya, Samejima, Karagiri, & Kawato, 2002). The suggestion that the basal ganglia consist of multiple separable loops also has a long history (Alexander et al., 1986; Alexander & Crutcher, 1990; Haber et al., 2000; Middleton & Strick, 2000), yet remains controversial (Graybiel, 2000; Parthasarathy, Schall, & Graybiel, 1992). The suggestion that these separate loops are indicative of separate discounting factors (Kurth-Nelson & Redish, 2004a; Tanaka et al., 2004) is, however, novel. More work needs to be done to confirm or reject that hypothesis. In any case, it is likely that the Tanaka et al. (2004) data reflect patterns of activity that could correspond to a parallel computation based on a continuum of discounting factors.

One important consequence of this multiple-exponential hypothesis is that shifts in the distribution of included exponentials would produce discounting functions that deviate from Equation 11. Although the hyperbolic fit for the animal behavior literature is often excellent (Mazur, 1985, 1997; Richards et al., 1997), the fit for the human decision literature is more variable—sometimes excellent (Vuchinich & Simpson, 1998) and sometimes less so (Reynolds, 2006), particularly for drug users (Madden et al., 1999; Mitchell, 1999). Schweighofer et al. (2006) reported that under specific conditions in which a single exponential discounting rate is optimal, humans can learn to match that factor and show an exponential discounting function.

Changes in serotonin levels have long been associated with impulsivity (with lower levels of serotonin correlating with more impulsivity; Carver & Miller, 2006; Chamberlain, Muller, Robbins, & Sahakian, 2006; Chamberlain & Sahakian, 2007). Rats with dorsal raphe (serotonin) lesions showed earlier indifference points on Mazur's (1997) adjusting-delay paradigm (Mobini et al., 2000; Wogar, Bradshaw, & Szabadi, 1993). These rats were still able to accurately time delays when no contrast was involved, so the change was not the result of loss of temporal recognition (Morrissey, Wogar, Bradshaw, & Szabadi, 1993). Changing levels of serotonin precursors (e.g., tryptophan) can change the measured discounting rates in human participants (Tanaka et al., 2007). Doya (2000a, 2002) has explicitly suggested that serotonin may control the discounting rate used in an exponential discounting module. Alternatively, serotonin may control the distribution of exponential components contributing to the behavior. These proposals still constitute a controversial hypothesis, and there is little direct evidence to support it; however, recent experiments in the Doya laboratory (Tanaka et al., 2007) have found that changes in serotonin precursors (e.g., tryptophan) can reduce activity in certain of the discounting slices seen by Tanaka et al. (2004) while enhancing activity in others.

A sum of internal exponential discounting functions will only produce hyperbolic discounting in the case of a uniform distribution of exponentials covering the entire available range. In general, a sum of internal exponential discounting functions will produce a power law behaviorally:

$$V_d(r) = r \int_{\kappa=0}^{\infty} g(\kappa) e^{-\kappa d} d\kappa, \tag{20}$$

where $g(\kappa)$ is the distribution of exponential discounting factors $0 < \kappa < \infty$. For simplicity, we assume $g(\kappa) = \kappa^\beta$, where β is a constant that controls the distribution of components. (In this formulation, $\beta = 0$ implies a flat distribution of exponentials, $\beta > 0$ implies more high-κ, faster discounting components, and $\beta < 0$ implies more low-κ, slower discounting components.) Under these assumptions, the integrated value function can be written analytically as

$$V_d(r) = r \cdot \frac{\alpha}{d^{(1+\beta)}}, \tag{21}$$

where α is a constant term and β is derived from the $g(\kappa)$ distribution. When $\beta = 0$, this corresponds to a hyperbolic $1/d$ discounting function. As β increases, this function deviates from hyperbolic to become more impulsive, and as β decreases, this function deviates from hyperbolic to become less impulsive (see Figure 5.7). Both group data and individual data are well fit by power laws such as Equation 21 (Redish, Landes, & Bickel, 2008), although it is not clear yet whether Equation 21 provides any better fit to the experimental data than do standard hyperbolic discounting analyses (e.g., Equation 11). Of course, the actual $g(\kappa)$ distribution could be any mix of exponential functions, and could potentially be variable under pharmacological or experimental control (Schweighofer, Tanaka, & Doya, 2007; Tanaka et al., 2007), including becoming a single exponential function under the right conditions (Schweighofer et al., 2006).

SUMMARY AND CONCLUSION

In making a decision between multiple choices, a complete description of the values of the two choices would require specification and integration over all potential possibilities, taking into account the uncertainty, risk, and investment opportunities with each decision. This infinite calculation is, of course, impossible to do with a finite decision process. A reasonable method of solving this problem is to discount delayed rewards. Humans and animals discount delayed rewards with functions better described as hyperbolic or power

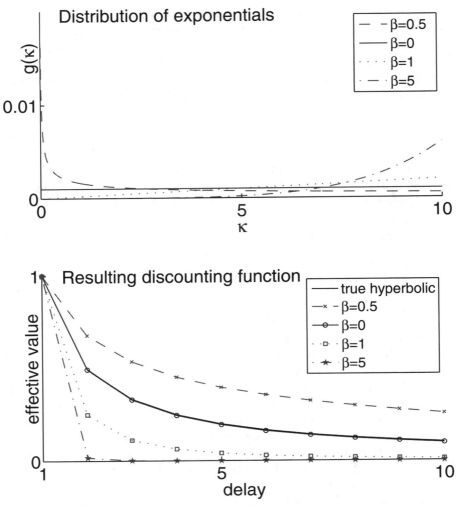

Figure 5.7. Top: Distributions of exponentials as the distribution of exponentials change. Bottom: The resulting value-discounting functions can become more or less impulsive with changing distributions of exponentials. A uniform distribution of exponential discounting functions (characterized by $\beta = 0$) produces a close match to hyperbolic discounting.

law functions (with changing discount rates over time) than as exponential functions (with constant discount rates). Four sets of neural models have been proposed to explain this discrepancy: (a) that agents are actually maximizing rates of reward, normalizing observed rewards by current expectations of average rates of reward; (b) that changes in time perception produce variations in underlying estimates of delays, leading to a spreading out of the exponential discounting function, which leads to a hyperbolic-like power law; and (c) and

(d) that neural systems include two (or more) subsystems that discount future rewards at different rates. The extensive neural data support the multiple subsystem hypothesis quite strongly; however, the number of subsystems and the identity of the specific components making up each subsystem remain unresolved. Although a number of specific algorithms have been proposed to underlay these subsystems, these proposals remain controversial. These multiple subsystems may also underlay complexities in temporal perception, as well as in general memory and behavioral processes. More work testing specific neural hypotheses under conditions that change discounting factors is needed.

REFERENCES

Acheson, A., Farrar, A. M., Patak, M., Hausknecht, K. A., Kieres, A. K., Choi, S., et al. (2006). Nucleus accumbens lesions decrease sensitivity to rapid changes in the delay to reinforcement. *Behavioural Brain Research, 173*, 217–228.

Ainslie, G. (1975). Specious reward: A behavioral theory of impulsiveness and impulse control. *Psychological Bulletin, 82*, 463–496.

Ainslie, G. (1992). *Picoeconomics.* Cambridge, England: Cambridge University Press.

Ainslie, G. (2001). *Breakdown of will.* Cambridge, England: Cambridge University Press.

Ainslie, G., & Monterosso, J. (2004, October 15). Behavior: A marketplace in the brain? *Science, 306*, 421–423.

Alexander, G. E., & Crutcher, M. D. (1990). Functional architecture of basal ganglia circuits: Neural substrates of parallel processing. *Trends in Neurosciences, 13*, 266–271.

Alexander, G. E., DeLong, M. R., & Strick, P. L. (1986). Parallel organization of functionally segregated circuits linking basal ganglia and cortex. *Annual Review of Neuroscience, 9*, 357–381.

Amiez, C., Joseph, J.-P., & Procyk, E. (2005). Anterior cingulate error-related activity is modulated by predicted reward. *European Journal of Neuroscience, 21*, 3447–3452.

Anderson, R. B., & Tweney, R. D. (1997). Artifactual power curves in forgetting. *Memory & Cognition, 25*, 724–730.

Barbas, H. (2007). Specialized elements of orbitofrontal cortex in primates. In G. Schoenbaum, J. A. Gottfried, E. A. Murray, & S. J. Ramus (Eds.), *Annals of the New York Academy of Sciences: Vol. 1121. Linking affect to action: Critical contributions of the orbitofrontal cortex* (pp. 10–32). New York: New York Academy of Sciences.

Bayer, H. M., & Glimcher, P. (2005). Midbrain dopamine neurons encode a quantitative reward prediction error signal. *Neuron, 47*, 129–141.

Bayer, H. M., Lau, B., & Glimcher, P. W. (2007). Statistics of midbrain dopamine neuron spike trains in the awake primate. *Journal of Neurophysiology, 98*, 1428–1439.

Bechara, A. (2005). Decision making, impulse control, and loss of willpower to resist drugs: A neurocognitive perspective. *Nature Neuroscience, 8*, 1458–1463.

Bechara, A., & van der Linden, M. (2005). Decision-making and impulse control after frontal lobe injuries. *Current Opinion in Neurology, 18*, 734–739.

Bellman, R. (1958). On a routing problem. *Quarterly Journal of Applied Mathematics, 16*, 87–90.

Beran, M. J., Savage-Rumbaugh, E. S., Pate, J. L., & Rumbaugh, D. M. (1999). Delay of gratification in chimpanzees (*Pan troglodytes*). *Developmental Psychobiology, 34*, 119–127.

Bernheim, B. D., & Rangel, A. (2004). Addiction and cue-triggered decision processes. *American Economic Review, 94*, 1558–1590.

Bertin, M., Schweighofer, N., & Doya, K. (2007). Multiple model-based reinforcement learning explains dopamine neuronal activity. *Neural Networks, 20*, 668–675.

Bickel, W. K., & Marsch, L. A. (2001). Toward a behavioral economic understanding of drug dependence: Delay discounting processes. *Addiction, 96*, 73–86.

Bickel, W. K., Miller, M. L., Yi, R., Kowal, B. P., Lindquist, D. M., & Pitcock, J. A. (2007). Behavioral and neuroeconomics of drug addiction: Competing neural systems and temporal discounting processes. *Drug and Alcohol Dependence, 90*(Suppl. 1), S85–S91.

Botvinick, M., Nystrom, L. E., Fissell, K., Carter, C. S., & Cohen, J. D. (1999, November 11). Conflict monitoring versus selection-for-action in anterior cingulate cortex. *Nature, 402*, 179–181.

Boysen, S. T., & Berntson, G. G. (1995). Responses to quantity: Perceptual versus cognitive mechanisms in chimpanzees (*Pan troglodytes*). *Journal of Experimental Psychology: Animal Behavior Processes, 21*, 82–86.

Brass, M., & Haggard, P. (2007). To do or not to do: The neural signature of self-control. *Journal of Neuroscience, 27*, 9141–9145.

Braver, T. S., Barch, D. M., Gray, J. R., Molfese, D. L., & Snyder, A. (2001). Anterior cingulate cortex and response conflict: Effects of frequency, inhibition, and errors. *Cerebral Cortex, 11*, 825–836.

Buzsáki, G. (2006). *Rhythms of the brain*. Oxford, England: Oxford University Press.

Cardinal, R. N. (2006). Neural systems implicated in delayed and probabilistic reinforcement. *Neural Networks, 19*, 1277–1301.

Cardinal, R. N., & Howes, N. J. (2005). Effects of lesions of the nucleus accumbens core on choice between small certain rewards and large uncertain rewards in rats. *BMC Neuroscience, 6*, 37.

Cardinal, R. N., Pennicott, D. R., Sugathapala, C. L., Robbins, T. W., & Everitt, B. J. (2001, May 24). Impulsive choice induced in rats by lesion of the nucleus accumbens core. *Science, 292*, 2499–2501.

Carver, C. S., & Miller, C. J. (2006). Relations of serotonin function to personality: Current views and a key methodological issue. *Psychiatry Research, 144*, 1–15.

Chamberlain, S. R., Muller, U., Robbins, T. W., & Sahakian, B. J. (2006). Neuropharmacological modulation of cognition. *Current Opinion in Neurology, 19*, 607–612.

Chamberlain, S. R., & Sahakian, B. J. (2007). The neuropsychiatry of impulsivity. *Current Opinion in Psychiatry, 20,* 255–261.

Clark, L., Manes, F., Antoun, N., Sahakian, B. J., & Robbins, T. W. (2003). The contributions of lesion laterality and lesion volume to decision-making impairment following frontal lobe damage. *Neuropsychologia, 41,* 1474–1483.

Courville, A. C., Daw, N. D., & Touretzky, D. S. (2006). Bayesian theories of conditioning in a changing world. *Trends in Cognitive Sciences, 10,* 294–300.

Crutcher, M. D., & Alexander, G. E. (1990). Movement-related neuronal activity selectively coding either direction or muscle pattern in three motor areas of the monkey. *Journal of Neurophysiology, 64,* 151–163.

Daw, N. D. (2003). *Reinforcement learning models of the dopamine system and their behavioral implications.* Unpublished doctoral dissertation, Carnegie Mellon University.

Daw, N. D., Courville, A. C., & Touretzky, D. S. (2002a). Dopamine and inference about timing. In *Proceedings of the IEEE Second International Conference on Development and Learning* (pp. 271–276). Washington, DC: IEEE Computer Society.

Daw, N. D., Courville, A. C., & Touretzky, D. S. (2002b). Timing and partial observability in the dopamine system. *NIPS, 15,* 99–106.

Daw, N. D., Courville, A. C., & Touretzky, D. S. (2006). Representation and timing in theories of the dopamine system. *Neural Computation, 18,* 1637–1677.

Daw, N. D., Niv, Y., & Dayan, P. (2005). Uncertainty-based competition between prefrontal and dorsolateral striatal systems for behavioral control. *Nature Neuroscience, 8,* 1704–1711.

Daw, N. D., O'Doherty, J. P., Dayan, P., Seymour, B., & Dolan, R. J. (2006). Cortical substrates for exploratory decisions in humans. *Nature, 441,* 876–879.

Daw, N. D., & Touretzky, D. S. (2000). Behavioral considerations suggest an average reward TD model of the dopamine system. *Neurocomputing, 32,* 679–684.

Doya, K. (2000a). Metalearning, neuromodulation, and emotion. In G. Hatano, N. Okada, & H. Tanabe (Eds.), *Affective minds* (pp. 101–104). New York: Elsevier.

Doya, K. (2000b). Reinforcement learning in continuous time and space. *Neural Computation, 12,* 219–245.

Doya, K. (2002). Metalearning and neuromodulation. *Neural Networks, 15,* 495–506.

Doya, K., Samejima, K., Katagiri, K.-I., & Kawato, M. (2002). Multiple model-based reinforcement learning. *Neural Computation, 14,* 1347–1369.

Estle, S. J., Green, L., Myerson, J., & Holt, D. D. (2007). Discounting of monetary and directly consumable rewards. *Psychological Science, 18,* 58–63.

Evans, T. A., & Beran, M. J. (2007). Delay of gratification and delay maintenance by rhesus macaques (Macaca mulatta). *Journal of General Psychology, 134,* 199–216.

Evenden, J. L. (1999). Varieties of impulsivity. *Psychopharmacology (Berlin), 146,* 348–361.

Fiorillo, C. D., Tobler, P. N., & Schultz, W. (2005). Evidence that the delay-period activity of dopamine neurons corresponds to reward uncertainty rather than backpropagating TD errors. *Behavioral and Brain Functions, 1,* 7.

Frederick, S., Loewenstein, G., & O'Donoghue, T. (2002). Time discounting and time preference: A critical review. *Journal of Economic Literature*, *40*, 351–401.

Gallistel, C. R. (1990). *The organization of learning*. Cambridge, MA: MIT Press.

Gallistel, C. R., & Gibbon, J. (2000). Time, rate, and conditioning. *Psychological Review*, *107*, 289–344.

Gibbon, J., Church, R. M., Fairhurst, S., & Kacelnik, A. (1988). Scalar expectancy theory and choice between delayed rewards. *Psychological Review*, *95*, 102–114.

Glimcher, P. W., Kable, J., & Louie, K. (2007). Neuroeconomic studies of impulsivity: Now or just as soon as possible? *American Economic Review*, *97*, 142–147.

Grace, R. C. (1999). The matching law and amount-dependent exponential discounting as accounts of self-control choice. *Journal of the Experimental Analysis of Behavior*, *1*, 27–44.

Grant, S., Contoreggi, C., & London, E. D. (2000). Drug abusers show impaired performance in a laboratory test of decision making. *Neuropsychologia*, *38*, 1180–1187.

Gray, J. A. (1982a). *The neuropsychology of anxiety: An enquiry into the functions of the septo-hippocampal system*. New York: Oxford University Press.

Gray, J. A. (1982b). Précis of *The Neuropsychology of Anxiety: An Enquiry into the Functions of the Septo-Hippocampal System*. *Behavioral and Brain Sciences*, *5*, 469–484; commentary and response, 484–534.

Gray, J., & McNaughton, N. (2000). *The neuropsychology of anxiety*. Oxford, England: Oxford University Press.

Graybiel, A. (2000). The basal ganglia. *Current Biology*, *10*, R509–R511.

Graybiel, A. M., Flaherty, A. W., & Gimenez-Amaya, J.-M. (1991). Striosomes and matrisomes. In G. Bernardi, M. B. Carpenter, & G. Di Chiara (Eds.), *The basal ganglia III* (pp. 3–12). New York: Plenum Press.

Green, L., & Myerson, J. (2004). A discounting framework for choice with delayed and probabilistic rewards. *Psychological Bulletin*, *130*, 769–792.

Green, L., Myerson, J., Holt, D. D., Slevin, J. R., & Estle, S. J. (2004). Discounting of delayed food rewards in pigeons and rats: Is there a magnitude effect? *Journal of the Experimental Analysis of Behavior*, *81*, 39–50.

Green, L., Myerson, J., & Macaux, E. W. (2005). Temporal discounting when the choice is between two delayed rewards. *Journal of Experimental Psychology: Learning, Memory, and Cognition*, *31*, 1121–1133.

Green, L., Myerson, J., & McFadden, E. (1997). Rate of temporal discounting decreases with amount of reward. *Memory & Cognition*, *25*, 715–723.

Haber, S. N., Fudge, J. L., & McFarland, N. R. (2000). Striatonigrostriatal pathways in primates form an ascending spiral from the shell to the dorsolateral striatum. *Journal of Neuroscience*, *20*, 2369–2382.

Isoda, M., & Hikosaka, O. (2007). Switching from automatic to controlled action by monkey medial frontal cortex. *Nature Neuroscience*, *10*, 240–248.

Johnson, M. W., & Bickel, W. K. (2002). Within-subject comparison of real and hypothetical money rewards in delay discounting. *Journal of the Experimental Analysis of Behavior*, *77*, 129–146.

Kacelnik, A. (1997). Normative and descriptive models of decision making: Time discounting and risk sensitivity. *Ciba Foundation Symposium, 208*, 51–66; discussion, 67–70.

Kacelnik, A., & Bateson, M. (1996). Risky theories—The effects of variance on foraging decisions. *American Zoologist, 36*, 402–434.

Kakade, S., & Dayan, P. (2002). Dopamine: Generalization and bonuses. *Neural Networks, 15*, 549–599.

Kalenscher, T., & Pennartz, C. M. A. (2008). Is a bird in the hand worth two in the future? The neuroeconomics of intertemporal decision-making. *Progress in Neurobiology, 84*, 284–315.

Kelley, A. E., & Berridge, K. C. (2002). The neuroscience of natural rewards: Relevance to addictive drugs. *Journal of Neuroscience, 22*, 3306–3311.

Kennerley, S. W., Walton, M. E., Behrens, T. E. J., Buckley, M. J., & Rushworth, M. F. S. (2006). Optimal decision making and the anterior cingulate cortex. *Nature Neuroscience, 9*, 940–947.

Kirby, K. N. (1997). Bidding on the future: Evidence against normative discounting of delayed rewards. *Journal of Experimental Psychology: General, 126*, 54–70.

Kurth-Nelson, Z., & Redish, A. D. (2004a). μagents: Action-selection in temporally-dependent phenomena using temporal difference learning over a collective belief structure. *Society for Neuroscience Abstracts, 29*, Program No. 207.1.

Kurth-Nelson, Z., & Redish, A. D. (2004b). [Hyperbolic and exponential discounting with μAgents]. Unpublished simulations.

Laibson, D. I. (1996). An economic perspective on addiction and matching. *Behavioral and Brain Sciences, 19*, 583–584.

Logothetis, N. (2002). The neural basis of the blood-oxygen-level-dependent functional magnetic resonance imaging signal. *Philosophical Transactions of the Royal Society of London B, 357*, 1003–1037.

Lubman, D. I., Yücel, M., & Pantelis, C. (2004). Addiction, a condition of compulsive behaviour? Neuroimaging and neuropsychological evidence of inhibitory dysregulation. *Addiction, 99*, 1491–1502.

Madden, G. J., Bickel, W. K., & Jacobs, E. A. (1999). Discounting of delayed rewards in opioid-dependent outpatients: Exponential or hyperbolic discounting functions? *Experimental and Clinical Psychopharmacology, 7*, 284–293.

Madden, G. J., Petry, N. M., Badger, G. J., & Bickel, W. K. (1997). Impulsive and self-control choices in opioid-dependent patients and non-drug-using control patients: Drug and monetary rewards. *Experimental and Clinical Psychopharmacology, 5*, 256–262.

Mazur, J. E. (1985). Probability and delay of reinforcement as factors in discrete-trial choice. *Journal of the Experimental Analysis of Behavior, 43*, 341–351.

Mazur, J. (1997). Choice, delay, probability and conditioned reinforcement. *Animal Learning and Behavior, 25*, 131–147.

Mazur, J. E. (2001). Hyperbolic value addition and general models of animal choice. *Psychological Review, 108*, 96–112.

Mazur, J. E. (2006). Choice between single and multiple reinforcers in concurrent-chains schedules. *Journal of the Experimental Analysis of Behavior, 86*, 211–222.

McClure, S. M., Berns, G. S., & Montague, P. R. (2003). Temporal prediction errors in a passive learning task activate human striatum. *Neuron, 38*, 339–346.

McClure, S. M., Ericson, K. M., Laibson, D. I., Loewenstein, G., & Cohen, J. D. (2007). Time discounting for primary rewards. *Journal of Neuroscience, 27*, 5796–5804.

McClure, S. M., Laibson, D. I., Loewenstein, G., & Cohen, J. D. (2004, October 15). Separate neural systems value immediate and delayed monetary rewards. *Science, 306*, 503–507.

Metcalfe, J., & Mischel, W. (1999). A hot/cool-system analysis of delay of gratification: Dynamics of willpower. *Psychological Review, 106*, 3–19.

Middleton, F. A., & Strick, P. L. (2000). Basal ganglia and cerebellar loops: Motor and cognitive circuits. *Brain Research Reviews, 31*, 236–250.

Mischel, W., & Underwood, B. (1974). Instrumental ideation in delay of gratification. *Child Development, 45*, 1083–1088.

Mitchell, S. H. (1999). Measures of impulsivity in cigarette smokers and non-smokers. *Psychopharmacology (Berlin), 146*, 455–464.

Mobini, S., Body, S., Ho, M.-Y., Bradshaw, C. M., Szabadi, E., Deakin, J. F. W., & Anderson, I. M. (2002). Effects of lesions of the orbitofrontal cortex on sensitivity to delayed and probabilistic reinforcement. *Psychopharmacology (Berlin), 160*, 290–298.

Mobini, S., Chiang, T. J., Al-Ruwaitea, A. S., Ho, M. Y., Bradshaw, C. M., & Szabadi, E. (2000). Effect of central 5-hydroxytryptamine depletion on inter-temporal choice: A quantitative analysis. *Psychopharmacology (Berlin), 149*, 313–318.

Morrissey, G., Wogar, M. A., Bradshaw, C. M., & Szabadi, E. (1993). Effect of lesions of the ascending 5-hydroxytryptaminergic pathways on timing behaviour investigated with an interval bisection task. *Psychopharmacology (Berlin), 112*, 80–85.

Murray, E. A., O'Doherty, J. P., & Schoenbaum, G. (2007). What we know and do not know about the functions of the orbitofrontal cortex after 20 years of cross-species studies. *Journal of Neuroscience, 27*, 8166–8169.

Myerson, J., & Green, L. (1995). Discounting of delayed rewards: Models of individual choice. *Journal of the Experimental Analysis of Behavior, 64*, 263–276.

Niv, Y., Duff, M. O., & Dayan, P. (2005). Dopamine, uncertainty, and TD learning. *Behavioral and Brain Functions, 1*, 6.

Noël, X., Van der Linden, M., d'Acremont, M., Bechara, A., Dan, B., Hanak, C., & Verbanck, P. (2007). Alcohol cues increase cognitive impulsivity in individuals with alcoholism. *Psychopharmacology (Berlin), 192*, 291–298.

Odum, A. L., & Rainaud, C. P. (2003). Discounting of delayed hypothetical money, alcohol, and food. *Behavioural Processes, 64*, 305–313.

Okano, K., & Tanji, J. (1987). Neuronal activities in the primate motor fields of the agranular frontal cortex preceding visually triggered and self-paced movement. *Experimental Brain Research, 66*, 155–166.

O'Keefe, J., & Nadel, L. (1978). *The hippocampus as a cognitive map*. Oxford, England: Clarendon Press.

Ong, E. L., & White, K. G. (2004). Amount-dependent temporal discounting? *Behavioural Processes, 66*, 201–212.

Padoa-Schioppa, C., & Assad, J. A. (2006, May 11). Neurons in the orbitofrontal cortex encode economic value. *Nature, 441*, 223–226.

Padoa-Schioppa, C., & Assad, J. A. (2008). The representation of economic value in the orbitofrontal cortex is invariant for changes of menu. *Nature Neuroscience, 11*, 95–102.

Parthasarathy, H., Schall, J., & Graybiel, A. (1992). Distributed but convergent ordering of corticostriatal projections: Analysis of the frontal eye field and the supplementary eye field in the macaque monkey. *Journal of Neuroscience, 12*, 4468–4488.

Pennartz, C. M. A., Groenewegen, H. J., & Lopes da Silva, F. H. (1994). The nucleus accumbens as a complex of functionally distinct neuronal ensembles: An integration of behavioural, electrophysiological, and anatomical data. *Progress in Neurobiology, 42*, 719–761.

Petry, N. M., Bickel, W. K., & Arnett, M. (1998). Shortened time horizons and insensitivity to future consequences in heroin addicts. *Addiction, 93*, 729–738.

Poldrack, R. A., & Packard, M. G. (2003). Competition among multiple memory systems: Converging evidence from animal and human studies. *Neuropsychologia, 41*, 245–251.

Price, J. L. (2007). Definition of the orbital cortex in relation to specific connections with limbic and visceral structures and other cortical regions. In G. Schoenbaum, J. A. Gottfried, E. A. Murray, & S. J. Ramus (Eds.), *Annals of the New York Academy of Sciences: Vol. 1121. Linking affect to action: Critical contributions of the orbitofrontal cortex* (pp. 54–71). New York: New York Academy of Sciences.

Ramus, S. J., Davis, J. B., Donahue, R. J., Discenza, C. B., & Waite, A. A. (2007). Interactions between the orbitofrontal cortex and hippocampal memory system during the storage of long-term memory. In *Annals of the New York Academy of Sciences, 1121*, 216–231. In G. Schoenbaum, J. A. Gottfried, E. A. Murray, & S. J. Ramus (Eds.), *Annals of the New York Academy of Sciences: Vol. 1121. Linking affect to action: Critical contributions of the orbitofrontal cortex* (pp. 216–231). New York: New York Academy of Sciences.

Read, D. (2001). Is time-discounting hyperbolic or subadditive? *Journal of Risk and Uncertainty, 23*, 5–32.

Redish, A. D. (1999). *Beyond the cognitive map: From place cells to episodic memory*. Cambridge, MA: MIT Press.

Redish, A. D. (2004, December 10). Addiction as a computational process gone awry. *Science, 306*, 1944–1947.

Redish, A. D., Jensen, S., & Johnson, A. (2008). A unified framework for addiction: Vulnerabilities in the decision process. *Behavioral and Brain Sciences, 31*, 415–487.

Redish, A. D., Jensen, S., Johnson, A., & Kurth-Nelson, Z. (2007). Reconciling reinforcement learning models with behavioral extinction and renewal: Implications for addiction, relapse, and problem gambling. *Psychological Review, 114*, 784–805.

Redish, A. D., & Johnson, A. (2007). A computational model of craving and obsession. In B. W. Balleine, K. Doya, J. O'Doherty, & M. Sakagami (Eds.), *Annals of the New York Academy of Sciences: Vol. 1104. Reward and decision making in corticobasal ganglia networks* (pp. 324–339). New York: New York Academy of Sciences.

Redish, A. D., Landes, R., & Bickel, W. K. (2008). [Quantitative measures of delay discounting]. Unpublished observations.

Reynolds, B. (2006). A review of delay-discounting research with humans: Relations to drug use and gambling. *Behavioural Pharmacology, 17*, 651–667.

Richards, J. B., Mitchell, S. H., de Wit, H., & Seiden, L. S. (1997). Determination of discount functions in rats with an adjusting-amount procedure. *Journal of the Experimental Analysis of Behavior, 67*, 353–366.

Rodriguez, M. L., & Logue, A. W. (1988). Adjusting delay to reinforcement: Comparing choice in pigeons and humans. *Journal of Experimental Psychology: Animal Behavior Processes, 14*, 105–117.

Roesch, M. R., Calu, D. J., Burke, K. A., & Schoenbaum, G. (2007). Should I stay or should I go? Transformation of time-discounted rewards in orbitofrontal cortex and associated brain circuits. In B. W. Balleine, K. Doya, J. O'Doherty, & M. Sakagami (Eds.), *Annals of the New York Academy of Sciences: Vol. 1104. Reward and decision making in corticobasal ganglia networks* (pp. 21–24). New York: New York Academy of Sciences.

Roesch, M. R., Taylor, A. R., & Schoenbaum, G. (2006). Encoding of time-discounted rewards in orbitofrontal cortex is independent of value representation. *Neuron, 51*, 509–520.

Rogers, A. R. (1997). Evolution and human choice over time. *Ciba Foundation Symposium, 208*, 231–248; discussion, 249–252.

Rubenstein, A. (2003). "Economics and psychology"? The case of hyperbolic discounting. *International Economic Review, 44*, 1207–1216.

Rubin, D. C., Hinton, S., & Wenzel, A. (1999). The precise time course of retention. *Journal of Experimental Psychology: Learning, Memory, and Cognition, 25*, 1161–1176.

Rubin, D. C., & Wenzel, A. E. (1996). One hundred years of forgetting: A quantitative description of retention. *Psychological Review, 103*, 734–760.

Rushworth, M. F. S., Buckley, M. J., Behrens, T. E. J., Walton, M. E., & Bannerman, D. M. (2007). Functional organization of the medial frontal cortex. *Current Opinion in Neurobiology, 17*, 220–227.

Rushworth, M. F. S., Walton, M. E., Kennerley, S. W., & Bannerman, D. M. (2004). Action sets and decisions in the medial frontal cortex. *Trends in Cognitive Sciences, 8*, 410–417.

Samuelson, P. A. (1937). A note on measurement of utility. *Review of Economic Studies, 4*, 155–161.

Schoenbaum, G., Setlow, B., Saddoris, M. P., & Gallagher, M. (2006). Encoding changes in orbitofrontal cortex in reversal-impaired aged rats. *Journal of Neurophysiology, 95*, 1509–1517.

Schoenbaum, G., & Shaham, Y. (2008). The role of orbitofrontal cortex in drug addiction: A review of preclinical studies. *Biological Psychiatry, 63*, 256–262.

Schweighofer, N., Shishida, K., Han, C. E., Okamoto, Y., Tanaka, S. C., Yamawaki, Y., & Doya, K. (2006). Humans can adopt optimal discounting strategy under real-time constraints. *PLoS Computational Biology, 2*, e152.

Schweighofer, N., Tanaka, S. C., & Doya, K. (2007). Serotonin and the evaluation of future rewards: Theory, experiments, and possible neural mechanisms. In B. W. Balleine, K. Doya, J. O'Doherty, & M. Sakagami (Eds.), *Annals of the New York Academy of Sciences: Vol. 1104. Reward and decision making in corticobasal ganglia networks* (pp. 289–300). New York: New York Academy of Sciences.

Sohn, J.-W., & Lee, D. (2007). Order-dependent modulation of directional signals in the supplementary and presupplementary motor areas. *Journal of Neuroscience, 27*, 13655–13666.

Sozou, P. D. (1998). On hyperbolic discounting and uncertain hazard rates. *Philosophical Transactions of the Royal Society London B, 265*, 2015–2020.

Squire, L. R. (1987). *Memory and brain.* New York: Oxford University Press.

Staddon, J. E. R., & Cerutti, D. T. (2003). Operant conditioning. *Annual Reviews of Psychology, 54*, 115–144.

Staddon, J. E. R., Chelaru, I. M., & Higa, J. J. (2002). Habituation, memory and the brain: The dynamics of interval timing. *Behavioural Processes, 57*, 71–88.

Staddon, J. E., & Higa, J. J. (1999). The choose-short effect and trace models of timing. *Journal of the Experimental Analysis of Behavior, 72*, 473–478.

Stephens, D. W., & Krebs, J. R. (1987). *Foraging theory.* Princeton, NJ: Princeton University Press.

Strick, P. L., Dum, R. P., & Picard, N. (1995). Macro-organization of the circuits connecting the basal ganglia with the cortical motor areas. In J. C. Houk, J. L. Davis, & D. G. Beiser (Eds.), *Models of information processing in the basal ganglia* (pp. 117–130). Cambridge, MA: MIT Press.

Strotz, R. H. (1955). Myopia and inconsistency in dynamic utility maximization. *Review of Economic Studies, 23*, 165–180.

Sugrue, L. P., Corrado, G. S., & Newsome, W. T. (2004, June 18). Matching behavior and the representation of value in the parietal cortex. *Science, 304*, 1782–1787.

Sutton, R. S., & Barto, A. G. (1998). *Reinforcement learning: An introduction.* Cambridge, MA: MIT Press.

Tanaka, S. C., Doya, K., Okada, G., Ueda, K., Okamoto, Y., & Yamawaki, S. (2004). Prediction of immediate and future rewards differentially recruits cortico-basal ganglia loops. *Nature Neuroscience, 7*, 887–893.

Tanaka, S. C., Schweighofer, N., Asahi, S., Shishida, K., Okamoto, Y., Yamawaki, S., & Doya, K. (2007). Serotonin differentially regulates short- and long-term prediction of rewards in the ventral and dorsal striatum. *PLoS ONE, 2*, e1333.

Tanji, J. (2001). Sequential organization of multiple movements: Involvement of cortical motor areas. *Annual Review of Neuroscience, 24,* 631–651.

Tiffany, S. T. (1990). A cognitive model of drug urges and drug-use behavior: Role of automatic and nonautomatic processes. *Psychological Review, 97,* 147–168.

Torregrossa, M. M., Quinn, J. J., & Taylor, J. R. (2008). Impulsivity, compulsivity, and habit: The role of orbitofrontal cortex revisited. *Biological Psychiatry, 63,* 253–255.

Tremblay, L., & Schultz, W. (1999). Relative reward preference in primate orbitofrontal cortex. *Nature, 398,* 704–708.

Vuchinich, R. E., & Simpson, C. A. (1998). Hyperbolic temporal discounting in social drinkers and problem drinkers. *Experimental and Clinical Psychopharmacology, 6,* 292–305.

Walton, M. E., Rudebeck, P. H., Bannerman, D. M., & Rushworth, M. F. S. (2007). Calculating the cost of acting in frontal cortex. In B. W. Balleine, K. Doya, J. O'Doherty, & M. Sakagami (Eds.), *Annals of the New York Academy of Sciences: Vol. 1104. Reward and decision making in corticobasal ganglia networks* (pp. 340–356). New York: New York Academy of Sciences.

Winstanley, C. A., Theobald, D. E. H., Cardinal, R. N., & Robbins, T. W. (2004). Contrasting roles of basolateral amygdala and orbitofrontal cortex in impulsive choice. *Journal of Neuroscience, 24,* 4718–4722.

Wittmann, M., Leland, D. S., & Paulus, M. P. (2007). Time and decision making: Differential contribution of the posterior insular cortex and the striatum during a delay discounting task. *Experimental Brain Research, 179,* 643–653.

Wixted, J. T., & Ebbesen, E. B. (1997). Genuine power curves in forgetting: A quantitative analysis of individual subject forgetting functions. *Memory & Cognition, 25,* 731–739.

Wogar, M. A., Bradshaw, C. M., & Szabadi, E. (1993). Effect of lesions of the ascending 5-hydroxytryptaminergic pathways on choice between delayed reinforcers. *Psychopharmacology (Berlin), 111,* 239–243.

Wörgötter, F., & Porr, B. (2005). Temporal sequence learning, prediction, and control—A review of different models and their relation to biological mechanisms. *Neural Computations, 17,* 245–319.

Yu, A., & Dayan, P. (2005). Uncertainty, neuromodulation, and attention. *Neuron, 46,* 681–692.

Zahm, D. S., & Brog, J. S. (1992). On the significance of subterritories in the accumbens part of the rat ventral striatum. *Neuroscience, 50,* 751–767.

Zermatten, A., Van der Linden, M., d'Acremont, M., Jermann, F., & Bechara, A. (2005). Impulsivity and decision making. *Journal of Nervous and Mental Disease, 193,* 647–650.

Zilli, E. A., & Hasselmo, M. E. (2008). Modeling the role of working memory and episodic memory in behavioral tasks. *Hippocampus, 18,* 193–209.

6

NEUROECONOMICS OF RISK-SENSITIVE DECISION MAKING

SARAH R. HEILBRONNER, BENJAMIN Y. HAYDEN,
AND MICHAEL L. PLATT

Uncertainty is ubiquitous, and adaptive behavior requires dealing with it in a biologically meaningful fashion. Our goal in this chapter is to describe current evidence concerning the mechanisms that allow decision makers to deal with the uncertainty that characterizes our world. A fundamental premise is that these mechanisms are embodied in neuronal and chemical events in the brain. We therefore advocate a neuroeconomic approach to understanding the mechanisms of risk-sensitive decision making (Glimcher, 2002; Sanfey, Loewenstein, McClure, & Cohen, 2006). This emphasis distinguishes our goals from those of behavioral psychologists, economists, and evolutionary biologists. Nonetheless, each of these other approaches offers valuable insights, so we consider evidence from these related fields (Glimcher, 2003).

A neuroeconomic approach has several appealing features. First, the brain is the biological basis of cognition and behavior; thus, any model of decision making must ultimately be valid at the neural level. Second, a more detailed understanding of the neural mechanisms underlying decision making will allow us to refine and elaborate on current models of behavior and cognition. Finally, the neuroeconomic approach brings us closer to developing treatments for mental disorders characterized by risky behavior and impulsivity, including compulsive gambling, addiction, obsessive–compulsive disorder, and attention-deficit/hyperactivity disorder. Accurate neural models will be crucial for resolving these pressing medical concerns.

Our specific goal in this chapter is to review current evidence regarding the brain mechanisms supporting decision making under economic risk. To do this, we discuss the relationship between risk and economic decision making more broadly, focusing on impulsivity and delay discounting. Because risk-sensitive decision making and delay discounting share several intuitive properties, there has been much speculation about how the two processes are related (Green & Myerson, 2004; Rachlin, 2000). Although it remains unclear whether these types of decisions share common neuronal mechanisms, we believe that the neuroeconomic approach provides a solid foundation on which a synthesis may be built.

RISK SENSITIVITY

If decision makers are simply trying to maximize reward, they should be indifferent to risk. That is, they should equally prefer two options offering the same average payoff, but with different probabilities and rewards for any given decision. In practice, however, humans and nonhuman animals reliably avoid or seek risk, often paying large penalties for their choices. For example, vendors of consumer electronics sell extended warranties that are only useful in the unlikely situation that the device breaks within a certain timeframe. Such warranties are known to be poor investments, yet their continuing popularity attests to people's willingness to pay money to reduce uncertainty.

In general, humans and other animals are risk averse (Kacelnik & Bateson, 1996; Kahneman & Tversky, 1979; Rabin, 2000); that is, they will reliably pay a premium to reduce risk. Risk sensitivity in humans is typically assessed by examining responses made to hypothetical questions concerning simple choices between two lotteries offering different reward payoffs with different probabilities. In such situations, people typically require a bonus, known as the *risk premium*, before they will choose the risky option. Studies of nonhuman animals have generally found that they, like humans, are risk averse (Kacelnik & Bateson, 1996). Given the constraints of working with nonlinguistic species, risk sensitivity in animals is generally tested by examining responses of animals trained to choose between two options presenting food rewards offered with different probabilities. Such tests have been performed on species as phylogenetically distinct as bees and rhesus macaques (Hayden & Platt, 2007; Shafir, Wiegmann, Smith, & Real, 1999). Despite the large differences between human and animal studies, the reliable observation of risk aversion in humans and animals suggests that it is widespread and divorced from experimental context (Kacelnik & Bateson, 1996).

A closer investigation, however, reveals that risk aversion is not ubiquitous. In fact, there are a surprisingly large number of situations that promote risk seeking. In general, it appears that risk preferences are highly dependent on context. For example, risk seeking is promoted by small stakes (Prelec & Loewenstein, 1991; Weber & Chapman, 2005), low probabilities (Kacelnik & Bateson, 1996), and framing as a loss (Tversky & Kahneman, 1981). In fact, the list of contexts that promote risk seeking is so extensive that these situations do not seem to be exceptions. Instead, it appears that risk preferences are fundamentally context dependent (see Table 6.1).

Utility Curve

Since the work of Daniel Bernoulli (1738/1954), economists have sought explanations for risk aversion. Bernoulli proposed that risk sensitivity could be explained by the shape of a hypothetical construct known as the utility curve (also see Von Neumann & Morgenstern, 1944). The utility curve indicates the subjective value (or *utility*) derived from a given quantity of a good. Bernoulli knew that the benefit one obtains from any particular good tends to decline as one obtains more of that good (the *law of diminishing marginal utility*). This law gives the utility curve its characteristic concave shape

TABLE 6.1
Situations That Promote Risk-Seeking Behavior

Situation	Study
Short intertrial intervals	Hayden and Platt (2007); McCoy and Platt (2005b)
Long intertrial intervals	Kaminski and Ator (2001)
Negative energy states	Caraco (1981)
Rich foraging environments	Gilby and Wrangham (2007)
Severe memory constraints	Dukas and Real (1993)
Lack of cultural norms concerning money	Henrich and McElreath (2002)
Decisions from experience	Hertwig, Barron, Weber, and Erev (2004)
Loss frames	Tversky and Kahneman (1981)
Losses	Kahneman and Tversky (1979)
Hypothetical payouts	Holt and Laury (2002)
Small rewards	Prelec and Loewenstein (1991); Weber and Chapman (2005)
Negative affect	Leith and Baumeister (1996)
Positive affect	Isen and Patrick (1983)
Anger	Lerner and Keltner (2001)
Variable delays	Kacelnik and Bateson (1996)
Low probability of gain	Tversky and Kahneman (1992)

Note. Although risk aversion is generally assumed to be universal for both humans and animals, the list of situations promoting risk seeking is surprisingly long. The length and heterogeneity of this list provides a challenge to general theories of risk, most of which assume that risk aversion is universal.

(see Figure 6.1, Panel A). The utility curve provides a satisfying explanation for risk aversion. With diminishing marginal utility, the utility of the safe outcome (the vertical line labeled *safe* in Panel A of Figure 6.1) is necessarily greater than the average utility of the two risky goods shown in the same panel (compare the two horizontal dashed lines). Thus, the concavity of the utility curve offers a satisfying, elegant explanation for risk aversion and helps to predict the appeal of a specific gamble to a particular individual.

The concave utility curve account of risk sensitivity has faced several major challenges. First, as noted earlier, risk aversion is not nearly as universal as is generally supposed. Second, in practice it is nearly impossible to estimate an individual's utility function without asking him or her questions about risk, a disturbingly circular approach. The impracticality of validly ascertaining an individual's utility curve makes it difficult to exploit the predictive power offered by the utility curve account. Another problem arises as a direct consequence of the weak assumption that utility curves are continuous and have monotonically decreasing derivatives. Given these assumptions, observed levels of risk aversion for small stakes necessarily lead to ridiculously large levels of risk aversion for larger stakes (Rabin, 2000; Rabin & Thaler, 2001). However, without these simple assumptions, the utility curve model loses much of its explanatory power. Finally, it is not clear that decisions regarding

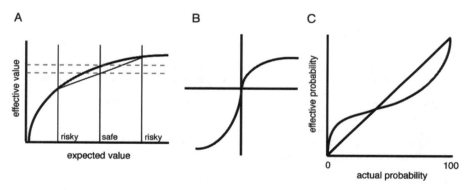

Figure 6.1. Utility-based models of risk. A: Hypothetical utility curve. Participants are assumed to value rewards in a way that differs systematically from the associated numerical values. Typically, the value of a reward rises more slowly than its numerical value. The distinction between a value and its utility can explain some forms of risk aversion. Although the expected value (abscissa) of the safe reward and the risky reward (i.e., the average of the two risky rewards) may be the same, the expected utility (ordinate) of these options may differ systematically. For a concave utility curve (such as that shown here), the expected utility of a gamble is smaller than the expected utility of a safe option. B: Utility curve and probability transform function according to prospect theory. Prospect theory hypothesizes a concave utility function for gains and a steeper convex utility function for losses. C: Prospect theory also hypothesizes that probabilities are weighted nonlinearly. High probabilities are underweighted, and low probabilities are overweighted.

hypothetical goods accurately reflect true individual preferences (Holt & Laury, 2002), or even whether people hold stable preferences that are expressed in their choice behavior (Ariely, Loewenstein, & Prelec, 2005). Such failures of the basic assumptions of economic theory make it impossible to satisfactorily explain risk sensitivity within the context of axiomatic economic principles such as utility theory.

Prospect Theory

Another major challenge to the traditional utility curve account comes from prospect theory (Kahneman & Tversky, 1979, 2000). Prospect theory encompasses three specific hypotheses. First, individuals make decisions with respect to changes in current wealth state rather than with respect to absolute wealth. Second, the utility curve has a characteristic shape that differs from the one proposed by Bernoulli (1738/1954). As shown in Figure 6.1, Panel B, the utility curve is concave for gains and convex for losses, has a steeper slope for losses, and is not continuously differentiable at the zero point. This characteristic shape leads to risk aversion for gains (as in Panel A) and risk seeking for losses (the latter occurring because the average of the risky losses is less aversive than the assured loss). Third, as shown in Figure 6.1, Panel C, decision makers transform reported probabilities according to a specific function that overweights low probabilities and underweights high probabilities. This property explains why a single person may both play the lottery (overweighting the low probability of winning the jackpot) and purchase disaster insurance (underweighting the high probability of avoiding disaster).

The aspect of prospect theory that has received the most attention is the asymmetry between the domains of gains and losses (Bernartzi & Thaler, 1995; Kahneman & Tversky, 1979; Tversky & Kahneman, 1991), a difference well illustrated by one of the original scenarios constructed by Tversky and Kahneman (1981). In the Asian Disease Problem, participants make a hypothetical choice between safe and risky medical interventions for an infected population (Tversky & Kahneman, 1981). In one condition, the choices are framed in terms of lives lost; in the other, choices are framed in terms of lives saved. Participants are risk seeking in the loss frame but risk averse in the gain frame, even though the facts about each intervention program remain identical across conditions. This framing effect has since been extended to a variety of scenarios and frame types; indeed, it has even been reported that some nonhuman animals are risk averse for gains but risk seeking for losses (Harder & Real, 1987). The ubiquity of risk aversion for gains and risk seeking for losses suggests that these behavior patterns reflect the operation of a mechanism that may be adaptive in many common natural environments (Gigerenzer, Todd, & Group, 1999; Kacelnik & Bateson, 1996; McNamara & Houston, 1986).

Prospect theory retains a great deal of predictive power, particularly in describing human behavior with regards to money (Kahneman & Tversky, 2000). However, in many ways it has fallen short as a complete theory of risk sensitivity. Most important, it does not fully encapsulate the range of risk-sensitive behavior observed in both humans and nonhuman animals. As discussed in the preceding and summarized in Table 6.1, risk seeking in the gains domain has been observed in a wide variety of species across a large array of contexts (Dukas & Real, 1993; Gilby & Wrangham, 2007; Kaminski & Ator, 2001; McCoy & Platt, 2005a). Furthermore, when gambles are framed as losses, nonhuman animals are not reliably risk seeking, further diminishing the predictive value of prospect theory (Kacelnik & Bateson, 1996; Marsh & Kacelnik, 2002).

Regret

Acknowledging these weaknesses in both prospect theory and expected utility theory, others have proposed cognitive accounts of risk sensitivity. For example, regret theory recasts risk aversion as regret minimization (Bell, 1982; Loomes & Sugden, 1982). *Regret* is operationally defined as the difference between the received outcome and the outcome of the forgone option and is distinct from *disappointment,* or the difference between the received outcome and the greatest alternative outcome from that option. Regret avoidance can induce both risk aversion (because of the possibility of losing) and risk seeking (because of the possibility of a forgone win), assuming the participant knows outcomes will be revealed after the gamble. In fact, knowledge of the alternative outcome can significantly influence people's choices: For example, people are more risk seeking when they will be forced to learn the outcome of the unchosen option than when they will not (Zeelenberg, 1999), suggesting that regret does regulate decisions (Humphrey, 2004). Recent studies of the neural mechanisms of regret have suggested that neural substrates of regret aversion are distinct from those that subserve disappointment aversion (Camille et al., 2004; Coricelli et al., 2005).

Scalar Utility Theory

Another explanation for risk sensitivity has emerged from behavioral ecology. Scalar utility theory explains risk preferences by the observed psychophysical properties of the representation of quantities (Hamm & Shettleworth, 1987; Kacelnik & Brito e Abreu, 1998; Perez & Waddington, 1996; Smallwood, 1996). According to Weber's law, perceptual variance scales with the mean of stimulus intensity. Thus, as the sizes of two different rewards (or delays) increase, they will be more and more difficult to discriminate. This property causes the expected probability distribution of a risky reward, derived from its history, to become positively skewed around the true mean, whereas the probability distribution of the fixed reward will be at the true mean. If decisions reflect the outcome of a competitive process between two samples randomly selected from the means of two reward distributions, a decision maker obeying Weber's law will sample more often from the smaller end of the x-axis and will thus prefer the safe option to the risky one (Kacelnik & Brito e Abreu, 1998). In the case of delays (or, presumably, any other losses or costs), participants seek to minimize the amount of time until food acquisition, so the risky outcome will be preferred. Scalar utility theory therefore predicts both risk aversion toward gains and risk seeking toward losses.

Evidence for scalar utility effects on risk sensitivity comes from the finding that humans and other animals typically adhere to Weber's law in perceptual discrimination of time and amount (Gibbon, 1977; Gibbon, Church, Fairhurst, & Kacelnik, 1988; but see Bizo, Chu, Sanabria, & Killeen, 2006, for counterevidence). However, mounting evidence for risk seeking in the gains domain (see Table 6.1) reduces the appeal of this model. Moreover, it is unclear whether proposed failures of memory are large enough to explain patterns of economic decision making for humans or nonhuman animals.

State Variables and Risk Sensitivity

Another explanation for risk-sensitive behavior derives from consideration of the impact of state variables like energy budgets on decision making. For example, some animals need to find enough food each day to survive to make another choice in the future. Thus, risk seeking for gains may be the only option for an organism that is on the brink of starvation (Caraco, 1981). This situation can be generalized to any in which the animal's utility function is convex over the range of possible gains. Although risk sensitivity theory, as these ideas are called, elegantly applies ideas drawn from foraging theory to risk-sensitive preferences, the required energy state is so narrow that it has proved difficult to reproduce in a laboratory setting or confirm in field studies (Kacelnik, 1997). Furthermore, risk seeking has been reliably observed in situations in which animals are far from starvation (Gilby & Wrangham, 2007; Heilbronner, Rosati, Stevens, Hare, & Hauser, 2008). As revealed in Kacelnik and Bateson's (1996) literature review, juncos (*Junco hyemalis*) in the original studies of state-dependent risk seeking (e.g., Caraco, 1981) may be more the exception than the rule. In contrast with songbirds, other animals may store excess energy as fat, and so may be able to survive for long periods of time without food. For these reasons, there has been little empirical evidence to support the theory's predictions.

Reward Salience and Risk Sensitivity

A final possible explanation for risk sensitivity is the relative salience of the possible outcomes of the gamble (e.g., Bechara, Damasio, Damasio, & Anderson, 1994), an account we call *biased anchoring*. A salient outcome may be more available to cognitive processes (memory, value representation, attention, etc.) and thus bias decisions (Tversky & Kahneman, 1973). Risk aversion may reflect the use of the loss (from a gamble) as an anchor by which to judge the expected utility of a given option. Likewise, risk seeking could result from using the win as an anchor, effectively overweighting the large payoff from a risky choice. For example, it is known that humans in a positive mood are more risk averse than controls (Isen & Geva, 1987). Despite their good mood, they exhibit a tendency to think more about the possibility of losing than do controls (Isen & Geva 1987). These participants' tendency to avoid risk may reflect a biased focus on the possibility of losing.

Summary

Although decision makers are risk averse in many circumstances, there are many other contexts in which decision makers are reliably risk seeking. We have summarized a few of the major models designed to explain the full range of risk-sensitive behaviors. Although each account explains risk-sensitive behavior in certain contexts, a single general account of risk sensitivity remains elusive. It is likely that a richer understanding of the neuronal mechanisms underlying risk sensitivity can lead to a greater understanding of behavior toward risk.

NEURAL SIGNATURES OF ECONOMIC RISK

Neuroscience offers the opportunity to carve decision making into component processes (Romo & Salinas, 2003; Schall, 2004). One central goal of the neuroeconomic study of risk-sensitive decision making is to determine where and how these processes are instantiated in the brain (Glimcher, 2002; Sanfey et al., 2006). In any risky decision, neural signals must exist that contain information about two or more options, and for at least one of them the associated uncertainty will have to be represented as well.

Representations of Expected Value and Risk

Several studies have probed the representation of uncertainty in the brain (reviewed in Knutson & Bossaerts, 2007; Platt & Huettel 2008). One neural substrate that has recently been implicated in this process is the dopamine system, which is generally linked to reward processing (Schultz, 2006). Dopamine neurons in the substantia nigra pars compacta and the ventral tegmental area project to the striatum and to the cortex (Schultz, 2006). Reward-predicting cues and unpredicted rewards generally elicit *phasic* (i.e., brief) responses from dopamine neurons, whereas failures to receive predicted rewards phasically suppress their activity (Bayer, Handel, & Glimcher, 2004; Schultz, Dayan, & Montague, 1997; Tobler, Fiorillo, & Schultz, 2005). Such responses are thought to encode a reward *prediction error*, or the difference between the expected and the obtained reward (Montague, Dayan, & Sejnowski, 1996; Schultz et al., 1997), information that is particularly useful for learning in uncertain environments (Sutton & Barto, 1998). (For discussions of dissenting views on dopamine function, see Redgrave & Gurney, 2006; Ungless, 2004.)

Explicit signals of expected and obtained rewards have obvious benefits to the decision maker. Dopamine's role in representing uncertain outcomes was examined directly in a study of the responses of dopaminergic neurons to conditioned stimuli associated with either fixed or risky rewards (Fiorillo, Tobler, & Schultz, 2003). Monkeys observed one of five visual stimuli, each associated with a specific likelihood of reinforcement (0%, 25%, 50%, 75%, and 100%). Then, after a delay, the reward was either given or withheld. The authors found that the population of dopamine neurons, as well as some single dopamine neurons, encoded both the expected value of the information and its uncertainty (which is maximized at a reward probability of 50%) in distinct ways. Brief phasic responses signaled the expected value of the reward, whereas subsequent tonic changes in activity matched the uncertainty associated with the stimulus.

These results suggest that dopamine neurons may contribute to the representation of both reward uncertainty and predicted reward value, an idea that was tested in a recent neuroimaging study (Preuschoff, Bossaerts, & Quartz, 2006). On each trial, human participants placed a bet on which of two playing cards ranging from 1 to 10 would have a higher numeric value. One card was then revealed, informing the participant of how likely he or she was to win (e.g., revealing a low number signals a high probability of winning if the participant guessed that the second card would be the larger of the two). The authors found that blood flow in the dorsal and ventral striatum (the primary target of dopamine neurons) was correlated with the expected value of the gamble (i.e., the signaled probability of a win), and blood flow in the ventral striatum, the midbrain, and the mediodorsal thalamus was correlated with risk (which was highest when the first card provided no information about the likelihood of a win). Notably, these two signals had different temporal dynamics: Expected value was encoded in the early part of the hemodynamic response, whereas risk was encoded in the late part of the response. Despite the large difference in the time scales between the firing rates of single neurons (milliseconds) and the hemodynamic response (seconds), these results are roughly consistent with the idea that dopamine neurons encode different forms of reward-related information in early and late portions of their responses.

To fully understand risk-sensitive decision making, we need to dissociate the neural correlates of risk and expected value. To do so, Knutson, Taylor, Kaufman, Peterson, and Glover (2005) used a version of the monetary incentive delay task. Each participant was presented with a cue indicating whether money would be won or lost, what the expected value of a win or loss was, and what the approximate probability of a win or loss would be. Then the participant had to press a button as fast as possible. If the participant responded quickly enough, the indicated amount was given (or taken away in the case of losses). Here, expected value was encoded by the nucleus accumbens (a structure that largely overlaps with the ventral striatum), whereas probability was associated with the blood oxygen level dependent (usually referred to as "BOLD") signal in the medial prefrontal cortex (MPFC). The authors inferred that emotional information is maintained within subcortical circuits that include the nucleus accumbens and then is transmitted to cortical circuits including MPFC, where it is combined with probability and can ultimately influence the decision.

Competing Systems for Losses and Gains

How is the gamble actually evaluated in a risky decision? For a risky option, multiple possible rewards must be combined into a single representation of value. One proposal is that this combined signal reflects the outcome of a competition between systems encoding the possibilities of winning and of losing. Given the importance of dopamine neurons for signaling reward prediction error, this system is a reasonable place to begin looking for a neural basis of this posited competition. However, at present, it remains unclear whether dopamine neurons are capable of representing negative reward predictions or outcomes (Bayer et al., 2004; Schultz, 2006). Neuronal signals consistent with negative reward prediction errors have been located within the lateral habenula, a structure within the diencephalon (Matsumoto & Hikosaka, 2007); these may provide a functional complement to dopamine neurons. In addition, several cortical regions, including the dorsolateral prefrontal cortex (DLPFC; Kobayashi et al., 2006), the amygdala (Gottfried, O'Doherty, & Dolan, 2003; Paton, Belova, Morrison, & Salzman, 2006), the posterior cingulate cortex (McCoy, Crowley, Haghighian, Dean, & Platt, 2003), and the orbitofrontal cortex (Gottfried, O'Doherty, & Dolan, 2002; Zald, Hagen & Pardo, 2002), contain heterogeneous populations of neurons whose responses code for both gains and losses (or for larger and smaller than expected wins).

Given that different structures may encode winning and losing, the valuation of a risky option could reflect the outcome of a compromise between signals carried by separate brain regions. This hypothesis has been tested in several neuroimaging studies. In one, participants made invest-ments in a simulated stock market (Kuhnen & Knutson, 2005). The exper-imenters found that risk-seeking decisions were preceded by activation in the ventral striatum. Because the ventral striatum is a primary target of dopamine neurons (discussed earlier in this chapter), activation there is likely correlated with dopamine release. In contrast, risk-averse and risk-neutral decisions were preceded by activation in the insula. In prior studies, the insula has been most reliably activated by aversive or unpleasant stimuli or by increasing effort. The authors hypothesized that risk seeking in this task is mediated by a brief positive affect associated with the gamble, whereas risk aversion is mediated by a brief negative affect. These ideas imply that the decision to gamble reflects the outcome of competition between distinct areas representing the possibility of winning and the possibility of losing.

A recent study has challenged the notion that separate anatomical areas mediate the representation of winning versus losing (Tom, Fox, Trepel, & Poldrack, 2007). Participants in each trial indicated their level of preference for a gamble offering equal probabilities of winning or losing money. To tempt the generally risk-averse participants into gambling, the average size of the gain was set to about twice the average size of the loss. To specifically isolate decision utility, the authors did not resolve the gambles until after a delay. It is surprising that although the authors found a standard set of areas exhibit-ing positive correlation with the size of the potential win, they did not find any brain region whose responses were positively correlated with possible losses. One explanation for this discrepancy reflects the difference between decision utility (the amount of utility expected at the time of the decision) and experienced utility (the amount of utility actually gained). The authors argued that their focus on decision utility, as opposed to experienced utility, allowed them to eliminate confounding factors such as prediction error. They suggested that earlier studies that found discrete brain regions activated for potential gains and losses may in fact reflect a combination of these confound-ing factors. These results indicate that the predecision competition between representations of the possibility of winning and of losing may take place within single brain areas rather than between different brain areas.

Whether the possibilities of winning and losing are encoded by the same or different brain areas, it is clear that seemingly extraneous factors, such as the way in which a gamble is framed, can bias the relative influence of poten-tial outcomes. One study has identified a neural substrate for the effects of framing on risk-sensitive decision making (De Martino, Kumaran, Seymour, & Dolan, 2006). De Martino et al. (2006) asked participants to make deci-sions in a series of gambles, some of which were framed as gains and others of which were framed as losses. The extent to which framing biased choices varied across individuals. The authors showed that individual susceptibility to framing was reflected in activation in the amygdala. Because the amygdala is associated with emotional information processing, they concluded that framing is fundamentally an emotional process. In contrast, they found that activation in the orbitofrontal and mediofrontal cortices was correlated with reduced susceptibility to framing.

Neurophysiological Correlates of Risky Decision Making

The neural mechanisms of calculating and storing evaluative information remain unknown. Previous studies have shown that the firing rates of single neurons in the lateral intraparietal area (LIP) of primate parietal cortex are positively correlated with the expected value of visual orienting movements (Platt & Glimcher, 1999). Monkeys in these types of studies are typically rewarded with a small squirt of juice for correct performance. When the likelihood of receiving the reward was instead set at 50%, the authors found that the expected value of the movement and the firing rate of the neurons decreased in concert. LIP neurons also encode expected value when it is determined by information gathered from recent trials (Sugrue, Corrado, & Newsome, 2004) or by the Nash equilibrium optimal strategy in a competitive game (Dorris & Glimcher, 2004).

The next obvious step in understanding this circuitry is to find the source of the reward information that modulates neuronal activity in LIP. Several studies from our lab have supported the hypothesis that one source of this information is the posterior cingulate cortex (CGp; Dean, Crowley, & Platt, 2004; Dean & Platt, 2006; McCoy et al., 2003; McCoy & Platt 2005a). CGp is a cortical structure that receives direct and indirect projections from several reward-related structures, including the orbitofrontal cortex, the anterior cingulate cortex, and the striatum (Vogt & Gabriel, 1993). CGp projects to the parietal cortex (Kobayashi & Amaral, 2003; Vogt & Gabriel, 1993) and to other areas contributing to action-based decision making (Dorris & Glimcher, 2004; Platt & Glimcher, 1999; Shadlen & Newsome, 2001; Sugrue et al., 2004; Yang & Shadlen 2007).

Our studies (Dean et al., 2004; McCoy et al., 2003) have indicated that individual CGp neurons respond with relatively long-lasting changes in activity after movements toward a target that predicts a reward (Figure 6.2, Panel C). Many of these neurons signal the value of the reward expected or experienced for executing the movement. This information appears to be encoded in positive or negative terms by separate populations of CGp neurons. In other words, CGp neurons are monotonically tuned for reward size in the same way that neurons in other parts of the brain are tuned for orientation, brightness, or motion direction. Notably, some CGp neurons are positively tuned (higher firing for larger rewards and lower firing for smaller rewards), and others are negatively tuned. This heterogeneity means that the aggregate neuronal signals from positively and negatively tuned neurons may

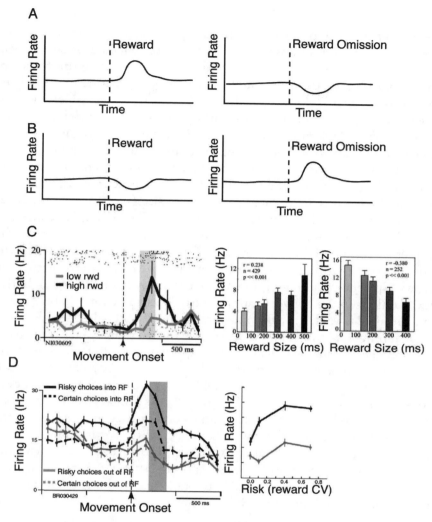

Figure 6.2. Neurophysiological correlates of reward and risk. A: Responses of a hypothetical positive reward prediction error neuron. When an unexpected reward occurs,
firing rate increases phasically. When a reward is expected but no reward occurs, firing
rate drops phasically. Responses of dopamine neurons are similar to these hypothetical
neurons, although the extent to which they encode expected reward omissions remains
unclear. B: Responses of hypothetical negative reward prediction error neurons. When
an unexpected reward occurs, firing rate falls phasically. When a reward is expected
but no reward occurs, firing rate rises phasically. Responses of habenula neurons
may instantiate negative reward prediction error signals. C: Responses of posterior
cingulate cortex neurons vary with reward (rwd) size. These neurons respond differentially to reward size both before and after the occurrence of the reward. Across
the population of neurons, some neurons are positively tuned for reward size, and
others are negatively tuned for reward size. D: Responses of posterior cingulate
cortex neurons vary with risk. These neurons respond more strongly to choices
of the risky option than choices of the safe option. In addition, these neurons
respond with higher tonic firing rates for higher risk levels (coefficient of variation
[CV]). RF = response field. Panel C from "Risk-Sensitive Neurons in Macaque Posterior
Cingulate Cortex," by A. N. McCoy and M. L. Platt, 2005, *Nature Neuroscience, 8,*
p. 1033. Copyright 2005 by Nature Publishing Group. Adapted with permission. Panel
D from "Saccade Reward Signals in Posterior Cingulate Cortex," by A. N. McCoy,
J. C. Crowley, G. Haghighian, H. L. Dean, and M. L. Platt, 2003, *Neuron, 40,* p. 1223.
Copyright 2003 by Cell Press. Adapted with permission.

average out and that the greater neuronal population may not encode reward size. This fact in turn means that CGp neuronal populations should project onto different downstream or readout neurons. Another interesting feature of this area is that many CGp neurons exhibit enhanced responses to unexpected omissions of rewards (McCoy et al., 2003). This response property is reminiscent of dopamine neurons (see earlier discussion in this chapter) and suggests that CGp monitors the consequences of actions to guide changes in behavior. In any case, the heterogeneity in reward encoding links CGp with other brain areas, including the amygdala, DLPFC, and orbitofrontal cortex (OFC), in which the activity of individual neurons is both positively and negatively correlated with reward size (Gottfried et al., 2002; 2003; Kobayashi et al., 2006; Paton et al., 2006; Zald et al., 2002).

These prior observations suggested that CGp might contribute to the computations underlying risk-sensitive decision making. To examine the contribution of CGp to risky decision making, we recorded the activity of single CGp neurons during a gambling task (McCoy & Platt, 2005b). In this task, monkeys chose between two targets: The safe target reliably offered a middle-sized reward; the risky target stochastically offered either a larger or a smaller reward. Monkeys strongly preferred the risky target even though the risky and safe options were matched for expected value. In fact, as risk level (defined as the variance of the two possible outcomes of the risky option; coefficient of variation in Figure 6.2, Panel D) increased, the monkeys' tendency to choose the risky option rose from 55% to 80%. As can be seen in Figure 6.2, Panel D, we found long-lasting (200-millisecond to 2-second) changes in the responses of these neurons that were correlated with risk. In addition, CGp neurons fired more vigorously after monkeys chose the risky option than after monkeys chose the safe option. These results suggest that CGp maintains representations of the value of uncertain options for use by downstream decision structures in the parietal lobe and elsewhere.

Expected and Unexpected Forms of Uncertainty

Most studies of risk-sensitive decision making have focused on tasks in which the level of risk is well defined to both the experimenter and the participant. That is, all parties are assumed to know that the outcome of any risky choice is fully stochastic and that no information can be gathered that will reduce the amount of uncertainty associated with the risky option. However, there is evidence that the brain deals with different forms of uncertainty in different ways.

Several authors have found it useful to divide uncertainty into measurable and unmeasurable forms (Ellsberg, 1961; Knight, 1921), two forms of uncertainty that are sometimes called *knowable* and *unknowable* or *expected* and *unexpected*. Whereas measureable uncertainty is characterized by a precise numerical description of the possible outcomes, unmeasurable uncertainty is characterized by probabilities that are not known or that cannot be known. Unmeasurable uncertainty sometimes includes the uncertainty associated with a single event drawn from a stochastic distribution (Knight, 1921). The terms *unmeasurable uncertainty*, *unexpected uncertainty*, and *ambiguity*, although perhaps used in subtly different ways, probably represent states along a continuum of uncertainty, and we do not strongly distinguish among them here.

In most studies of decision making in humans, participants are presented with precise numerical descriptions of the different probabilities associated with different outcomes; this form of uncertainty is known. Likewise, in most animal studies, subjects are so well trained that the animal can be assumed to have a stable internal representation of the likelihood of outcomes, so risk is thought to be known. However, many situations, especially those outside the laboratory, present unmeasurable uncertainty (Knight, 1921). In such situations, decision makers need to pay more attention, learn more quickly, and search for sources of information that will allow them to gain information about contingencies in their environment (Yu & Dayan, 2005).

Measurable and unmeasurable forms of uncertainty have some intuitive linkage with expected and unexpected forms of uncertainty discussed in neuroscience. Separate neuronal systems may mediate expected and unexpected forms of uncertainty (Yu & Dayan, 2005). Specifically, it has been speculated that the acetylcholine system signals the expected uncertainty in a given situation (Yu & Dayan, 2002), and the norepinephine system signals unexpected uncertainty (Aston-Jones & Cohen, 2005; Dayan & Yu, 2006). These two neuromodulators are thus thought to have complementary roles in decision making. Acetylcholine and norepinephrine both act by biasing cortical processing from feedback-driven (top-down) to stimulus-driven (bottom-up) responses by suppressing the activity of intracortical neurons (Aston-Jones & Cohen, 2005; Usher, Cohen, Servan-Schreiber, Rajkowski, & Aston-Jones, 1999), thereby facilitating responsiveness to changes in the environment and stimulating learning (Yu & Dayan, 2005). The precise mechanisms by which these transmitters act may allow them to specifically potentiate the differential responses to unexpected and expected forms of uncertainty (Yu & Dayan, 2005).

In economics, the distinction between risk and ambiguity is exemplified by the Ellsberg (1961) paradox. Consider two bags full of red and blue balls. Bag 1 holds 50 red and 50 blue balls. Bag 2 contains n red and $100 - n$ blue balls, where n is randomly chosen between 0 and 100. One ball will be chosen at random from one of the bags, and a payoff of $10 will be given for the red and a payoff of $1 for the blue. Although the expected value of the two bags is identical, most participants will prefer the first (risky) bag to the second (ambiguous) bag. This predilection for choosing the option with a known uncertainty is referred to as *ambiguity aversion*.

In a study by Hsu, Bhatt, Adolphs, Tranel, and Camerer (2005), the neural correlates of ambiguity aversion were assessed using three complementary methods. In one, participants chose between a risky and an ambiguous decision using cards. In another, participants gambled on topics about which they felt that they had more or less background information ("Was the temperature in New York/Bishkek greater than 60 degrees on October 15th last year at 5 p.m.?"). In the third condition, they competed against players with more information than they had in a gambling game. The authors found that across the three conditions, the level of ambiguity was positively correlated with the level of activation in the OFC and the amygdala and negatively correlated with the level of activity in the striatum. In addition, participants with OFC lesions were insensitive to the level of ambiguity in a gamble. These convergent results suggest that the OFC contributes directly to ambiguity aversion.

Ambiguity preferences were also studied in a second neuroimaging study (Huettel, Stowe, Gordon, Warner, & Platt, 2006). On each trial, participants chose between two gambles, each identified by a circle on a screen. Gambles were certain (a full circle), risky (with circle portions corresponding to the probabilities of the two outcomes), or ambiguous (empty circle). Behavioral data for each participant were fit with separate parameters for risk and ambiguity preference levels. Each individual's ambiguity seeking was most strongly predicted by activation in the lateral prefrontal cortex. Because activation in this region is associated with cognitive control, it was inferred that ambiguity preference reflects successful control of the prepotent urge to avoid ambiguity. Furthermore, activation in this area was negatively correlated with a clinical measure of impulsivity. In contrast, risk preference correlated with activity in the parietal cortex, a finding that is reminiscent of findings from other physiological studies that the parietal cortex represents quantitative information in contexts with low uncertainty (Platt & Glimcher, 1999; Roitman, Brannon, & Platt, 2007; Sugrue et al., 2004).

Summary

Researchers are in the early stages of identifying the neural substrates responsible for integrating information about current needs and reward history and using this information to select appropriate behaviors. Such areas appear to be critical for decision making in risky contexts because they estimate and represent the likelihood of different outcomes and participate in selecting specific options. Critical brain regions include the striatum, the orbitofrontal cortex, and the cingulate cortex. Dopamine, which signals expected reward, is a particularly important neuromodulator regulating both risky and certain decisions. Future studies will focus on identifying the specific roles of these areas and brain chemicals in different aspects of risky decision making.

FUNCTIONAL MANIPULATION OF RISK PREFERENCES

Manipulating decision-making processes directly tests theories about their underlying neural mechanisms, permitting us to distinguish effects correlated with behavior from those that cause behavior. Moreover, manipulation represents one of the ultimate goals of this research: Given the ubiquity of failures to accurately deal with uncertainty in several psychiatric disorders, treatments for suboptimal risky decision making are a potential target for therapies.

Affect influences one's propensity to gamble. Positive affect is a cognitive state characterized by a positive outlook, greater engagement in the environment, and a general tendency to experience good moods. It can be induced via participant gifts, winning at competitive games, or even autobiographical recall of positive events. Participants in a positive state typically exhibit a greater optimism about their prospects in a gambling situation (Nygren, Isen, Taylor, & Dulin, 1996). They overestimate the likelihood of rare positive events and underestimate the likelihood of rare negative events. Paradoxically, these participants have a reduced tendency to accept any gamble. Consistent with this observation, they require a greater probability of winning than do control participants to induce risk-seeking behavior (Isen & Geva, 1987).

Risk aversion among participants with positive affect is certainly puzzling. These participants showed reduced utility for gains and increased disutility for losses (Isen, Nygren, & Ashby, 1988). Although participants with positive affect are reliably more optimistic than control participants and focus more on positive thoughts and memories (Mischel, Ebbesen, & Zeiss, 1973), they show a greater tendency to list thoughts about loss, suggesting that their decisions are anchored to the possibility of losing (Isen & Geva, 1987). These results suggest that participants with positive affect enjoy their state, are aware of its lability, and will adopt cognitive and behavioral strategies designed to maintain their affect.

Negative affect is a cognitive state characterized by a negative orientation toward the present situation and life in general, by recurring negative and pessimistic thoughts that often cause distress, and by a tendency toward bad moods. Participants in whom negative affect has been induced exhibit greater pessimism about their likelihood of winning gambles but are more risk seeking. This tendency is especially pronounced in situations with low probabilities of winning (lotteries) and in situations in which one possible outcome (such as a loud annoying sound) is aversive (Leith & Baumeister, 1996). In general, the behavioral consequences of negative affect and depression tend to overlap. Even though they are thought to be generated by different processes (Hartlage, Alloy, Vazquez, & Dykman, 1993), understanding negatively motivated risk sensitivity may help us treat depression.

Another method of inducing risk sensitivity is direct manipulation or activation of neural tissue. The simplest way to do this is to provide transcranial magnetic stimulation to the scalp, which, depending on the stimulation condition, can activate or inactivate underlying populations of neurons. Two studies of this kind examined the role of the dorsolateral prefrontal cortex in risk-sensitive decision making. Transcranial magnetic stimulation–induced deactivation of right DLPFC promoted risk seeking, even when it was financially disadvantageous (Knoch et al., 2006). Although this effect may be explained by a transient induction of negative affect (Gershon, Dannon, & Grunhaus, 2003), the authors argued that the right DLPFC normally suppresses the tendency to choose the more seductive risky option, and disruption of this brain area leads to a release from suppression of this risk-averse tendency. Notably, this hypothesis provides a nice link between the concepts of self-control and risk. Consistent with this idea, activation of the DLPFC through transcranial direct current stimulation promotes risk aversion (Fecteau et al., 2007). Such results are especially interesting given the observed activation of these areas in decision making under ambiguity (Huettel et al., 2006).

Summary

Risk preferences are not static. Instead, they are highly labile and depend on a variety of circumstances. Experimenters can manipulate these circumstances to predictably alter risk preferences. Such manipulations provide strong tests of the validity of neural models of risky decision making.

IMPULSIVITY AND RISK SENSITIVITY

Just as decisions deviate from normative ideals when options are uncertain, so too do decisions deviate when options are delayed. Humans and other animals generally exhibit a preference for immediacy, preferring sooner rewards to later ones and seeking to defer unpleasant outcomes (but see Frederick, Loewenstein, & O'Donoghue, 2002). Such behavioral impulsiveness has long been associated with risk sensitivity. Nonetheless, the precise relationship between these two behavioral patterns and the relationships between their underlying neural mechanisms remain obscure.

Two distinct ideas about the relationship between impulsivity and risk sensitivity have emerged. In one view, "general impulsivity" is a personality trait that encompasses a suite of potentially maladaptive behaviors, including both risk seeking and high devaluation of future rewards (see Myerson, Green, Hanson, Holt, & Estle, 2003). Impulsive individuals are risk seeking, fail to fully consider the consequences of decisions, and do not accurately weigh costs and benefits. General impulsivity has been implicated in a variety of psychiatric disorders, including drug and gambling addiction (e.g., Mitchell, 1999), the manic phase of bipolar disorder, schizophrenia, attention-deficit/hyperactivity disorder, and even some personality disorders (Henry et al., 2001; Oades, Slusarek, Velling, & Bondy, 2002).

Performance on a delay-discounting task, a measure of impulsivity, can also predict academic performance, social competence, and successful handling of stressful situations (Mischel, Shoda, & Rodriguez, 1989), suggesting that general impulsivity influences all of these behavioral tendencies. Thus, short time horizons and risk-seeking behavior (to the point of obsessive gambling) may be comorbid, implying a common underlying cause. Studies of human pathologies have provided some empirical support for this linkage. For example, addicted smokers are more impulsive than nonsmokers on a delay-discounting task (Mitchell, 1999), and they are also more likely to be problem gamblers (Petry & Oncken, 2002).

In contrast to the idea of general impulsivity, the relationship between impulsivity and risk sensitivity may be explained by interruption or collection risk. The future is inherently uncertain: A delayed reward is riskier than its more immediate counterpart. When thinking about a future reward, an individual may consider the chance that its value will change in an unpredictable manner. That is, something may cause the original reward offer to be unavailable or greatly reduced by the time it is actually collected. For example, a monkey considering whether to eat an unripe fruit now or wait until it has ripened in a week needs to account for whether another monkey will steal the fruit in the meantime. Any number of events may devalue a delayed reward—the market could drastically change, food could rot, a giver could renege on his or her offer, the chooser's energy or monetary demands may change, and so forth (McNamara & Houston, 1986). One simple prediction of the idea that risk mediates impulsivity is that devaluation of future rewards should be consistent across equal time spans because the possible risk is, on average, the same across periods. However, humans and nonhuman animals do not exhibit such behavior (e.g., Ainslie & Haslam, 1992; Madden, Begotka, Raiff, & Kastern, 2003; Mazur, 1987). Instead, their behavior is time inconsistent: They act as if risk is not the same across time periods. This leads to *preference reversals*: In a choice between $5 now and $6 in a month, participants may prefer the $5, but if the choice is between $5 in 12 months and $6 in 13 months, they are likely to prefer the $6. However, the collection risk difference associated with the two choices is the same: It is the risk associated with a single month's delay. This behavioral inconsistency demonstrates that impulsivity must reflect more than just interruption risk. Nevertheless, uncertainty is probably still a major force behind impulsivity in intertemporal choice (Rachlin, 2000). This perspective offers the counterintuitive prediction that individuals who are more willing to wait for delayed rewards should be more risk seeking. It is interesting that in a straightforward questionnaire, human participants were slightly more likely to take a risk if they were relatively patient in a delay-discounting task (Myerson et al., 2003).

Additionally, participants may perceive choices between engaging in risk-seeking and risk-averse strategies as ones that they will follow for several trials. If participants construe the risky option to be virtually certain to pay off at some point, then their attitudes about the relative appeal of sooner and later rewards become important (Rachlin, 2000; Rachlin, Raineri, & Cross, 1991). Our lab recently found that by varying the time between choices (the *intertrial interval*), we could influence the likelihood that monkeys would gamble in a sequential choice task (Figure 6.3; Hayden & Platt, 2007). Specifically, monkeys were risk seeking with short intertrial intervals and risk neutral with long intertrial intervals (Figure 6.3, Panel C). Moreover, the precise level of risk seeking was predicted by the hyperbolic discount function inferred from intertemporal choice data. Such results are predicted by Rachlin's (2000) string theory, which argues that gambles may be construed as a series of outcomes in the future (Figure 6.3, Panels A and B). If the possibility of winning is more salient than the possibility of losing, then future outcomes may be grouped into strings of losses followed by a win. Such a construal biases the subjective likelihood of winning. These results imply that choices about risky options have an important temporal component and that preferences and perceptions about reward rates help to shape preferences.

Although a comprehensive review of the mechanisms supporting impulsive decision making is beyond the scope of this chapter (see chaps. 4 and 5 of this volume), we highlight just two of the important areas of convergence between studies of the neural mechanisms of risk and impulsivity. We can ask first whether there are patients with brain damage who show abnormal risk preferences or delay-discounting rates. Likely candidates are those with damage to the ventromedial prefrontal cortex (VMPFC). Although such patients typically lie within a normal range of performance on most cognitive tasks, they exhibit deviant decision-making patterns. For example, on the Iowa Gambling Task participants repeatedly choose among decks of cards with different reward and probability parameters. VMPFC patients will continue to pick a deck that is disadvantageous in the long term but offers occasional large payoffs (Bechara, Damasio, Tranel, & Damasio, 1997). These failures have been attributed to myopia for future rewards (Bechara, Damasio, Damasio, & Anderson, 1994; Bechara, Tranel, & Damasio, 2000). Although VMPFC patients do not exhibit deviant patterns of delay discounting, they do show shorter time perspectives (a measure of how far into the future one regularly considers) than do control participants (Fellows & Farah, 2005). Furthermore, in addition to being future myopic, the patients' behavior on the Iowa Gambling Task could be interpreted as risk seeking, perhaps attributable to hypersensitivity to wins (but see Bechara et al., 2000). Indeed, in a traditional gambling task, VMPFC patients are relatively risk seeking (Sanfey,

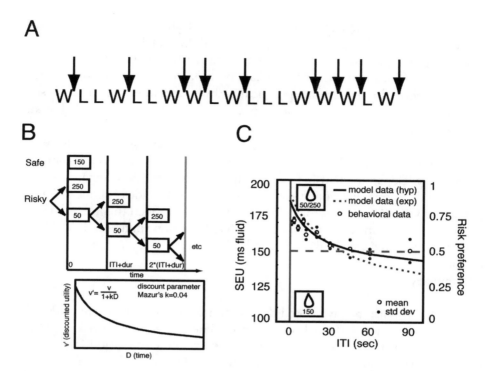

Figure 6.3. Risk and impulsivity: one model. A: According to Rachlin's (2000) string theory, repeated gambles may be construed as a series of outcomes in the future. If the possibility of winning is more salient than the possibility of losing, then future outcomes may be grouped into strings of losses (Ls) followed by a win (W). Such a conception biases the subjective likelihood of winning. B: Future outcomes are discounted according to a hyperbolic decay function. Strings of losses followed by a win may not be evaluated until the end of the string. By this process, the delay between sequential trials may influence the utility of the prospect of a gamble. C: One way to test this possibility is to examine the influence of the delay between trials on risky behavior. We have recently shown that monkeys' propensity to gamble is a decreasing function of the delay between trials in a sequence. These results link together the concepts of risk and impulsivity. ITI = intertrial interval; dur = duration; hyp = hypothesis; exp = experiment; SEU = subjective expected utility; hyp = hyperbolic; exp = exponential; std dev = standard deviation; ms = milliseconds; sec = seconds. From "Temporal Discounting Predicts Risk Sensitivity in Rhesus Macaques," by B. Y. Hayden and M. L. Platt, 2007, *Current Biology, 17,* p. 51. Copyright 2007 by Elsevier. Adapted with permission.

Hastie, Colvin, & Grafman, 2003). The co-occurrence of abnormal time perspectives and risk seeking suggests that the VMPFC may subserve both types of decisions.

Future studies of the relationship between impulsivity and risk sensitivity may focus on dopamine. Although no study has investigated the idea that dopamine mediates both impulsivity and risk sensitivity, the evidence is tantalizing. Dopamine agonists used to treat Parkinson's disease may induce pathological gambling (Dodd et al., 2005), and abnormal dopamine functioning may produce impulsivity (Cardinal, Pennicott, Sugathapala, Robbins, & Everitt, 2001). Dopamine may mediate both processes by activating cortex, both directly through the mesocortical pathway and indirectly through striatal projections. Such activations may induce general approach behavior, both to risky options and to immediate options (Schultz, 2006).

The common role of dopamine in both risk seeking and impulsivity is consistent with the idea that dopamine serves as a general reward-signaling molecule. Dopamine may in fact participate in hypothesized domain-general reward decisions. Economic theories elegantly unite ideas about different types of valuation into a single common framework. Such theories allow the direct comparison of possible outcomes that differ along different dimensions, such as expected value, risk level, and delay.

Summary

Many authors have noted that responses to probabilistic rewards and delayed rewards have much in common. The fact that both risky options and delayed options tend to be discounted provides a second impetus to develop a common framework to explain the effects of both factors on decision making. Determining the mechanistic bases of these types of decisions remains a central goal of neuroeconomics.

REFERENCES

Ainslie, G., & Haslam, N. (1992). Hyperbolic discounting. In G. Loewenstein & J. Elster (Eds.), *Choice over time* (pp. 57–92). New York: Russell Sage Foundation.

Ariely, D., Loewenstein, G., & Prelec, D. (2005). Tom Sawyer and the construction of value. *Journal of Economic Behavior & Organization, 60,* 1–10.

Aston-Jones, G., & Cohen, J. D. (2005). An integrative theory of locus coeruleus-norepinephrine function: Adaptive gain and optimal performance. *Annual Review of Neuroscience, 28,* 403–450.

Bayer, H. M., Handel, A., & Glimcher, P. W. (2004). Eye position and memory saccade related responses in substantia nigra pars reticulata. *Experimental Brain Research, 154,* 428–441.

Bechara, A., Damasio, A. R., Damasio, H., & Anderson, S. W. (1994). Insensitivity to future consequences following damage to human prefrontal cortex. *Cognition, 50,* 7–15.

Bechara, A., Damasio, H., Tranel, D., & Damasio, A. R. (1997, February 28). Deciding advantageously before knowing the advantageous strategy. *Science, 275,* 1293–1295.

Bechara, A., Tranel, D., & Damasio, H. (2000). Characterization of the decision-making deficit of patients with ventromedial prefrontal cortex lesions. *Brain, 123*(Pt. 11), 2189–2202.

Bell, D. E. (1982). Regret in decision making under uncertainty. *Operations Research, 30*, 961–981.

Benartzi, S., & Thaler, R. (1995). Myopic loss aversion and the equity premium puzzle. *Quarterly Journal of Economics, 100*, 73–92.

Bernoulli, D. (1954). Specimen theoriae novae de mensura sortis [Exposition of a new theory on the measurement of risk]. *Econometrica, 5*, 22–36. (Original work published 1738)

Bizo, L. A., Chu, J. Y., Sanabria, F., & Killeen, P. R. (2006). The failure of Weber's law in time perception and production. *Behavioural Processes, 71*, 201–210.

Camille, N., Coricelli, G., Sallet, J., Pradat-Diehl, P., Duhamel, J. R., & Sirigu, A. (2004, May 21). The involvement of the orbitofrontal cortex in the experience of regret. *Science, 304*, 1167–1170.

Caraco, T. (1981). Energy budgets, risk and foraging preferences in dark-eyed juncos (*Junco hyemalis*). *Behavioral Ecology and Sociobiology, 8*, 213–217.

Cardinal, R. N., Pennicott, D. R., Sugathapala, C. L., Robbins, T. W., & Everitt, B. J. (2001, May 24). Impulsive choice induced in rats by lesions of the nucleus accumbens core. *Science, 292*, 2499–2501.

Coricelli, G., Critchley, H. D., Joffily, M., O'Doherty, J. P., Sirigu, A., & Dolan, R. J. (2005). Regret and its avoidance: A neuroimaging study of choice behavior. *Nature Neuroscience, 8*, 1255–1262.

Dayan, P., & Yu, A. J. (2006). Phasic norepinephrine: A neural interrupt signal for unexpected events. *Network, 17*, 335–350.

Dean, H. L., Crowley, J. C., & Platt, M. L. (2004). Visual and saccade-related activity in macaque posterior cingulate cortex. *Journal of Neurophysiology, 92*, 3056–3068.

Dean, H. L., & Platt, M. L. (2006). Allocentric spatial referencing of neuronal activity in macaque posterior cingulate cortex. *Journal of Neuroscience, 26*, 1117–1127.

De Martino, B., Kumaran, D., Seymour, B., & Dolan, R. J. (2006, August 4). Frames, biases, and rational decision-making in the human brain. *Science, 313*, 684–687.

Dodd, M. L., Klos, K. J., Bower, J. H., Geda, Y. E., Josephs, K. A., & Ahlskog, J. E. (2005). Pathological gambling caused by drugs used to treat Parkinson disease. *Archives of Neurology, 62*, 1377–1381.

Dorris, M. C., & Glimcher, P. W. (2004). Activity in posterior parietal cortex is correlated with the relative subjective desirability of action. *Neuron, 44*, 365–378.

Dukas, R., & Real, L. A. (1993). Effects of recent experience on foraging decisions by bumble bees. *Oecologia, 94*, 244–246.

Ellsberg, D. (1961). Risk, ambiguity, and the savage axioms. *Quarterly Journal of Economics, 75*, 643–669.

Fecteau, S., Pascual-Leone, A., Zald, D. H., Liguori, P., Theoret, H., Boggio, P. S., & Fregni, F. (2007). Activation of prefrontal cortex by transcranial direct current stimulation reduces appetite for risk during ambiguous decision making. *Journal of Neuroscience, 27*, 6212–6218.

Fellows, L. K., & Farah, M. J. (2005). Dissociable elements of human foresight: A role for the ventromedial frontal lobes in framing the future, but not in discounting future rewards. *Neuropsychologia, 43*, 214–1221.

Fiorillo, C. D., Tobler, P. N., & Schultz, W. (2003, March 21). Discrete coding of reward probability and uncertainty by dopamine neurons. *Science, 299*, 1898–1902.

Frederick, S., Loewenstein, G., & O'Donoghue, T. (2002). Time discounting and time preference: A critical review. *Journal of Economic Literature, 40*, 351–401.

Gershon, A. A., Dannon, P. N., & Grunhaus, L. (2003). Transcranial magnetic stimulation in the treatment of depression. *American Journal of Psychiatry, 160*, 835–845.

Gibbon J. (1977). Scalar expectancy theory and Weber's law in animal timing *Psychological Review, 84*, 279–325.

Gibbon, J., Church, R. M., Fairhurst, S., & Kacelnik, A. (1988). Scalar expectancy theory and choice between delayed rewards. *Psychological Review, 95*, 102–114.

Gigerenzer, G., Todd, P. M., & Group, A. (1999). *Simple heuristics that make us smart.* Oxford, England: Oxford University Press.

Gilby, I. C., & Wrangham, R. W. (2007). Risk-prone hunting by chimpanzees (*Pan troglodytes schweinfurthii*) increases during periods of high diet quality. *Behavioral Ecology and Sociobiology, 61*, 1771–1779.

Glimcher, P. (2002). Decisions, decisions, decisions: Choosing a biological science of choice. *Neuron, 36*, 323–332.

Glimcher, P. W. (2003). The neurobiology of visual-saccadic decision making. *Annual Review of Neuroscience, 26*, 133–179.

Gottfried, J. A., O'Doherty, J., & Dolan, R. J. (2002). Appetitive and aversive olfactory learning in humans studied using event-related functional magnetic resonance imaging. *Journal of Neuroscience, 22*, 10829–10837.

Gottfried, J. A., O'Doherty, J., & Dolan, R. J. (2003, August 22). Encoding predictive reward value in human amygdala and orbitofrontal cortex. *Science, 301*, 1104–1107.

Green, L., & Myerson, J. A. (2004). Discounting framework for choice with delayed and probabilistic rewards. *Psychological Bulletin, 130*, 769–792.

Hamm, S. L., & Shettleworth, S. J. (1987). Risk aversion in pigeons. *Journal of Experimental Psychology, 13*, 376–383.

Harder, L. D., & Real, L. A. (1987). Why are bumble bees risk averse? *Ecology, 68*, 1104–1108.

Hartlage, S., Alloy, L. B., Vazquez, C., & Dykman, B. (1993). Automatic and effortful processing in depression. *Psychological Bulletin, 113*, 247–278.

Hayden, B. Y., & Platt, M. L. (2007). Temporal discounting predicts risk sensitivity in rhesus macaques. *Current Biology, 17,* 49–53.

Heilbronner, S. R., Rosati, A. G., Stevens, J. R., Hare, B., & Hauser, M. D. (2008). A fruit in the hand or two in the bush? Divergent risk preferences in chimpanzees and bonobos. *Biology Letters, 4,* 246–249.

Henrich, J., & McElreath, R. (2002). Are peasants risk-averse decision makers? *Current Anthropology, 43,* 178–181.

Henry, C., Mitropoulou, V., New, A. S., Koenigsberg, H. W., Silverman, J., & Siever, L. J. (2001). Affective instability and impulsivity in borderline personality and bipolar II disorders: Similarities and differences. *Journal of Psychiatric Research, 35,* 307–312.

Hertwig, R., Barron, G., Weber, E. U., & Erev, I. (2004). Decisions from experience and the effect of rare events in risky choice. *Psychological Science, 15,* 534–539.

Holt, C. A., & Laury, S. K. (2002). Risk aversion and incentive effects. *American Economic Review, 92,* 1644–1655.

Hsu, M., Bhatt, M., Adolphs, R., Tranel, D., & Camerer, C. F. (2005, December 9). Neural systems responding to degrees of uncertainty in human decision-making. *Science, 310,* 1680–1683.

Huettel, S. A., Stowe, C. J., Gordon, E. M., Warner, B. T., & Platt, M. L. (2006). Neural signatures of economic preferences for risk and ambiguity. *Neuron, 49,* 765–775.

Humphrey S. J. (2004). Feedback-conditional regret theory and testing regret-aversion in risky choice. *Journal of Economic Psychology, 25,* 839–857.

Isen, A. M., & Geva, N. (1987). The influence of positive affect on acceptable level of risk: The person with a large canoe has a large worry. *Organizational Behavior and Human Decision Processes, 39,* 145–154.

Isen, A. M., Nygren, T. E., & Ashby, F. G. (1988). Influence of positive affect on the subjective utility of gains and losses: It is just not worth the risk. *Journal of Personality and Social Psychology, 55,* 710–717.

Isen, A. M., & Patrick, R. (1983). The effect of positive feelings on risk taking: When the chips are down. *Organizational Behavior and Human Performance, 31,* 194–202.

Kacelnik, A. (1997). Normative and descriptive models of decision making: Time discounting and risk sensitivity. *Ciba Foundation Symposium, 208,* 51–67; discussion 67–70.

Kacelnik, A., & Bateson, M. (1996). Risky theories—The effects of variance on foraging decisions. *American Zoologist, 36,* 402–434.

Kacelnik, A., & Brito e Abreu, F. (1998). Risky choice and Weber's law. *Journal of Theoretical Biology, 194,* 289–298.

Kahneman, D., & Tversky, A. (1979). Prospect theory: An analysis of decision under risk. *Econometrica, 47,* 263–291.

Kahneman, D., & Tversky, A. (2000). *Choices, values, and frames.* Cambridge, England: Cambridge University Press.

Kaminski, B. J., & Ator, N. A. (2001). Behavioral and pharmacological variables affecting risky choice in rats. *Journal of the Experimental Analysis of Behavior, 75,* 275–297.

Knight, F. H. (1921). *Risk, uncertainty, and profit.* Boston: Houghton Mifflin.

Knoch, D., Gianotti, L. R., Pascual-Leone, A., Treyer, V., Regard, M., Hohmann, M., & Brugger, P. (2006). Disruption of right prefrontal cortex by low-frequency repetitive transcranial magnetic stimulation induces risk-taking behavior. *Journal of Neuroscience, 26,* 6469–6472.

Knutson, B., & Bossaerts, P. (2007). Neural antecedents of financial decisions. *Journal of Neuroscience, 27,* 8174–8177.

Knutson, B., Taylor, J., Kaufman, M., Peterson, R., & Glover G. (2005). Distributed neural representation of expected value. *Journal of Neuroscience, 25,* 4806–4812.

Kobayashi, S., Nomoto, K., Watanabe, M., Hikosaka, O., Schultz, W., & Sakagami, M. (2006). Influences of rewarding and aversive outcomes on activity in macaque lateral prefrontal cortex. *Neuron, 51,* 861–870.

Kobayashi, Y., & Amaral, D. G. (2003). Macaque monkey retrosplenial cortex: II. Cortical afferents. *Journal of Comparative Neurology, 466,* 48–79.

Kuhnen, C. M., & Knutson, B. (2005). The neural basis of financial risk taking. *Neuron, 47,* 763–770.

Leith, K. P., & Baumeister, R. F. (1996). Why do bad moods increase self-defeating behavior? Emotion, risk taking, and self-regulation. *Journal of Personality and Social Psychology, 71,* 1250–1267.

Lerner, J. S., & Keltner, D. (2001). Fear, anger, and risk. *Journal of Personality and Social Psychology, 81,* 146–159.

Loomes, G., & Sugden, R. (1982). Regret theory: An alternative theory of rationality under uncertainty. *Economic Journal, 92,* 805–824.

Madden, G. J., Begotka, A. M., Raiff, B. R., & Kastern, L. L. (2003). Delay discounting of real and hypothetical rewards. *Experimental and Clinical Psychopharmacology, 11,* 139–145.

Marsh, B., & Kacelnik, A. (2002). Framing effects and risky decisions in starlings. *Proceedings of the National Academy of Sciences USA, 99,* 3352–3355.

Matsumoto, M., & Hikosaka, O. (2007). Lateral habenula as a source of negative reward signals in dopamine neurons. *Nature, 447,* 1111–1115.

Mazur, J. E. (1987). An adjusting procedure for studying delayed reinforcement. In M. L. Commons, J. E. Mazur, J. A. Nevin, & H. Rachlin (Eds.), *Quantitative analyses of behavior: Vol. 5. The effect of delay and intervening events on reinforcement value* (pp. 55–73). Mahwah, NJ: Erlbaum.

McCoy, A. N., Crowley, J. C., Haghighian, G., Dean, H. L., & Platt, M. L. (2003). Saccade reward signals in posterior cingulate cortex. *Neuron, 40,* 1031–1040.

McCoy, A. N., & Platt, M. L. (2005a). Expectations and outcomes: Decision-making in the primate brain. *Journal of Comparative Physiology A: Neuroethology, Sensory, Neural, and Behavioral Physiology, 191,* 201–211.

McCoy, A. N., & Platt, M. L. (2005b). Risk-sensitive neurons in macaque posterior cingulate cortex. *Nature Neuroscience, 8,* 1220–1227.

McNamara, J. M., & Houston, A. I. (1986). The common currency for behavioral decisions. *American Naturalist, 127,* 358–378.

Mischel, W., Ebbesen, E. B., & Zeiss, A. R. (1973). Selective attention to the self: Situational and dispositional determinants. *Journal of Personality and Social Psychology, 27,* 129–142.

Mischel, W., Shoda, Y., & Rodriguez, M. I. (1989, May 26). Delay of gratification in children. *Science, 244,* 933–938.

Mitchell, S. H. (1999). Measures of impulsivity in cigarette smokers and non-smokers. *Psychopharmacology (Berlin), 146,* 455–464.

Montague, P. R., Dayan, P., & Sejnowski, T. J. (1996). A framework for mesencephalic dopamine systems based on predictive Hebbian learning. *Journal of Neuroscience, 16,* 1936–1947.

Myerson, J., Green, L., Hanson, J. S., Holt, D. D., & Estle, S. J. (2003). Discounting delayed and probabilistic rewards: Processes and traits. *Journal of Economic Psychology, 24,* 619–635.

Nygren, T. E., Isen, A. M., Taylor, P. J., & Dulin, J. (1996). The influence of positive affect on the decision rule in risk situations: Focus on outcome (and especially avoidance of loss) rather than probability. *Organizational Behavior and Human Decision Processes, 66,* 59–72.

Oades, R. D., Slusarek, M., Velling, S., & Bondy, B. (2002). Serotonin platelet-transporter measures in childhood attention-deficit/hyperactivity disorder (ADHD): Clinical versus experimental measures of impulsivity. *World Journal of Biological Psychiatry, 3,* 96–100.

Paton, J. J., Belova, M. A., Morrison, S. E., & Salzman, C. D. (2006). The primate amygdala represents the positive and negative value of visual stimuli during learning. *Nature, 439,* 865–870.

Perez, S. M., & Waddington, K. D. (1996). Carpenter bee (*Xylocopa micans*) risk indifference and a review of nectarivore risk-sensitivity studies. *American Zoologist, 36,* 435–446.

Petry, N. M., & Oncken, C. (2002). Cigarette smoking is associated with increased severity of gambling problems in treatment-seeking gamblers. *Addiction, 97,* 745–753.

Platt, M. L., & Glimcher, P. W. (1999). Neural correlates of decision variables in parietal cortex. *Nature, 400,* 233–238.

Platt, M. L., & Huettel, S. A. (2008). Risky business: The neuroeconomics of decision-making under uncertainty. *Nature Neuroscience, 11,* 398–403.

Prelec, D., & Loewenstein, G. (1991). Decision making over time and under uncertainty: A common approach. *Management Science, 37,* 770–786.

Preuschoff, K., Bossaerts, P., & Quartz, S. R. (2006). Neural differentiation of expected reward and risk in human subcortical structures. *Neuron, 51,* 381–390.

Rabin, M. (2000). Risk aversion and expected-utility theory: A calibration theorem. *Econometrica, 68,* 1281–1292.

Rabin, M., & Thaler, R. H. (2001). Risk aversion. *Journal of Economic Perspectives*, *15*, 219–232.

Rachlin H. (2000). *The science of self-control*. Cambridge, MA: Harvard University Press.

Rachlin, H., Raineri, A., & Cross, D. (1991). Subjective probability and delay. *Journal of the Experimental Analysis of Behavior*, *55*, 233–244.

Redgrave, P., & Gurney, K. (2006). The short-latency dopamine signal: A role in discovering novel actions? *Nature Reviews Neuroscience*, *7*, 967–975.

Roitman, J. D., Brannon, E. M., & Platt, M. L. (2007). Monotonic coding of numerosity in macaque lateral intraparietal area. *PLoS Biology*, *5*, e208.

Romo, R., & Salinas, E. (2003). Flutter discrimination: Neural codes, perception, memory and decision making. *Nature Reviews Neuroscience*, *4*, 203–218.

Sanfey, A. G., Hastie, R., Colvin, M. K., & Grafman, J. (2003). Phineas gauged: Decision-making and the human prefrontal cortex. *Neuropsychologia*, *41*, 1218–1229.

Sanfey, A. G., Loewenstein, G., McClure, S. M., & Cohen, J. D. (2006). Neuroeconomics: Cross-currents in research on decision-making. *Trends in Cognitive Science*, *10*, 108–116.

Schall, J. D. (2004). On building a bridge between brain and behavior. *Annual Review of Psychology*, *55*, 23–50.

Schultz, W. (2006). Behavioral theories and the neurophysiology of reward. *Annual Review of Psychology*, *57*, 87–115.

Schultz, W., Dayan, P., & Montague, P. R. (1997, March 14). A neural substrate of prediction and reward. *Science*, *275*, 1593–1599.

Shadlen, M. N., & Newsome, W. T. (2001). Neural basis of a perceptual decision in the parietal cortex (area LIP) of the rhesus monkey. *Journal of Neurophysiology*, *86*, 1916–1936.

Shafir, S., Wiegmann, D. D., Smith, B. H., & Real, L. A. (1999). Risk-sensitive foraging: Choice behaviour of honeybees in response to variability in volume of reward. *Animal Behavior*, *57*, 1055–1061.

Smallwood, P. (1996). An introduction to risk sensitivity: The use of Jensen's inequality to clarify evolutionary arguments of adaptation and constraint. *American Zoologist*, *36*, 392–401.

Sugrue, L. P., Corrado, G. S., & Newsome, W. T. (2004, June 18). Matching behavior and the representation of value in the parietal cortex. *Science*, *304*, 1782–1787.

Sutton, R. S., & Barto, A. G. (1998). *Reinforcement learning: An introduction*. Cambridge, MA: MIT Press.

Tobler, P. N., Fiorillo, C. D., & Schultz, W. (2005, March 11). Adaptive coding of reward value by dopamine neurons. *Science*, *307*, 1642–1645.

Tom, S. M., Fox, C. R., Trepel, C., & Poldrack, R. A. (2007, January 26). The neural basis of loss aversion in decision-making under risk. *Science*, *315*, 515–518.

Tversky, A., & Kahneman, D. (1973). Availability: A heuristic for judging frequency and probability. *Cognitive Psychology, 5*, 207–232.

Tversky, A., & Kahneman, D. (1981, January 30). The framing of decisions and the psychology of choice. *Science, 211*, 453–458.

Tversky, A., & Kahneman, D. (1991). Loss aversion in riskless choice: A reference-dependent model. *Quarterly Journal of Economics, 106*, 1039–1061.

Tversky, A., & Kahneman, D. (1992). Advances in prospect theory: Cumulative representation of uncertainty. *Journal of Risk and Uncertainty, 5*, 297–323.

Ungless, M. A. (2004). Dopamine: The salient issue. *Trends in Neuroscience, 27*, 702–706.

Usher, M., Cohen, J. D., Servan-Schreiber, D., Rajkowski, J., & Aston-Jones, G. (1999, January 22). The role of locus coeruleus in the regulation of cognitive performance. *Science, 283*, 549–554.

Vogt, B. A., & Gabriel, M. (1993). *Neurobiology of cingulate cortex and limbic thalamus*. Boston: Birkhauser.

Von Neumann, J. V., & Morganstern, O. (1944). *Theory of games and economic behavior*. Princeton, NJ: Princeton University Press.

Weber, B. J., & Chapman, G. B. (2005). Playing for peanuts: Why is risk seeking behavior more common for low-stakes gambles? *Organizational Behavior and Human Decision Processes, 97*, 31–46.

Yang, T., & Shadlen, M. N. (2007). Probabilistic reasoning by neurons. *Nature, 447*, 1075–1080.

Yu, A. J., & Dayan, P. (2002). Acetylcholine in cortical inference. *Neural Network, 15*, 719–730.

Yu, A. J., & Dayan, P. (2005). Uncertainty, neuromodulation, and attention. *Neuron, 46*, 681–692.

Zald, D. H., Hagen, M. C., & Pardo, J. V. (2002). Neural correlates of tasting concentrated quinine and sugar solutions. *Journal of Neurophysiology, 87*, 1068–1075.

Zeelenberg, M. (1999). Anticipated regret, expected feedback and behavioral decision making. *Journal of Behavioral Decision Making, 12*, 93.

III

DISCOUNTING AND ADDICTIVE DISORDERS

7

DELAY DISCOUNTING AND SUBSTANCE ABUSE–DEPENDENCE

RICHARD YI, SUZANNE H. MITCHELL, AND WARREN K. BICKEL

According to the *Diagnostic and Statistical Manual of Mental Disorders* (4th ed.; *DSM–IV*; American Psychiatric Association, 1994), substance abuse is characterized by maladaptive and recurrent substance use resulting in physical, legal, and/or interpersonal problems. Significant in this definition are the cross-temporal outcomes, both immediate and delayed, associated with substance abuse. The choice to consume a substance of abuse presumably results in an immediate rush or high, removal of withdrawal symptoms (for the substance-dependent individual), or both. In fact, greater immediacy in the reinforcing effects of the substance (faster onset of action via route of administration) is associated with greater severity of dependence (Gossop, Griffiths, Powls, & Strange, 1994) and withdrawal effects (Smolka & Schmidt, 1999). Unfortunately, repeated consumption of a substance of abuse is also likely to result in delayed deterioration of health and social relationships as well as legal repercussions.

The substance abuser is typically confronted throughout the day with the choice of consuming or not consuming the substance of abuse; such

This research and preparation of this chapter were supported by National Institutes of Health Grants DA11692, DA021707, DA015543, DA016727, and DA022386.

choices may be punctuated by encountering drug-related cues. Reinforcement for drug consumption is relatively small and immediate or nearly immediate relative to reinforcement for nonconsumption (sobriety, improved health, vocational success, and social relationships). The substance abuser's repeated drug taking indicates that the subjective value of drug consumption is greater than the subjective value of nonconsumption or abstinence. Assuming that the subjective value of nonconsumption is reduced as a function of the delay to its reinforcing effects, the construct of delay discounting is particularly suited to the study of substance abuse and dependence.

The following sections represent the current understanding of delay discounting as applied to substance abuse. We begin with studies that have compared delay discounting of outcomes in the future (which we refer to here as *delay discounting*) by substance-abusing populations and nonusing controls. Noteworthy is that much of the literature reviewed used immediate and delayed money outcomes as choice alternatives. Although the substance abuser is not nominally choosing between money outcomes when deciding to consume or not to consume a substance of dependence, the substance abuser is exhibiting a general choice bias favoring immediate reinforcement in lieu of larger, delayed reinforcement. Given the generality of this choice bias across a variety of commodities (including money, drugs, and health) and the relative precision of monetary units, the discounting of money is the prevalent modus operandi in human discounting research on substance abuse and dependence.

We also report on the current understanding of *probability discounting*, a construct thought to have some behavioral overlap with delay discounting (although different neural substrates appear to be involved). We examine the effect of long-term abstinence on delay discounting as well as the utility of delay-discounting measures as predictive tools. Finally, we speculate on more global features of time, incorporating the new construct of *past discounting* and a developmental perspective on substance abuse and discounting.

DELAY DISCOUNTING AND SUBSTANCE ABUSE

Individual differences in delay discounting provide a framework for understanding why the substance abuser reliably and consistently chooses to consume the substance of abuse, whereas the teetotaler or recreational user reliably and consistently (for the most part) chooses not to consume the substance of abuse. Thus, the theoretical application of delay discounting to the study of substance abuse requires confirmation that substance-abusing individuals place a relatively greater emphasis on the present and near-present outcomes, resulting in more discounting of future outcomes than by individuals who do not engage in substance abuse. Numerous studies have compared delay discounting by substance-abusing and nonabusing populations, and nearly all of the published literature has confirmed that substance-abusing individuals have higher rates of delay discounting than do matched controls. Given the robustness of this finding, there appears to be a general consensus that substance abusers discount delayed outcomes more than do nonabusers.

Cigarettes and Nicotine

At this time, the population of substance abusers who have been most examined using delay-discounting procedures are cigarette smokers. In one of the first comparisons of discounting by cigarette smokers and never-smokers, S. H. Mitchell (1999) collected indifference points for $10 that was delayed between 0 days and 1 year (0, 7, 30, 90, 180, and 365 days): Twenty moderate smokers (15-plus cigarettes daily) and 20 never-smokers (0 lifetime cigarettes) made binary choices between a delayed $10 and a smaller, immediate amount of money. Median indifference points for cigarette smokers were lower than those of never-smokers at four of five delays and significantly different at 1 week and 1 month (via nonparametric analyses). The rate of delay discounting was calculated using Mazur's (1987) hyperbolic model of discounting (see chap. 1, this volume), revealing a trend of higher discount rates for smokers than for never-smokers.

Concurrently, Bickel, Odum, and Madden (1999) compared delay discounting by 23 cigarette smokers (20-plus cigarettes daily for the past 5 years), 22 never-smokers (0 lifetime cigarettes), and 21 ex-smokers (at least 1 year of cigarette abstinence after >20 cigarettes daily for at least 5 years). Participants chose between hypothetically receiving $1,000 (delayed between 1 week and 25 years) and a smaller, immediate sum of money. Comparison of discounting rates between groups revealed that cigarette smokers discount delayed rewards more than never-smokers and ex-smokers and that the latter groups do not discount delayed rewards differently. Additional research on delay discounting by cigarette smokers has expanded the generality of this difference in discounting between cigarette smokers and nonsmokers since these early reports. Odum, Madden, and Bickel (2002) found that cigarette smokers discount future health outcomes (both improvement and deterioration) more than never-smokers, with ex-smokers intermediate between these. Baker, Johnson, and Bickel (2003) further added to the growing body of knowledge with a study comparing discounting by cigarette smokers and never-smokers of future money gains and losses; future cigarette gains and losses, all at multiple magnitudes; and future health gains and losses. The overall pattern of results indicated that cigarette smokers discount future outcomes of many types more than never-smokers regardless of the domain, magnitude, or valence of the choice alternatives. Other studies have continued to replicate the basic finding that greater discounting of future outcomes is observed in cigarette smokers than in nonsmokers (e.g., Reynolds, Richard, Horn, & Karraker, 2004).

Work by Ohmura, Takahashi, and Kitamura (2005) has suggested that the smoker–nonsmoker difference in delay discounting is actually a continuum based on cigarette consumption. Delay discounting was assessed in a diverse group of smokers ($M = 14.4$ cigarettes daily, $SD = 6.7$) and in 23 never-smokers (0 lifetime cigarettes), and a positive correlation was observed between the discounting of future money gains and rate of smoking (identified as either number of cigarettes smoked per day, $r = -.66$, or estimated daily nicotine intake, $r = -.57$). This sheds light on the more equivocal results seen in studies of light smokers. Heyman and Gibb (2006), for example, examined delay discounting by college students who were regular smokers (40-plus cigarettes weekly), chippers, or nonsmokers (fewer than 100 lifetime cigarettes). *Chippers* were defined as nonaddicted cigarette smokers who smoke fewer than 20 cigarettes weekly, typically on weekends and within social contexts (out with friends). They found that chippers discounted future outcomes like nonsmokers and unlike regular smokers, that is, less than regular smokers and equal to nonsmokers. In contrast, Johnson, Bickel, and Baker (2007) found that light smokers discounted future outcomes like smokers (20-plus cigarettes daily) and unlike nonsmokers (0 lifetime cigarettes). These light smokers were demographically diverse and smoked up to 10 cigarettes daily (70 cigarettes weekly). Phenotypically, the college chippers (Heyman & Gibb, 2006) were more similar to nonsmokers, and the light smokers (Johnson et al., 2007) were more similar to regular smokers. Given that rate of discounting appears to be a function of the rate of cigarette smoking, a reasonable explanation for these disparate results is this categorization difference. Although no correlations were reported in Heyman and Gibb or in Johnson et al., one would expect at least a positive trend for rate of discounting and cigarette smoking.

Alcohol

Like cigarettes, the discounting of future outcomes by people with alcoholism and problem drinkers compared with light drinkers has received substantial attention. Although the control or comparison population in these studies has been light or social drinkers rather than nondrinkers, the results have largely mirrored those of studies of cigarette smoking: greater discounting of future outcomes in those with alcoholism or problem drinkers than in light drinkers. In the first study examining delay discounting as a function of alcohol consumption, Vuchinich and Simpson (1998) compared delay discounting of hypothetical $1,000 gains by college students categorized as light social drinkers, heavy social drinkers, or problem drinkers. Categorization was based on an index of estimated alcohol consumption in the previous year: Light drinkers were at the low end of the distribution (excluding nondrinkers), heavy drinkers were at the high end of the distribution without alcohol-associated problems, and problem drinkers were at the high end of the distribution with alcohol-associated problems. A computerized choice procedure determined indifference points for future hypothetical money gains, and the estimated discounting rates indicated that both heavy drinkers and problem drinkers discounted more than did light drinkers. Although no direct comparison was conducted between heavy drinkers and problem drinkers, the authors did report that the difference between light drinkers and problem drinkers was larger than the difference between light drinkers and heavy drinkers. This suggests that heavy drinkers with alcohol-associated problems may discount delayed rewards more than do heavy drinkers without alcohol-associated problems, indicating that high alcohol consumption and the consequences associated with this consumption have a somewhat additive effect on delay discounting.

Additional research on people with alcoholism has confirmed this early finding that heavy alcohol consumption is associated with high rates of delay discounting. Petry (2001) compared delay discounting of money and alcohol by 19 people with active alcoholism (met current DSM–IV dependence criteria), 12 people with abstinent alcoholism (met lifetime dependence criteria without alcohol consumption to intoxication in the past 30 days), and 15 controls with no history of alcohol problems. The overall trend observed across different magnitudes and commodities was that those with active alcoholism discounted future outcomes in general more than did controls, and those with abstinent alcoholism discounted somewhere between these groups. In contrast, Kirby and Petry (2004) found no difference between those with alcoholism and controls and no difference between those with active alcoholism and those who were currently abstinent. The lack of group difference observed between those with alcoholism and controls, however, may be because of the relatively lenient inclusion criteria for those with alcoholism in Kirby and Petry (2004), namely, lifetime history of a 1-year regular pattern of thrice-weekly alcohol consumption to intoxication and experience of some problems associated with consumption. These criteria fall substantially short of the current DSM–IV criteria for alcohol dependence used by Petry and may be phenotypically more similar to the controls of Petry or social drinkers of Vuchinich and Simpson (1998).

Research evaluating individuals receiving treatment for alcoholism has continued to confirm group differences. Bjork, Hommer, Grant, and Danube (2004) compared delay discounting of $10 gains by 130 alcohol-dependent patients at an inpatient treatment facility for alcohol abuse (thus abstinent at time of measurement) and 41 controls with no history of alcohol dependence, finding a higher rate of discounting in the former group. Although data analysis was conducted somewhat differently than in previous studies of delay discounting, J. M. Mitchell, Fields, D'Esposito, and Boettiger (2005) confirmed the observation that abstinent people with alcoholism (minimum

2 weeks) discounted future outcomes more than did nondrinking controls. Dom, D'haene, Hulstijn, and Sabbe (2006) compared 42 people with early-onset alcoholism (EOA) and 46 people with late-onset alcoholism (LOA) in a treatment facility for alcoholism with a group of 54 control participants with no history of substance abuse. All those with EOA and LOA met *DSM–IV* criteria for alcohol abuse or dependence, and delay discounting of hypothetical money assessments was collected after admission into the treatment facility and detoxification; individuals with EOA and LOA were defined as those with alcoholism onset before and after the age of 25, respectively. It is interesting that those with EOA were found to discount future money more than did those with LOA and nonalcoholic controls, once again suggesting that different phenotypes can be differentiated with delay-discounting measures. In contrast to most previous published research, however, those with LOA and controls did not differ on rate of delay discounting. We can offer no firm explanation for this outcome other than a possible interaction of detoxification and alcoholism subtype (EOA and LOA), resulting in a phenotype similar to controls for those with LOA only. Another possibility is related to the cigarette smoking status of control participants. This group was screened for alcohol consumption and abuse of illicit substances, but cigarette smoking was not evaluated. If a substantial number of these individuals were cigarette smokers, we might expect to find no difference between controls and either the EOA or the LOA groups. The smoking status of abstinent individuals with alcoholism in the Bjork et al. and Mitchell et al. studies is also unreported. Thus, it becomes unclear whether heightened discounting in these abstinent people with alcoholism is attributable to prolonged effects of past alcohol use and abuse, to differences in continued cigarette smoking, or to a combination of the two factors.

Opioids, Cocaine, and Methamphetamine

To the best of our knowledge, the Madden, Petry, Badger, and Bickel (1997) study is the first published study to compare the discounting of future outcomes in substance-abusing and control populations. Delay discounting of hypothetical $1,000 and heroin was assessed in 18 opioid-dependent individuals (9.4 mean years of heroin use before entering treatment) receiving buprenorphine pharmacotherapy and 38 nondependent matched (on demographic variables such as age and gender) controls. Consistent with the perspective that substance-abusing individuals express relatively greater preference for immediate outcomes, opioid-dependent individuals discounted future money more than did controls (replicated in Kirby, Petry, & Bickel, 1999). Furthermore, opioid-dependent individuals in the Madden et al. study discounted $1,000 worth of heroin more than they did $1,000. Kirby and Petry (2004) also found that heroin-dependent individuals discounted future money more than did controls and that actively using heroin-dependent individuals discounted more than did abstinent heroin-dependent individuals. There also appear to be different subgroups within the opioid-dependent population. Odum, Madden, Badger, and Bickel (2000) assessed delay discounting of hypothetical money and heroin outcomes and a willingness to share a needle to inject heroin in 32 heroin abusers. Approximately half of these participants said that they would share a needle rather than wait to obtain a clean needle. These participants discounted future money outcomes more than did participants unwilling to share needles.

The same pattern of results has been obtained in the study of stimulants. Coffey, Gudleski, Saladin, and Brady (2003) compared discounting of hypothetical $1,000 by 12 in-treatment crack- and cocaine-dependent individuals (meeting *DSM–IV* criteria, mean cocaine abstinence for 13 days) and 13 matched controls (no drug dependence other than nicotine). As in previous studies of substance-dependent individuals, cocaine-dependent individuals discounted future money gains more than did controls and discounted future cocaine gains more than a comparable amount of money. Heil, Johnson, Higgins, and Bickel (2006) conducted a similar study with actively using cocaine-dependent individuals (within the past month), abstinent cocaine-dependent individuals (for at least 1 month), and controls. Overall, greater discounting was observed in cocaine-dependent individuals than in controls. Furthermore, no difference was observed between actively using and abstinent individuals. This result has also been observed in Kirby and Petry (2004), who also found no difference between actively using (cocaine use in the past 2 weeks) and abstinent cocaine-dependent (no use in the past 2 weeks) individuals. As with cocaine, published studies comparing delay discounting by methamphetamine (MA)-dependent individuals and matched controls have continued to find greater discounting in the former group. This result has been observed in currently abstinent MA-dependent individuals receiving treatment (Hoffman et al., 2006) and actively using non–treatment-seeking MA-dependent individuals (Monterosso et al., 2007).

Gambling

Some of the principal behavioral features of addiction (e.g., compulsion, loss of control) can exist even in the absence of a substance of abuse. The *DSM–IV* characterization of pathological gambling, for instance, overlaps substantially with substance abuse disorders. And like substance abusers, the pathological gambler must choose between the immediate reinforcement for engaging in the maladaptive activity (gambling) and the delayed reinforcement for not engaging in the maladaptive activity (e.g., financial and interpersonal health). Therefore, the same immediate–delayed intertemporal conflict for substance abusers applies to pathological gamblers, with choice bias favoring immediate rather than delayed rewards. The research with delay-discounting procedures supports this conceptualization.

Comparisons between pathological gamblers and matched controls with measures of delay discounting have indicated that pathological gamblers discount future outcomes more steeply than do controls. Petry (2001), for instance, compared 60 pathological gamblers (met *DSM–IV* criteria for pathological gambling) enrolled in a treatment trial with 26 matched controls (no lifetime history of illicit drug or alcohol abuse). Pathological gamblers discounted hypothetical $1,000 more than did controls. This result was replicated with non–treatment-seeking, active pathological gamblers in Dixon, Marley, and Jacobs (2003). For more comprehensive coverage of this topic, see chapter 10 (this volume).

PROBABILITY DISCOUNTING AND SUBSTANCE ABUSE

Probability discounting is the idea that the subjective value of outcomes that are less probable will be lower than that of outcomes that are more probable and that the subjective value of an outcome will decline as a systematic function of its decreasing probability. A number of early studies demonstrated that this was indeed the case and that if probability was expressed in terms of the odds against $(1 - p)/p$, a hyperbolic function like that used to describe delay discounting would account for the data well (e.g., Rachlin, Raineri, & Cross, 1991). Although some have referred to probability discounting as *uncertainty discounting* (e.g., S. H. Mitchell, 2004a), this terminology is probably best avoided because uncertainty does not vary directly with probability but is maximal at $p = .5$.

Parallels between probability discounting and delay discounting have been drawn on a number of bases. First, the methodology used to examine both is very similar. In most studies, participants are asked whether they prefer X or Y. In typical delay- and probability-discounting paradigms, X will be an amount of reward available immediately and for sure (often money but also a drug [e.g., Baker et al., 2003] or another consumable [e.g., Estle, Green, Myerson, & Holt, 2007]). In delay-discounting paradigms, Y is an amount of reward available at some time in the future, whereas in probability-discounting paradigms, Y is some amount of reward available with some probability. Second, from a theoretical standpoint, both delay and probability can be viewed as economic costs. Thus, waiting time is widely viewed as a significant cost variable in economic models of various behaviors, for example, in the animal foraging literature (Stephens & Krebs, 1986). Probability has been viewed as providing information about the number of times that a behavior might have to be performed before a particular outcome is achieved in a repeated-gambles situation (Rachlin, Siegel, & Cross 1994), implying higher degrees of effort and time before a desired outcome is secured. This view has caused some researchers to speculate that delay discounting is a special case of probability discounting because the longer the delay, the higher the probability that an outcome might not occur (Rachlin et al., 1991). Third, the ability of a hyperbolic function (e.g., Mazur, 1987) to describe data well from both paradigms has been viewed as suggesting a link between the two. Fourth, a number of studies have assessed both delay discounting and probability discounting within the same participants (e.g., S. H. Mitchell, 1999; Richards, Zhang, Mitchell, & de Wit, 1999). These studies reported statistically significant positive correlations (but also see Ohmura et al., 2005; Reynolds et al., 2004), suggesting that similar neuropsychological processes are involved in each type of decision.

These commonalities lead naturally to the hypothesis that probability discounting should be heightened in drug users as compared with nonusers in the same way that delay discounting differs between these groups. Surprisingly few studies have examined this question, and all have focused on cigarette smokers. The earliest study (S. H. Mitchell, 1999) compared moderate and never-smokers in a probability-discounting task in which participants chose between $10 available with various probabilities (1.00, .90, .75, .50, .25, .10) and certain amounts of money ranging from $10.50 to $0.01. She quantified the degree of probability discounting for individual participants in each group and then used nonparametric statistics to evaluate group differences. None were found, although measures of delay discounting performed on the same participants were able to distinguish between the groups. Ohmura et al. (2005) also reported no difference in probability discounting in their comparison of light-moderate smokers and never-smokers. These researchers used a task in which the amounts were larger than those used in S. H. Mitchell (1999), but the probabilities were similar. That is, participants chose between a hypothetical ¥100,000 (approximately $1,000) available with probabilities of 0.9, 0.7, 0.5, 0.3, and 0.1 and a certain amount ranging from ¥100,000 to ¥5,000.

These failures to observe a smoking-related difference in probability discounting stand in contrast to data collected by Reynolds et al. (2004), using 25 heavy smokers (20-plus cigarettes daily) and 29 never-smokers. Using tasks similar to those used by S. H. Mitchell (1999), participants chose between a hypothetical $10 available with a probability of 1.00, .90, .75, .50, and .25 and a certain reward. Comparisons of the area under the curve (Myerson, Green, Hanson, Holt, & Estle, 2001) and the gradients of the discount functions revealed that smokers discounted probabilistic rewards more than did never-smokers, although the effect size of this result was not as large as that obtained when delay discounting was assessed in the same participants. Reynolds et al. speculated that their results might have differed from those of S. H. Mitchell (1999) because Mitchell's participants were lighter smokers than those sampled by Reynolds et al. This explanation could also be applied to the Ohmura et al. (2005) findings because they recruited participants who were lighter smokers than were the Reynolds et al. participants.

Data recently collected by Yi, Chase, and Bickel (2007) supported this argument to some degree. In their study, 30 heavy smokers (20-plus cigarettes daily) and 29 nonsmokers (0 cigarettes in the past 12 months) performed several tasks in which participants chose between a hypothetical monetary amount ($10, $100, and $1,000) available with a probability of .95, .75, .50, .25, .10, .05, and .01 and amounts of money available with a probability of 1.0. Initial analyses of the area under the curve and the gradients of the discount curve revealed no differences in probability discounting between smokers and nonsmokers. However, further inspection of the data revealed that for the larger probabilities (.95, .75, and .50) in the $100 and $1,000 task variants, smokers discounted the probabilistic outcomes more than did nonsmokers. Reynolds et al. did not provide data that would allow comparison of indifference points between smokers and nonsmokers at high probabilities. However, it is worth noting that the task used by these researchers had no probability value lower than .25, allowing the higher values to have more influence on the fitted function than did the S. H. Mitchell and the Ohmura et al. studies. Thus, smokers appear to discount probabilistic outcomes to a greater degree than do nonsmokers, but only if they are heavy smokers and only at probabilities of .50 and higher. Studies examining users of other drugs of abuse are unavailable, so the question remains as to the generalizability of these findings.

The conclusion that differences are only observed at higher levels of drug use is consistent with data from Ohmura et al. (2005) and Kollins (2003) with delay-discounting assessments. These researchers reported that delay discounting was steeper in individuals who smoked more or had more substantive patterns of drug use than in individuals who smoked less or did not use drugs; rate of delay discounting was a function of rate of drug consumption. This in turn implies that tasks assessing probability discounting are not as sensitive to differences in drug use as are delay-discounting tasks. Although this is not inconsistent with the idea that delay and probability discounting are part of the same neuropsychological process, a number of researchers have suggested that different processes underlie performance on the two types of task (e.g., Myerson et al., 2003). Furthermore, data from the animal literature have strongly supported the idea that although there is some overlap, the neural substrates of delay and probability discounting are not identical (e.g., Acheson et al., 2006).

From a theoretical standpoint, heightened probability discounting in smokers compared with nonsmokers is intriguing. Probability-discounting performance is analyzed by converting probabilities to odds against, as described earlier. Thus, the steeper the discount function, the more risk averse and less risk prone the individual is ($h < 1$, risk averse; $h > 1$, risk prone). Thus, the finding that smokers show steeper discounting suggests that they are less risk prone than nonsmokers. It may be difficult to reconcile this conclusion with the personality literature indicating that smokers are higher on scales of extraversion, sensation seeking, and risk taking (e.g., Munafo, Zetteler, & Clark, 2007) and may call for a reassessment of what probability-discounting tasks are measuring.

EFFECT OF ABSTINENCE ON DELAY DISCOUNTING

The higher rates of delay discounting observed in drug-dependent individuals relative to controls begs the question of the effect of long-term drug abstinence on delay discounting. Given the relationship observed between rate of drug consumption and rate of discounting (Kollins, 2003; Ohmura et al., 2005), one would predict that discounting rate would be lower after prolonged drug abstinence than during active substance abuse. The significance of determining the rate of discounting future outcomes of formerly drug-dependent individuals lies in the implications for treatment and for understanding possible long-term consequences of substance abuse. For instance, elevated delay discounting after substance abuse and long-term abstinence implies either that substance abuse chronically increases the rate at which future events are discounted or that substance abusers have preexisting and immutable high rates of delay discounting that render them susceptible to drug use or abuse. Reduced delay discounting as a function of long-term drug abstinence would indicate either that long-term abstinence results in recovery of delay discounting to lower preabuse levels or that an individual's ability to abstain is related to a relatively lower preexisting rate of delay discounting that was unaffected by drug use or abstinence.

A small handful of studies have compared delay discounting of drug-dependent and formerly dependent individuals. Some of the research reviewed previously used drug-dependent individuals who were receiving treatment at the time of assessment (and had presumably been abstinent for some duration of time). Bickel et al. (1999) compared delay discounting of current smokers, ex-smokers, and never-smokers. Ex-smokers were individuals who had likely been dependent for at least 5 years during their active smoking and abstinent for at least the most recent 1-year period. Ex-smokers discounted a hypothetical future $1,000 less than did active smokers and no differently than never-smokers. If rate of delay discounting is largely a state variable and can change as a function of drug use status, this result implies that the increase in delay discounting resulting from chronic cigarette smoking can be reversed with sustained cigarette abstinence. If rate of delay discounting is largely a trait variable, this result implies that individuals who smoke and have lower rates of delay discounting are more likely to quit smoking and remain abstinent compared with smokers who have higher rates of delay discounting.

Bretteville-Jensen (1999) defined an *ex-user* as someone self-reporting previous heroin or amphetamine misuse, without specification of the duration of abstinence. Active misusers discounted hypothetical money gains more than did former misusers, who discounted more than nonmisusers with no history of amphetamine use. With former misusers intermediate between active and non-misusers, these findings remain equally consistent with a state interpretation (as abstinence duration increases, delay discounting should recover to rates comparable to those of the nonmisusers) or a trait interpretation (preexisting discounting rate is responsible for the more moderate duration of misuse).

Heil et al. (2006) found no difference between delay discounting of hypothetical money by active and abstinent cocaine-dependent participants, although this may be a function of the active–abstinent classification. All participants were in treatment for cocaine dependence, with active individuals having used cocaine once in the past month and abstinent individuals not having used any cocaine in the past month; thus, a single instance of drug use in the previous 30 days differentiated active and abstinent groups. If delay discounting is a state variable, the phenotypic differentiation between these groups may have been insufficient to detect group differences in rate of delay discounting. As a point of contrast, the phenotypic differentiation of active versus abstinent smokers in Bickel et al. (1999) was heavy, daily smoking versus no smoking at all in the previous year. To the extent that delay discounting is a trait variable, delay discounting rate could be used as a predictor variable for the unreported long-term treatment outcomes of the participants in Heil et al. (2006).

Finally, the MA-dependent participants in Hoffman et al.'s (2006) study were all in treatment and technically abstinent for at least 2 weeks at the time of testing. Given that these participants discounted future hypothetical money more than did nondependent controls, it may be the case that the 2-week abstinent group is phenotypically not different from an active MA group (e.g., those participants in Monterosso et al., 2007). In fact, the relatively divergent results in this review of delay discounting as a function of abstinence may be due to different drug-specific patterns of use and abuse, as well as the diverse criteria for abstinence used in these studies. For instance, 1 week of reinforced cigarette reduction resulted in a decrease in delay discounting in cigarette smokers (Yi et al., 2008). Clearly, standardized criteria for active and former substance abuse classifications are necessary to get a more conclusive understanding of long-term drug abstinence and discounting.

PAST DISCOUNTING

Philosopher George Santayana famously tied people's ability to control their future to their recollection and understanding of the past. Historians, zoologists, and paleoclimatologists (and of course many more) take this to heart in their everyday work and know implicitly the connection between the past and future. The past–future connection certainly applies in the study of psychology and psychiatry, and their relationship has received some direct attention. In a study of self-control and impulsiveness, Rachlin (2000) proposed that estimates of time left in delay-of-gratification studies are an increasing function of time already elapsed. Trope and Liberman's (2003) temporal construal theory proposed that the same factors that affect mental representations of future events affect mental representations of past events (and other dimensions of psychological distance); events of substantial distance from the present (in the past or future) tend to be construed at a higher, abstract, superordinate level and events of immediate distance from the present tend to be construed at a lower, concrete, subordinate level.

Buckner and Carroll (2007) speculated that the ability to project oneself into the future (prospection, relevant to delay discounting) and remembering one's past (episodic memory) work on a common brain network; both processes "require projection of oneself from the immediate environment to alternative perspectives" (p. 29). There is some preliminary evidence that memory affects delay discounting: Putting a load on an individual's short-term memory results in an increase in delay discounting (Hinson, Jameson, & Whitney, 2003). An implication of these perspectives is that an individual's projection of the future mirrors that individual's perception of the past. If this were the case, the rate of decline in subjective value of an outcome would be similar as the outcome moves temporally further in the future and the past.

Informed by these perspectives, Yi, Gatchalian, and Bickel (2006) advanced the construct of *past discounting*—the idea that just as outcomes in the distant future are discounted as a function of time from the present, outcomes in the distant past are also discounted as a function of duration of time from the immediate. This construct was tested and confirmed with a control population. College students were asked to indicate preference between two outcomes: one occurring in the distant past and another occurring in the immediate past. The principal watermarks of delay discounting were observed in past discounting: namely, hyperbolic discounting, the *sign effect* (greater discounting of gains than losses), and the *magnitude effect* (greater discounting of small-magnitude than of large-magnitude rewards). Furthermore, significant correlations were observed between delay- and past-discounting conditions. To date, a single study has examined past discounting by a substance-abusing population. Bickel, Yi, Gatchalian, and Kowal (2008) compared delay and past discounting of hypothetical money gains by 30 heavy cigarette smokers (20-plus cigarettes daily and met *DSM–IV* criteria for nicotine dependence) and 29 control nonsmokers. Consistent with previous findings, they recorded higher rates of delay discounting in smokers when compared with controls. They found that smokers also discounted past outcomes at a higher rate than did controls and that delay and past discounting rates were significantly correlated. Similar results obtained with other drugs of abuse (e.g., alcohol) would perhaps illuminate why individuals engaged in substance abuse appear not to learn from previous mistakes.

PREDICTION OF DRUG RELAPSE USING
DISCOUNTING METHODOLOGIES

Differentiation of substance-abusing individuals and controls with discounting methodologies provides unique theoretical insights into substance abuse. However, recent studies have indicated that discounting assessments can have substantial clinical value as well. As of this date, two published studies have suggested that delay discounting may predict when an abstinent individual will relapse or, in other words, the duration of an abstinence effort. Dallery and Raiff (2007) evaluated the effect of a nicotine patch on smokers' ability to remain abstinent in a laboratory model of relapse. Thirty cigarette smokers (20-plus cigarettes daily with no intention to quit in the immediate future) were given a nicotine or placebo patch before the laboratory test of abstinence. During this test, smoking was allowed during 10-minute smoking intervals separated by 20-minute no-smoking periods. During the smoking intervals, participants were given a progressively larger amount of money for every 30 seconds they went without smoking. Taking a puff (relapse) reset the monetary reward to what it was at the beginning of the smoking interval. The nicotine patch did not affect relapse rates. However, presession assessments of delay discounting (hypothetical $100 gains) predicted whether a participant would relapse or abstain throughout the 2-hour session.

Similar findings were reported by Yoon et al. (2007), who examined delay discounting as a predictor of smoking relapse. Rate of delay discounting of delayed hypothetical $1,000 rewards was assessed in a sample of spontaneous quitters—those who quit smoking on pregnancy without therapeutic aid. When asked at 24 weeks postpartum, those with high baseline (during pregnancy) rates of delay discounting were more likely to have relapsed than those with lower rates of discounting. These two studies suggested that discounting rate can dichotomize those who maintain abstinence and those who do not on the basis of a somewhat arbitrary threshold (end of 2-hour session in Dallery & Raiff, 2007, and 24 weeks postpartum in Yoon et al., 2007). Continued research may indicate a more continuous relationship between the variables.

DISCOUNTING AND SUBSTANCE ABUSE FROM A
DEVELOPMENTAL PERSPECTIVE

Only a few studies have examined whether delay discounting changes as a function of age, but all have suggested that discounting decreases across the life span. In a series of studies by Leonard Green and his colleagues (Green, Fry, & Myerson, 1994; Green, Myerson, Lichtman, Rosen,

& Fry, 1996, 1999), older adults (approximate age = 70 years) discounted hypothetical amounts of money less than did adults (approximate age = 33 years), who in turn discounted less than children (approximate age = 12 years). Similarly, Olson, Hooper, Collins, and Luciana (2007) reported that area under the discount curve (Myerson, Green, & Warusawitharana, 2001) was significantly positively correlated with age in participants ages 9–23 ($N = 80, r = .37$); that is, the discount curve was steeper, resulting in a smaller area under the curve for younger participants than for older participants. These studies are provocative, yet several limitations should be acknowledged, including their cross-sectional nature, differences in the inherent value of the rewards being discounted over and above differences arising from economic status of participants, and possible differences in drug use history. Large-scale longitudinal studies are required to determine definitively whether delay discounting changes over the life span and the biological and socioeconomic factors responsible for any changes.

The heightened delay discounting observed in adolescents relative to adults is consistent with the notion that this period is a time of heightened vulnerability to drug use initiation. However, data provided by Reynolds, Karraker, Horn, and Richards (2003) have suggested no difference in rates of delay discounting between adolescents (14–16 years old) who smoked cigarettes at least once a week for 6 or more months ($N = 19$), those experimenting with smoking ($N = 17$; one to six cigarettes smoked in prior 6 months), and never-smokers ($N = 19$; 0 lifetime cigarettes smoked). More recently, Reynolds et al. (2007) reported that 14- to 18-year-old adolescent daily smokers who smoked more regularly ($N = 25$; 8.6 cigarettes daily) discounted delayed rewards more than same-age never-smokers ($N = 26$; 0 lifetime cigarettes smoked). Together, these data suggest that the extent of delay discounting is strongly correlated with the number of cigarettes smoked, which is in accord with data gathered from adult smokers (e.g., Ohmura et al., 2005) and the more recent finding that adult heavy drinkers discount more than do light-drinking adolescents (Field, Christiansen, Cole, & Goudie, 2007). Although additional studies are needed, these data suggest that discounting rate is not predictive of problem drug use. This suggestion may be somewhat controversial because a number of researchers have theorized that differences in delay discounting may somehow predict future drug use initiation (e.g., S. H. Mitchell, 2004b), and some research using animals has supported such a link (e.g., chap. 9, this volume; Perry, Larson, German, Madden, & Carroll, 2005; Poulos, Le, & Parker, 1995). Given evidence that normal function in brain regions associated with intertemporal decision making (McClure, Ericson, Laibson, Loewenstein, & Cohen, 2007; McClure, Laibson, Loewenstein, & Cohen, 2004) is altered in chronic drug use (Bolla et al., 2004; Martinez et al., 2007), our hypothesis is that changes in delay discounting are occasioned by the neuroadaptations associated with prolonged drug use. Nonetheless, this does not preclude the possibility that relatively high delay discounting in adolescence may lead to later drug use and abuse.

THEORETICAL CONTRIBUTIONS OF DISCOUNTING RESEARCH TO UNDERSTANDING SUBSTANCE ABUSE

Recently, the application of brain imaging techniques has contributed to theoretical hypotheses that apply discounting research to our understanding of the nature of substance abuse (e.g., chap. 5, this volume). Functional brain imaging during delay-discounting tasks has identified regions of the brain involved in evaluating immediate and delayed rewards. The results of two studies by McClure et al. (2004, 2007; but also see Monterosso et al., 2007) have suggested greater relative activation of limbic regions in choice involving immediate outcomes and greater relative activation in frontal and parietal regions in choice involving delayed outcomes. These data support the proposals of numerous investigators (Bechara, 2005; Bickel et al., 2007; Jentsch & Taylor, 1999) emphasizing the influence of two competing brain regions in the valuation of immediate and delayed outcomes, that is, affecting the individual's rate of discounting as well as his or her likelihood of engaging in substance abuse.

This conceptualization of substance abuse as influenced by the interplay between regions of the brain responsible for immediate (limbic regions) and delayed (frontal regions) outcomes has significant implications for therapeutic interventions for substance abuse. It may be possible that greater relative control by the frontal regions of the brain might be necessary for the advantageous cross-temporal organization of behavior associated with nonpathological substance use or abstinence. Rehabilitation of diminished cross-temporal control and related executive function in substance-abusing populations might then serve as treatment for substance abuse or improve the efficacy of other interventions.

To date, we are aware of one published study applying functional brain imaging technology to discounting by substance abusers (MA, in Monterosso et al., 2007). Although a different pattern of activation was observed in certain prefrontal and parietal regions of the brain between MA-dependent individuals and controls as a function of choice difficulty, the overall prediction based on McClure et al. (2004) was not supported: No differences were observed in prefrontal activation between MA-dependent individuals and controls. Given substantial procedural differences between McClure et al. and Monterosso et al. (2007), it is difficult to speculate on the reason for this discord. Certainly, current and future brain imaging studies should use more unified procedures to greatly expand our nascent understanding of brain activation, intertemporal choice, and substance abuse.

SUMMARY AND CONCLUSIONS

The extensive research on delay discounting confirms that individuals who abuse drugs discount delayed outcomes more than those who do not. This appears to be the case whether the drug of abuse is licit (cigarettes, alcohol) or illicit (heroin, cocaine). Recent research has further indicated that rate of delay discounting may be a function of the frequency of use. The early research on past discounting suggested that individuals who abuse drugs may discount past outcomes more than those who do not; continued research on this topic and confirmation of the preliminary results may have a direct theoretical impact on our understanding of substance abuse disorders. For instance, does diminished memory play a role in development and maintenance of substance abuse disorders, and can something be done to remediate this? Some very promising research has indicated that rate of discounting may be able to predict treatment outcome. This may have substantial clinical significance because we can use the knowledge of who is and is not likely to respond to treatment to adjust treatment strategies a priori. Finally, functional MRI and other brain imaging technologies promise to be valuable tools in our understanding of the overvaluation of immediate outcomes (high discounting) observed in substance abuse.

Discounting research offers a unique perspective on the seemingly irrational behavior of individuals who pathologically engage in behavior that is detrimental in the long term. There may be no better or socially important archetype of this than substance abuse. We expect that continued research in discounting will lead to greater understanding of substance abuse and dependence, influencing prevention and intervention strategies long into the future.

REFERENCES

Acheson, A., Farrar, A. M., Patak, M., Hausknecht, K. A., Kieres, A. K., Choi, S., et al. (2006). Nucleus accumbens lesions decrease sensitivity to rapid changes in the delay to reinforcement. *Behavioural Brain Research, 173,* 217–228.

American Psychiatric Association. (1994). *Diagnostic and statistical manual of mental disorders* (4th ed.). Washington, DC: Author.

Baker, F., Johnson, M. W., & Bickel, W. K. (2003). Delay discounting differs between current and never-smokers across commodities, sign, and magnitudes. *Journal of Abnormal Psychology, 112,* 382–392.

Bechara, A. (2005). Decision making, impulse control, and loss of willpower to resist drugs: A neurocognitive perspective. *Nature Neuroscience, 8,* 1458–1463.

Bickel, W. K., Miller, M. L., Yi, R., Kowal, B. P., Lindquist, D. M., & Pitcock, J. A. (2007). Behavioral- and neuro-economics of drug addiction: Competing neural systems and temporal discounting processes. *Drug and Alcohol Dependence*, 90(Suppl. 1), S85–S91.

Bickel, W. K., Odum, A. L., & Madden, G. J. (1999). Impulsivity and cigarette smoking: Delay discounting in current, never-, and ex-smokers. *Psychopharmacology (Berlin)*, 146, 447–454.

Bickel, W. K., Yi, R., Gatchalian, K. M., & Kowal, B. P. (2008). Past discounting by cigarette smokers. *Drug and Alcohol Dependence*, 96, 256–262.

Bjork, J. M., Hommer, D. W., Grant, S. J., & Danube, C. (2004). Impulsivity in abstinent alcohol-dependent patients: Relation to control subjects and Type 1-/Type 2-like traits. *Alcohol*, 34, 133–150.

Bolla, K., Ernst, M., Kiehl, K., Mouratidis, M., Eldreth, D., Contoreggi, C., et al. (2004). Prefrontal cortical dysfunction in abstinent cocaine abusers. *Journal of Neuropsychiatry and Clinical Neurosciences*, 16, 456–464.

Bretteville-Jensen, A. L. (1999). Addiction and discounting. *Journal of Health Economics*, 18, 393–407.

Buckner, R. L. & Carroll, D. C. (2007). Self-projection and the brain. *Trends in Cognitive Sciences*, 11, 49–57.

Coffey, S. F., Gudleski, G. D., Saladin, M. E., & Brady, K. T. (2003). Impulsivity and rapid discounting of delayed hypothetical rewards in cocaine-dependent individuals. *Experimental and Clinical Psychopharmacology*, 11, 18–25.

Dallery, J., & Raiff, B. R. (2007). Delay discounting predicts cigarette smoking in a laboratory model of abstinence reinforcement. *Psychopharmacology (Berlin)*, 190, 485–496.

Dixon, M. R., Marley, J., & Jacobs, E. A. (2003). Delay discounting by pathological gamblers. *Journal of Applied Behavior Analysis*, 36, 449–458.

Dom, G., D'haene, P. D., Hulstijn, W., & Sabbe, B. (2006). Impulsivity in abstinent early- and late-onset alcoholics: Differences in self-report measures and a delay discounting task. *Addiction*, 101, 50–59.

Estle, S. J., Green, L., Myerson, J., & Holt, D. D. (2007). Discounting of monetary and directly consumable rewards. *Psychological Science*, 18, 58–63.

Field, M., Christiansen, P., Cole, J., & Goudie, A. (2007). Delay discounting and the alcohol Stroop in heavy drinking adolescents. *Addiction*, 102, 579–586.

Gossop, M., Griffiths, P., Powls, B., & Strange, J. (1994). Cocaine: Patterns of use, route of administration, and severity of dependence. *British Journal of Psychiatry*, 164, 660–664.

Green, L., Fry, A. F., & Myerson, J. (1994). Discounting of delayed rewards: A lifespan comparison. *Psychological Science*, 5, 33–36.

Green, L., Myerson, J., Lichtman, D., Rosen, S., & Fry, A. (1996). Temporal discounting in choice between delayed rewards: The role of age and income. *Psychology and Aging*, 11, 79–84.

Green, L., Myerson, J., Lichtman, D., Rosen, S., & Fry, A. (1999). Amount of reward has opposite effects on the discounting of delayed and probabilistic outcomes. *Journal of Experimental Psychology: Learning, Memory, and Cognition*, 25, 418–427.

Heil, S. H., Johnson, M. W., Higgins, S. T., & Bickel, W. K. (2006). Delay discounting in currently using and currently abstinent cocaine-dependent outpatients and non-drug-using matched controls. *Addictive Behaviors, 31,* 1290–1294.

Heyman, G. M., & Gibb, S. P. (2006). Delay discounting in college cigarette chippers. *Behavioural Pharmacology, 17,* 669–679.

Hinson, J. M., Jameson, T. L., & Whitney, P. (2003). Impulsive decision making and working memory. *Journal of Experimental Psychology: Learning, Memory, and Cognition, 29,* 298–306.

Hoffman, W. F., Moore, M., Templin, R., McFarland, B., Hitzemann, R. J., & Mitchell, S. H. (2006). Neuropsychological function and delay discounting in methamphetamine-dependent individuals. *Psychopharmacology (Berlin), 188,* 162–170.

Jentsch, J. D., & Taylor, J. R. (1999). Impulsivity resulting from frontostriatal dysfunction in drug abuse: Implications for the controls of behavior controlled by reward-related stimuli. *Psychopharmacology (Berlin), 146,* 373–390.

Johnson, M. W., Bickel, W. K., & Baker, F. (2007). Moderate drug use and delay discounting: A comparison of heavy, light, and never smokers. *Experimental and Clinical Psychopharmacology, 15,* 187–194.

Kirby, K. N., & Petry, N. M. (2004). Heroin and cocaine abusers have higher discount rates for delayed rewards than alcoholics or non-drug-using controls. *Addiction, 99,* 461–471.

Kirby, K. N., Petry, N. M., & Bickel, W. K. (1999). Heroin addicts have higher discounting rates for delayed rewards than non-drug using controls. *Journal of Experimental Psychology: General, 128,* 78–87.

Kollins, S. H. (2003). Delay discounting is associated with substance use in college students. *Addictive Behaviors, 28,* 1167–1173.

Madden, G. J., Petry, N. M., Badger, G., & Bickel, W. K. (1997). Impulsive and self-control choices in opioid-dependent subjects and non-drug using controls: Drug and monetary rewards. *Experimental and Clinical Psychopharmacology, 5,* 256–262.

Martinez, D., Narendran, R., Foltin, R. W., Slifstein, M., Hwang, D. R., Broft, A., et al. (2007). Amphetamine-induced dopamine release: Markedly blunted in cocaine dependence and predictive of the choice to self-administer cocaine. *American Journal of Psychiatry, 164,* 622–629.

Mazur, J. E. (1987). An adjusting procedure for studying delayed reinforcement. In M. L. Commons, J. E. Mazur, J. A. Nevin, & H. Rachlin (Eds.), *The effect of delay and of intervening event on reinforcement value: Quantitative analyses of behavior* (pp. 55–73). Mahwah, NJ: Erlbaum.

McClure, S. M., Ericson, K. M., Laibson, D. I., Loewenstein, G., & Cohen, J. D. (2007). Tie discounting for primary rewards. *Journal of Neuroscience, 27,* 5796–5804.

McClure, S. M., Laibson, D. I., Loewenstein, G., & Cohen, J. D. (2004, October 15). Separate neural systems value immediate and delayed monetary rewards. *Science, 306,* 503–507.

Mitchell, J. M., Fields, H. L., D'Esposito, M., & Boettiger, C. A. (2005). Impulsive responding in alcoholics. *Alcoholism: Clinical and Experimental Research, 29,* 2158–2169.

Mitchell, S. H. (1999). Measures of impulsivity in cigarette smokers and non-smokers. *Psychopharmacology (Berlin), 146,* 455–464.

Mitchell, S. H. (2004a). Effects of short-term nicotine deprivation on decision-making: Delay, uncertainty and effort discounting. *Nicotine & Tobacco Research, 6,* 819–828.

Mitchell, S. H. (2004b). Measuring impulsivity and modeling its association with cigarette smoking. *Behavioral and Cognitive Neuroscience Reviews, 3,* 261–275.

Monterosso, J. R., Ainslie, G., Xu, J., Cordova, X., Domier, C. P., & London, E. D. (2007). Frontoparietal cortical activity of methamphetamine-dependent and comparison subjects performing a delay discounting task. *Human Brain Mapping, 28,* 383–393.

Munafo, M. R., Zetteler, J. I., & Clark, T. G. (2007). Personality and smoking status: A meta-analysis. *Nicotine & Tobacco Research, 9,* 405–413.

Myerson, J., Green, L., Hanson, J. S., Holt, D. D., & Estle, S. J. (2003). Discounting delayed and probabilistic rewards: Processes and traits. *Journal of Economic Psychology, 24,* 619–635.

Myerson, J., Green, L., & Warusawitharana, M. (2001). Area under the curve as a measure of discounting. *Journal of the Experimental Analysis of Behavior, 76,* 235–243.

Odum, A. L., Madden, G. J., Badger, G. J., & Bickel, W. K. (2000). Needle sharing in opioid-dependent outpatients: Psychological processes underlying risk. *Drug and Alcohol Dependence, 60,* 259–266.

Odum, A. L., Madden, G. J., & Bickel, W. K. (2002). Discounting of delayed health gains and losses by current, never-, and ex-smokers of cigarettes. *Nicotine & Tobacco Research, 4,* 295–303.

Ohmura, Y., Takahashi, T., & Kitamura, N. (2005). Discounting delayed and probabilistic monetary gains and losses by smokers of cigarettes. *Psychopharmacology (Berlin), 182,* 508–515.

Olson, E. A., Hooper, C. J., Collins, P., & Luciana, M. (2007). Adolescents' performance on delay and probability discounting tasks: Contributions of age, intelligence, executive functioning, and self-reported externalizing behavior. *Personality and Individual Differences, 43,* 1886–1897.

Perry, J. L., Larson, E. B., German, J. P., Madden, G. J., & Carroll, M. E. (2005). Impulsivity (delay discounting) as a predictor of acquisition of IV cocaine self-administration in female rats. *Psychopharmacology (Berlin), 178,* 193–201.

Petry, N. M. (2001). Delay discounting of money and alcohol in actively using alcoholics, currently abstinent alcoholics, and controls. *Psychopharmacology (Berlin), 154,* 243–250.

Poulos, C. X., Le, A. D., & Parker, J. L. (1995). Impulsivity predicts individual susceptibility to high levels of alcohol self-administration. *Behavioural Pharmacology, 6,* 810–814.

Rachlin, H. (2000). *The science of self-control.* Cambridge, MA: Harvard University Press.

Rachlin, H., Raineri, A., & Cross, D. (1991). Subjective probability and delay. *Journal of the Experimental Analysis of Behavior, 55,* 233–244.

Rachlin, H., Siegel, E., & Cross, D. (1994). Lotteries and the time horizon. *Psychological Science, 5,* 390–393.

Reynolds, B., Karraker, K., Horn, K., & Richards, J. B. (2003). Delay and probability discounting as related to different stages of adolescent smoking and non-smoking. *Behavioural Processes, 64,* 333–344.

Reynolds, B., Patak, M., Shroff, P., Penfold, R. B., Melanko, S., & Duhig, A. M. (2007). Laboratory and self-report assessments of impulsive behavior in adolescent daily smokers and nonsmokers. *Experimental and Clinical Psychopharmacology, 15,* 264–271.

Reynolds, B., Richards, J. B., Horn, K., & Karraker, K. (2004). Delay and probability discounting as related to cigarette smoking status in adults. *Behavioural Processes, 65,* 35–42.

Richards, J. B., Zhang, L., Mitchell, S. H., & de Wit, H. (1999). Delay or probability discounting in a model of impulsive behavior: Effect of alcohol. *Journal of the Experimental Analysis of Behavior, 71,* 121–143.

Smolka, M., & Schmidt, L. G. (1999). The influence of heroin dose and route of administration on the severity of the opiate withdrawal syndrome. *Addiction, 94,* 1191–1198.

Stephens, D. W., & Krebs, J. R. (1986). *Foraging theory.* Princeton, NJ: Princeton University Press.

Trope, Y., & Liberman, N. (2003). Temporal construal. *Psychological Review, 110,* 403–421.

Vuchinich, R., & Simpson, C. (1998). Hyperbolic temporal discounting in social drinkers and problem drinkers. *Experimental and Clinical Psychopharmacology, 6,* 292–305.

Yi, R., Chase, W. D., & Bickel, W. K. (2007). Probability discounting among cigarette smokers and nonsmokers: Molecular analysis discerns group differences. *Behavioral Pharmacology, 18,* 633–639.

Yi, R., Gatchalian, K. M., & Bickel, W. K. (2006). Discounting of past outcomes. *Experimental and Clinical Psychopharmacology, 14,* 311–317.

Yi, R., Johnson, M. W., Giordano, L. A., Landes, R. D., Badger, G. J., & Bickel, W. K. (2008). The effects of reduced cigarette smoking on discounting future rewards: An initial evaluation. *Psychological Record, 58,* 163–174.

Yoon, J. H., Higgins, S. T., Heil, S. H., Sugarbaker, R. J., Thomas, C. S., & Bader, G. J. (2007). Delay discounting predicts postpartum relapse to cigarette smoking among pregnant women. *Experimental and Clinical Psychopharmacology, 15,* 176–186.

8

DRUG EFFECTS ON DELAY DISCOUNTING

HARRIET DE WIT AND SUZANNE H. MITCHELL

There are multiple, bidirectional relationships between drug use and impulsive behaviors such as delay discounting (de Wit, 2009; Perry & Carroll, 2008). Not only may impulsive behavioral tendencies increase the likelihood of initiating drug use, but use of drugs, either chronic or acute, may increase the tendency to make impulsive choices. Comparisons of human drug users and nonusers have confirmed that drug users exhibit a stronger preference for immediate reward compared with nonusers (Bickel, Marsch, & Carroll, 2000), but it is difficult to determine the origin of this relationship, that is, whether the preference preceded the use of drugs or whether it resulted from drug use, perhaps through neuroadaptations related to drug exposure (e.g., Cardinal, 2006). Studies with laboratory animals can partially address this issue because there is now a large literature documenting the effects of drugs on measures of delay discounting. Most of these have examined acute doses of drugs, but some have also examined the effects of chronic exposure. A smaller literature exists with humans, including studies examining the acute effects of abused drugs on measures of delay discounting. In this chapter, we review findings from nonhuman

Preparation of this chapter and some of the research reported in this review were supported by National Institute on Drug Abuse Grants DA09133, 015543, and 016727.

and human studies on the effects of drugs of abuse on discounting. An important issue that arises in the review of this literature is the methodological details of the discounting procedures used, including the differences between the procedures used with humans versus nonhumans. Therefore, we discuss these methodological issues to attempt to resolve apparent discrepancies.

ANIMAL DELAY DISCOUNTING

Studies using animal models are uniquely able to assess the effects of drugs of abuse because the drug-naive state of subjects can be assured at the outset of the study. Accordingly, a number of investigators have examined how acute and chronic exposure to drugs affect delay discounting. Many other studies have been conducted with laboratory animals to investigate the neural bases of discounting, using either challenge drugs that are not abused (e.g., Robinson et al., 2007; Winstanley, Theobald, Dalley, Cardinal, & Robbins, 2006) or lesions of specific structures thought to be involved in the behavior (e.g., Acheson, Farrar, et al., 2006; chap. 4, this volume; Kheramin et al., 2004; Mobini et al., 2002). However, this chapter is limited to a review of delay-discounting studies examining drugs with abuse potential (d-amphetamine, methamphetamine, cocaine, nicotine, methylphenidate, ethanol, diazepam, morphine).

Comparisons across studies of delay discounting are limited by the extent to which the studies used comparable procedures. First, most but not all of the studies have used rats as subjects. For example, only two studies have examined the effects of d-amphetamine in mice (Helms, Reeves, & Mitchell, 2006; Isles, Humby, & Wilkinson, 2003), and just one study used pigeons (Pitts & Febbo, 2004). Thus, possible species differences must be considered when interpreting the general effects of these drugs on discounting. Second, the behavioral tasks used to measure delay discounting vary across studies in ways that could influence their outcome and interpretation. The most frequently used procedure for examining delay discounting is a within-sessions procedure, initially described by Evenden and Ryan (1996), in which subjects choose between a smaller–sooner and a larger–later reward, usually food, across several blocks of trials. In the first block, rats choose between receiving an immediate small reward (e.g., one food pellet) and an immediate large reward (e.g., four food pellets) by making the appropriate response (e.g., lever press, nose poke). In subsequent trial blocks, the delay to the delivery of the larger reward is systematically increased, typically through delays of 10, 20, 40, and 60 seconds. Blocks begin with a series of forced-choice trials (e.g., four trials in which the animal may select only one alternative per trial), which are followed by free-choice trials (e.g., six trials) during which subjects select the preferred alternative. A postreinforcer intertrial interval (usually a blackout) ensures that each trial lasts 100 seconds regardless of the rat's choice. The primary dependent variable, the number of choices of the larger reward alternative, usually declines systematically as a function of the length of the delay to the receipt of the reward. Although various manipulation checks can be used to verify that choice is controlled by both the reward size and the delay (e.g., reversing the lever to which the smaller–sooner and larger–later rewards are assigned), few studies in this review have included these control procedures (but see Evenden & Ryan, 1996; Isles et al., 1999; Pitts & McKinney, 2005). Unfortunately, inclusion of these control procedures requires additional sessions and additional drug exposure, which could blur the distinction between the acute and chronic effects of the drug when interpreting any observed drug effects.

Another procedure frequently used to assess delay discounting is the *adjusting-amount procedure* (Richards, Mitchell, de Wit, & Seiden, 1997), in which one reward is systematically adjusted depending on the subject's recent choices. That is, if the subject chooses the larger–later reward on one trial, then on the next trial the size of the smaller–sooner reward is increased. Conversely, if the subject chooses the smaller–sooner reward, then on the next trial the size of this reward is decreased. This is continued until a point is reached at which the subject is indifferent between the alternatives; that is, the size of the smaller–sooner reward is equivalent in value to that of the larger–later reward. In this procedure, unlike the Evenden and Ryan (1996) within-sessions procedure, the effects of different delays on choice must be assessed in different sessions, potentially increasing both the time required to complete a study and the subject's exposure to the drugs under examination.

A third, less widely used procedure for assessing delay discounting is the *adjusting-delay procedure* (Mazur, 1987, 1988). This procedure is similar to the adjusting-amount procedure in that choices on one trial dynamically affect the alternatives offered on the next trial. However, as indicated by the name, in the adjusting-delay procedure the time to the larger–later reward is varied rather than the amount of the smaller–sooner reward. Typically, if the subject chooses the larger–later alternative on two consecutive trials, the length of the delay to this reward increases on the next trial. Conversely, two consecutive choices of the smaller–sooner alternative causes the delay to the larger–later reinforcer to shorten until an indifference point between the alternatives is reached. This procedure is not widely used in the study of drug effects on delay discounting for at least two reasons. First, it requires a considerable number of sessions for choices to stabilize, and once stable indifference is reached, only a single point on the delay discount function is obtained; the remainder of the function must be obtained in subsequent conditions. Therefore, this procedure requires considerably more time relative to the ones described earlier. Second, the two alternatives differ in both reward size and delay duration, making it difficult to determine whether a drug's effects on delay discounting are attributable to changes in sensitivity to reward size or changes in timing processes affecting sensitivity to delay. This is also a concern with other procedures but arguably less so because in the within-sessions procedure and the adjusting-amount procedure, one of the alternatives has a 0-second delay.

How the differences separating these three procedures have influenced measures of delay discounting is unclear. The three procedures probably vary in the extent to which they involve related underlying neuropsychological processes (e.g., attention, working memory). For example, the within-session procedure, in which forced-choice trials are followed by 4 to 10 free-choice trials separated by intertrial intervals of 30 to 100 seconds, arguably imposes greater working memory demands than do the dynamically adjusting procedures. In the next sections, we review the results of studies exploring the effects of various commonly abused drugs on delay discounting in laboratory animals. As we show, there is no clear evidence that the three procedures produce consistently different results, although the relatively small number of studies make such comparisons difficult.

The largest number of studies, by far, have been conducted with amphetamine, allowing investigators to examine the role of other, more salient design factors, such as dose response functions, acute versus chronic dosing, and the importance of a stimulus during the delay. Tables 8.1–8.5 provide summaries of the different studies that are discussed in this chapter, grouped according to the drug administered: d-amphetamine, methamphetamine, and methylphenidate (Table 8.1); cocaine and nicotine (Table 8.2); ethanol (Table 8.3); diazepam (Table 8.4); and morphine (Table 8.5). Each table outlines the delay-discounting procedure used (within sessions, adjusting amount, or adjusting delay), the delays assessed, whether a unique cue was associated with the delay interval, the dose of drug administered, the dosing characteristics, the type of subjects (rats, mice, pigeons; strains and sexes), and the study reference information. Within each table, studies are grouped according to the delay-discounting procedure used for easy comparisons between studies using the same basic procedures.

Amphetamine, Methamphetamine and Methylphenidate

As shown in Table 8.1, most of the studies that have examined the impact of acute doses of drugs on delay discounting have examined d-amphetamine. Eleven studies have been published on the effects of d-amphetamine that vary in their procedural details and in drug administration protocols. As can be seen from the Results column of Table 8.1, the data from these 11 studies have been mixed: In 6 studies, d-amphetamine increased choice of the larger–later reward; in 2 studies, the drug decreased these choices; and in 3 studies, the drug had either no effect or mixed increases and decreases depending on the conditions (summary provided in Table 8.6). The reasons for the differences across studies are not clear, but the results summarized in Table 8.1 suggest that they were

TABLE 8.1

Characteristics of the d-Amphetamine, Methamphetamine, and Methylphenidate Studies

Discounting procedure; delay(s)	Delay interval stimulus	Drug administration characteristics	Dose (mg/kg)	Results	Species[a] and strain	Authors
			d-Amphetamine			
Within session; 0, 10, 20, 40, 60	No	Intraperitoneal injection Tuesday and Friday; 3× per dose	0.03 0.1	No effect Decrease	Rats; Sprague-Dawley	Evenden and Ryan (1996)
Within session; 0, 10, 20, 40, 60	No	Intraperitoneal injections on alternate days; 3× per dose	0.3 1.0 1.6	No effect Decrease No effect	Rats; Lister hooded	Cardinal et al. (2000)
Within session; 0, 10, 20, 40, 60	Yes	Intraperitoneal injections on alternate days; 3× per dose	0.3 1.0 1.6	Increase No effect No effect	Rats; Lister hooded	Cardinal et al. (2000)
Within session; 0.5–8	Not reported	Daily injection (route unknown); alternating vehicle then drug; 1× per dose	0.25 0.5	Increase No effect	Rats; Long-Evans	Floresco et al. (2007)
Within session; 0, 3, 6, 12, 24	Tray light	Daily intraperitoneal injections; no randomization; 3× per dose	0.15 0.3	No effect No effect	Rats; Harlan Sprague-Dawley	Uslaner & Robinson (2006)
Within session; 0, 10, 20, 40, 60	No	Intraperitoneal injections; ascending dose order; × per dose unspecified	0.2 0.5 1.0	Increase Increase Increase	Rats; Wistar	Van Gaalen et al. (2006)
Within session; 0, 10, 20, 40, 60	No	Intraperitoneal injections; vehicle then drug; ascending doses until 3× per dose; 10 days between ascending series Then vehicle–high dose 3× with 5 days between vehicle–drugs sets	0.3 1.0 1.5 2.3	Increasing trend Increasing trend Increasing trend Increase Effects less apparent in animals who were less impulsive to begin with	Rats; Lister hooded	Winstanley et al. (2003, Experiment 1)

(continues)

TABLE 8.1

Characteristics of the d-Amphetamine, Methamphetamine, and Methylphenidate Studies   *(Continued)*

Discounting procedure; delay(s)	Delay interval stimulus	Drug administration characteristics	Dose (mg/kg)	Results	Species[a] and strain	Authors
		d-Amphetamine				
Within session; 0, 10, 20, 40, 60	No	Intraperitoneal injections; vehicle then drug; ascending doses until 3× per dose; 10 days between ascending series	1.0 1.5	Increase Increase (Replicate Experiment 1)	Rats; Lister hooded	Winstanley et al. (2003, Experiment 2)
Within session; 0, 10, 20, 40, 60	No	Unknown route; vehicle then drug; ascending doses until 3× per dose; 10 days between ascending series	0.3 1.0 1.5	Increase Increase Increase (Replicate Winstanley et al., 2003). No post hoc tests for dose	Rats; Lister hooded	Winstanley et al. (2005, Experiment 1)
Within session; 0, 2, 4, 8, 12	No	Systemic injection every 4 days; 4× per dose	0.4 0.6 0.8 1.0	Increase Increase Decrease Larger–later never chosen	Mice; F2 cross of C57BL and DBA strains	Isles et al. (2003)
Adjusting amount	Tone	Intraperitoneal injections Tuesday and Friday; 3× per dose	0.5 1.0	No effect Increase	Rats; Sprague-Dawley	Wade et al. (2000)
Adjusting amount	Tone	Intraperitoneal injections Tuesday and Friday; 4× per dose	0.4 0.8 1.2	No effects Decrease both strains Decrease both strains	Mice; C57BL/6J and DBA/2J	Helms et al. (2006)

	Methamphetamine				
Adjusting amount	Tone	0.5 1.0 2.0 4.0	No effect Increase Increase No responding	Rats; Holtzman and Sprague-Dawley	Richards, Sabol, and de Wit (1999)
Adjusting amount	Tone	4.0	Decrease	Rats; Holtzman and Sprague-Dawley	Richards, Sabol, and de Wit (1999)
Concurrent chain schedules	Light specific to choice	0.3 1.0 1.7 3.0	Decreased response rate during initial links to stimulus associated with long delay terminal link at the 1.0 and 1.7 mg/kg doses only	Pigeons; White Carneau	Pitts and Febbo (2004)
	Methylphenidate				
Within session; 0, 5, 10, 20, 30, 40, 50	Blinking light	0 1 3 5.6 10 17 ($N = 1$)	Increase in larger–later choice highly variable; statistics not provided	Rats; Holtzman and Sprague-Dawley	Pitts and McKinney (2005)

The second column also contains procedural descriptions below each stimulus:
- "Intraperitoneal injections Tuesday and Friday; 1× per dose"
- "Intraperitoneal injections daily 14 days (saline & methamphetamine counterbalanced), testing throughout"
- "Intramuscular (breast) injections Tuesday and Friday; order unspecified; at least 2× per dose"
- "Friday intraperitoneal injection; order unspecified; 2–4× per dose"

(continues)

TABLE 8.1
Characteristics of the d-Amphetamine, Methamphetamine, and Methylphenidate Studies *(Continued)*

Discounting procedure; delay(s)	Delay interval stimulus	Drug administration characteristics	Dose (mg/kg)	Results	Species[a] and strain	Authors
		Methylphenidate				
Within session; 0, 10, 20, 40, 60	No	Intraperitoneal injections, interval unspecified; ascending doses; × per dose unspecified	0.3 1.0 3.0	Increase Increase Increase	Rats; Wistar	van Gaalen et al. (2006)
Modified within session using a T-maze; 30	No	Route unspecified; 2× consecutive days	Adults: 3.0 Juveniles: 1.0 3.0 5.0 10.0	No effect No effect Increase Increase No effect	Rats Adults: Wistar, Wistar Kyoto, Spontaneously Hypertensive Rats Juveniles: Wistar	Bizot et al. (2007)

Note. × = times.

[a]All subjects were male except those from Richards, Sabol, and de Wit (1999) and Wade et al. (2000), in which sex was unspecified.

not because of differences between the within-sessions and adjusting-amount procedures or the lengths of delay assessed. We discuss two possible procedural differences that could contribute to these discrepant results, the inclusion of a stimulus during the delay and dose-related differences.

In the two earliest studies, Evenden and Ryan (1996) reported that d-amphetamine (0.1 mg/kg) decreased choice of the large delayed reward, whereas Wade, de Wit, and Richards (2000) reported that d-amphetamine (1.0 mg/kg) increased choice of the large reward. Evenden and Ryan (1996) used the within-session procedure described earlier, whereas Wade et al. used the adjusting-amount procedure (Richards et al., 1997). There are several differences between these studies, including methodological differences between the within-session and adjusting-amount procedures, as well as the doses at which the effects were observed. As noted by Cardinal, Robbins, and Everitt (2000), one methodological difference between the within-session procedure used by Evenden and Ryan and the adjusting-amount procedure used by Wade et al. was the presence of a unique stimulus during the delay interval. That is, in the Evenden and Ryan study, no stimulus bridged the delay interval, whereas in the Wade et al. study, a tone immediately followed the choice of the larger–later reward and remained on until the reward was presented.

Pavlovian conditioning principles suggest that repeatedly presenting a stimulus moments before the delivery of food (at the end of the delay in this situation) will cause the stimulus to become a conditioned reinforcer. Richards, Sabol, and de Wit (1999) hypothesized that in delay-discounting procedures that include such a stimulus, a conditioned reinforcer is added to the delayed reward, thereby increasing the subjective value of the delayed alternative and subsequently choice of that alternative. Furthermore, d-amphetamine is believed to specifically enhance the efficacy of conditioned reinforcers, and so the drug would disproportionately increase the value of the delayed reward when combined with a conditioned stimulus. In a test of this intriguing idea, Cardinal et al. (2000) reported that d-amphetamine increased preference for the larger–later alternative when the delay included a delay-bridging cue and had the opposite effect when no cue was presented. However, these effects were only found at specific doses (0.3 mg/kg for the increase and 1.0 mg/kg for the decrease). Additional data suggesting that the simple presence or absence of a delay-bridging cue could not account for the different effects of d-amphetamine have accumulated more recently. In one study, using inbred strains of mice, d-amphetamine decreased choice of the larger–later alternative despite the presence of a cue during the delay (Helms et al., 2006). Subsequent studies from the Robbins laboratory also produced contradictory outcomes because d-amphetamine increased preference for the larger–later reinforcer when no cue was presented during the delay (e.g., Winstanley, Dalley, Theobald, & Robbins, 2003; Winstanley, Theobald, Dalley, & Robbins, 2005).

Dose of drug administered is another possible source of the differences in the effects of d-amphetamine on delay discounting. For example, Isles et al. (2003) reported that low doses of amphetamine (0.4 and 0.6 mg/kg) increased choice of the larger–later alternative in mice, whereas higher doses (0.8 and 1.0 mg/kg) decreased delayed reward choice in F2 C57BL/6 × CBA/Ca F2 mice. Similar effects were reported by Cardinal et al. (2000) using outbred rats. Although these findings raise the possibility that amphetamine may have biphasic, dose-related effects on delay discounting, inspection of Table 8.1 shows that dose alone does not account for the differences.

Another possible source of the differences across studies is the number of administrations of drug and days between successive drug administrations. Richards, Sabol, and de Wit (1999) reported that a single injection of methamphetamine at either 1.0 mg/kg or 2.0 mg/kg separated by at least 2 days increased choice of the larger–later reward relative to placebo (but see Pitts & Febbo, 2004), whereas daily injections of 4.0 mg/kg over a 14-day period resulted in decreases in delayed reward choice. These data suggest that neuroadaptations induced by the different dosing regimes could influence the outcome of some of these studies with repeated amphetamine administration, although data relating to this idea are lacking. In sum, there is no clear explanation for the divergent findings on the effects of amphetamine on delay discounting.

Methylphenidate

Only three studies have examined the effects of methylphenidate on delay discounting (Bizot et al., 2007; Pitts & McKinney, 2005; van Gaalen, van Koten, Schoffelmeer, & Vanderschuren, 2006). The former used a T-maze–based procedure and a single delay length, and the others used a within-sessions procedure. Delay intervals were signaled in Pitts and McKinney (2005) but unsignaled in the other studies. Although Bizot et al. (2007) reported no effects of methylphenidate on adult rats, methylphenidate increased choice of the larger–later reward in juveniles. In contrast, both studies using the within-session procedure reported increased choice of the large–later reward, although the data provided by Pitts and McKinney appear more variable, perhaps because of the smaller number of subjects and the presentation of data for individuals.

Cocaine

In contrast to the amphetamine literature, in which most studies have focused on the acute effects of the drug, all of the studies examining cocaine have examined changes in delay discounting after a prolonged period of drug exposure (see Table 8.2). The first study examining the effects of cocaine

TABLE 8.2
Characteristics of Studies Examining Cocaine and Nicotine

Discounting procedure; delay(s)	Delay interval stimulus	Drug administration characteristics	Dose (mg/kg)	Results	Species[a] and strain	Authors
Cocaine						
Within session; 0, 10, 20, 40, 60	No	14 daily intraperitoneal injections; assessment: 3 weeks after final injection	30	Decrease	Rats; Long-Evans	Simon et al. (2007)
Within session; 0, 10, 20, 40, 60	No	3 injections per day for 14 days (route unspecified)	15	Decrease	Rats; Long-Evans	Paine et al. (2003)
Adjusting delay	Houselight color changed	10–36 daily intraperitoneal injections; assessment: last 5 days then 10–36 days after final injection	15	Decrease	Rats; hooded	Logue et al. (1992)
Nicotine						
Adjusting delay	Light above lever	Acute: subcutaneous injections Wed. and Sun.; 2× per dose; descending order for each cycle	0.03 0.1 0.3 1.0	Decrease, but variable effect sizes across doses	Rats; Harlan Sprague-Dawley	Dallery and Locey (2005)
Adjusting delay	Light above lever	65 days 0.3 mg/kg subcutaneous (1 mg/kg: N = 1), then doses as in acute study (with Wed. and Sun. injections but 0.3 on other days)	0.03 0.1 0.3 1.0	Decrease in larger–later choice, returning to predrug baseline within 70 sessions (no post hoc tests)	Rats; Harlan Sprague-Dawley	Dallery and Locey (2005)

Note. × = times.
[a]All subjects were male.

was reported by Logue et al. (1992) using an adjusting-delay procedure. They found that cocaine (15 mg/kg intraperitoneal) administered daily for 10 to 36 days decreased the rats' preference for larger–later rewards. Similar shifts away from choice of the more delayed reward were reported using the within-session procedure and 14 days of drug administration by Paine, Dringenberg, and Olmstead (2003; 15 mg/kg 3 times daily) and Simon, Mendez, and Setlow (2007; 30 mg/kg). It is interesting that in the latter study, the data were collected 3 weeks after cocaine injections ceased, suggesting that the increased discounting of the delayed reward reported by Logue et al. is a long-lasting effect.

When cocaine-exposed rats in the Logue et al. (1992) study received repeated saline injections after their cocaine experience, their choice behavior returned to levels seen before cocaine exposure. The finding that behavior returns to normal is consistent with the human literature comparing current and former drug users (e.g., Bickel, Odum, & Madden, 1999). Thus, it appears that prolonged, chronic cocaine exposure resulted in increased delay discounting (consistent with the Richards, Sabol, & de Wit, 1999, report examining chronic methamphetamine exposure). However, cessation of use allows behavior to return to baseline levels.

Nicotine

This return to baseline levels after cessation of long-term use of cocaine is consistent with data provided by Dallery and Locey (2005) examining the effects of nicotine on delay discounting. Like Logue et al. (1992), they used an adjusting-delay procedure and reported systematically decreased choice of the larger–later reinforcer when nicotine doses were administered with at least 2 days between injections. When rats had been exposed to nicotine every day for 65 successive days, choice of the larger–later reinforcer was rare at every dose tested (including vehicle injections). In summary, prolonged exposure to cocaine or nicotine caused a decrease in choice of larger–later rewards. Moreover, choices slowly returned to baseline after drug administration had been discontinued.

Ethanol

In contrast to research examining stimulant drugs, fewer studies have examined other drug classes. Table 8.3 shows the three published studies that have examined the impact of ethanol on delay discounting. In an early study, Poulos, Parker, and Le (1998) used a T-maze to assess rats' choices between larger–later and smaller–sooner rewards. The goal box at the end of one arm provided 2 food pellets immediately, and the other provided 12 pellets delivered after a 12-second confinement period. Higher doses of ethanol decreased

TABLE 8.3

Characteristics of Studies Examining Ethanol

Discounting procedure; delay(s)	Delay interval stimulus	Drug administration characteristics	Dose (mg/kg)	Results	Species[a] and strain	Authors
Within session; 0, 1, 2, 5, 15	No	Intraperitoneal injections Tuesday and Friday; 3× per dose	0.3 1.0	No effect Decrease	Rats; Sprague-Dawley	Evenden and Ryan (1999)
Within session; 0, 10, 20, 40, 60	No	Intraperitoneal injections 2× per week in the following sequence: 0.5, 0.25, 1.0, 1.5	0.25 0.5 1.0 1.5	Biphasic effect, with more impulsive-like behavior induced by intermediate ethanol doses	Rats; Long-Evans	Tomie et al. (1998)
Modified within session using a T-maze; 5	Stimuli associated with goal box	Daily intraperitoneal injections; order randomized; 2× per dose	0.6 0.9 1.2 1.8	Decrease Decrease Decrease Decrease	Rats; Wistar	Poulos et al. (1998)
Modified within session using a T-maze; 5, 10, 15	Stimuli associated with goal box	Daily intraperitoneal injections; order unspecified; 2× per dose	0.6 0.9 1.2 1.8	Decrease Decrease Decrease Decrease	Rats, Long-Evans	Olmstead et al. (2006)

Note. × = times.
[a]All subjects were male.

choice of the larger–later alternative. This result was replicated by Olmstead, Hellemans, and Paine (2006) in a very similar study using a T-maze, the same doses of ethanol, and similar reinforcer sizes and delays and in one by Evenden and Ryan (1999) using the within-session procedure. Interestingly, on the basis of a pre-ethanol exposure screening, Poulos et al. performed a median split to create a group of "low reactives," that is, the 8 rats that selected the larger–later alternative the most, and a group of "high reactives," the remaining 8 rats that selected it the least. Ethanol decreased choice of the delayed rewards in both groups, suggesting that preexisting individual differences in delay discounting do not change the effect of ethanol on the processes responsible for delay discounting. Similar data were reported by Tomie, Aguado, Pohorecky, and Benjamin (1998) for rats, which showed decreased choice of larger–later rewards as the delay lengthened during the pre-ethanol assessment, whereas no effect of ethanol was observed for rats previously classified as "insensitive" to the effects of delay. In summary, all of the published studies with ethanol have indicated that where an effect of ethanol was observed, this drug decreased choices of the large, delayed reward.

Diazepam

Two studies have examined the acute effects of diazepam on delay discounting (Table 8.4). Thiebot, le Bihan, Soubrie, and Simon (1985) used a T-maze procedure to examine the effects of benzodiazepines, including diazepam, on preference for two food pellets available immediately versus eight pellets available after a delay (0, 15, or 30 seconds) using a design in which delay varied between groups. Compared with placebo, 2 mg/kg and 4 mg/kg doses of diazepam systematically decreased choice of the larger–later reward when it was delayed by 15 or 30 seconds. In contrast, Evenden and Ryan (1996) reported that smaller doses of diazepam (0.3 mg/kg and 1.0 mg/kg) increased choice of the larger–later reward in a within-session paradigm. No studies have been completed in which an overlapping dose range has been assessed, so it is impossible to determine whether the differences between the studies can be attributed simply to dose. In summary, high doses of diazepam caused decreases in larger–later reward choice, whereas a study using lower doses reported the opposite effect.

Morphine

Two studies have examined the effects of morphine on delay discounting in rats (Table 8.5). Kieres et al. (2004) reported that 1.8 mg/kg morphine, but not lower doses, decreased choice of the larger–later reward in an adjusting-amount procedure. Pitts and McKinney (2005) tested the effects of a wider range of doses of morphine using a within-sessions procedure and reported that

TABLE 8.4
Characteristics of Studies Examining Diazepam

Discounting procedure; delay(s)	Delay interval stimulus	Drug administration characteristics	Dose (mg/kg)	Results	Species[a] and strain	Authors
Within session; 0, 10, 20, 40, 60	No	Intraperitoneal injections Tuesday and Friday; 3× per dose	0.3 1.0	Increase Increase	Rats; Sprague-Dawley	Evenden and Ryan (1996)
Modified within session using a T-maze; 0, 15, 30, 60	No	Intraperitoneal injections; interval unspecified; order unspecified; 2× per dose	2.0 4.0	Decrease Decrease	Rats; Wistar	Thiebot et al. (1985)

Note. × = times.
[a]All subjects were male.

TABLE 8.5
Characteristics of Studies Examining Morphine

Discounting procedure; delay(s)	Delay interval stimulus	Drug administration characteristics	Dose (mg/kg)	Results	Species[a] and strain	Authors
Within session; 0, 5, 10, 20, 30, 40, 50	Blinking light	Friday intraperitoneal injection; order unspecified; 2–4× per dose	0.3 (N = 1) 1 3 5.6 10 (N = 2) 17 (N = 2)	Inconsistent results possibly decreased larger-later choice, no statistics provided	Rats; Holtzman Sprague-Dawley	Pitts and McKinney (2005)
Adjusting amount	Tone and light above food dispenser	Subcutaneous injections; Tuesday and Friday; ascending dose order; 2× per dose	0.3 1.0 1.8	No effect No effect Decrease	Rats; Sprague-Dawley	Kieres et al. (2004)

Note. × = times.
[a]All subjects were male.

the drug produced highly variable responses across individual animals; however, choice of the large, delayed reinforcer during the saline condition was low, raising the possibility that no reliable effect of morphine was seen in this study because of a floor effect. In summary, morphine had inconsistent effects: At one dose, it decreased choice of the larger–later reward, but in another study its effects were inconsistent.

Summary

A number of studies have used animal models to examine the effects of drugs of abuse on choice of larger–later versus smaller–sooner rewards in a delay-discounting paradigm (Table 8.6). Although we recognize that this sample may be biased by selective publication, most of these studies have reported effects of acute administration of drugs of abuse (at least at some doses). Whereas some of the studies using d-amphetamine, methylphenidate, and methamphetamine have reported increased choice of the delayed option, most studies have indicated that drugs of abuse decrease choices of the larger–later rewards, that is, they increase impulsivity. Although the results of studies with amphetamine are less consistent, there are also more of these studies, compared with studies with other drugs, and they have used more disparate methods. Ultimately, careful application of these sensitive procedures will reveal the effects of different doses of each of the drugs, the relative effects of acute or chronic administration, the importance of stimuli presented during the

TABLE 8.6
Summary of Changes in Choice of the Larger–Later (LL)
Reward After Administration of Each Type of Drug

Drug	No. studies	Decrease in LL choice	Increase in LL choice	Mixed effects	No effect
d-amphetamine	11	2	6	2[a]	1
Methamphetamine	3[b]	2	1		
Methylphenidate	3		2	1	
Cocaine	3	3			
Nicotine	2[c]	2			
Ethanol	4	3		1	
Diazepam	2	1	1		
Morphine	2	1		1	

[a]For one of these studies (Cardinal et al., 2000), the effects were dependent on the stimulus occurring during the delay: Without a stimulus, decreases in LL reward choice were observed; with a stimulus, increases were observed.
[b]Richards, Sabol, and de Wit (1999) included two studies. In one study, rats received methamphetamine acutely; in the other, the same subjects received chronic, daily administration of methamphetamine. The different administration schedules had opposite effects on LL reward choice (see Table 8.1).
[c]Dallery and Locey (2005) included two studies. In one study, rats received nicotine acutely; in the other, the same subjects received chronic, daily administration of nicotine. The different administration schedules had the same effects on LL reward choice (see Table 8.2).

delays, and the importance of other key methodological differences between the various procedures.

HUMAN DELAY DISCOUNTING

Relatively few studies have examined the direct effects of drugs or acute abstinence from drugs on delay discounting in humans, and these studies have suggested that it is surprisingly difficult to detect acute, drug-induced increases in delay discounting (Table 8.7). This inability to show drug-induced discounting is surprising in view of the common impression that certain drugs, such as alcohol, make individuals more reactive to immediate and salient rewards compared with more distant ones (*alcohol myopia*; Duffy, 1995; Graham, 1980; Steele & Josephs, 1990). It is also not consistent with studies with nonhumans, using comparable doses of drugs and similar procedures, that have consistently shown increases or decreases in discounting. It is likely that the failure to detect acute, drug-induced changes in discounting in humans is related to certain features of the human discounting tasks. Key differences in the procedures used in humans and nonhumans probably explain the species differences in drug effects in discounting.

Ethanol

One of the earliest studies to examine the effects of a drug on delay discounting assessed the effects of moderate doses of ethanol in nonproblem social drinkers (Richards, Zhang, Mitchell, & de Wit, 1999). In this study, 24 young adults participated in two sessions in which they received ethanol (0.5 g/kg, $N = 12$, or 0.8 g/kg, $N = 12$) or placebo beverages under double-blind conditions. Twenty minutes after ingesting the beverage, participants completed an adjusting-amount procedure designed to measure delay discounting. In this procedure, the delayed option was always $10 and the immediate option was a smaller amount of money, which varied systematically across trials depending on the participant's last choice until an indifference point was reached. Indifference points were determined for delays of 0, 2, 30, 180, and 365 days. The options were presented as questions on a computer screen. Questions relating to the different delays were intermixed, and they were also mixed with questions regarding different probabilities of outcome. This mixture of questions reduced the chance of a bias relating either to memory of previous responses or to systematic increases or decreases in the value of the immediate option. A single trial was selected at random at the end of each session, and the outcome of the selected choice on that trial was delivered (i.e., the money was provided immediately or made available later). Delay discounting was assessed by calcu-

TABLE 8.7

Acute Effects of Drugs on Choice of the Larger–Later Reward in a Delay-Discounting Task With Human Participants

Drug	Dose	Subjects	Immediate reinforcer	Procedure	Delay range	Results	Authors
Ethanol	0, 0.5, 0.8 g/kg	Social drinkers	$10, real	Adjusting amount	0–365 days	No effect	Richards, Zhang, et al. (1999)
Ethanol	0, 0.7 g/kg	Students	$10, real	Mixed trials	0–365 days	No effect	Ortner et al. (2003)
Ethanol	0, 0.4, 0.8 g/kg	Social drinkers	$0.30; delayed with 35% probability	Experiential discounting; adjusting amount	0–60 s	0.8 g/kg increased discounting	Reynolds et al. (2006)
THC	0, 7.5, 15 mg	Marijuana users	$10, real	Adjusting amount	0–365 days	No effect	McDonald et al. (2003)
Diazepam	5, 10, 20 mg	Healthy volunteers	$10, real	Adjusting amount	0–365 days	No effect	Reynolds et al. (2004)
Bupropion	150 mg	Healthy volunteers	$10, real	Adjusting amount	0–365 days	No effect	Acheson, Reynolds, et al. (2006) Acheson and de Wit (2008)
d-amphetamine	20 mg	Healthy volunteers	$10, real	Adjusting amount	0–365 days	No effect or small decrease	Acheson and de Wit (2008); de Wit et al. (2002)
Naltrexone	50 mg	Healthy volunteers	$100, hypo-thetical	Mixed trials	0–180 days	No effect	J. M. Mitchell et al. (2007)

Note. THC = tetrahydrocannabinol.

lating the value of the k variable in the Mazur (1987) hyperbolic formula (for details, see chap. 1, this volume). Although ethanol ingestion was verified with breath alcohol levels and the drug produced its expected effects on subjective state (e.g., ratings of "feel a drug effect"), neither dose of ethanol increased discounting relative to placebo. Ortner, MacDonald, and Olmstead (2003) studied the effects of ethanol (0.7 g/kg) in healthy undergraduates ($N = 76$) in a procedure that also included a test of a salient cue that was expected to increase the motivation to drink. Discounting was assessed using a procedure described by S. H. Mitchell (1999), in which participants made choices between \$10 delivered after 0, 7, 30, 90, 180, or 365 days or smaller amounts of money now. Consistent with the Richards, Zhang, et al. (1999) study, alcohol did not increase discounting, and the cue had no effect.

Several procedural considerations may have contributed to the lack of an alcohol effect on discounting in the Richards, Zhang, et al. (1999) and Ortner et al. (2003) studies. The first is a key concern with many of the studies with humans: that participants do not experience the delays or the delayed rewards within the experimental session. For example, while they are in the intoxicated state, they make choices between one amount of money now versus another amount available after a delay of up to a year. Thus, neither the delay period nor the delivery of either reward are experienced during the session while choices are made in the drugged state. Even if immediate monetary rewards were delivered, nothing was available for immediate purchase and consumption in these laboratories. This is in contrast to animal discounting procedures, in which the animal experiences the delay under the effects of the drugs. The animals also experience both the immediate and the delayed rewards while they are under the influence of the drug. Thus, one possible reason for the lack of effect of alcohol on discounting in these human studies is that the participants did not experience the delays and delayed rewards while intoxicated. A second possible reason is that impulsive choices did not result in immediate consumable rewards; instead, all monetary consequences are delivered at the end of the session after all choices were made. Another methodological concern is that participants may remember the choices they made in previous sessions and make the same choices in subsequent sessions. Such fixed response patterns would decrease the sensitivity of the task to state changes, thereby masking any potential effect of the drug. This seems somewhat unlikely, however, because the different delays were presented in random order and intermixed with questions about probabilities.

Another study examined the acute effects of ethanol on discounting using a different procedure designed to ensure that the delays and delayed rewards are experienced in the drugged state (Reynolds & Schiffbauer, 2002). Reynolds, Richards, and de Wit (2006) used this experiential discounting task in which participants chose between a certain amount of money delivered immediately or a larger, probabilistic amount delivered after a delay of 0, 15, 30, or 60 seconds. The money was dispensed in coins immediately when it was available, and the delayed amount was delivered with a 35% chance of delivery. Healthy social drinkers ($N = 24$) were tested under three conditions: placebo, 0.4 g/kg ethanol, and 0.8 g/kg ethanol. In this procedure, in which the delays and delayed rewards are experienced in the intoxicated state, ethanol (0.8 g/kg) increased discounting. Although these findings are promising insofar as they support the common conception that alcohol increases impulsivity, the procedure has some shortcomings that raise questions about the interpretation. First, consistent selection of the more immediate option in this procedure can result in a shorter session, raising the possibility that ethanol simply affected the participants' tendency to end the session as soon as possible. Indeed, Scheres et al. (2006) have demonstrated that adding intertrial intervals to compensate for this effect results in less discounting. Second, the delayed option was provided on a probabilistic basis, raising the possibility that alcohol affected participants' sensitivity to reward probability rather than delay to reward delivery. Despite these shortcomings, the experiential discounting task is a valuable addition to the literature and may lead to a procedure that is sensitive to drug effects without these methodological confounds.

Other Drugs

The Richards, Zhang, et al. (1999) procedure described earlier has also been used to test acute effects of several other drugs; however, these studies also found no effects or modest drug effects. Drugs that did not alter discounting include tetrahydrocannabinol (7.5 milligrams, 15 milligrams; McDonald, Schleifer, Richards, & de Wit, 2003), diazepam (5, 10, and 20 milligrams; Acheson, Reynolds, Richardson, & de Wit, 2006; Reynolds, Richards, Dassenger, & de Wit, 2004), and bupropion (Acheson & de Wit, 2008). The effects of d-amphetamine were inconsistent: de Wit, Enggasser, and Richards (2002) found that d-amphetamine (20 milligrams) slightly decreased k values in 36 healthy young adults, compared with a placebo condition, but in a more recent study (Acheson & de Wit, 2008) d-amphetamine (20 milligrams) had no effect on k values in a similar population. A decrease in impulsivity after a stimulant drug such as amphetamine is consistent with the clinical effectiveness of stimulants to decrease impulsive symptoms in children with attention-deficit/hyperactivity disorder (American Psychiatric Association, 1994). One other study has examined the effect of an acute drug on delay discounting (J. M. Mitchell et al., 2007). These investigators tested the effect of the opioid antagonist naltrexone on discounting in people with alcoholism and healthy controls. Participants received naltrexone (50 milligrams) or placebo 3 hours before session. They were given a choice between varying amounts of money ($1, $2, $5, $10, $20, or $100) after a delay (1 week, 2 weeks, 1 month, 3 months, or 6 months) or a fraction of that amount immediately (70%, 85%, 90%, or 95%). In this study, the rewards were hypothetical, and the outcome measure was the proportion of immediate choices. As reported previously (Vuchinich & Simpson, 1998), those with alcoholism discounted more than did controls; however, naltrexone did not decrease discounting in either group.

Drug Abstinence

Several studies have examined the effects of acute abstinence from a drug (heroin or nicotine) on discounting (Table 8.8). S. H. Mitchell (2004) studied smokers ($N = 11$) after a 24-hour abstinence or normal smoking. These participants completed two delay-discounting tasks, one assessing choices between cigarettes and money and the other assessing choices between different amounts of money. Their options in the first task were $10 after 0, 7, 30, 90, 180, or 365 days or cigarettes (0–60) now, and their choices in the second task were $10 after the same range of delays or smaller amounts now, varied in $0.50 increments. These trials were intermixed with other questions assessing the effects of varying probability and amount of effort required to obtain a reward. Participants were required to remain in the laboratory for 6 hours after the task so that the opportunity to smoke after the session would not influence their responses. In the first task, cigarette withdrawal increased preference for immediate cigarettes over delayed money. In the second task, however, abstinence did not affect discounting of delayed money when the immediate alternative was money. These findings led S. H. Mitchell to conclude that withdrawal increased the value of cigarettes to smokers, but it did not increase discounting or aversion to delay more generally.

More recently, Field, Santarcangelo, Sumnall, Goudie, and Cole (2006) assessed discounting in cigarette smokers ($N = 30$) after a 13-hour abstinence or normal smoking. This study used hypothetical rewards and involved choices between two amounts of money now or later as well as between varying numbers of cigarettes now or later. Participants had a choice between £500 after a delay (1 week, 2 weeks, 1 month, 6 months, 1 year, 5 years, and 25 years in sequence) or a smaller amount of money now (beginning with 100% and systematically decreasing to 1% in 5% steps). Participants were also given choices between smaller–sooner and larger–later cigarette rewards. Measures of delay discounting indicated that smokers discounted cigarettes more than money, although this could have been related to difference in the size of the rewards (£500 vs. several cigarettes) because humans tend to discount large rewards at a lower rate than smaller rewards (see review by Green & Myerson, 2004). More important, Field et al. found that cigarette abstinence significantly increased discounting of both money and cigarettes. These authors provided a

TABLE 8.8
Effects of Acute Drug Abstinence on Choice of a Larger–Later Reward in a Delay-Discounting Task With Human Participants

Withdrawn drug	Duration of abstinence	Reward	Procedure	Delay range	Results	Authors
Nicotine	24 hour versus no abstinence	Money ($10) versus cigarettes	Mixed trials	0–365 days	Withdrawal increased value of cigarettes	S. H. Mitchell (2004)
Nicotine	24 hour versus no abstinence	Money ($10) versus money	Mixed trials	0–365 days	Withdrawal did not affect discounting	S. H. Mitchell (2004)
Nicotine	13 hour versus no abstinence	Hypothetical money (£500); cigarettes	Systematically descending immediate amounts	1 week to 25 years	Deprivation increased discounting of both money and cigarettes	Field et al. (2006)
Nicotine	3 hours, with or without nicotine patch	Hypothetical money, $100	Adjusting amount	0–10 years	No effect	Dallery and Raiff (2007)
Opioid	5 days after buprenorphine[a]	Heroin; hypothetical money, $10,000	Adjusting amount	0–25 years	Withdrawal increased discounting of both money and heroin	Giordano et al. (2002)

[a]Opiate-dependent patients received a quintuple maintenance dose of buprenorphine 5 days before the session.

thoughtful discussion of the possible reasons for the apparent discrepancy between their study and the S. H. Mitchell (2004) study, including sample size, severity of dependence, and numerous methodological differences between the studies.

A third study (Dallery & Raiff, 2007) assessed the effect of 3-hour nicotine deprivation on delay discounting. Smokers not planning to quit received nicotine (14 milligrams) or placebo patches ($n = 15$ per group) while they abstained from smoking for 3 hours. Then they completed a delay-discounting task as well as measures of mood state. The delay-discounting task was an adjusting-amount procedure with a hypothetical delayed amount of $100 (delays ranged from 1 week to 10 years with the questions presented in random order). The authors used the adjusting-amount algorithm of Johnson and Bickel (2002) to determine the discounted value of each delayed reward. Although the nicotine patch decreased negative affect, it did not significantly affect delay discounting or smoking. Whether the 3-hour deprivation period was sufficient to produce a behaviorally significant deprivation effect or whether the nicotine patch had the same effect as cigarette smoking would have had during this period is not known. Thus, one of three studies has found more extreme discounting of delayed outcomes after acute withdrawal from cigarettes. This suggests either that the effect is relatively modest and may depend on the severity of withdrawal or that procedural differences separating the existing studies hold clues about the conditions under which discounting is and is not affected by drug abstinence.

Finally, one study examined delay discounting of heroin and money in heroin abusers who were in mild opioid withdrawal (Giordano et al., 2002). Heroin abusers ($N = 13$) maintained on buprenorphine were tested 5 days after a quintuple daily dose of buprenorphine, at a time when withdrawal symptoms were beginning to appear. In separate conditions, participants were asked to choose between immediate and delayed hypothetical heroin or monetary rewards (three different magnitudes of each reward type). The amount of the immediate reward was adjusted until indifference was reached at delays ranging from 1 week to 25 years. Heroin abusers discounted heroin more than they discounted money, and when they were tested during acute withdrawal they exhibited even more pronounced discounting for both heroin and money.

Summary

Taken together, these findings provide a mixed picture of the usefulness of existing procedures to detect acute drug effects on human delay discounting. Although ethanol has generally increased discounting of delayed food rewards in laboratory rats (see Table 8.3), it has thus far not produced comparable effects in humans. This may be because human participants were asked to make decisions with no experience with the delayed rewards and no immediate outcome comparable to a food pellet that the rat may consume immediately after making an impulsive choice. Instead, the outcomes of the human's choice, if delivered at all, were delivered after the session when participants were no longer intoxicated. Although these variables may influence the sensitivity of the procedures, it should be noted that the decisions made by intoxicated humans in nonlaboratory settings may also often share this feature: Drug users make choices while intoxicated that affect their lives well into the future, when they may not be under the influence of the drug. The studies reviewed earlier also address the interesting possibility that acute abstinence may increase impulsive behavior in humans. As noted by Giordano et al. (2002), this increased propensity to make impulsive decisions during withdrawal may be an important obstacle to drug users' success in abstaining. The studies described earlier illustrate the problems associated with different delay-discounting procedures used with humans and point to the importance of developing improved, state-sensitive variations of these procedures.

CONCLUSIONS AND FUTURE DIRECTIONS

This review raises a number of methodological and theoretical issues. One key issue is whether the delay-discounting procedures in nonhumans measure the same underlying processes as delay-discounting procedures in humans (Heyman 2003; Tesch & Sanfey, 2008). For example, the time frame of delays typically used in animal studies (seconds to minutes) is very different from the days to years used in most human studies. Decisions involving these different time parameters may involve different processes. Animal studies use primary rewards such as food or sucrose, whereas human studies usually use money. These may recruit fundamentally different neural processes. And, as discussed earlier, for various reasons the human procedures may not be sensitive to state changes in impulsivity. Thus, there is an urgent need for sensitive and valid procedures to measure delay discounting in humans using procedures that are directly comparable to those used with animals. This would allow us to conduct further investigations of the genetic basis, and the neural mechanisms, underlying discounting.

REFERENCES

Acheson, A., & de Wit, H. (2008). Bupropion improves attention but does not affect impulsive behavior in healthy adults. *Experimental and Clinical Psychopharmacology, 16,* 113–123.

Acheson, A., Farrar, A. M., Patak, M., Hausknecht, K. A., Kieres, A. K., Choi, S., et al. (2006). Nucleus accumbens lesions decrease sensitivity to rapid changes in the delay to reinforcement. *Behavioural Brain Research, 173*, 217–228.

Acheson, A., Reynolds, B., Richards, J. B., & de Wit, H. (2006). Diazepam impairs behavioral inhibition but not delay discounting or risk taking in healthy adults. *Experimental and Clinical Psychopharmacology, 14*, 190–198.

American Psychiatric Association. (1994). *Diagnostic and statistical manual of mental disorders* (4th ed.). Washington, DC: Author.

Bickel, W. K., Marsch, L. A., & Carroll, M. E. (2000). Deconstructing relative reinforcing efficacy and situating the measures of pharmacological reinforcement with behavioral economics: A theoretical proposal. *Psychopharmacology (Berlin), 153*, 44–56.

Bickel, W. K., Odum, A. L., & Madden, G. J. (1999). Impulsivity and cigarette smoking: Delay discounting in current, never-, and ex-smokers. *Psychopharmacology (Berlin), 146*, 447–454.

Bizot, J.-C., Chenault, N., Houzé, B., Herpin, A., David, S., Pothion, S., & Trovero, F. (2007). Methylphenidate reduces impulsive behaviour in juvenile Wistar rats, but not in adult Wistar, SHR, and WKY rats. *Psychopharmacology (Berlin), 193*, 215–223.

Cardinal, R. N. (2006). Neural systems implicated in delayed and probabilistic reinforcement. *Neural Networks, 19*, 1277–1301.

Cardinal, R. N., Robbins, T. W., & Everitt, B. J. (2000). The effects of d-amphetamine, chlordiazepoxide, alpha-flupenthixol and behavioural manipulations on choice of signalled and unsignalled delayed reinforcement in rats. *Psychopharmacology (Berlin), 152*, 362–375.

Dallery, J., & Locey, M. L. (2005). Effects of acute and chronic nicotine on impulsive choice in rats. *Behavioral Pharmacology, 16*, 15–23.

Dallery, J., & Raiff, B. R. (2007). Delay discounting predicts cigarette smoking in a laboratory model of abstinence reinforcement. *Psychopharmacology (Berlin), 190*, 485–496.

de Wit, H. (2009). Impulsivity as a determinant and consequence of drug use: A review of underlying processes. *Addiction Biology, 14*, 22–31.

de Wit, H., Enggasser, J. L., & Richards, J. B. (2002). Acute administration of d-amphetamine decreases impulsivity in healthy volunteers. *Neuropsychopharmacology, 27*, 813–825.

Duffy, J. D. (1995). The neurology of alcoholic denial: Implications for assessment and treatment. *Canadian Journal of Psychiatry, 40*, 257–263.

Evenden, J. L., & Ryan, C. N. (1996). The pharmacology of impulsive behavior in rats: The effects of drugs on response choice with varying delays of reinforcement. *Psychopharmacology (Berlin), 128*, 161–170.

Evenden, J. L., & Ryan, C. N. (1999). The pharmacology of impulsive behavior in rats VI: The effects of ethanol and selective serotonergic drugs on response choice with varying delays of reinforcement. *Psychopharmacology (Berlin)*, *146*, 413–421.

Field, M., Santarcangelo, M., Sumnall, H., Goudie, A., & Cole, J. (2006). Delay discounting and the behavioural economics of cigarette purchases in smokers: The effects of nicotine deprivation. *Psychopharmacology (Berlin)*, *186*, 255–263.

Floresco, S. B., Tse, M. T., & Ghods-Sharifi, S. (2007). Dopaminergic and glutamatergic regulation of effort- and delay-based decision making. *Neuropsychopharmocology*, *30*, 1–14.

Giordano, L. A., Bickel, W. K., Loewenstein, G., Jacobs, E. A., Marsch, L., & Badger, G. J. (2002). Mild opioid deprivation increases the degree that outpatients discount delayed heroin and money. *Psychopharmacology (Berlin)*, *163*, 174–182.

Graham, K. (1980). Theories of intoxicated aggression. *Canadian Journal of Behavior Science*, *12*, 141–158.

Green, L., & Myerson, J. (2004). A discounting framework for choice with delayed and probabilistic rewards. *Psychological Review*, *130*, 769–792.

Helms, C. M., Reeves, J. M., & Mitchell, S. H. (2006). Impact of strain and D-amphetamine on impulsivity (delay discounting) in inbred mice. *Psychopharmacology (Berlin)*, *188*, 144–151.

Heyman, G. M. (2003). The remarkable agreement between people and pigeons concerning rewards delayed: Comments on Suzanne Mitchell's paper. In N. Heather, & R. Vuchinich (Eds.), *Choice, behavioral economics, and addiction* (pp. 358–362). New York: Elsevier.

Isles, A. R., Humby, T., & Wilkinson, L. S. (2003). Measuring impulsivity in mice using a novel operant delayed reinforcement task: Effects of behavioural manipulations and d-amphetamine. *Pharmacology*, *170*, 376–382.

Johnson, M. W., & Bickel, W. K. (2002). Within-subject comparison of real and hypothetical money rewards in delay discounting. *Journal of the Experimental Analysis of Behavior*, *77*, 129–146.

Kheramin, S., Body, S., Ho, M. Y., Velazquez-Martinez, D. N., Bradshaw, C. M., Szabadi, E., et al. (2004). Effects of orbital prefrontal cortex dopamine depletion on inter-temporal choice: A quantitative analysis. *Psychopharmacology (Berlin)*, *175*, 206–214.

Kieres, A. K., Hausknecht, K. A., Farrar, A. M., Acheson, A., de Wit, H., & Richards, J. B. (2004). Effects of morphine and naltrexone on impulsive decision making in rats. *Psychopharmacology (Berlin)*, *173*, 167–174.

Logue, A. W., Tobin, H., Chelonis, J. J., Wang, R. Y., Geary, N., & Schachter, S. (1992). Cocaine decreases self-control in rats: A preliminary report. *Psychopharmacology (Berlin)*, *109*, 245–247.

Mazur, J. E. (1987). An adjusting procedure for studying delayed reinforcement. In M. L. Commons, J. E. Mazur, J. A. Nevin, & H. Rachlin (Eds.), *Quantitative analyses of behavior: V. The effect of delay and of intervening events on reinforcement value* (pp. 55–73). Hillsdale, NJ: Erlbaum.

Mazur, J. E. (1988). Estimation of indifference points with an adjusting-delay procedure. *Journal of the Experimental Analysis of Behavior, 49*, 37–47.

McDonald, J., Schleifer, L., Richards, J. B., & de Wit, H. (2003). Effects of THC on behavioral measures of impulsivity in humans. *Neuropsychopharmacology, 28*, 1356–1365.

Mitchell, J. M., Fields, H. L., White, R. L., Meadoff, T. M., Joslyn, G., Rowbothem, M. C. (2007). The Asp40 μ-opioid receptor allele does not predict naltrexone treatment efficacy in heavy drinkers. *Journal of Clinical Psychology, 27*, 112–115.

Mitchell, S. H. (1999). Measures of impulsivity in cigarette smokers and non-smokers. *Psychopharmacology (Berlin), 146*, 455–464.

Mitchell, S. H. (2004). Effects of short-term nicotine deprivation on decision-making: Delay, uncertainty and effort discounting. *Nicotine & Tobacco Research, 6*, 819–28.

Mobini, S., Body, S., Ho, M. Y., Bradshaw, C. M., Szabadi, E., Deakin, J. F., & Anderson, I. M. (2002). Effects of lesions of the orbitofrontal cortex on sensitivity to delayed and probabilistic reinforcement. *Psychopharmacology (Berlin), 160*, 290–298.

Olmstead, M. C., Hellemans, K. G. C., & Paine, T. A. (2006). Alcohol-induced impulsivity in rats: An effect of cue salience? *Psychopharmacology (Berlin), 184*, 221–228.

Ortner, C. N. M., MacDonald, T. K., Olmstead, M. C. (2003). Alcohol intoxication reduces impulsivity in the delay-discounting paradigm. *Alcohol and Alcoholism, 38*, 151–156.

Paine, T. A., Dringenberg, H. C., & Olmstead, M. C. (2003). Effects of chronic cocaine on impulsivity: Relation to cortical serotonin mechanisms. *Behavioural Brain Research, 147*, 135–147.

Perry, J. L., & Carroll, M. E. (2008). The role of impulsive behavior in drug abuse. *Psychopharmacology (Berlin), 200*, 1–26.

Pitts, R. C., & Febbo, S. M. (2004). Quantitative analyses of methamphetamine's effects on self-control choices: Implications for elucidating behavioral mechanisms of drug action. *Behavioural Processes, 66*, 213–233.

Pitts, R. C., & McKinney, A. P. (2005). Effects of methylphenidate and morphine on delay-discounting functions obtained within sessions. *Journal of the Experimental Analysis of Behavior, 83*, 297–314.

Poulos, C. X., Parker, J. L., & Le, D. A. (1998). Increased impulsivity after injected alcohol predicts later alcohol consumption in rats: Evidence for loss-of-control drinking and marked individual differences. *Behavioral Neuroscience, 112*, 1247–1257.

Reynolds, B., Richards, J. B., Dassinger, M., & de Wit, H. (2004). Therapeutic doses of diazepam do not increase impulsive behavior in humans. *Pharmacology Biochemistry and Behavior, 79*, 17–24.

Reynolds, B., Richards, J. B., & de Wit, H. (2006). Acute alcohol effects on laboratory measures of impulsive behavior in humans. *Pharmacology Biochemistry and Behavior, 83*, 194–202.

Reynolds, B., & Schiffbauer, R. (2002). Measuring state changes in human delay discounting: An experiential discounting task. *Behavioral Processes, 67*, 343–356.

Richards, J. B., Mitchell, S. H., de Wit, H., & Seiden, L. S. (1997). Determination of discount functions in rats with an adjusting-amount procedure. *Journal of the Experimental Analysis of Behavior, 67*, 353–366.

Richards, J. B., Sabol, K. E., & de Wit, H. (1999). Effects of methamphetamine on the adjusting amount procedure: A model of impulsive behavior in rats. *Psychopharmacology (Berlin), 146*, 432–439.

Richards, J., Zhang, L., Mitchell, S. H., & de Wit, H. (1999). Discounting by delay and probability in a model of impulsive behavior: Effects of alcohol. *Journal of the Experimental Analysis of Behavior, 71*, 121–143.

Robinson, E. S., Eagle, D. M., Mar, A. C., Bari, A., Banerjee, G., Jiang, X., et al. (2007). Similar effects of the selective noradrenaline reuptake inhibitor atomoxetine on three distinct forms of impulsivity in the rat. *Neuropsychopharmacology, 33*, 1028–1037.

Scheres, A., Dijkstra, M., Ainslie, E., Balkan, J., Reynolds, B., Sonuga-Barke, E., & Castellanos, F. X. (2006). Temporal and probabilistic discounting of rewards in children and adolescents: Effects of age and ADHD symptoms. *Neuropsychologia, 44*, 2092–2103.

Simon, N. W., Mendez, I. A., & Setlow, B. (2007). Cocaine exposure causes long-term increases in impulsive choice. *Behavioral Neuroscience, 121*, 543–549.

Steele, C. M., & Josephs, R. A. (1990). Alcohol myopia: Its prized and dangerous effects. *American Psychologist, 45*, 921–933.

Tesch, A. D., & Sanfey, A. G. (2008). Models and methods in delay discounting. In W. T. Tucker, S. Ferson, A. M. Finkel, & D. Slavin (Eds.), *Annals of the New York Academy of Sciences: Vol. 1128. Strategies for risk communication: Evolution, evidence, experience* (pp. 90–94). New York: New York Academy of Sciences.

Thiebot, M. H., le Bihan, C., Soubrie, P., & Simon, P. (1985). Benzodiazepines reduce the tolerance to reward delay in rats. *Psychopharmacology (Berlin), 86*, 147–152.

Tomie, A., Aguado, A. S., Pohorecky, L. A., & Benjamin, D. (1998). Ethanol induces impulsive-like responding in a delay-of-reward operant choice procedure: Impulsivity predicts autoshaping. *Psychopharmacologia, 139*, 376–382.

Uslaner, J. M., & Robinson, T. E. (2006). Subthalamic nucleus lesions increase impulsive action and decrease impulsive choice—Mediation by enhanced incentive motivation? *European Journal of Neuroscience, 24*, 2345–2354.

van Gaalen, M. M., van Koten, R., Schoffelmeer, A. N. M, & Vanderschuren, L. J. M. J. (2006). Critical involvement of dopaminergic neurotransmission in impulsive decision making. *Biological Psychiatry, 60*, 66–73.

Vuchinich, R. E., & Simpson, C. A. (1998). Hyperbolic temporal discounting in social drinkers and problem drinkers. *Experimental and Clinical Psychopharmacology*, 6, 292–305.

Wade, T. R., de Wit, H., & Richards, J. B. (2000). Effects of dopaminergic drugs on delayed reward as a measure of impulsive behavior in rats. *Psychopharmacology (Berlin)*, 150, 90–101.

Winstanley, C. A., Dalley, J. W., Theobald, D. E. H., & Robbins, T. W. (2003). Global 5-HT depletion attenuates the ability of amphetamine to decrease impulsive choice on a delay-discounting task in rats. *Psychopharmacology (Berlin)*, 170, 320–331.

Winstanley, C. A., Theobald, D. E. H., Dalley, J. W., Cardinal, R. N., & Robbins, T. W. (2006). Double dissociation between serotonergic and dopaminergic modulation of medial prefrontal and orbitofrontal cortex during a test of impulsive choice. *Cerebral Cortex*, 16, 106–114.

Winstanley, C. A., Theobald, D. E. H., Dalley, J. W., & Robbins, T. W. (2005). Interactions between serotonin and dopamine in the control of impulsive choice in rats: Therapeutic implications for impulse control disorders. *Neuropsychopharmacology*, 30, 669–682.

9

DELAY DISCOUNTING AS A PREDICTOR OF DRUG ABUSE

MARILYN E. CARROLL, JUSTIN J. ANKER, JAMI L. MACH,
JENNIFER L. NEWMAN, AND JENNIFER L. PERRY

Chapter 8 of this volume describes how drugs of abuse affect delay discounting. In this chapter, we take a complementary approach and discuss how impulsivity, as determined by delay discounting, affects and predicts drug-seeking behavior (e.g., chap. 7, this volume; Perry & Carroll, 2008); we focus on impulsive choice in the form of delay discounting but briefly mention other models that represent impulsive behavior (e.g., impaired inhibition) when both types of assessments can be discussed regarding particular aspects of drug abuse. We also compare several forms of drug-seeking behavior because they serve as models of drug abuse in humans, including acquisition of initial use (vulnerability to drug abuse); steady-state or maintenance of drug taking (regulated use); escalation of intake (dysregulated, binge use), a hallmark of addiction; extinction (withdrawal, abstinence) characterized by continued responding (drug seeking, craving) when drug access has been terminated; and the most challenging phase for treatment of drug abuse, reinstatement of drug seeking, generated by reexposure to the drug and/or drug-associated cues. Finally, we consider potential treatments for drug abuse that reduce impulsivity for drugs.

The writing of this chapter was supported by National Institute on Drug Abuse Grants K05 DA15267, P20 DA 024196, R01 DA02486, and R01 DA03240.

The studies reviewed in this chapter and the previous one suggest a strong relationship between impulsive choice and drug abuse. Animal models allow us to test several possible hypotheses, including the following. First, a *trait-based* perspective holds that an impulsive predisposition (delay discounting) precedes and determines the extent of drug abuse (this chapter; chap. 2, this volume). Second, a *drug-induced state* view holds that drug use increases or decreases the probability of impulsive choice in a delay-discounting paradigm (chap. 8, this volume). Third, a *third-variable* hypothesis proposes that impulsive choice and drug abuse are associated with another factor (e.g., sex, novelty reactivity, dietary proclivities) that underlies both impulsivity and drug-seeking behavior. In this review, we show how the behavioral context, such as the response requirements for drug access and the magnitude of drug reinforcement, can be manipulated to increase or decrease impulsive choice. We also show how environmental and biological factors function independently and additively to exert an influence on drug-seeking behavior at several stages of the addiction process in humans. As it becomes clearer that impulsivity appears to be a major factor contributing to problems of drug abuse, it is necessary to understand the role of impulsivity among other important predictor variables when developing prevention or treatment strategies for drug abuse and addictive behavior in general.

The chapter is organized into sections discussing (a) delay discounting for food reinforcement as a predictor of drug-seeking behavior, (b) treatment of impulsive drug use (nondrug incentives), (c) delay discounting for drug reinforcement, (d) environmental factors related to impulsivity and drug seeking, and (e) biological factors related to impulsivity and drug seeking.

DELAY DISCOUNTING FOR FOOD REINFORCEMENT AS A PREDICTOR OF DRUG-SEEKING BEHAVIOR

The role of impulsivity, assessed by delay discounting and other measures, has been shown to predict drug-seeking behavior at several phases of the addiction process. These include acquisition, maintenance, escalation, extinction, reinstatement, and ultimately treatment of drug abuse. Consideration of the separate phases is necessary because interventions that are effective in one phase may be ineffective or increase drug taking in another phase. Other measures of impulsivity, producing results that are consistent with delay discounting in relation to drug-seeking behavior, are discussed as well. Accumulating evidence has suggested that there is some agreement between impulsivity determined by different behavioral measures and subsequent drug-rewarded behavior (de Wit & Richards, 2004; Perry & Carroll, 2008), but the basic measures of impulsive choice and impaired inhibition likely measure different aspects of impulsivity (Wilhelm, Reeves, Phillips, & Mitchell, 2007). Because it is difficult to prospectively study the etiology of drug abuse in humans, our primary focus in this review is animal laboratory data, although we note relevant accounts from the human literature.

Acquisition

The *acquisition* phase of drug self-administration is defined as initial use that eventually stabilizes over a period of days to weeks to produce a steady rate of drug intake over time. In one of the first studies to examine whether impulsivity predicts drug intake in rats, Poulos, Le, and Parker (1995) allowed rats to choose between 2 food pellets that were presented immediately or 12 pellets delivered after a 15-second delay. They identified rats as high, medium, or low impulsive if they chose the smaller–sooner reward on at least 75%, 45%–60%, or 5%–30% of the trials, respectively. The high-impulsive rats subsequently consumed significantly more of a 12% ethanol solution than did the groups designated as medium- or low-impulsive. Another study using a behavioral inhibition task for food showed that mice that were more impulsive (i.e., failed to inhibit a response) subsequently consumed more ethanol than mice that were less impulsive (S. Logue, Swartz, & Wehner, 1998).

The results from the delay-discounting study (Poulos et al., 1995) were extended to female rats initially screened for high or low impulsivity using an adjusting-delay operant task (Perry, Larson, German, Madden, & Carroll, 2005). Under this schedule, adapted from Mazur (1987), choosing the larger–later food reward increased the delay to this reward on subsequent choice trials, whereas selecting the smaller–sooner reward decreased the delay to the larger–later reward. The stable mean adjusted delay (MAD) provided a measure of the average delay each rat would tolerate before switching to the smaller–sooner reward. High impulsivity (HiI) was defined as a MAD of 9 seconds or fewer, and low impulsivity (LoI) was defined as MAD of 13 seconds or more, based on empirically determined values that resulted in a bimodal distribution in a pilot study. Subsequently, HiI and LoI rats were given the opportunity to intravenously self-administer cocaine. Consistent with a trait account, a higher percentage of HiI rats than of LoI rats met the criteria for acquisition of cocaine self-administration, and the HiI rats also met the criteria in significantly fewer days ($M = 17.1$) than did the LoI rats ($M = 27.0$). Thus, high rates of delay discounting were predictive of subsequent cocaine self-administration.

This work was recently extended to compare male to female HiI and LoI rats on the acquisition of cocaine self-administration, with the inclusion of MAD distributions (Perry, Nelson, & Carroll, 2008). The frequency distribution of MAD values was similar in males and females, and it was characterized by a unimodal, skewed (right) distribution (Figure 9.1, Panel A), with 70% of both males and females having MADs of less than 9 seconds (HiI), whereas no more than 24% of either sex's MADs were equal to or greater than 13 seconds

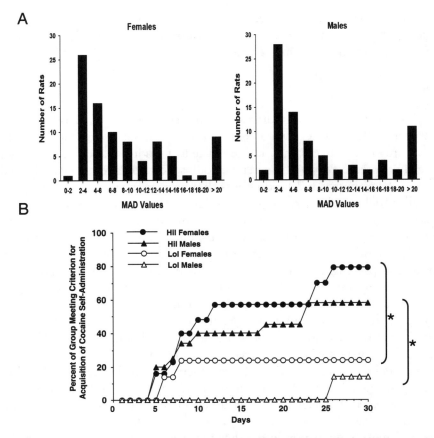

Figure 9.1. A: Distribution of rats by mean adjusted delay (MAD) value in female (left) and male (right) groups. B: Cumulative percentage of rats in each group acquiring cocaine (0.4 mg/kg) self-administration during 6-hour self-administration sessions over a 30-day acquisition period. Asterisks and brackets indicate that high-impulsivity (HiI) male and female rats acquired cocaine self-administration faster and in greater numbers per group than did their low-impulsivity (LoI) counterparts ($p < .05$). From "Impulsivity (Delay Discounting) as a Predictor of Acquisition and Reinstatement of IV Cocaine Self-Administration in Male and Female Rats," by J. L. Perry, S. E. Nelson, and M. E. Carroll, 2008, *Experimental and Clinical Psychopharmacology, 16,* pp. 168, 171. Copyright 2008 by the American Psychological Association. Reprinted with permission of the authors.

(LoI). Thus, a large proportion of the animals were considered by this definition to be high (vs. low) impulsive. These results agreed with other reports that rats are generally impulsive under a delay-discounting task in contrast to less impulsive human and nonhuman primates, although results may be dependent on specific discounting procedures and reinforcers used (Green & Estle, 2003; Tobin & Logue, 1994; Tobin, Logue, Chelonis, Ackerman, & May, 1996).

Groups of male and female HiI and LoI rats were tested for acquisition of cocaine self-administration, and HiI rats acquired faster than their LoI counterparts (Figure 9.1, Panel B). Because locomotor activity is also a predictor of acquisition of drug self-administration (Piazza, Deminiere, Le Moal, & Simon, 1989), open-field activity was measured in the HiI and LoI rats; however, they did not differ, suggesting that differences in impulsivity for food in the HiI and LoI groups were not accounted for by differences in locomotor activity (Perry et al., 2008). A recent report indicated that locomotor activity is related to acquisition of drug self-administration but not to the subsequent development of impulsive and compulsive aspects of drug addiction (Belin, Mar, Dalley, Robbins, & Everitt, 2008). The data on acquisition of cocaine self-administration obtained with delay-discounting procedures are in agreement with recent results using a five-choice serial reaction time test (5CSRT) of impulsive behavior (response inhibition) and subsequent acquisition of intravenous cocaine self-administration (Dalley et al., 2007). Impulsivity was defined as high levels of anticipatory responding before the presentation of a brief light stimulus that predicted food access. Dalley et al. (2007) and Perry et al. (2005) both found that HiI rats self-administered cocaine infusions in a shorter period of time than did LoI rats, and HiI rats had more lever responses than did LoI rats on many of the acquisition days. In the Dalley et al. study, however, infusions were limited by number and the amount of time the drug was available. With these limitations, the acquisition rates of self-administered infusions did not significantly differ in HiI versus LoI rats.

Another important finding of the Dalley et al. (2007) study was that before receiving access to cocaine self-administration, HiI and LoI rats were scanned by micro-positron emission tomography for dopamine D2/3 receptor availability in the ventral and dorsal striatum to determine whether neurochemical status differed in rats that were ultimately designated as HiI and LoI. A negative correlation was found between receptor availability in the ventral striatum and impulsivity characterized by inhibitory failure. Thus, not only did impulsivity predict more rapid cocaine self-administration, but there were preexisting neurobiological correlates. These results support the trait hypothesis that individual differences in impulsivity precede and predict vulnerability to drug abuse, but they can also be interpreted in terms of the third-variable hypothesis (e.g., that reactivity to novelty may be related to both impulsivity and cocaine self-administration; Uhl, 2007). More important, in these studies (Belin et al., 2008; Dalley et al. 2007; Perry et al., 2005, 2008) neither impulsivity nor cocaine self-administration were related to novelty-induced locomotor activity, leaving the third-variable hypothesis untenable for these studies.

These initial findings strongly suggest that impulsivity (Dalley et al., 2007; Perry et al., 2005, 2008) and nucleus accumbens dopamine D2/3 receptor availability (Dalley et al., 2007) predate the acquisition of cocaine self-administration, supporting the importance of impulsivity as a trait or endophenotype in the acquisition of drug-reinforced behavior (Dalley et al., 2007). Longitudinal studies of humans have supported this view by showing that impulsive choice in preschoolers was later correlated with adolescent social difficulties and problems associated with drug abuse (e.g., Giancola & Mezzich, 2003).

Maintenance

After acquisition of drug self-administration, there is a *maintenance* phase during which intake remains stable for extended periods depending on the length of drug availability each day. With certain drugs such as nicotine, stable intake can be maintained; however, with drugs such as psychomotor stimulants, opioids, and alcohol, intake escalates over time. There are a few studies comparing differences in impulsivity (HiI vs. LoI) during maintenance using either delay discounting (Perry et al., 2008) or the 5CSRT task (Dalley et al., 2007), and these studies have consistently shown only modest differences in drug self-administration across HiI and LoI rats. For example, both male and female groups showed no significant HiI versus LoI differences in cocaine infusions (not shown) during maintenance, and there were only slight differences in responses (LoI > HiI) in females (Figure 9.2, Panel A) on the last 2 days of maintenance (Perry et al., 2008). Similarly, more impulsive rats in the 5-CSRT task showed more responses (but not number of infusions) than did LoI rats during 15 days of acquisition (Dalley et al., 2007). In both studies, response measures showed a greater disparity (generally HiI > LoI) than did the infusion measures because of responding during cocaine infusions. This inappropriate responding may be a form of impaired inhibition. Later, in the Dalley et al. (2007) study, when cocaine dose was varied during maintenance, there was a vertical shift upward in the dose–response function in HiI rats compared with LoI rats, and the greatest HiI > LoI differences occurred at a low cocaine dose (0.25 milligram/infusion). In summary, because of the short daily access times used to study maintenance using both the adjusting-delay (Perry et al., 2008) and the 5CSRT (Dalley et al., 2007) task and/or the use of higher doses that produce ceiling effects, there were only small and inconsistent differences across studies in cocaine self-administration during the maintenance phase.

Escalation

This phase in humans is considered a hallmark of drug abuse characterized by a transition from a steady level of intake to an accelerated level of drug-seeking behavior, and it can consist of periods of dysregulated (Lynch, Arizzi, & Carroll, 2000) or binge drug use (Shaffer & Eber, 2002). *Escalation* may be defined as a significant increase in drug intake over time (e.g., 3 weeks). Drug-induced-state impulsivity may be what triggers or initiates the escalation of drug-seeking behavior, eventually resulting in compulsive repetition of the bingelike patterns (Ahmed & Koob, 1999). Escalation of drug intake can be

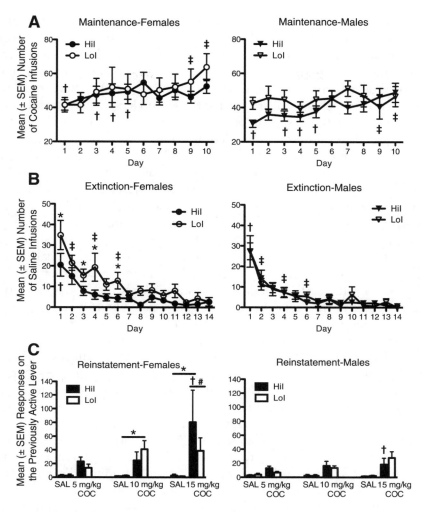

Figure 9.2. A: Mean (±*SEM*) cocaine infusions self-administered during a 10-day maintenance period in female (left) and male (right) high-impulsivity (HiI) and low-impulsivity (LoI) groups. Crosses indicate sex differences in HiI groups and double crosses represent sex differences in LoI groups, each significant at *p* < .05, and there were no phenotype differences. B: Mean (±*SEM*) saline infusions on the previously active, cocaine-paired lever during the 14-day extinction period in female (left) and male (right) HiI and LoI rats. Crosses and double crosses are described in A. C: Mean (±*SEM*) responses on the previously active, cocaine-paired lever during the reinstatement period in female (left) and male (right) HiI and LoI rats after three randomly presented priming doses of cocaine (5, 10, and 15 mg/kg), each preceded by a saline-priming injection. Asterisks indicate a cocaine (COC) versus saline (SAL) priming effect, a pound sign indicates a HiI versus LoI difference, and a plus sign shows a sex difference, all significant at *p* < .05. Adapted from "Impulsivity (Delay Discounting) as a Predictor of Acquisition and Reinstatement of IV Cocaine Self-Administration in Male and Female Rats," by J. L. Perry, S. E. Nelson, and M. E. Carroll, 2008, *Experimental and Clinical Psychopharmacology, 16,* pp.173–174. Copyright 2008 by the American Psychological Association. Adapted with permission of the authors.

modeled by providing laboratory animals with extended daily access to drug (e.g., 5–12 hours; Ahmed & Koob, 1999; Roth & Carroll, 2004). Recent studies have shown that HiI rats are more likely to escalate drug intake than are LoI rats and to respond at a higher rate when the period of drug access is subsequently reduced. For example, in the Dalley et al. (2007) study, once rats acquired cocaine self-administration and the session length was increased from 5 to 8 hours, the rats that were more impulsive on the 5CSRT task also showed a greater tendency for escalation of cocaine intake compared with their LoI counterparts. Thus, high impulsivity on the 5CSRT task was linked to higher maintenance and escalation of cocaine self-administration.

In a recent study in our laboratory, rats were preselected for HiI and LoI on the basis of MADs lower than 9 seconds and higher than 13 seconds, respectively, and a different cocaine escalation procedure was used. Figure 9.3, Panel A, shows that comparisons of the first block of 3 days to the last three blocks of 3 days during a 21-day period of 6-hour daily access revealed a significant escalation effect in the HiI group but not in the LoI group (Anker, Perry, & Carroll, 2009). In addition, before and after the 21-day escalation phase, the rats in the Anker et al. (2009) study self-administered cocaine in 2-hour sessions in which drug was available under a fixed-ratio (FR) 1 schedule. HiI rats showed a significant increase in cocaine infusions from pre- to postescalation, but LoI rats did not (Figure 9.3B). Finally, Anker et al. found that the HiI rats' postescalation cocaine infusions under a progressive ratio schedule were higher at the 0.8 mg/kg dose than during preescalation, but there was no difference in LoI rats.

The HiI versus LoI cocaine escalation results (Anker et al., 2009) concur with those of previous studies showing postescalation increases in short-access drug intake under a progressive ratio schedule in groups that escalated their drug intake, such as female rats with regular hormonal cycles (Roth & Carroll, 2004), rats with endogenous or administered estrogen (Larson, Anker, Gliddon, & Carroll, 2007), or monkeys self-administering phencyclidine (Carroll, Batulis, Landry, & Morgan, 2005). The enduring postescalation elevations in drug intake under the progressive ratio schedule suggest that escalation has produced an increase in the reward value of cocaine. Thus, if escalation of drug intake was initially attributable to impulsivity, it is possible that highly impulsive individuals are more sensitive to the rewarding effects or reward-sensitizing effects of drugs. For example, mice and rats screened as impulsive on a delay-discounting task exhibited greater locomotor sensitization after repeated exposure to ethanol (Mitchell, Reeves, Li, & Phillips, 2006) and d-amphetamine (Perry & Bardo, 2007), respectively. Also, in human participants, high levels of impulsivity predicted an enhanced euphoric response (e.g., "feel high," "feel good") to cocaine compared with low levels of impulsivity based on personality inventories (Cascella et al., 1994). Alternatively, the increased drug intake during escalation (a drug-induced state

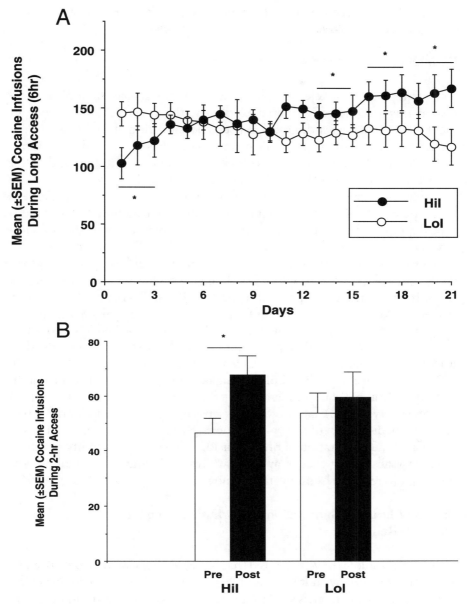

Figure 9.3. A: Mean (±*SEM*) cocaine (0.4 mg/kg) infusions over 21 days of extended access (6-hour sessions) for high-impulsivity (HiI) and low-impulsivity (LoI) groups selected on the basis of mean adjusted delay values of 9 seconds or less or 13 seconds or more, respectively. Horizontal bars indicate that the last three 3-day blocks were significantly higher than the first 3-day block in the HiI group. B: Mean (±*SEM*) cocaine (0.4 mg/kg) infusions compared during short-access (2 hour) sessions before and after the 21-day long-access (6-hour) period. The asterisk indicates that the HiI group showed a significant (*p* < .05) increase from pre– to post–long access (Anker, Perry, & Carroll, 2009).

that may have been engendered by impulsivity) could have conferred greater reward value to cocaine.

Extinction, Abstinence, and Withdrawal

This phase is modeled after the human condition of abstinence or cessation of drug use followed by a brief exposure to the drug itself and/or environmental cues that trigger drug-seeking behavior and ultimately relapse. In the model of relapse used in rats, after a maintenance phase (e.g., 14 days) of intravenous drug self-administration, saline, or vehicle is substituted for drug for 2–3 weeks while drug-seeking behavior extinguishes. Thus, responding on the active lever produces a saline infusion and infusion-paired stimuli. There is then a period of saline- or drug-primed reinstatement using different intraperitoneal drug doses or saline on alternating days. When this procedure was followed in rats that were previously selected as HiI (MAD < 9 seconds) and LoI (MAD > 13 seconds) by means of the adjusting-delay task (reinforced by food pellets), there were no HiI versus LoI differences in cocaine infusions during the 2-hour maintenance period. Figure 9.2, Panel B, indicates that when shifted to drug extinction, saline infusions were higher in LoI females than in HiI females and in males (vs. females) on Day 1, but reached low and stable levels in all groups by 7 to 8 days into extinction. The extinction response data (LoI > HiI and male > female) stand in contrast to the findings of Perry et al. (2008) for acquisition (HiI > LoI and female > male). A possible explanation for this reversal of acquisition and extinction responding is that HiI (vs. LoI) and female (vs. male) rats were more sensitive to drug and external cues, enabling them to learn the lever–drug contingency and achieve higher rates of cocaine self-administration during acquisition. Their greater ability to attend to cues (or absence of cues) may also have resulted in faster extinction when the drug was replaced by saline, thus removing the drug cues.

Effects of Drug Withdrawal on Delay Discounting for a Nondrug Reinforcer

Several studies have suggested that increased impulsivity may be a characteristic of a drug withdrawal state. Studies using laboratory animals and response inhibition models such as the 5CSRT task (e.g., Winstanley, 2007) have indicated that impulsivity increases during withdrawal from the drug state. Recent findings from our laboratory have suggested increased discounting of delayed saccharin rewards during withdrawal from orally delivered phencyclidine (PCP). In this study, male and female monkeys were tested using a two-component PCP–saccharin self-administration delay-discounting procedure. During the first component of the session, monkeys chose between orally self-administered PCP and water that were available under concurrent and independent FR 16 schedules. During the second component, discounting of a delayed saccharin liquid reinforcer was measured using an adjusting-delay procedure. After PCP self-administration stabilized, PCP was replaced with water for 14 days and discounting of delayed saccharin was measured as before. Licks at the PCP spout declined significantly when water was substituted for PCP and returned to baseline levels when PCP was reintroduced (Figure 9.4, Panel A), indicating that PCP functioned as a reinforcer. As shown in Figure 9.4, Panel B, during PCP withdrawal (water substitution) the MAD for saccharin significantly decreased, indicating increased impulsivity,

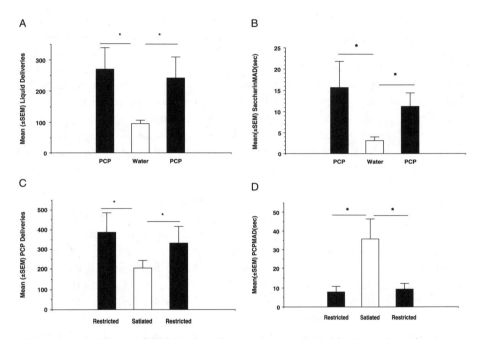

Figure 9.4. A: Mean (±*SEM*) liquid deliveries are presented for 8 monkeys for sequential conditions of phencyclidine (PCP; 0.5 mg/ml) access, PCP withdrawal (water substitution), and reinstatement of PCP access. B: Mean (±*SEM*) mean adjusted delay (MAD) values for saccharin (0.3% v/v) that was available under an adjusting-delay schedule. The asterisks indicate significant decreases in liquid deliveries (A) and MAD values (B) during PCP withdrawal (Carroll, Mach, & Newman, 2009). C: Mean (±*SEM*) total PCP deliveries per session from both the smaller–sooner (1 delivery) and the larger–later (12 deliveries) choices for 8 monkeys that orally self-administered PCP (0.25 mg/ml) under an adjusting-delay procedure during sequential periods of food restriction (85% of free-feeding body weight), satiation (ad libitum access to food), and food restriction for 2–3 weeks per condition. The asterisks indicate a significant ($p < .05$) decrease in PCP intake due to food satiation. D: MAD (±SEM) values corresponding to PCP self-administration in C. The asterisks indicate that the MAD during the satiation condition was significantly ($p < .05$) higher than the restriction conditions, indicating lower impulsivity for PCP during the food satiation condition (Carroll, Mach, & Newman, 2009).

and it returned to previous levels when PCP was reinstated. There was no significant withdrawal effect (decreased MAD for saccharin) in female monkeys (not shown), and this was consistent with earlier work showing PCP withdrawal deficits on an operant food-rewarded task with males but not with females (Perry, Normile, Morgan, & Carroll, 2006). These results concur with previous preclinical findings that impulsivity is increased during drug withdrawal (Field, Santarcangelo, Sumnall, Goudie, & Cole, 2006; Giordano et al., 2002).

Reinstatement and Relapse

Relapse to drug-seeking behavior after a period of abstinence or withdrawal is one of the most challenging aspects of drug abuse treatment in humans. A recent study by Perry et al. (2008) used the adjusting-delay procedure with food rewards to compare HiI and LoI male and female rats on reinstatement of cocaine-seeking behavior. After the extinction phase (Figure 9.2, Panel B), rats were given intraperitoneal saline or cocaine priming injections on 6 alternating days, whereas daily cocaine doses (5 mg/kg, 10 mg/kg, 15 mg/kg) were varied nonsystematically. HiI females pressed the cocaine-associated lever at significantly higher rates after 15 mg/kg cocaine-priming injections than did LoI females and both HiI and LoI males, which did not differ from each other (Figure 9.2, Panel C). Thus, high rates of delay discounting and female sex were the characteristics most predictive of reinstatement (relapse).

These results bear some similarity to the finding that response-inhibition-impulsive rats (as assessed by the go/no-go task) showed enhanced rates of responding during cocaine-primed reinstatement compared with rats with no inhibitory deficits (Deroche-Gamonet, Belin, & Piazza, 2004). In a recent study, Diergaarde et al. (2008) reported that rats selected for high (vs. low) impulsivity, using both the delay-discounting task and a test of impaired inhibition (5CSRT), showed enhanced reinstatement of nicotine-seeking behavior. Together, these findings suggest that impulsive individuals, as defined by deficits in delay discounting or impaired inhibition, may be particularly vulnerable to relapse to drug use.

The relation between delay discounting and relapse has been shown in the human literature as well. Individuals who discount delayed monetary rewards at a high rate may have a difficult time resisting abstinence-ending temptations. For example, some evidence has suggested that high rates of delay discounting are predictive of greater craving after environmental and smoking cues (Doran, Spring, & McChargue, 2007). More directly, Yoon et al. (2007) reported that rates of delay discounting were inversely related to smoking abstinence in postpartum women participating in a 1-year abstinence-contingent, voucher-based incentive program. Similar findings were reported in a clinical laboratory model of smoking relapse; participants who discounted delayed rewards at a higher rate were more likely to forgo monetary rewards for the opportunity to smoke (Dallery & Raiff, 2007). Likewise, some evidence has suggested that personality measures of impulsivity such as the Barratt Impulsivity Scale may be inversely related to retention in drug treatment (Moeller et al., 2001).

TREATMENT OF IMPULSIVE DRUG USE: NONDRUG INCENTIVES

In humans, successful treatment would be the final phase of drug abuse, and many behavioral and pharmacological approaches to treatment have been modeled with animal studies of drug abuse (e.g., Carroll, Bickel, & Higgins, 2001). Because impulsivity has a strong relationship to drug abuse, there may be advantages in having a model that considers the role of impulsivity in the treatment of drug abuse in HiI versus LoI individuals. Recent studies have shown that individuals with differing vulnerability to drug abuse respond differently to treatment. For example, female rats and monkeys (like HiI rats) show more robust acquisition (Carroll, Roth, Voeller, & Nguyen, 2000; Lynch & Carroll, 1999), escalation (Roth & Carroll, 2004), and reinstatement (Perry et al., 2008) of drug-seeking behavior than do males, but paradoxically, females are also more responsive than males to both behavioral (e.g., Cosgrove & Carroll, 2003) and pharmacological (e.g., Cosgrove & Carroll, 2002) treatments. Because impulsivity and sex appear to be additive vulnerability factors (Perry, Nelson, Anderson, Morgan, & Carroll, 2007), one might hypothesize that HiI rats would be more affected than LoI rats by treatment attempts. However, initial clinical data have shown better treatment outcome in less impulsive individuals (Dallery & Raiff, 2007; Yoon et al., 2007). Further investigation of the role of impulsivity in treatment using animal models is needed.

In a recent study, an initial attempt was made to alter impulsivity for drug reward in monkeys by providing a nondrug incentive, food. Rhesus monkeys were exposed to the adjusting-delay procedure with oral PCP deliveries used as the smaller–sooner and larger–later reinforcers. In the first phase, monkeys were food restricted (85% of free-feeding weight), and stable MAD values were determined. For the next 2 weeks, monkeys were given ad libitum access to food when not in their 3-hour PCP delay-discounting sessions, and MADs were redetermined. In the final phase, the monkeys were returned to restricted feeding, and stable MADs were reassessed. The results (Figure 9.4, Panel C) show that food satiation significantly decreased total PCP intake and the MAD values were elevated, indicating greater ability to wait for delayed PCP reinforcement (Figure 9.4, Panel D). During the subsequent food restriction phase, PCP intake and MAD values returned to presatiation values, indicating that the results were because of the feeding conditions and not changes in behavior over time. These findings with food suggest that access to nondrug substances (e.g., food) reduces drug intake and impulsivity directed toward drug consumption.

DELAY DISCOUNTING FOR DRUG REINFORCEMENT

Most of the animal studies discussed earlier using delay discounting as a predictor of drug-seeking behavior have been conducted with food rewards, yet a useful model of human drug addiction would include preclinical delay discounting in which a drug of abuse serves as the reinforcer. Interpreting data from such experiments may be difficult because the self-administered drug may alter the rate of delay discounting (see chap. 8, this volume); however, results from studies combining discounting of delayed drug with other factors that affect drug taking (e.g., sex, sweet preference) may yield important information regarding interactions among these vulnerability factors. For example, a recent study conducted in our laboratory examined the rates at which delayed cocaine and food were discounted by male and female rats selectively bred for high saccharin (HiS) versus low saccharin (LoS) intake (Perry et al., 2007). An adjusting-delay procedure was used (as described earlier), and comparisons of discounting of food and cocaine were made across HiS and LoS groups. The immediate amount was one delivery, and the delayed amounts were varied systematically over three magnitudes, each tested separately. For the food groups, there were significant sex and HiS versus LoS differences in MADs. HiS rats were more impulsive than LoS rats, and female LoS rats were more impulsive than male LoS rats. In the cocaine groups, however, there were no sex or HiS and LoS differences in impulsivity (data not shown). Instead, all rats produced MAD values in the range observed with LoS rats in the food groups. The cocaine may have differentially reduced impulsivity in HiS and LoS rats (more in HiS than in LoS rats and in females than males) because HiS and female rats consumed more cocaine than did LoS and males, respectively.

Woolverton, Myerson, and Green (2007) studied discounting of delayed intravenous cocaine self-administration in rhesus monkeys. Using an adjusting-amount procedure, they determined the subjective value of a larger–later (0.2 mg/kg) cocaine infusion delivered after a range of delays. The decline in subjective value of delayed cocaine was well described by Mazur's (1987) hyperbolic discounting function, a finding consistent with extensive animal studies using food reward (e.g., Green, Myerson, Holt, Slevin, & Estle, 2004) and human studies using hypothetical and actual choices of monetary and drug reinforcers (e.g., Madden, Begotka, Raiff, & Kastern, 2003). Woolverton et al. reported that primate discounting rates were lower than those reported with rats and pigeons; however, direct comparisons are limited by the use of different procedures and reinforcers (A. W. Logue, 1988; Mazur & Logue, 1978). Thus, nonhuman primates may more closely represent a model of human impulsivity and drug abuse than rodents.

ENVIRONMENTAL FACTORS RELATED TO IMPULSIVITY AND DRUG SEEKING

In humans, environmental conditions may determine the extent to which a relationship exists between impulsivity and the development of drug abuse. In animals, the studies discussed below illustrate the importance of environmental conditions and contingencies for the extent to which impulsivity influences drug-seeking behavior.

Response Requirements

Experiments have demonstrated that impulsive choices were reduced by adding equal delays to both the immediate and the delayed reinforcers (e.g., Rachlin & Green, 1972). In a study conducted in our laboratory, we sought to determine whether similar preference reversals would be observed if equivalent amounts of work were added to the effort required to obtain immediate and delayed PCP deliveries (Newman, Perry, & Carroll, 2008). Male monkeys responded under the adjusting-delay procedure, and the FR required for both the smaller–sooner and the larger–later PCP rewards was varied from FR 8 to FR 96. At FRs 8 and 16, responding was highly impulsive (MAD = 4 seconds); however, as the FR requirement was progressively raised (from 32 to 64, and then to 96), the MAD steadily increased to nearly 40 seconds (Figure 9.5, Panel A). When the FR 8 condition was repeated after the higher FRs had been tested, MAD values significantly increased from the initial 4 seconds to 8 seconds (Figure 9.5, Panel A). This difference suggests that gradually increasing the response requirement (thus additively increasing the delay to the larger and smaller PCP delivery) may have served to train the monkeys to better tolerate delays to the larger–later outcome (cf. Mazur & Logue, 1978). Similar delay tolerance training has been successfully used in impulsive children (Schweitzer & Sulzer-Azaroff, 1988).

To control for experience with the discounting schedule, an additional group of monkeys was tested with an increase in FR values for PCP deliveries over the following progression: 8, 16, 32, 64, 96, 128, 192, and 256. This study differed from the previous one because this group had only approximately 4 to 6 weeks of experience on the delay discounting at FR 8 schedule before the FR increases began, whereas the initial group tested had a minimum of 78 weeks of training on the discounting schedule. The newer group with shorter training started at a MAD of 10 seconds for FR 8 and progressed

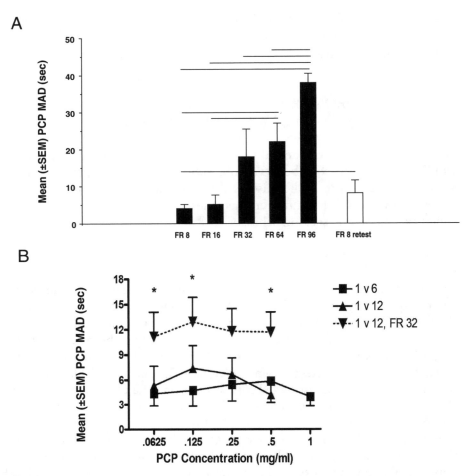

Figure 9.5. A: Mean adjusted delays (MADs; ±SEM) for phencyclidine (PCP; 0.25 mg/ml) deliveries under an adjusting-delay procedure for smaller–sooner (1 0.6-milliliter) versus larger–later (12 0.6-milliliter) PCP deliveries whereby each delivery was contingent on an fixed-ratio (FR) schedule of lip contacts on the lip-activated drinking spout. FR values for the liquid deliveries were changed from 8 to 16, 32, 64, and 96 in ascending order. Horizontal lines indicate significant differences between the FR conditions ($p < .05$). The initial FR 8 condition is compared with a retest condition under FR 8 (white bar), and the dashed line indicates a significantly higher MAD when the FR 8 condition was retested after exposure to the ascending FRs (redrawn from Newman et al., 2008). B: MADs (±*SEM*) for PCP at five concentrations (0.0625, 0.125, 0.25, 0.5, and 1.0 mg/ml) under an adjusting-delay procedure for smaller–sooner (1 0.6-milliliter) versus larger–later (6 or 12 0.6-milliliter) deliveries in rhesus monkeys that were offered a choice of 1 versus 6 deliveries (squares) or 1 versus 12 deliveries (triangles and inverted triangles). The FR for each PCP delivery was FR 8 (squares, triangles) or FR 32 (inverted triangles). Asterisks indicate a significant increase in MAD values under the 1- versus 12-delivery condition with the FR 32 per each delivery (redrawn from Newman et al., 2008).

to 15 seconds at FR 256. There was a steady increase in MAD (decreased impulsivity) as the FR for PCP increased (not shown), but it was not as dramatic as in monkeys that had longer experience with delay discounting (78 weeks). Thus, in animals with extensive schedule and drug experience, increasing the FR lowered impulsivity while only slightly reducing impulsivity in monkeys with less training. Studies have shown that training pigeons with long delays between responding and food reinforcement, and using a fading procedure to gradually reduce the delay, trains them to tolerate long delays when the training conditions have ended (Mazur & Logue, 1978). Similar behavioral modifications have been made to establish tolerance to delays to reinforcement in humans (e.g., Dixon, Rehfeldt, & Randich, 2003).

Magnitude of Reinforcement

Studies conducted with human participants have suggested that rate of delay discounting decreases as the magnitude of the larger–later reinforcer increases (i.e., an inverse relation between impulsivity and reinforcer magnitude; e.g., Johnson & Bickel, 2002). When applied to discounting of delayed drugs, one might expect lower rates of discounting with higher doses of drugs, but studies with animals have not always shown a reliable magnitude effect (Green et al., 2004; Perry et al., 2007; Richards, Mitchell, de Wit, & Seiden, 1997).

The effect of changing dose on delay discounting has been examined in nonhuman primates using a fixed-delay choice model. Anderson and Woolverton (2003) found that the value of a higher dose of cocaine was discounted less than that of smaller doses. However, using the adjusting-delay procedure, Newman et al. (2008) failed to show that MADs were affected by reinforcer magnitude determined either by concentration of PCP (0.0625–1.0 mg/ml) or the number of the delayed reinforcers (i.e., 6 deliveries vs. 12 deliveries; Figure 9.5, Panel B). However, when the FR value was increased from 8 to 32, a significant upward shift in the concentration–MAD curve was observed (Figure 9.5, Panel B). Additionally, at FR 32 (vs. FR 8) there was a significantly higher percentage of delayed (vs. immediate) choices across all four PCP concentrations, suggesting that the additional delay (on both immediate and delayed sides) imposed by a higher FR requirement may have trained the monkeys to accept longer delays and exhibit less impulsivity (Newman et al., 2008).

Reward-Associated Cues

The role of environmental stimuli in drug-seeking behavior is well documented throughout the literature, and the neural basis underlying environment, drug abuse, and behavioral inhibition has been addressed (Jentsch & Taylor, 1999). Using operant tasks such as the go/no-go procedure (Noel et al.,

2007) and the 5CSRT task (Paine, Tomasiewicz, Zhang, & Carlezon, 2007), the effects of drugs on impulsive reactions to environmental stimuli have been examined. In addition, preclinical research has also been conducted on the effects of drug-associated cues as they affect delay discounting related to drug-seeking behaviors. For example, in some studies when the delays to the larger reinforcer were not signaled, stimulants increased impulsivity in rats (e.g., Charrier & Thiebot, 1996; Evenden & Ryan, 1996; A. W. Logue et al., 1992); in others, when the delays were cued, stimulants decreased impulsivity (Richards, Sabol, & de Wit, 1999; Wade, de Wit, & Richards, 2000). However, the relation between delay-bridging stimulus cues and amphetamine effects on impulsivity are not always this clear (see chap. 8, this volume).

A few clinical studies conducted to date have shown that cigarette smokers (Doran, McChargue, & Spring, 2007; Doran, Spring, & McChargue, 2007) and alcohol-dependent participants (Noel et al., 2007) showed increased impulsive reactivity to drug-associated cues. Individuals identified as high impulsive by behavioral and personality measures are more aware, more affected by, and less resistant to reward cues than those who are less impulsive (e.g., Jentsch & Taylor, 1999). In a recent study by Doran, Spring, and McChargue (2007), a delay-discounting task was used with smokers, offering them 10 choices of 1 cigarette immediately or 2, 3, 4, 5, 6, 8, 10, 12, 15, or 20 cigarettes after a 1-hour delay. Both actual and hypothetical choices were compared, and each type of choice was studied after a neutral cue and a smoking cue had been presented, with the order of conditions counterbalanced. Impulsivity was significantly correlated with craving scores, particularly after the smoking (vs. neutral) cue, and similar results were found across the hypothetical and actual outcome conditions. These results with delay discounting are in contrast to those found by Field, Rush, Cole, and Goudie (2007), who reported that smoking cues had no effect on delay discounting, although they did increase craving. Perhaps the impulsive smokers' preference for the smaller–sooner reward is mediated by a stronger craving response such that cue exposure in impulsive smokers renders them less resistant to the immediate reward. Alternatively, there may be a third underlying neurobiological variable such as impaired dopamine, glutamate, or GABA function that mediates both the cue-related craving and impulsive choice for cigarettes.

BIOLOGICAL FACTORS RELATED TO IMPULSIVITY AND DRUG ABUSE: ADDITIVE VULNERABILITY

Selective Breeding for Sweet Preference

Reactivity to nondrug rewards such as sweet substances (Carroll, Morgan, Anker, & Perry, 2008) or physical activity (e.g., wheel running) in rats (Larson

& Carroll, 2005) can be a strong predictor of drug-seeking behavior similar to high versus low impulsivity. These studies have agreed with reports in humans showing a relationship between drug abuse, impulsivity, and reactivity to nondrug incentives (Volkow & Wise, 2005). However, in humans it is unclear whether drug abuse precedes and augments these behavioral characteristics, whether impulsivity and reward reactivity precede and facilitate drug abuse, whether the conditions coexist, or whether there is a third factor such as stress, aggression, or negative affect that explains impulsivity and its effects on drug abuse and reward seeking (e.g., Verdejo-Garcia, Bechara, Recknor, & Perez-Garcia, 2007).

In an attempt to address these questions with laboratory animals, delay discounting has been used to compare drug-seeking behavior in preselected HiI and LoI rats as well as rats that have been selectively bred for HiS and LoS intake. A proclivity for sweetened substances predicts many aspects of drug abuse (Perry et al., 2006a). For example, HiS rats consumed more ethanol than did LoS rats (Dess, Badia-Elder, Thiele, Kiefer, & Blizard, 1998). HiS rats acquired cocaine self-administration faster than did LoS rats (Carroll, Morgan, Lynch, Campbell, & Dess, 2002), and HiS rats exhibited higher levels of escalation (Perry et al., 2006a) and dysregulation (Carroll, Anderson, & Morgan, 2007) of intravenous cocaine self-administration than did LoS rats. They also reinstated cocaine-seeking behavior after a period of extinction (withdrawal) to a greater extent than did LoS rats (Perry, Morgan, Anker, Dess, & Carroll, 2006). Therefore, in many ways HiS and LoS rats show similarities to HiI and LoI rats, respectively, in drug-seeking behavior across several phases of drug abuse.

In a study recently conducted to determine whether dietary preference would interact with delay discounting and sex on measures obtained with both food and cocaine rewards (Perry et al., 2007), HiS female rats were more impulsive for food than were LoS females and both HiS and LoS males, but they did not differ for cocaine reinforcement. HiS and LoS male and female rats were also compared in a go/no-go procedure for intravenous cocaine reward to measure impaired inhibition (Anker & Carroll, 2008). In a procedure similar to that of Deroche-Gamonet et al. (2004), three 45-minute go components (cocaine self-administration at FR 1) were separated by 15-minute no-go components (extinction), with different stimuli signaling the go and no-go components. Responding during the no-go components was used as a measure of impaired inhibition impulsivity, and results were similar to the delay-discounting task. HiS rats responded more than LoS rats, especially females, and females exceeded males in the HiS groups, but there were no sex differences in LoS groups. Thus, selective breeding for HiS intake (HiS) and sex (female) additively predicted higher cocaine intake and higher impulsivity for cocaine. Others have demonstrated a relationship between avidity for sweetened dietary substances and impulsivity in both rats and humans using different procedures (Vaidya, Grippo, Johnson, & Watson, 2004).

Sex

In recent years, sex has emerged as an important variable in both human drug abuse patterns and in animal models of drug abuse (for reviews, see Carroll, Lynch, Roth, Morgan, & Cosgrove, 2004; Festa & Quinones-Jenab, 2004). Adult men are more likely than women to use drugs, but adolescent boys and girls are nearly equivalent in their use patterns (Substance Abuse and Mental Health Services Administration, 2006). Although men are more likely to have opportunities for drug use, once the opportunity occurs, women are more likely than men to transition from occasional to continued abuse (e.g., Hernandez-Avila, Rounsaville, & Kranzler, 2004).

Preclinical animal studies have indicated that females exceed males in nearly all phases of drug abuse, including acquisition, escalation, dysregulation of self-selected dose, extinction, and reinstatement (Carroll et al., 2004). In fact, the only phase in which males exceed females is in the severity of withdrawal during extinction or abstinence. For example, initial studies have suggested that male monkeys show greater withdrawal effects from PCP than do females (Perry, Normile, et al., 2006), morphine-exposed male rats show more severe physical withdrawal signs than do females (Cicero, Nock, & Meyer, 2002), and male rats show greater withdrawal from ethanol than do females (Devaud & Chadda, 2001; Gatch & Lal, 2001; Varlinskaya & Spear, 2004). In a human study, men had more evidence of alcohol withdrawal than did women (Woodstock-Striley, Cottler, & Ben Abdallah, 2004); however, in other animal studies there were no sex differences (Wessinger, 1995), opposite-sex differences (Suzuki, Koike, Yoshii, & Yanaura, 1985), or mixed results (Wessinger & Owens, 1991). Hormonal status is the major factor that explains sex differences in drug abuse. In rats, estrogen facilitated drug-seeking behavior (e.g., Anker, Larson, Gliddon, & Carroll, 2007; Larson et al., 2007), and progesterone attenuated estrogen's facilitatory effects (Anker et al., 2007; Jackson, Robinson, & Becker, 2006; Larson et al., 2007).

Although sex, hormonal influences, and impulsivity appear to have a major influence on drug-reinforced behavior, there are very few preclinical studies of sex differences in impulsivity, especially as it relates to drug abuse. In adjusting-delay procedure studies with rats responding for food pellets (Perry et al., 2007), there were no sex differences in MADs or in the number of reinforcers delivered. However, in rats selectively bred for HiS or LoS intake, sex differences emerged only in LoS rats (females > male) self-administering food but not cocaine (Perry et al., 2007). Van Haaren, van Hest, and van de Poll (1988) have also found that female rats discounted delayed food reinforcers more than did males, but this study was not related to drug self-administration.

In the drug-related studies, sex was not predictive of impulsivity, but sex, impulsivity, and saccharin intake were all strongly predictive of drug-seeking behavior. A similar study was conducted with male and female rhesus monkeys self-administering oral PCP under an adjusting-delay choice schedule (Newman et al., 2008). Consistent with the findings with cocaine and rats (Perry et al., 2007), no sex differences were found in the impulsivity measures' (MAD) values. Thus, on the basis of the initial preclinical results, it can be tentatively concluded that although sex and impulsivity are both strongly related to drug abuse, they may be only weakly related or unrelated to each other.

Clinical studies of sex differences in impulsivity have also produced inconclusive results. For example, women have lower (Kirby & Marakovic, 1996), higher (Wallace, 1979), or the same (Fillmore & Weafer, 2004; Reynolds, Richards, Dassinger, & de Wit 2004; Skinner, Aubin, & Berlin, 2004) discounting rates as men. Others have shown that women discounted hypothetical reinforcers at a higher rate than men, but they discounted actual reinforcers less than did men (Heyman & Gibb, 2006). Testing methods, stimulus conditions, and other experimental procedures may influence sex differences in impulsive behavior.

Age may also influence the ability of impulsivity to predict drug abuse in males versus females. For example, Labouvie and McGee (1986) showed that in adolescents, but not in adults, personality measures of impulsivity and drug abuse were more closely related in males than in females. Others have found that sex differences and impulsivity related to drug abuse are drug specific. For example, higher impulsivity has been reported in females (vs. males) who used nicotine, whereas impulsivity in males (but not females) was associated with elevated caffeine and alcohol use (Waldeck & Miller, 1997). Some have found no sex differences in the relationship between impulsivity and drug use (Nagoshi, Wilson, & Rodriguez, 1991), and others have reported that men showed more alcohol-induced impaired inhibition than did women (Fillmore & Weafer, 2004). Many procedural differences may account for discrepancies in the results of these studies, but the preclinical and clinical data have suggested that sex as a variable predicting drug abuse may operate independently of impulsivity.

CONCLUSION

The studies discussed in this review indicate that impulsivity is a major individual behavioral characteristic that predicts drug-seeking behavior throughout several phases of drug abuse that occur in humans and are modeled in animals. Other variables have also emerged as strong predictors, such as sex, novelty reactivity, activity level, and sweet preferences; however, some of these variables seem to be synergistic with impulsivity to produce an additive vulnerability to drug abuse (e.g., sweet preference), whereas others seem to operate independently of impulsivity (e.g., sex, novelty reactivity, and loco-motor activity).

Impulsivity has also been strongly related to other addictive behaviors such as gambling (e.g., Brewer & Potenza, 2007; Petry, 2007; Potenza, 2007) and ingestive addictive behaviors such as binge eating or other eating dis-orders (e.g., Dawe & Loxton, 2004). Drug abuse and eating disorders may share neurobiological mechanisms (e.g., Corwin & Hajnal, 2005; Grigson, 2002; Nestler, 2005; Volkow & Wise, 2005). Thus, there may be other factors underlying impulsivity that determine the relation between delay discount-ing and drug abuse, such as reactivity to drug-related cues and sweet substances and attention, memory, and learning ability. Goals for future research are to investigate the key factors responsible for the ability of impulsive behavior to predict drug-seeking behavior and to design intervention and treatment strate-gies that will reduce drug abuse and other addictions through management of impulsive behavior.

REFERENCES

Ahmed, S. H., & Koob, G. F. (1999). Long-lasting increase in the set point for cocaine self-administration after escalation in rats. *Psychopharmacology (Berlin)*, *146*, 303–312.

Anderson, K. G., & Woolverton, W. L. (2003). Effects of dose and infusion delay on cocaine self-administration choice in rhesus monkeys. *Psychopharmacology (Berlin)*, *167*, 424–430.

Anker, J. J., & Carroll, M. E. (2008). Impulsivity on a go/no-go task for i.v. cocaine and food in male and female rats selectively bred for high and low saccharin intake. *Behavioural Pharmacology*, *19*, 615–629.

Anker, J. J., Larson, E. B., Gliddon, L. A., & Carroll, M. E. (2007). Effects of prog-esterone and estrogen on reinstatement of cocaine-seeking behavior in female rats. *Experimental and Clinical Psychopharmacology*, *15*, 472–480.

Anker, J. J., Perry, J. L., & Carroll, M. E. (2009). *Impulsivity predicts the escalation of cocaine self-administration in rats*. Manuscript under review.

Belin, D., Mar, A. C., Dalley, J. W., Robbins, T. W., & Everitt, B. J. (2008, June 6). High impulsivity predicts the switch to compulsive cocaine-taking. *Science*, *320*, 1352–1355.

Brewer, J. A., & Potenza, M. N. (2007). The neurobiology and genetics of impulse control disorders: Relationships to drug addictions. *Biochemical Pharmacology*, *75*, 63–75.

Carroll, M. E., Anderson, M. M., & Morgan, A. D. (2007). Regulation of intra-venous cocaine self-administration in rats selectively bred for high (HiS) and low (LoS) saccharin intake. *Psychopharmacology (Berlin)*, *190*, 331–341.

Carroll, M. E., Batulis, D., Landry, K., & Morgan, A. D. (2005). Sex differences in the escalation of oral phencyclidine (PCP) self-administration under FR and PR schedules in rhesus monkeys. *Psychopharmacology (Berlin)*, *180*, 414–426.

Carroll, M. E., Bickel, W. K., & Higgins, S. T. (2001). Nondrug incentives to treat drug abuse: Laboratory and clinical developments. In M. E. Carroll & J. B. Overmier (Eds.), *Animal research and human psychological health: Advancing human welfare through behavioral science* (pp. 139–154). Washington, DC: American Psychological Association.

Carroll, M. E., Lynch, W. J., Roth, M. E., Morgan, A. D., & Cosgrove, K. P. (2004). Sex and estrogen influence drug abuse. *Trends in Pharmacological Science*, *25*, 273–279.

Carroll, M. E., Mach, J., & Newman, J. L. (2009). *Interactive effects of drug and nondrug rewards and their withdrawal on impulsive behavior for drug and nondrug rewards in rhesus monkeys*. Manuscript under revision.

Carroll, M. E., Morgan, A. D., Anker, J. J., & Perry, J. L. (2008) Selective breeding for differential saccharin intake as an animal model of drug abuse. *Behavioural Pharmacology*, *19*, 435–460.

Carroll, M. E., Morgan, A. D., Lynch, W. J., Campbell, U. C., & Dess, N. K. (2002). Intravenous cocaine and heroin self-administration in rats selectively bred for differential saccharin intake: Phenotype and sex differences. *Psychopharmacology (Berlin)*, *161*, 304–313.

Carroll, M. E., Roth, M. E., Voeller, R. K., & Nguyen, P. D. (2000). Acquisition of oral phencyclidine self-administration in rhesus monkeys: Effect of sex. *Psychopharmacology (Berlin)*, *149*, 401–408.

Cascella, N. G., Nagoshi, C. T., Muntaner, C., Walter, D., Haertzen, C. A., & Kumor, K. M. (1994). Impulsiveness and subjective effects of intravenous cocaine administration in the laboratory. *Journal of Substance Abuse*, *6*, 355–366.

Charrier, D., & Thiebot, M. H. (1996). Effects of psychotropic drugs on rat responding in an operant paradigm involving choice between delayed reinforcers. *Pharmacology Biochemistry and Behavior*, *54*, 149–57.

Cicero, T. J., Nock, B., & Meyer, E. R. (2002). Gender-linked differences in the expression of physical dependence in the rat. *Pharmacology Biochemistry and Behavior*, *72*, 691–697.

Corwin, R. L., & Hajnal, A. (2005). Too much of a good thing: Neurobiology of non-homeostatic eating and drug abuse. *Physiology & Behavior*, *86*, 5–8.

Cosgrove, K. P., & Carroll, M. E. (2002). Effects of bremazocine on the oral self-administration of smoked cocaine base, and orally delivered ethanol, phencyclidine, saccharin and food in rhesus monkeys: A behavioral economic analysis. *Journal of Pharmacology and Experimental Therapeutics*, *301*, 993–1002.

Cosgrove, K. P., & Carroll, M. E. (2003). Differential effects of a nondrug reinforcer, saccharin, on oral self-administration of phencyclidine (PCP) in male and female rhesus monkeys. *Psychopharmacology (Berlin)*, *170*, 9–16.

Dalley, J. W., Fryer, T. D., Brichard, L., Robinson, E. S., Theobald, D. E., Laane, K., et al. (2007, March 2). Nucleus accumbens D2/3 receptors predict trait impulsivity and cocaine reinforcement. *Science*, *315*, 1267–70.

Dallery, J., & Raiff, B. R. (2007). Delay discounting predicts cigarette smoking in a laboratory model of abstinence reinforcement. *Psychopharmacology (Berlin)*, *190*, 485–496.

Dawe, S., & Loxton, N. J. (2004). The role of impulsivity in the development of substance use and eating disorders. *Neuroscience and Biobehavioral Reviews*, *28*, 343–351.

Deroche-Gamonet, V., Belin, D., & Piazza, P. V. (2004, August 13). Evidence for addiction-like behavior in the rat. *Science*, *305*, 1014–1017.

Dess, N. K., Badia-Elder, N. E., Thiele, T. E., Kiefer, S. W., & Blizard, D. A. (1998). Ethanol consumption in rats selectively bred for differential saccharin intake. *Alcohol*, *16*, 275–278.

Devaud, L. L., & Chadda, R. (2001). Sex differences in rats in the development of and recovery from ethanol dependence assessed by changes in seizure suscepti-bility. *Alcoholism: Clinical and Experimental Research*, *25*, 1689–96.

de Wit, H., & Richards, J. B. (2004). Dual determinants of drug use in humans: Reward and impulsivity. In R. A. Bevins & M. T. Bardo (Eds.), *Nebraska Symposium on Motivation: Vol. 50. Motivational factors in the etiology of drug abuse* (pp. 19–55). Lincoln: University of Nebraska Press.

Diergaarde, L., Pattij, T., Poortvliet, I., Hogenbood, F., de Vries, W., Schoffelmeer, A. N. M., & de Vries, T. J. (2008). Impulsive choice and impulsive action predict vulnerability to distinct stages of nicotine seeking in rats. *Biological Psychiatry*, *63*, 301–308.

Dixon, M. R., Rehfeldt, R. A., & Randich, L. (2003). Enhancing tolerance to delayed reinforcers: The role of intervening activities. *Journal of Applied Behavior Analysis* *36*, 263–266.

Doran, N., McChargue, D., & Spring, B. (2007). Effect of impulsivity on cardiovas-cular and subjective reactivity to smoking cues. *Addictive Behavior*, *33*, 167–172.

Doran, N., Spring, B., & McChargue, D. (2007). Effect of impulsivity on craving and behavioral reactivity to smoking cues. *Psychopharmacology (Berlin)*, *194*, 279–288.

Evenden, J. L., & Ryan, C. N. (1996). The pharmacology of impulsive behaviour in rats: The effects of drugs on response choice with varying delays of reinforce-ment. *Psychopharmacology*, *128*, 161–170.

Festa, E. D., & Quinones-Jenab, V. (2004). Gonadal hormones provide the biologi-cal basis for sex differences in behavioral responses to cocaine. *Hormones and Behavior*, *46*, 509–519.

Field, M., Rush, M., Cole, J., & Goudie, A. (2007). The smoking Stroop and delay discounting in smokers: Effects of environmental smoking cues. *Journal of Psychopharmacology*, *21*, 603–610.

Field, M., Santarcangelo, M., Sumnall, H., Goudie, A., & Cole, J. (2006). Delay dis-counting and the behavioural economics of cigarette purchases in smokers: The effects of nicotine deprivation. *Psychopharmacology (Berlin)*, *186*, 255–263.

Fillmore, M. T., & Weafer, J. (2004). Alcohol impairment of behavior in men and women. *Addiction*, *99*, 1237–1246.

Gatch, M. B., & Lal, H. (2001). Animal models of the anxiogenic effects of ethanol withdrawal. *Drug Development Research, 54*, 95–115.

Giancola, P. R., & Mezzich, A. C. (2003). Executive functioning, temperament, and drug use involvement in adolescent females with a substance use disorder. *Journal of Child Psychology and Psychiatry, 44*, 857–866.

Giordano, L. A., Bickel, W. K., Loewenstein, G., Jacobs, E. A., Marsch, L., & Badger, G. J. (2002). Mild opioid deprivation increases the degree that opioid-dependent outpatients discount delayed heroin and money. *Psychopharmacology (Berlin), 163*, 174–182.

Green, L., & Estle, S. J. (2003). Preference reversals with food and water reinforcers in rats. *Journal of the Experimental Analysis of Behavior, 29*, 233–242.

Green, L., Myerson, J., Holt, D. D., Slevin, J. R., & Estle, S. J. (2004). Discounting of delayed food rewards in pigeons and rats: Is there a magnitude effect? *Journal of the Experimental Analysis of Behavior, 81*, 39–50.

Grigson, P. S. (2002). Like drugs for chocolate: Separate rewards modulated by common mechanisms? *Physiology & Behavior, 76*, 389–95.

Hernandez-Avila, C. A., Rounsaville, B. J., & Kranzler, H. R. (2004). Opioid-, cannabis- and alcohol-dependent women show more rapid progression to substance abuse treatment. *Drug and Alcohol Dependence, 74*, 265–272.

Heyman, G. M., & Gibb, S. P. (2006). Delay discounting in college cigarette chippers. *Behavioural Pharmacology, 17*, 669–679.

Jackson, L. R., Robinson, T. E., & Becker, J. B. (2006). Sex differences and hormonal influences on acquisition of cocaine self-administration in rats. *Neuropsychopharmacology, 31*, 129–138.

Jentsch, J. D., & Taylor, J. R. (1999). Impulsivity resulting from frontostriatal dysfunction in drug abuse: Implications for the control of behavior by reward-related stimuli. *Psychopharmacology (Berlin), 146*, 373–390.

Johnson, M. W., & Bickel, W. K. (2002.) Within-subject comparison of real and hypothetical money rewards in delay discounting. *Journal of the Experimental Analysis of Behavior, 77*, 129–146.

Kirby, K. N., & Marakovic, N. N. (1996). Delay-discounting probabilistic rewards: Rates decrease as amounts increase. *Psychonomic Bulletin & Review, 3*, 100–104.

Labouvie, E. W., & McGee, C. R. (1986). Relation of personality to alcohol and drug use in adolescence. *Journal of Consulting and Clinical Psychology, 54*, 289–293.

Larson, E. B., Anker, J. J., Gliddon, L. A., & Carroll, M. E. (2007). Effects of estrogen and progesterone on the escalation of cocaine self-administration in female rats during extended access. *Experimental and Clinical Psychopharmacology, 15*, 461–471.

Larson, E. B., & Carroll, M. E. (2005). Wheel running as a predictor of cocaine self-administration and reinstatement in rats. *Pharmacology Biochemistry and Behavior, 82*, 590–600.

Logue, A. W. (1988). Research on self-control: An integrating framework. *Behavior and Brain Sciences, 11*, 665–709.

Logue, A. W., Tobin, H., Chelonis, J. J., Wang, R. Y., Geary, N., & Schachter, S. (1992). Cocaine decreases self-control in rats: A preliminary report. *Psychopharmacology, 109*, 245–247.

Logue, S., Swartz, R. J., & Wehner, J. M. (1998). Genetic correlation between performance on an appetitive-signaled nosepoke task and voluntary ethanol consumption. *Alcoholism: Clinical and Experimental Research, 22*, 1912–1920.

Lynch, W. J., Arizzi, M. N., & Carroll, M. E. (2000). Effects of sex and the estrous cycle on regulation of intravenously self-administered cocaine in rats. *Psychopharmacology, 152*, 32–39.

Lynch, W. J., & Carroll, M. E. (1999). Sex differences in the acquisition of intravenously self-administered cocaine and heroin in rats. *Psychopharmacology, 144*, 77–82.

Madden, G. J., Begotka, A. M., Raiff, B. R., & Kastern, L. L. (2003). Delay discounting of real and hypothetical rewards. *Experimental and Clinical Psychopharmacology, 11*, 139–145.

Mazur, J. E. (1987). An adjusting procedure for studying delayed reinforcement. In M. L. Commons, J. E. Mazur, J. A. Nevin, & H. Rachlin (Eds.), *Qualitative analyses of behavior: The effect of delay and of intervening events on reinforcement value* (pp. 55–73). Hillsdale, NJ: Erlbaum.

Mazur, J. E., & Logue, A. (1978). Choice in a self-control paradigm: Effects of a fading procedure. *Journal of Experimental and Analytical Behavior, 30*, 11–17.

Mitchell, S. H., Reeves, J. M., Li, N., & Phillips, T. J. (2006) Delay discounting predicts behavioral sensitization to ethanol in outbred WSC mice. *Alcoholism: Clinical and Experimental Research, 30*, 429–437.

Moeller, F. G., Dougherty, D. M., Barratt, E. S., Schmitz, J. M., Swann, A. C., & Grabowski, J. (2001). The impact of impulsivity on cocaine use and retention in treatment. *Journal of Substance Abuse and Treatment, 21*, 193–198.

Nagoshi, C. T., Wilson, J. R., & Rodriguez, L. A. (1991). Does psychomotor sensitivity to alcohol predict subsequent alcohol use? *Alcohol: Clinical and Experimental Research, 15*, 661–667.

Nestler, E. J. (2005). Is there a common molecular pathway for addiction? *Nature Neuroscience, 8*, 1445–1449.

Newman, J. L., Perry, J. L., & Carroll, M. E. (2008). Effects of altering reinforcer magnitude and reinforcement schedule on phencyclidine (PCP) self-administration in monkeys using an adjusting delay task. *Pharmacology Biochemistry and Behavior, 90*, 778–786.

Noel, X., Van der Linden, M., d'Acremont, M., Bechara, A., Dan, B., Hanak, C., & Verbanck, P. (2007). Alcohol cues increase cognitive impulsivity in individuals with alcoholism. *Psychopharmacology (Berlin), 192*, 291–298.

Paine, T. A., Tomasiewicz, H. C., Zhang, K., & Carlezon, W. A., Jr. (2007). Sensitivity of the five-choice serial reaction time task to the effects of various psychotropic drugs in Sprague-Dawley rats. *Biological Psychiatry, 62*, 687–693.

Perry, J. L., & Bardo, M. T. (2007). [Delay discounting and sensitization to the locomotor-activating effects of d-amphetamine]. Unpublished raw data.

Perry, J. L., & Carroll, M. E. (2008). The role of impulsive behavior in drug abuse. *Psychopharmacology, 200,* 1–26.

Perry, J. L., Larson, E. B., German, J. P., Madden, G. J., & Carroll, M. E. (2005). Impulsivity (delay discounting) as a predictor of acquisition of IV cocaine self-administration in female rats. *Psychopharmacology, 178,* 193–201.

Perry, J. L., Morgan, A. D., Anker, J. J., Dess, N. K., & Carroll, M. E. (2006). Escalation of i.v. cocaine self-administration and reinstatement of cocaine-seeking behavior in rats bred for high and low saccharin intake. *Psychopharmacology, 186,* 235–245.

Perry, J. L., Nelson, S. E., Anderson, M. M., Morgan, A. D., & Carroll, M. E. (2007). Impulsivity (delay discounting) for food and cocaine in male and female rats selectively bred for high and low saccharin intake. *Pharmacology Biochemistry and Behavior, 86,* 822–837.

Perry, J. L., Nelson, S. E., & Carroll, M. E. (2008). Impulsivity (delay discounting) as a predictor of acquisition and reinstatement of IV cocaine self-administration in male and female rats. *Experimental and Clinical Psychopharmacology, 16,* 165–177.

Perry, J. L., Normile, L. M., Morgan, A. D., & Carroll, M. E. (2006). Sex differences in physical dependence on orally self-administered phencyclidine (PCP) in rhesus monkeys (*Macaca mulatta*). *Experimental and Clinical Psychopharmacology, 14,* 68–78.

Petry, N. M. (2007). Concurrent and predictive validity of the Addiction Severity Index in pathological gamblers. *American Journal of Addiction, 16,* 272–282.

Piazza, P. V., Deminiere, J. M., Le Moal, M., & Simon, H. (1989, September 29). Factors that predict individual vulnerability to amphetamine self-administration. *Science, 245,* 1511–1513.

Potenza, M. N. (2007). Impulsivity and compulsivity in pathological gambling and obsessive-compulsive disorder. *Review of Brazilian Psychiatry, 29,* 105–16.

Poulos, C. X., Le, A. D., & Parker, J. L. (1995). Impulsivity predicts individual susceptibility to high levels of alcohol self-administration. *Behavioral Pharmacology, 6,* 810–814.

Rachlin, H., & Green, H. (1972). Commitment, choice, and self-control. *Journal of the Experimental Analysis of Behavior, 17,* 15–22.

Reynolds, B., Richards, J. B., Dassinger, M., & de Wit, H. (2004). Therapeutic doses of diazepam do not alter impulsive behavior in humans. *Pharmacology Biochemistry and Behavior, 79,* 17–24.

Richards, J. B., Mitchell, S. H., de Wit, H., & Seiden, L. S. (1997). Determination of discount functions in rats with an adjusting-amount procedure. *Journal of the Experimental Analysis of Behavior, 67,* 353–366.

Richards, J. B., Sabol, K. E., & de Wit, H. (1999). Effects of methamphetamine on the adjusting amount procedure, a model of impulsive behavior in rats. *Psychopharmacology (Berlin), 146,* 432–439.

Roth, M. E., & Carroll, M. E. (2004). Sex differences in the escalation of intravenous cocaine intake following long- or short-access to cocaine self-administration. *Pharmacology Biochemistry and Behavior, 78,* 199–207.

Schweitzer, J. B., & Sulzer-Azaroff, B. (1988) Self-control: Teaching tolerance for delay in impulsive children. *Journal of the Experimental Analysis of Behavior, 50,* 173–186.

Shaffer, H. J., & Eber, G. B. (2002). Temporal progression of cocaine dependence symptoms in the US National Comorbidity Survey. *Addiction, 97,* 543–4.

Skinner, M. D., Aubin, H. J., & Berlin, I. (2004). Impulsivity in smoking, nonsmoking, and ex-smoking alcoholics. *Addictive Behavior, 29,* 973–978.

Substance Abuse and Mental Health Services Administration. (2006). *Results from the 2005 National Household Survey on Drug Use and Health: Vol. 1. Summary of national findings* (NSDUH Series H-13, DHHS Publication No. SMA 05 4062). Rockville, MD: Substance Abuse and Mental Health Services Administration, Office of Applied Studies.

Suzuki, T., Koike, Y., Yoshii, T. K., & Yanaura, S. (1985). Sex differences in the induction of physical dependence on pentobarbital in the rat. *Japanese Journal of Pharmacology, 39,* 453–459.

Tobin, H., & Logue, A. W. (1994). Self-control across species (*Columba livia, Homo sapiens,* and *Rattus norvegicus*). *Journal of Comparative Psychology, 108,* 126–133.

Tobin, H., Logue, A. W., Chelonis, J. J., Ackerman, K. T., & May, J. G., III (1996). Self-control in the monkey *Macaca fascicularis. Animal Learning and Behavior, 24,* 168–74.

Uhl, G. (2007). Premature poking: Impulsivity, cocaine and dopamine. *Nature Medicine, 13,* 413–414.

Vaidya, J. G., Grippo, A. J., Johnson, A. K., & Watson, D. (2004). A comparative developmental study of impulsivity in rats and humans: The role of reward sensitivity. In R. E. Dahl & L. P. Spear (Eds.), *Annals of the New York Academy of Sciences: Vol. 1021. Adolescent brain development: Vulnerabilities and opportunities* (pp. 395–398). New York: New York Academy of Sciences.

Van Haaren, F., van Hest, A., & van de Poll, N. E. (1988). Self-control in male and female rats. *Journal of the Experimental Analysis of Behavior, 49,* 210–211.

Varlinskaya, E. I., & Spear, L. P. (2004). Changes in sensitivity to ethanol-induced social facilitation and social inhibition from early to late adolescence. In R. E. Dahl & L. P. Spear (Eds.), *Annals of the New York Academy of Sciences: Vol. 1021. Adolescent brain development: Vulnerabilities and opportunities* (pp. 459–461). New York: New York Academy of Sciences.

Verdejo-Garcia, A., Bechara, A., Recknor, E. C., & Perez-Garcia, M. (2007). Negative emotion-driven impulsivity predicts substance dependence problems. *Drug and Alcohol Dependence, 91,* 213–19.

Volkow, N. D., & Wise, R. A. (2005). How can drug addiction help us understand obesity? *Nature Neuroscience, 8,* 555–560.

Wade, T. R., de Wit, H., & Richards, J. B. (2000). Effects of dopaminergic drugs on delayed reward as a measure of impulsive behavior in rats. *Psychopharmacology, 150,* 90–101.

Waldeck, T. L., & Miller, L. S. (1997). Gender and impulsivity differences in licit substance use. *Journal of Substance Abuse, 9,* 269–275.

Wallace, C. J. (1979). The effects of delayed rewards, social pressure, and frustration on the responses of opiate addicts. *NIDA Research Monograph, 25*, 6–25.

Wessinger, W. D. (1995). Sexual dimorphic effects of chronic phencyclidine in rats. *European Journal of Pharmacology, 277*, 107–112.

Wessinger, W. D., & Owens, S. M. (1991). Phencyclidine dependence: The relationship of dose and serum concentrations to operant behavioral effects. *Journal of Pharmacology and Experimental Therapeutics, 258*, 207–215.

Wilhelm, C. J., Reeves, J. M., Phillips, T. J., & Mitchell, S. H. (2007). Mouse lines selected for alcohol consumption differ on certain measures of impulsivity. *Alcoholism: Clinical and Experimental Research, 31*, 1839–1845.

Winstanley, C. A. (2007). The orbitofrontal cortex, impulsivity and addiction: Probing orbitofrontal dysfunction at the neural, neurochemical and molecular level. In G. Schoenbaum, J. A. Gottfried, E. A. Murray, & S. J. Ramus (Eds.), *Annals of the New York Academy of Sciences: Vol. 1121. Linking affect to action: Critical contributions of the orbitofrontal cortex* (pp. 639–655). New York: New York Academy of Sciences.

Woodstock-Striley, C., Cottler, L. B., & Ben Abdallah, A. (2004, June). *Females have less physiological dependence to alcohol than men.* Abstract presented at the 66th Annual Meeting of the College on Problems of Drug Dependence, San Juan, Puerto Rico.

Woolverton, W. L., Myerson, J., & Green, L. (2007). Delay discounting of cocaine by rhesus monkeys. *Experimental and Clinical Psychopharmacology, 15*, 238–244.

Yoon, J. H., Higgins, S. T., Heil, S. H., Sugarbaker, R. J., Thomas, C. S., & Badger, G. J. (2007). Delay discounting predicts postpartum relapse to cigarette smoking among pregnant women. *Experimental and Clinical Psychopharmacology, 15*, 176–186.

10

DISCOUNTING AND PATHOLOGICAL GAMBLING

NANCY M. PETRY AND GREGORY J. MADDEN

Pathological gambling is a disorder characterized by excessive gambling. It often occurs in conjunction with substance use disorders, and research is beginning to examine the association between these disorders, especially with regard to impulsivity and discounting. In this chapter, we initially review the diagnosis and prevalence rates of pathological gambling, including its comorbidity with substance use disorders. We then describe relations between personality measures of impulsivity and pathological gambling. Gamblers' patterns of choices on the Iowa Gambling Task (IGT) and measures of delay and probability discounting are covered in depth, and we discuss the degree to which these choices are uniquely associated with a gambling disorder rather than a comorbid substance use disorder. Recent theories regarding the role of discounting in the etiology of pathological gambling are described, as are suggestions for future research.

Preparation of this chapter was supported in part by National Institutes of Health Grants R01-MH60417, R01-MH60417-Supp, R01-MH61346-Suppl, R01-DA021567, R01-DA13444, R01-DA018883, R01-DA016855, R21-DA023564, P50-AA03510, and P50-DA09241.

PATHOLOGICAL GAMBLING DIAGNOSIS AND PREVALENCE

The *Diagnostic and Statistical Manual of Mental Disorders* (4th ed.; American Psychiatric Association, 1994) classified pathological gambling as an impulse control disorder. This disorder involves persistent and recurrent gambling that is disruptive to one's personal life, family, or vocation. To receive a diagnosis, an individual must endorse at least 5 out of 10 criteria, which include (a) preoccupation with gambling; (b) need to gamble with increasing amounts of money to maintain excitement; (c) repeated unsuccessful attempts to stop or reduce gambling; (d) restlessness and/or irritability when attempting to reduce or stop gambling; (e) gambling as a way to escape unpleasant emotions; (f) chasing losses; (g) lying to others to hide the extent of gambling; (h) committing illegal acts to finance gambling or repay debts; (i) placing a relationship, job, educational, or other opportunity in jeopardy by gambling; and (j) seeking assistance from others to relieve a dire financial situation caused by gambling.

Although not a formal diagnostic category, *problem gambling* is a term commonly used for individuals who meet some of the diagnostic criteria for pathological gambling but who do not meet five criteria necessary for a diagnosis (Petry, 2005). We use the phrase *disordered gambling* throughout this chapter to refer to the combined group of both pathological and problem gamblers.

Shaffer, Hall, and Vander Bilt (1999) published a meta-analysis of North American prevalence studies of disordered gambling conducted before 1997. Most of these surveys were conducted in specific states, geographical regions, or patient populations. They found lifetime prevalence rates of pathological gambling among adults to be 1.6% and lifetime rates of problem gambling to be 3.9%. Past-year prevalence rates were 1.1% for pathological gambling and 2.8% for problem gambling.

Three more recent, and nationally representative, surveys of prevalence rates of pathological gambling have found similar or somewhat lower prevalence rates, ranging from 0.4% to 2.0% (Gerstein et al., 1999; Petry, Stinson, & Grant, 2005; Welte, Barnes, Wieczorek, Tidwell, & Parker, 2001). In the National Gambling Impact Study, Gerstein et al. (1999) surveyed 2,417 randomly selected residents by phone. They found the lifetime prevalence rate of pathological gambling to be 0.8%, with 1.3% having lifetime problem gambling. Past-year rates were 0.1% for pathological gambling and 0.4% for problem gambling. In another phone survey of 2,638 adults throughout the country, Welte et al. (2001) found lifetime prevalence rates of pathological and problem gambling of 2.0% and 2.8%, respectively, and past-year rates of 1.3% and 2.2%. The most recent survey (Petry et al., 2005), from the National Epidemiological Survey on Alcohol and Related Disorders, is also the largest to date. This in-person survey of more than 43,000 randomly selected adults throughout the United States estimated the lifetime prevalence rate of pathological gambling at 0.4%.

COMORBIDITY OF GAMBLING AND SUBSTANCE USE DISORDERS

These national surveys also examined the associations between pathological gambling and other psychiatric conditions. In the National Gambling Impact Study, Gerstein et al. (1999) found that 9.9% of those with lifetime pathological gambling also had a lifetime diagnosis of alcohol dependence, compared with 1.1% of nongamblers. Welte et al. (2001) noted that an even higher percentage of lifetime pathological gamblers (25%) had current alcohol dependence, compared with 1.4% of nongamblers. Similarly, the National Epidemiological Survey on Alcohol and Related Disorders study (Petry et al., 2005) reported that alcohol dependence was five times higher in pathological gamblers than in nonpathological gamblers. Beyond alcohol dependence, Petry et al. (2005) found that pathological gambling increased the odds of an illicit drug use disorder by 4.4-fold, with 38.1% of lifetime pathological gamblers having one or more illicit substance use disorder compared with 8.8% of nongamblers. Thus, these three nationally representative epidemiology studies found strong evidence for an association between pathological gambling and substance use disorders.

High rates of comorbidity are noted in treatment-seeking samples as well. Shaffer et al.'s (1999) meta-analysis provided estimates of rates of pathological gambling among substance abusers. In 18 surveys of adults in treatment for substance use disorders, lifetime rates of pathological gambling were estimated at 14%, significantly higher than the 0.4% to 2.0% rate of lifetime pathological gambling found in general population surveys (Gerstein et al., 1999; Petry et al., 2005; Welte et al., 2001). Several more recent studies have reported similar proportions, with generally 10% to 13% of substance-dependent treatment-seeking individuals also meeting diagnostic criteria for pathological gambling (e.g., Cunningham-Williams, Cottler, Compton, Spitznagel, & Ben-Abdallah, 2000; Langenbucher, Bavly, Labouvie, Sanjuan, & Martin, 2001; Toneatto & Brennan, 2002). Likewise, individuals seeking treatment for pathological gambling either through Gamblers Anonymous or through a professional treatment provider are more likely to meet the diagnostic criteria for a substance use disorder than the population at large (Ibanez et al., 2001; Ladd & Petry, 2003; Maccallum & Blaszczynski, 2002; Specker, Carlson, Edmonson, & Johnson, 1996). Thus, substantial evidence, and no contradictory data, has indicated that substance use and gambling disorders co-occur. One explanation for the co-occurrence of these disorders is that both conditions may be manifestations of an underlying disorder of impulse control.

PERSONALITY MEASURES OF IMPULSIVITY IN DISORDERED GAMBLERS AND SUBSTANCE ABUSERS

Longitudinal studies have identified impulsivity in children as a risk factor for later development of substance abuse and gambling problems (Dawes, Tarter, & Kirisci, 1997; Vitaro, Arseneault, & Tremblay, 1997, 1999; White et al., 1994), and cross-sectional studies have shown that levels of impulsiveness are associated with substance use and abuse, as well as gambling, in college students (Jaffe & Archer, 1987). Numerous cross-sectional studies have demonstrated that substance-dependent patients score higher than controls on personality inventories of impulsivity (Allen, Moeller, Rhoades, & Cherek, 1998; Chalmers, Olenick, & Stein, 1993; Cookson, 1994; Eisen, Youngman, Grob, & Dill, 1992; McCormick, Taber, Kruedelbach, & Russo, 1987; Patton, Stanford, & Barratt, 1995; Rosenthal, Edwards, Ackerman, Knott, & Rosenthal, 1990; Sher & Trull, 1994). Although pathological gambling is classified as a disorder of impulse control, the relation between impulsivity and this disorder is mixed. Although some research has found high levels of impulsivity on standardized personality measures in pathological gamblers (Blaszczynski, Steel, & McConaghy, 1997; Carlton & Manowitz, 1994; McCormick et al., 1987; Steel & Blaszczynski, 1998), other research has reported either no difference or even lower scores on personality scales assessing impulsivity and related traits (Allcock & Grace, 1988; Blaszczynski, McConaghy, & Frankova, 1990; Blaszczynski, Wilson, & McConaghy, 1986; Dickerson, Hinchy, & Fabre, 1987). These discrepancies might be expected if impulsivity is correlated with substance-use disorders but not with pathological gambling. Because up to 50% of pathological gamblers have a history of drug or alcohol use disorders (Petry et al., 2005), those studies reporting a relation between impulsivity and pathological gambling may simply have drawn a larger sample of substance-dependent gamblers than other studies. Failure to report drug use histories makes it difficult to assess this hypothesis with existing data.

Another possible explanation for the discrepant findings across studies is that impulsiveness is a multidimensional construct (Gerbing, Ahadi, & Patton, 1987) that includes orientation toward the present, diminished ability to delay gratification, behavioral disinhibition, risk taking, sensation seeking, boredom proneness, reward sensitivity, hedonism, and poor planning. Some types of impulsiveness may be characteristic of substance use disorders, such as sensation seeking, and other aspects may be more closely related to pathological gambling, such as sensitivity to probabilistic rewards. Other aspects of impulsiveness may be representative of both disorders, such as present orientation, disinhibition, and poor planning (e.g., Vitaro et al., 1999). To date, sufficient data are not available examining these multiple aspects of impulsivity in pathological gamblers both with and without substance use problems.

The use of behavioral tasks to assess impulsivity may have some benefits over personality inventories in uncovering the nature of impulsivity and its relation to various other disorders. Compared with personality questionnaires, behavioral tasks may serve as more construct-relevant indicators of impulsivity. In the next sections, we describe some behavioral measures of impulsivity that have been examined in pathological gamblers both with and without substance use disorders.

IOWA GAMBLING TASK

One specific aspect of impulsiveness that can be measured behaviorally is the inability to tolerate long delays to reinforcer presentation, or preference for smaller, more immediate rewards over larger, more delayed rewards (Rachlin & Green, 1972). Ainslie (1975) extended this behavioral definition of impulsivity to include preferences for small, more immediate rewards at the expense of large delayed losses. This definition seems to characterize both substance abuse and pathological gambling. The choice to use drugs or gamble excessively may produce immediate pleasurable sensations or excitement, but these most often come at the expense of substantial long-term deterioration in legal, financial, and social status.

Bechara, Damasio, Damasio, and Anderson (1994) and Bechara, Damasio, Tranel, and Damasio (1997) developed a task that appears to capture some of Ainslie's (1975) definition of impulsiveness and has surface similarities to the long-term losses associated with heavy substance use and gambling. In the IGT, participants select cards from four different decks ranging in probability and magnitude of gains and losses. Drawing from two of the decks periodically yields a large gain (e.g., $100) but continuing to choose from these decks results in a long-term net loss because of occasional substantial losses (e.g., $150–$1,250). Selecting these decks may reflect hypersensivity to large gains and/or insensitivity to large losses—two characteristics of addictive disorders. Cards drawn from the other two decks provide smaller gains (e.g., $50) but result in a long-term net gain because the low-probability losses are more modest (e.g., $25–$250). A number of substance-abusing populations make more impulsive choices on this task than do controls, including heroin-dependent (Petry, Bickel, & Arnett, 1998), alcohol-dependent (Dom, De Wilde, Hulstijn, van den Brink, & Sabbe, 2006), and polydrug-dependent individuals (Verdejo-Garcia, Perales, & Perez-Garcia, 2007).

Several groups of investigators have administered the IGT with disordered gamblers. In the first of these studies, Petry (2001c) evaluated the performance on this task of disordered gambling substance abusers ($n = 27$), nondisordered gambling substance abusers ($n = 63$), and nondisordered gambling, non–substance-abusing controls ($n = 21$). In addition to the IGT, participants completed other measures including the Eysenck Personality Questionnaire (Eysenck & Eysenck, 1978) and Barratt Impulsiveness Scale (Patton et al., 1995), two commonly used personality measures of impulsivity. Principal-components analyses revealed that these personality inventories measured three distinct aspects of impulsiveness: impulse control, novelty seeking, and time orientation. Choices on the IGT tapped a different dimension of impulsivity and loaded on a unique factor.

In this study (Petry, 2001c), and congruent with other research (Dom et al., 2006; Petry et al., 1998; Verdejo-Garcia et al., 2007), substance abusers, regardless of gambling histories, were more likely than controls to select cards from decks containing large gains but resulting in net losses (i.e., disadvantageous decks). Disordered gambling substance abusers selected cards from these disadvantageous decks significantly more often than their nondisordered gambling counterparts. The presence of disordered gambling and substance abuse had an additive effect on scores on the personality inventories of impulsivity as well. These effects may represent a hypersensitivity to reward on the part of those with addictive disorders because they preferred the decks with higher immediate payoff. They may also reflect a relative insensitivity to punishment because these high-payoff decks were associated with greater overall losses.

Pathological gamblers without drug use disorders were not evaluated in the Petry (2001c) study, and some have suggested they may constitute a population distinct from those with substance use disorders (Blaszczynski & Nower, 2003). Recently, Goudriaan, Oosterlaan, de Beurs, and van den Brink (2006) reported that pathological gamblers with no history of drug or alcohol dependence chose from the IGT's disadvantageous decks significantly more often than did nondisordered gambling controls. Compared with controls, pathological gamblers also had a reduced skin conductance response before selecting cards from the disadvantageous decks, and they had a lower heart rate before selecting a card from an advantageous deck. After a card was selected and the winning or losing consequence revealed, all participants' heart rates decreased after a loss, but only controls evidenced an increased heart rate after drawing a winning card. The authors interpreted these differences as a reduction in reward sensitivity among the pathological gamblers.

DELAY DISCOUNTING

As noted earlier, and throughout this book, an important component of impulsivity is preference for a smaller–sooner over a larger–later reward. Such a preference suggests that the value of the larger–later reward is subjectively discounted because of the delay to its delivery. In human studies that measure the discounting of delayed rewards, participants choose between a larger–later reward and an immediate reward, the magnitude of which is adjusted until the participant is indifferent between the two. At the indifference point, the magnitude of the smaller–sooner reward provides the subjective value of the larger–later reward. When indifference points are determined across a range of delay intervals, a curve can be plotted, describing the rate at which the value of a reward decreases with increasing delays to its receipt.

A hyperbolic function generally provides a good fit of these indifference points and is an easily interpreted description of delay discounting (Mazur, 1987):

$$V_d = A/(1 + kd). \tag{1}$$

In this equation, V_d is the present value of the delayed reward (indifference point), A is the amount of the delayed reward, d is the delay duration, and k is an empirically derived constant proportional to the degree of delay discounting.

The rate at which substance abusers discount delayed outcomes has been extensively studied and is covered more comprehensively by Yi, Mitchell, and Bickel in chapter 7 of this volume. Here it is important to note only that substance abusers discount delayed rewards more rapidly than controls. For example, Madden, Petry, Badger, and Bickel (1997); Bickel, Odum, and Madden (1999); and Vuchinich and Simpson (1998) found that heroin addicts, cigarette smokers, and heavy drinkers, respectively, discounted hypothetical amounts of money more rapidly than did controls. Similar findings have been reported when there is a chance that one of the rewards selected will actually be delivered (e.g., Kirby, Petry, & Bickel, 1999).

A number of studies have examined the relation between delay discounting and pathological gambling. The first of these studies produced evidence suggesting that pathological gambling and substance use disorders have additive effects on rate of delay discounting (i.e., the value of k in Equation 1). Petry and Casarella (1999) investigated delay discounting of hypothetical monetary rewards among disordered gambling substance abusers, substance abusers with no history of gambling problems, and controls. Groups with one or more addictive disorders discounted the delayed rewards significantly more than did the controls. Furthermore, substance abusers with gambling problems discounted delayed rewards at about 3 times the rate of substance abusers without gambling problems and at nearly 10 times the rate of controls.

More recent studies have examined rates of delay discounting in disordered gamblers and nongambling control groups. Two of these studies reported that disordered gamblers discounted the value of delayed hypothetical monetary rewards at a higher rate than did a nongambling control group (Dixon, Marley, & Jacobs, 2003; MacKillop, Anderson, Castelda, Mattson, & Donovick, 2006), and one study reported no difference (Holt, Green, & Myerson, 2003). The reasons behind these discrepant findings are unclear.

Dixon et al. (2003) asked their gambling group to complete the delay-discounting task in an off-track betting parlor, and their later research (Dixon, Jacobs, & Sanders, 2006) suggested that this setting may increase rates of delay discounting when compared with the nongambling settings in which control data were collected in their earlier study. To determine whether disordered gamblers discount delay rewards more than nongamblers when data are collected in comparable settings, we compared discounting measures in the two Dixon et al. (2003, 2006) studies and found that even when disordered gamblers completed the discounting task in a nongambling setting, they discounted delayed monetary rewards at a significantly higher rate than did nongambling controls (one-way analysis of variance, $p < .001$).

A shortcoming of each of these studies is that none of them reported prevalence of substance use disorders in their samples. This is concerning because of the high rates of comorbidity outlined earlier and the known association between substance use disorders and delay discounting. Thus, across-study differences in prevalence of substance use disorders may underlie the discontinuity between some of these studies. For example, if disordered gamblers recruited in off-track betting facilities are more likely to abuse drugs or alcohol, then this might help to explain why Dixon et al. (2003) found such high rates of delay discounting in these gamblers despite their having relatively low scores on the South Oaks Gambling Screen (SOGS; Lesieur & Blume, 1987), a common measure of gambling problems.

Other studies have examined the relation between delay discounting and pathological gambling while controlling for substance use status. For example, Petry (2001b) examined discounting rates in individuals with a primary diagnosis of pathological gambling separated into groups with and without substance use problems. Discounting rates were compared between the two groups of gamblers, as well as with a control group. As in the Petry and Casarella (1999) study, both groups of pathological gamblers evidenced higher delay-discounting rates than did controls, and gamblers with substance use disorders had the highest discounting rates. It is striking that these two studies, consisting of entirely different patient samples, had nearly identical k values for individuals with the dual addictive disorders, whether their primary problem was pathological gambling or substance use. Pathological gamblers with a history of substance use disorders had median k values of 0.29 compared with 0.26 for the group with a substance use diagnosis who were identified as also having significant gambling problems. Likewise, median k values obtained from participants with one disorder (either pathological gambling or substance use) were almost identical (0.06 for "pure" pathological gamblers and 0.05 for "pure" substance abusers).

Together, these data lend some credence to the hypothesis that pathological gambling and substance use disorders lie along a continuum of delay discounting. That is, moderately high rates of discounting may be a risk factor for developing a problem with either drugs or gambling. Still higher rates of discounting might be expected to put an individual at risk of developing multiple impulse control problems such as pathological gambling and substance abuse (see chap. 9, this volume).

Alessi and Petry (2003) reanalyzed data from the 62 treatment-seeking pathological gamblers who participated in the Petry and Casarella (1999) and Petry (2001b) studies. They evaluated the hypothesis that degree of delay discounting is associated with severity of gambling disorder as measured by the SOGS. In a regression analysis, the best predictor of delay discounting, even after controlling for demographics and substance use, was SOGS scores, which accounted for 12% of the variance in k values. Similar findings were reported by MacKillop et al. (2006), who reported significant or near significant ($p = .06$) differences in k values in groups separated by gambling severity. These results suggest that severity of gambling problems is closely linked with delay discounting.

Role of Delay Discounting in Pathological Gambling

A number of researchers have hypothesized how delay-discounting rates might be predictive of substance use disorders (chaps. 7 and 9, this volume), and some of these proposals may be equally applicable to pathological gambling. For example, if the delayed aversive outcomes typically associated with pathological gambling (e.g., loss of income, deterioration of social relations, legal difficulties) are substantially discounted, then their diminished negative value may fail to deter gambling in much the same way that the long-term consequences of cigarette smoking or drug use fail to deter these behaviors in drug-dependent individuals (Odum, Madden, Badger, & Bickel, 2000; Odum, Madden, & Bickel, 2002).

As noted in chapter 1 of this volume, the hyperbolic shape of the delay-discounting function (Equation 1) predicts preference reversals between self-control and impulsive choices. That is, tendencies toward self-control (e.g., going to the movies instead of the casino with the intention of having enough money to pay the rent at the end of the month) give way to impulsive choices as the benefits of these choices become more immediately available (e.g., while driving past the casino on the way to the theater). With the immediate thrills of gambling only moments away, their value outweighs the discounted value of having enough money to pay rent at the end of the month. Because, according to Equation 1, higher rates of delay discounting increase the probability of preference reversals, pathological gamblers' delay intolerance would appear to make their road to recovery a difficult journey, filled with good intentions and frequent relapses.

A related, complementary account of the importance of delay-discounting rate in the origin of pathological gambling is Rachlin's (1990, 2000) string theory. According to this theory, gamblers take account of their wins and losses after wins. Sometimes wins occur after the first bet, and because they are immediate, they retain their full reward value. Other wins follow a string of losses such that the net income at the end of the string is a negative value. If these negative value strings were only modestly discounted, then they would deter gambling. However, high discounting rates characteristic of pathological gamblers render the delayed net loss inert. That is, when gamblers take a mental accounting of the sums of immediate undiscounted gains and delayed (and discounted) losses, the net value of gambling is substantially positive. In contrast, individuals who discount delayed outcomes at a lower rate are more likely to be affected by the net loss of funds after the long strings of losses leading up to a win. Their accounting may be closer to the reality that gambling is a net-loss activity, and this may be sufficient to keep them out of gambling settings altogether.

A final hypothesis is that the shape of the hyperbolic delay-discounting function (i.e., Equation 1) predisposes individuals with high rates of discounting to favor gambling rewards over more predictable sources of income (Madden, Ewan, & Lagorio, 2007). This account, illustrated in Figure 10.1, focuses on the unpredictable time intervals separating gambling wins. Although the time to the next gambling win is unpredictable and can fall anywhere along the x-axes of Figure 10.1, for the sake of simplicity we have plotted just five of these unpredictably delayed monetary rewards in each panel. In our laboratory, these five different delays would be equally probable—what researchers refer to as a variable-time schedule of reinforcement. The discounted values of these unpredictably delayed rewards fall along a hyperbolic discounting curve. In the top panel, the curve was plotted using Equation 1 where k was set equal to the median reported for non–drug-abusing pathological gamblers by Petry (2001b): $k = 0.07$. The lower curve was drawn using a k typical of nongambling, non–drug-abusing humans ($k = 0.003$; see Kirby, 1997). The square data point in each panel corresponds to the discounted value of a reward of equivalent magnitude delivered after a predictable delay—a delay equivalent to the average of the five unpredictable delays.

Mazur (1989) demonstrated with pigeons that the value of an unpredictably delayed reward was given by the following variant of Equation 1,

$$V_u = \sum_{i=1}^{n} P_i \left(\frac{A}{1 + kD_i} \right),$$ (2)

where V_u is the discounted value of unpredictably delayed rewards, D_i, each obtained at probability P. Because all of the delays shown in Figure 10.1 are equally probable, Equation 2 holds that the value of the five unpredictably delayed rewards is equal to the average discounted value of these rewards. This

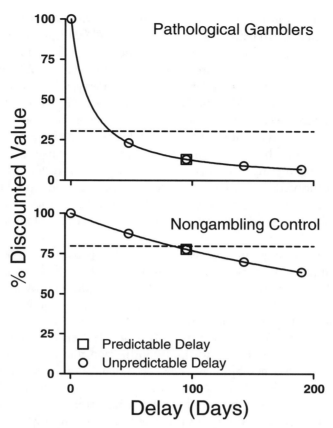

Figure 10.1. Hyperbolic discounting functions drawn using *k*s reported for non–drug-abusing pathological gamblers and nongambling non–drug-abusing controls. The average value of the unpredictably delayed (gambling-like) rewards is given by the dashed line in each panel. For pathological gamblers, the discounted value of gambling-like rewards exceeds that of the predictably delayed reward. The same is not true of controls with their lower rate of delay discounting.

average is shown as the horizontal dashed line in each panel of Figure 10.1. Because of the deeply bowed shape of the pathological gamblers' hyperbolic function, the average discounted value of the unpredictably delayed gambling rewards is 133% greater than the value of the same reward delivered after a predictable delay. Thus, Equation 1 predicts that individuals who discount delayed rewards at a high rate will view gambling rewards as substantially more valuable than the benefits of waiting a predictable amount of time to obtain the same reward (e.g., 2 weeks until the next paycheck). By contrast, the nongamblers' lower discounting rate renders their function approximately linear. For these individuals, the average of the unpredictably delayed rewards is only 2.5% greater than the predictable reward. We might, therefore, expect gambling to be an enjoyable activity, but one that is more easily forgone.

Figure 10.2 illustrates for a wide range of delay discounting rates (*ks*) the percentage increase in value obtained by choosing the unpredictably delayed gambling reward over the same reward obtained after a predictable delay. For the delay range shown in Figure 10.1 and at *ks* of 0.03 to 0.43 (the range reported for pathological gamblers by Alessi & Petry, 2003), the individual obtains a 55% to 820% added subjective reward value by choosing to gamble. This increase in the value of the gambling reward occurs because as *k* increases, the deeply bowed shape of the hyperbolic discounting curve becomes more bowed. The bowed shape of the discounting curve is responsible for enhanced preference for gambling rewards, and as this shape is accentuated, so too is the value of the unpredictably delayed reward. Thus, Equation 2 predicts that all else being equal, discounting rates are predictive of the decision to gamble and those with higher discounting rates are at greater risk of developing pathological gambling.

Several findings are consistent with this prediction. For example, pigeons tend to have very high discounting rates (usually *k* = 1.0), and this species is known to strongly prefer unpredictably delayed over predictably delayed food rewards (e.g., Mazur, 2007). Pigeons are also known to prefer the contingencies of reinforcement arranged by slot machines over predictable amounts of work to obtain food rewards (e.g., Madden & Hartman, 2006). Equation 2, which is critical to the hypothesized relation between delay-discounting rate and gambling, has been empirically verified with animal subjects (e.g., Mazur, 1991; Mazur & Romano, 1992) but has yet to be tested with humans; nevertheless, substantial evidence has indicated that Equation 1 well describes delay discounting in humans (see Green & Myerson, 2004). An important test of Equation 2 will determine whether higher rates of delay

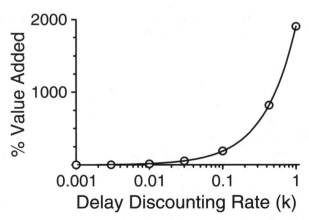

Figure 10.2. Predicted discounted value-added by selecting unpredictably delayed rewards over predictably delayed rewards. Value added is shown as a function of the rate at which delayed rewards are discounted.

discounting are predictive of stronger preferences for unpredictably delayed rewards and slot machine contingencies of reinforcement (i.e., random-ratio schedules). This research is currently underway in our laboratory.

Probability Discounting

Perhaps of even more relevance to the study of pathological gambling is probability discounting. Probability discounting refers to the devaluing of a chance outcome, and it is typically studied in humans by presenting participants with a series of choices between some amount of guaranteed money (real or hypothetical) and a larger amount of money with varying probabilities of receipt. For example, participants may choose between $20 guaranteed and a 40% chance of receiving $40. Rachlin, Raineri, and Cross (1991) proposed a hyperbolic equation that fits probabilistic discounting, in which Θ refers to the odds against, $(1 - p) / p$, receiving the probabilistic reward:

$$V = \frac{A}{1 + h\Theta}. \tag{3}$$

As in the delay-discounting equation, this equation contains a single free parameter, h, that quantifies probability discounting rate. As the free-parameter value increases, the subjective value of the outcome is more steeply discounted.

One might predict that probabilistic monetary outcomes would be discounted less in those who gamble more. That is, probabilistic rewards should retain more of their subjective value in individuals prone to gambling than in nondisordered gamblers. The single published study that has examined this hypothesis found that college-student disordered gamblers discounted probabilistic rewards less steeply than nondisordered gambling college students (Holt et al., 2003). Indices of delay discounting and probabilistic discounting were not significantly correlated, suggesting that the two indices of discounting measured unique constructs.

We recently examined probability discounting in 19 male treatment-seeking pathological gamblers (mean SOGS score = 13.3 ± 3.4). We included only those pathological gamblers without a history of substance use problems to control for any putative effect of substance use on probability discounting. We compared probability discounting between these pathological gamblers and a group of 19 nongambling, non–drug-using men matched on age, education, and income. Consistent with the study that used a less severe population of disordered gamblers (Holt et al., 2003), we found that pathological gamblers discounted probabilistic monetary wins significantly less than did controls (Madden, Petry, & Johnson, 2009). Unfortunately, across-study comparison of probability-discounting values was impossible because the two studies arranged different reward amounts and probabilities and used different methods of quantifying probability-discounting rates. Given the small number of studies that have examined probability discounting in disordered gambling populations, strong statements about the role of this process in gambling decisions must await further empirical investigations.

SUMMARY AND FUTURE DIRECTIONS

To summarize, most of the available data have suggested that pathological gambling is associated with steep discounting of delayed rewards and less steep discounting of probabilistic rewards. Some evidence has suggested that more pronounced between-group differences in delay discounting are correlated with gambling severity, and this outcome is predicted by Rachlin's (2000) string theory of gambling and by Equation 2 (Madden et al., 2007). As noted throughout this volume, substance use disorders are associated with higher rates of delay discounting and individuals with dual addictive disorders (pathological gambling and substance use disorders) have increased delay discounting compared with those with only one of the disorders. Although this relationship has not been examined with respect to probability discounting, most of the available data have suggested that the two forms of discounting are not closely associated and likely reflect different constructs of impulsivity (see chap. 3, this volume).

More important, the IGT and delay- and probability-discounting measures may be helpful in elucidating the relation between impulsivity–discounting and the development of clinical disorders. One model for this work is Walter Mischel's longitudinal studies, which suggested that the duration a 4- to 5-year-old child would wait for a large reward was predictive of social and academic competencies more than 10 years later (Mischel, Shoda, & Peake, 1988; Shoda, Mischel, & Peake, 1990). Longitudinal studies examining the relation between impulsivity and disordered gambling are thus far quite limited. One study (Vitaro et al., 1999) found that impulsivity, measured by a self-report questionnaire and a card-sorting task in early adolescence, predicted development of disordered gambling at age 17. Because questionnaire measures of impulsivity do not reliably correlate with delay discounting (e.g., Monterosso, Ehrman, Napier, O'Brien, & Childress, 2001), the role of early delay gratification abilities and subsequent development of disordered gambling remains an unstudied relation.

Tolerance for delays can be assessed in preschool children (Mischel & Metzner, 1962), and perhaps even in infants (Darcheville, Riviere, & Wearden, 1993). Therefore, the means for conducting longitudinal studies focused on predicting addictive behaviors are available and may prove an important area of future research.

To date, the study of the relation between discounting and addictive behaviors has largely taken a trait approach (i.e., documenting the correlation between discounting and the variety of addictive disorders), but there is also evidence that experiential variables can affect discounting rates (see chap. 2, this volume). Some researchers have speculated that high rates of delay discounting may be adaptive in environments in which delayed rewards are unlikely to be available after the delay (chap. 13, this volume; Williams & Dayan, 2005). Thus, a lifetime of learning not to trust others to deliver what they promise in the future may play a role in delay-discounting rates (Takahashi, Ikeda, & Hasegawa, 2007), and the tendency to take whatever is immediately available may be important in the decision to gamble or use drugs (Reynolds, Patak, & Shroff, 2007).

Consistent with a role of learning in discounting, Mischel's work has suggested that a number of cognitive strategies may help children better tolerate delays to a larger reward (Mischel, Shoda, & Rodriguez, 1989). Research conducted with animals likewise suggests that long-lasting patterns of delay tolerance can be taught even without mediating verbal strategies (e.g., Mazur & Logue, 1978), and at least one study has supported the use of a similar teaching strategy with children at risk for attention deficit/hyperactivity disorder (Schweitzer & Sulzer-Azaroff, 1988). That substance users might acquire self-control skills leading up to a successful quit attempt is supported to some extent by data suggesting that currently abstinent cigarette smokers, intravenous drug users, and people with alcoholism have lower delay-discounting rates compared with active users (Bickel et al., 1999; Bretteville-Jensen, 1999; Petry, 2001a). Further evidence for this comes from two studies demonstrating that prequit delay-discounting rates are predictive of success in interventions designed to promote cigarette abstinence (Dallery & Raiff, 2007; Yoon et al., 2007). The same hypothesis might be forwarded about the correlation between recent gambling frequency and rates of delay discounting. That is, acquired delay-tolerance skills leading up to a quit attempt might be predictive of success.

Of course, an equally viable trait-based interpretation of these findings is that some individuals with lower discounting rates will, for unrelated reasons, develop a substance use or gambling disorder, and their lower rate of discounting enhances their chances of a successful quit attempt. Whether more adaptive delay- or probability-discounting rates can be systematically taught, and the effects of such learning on clinical outcomes in pathological gambling, are important topics for future research.

A better understanding of how individuals discount rewards delayed in time and probabilistic outcomes may also serve as a theoretical construct for understanding pathological gambling. A wide literature has demonstrated that humans discount small rewards more rapidly than they do large rewards (Kirby et al., 1999; Myerson & Green, 1995; Raineri & Rachlin, 1993). By the nature of gambling, the value of an individual bet is substantially lower than the value of a win, and therefore may be discounted much more rapidly. In other words, a $1 bet may lose half its subjective value in a matter of minutes, whereas a $1,000 win will not lose half its subjective value for 1 year or more. The studies by Petry and Cassarella (1999), Petry (2001a), and Holt et al. (2003) all found disordered gamblers had greater discounting for smaller than for larger monetary rewards. As Rachlin (1990) proposed, gamblers bet in "strings," in which subjective losses are not considered until the next win occurs. Within each string, the cumulative effects of previous bets may be greatly devalued as a result of the rapid discounting of these relatively small monetary amounts.

Also of potential importance to Rachlin's (1990) string theory of gambling is how delayed losses are discounted. Some studies (Goudriaan, Oosterlaan, de Beurs, & van den Brink, 2005; Goudriaan et al., 2006; Petry, 2001b; Petry et al., 1998) have suggested that substance abusers and pathological gamblers are relatively insensitive to delayed losses. This sign effect, that gains are discounted at higher rates than losses, has not been widely investigated in substance-abusing or pathological gambling populations. However, Baker, Johnson, and Bickel (2003) found that current smokers discounted both gains and losses more rapidly than never-smokers. If pathological gamblers discount delayed losses at a particularly high rate, string theory predicts that this will make them all the more likely to gamble because the negative value of long strings of losses followed by a single win is so substantially discounted. Future examination of the sign effect in pathological gamblers, along with individuals with substance use disorders, is needed to better understand these associations.

The study of impulsivity, delay discounting, and probability discounting and their relation to disordered gambling is in its infancy. Important tests of how these processes might affect the decision to gamble have yet to be conducted. Should a particular type of discounting be shown to be an important factor in pathological gambling, then new avenues of research investigating biological, pharmacological, and learning processes may help to establish effective interventions for this disorder.

REFERENCES

Ainslie, G. (1975). Specious reward: A behavioral theory of impulsiveness and impulse control. *Psychological Bulletin, 82,* 463–496.

Alessi, S. M., & Petry, N. M. (2003). Pathological gambling severity is associated with impulsivity in a delay discounting procedure. *Behavioural Processes, 64,* 345–354.

Allcock, C. C., & Grace, D. M. (1988). Pathological gamblers are neither impulsive nor sensation-seekers. *Australian and New Zealand Journal of Psychiatry, 22,* 307–311.

Allen, T. J., Moeller, F. G., Rhoades, H. M., & Cherek, D. R. (1998). Impulsivity and history of drug dependence. *Drug and Alcohol Dependence, 50,* 137–145.

American Psychiatric Association. (1994). *Diagnostic and statistical manual of mental disorders* (4th ed.). Washington, DC: American Psychiatric Association.

Baker, F., Johnson, M. W., & Bickel, W. K. (2003). Delay discounting in current and never-before cigarette smokers: Similarities and differences across commodity, sign, and magnitude. *Journal of Abnormal Psychology, 112,* 382–392.

Bechara, A., Damasio, A. R., Damasio, H., & Anderson, S. W. (1994). Insensitivity to future consequences following damage to human prefrontal cortex. *Cognition, 50,* 7–15.

Bechara, A., Damasio, H., Tranel, D., & Damasio, A. R. (1997, February 28). Deciding advantageously before knowing the advantageous strategy. *Science, 275,* 1293–1295.

Bickel, W. K., Odum, A. L., & Madden, G. J. (1999). Impulsivity and cigarette smoking: Delay discounting in current, never, and ex-smokers. *Psychopharmacology (Berlin), 146,* 447–454.

Blaszczynski, A., McConaghy, N., & Frankova, A. (1990). Boredom proneness in pathological gambling. *Psychological Reports, 67,* 35–42.

Blaszczynski, A., & Nower, L. (2003). Imaginal desensitisation: A relaxation-based technique for impulse control disorders. *Journal of Clinical Activities, 2,* 1–14.

Blaszczynski, A., Steel, Z., & McConaghy, N. (1997). Impulsivity in pathological gambling: The antisocial impulsivist. *Addiction, 92,* 75–87.

Blaszczynski, A. P., Wilson, A. C., & McConaghy, N. (1986). Sensation seeking and pathological gambling. *British Journal of Addiction, 81,* 113–117.

Bretteville-Jensen, A. L. (1999). Addiction and discounting. *Journal of Health Economics, 18,* 393–407.

Carlton, P. L., & Manowitz, P. (1994). Factors determining the severity of pathological gambling in males. *Journal of Gambling Studies, 10,* 147–157.

Chalmers, D., Olenick, N. L., & Stein, W. (1993). Dispositional traits as risk in problem drinking. *Journal of Substance Abuse, 5,* 401–410.

Cookson, H. (1994). Personality variables associated with alcohol use in young offenders. *Personality and Individual Differences, 16,* 179–182.

Cunningham-Williams, R. M., Cottler, L. B., Compton, W. M., Spitznagel, E. L., & Ben-Abdallah, A. (2000). Problem gambling and comorbid psychiatric and substance use disorders among drug users recruited from drug treatment and community settings. *Journal of Gambling Studies, 16,* 347–376.

Dallery, J., & Raiff, B. R. (2007). Delay discounting predicts cigarette smoking in a laboratory model of abstinence reinforcement. *Psychopharmacology (Berlin), 190,* 485–496.

Darcheville, J. C., Riviere, V., & Wearden, J. H. (1993). Fixed-interval performance and self-control in infants. *Journal of the Experimental Analysis of Behavior, 60,* 239–254.

Dawes, M. A., Tarter, R. E., & Kirisci, L. (1997). Behavioral self-regulation: Correlates and 2 year follow-ups for boys at risk for substance abuse. *Drug and Alcohol Dependence, 45,* 165–176.

Dickerson, M., Hinchy, J., & Fabre, J. (1987). Chasing, arousal and sensation seeking in off-course gamblers. *British Journal of Addiction, 82,* 673–680.

Dixon, M. R., Jacobs, E. A., & Sanders, S. (2006). Contextual control of delay discounting by pathological gamblers. *Journal of Applied Behavior Analysis, 39,* 413–422.

Dixon, M. R., Marley, J., & Jacobs, E. A. (2003). Delay discounting by pathological gamblers. *Journal of Applied Behavior Analysis, 36,* 449–458.

Dom, G., De Wilde, B., Hulstijn, W., van den Brink, W., & Sabbe, B. (2006). Behavioural aspects of impulsivity in alcoholics with and without a cluster-B personality disorder. *Alcohol and Alcoholism, 41,* 412–420.

Eisen, S. V., Youngman, D. J., Grob, M. C., & Dill, D. L. (1992). Alcohol, drugs, and psychiatric disorders: A current view of hospitalized adolescents. *Journal of Adolescent Research, 7,* 250–265.

Eysenck, S. B. G., & Eysenck, H. J. (1978). Impulsiveness and venturesomeness: Their position in a dimensional system of personality description. *Psychological Reports 43,* 1247–1255.

Gerbing, D. W., Ahadi, S. A., & Patton, J. H. (1987). Toward a conceptualization of impulsivity: Components across the behavioral and self-report domains. *Multivariate Behavioral Research, 22,* 357–379.

Gerstein, D. R., Volberg, R. A., Toce, M. T., Harwood, H., Johnson, R. A., Buie, T., et al. (1999). *Gambling Impact and Behavior Study: Report to the National Gambling Impact Study Commission.* Chicago: University of Chicago, National Opinion Research Center.

Goudriaan, A. E., Oosterlaan, J., de Beurs, E., & van den Brink, W. (2005). Decision making in pathological gambling: A comparison between pathological gamblers, alcohol dependents, persons with Tourette syndrome, and normal controls. *Cognitive Brain Research, 23,* 137–151.

Goudriaan, A. E., Oosterlaan, J., de Beurs, E., & van den Brink, W. (2006). Psychophysiological determinants and concomitants of deficient decision making in pathological gamblers. *Drug and Alcohol Dependence, 84,* 231–239.

Green, L., & Myerson, J. (2004). A discounting framework for choice with delayed and probabilistic rewards. *Psychological Bulletin, 130,* 769–792.

Holt, D. D., Green, L., & Myerson, J. (2003). Is discounting impulsive? Evidence from temporal and probability discounting in gambling and non-gambling college students. *Behavioural Processes, 64,* 355–367.

Ibanez, A., Blanco, C., Donahue, E., Lesieur, H. R., Perez de Castro, I., Fernandez-Piqueras, J., et al. (2001). Psychiatric comorbidity in pathological gamblers seeking treatment. *American Journal of Psychiatry, 158,* 1733–1735.

Jaffe, L. T., & Archer, R. P. (1987). The prediction of drug use among college students from MMPI, MCMI, and sensation seeking scales. *Journal of Personality Assessment, 51,* 243–253.

Kirby, K. N. (1997). Bidding on the future: Evidence against normative discounting of delayed rewards: Rates decrease as amounts increase. *Journal of Experimental Psychology: General, 126,* 54–70.

Kirby, K. N., Petry, N. M., & Bickel, W. K. (1999). Heroin addicts have higher discount rates for delayed rewards than non-drug-using controls. *Journal of Experimental Psychology: General, 128,* 78–87.

Ladd, G. T., & Petry, N. M. (2003). A comparison of pathological gamblers with and without substance abuse treatment histories. *Experimental and Clinical Psychopharmacology, 11,* 202–209.

Langenbucher, J., Bavly, L., Labouvie, E., Sanjuan, P. M., & Martin, C. S. (2001). Clinical features of pathological gambling in an addictions treatment cohort. *Psychology of Addictive Behaviors, 15,* 77–79.

Lesieur, H. R., & Blume, S. B. (1987). The South Oaks Gambling Screen (SOGS): A new instrument for the identification of pathological gamblers. *American Journal of Psychiatry, 144,* 1184–1188.

Maccallum, F., & Blaszczynski, A. (2002). Pathological gambling and comorbid substance use. *Australian and New Zealand Journal of Psychiatry, 36,* 411–415.

MacKillop, J., Anderson, E. J., Castelda, B. A., Mattson, R. E., & Donovick, P. J. (2006). Divergent validity of measures of cognitive distortions, impulsivity, and time perspective in pathological gambling. *Journal of Gambling Studies, 22,* 339–354.

Madden, G. J., Ewan, E. E., & Lagorio, C. H. (2007). Toward an animal model of gambling: Delay discounting and the allure of unpredictable outcomes. *Journal of Gambling Studies, 23,* 63–83.

Madden, G. J., & Hartman, E. C. (2006). A steady-state test of the demand curve analysis of relative reinforcer efficacy. *Experimental and Clinical Psychopharmacology, 14,* 79–86.

Madden, G. J., Petry, N. M., Badger, G. J., & Bickel, W. K. (1997). Impulsive and self-control choices in opioid-dependent patients and non-drug-using control participants: Drug and monetary rewards. *Experimental and Clinical Psychopharmacology, 5,* 256–262.

Madden, G. J., Petry, N. M., & Johnson, P. (2009). *Pathological gamblers discount probabilistic rewards at lower rates than matched controls.* Manuscript submitted for publication.

Mazur, J. E. (1987). An adjusting procedure for studying delayed reinforcement. In M. L. Commons, J. E. Mazur, J. A. Nevin, & H. Rachlin (Eds.), *Quantitative analysis of behavior: Vol. 5. The effect of delay and of intervening events of reinforcement value* (pp. 55–73). Hillsdale, NJ: Erlbaum.

Mazur, J. E. (1989). Theories of probabilistic reinforcement. *Journal of the Experimental Analysis of Behavior, 51,* 87–99.

Mazur, J. E. (1991). Choice with probabilistic reinforcement: Effects of delay and conditioned reinforcers. *Journal of the Experimental Analysis of Behavior, 55,* 63–77.

Mazur, J. E. (2007). Choice in a successive-encounters procedure and hyperbolic decay of reinforcement. *Journal of the Experimental Analysis of Behavior, 88,* 73–85.

Mazur, J. E., & Logue, A. W. (1978). Choice in a "self-control" paradigm: Effects of a fading procedure. *Journal of the Experimental Analysis of Behavior, 30,* 11–17.

Mazur, J. E., & Romano, A. (1992). Choice with delayed and probabilistic reinforcers: Effects of variability, time between trials, and conditioned reinforcers. *Journal of the Experimental Analysis of Behavior, 58,* 513–525.

McCormick, R. A., Taber, J., Kruedelbach, N., & Russo, A. (1987). Personality profiles of hospitalized pathological gamblers: The California Personality Inventory. *Journal of Clinical Psychology, 43,* 521–527.

Mischel, W., & Metzner, R. (1962). Preference for delayed reward as a function of age, intelligence, and length of delay interval. *Journal of Abnormal Social Psychology, 64,* 425–431.

Mischel, W., Shoda, Y., & Peake, P. K. (1988). The nature of adolescent competencies predicted by preschool delay of gratification. *Journal of Personality and Social Psychology, 54,* 687–696.

Mischel, W., Shoda, Y., & Rodriguez, M. I. (1989, May 26). Delay of gratification in children. *Science, 244,* 933–938.

Monterosso, J., Ehrman, R., Napier, K. L., O'Brien, C. P., & Childress, A. R. (2001). Three decision-making tasks in cocaine-dependent patients: Do they measure the same construct? *Addiction, 96,* 1825–1837.

Myerson, J., & Green, L. (1995). Discounting of delayed rewards: Models of individual choice. *Journal of the Experimental Analysis of Behavior, 64,* 263–276.

Odum, A. L., Madden, G. J., Badger, G. J., & Bickel, W. K. (2000). Needle sharing in opioid-dependent outpatients: Psychological processes underlying risk. *Drug and Alcohol Dependence, 60,* 259–266.

Odum, A. L., Madden, G. J., & Bickel, W. K. (2002). Discounting of delayed health gains and losses by current, never-, and ex-smokers of cigarettes. *Nicotine and Tobacco Research, 4,* 295–303.

Patton, J. H., Stanford, M. S., & Barratt, E. S. (1995). Factor structure of the Barratt Impulsiveness Scale. *Journal of Clinical Psychology, 51,* 768–774.

Petry, N. M. (2001a). Delay discounting of money and alcohol in actively using alcoholics, currently abstinent alcoholics, and controls. *Psychopharmacology (Berlin), 154,* 243–250.

Petry, N. M. (2001b). Pathological gamblers, with and without substance use disorders, discount delayed rewards at high rates. *Journal of Abnormal Psychology, 110,* 482–487.

Petry, N. M. (2001c). Substance abuse, pathological gambling, and impulsiveness. *Drug and Alcohol Dependence, 63,* 29–38.

Petry, N. M. (2005). *Pathological gambling: Etiology, comorbidity, and treatment*. Washington, DC: American Psychological Association.

Petry, N. M., Bickel, W. K., & Arnett, M. (1998). Shortened time horizons and insensitivity to future consequences in heroin addicts. *Addiction, 93*, 729–738.

Petry, N. M., & Casarella, T. (1999). Excessive discounting of delayed rewards in substance abusers with gambling problems. *Drug and Alcohol Dependence, 56*, 25–32.

Petry, N. M., Stinson, F. S., & Grant, B. F. (2005). Comorbidity of DSM-IV pathological gambling and other psychiatric disorders: Results from the National Epidemiologic Survey on Alcohol and Related Conditions. *Journal of Clinical Psychiatry, 66*, 564–574.

Rachlin, H. (1990). Why do people gamble and keep gambling despite heavy losses? *Psychological Science, 1*, 294–297.

Rachlin, H. (2000). *The science of self-control*. Cambridge, MA: Harvard University Press.

Rachlin, H., & Green, L. (1972). Commitment, choice, and self-control. *Journal of the Experimental Analysis of Behavior, 17*, 15–22.

Rachlin, H., Raineri, A., & Cross, D. (1991). Subjective probability and delay. *Journal of the Experimental Analysis of Behavior, 55*, 233–244.

Raineri, A., & Rachlin, H. (1993). The effect of temporal constraints on the value of money and other commodities. *Journal of Behavioral Decision Making, 6*, 77–94.

Reynolds, B., Patak, M., & Shroff, P. (2007). Adolescent smokers rate delayed rewards as less certain than adolescent nonsmokers. *Drug and Alcohol Dependence, 90*, 301–303.

Rosenthal, T. L., Edwards, N. B., Ackerman, B. J., Knott, D. H., & Rosenthal, R. H. (1990). Substance abuse patterns reveal contrasting personal traits. *Journal of Substance Abuse, 2*, 255–263.

Schweitzer, J. B., & Sulzer-Azaroff, B. (1988). Self control: Teaching tolerance for delay in impulsive children. *Journal of the Experimental Analysis of Behavior, 50*, 173–186.

Shaffer, H. J., Hall, M. N., & Vander Bilt, J. (1999). Estimating the prevalence of disordered gambling behavior in the United States and Canada: A research synthesis. *American Journal of Public Health, 89*, 1369–1376.

Sher, K. J., & Trull, T. J. (1994). Personality and disinhibitory psychopathology: Alcoholism and antisocial personality disorder. *Journal of Abnormal Psychology, 103*, 92–102.

Shoda, Y., Mischel, W., & Peake, P. K. (1990). Predicting adolescent cognitive and self-regulatory competencies from preschool delay of gratification: Identifying diagnostic conditions. *Developmental Psychology, 26*, 978–986.

Specker, S. M., Carlson, G. A., Edmonson, K. M., & Johnson, P. E. (1996). Psychopathology in pathological gamblers seeking treatment. *Journal of Gambling Studies, 12*, 67.

Steel, Z., & Blaszczynski, A. (1998). Impulsivity, personality disorders, and pathological gambling severity. *Addiction, 93*, 895–905.

Takahashi, T., Ikeda, K., & Hasegawa, T. (2007). A hyperbolic decay of subjective probability of obtaining delayed rewards. *Behavioral Brain Functioning, 3*, 52.

Toneatto, T., & Brennan, J. (2002). Pathological gambling in treatment-seeking substance abusers. *Addictive Behaviors, 27*, 465–469.

Verdejo-Garcia, A. J., Perales, J. C., & Perez-Garcia, M. (2007). Cognitive impulsivity in cocaine and heroin polysubstance abusers. *Addictive Behaviors, 32*, 950–966.

Vitaro, F., Arseneault, L., & Tremblay, R. E. (1997). Dispositional predictors of problem gambling in male adolescents. *American Journal of Psychiatry, 154*, 1769–1770.

Vitaro, F., Arseneault, L., & Tremblay, R. E. (1999). Impulsivity predicts problem gambling in low SES adolescent males. *Addiction, 94*, 565–575.

Vuchinich, R. E., & Simpson, C. A. (1998). Hyperbolic temporal discounting in social drinkers and problem drinkers. *Experimental and Clinical Psychopharmacology, 6*, 292–305.

Welte, J., Barnes, G., Wieczorek, W., Tidwell, M. C., & Parker, J. (2001). Alcohol and gambling pathology among U.S. adults: Prevalence, demographic patterns, and comorbidity. *Journal of Studies on Alcohol, 62*, 706–712.

White, J. L., Moffitt, T. E., Caspi, A., Bartusch, D. J., Needles, D. J., & Stouthamer-Loeber, M. (1994). Measuring impulsivity and examining its relationship to delinquency. *Journal of Abnormal Psychology, 103*, 192–205.

Williams, J., & Dayan, P. (2005). Dopamine, learning, and impulsivity: A biological account of attention-deficit/hyperactivity disorder. *Journal of Child and Adolescent Psychopharmacology, 15*, 160–179.

Yoon, J. H., Higgins, S. T., Heil, S. H., Sugarbaker, R. J., Thomas, C. S., & Badger, G. J. (2007). Delay discounting predicts postpartum relapse to cigarette smoking among pregnant women. *Experimental and Clinical Psychopharmacology, 15*, 176–186.

IV

DISCOUNTING AND THE HUMAN CONDITION

11

ROLE OF TIME AND DELAY IN HEALTH DECISION MAKING

JALIE A. TUCKER, CATHY A. SIMPSON, AND YULIA A. KHODNEVA

Health-related decisions involve making choices among a wide range of options that shift over the life span and have variable, uncertain, and often complex consequences over future intervals ranging from days to months to years. Stakeholders involved in these choices typically include the individual whose health is in question, his or her family and other concerned social network members, and the immediate health care providers. As managed care organizations have come to dominate health care in the United States, a growing number of forces are also at play. These include health care access and coverage; health economic market forces; pertinent employer, hospital, state, and federal regulations; and, increasingly, guidelines for evidence-based practice.

Clearly, an organizing framework is needed to approach the complex set of variables that span micro to meso- to macrolevel influences on stakeholder choices (Tucker, Klapow, & Simpson, 2003). No single discipline can address the breadth of relevant issues and influences, although several have made

Manuscript preparation was supported in part by National Institutes of Health/National Institute on Alcohol Abuse and Alcoholism Grant R01 AA08972 and National Institutes of Health/National Institute on Drug Abuse Grant R21 DA021524.

important contributions, including health economics, medical sociology, health psychology, and behavioral economics (Berns, Laibson, & Loewenstein, 2007; Bickel & Vuchinich, 2000; Loewenstein, Brennan, & Volpp, 2007). In this chapter, we review the contributions of behavioral economics to understanding health decision making from multiple stakeholder perspectives, ranging from individuals to health systems to public health policy. Behavioral economics emphasizes how patterns of choice vary as a function of environmental features and, as applied to health, focuses on "now-versus-later" dynamic relationships between health states and outcomes, health protective and risk behaviors, and health services utilization (Simpson & Vuchinich, 2000; Tucker & Davison, 2000). This chapter touches on related bodies of work, such as medical decision making (e.g., Drummond, Sculpher, Torrance, O'Brien, & Stoddart, 2005), which has roots in health economics and has contributed methodologies used in behavioral economic and psychological research on health-related decisions.

The chapter is organized as follows: In the first section, we discuss how the commodity of interest, health, has been conceptualized and studied and briefly summarize health economic influences on health decision making. This provides necessary background for the review of behavioral economic and related research on health decision making from the perspective of the individual. A rapidly emerging generalization is that a host of potential "biases" influence health-related decisions that involve intertemporal choice under conditions of uncertainty in a manner consistent with research on intertemporal choice of commodities that are not health related (Berns et al., 2007; Ortendahl & Fries, 2005). After discussing implications of the research for behavioral health practices, in the final sections we selectively review studies on intertemporal choice at the public health or health care system levels, with an eye toward using behavioral economic concepts to develop broader research questions that address public health, health plan, and health policy applications. We conclude that a behavioral economic view of health as a commodity that may be chosen and toward whose acquisition resources may be directly allocated (Simpson & Vuchinich, 2000) offers a powerful organizing framework for understanding the role of delay in decision making at the individual, health systems, and health policy levels.

HEALTH AS AN ECONOMIC COMMODITY

Behavioral economics and health economics share a common view of health as a commodity subject to many of the same determinants that influence choices of other commodities requiring consumer allocation of resources (Fuchs, 1987, 1993; Grossman, 1972; Simpson & Vuchinich, 2000). This view of health follows a related reconceptualization in health economics that views demand for health care as a "normal good" with orderly price sensitivities once the distorting effects of insurance coverage on demand have been taken into account (Morrisey, 1992). Previously, demand for health care was viewed as largely inelastic and not subject to the same market forces that otherwise determine supply and demand for a normal good. This reconceptualization of health care and, by extension, health states and outcomes as commodities that may be chosen and toward whose acquisition resources may be directly allocated, continues to have conceptual and empirical viability in economic research on demand for health care. That literature has yielded robust generalizations about the influence of price and time costs on utilization patterns that continue to guide health plan configurations, benefits, and copayments; provider incentives; and reimbursement schemes, among other applications (e.g., Minott, 2007; Wagner & Bledsoe, 1990).

Despite the usefulness of this orienting perspective, unsettled issues remain about viewing health as a commodity that have implications for health-related decision making (Lazaro, Barberan, & Rubio, 2001; Tucker & Simpson, 2003). The first question concerns the functional properties of health that may influence resource allocation to obtain it. In an early and still relevant argument, Grossman (1972) contended that good health should not be viewed as an end in itself, but should be regarded as an intermediate state that allows individuals to seek out and engage in valued activities and commodities. In contrast, ill health consumes time and resources, thereby preventing one from engaging in valued activities. From this perspective, health is regarded as a summary variable that predicts access to or loss of future reinforcers. This places emphasis on the functional value (utility) of health states rather than defining them in physical or medical terms.

A second aspect of health that differs from normal goods is that "health capital" changes and eventually declines over the life span. Some changes are predictable if not inevitable (e.g., loss of near vision, menopause), and others are not. Health capital cannot be saved indefinitely or invested like money. But within a normal human life span, maintaining good health preserves present and future behavioral allocation opportunities (Simpson & Vuchinich, 2000).

Third, many decisions involving health occur as a series of choices over an extended, molar choice framework. In a *molar choice framework*, choices and outcomes may be quite separated over time, and choices may have uncertain outcomes that occur over variable time horizons. Despite this complexity, experimental research has shown that individuals can make choices that involve trade-offs between future health or life expectancy for the immediate receipt of desirable nonhealth goods and commodities (Redelmeir & Heller, 1993; Simpson & Vuchinich, 2000). For example, in a seminal study (Chapman & Johnson, 1995), healthy young adults evaluated exchanges between hypothetical amounts of life expectancy and valuable nonhealth commodities to be received immediately. They were willing to swap days and weeks of life for durable goods like televisions or cars and for immediately consumable goods like beer or snacks.

Thus, when outcomes are described clearly, individuals can evaluate their own health as an open-market commodity for trade. Whether this should be regarded as evidence that health is a normal good remains arguable (Lazaro, 2002), but as the following review shows, viewing health as a commodity has provided an organizing heuristic for research and has yielded results indicating that choices involving health function much like choices involving other commodities.

HEALTH-RELATED DECISIONS INVOLVING INTERTEMPORAL CHOICE

Behavioral economics provides a useful way to conceptualize and study the intertemporal trade-offs in health-related choices that have positive and negative consequences over different future intervals. Behavioral economic models of such intertemporal choices use empirically derived hyperbolic discount functions that decay rapidly in the short run and flatten out over the long run (Ainslie, 1975; Mazur, 1987). In contrast to the exponential discounting models favored in health economics, hyperbolic models predict and describe preference reversals over time and better fit animal and human data on intertemporal choice (Ainslie, 1975).

In this section, we selectively review the multidisciplinary research on health-related decision making from the perspective of the individual. The bulk of evidence comes from recent behavioral economic studies involving health-related commodities and delay discounting and adds to health-related evidence previously reviewed by us (e.g., Simpson & Vuchinich, 2000; Tucker & Davison, 2000; Tucker & Simpson, 2003) and by others (e.g., Chapman, 2005; Loewenstein, 2005a, 2005b). Additional relevant research comes from studies of health-related time preferences (e.g., Van der Pol & Cairns, 2000, 2001) and medical decision-making studies of time trade-offs between health states and outcomes (e.g., Chapman, 1996; Lazaro, 2002).

Methods Used to Study Health-Related Decisions

The standard gamble and the time trade-off (TTO) procedures pioneered in the medical decision-making literature continue to be used to assess preferences for health outcomes (Drummond et al., 2005; Sox, Blatt, Higgins, & Marton, 1988). Both present participants with choices between mutually exclusive hypothetical health outcomes, each with different associated probabilities over different intervals (e.g., poor health for more years of remaining life vs. full health for fewer years). The two methods yield similar, although not identical, utilities, which tend to be higher using the standard gamble procedure (Sox et al., 1988).

Because the standard gamble procedure involves comparisons of probabilities that can be confusing to participants, psychological and behavioral economic studies of health preferences have relied almost exclusively on variations of the TTO method (e.g., Chapman, 2002; Locadia et al., 2006). The TTO method assesses the length of time in good health that participants consider equivalent to a period of time in bad health, typically followed by death. The time in ill health is systematically varied until the participant is indifferent between the alternatives. The choice can be framed in terms of either the number of years in full health or the number of years the individual is willing to give up to be in full health (Torrance, 1997). The length of life in a given health state can be explicitly adjusted to reflect its quality (quality-adjusted life years).

Behavioral economic studies on discounting of delayed outcomes have often used an adaptation of a titration method developed in empirical work with animals (e.g., Mazur, 1987). In an adaptation to humans developed by Rachlin, Raineri, and Cross (1991), participants were presented with repeated choices between smaller–sooner and larger–later hypothetical monetary rewards, and the smaller–sooner reward amount was varied until participants were indifferent between them. As applied to health outcomes, participants typically read TTO-style scenarios in which they are to imagine they have a disease or symptom (e.g., painful arthritis). Participants choose between treatments that would reduce or eliminate the symptoms either sooner for a shorter period of time (smaller–sooner reward) or for a longer period of time after a delay (larger–later reward; e.g., Chapman, 2002). As in animal studies, the "amounts" (e.g., length of time "cured" or symptoms relieved) of the smaller–sooner health gain are adjusted until the participant is indifferent between the two treatments. This adjusting procedure may be used to quantify the discounted value of the delayed treatment outcome. A variation may be used to study the discounting of delayed aversive events (e.g., "Would you prefer to be ill for 10 months starting today or for 12 months in 25 years?"; Chapman & Elstein, 1995; Petry, 2003).

Although these health procedures are conceptually similar to those used to measure delay discounting of money and other durable goods, the latter assessments do not require narratives (*scenarios*) and instead present participants with a series of choices between precisely quantified amounts of money or other durable goods available over specified delays. Health-related scenarios variously describe treatments, length and quality of life, and health states and outcomes. Scenario detail and clarity, and participant understanding and interpretation, cannot be assumed, and participants generally have more direct experience with monetary than with health-related exchanges, which are often novel. Thus, in research on delay discounting of different commodities like health and money, there is often a confound between method and commodity domain. As discussed later, this presents problems in interpreting findings that compare discounting and time preferences across money, health, and other commodities.

Delay Discounting of Health Outcomes

Understanding the devaluing effects of time on future outcomes is basic to understanding health decision making (Bickel & Marsch, 2001; Chapman, 2005; Critchfield & Kollins, 2001). Using procedures similar to those just outlined, researchers have found that what is true of delayed monetary outcomes is also true of delayed health outcomes (gains and losses): The value of these delayed outcomes declines according to a hyperbolic discounting function (e.g., Baker, Johnson, & Bickel, 2003; Johnson, Bickel, & Baker, 2007). For example, Baker et al. (2003) asked current and never-before smokers to specify the duration of a 10% health gain that would be equivalent to having $1,000 now. The duration specified was considered to be $1,000 worth of health. Participants then completed an adjusting-amount procedure in which choices were made between $1,000 worth of health in the future and a smaller (adjusted) amount of health now. As expected, the value of delayed health gains decayed according to a hyperbolic discounting function. A similar function described the discounting of a $1,000 health loss.

In addition to the effects of delay on health choices, discounting rates have been reliably related to demographic and personality variables that are pertinent to characterizing the context of choice surrounding many health decisions. Steeper discounting is associated with lower income (Green, Myerson, Lichtman, Rosen, & Fry 1996) and education (Jaroni, Wright, Lerman, & Epstein, 2004) and younger age until established adulthood, when rates tend to stabilize (Green, Fry, & Myerson, 1994). Discounting, however, has not been reliably related to gender (Epstein et al., 2003; Kirby & Maracovic, 1996) or to personality measures of impulsiveness (Swann, Bjork, Moeller, & Dougherty, 2002). Most studies have not examined the effects of race or ethnicity on delay discounting; however, there is no empirical reason to expect differences after controlling for education and income.

Sign, Magnitude, Duration, and Sequence Effects

In addition to the evidence of delay discounting in health decisions, other research summarized in Table 11.1 has revealed consistent biases in health-related choices, such as sign, magnitude, duration, and sequence effects (Berns et al., 2007; Chapman, 1996, 2005; Ortendahl & Fries, 2005). With a few qualifications, these biases or deviations from expected utility have been observed in health-related choices in a manner similar to choices involving

TABLE 11.1
Potential Biases in Health Decision Making Involving Intertemporal Choice Under Conditions of Uncertainty

Bias	Definition	Examples involving health choices
Sign (instant endowment) effect	Positive outcomes are discounted more than negative outcomes.	Greater discounting of health gains than health losses in smokers and controls (Baker et al., 2003; Johnson et al., 2007).
Magnitude effect	Holding delay constant, discount rates are lower for larger magnitude outcomes; may interact with the domain effect.	Health discount rates are inversely related to magnitude of outcomes and length of delay (Chapman & Elstein, 1995).
Duration (dynamic inconsistency) effect	Discount rates are not constant over time and are smaller for distant than for proximal future intervals.	Hypothetical public outcomes over very long delays (30–900 years) are discounted less than those for shorter delays (1–30 years; Chapman, 2001).
Sequence effect	Sequences of outcomes that end in gains are preferred to those that end in losses, even when the overall utility of the sequences is the same.	Sequences involving improving years of health as an aggregate choice are preferred over sequences that were stable or involved health declines over time (Chapman, 1996).
Domain effect	Discount rates show independence across commodity classes (e.g., health, money) that cannot be attributed to differing utility functions.	Higher discount rates found for hypothetical money choices compared with health choices over similar delays (Chapman, 1996; Petry, 2003).
Role of affective states	"Hot" versus "cold" affective states affect health decision making in asymmetrical ways.	In hot states, persistence of current preferences overestimated; in cold states, effects of pain, fear, and deprivation on preferences underestimated (Loewenstein, 2005a).
Projection bias	Current preferences and affective states are projected onto points in the future when they are irrelevant.	Cancer patients making health care decisions exaggerate and expect current negative feelings to persist while overlooking positive aspects of longer life (Loewenstein, 2005b).
Role of health status	Poor health status is associated with higher valuation of quality of life and lower discount rates as compared with healthy status.	Respondents who rated their health as fair or poor tended to discount nonfatal health status losses at a lower rate than those who rated their health as good or better (Van der Pol & Cairns, 2001).
Income effect	Lower incomes are associated with steeper discounting.	Time preferences for health outcomes in developing countries are shorter than those in wealthier developed countries (Robberstad, 2005).

Note. Based on Ortendahl and Fries (2005), with select input from Baker et al. (2003), Chapman (2005), Loewenstein (2005a, 2005b), and the references cited as examples. Table order follows that of discussion in the text.

money and other commodities, adding further support for viewing health as an economic commodity.

For example, MacKeigan, Larson, Drugalis, Bootman, and Burns (1993) demonstrated the *sign effect* (i.e., steeper discounting of gains than losses) by showing that individuals randomly assigned to different health-gain and health-loss conditions for a hypothetical diagnosis of arthritis discounted health gains more steeply than health losses. Baker et al. (2003) found similar results in a study of smokers and lifetime nonsmokers. Health gains were discounted at a higher rate than health losses. Thus, the prospect of losing one's health may control more behavior than the prospect of a health gain.

Also consistent with research using money and other nonhealth commodities (e.g., Green et al., 1994), health discounting demonstrates the *magnitude effect,* such that longer durations of health are discounted at a lower rate than are shorter durations (e.g., Chapman, 1996; Chapman & Elstein, 1995). Chapman and Elstein (1995) assessed preferences between various choices involving immediate and delayed health outcomes that differed in amount; for example, participants were asked to imagine they were in poor health and then made choices between treatments that could return them to full health for varying intervals either immediately or after varying delays. Similar to results for money, shorter health durations were discounted more heavily than longer health durations. The highest rates were found for health intervals from 0 to 6 months, and rates declined over longer intervals of 1 to 4 years.

The *duration effect* (also termed the *dynamic inconsistency effect;* Ortendahl & Fries, 2005) refers to the finding that amounts of health to be received at shorter delays are more heavily discounted than are amounts available in the future (Chapman, 1996), including outcomes many years hence (Chapman, 2001). This effect may be considered either as a bias in choice over time or as a functional characteristic of the deeply bowed hyperbola associated with descriptions of choice over time. Regardless, the effect of duration on choice is quite relevant to real-world health decisions at the health system and policy levels, which can involve resource allocation toward uncertain outcomes that are years or decades away.

For example, Chapman (1996) found that across delays of 1, 3, 6, and 12 years, participants discounted health gains more sharply at shorter than longer delays. In a later investigation (Chapman, 2001) of time preferences over the very long term (30 to 900 years), a series of three experiments variously manipulated whether participants' choices affected present or future generations and whether they involved saving lives, improving health, or financial benefits. The study used a variation of the TTO technique described earlier. Across studies, the discount rate was lower for longer delays. However, holding delay constant, value was not affected by outcome type or whether the choice was inter- or intragenerational. The latter findings run counter to conventional ideas that people will be self-serving and make choices that favor themselves, others like themselves, or their generation. Although the negative results should be viewed cautiously because of the small samples and questionnaire data collection, they suggest that health care proxies and providers can make fairly unbiased decisions for others.

Other research has found evidence for a sequence effect in health decision making that is similar to that observed for non–health-related choices. Sequences of outcomes that end in a gain are generally preferred over sequences that end in a loss, even if the overall utilities of the sequences as a whole are equivalent (Loewenstein & Prelec, 1993). For example, Chapman (1996) had participants choose between temporally extended health states in which potential health status (e.g., full health, 80% of full health) for each year of an extended time frame (e.g., 3 years, 5 years) were presented as the height of a bar on a graph. The total health for the interval was held constant, but the slopes of the health profiles were either increasing or decreasing. Over intervals of less than 25 years, participants preferred increasing rather than decreasing amounts of health. Such findings indicated that contextualizing choices as cohesive, temporally extended series of events significantly increased the value of future outcomes over that found in choices between brief discrete events (Chapman, 1996; Loewenstein & Prelec, 1993).

In summary, health-related choices are influenced in a manner similar to choices involving money and other commodities. How the biases may interact remains to be determined (Baker et al., 2003), but this is a general empirical limitation not specific to the health literature.

Domain Effects: Artifact or Substantive Finding?

Although similarities in form (hyperbolic decay function) and biases (e.g., sign, magnitude, duration) have been shown for temporal discounting of health, monetary, and other rewards, a somewhat puzzling domain independence has been reported in which discounting rates are unique to each delayed commodity. High rates of discounting health outcomes may not be predictive of high rates of discounting delayed money, cigarettes, and other commodities, or vice versa (e.g., Baker et al., 2003; Chapman, 1996; Petry, 2003).

Some studies have found higher rates of discounting delayed health outcomes when compared with other commodities, including money and durable goods (e.g., Chapman, 1996; Petry, 2003). Although Chapman (2002) suggested such outcomes might be because of the verbal framing of hypothetical outcome scenarios, more recent findings have suggested that delayed health outcomes are more heavily discounted than delayed money even when attempts have been made to equate the magnitudes of health and money (e.g., Johnson et al., 2007). In an exception to this rule, Baker et al. (2003) found higher discounting of money losses than of health losses in smokers but no significant differences in discounting of money and health gains.

Another study (Chapman, 2002) suggested that domain independence varied depending on whether choices did or did not involve direct trades between health and money. When TTO scenarios put the responsibility on participants to buy medication to end (hypothetical) migraine headaches now or in the future, they generated orderly data in their exchanges of money for direct health outcomes that were consistent with studies of exchanges of durable commodities (e.g., Raineri & Rachlin, 1993), and discounting in the health and in the money domains were positively correlated. When they completed the same health and money TTO choices and were told that medication access was controlled by an insurance company, there was little association between discount rates for health and money.

Another possible contributor to domain independence may be differences in how health and other commodities are "consumed." In nonhealth domains, greater discounting has been found for more immediately consumable commodities (Odum & Rainaud, 2003); for example, legal (cigarettes, alcohol) and illegal (cocaine, heroin) drugs tend to be discounted more steeply by active substance users than does money (e.g., Madden, Bickel, & Jacobs, 1999; Odum, Madden, Badger, & Bickel, 2000; Petry, 2001). Odum and Baumann (2007) extended this result by comparing delay discounting of (hypothetical) money, cigarettes, and food that were approximately equated in value. They found that both consumable options were discounted at a similar rate that was steeper than the discount rate for monetary rewards.

In summary, research on domain independence is inconsistent about the direction of differences between discounting of health and other commodities. The reasons remain to be determined and may reflect inherent functional differences between commodities, methodological differences in assessing health and other commodity preferences, or both.

Negative Time Preferences

Individual differences in time preferences for undesirable health outcomes also question rational economic views of intertemporal choice (Loewenstein & Prelec, 1991; van der Pol & Cairns, 2000, 2001). Discounting utility theory assumes that people prefer to delay negative outcomes, such that health is discounted at a positive rate (Berns et al., 2007). Some people, however, show negative time preferences and prefer ill health sooner than later, perhaps to diminish unpleasant anticipation (dread). In a study of preferences for nonfatal health outcomes over three delay intervals (2–5, 6–9, and 10–13 years), 67% of participants had positive time perspectives, and the rest had zero or negative time preferences (van der Pol & Cairns, 2000). Another study showed that a sizable minority of HIV-positive patients wanted to start highly active antiretroviral therapy earlier than recommended by treatment guidelines, even though it often has severe side effects (Locadia et al., 2006). Negative time preferences have also been associated with accepting flu shots and perceiving health outcomes as more serious, whereas positive time preferences have been associated with older age (Chapman et al., 2001; Shleinitz, DePalo, Blume, & Stein, 2006). Negative time preferences help explain why some women with a family history of breast cancer undergo elective mastectomies (van der Pol & Cairns, 2000).

Discounting, Time Preferences, and Real-World Health Behaviors

The research discussed so far has been largely based on hypothetical choices involving health outcomes, and although significant regularities have been observed, the generality of relationships to real-world health behaviors remains to be addressed. Although research on this issue is not abundant, three lines of investigation have begun to illuminate how health discounting and time preferences correlate with, predict, or are influenced by actual health behavior patterns, health status, and emotional states in healthy and clinical samples.

Relationships Between Hypothetical and Real Health Choices and Behaviors

Discounting of hypothetical monetary rewards has repeatedly been associated with individuals' health behaviors, such as substance use (Bickel & Marsch, 2001; Petry 2003; Vuchinich & Simpson, 1998), risky sexual behavior (Farr, Vuchinich, & Simpson, 1998), and injection drug use (Odum et al., 2000). Results have been less clear regarding relationships between laboratory-derived health-discounting rates and real-world health behaviors that are not specific to substance use or related high-risk behaviors (e.g., Chapman & Coups, 1999; Chapman et al., 2001).

In a series of three studies, Chapman et al. (2001) examined the relationship of time preferences assessed using the TTO method and several health behaviors. As noted earlier, this method has conceptual similarities to delay discounting and some methodological overlap, but the procedures are not identical. In Study 1, university employees' monetary- and health-related time preferences were compared with whether they elected to receive a free flu shot. To obtain monetary time preferences, participants made choices between a constant immediate monetary fine and fines that varied in amount and delay. To obtain health time preferences, participants chose between having a 7-day flu now or remaining healthy for 1 to 12 days and then having the flu for 7 days. Monetary time preferences had a modest positive association with taking the flu shot, but health time preferences did not. Studies 2 and 3 assessed the health-related time preferences of older adults who were taking hypertension or cholesterol medications, respectively. Time preferences showed little relationship with self-reported medication adherence in either study. Time preferences have also been reported to have a weak relationship with exercise (Chapman, 1998) and other health behaviors (Chapman, 2005).

Role of Health and Affective States

As summarized in Table 11.1, health and affective states influence and can bias health decisions. People generally discount future health outcomes more steeply when they are in "hot" emotional or deprived states (craving a drug, hungry) than when they are in "cold" states (Chapman, 2005; Loewenstein, 2005a). In hot states, they tend to overestimate the extent to which their current preferences will persist into the future, whereas in cold states, an "empathy gap" exists such that they fail to appreciate fully how hot states will affect their preferences and behavior. This bias is important because medical decisions are often made when people have received bad health news or are in pain or discomfort.

Poor health status is also associated with relatively lower health-related discount rates (Van der Pol & Cairns, 2001). Although quite preliminary, other research has found similarities between decision making and risk preferences on laboratory tasks between substance users and individuals with brain lesions in areas that impair emotional regulation (Shiv, Loewenstein, & Bechara, 2005). Studies have also found that individuals tend to project current preferences onto points in the future when the preferences should be irrelevant to decision making (Loewenstein, 2005b), a tendency termed *projection bias*. They are inclined to exaggerate the duration of current unpleasant feelings, thereby increasing the likelihood of taking actions with long-term consequences on the basis of short-term preferences. Overall, the role of health states and affective biases in health decision making is complex and requires further study, particularly in ways that link basic science findings with questionnaire and observational data.

Research Implications for Promoting Sound Health Decisions and Behavioral Health Practices

Despite unresolved conceptual and methodological complexities about how to assess health-related preferences, particularly in relation to other commodities like money, the research reviewed offers a fairly coherent perspective on health decision making. Health-related choices are influenced by many of the same variables and choice biases that affect intertemporal choices that involve (hypothetical) money and other tangible commodities, and patterns of choice as a function of delay can be described by a common hyperbolic discount function. The generality of key relationships to the health domain seems well established empirically and extends the utility of a behavioral economic analysis to health choices, thereby offering common strategies and tactics with which to study the trade-offs between time, health, and money or other valuable commodities that are involved in many health choices at the individual level.

Given that individuals discount health outcomes and make short-term choices that are often not beneficial over the long term, what can the findings tell us about how to facilitate better health decisions, pro-health behaviors, and positive health outcomes? Two basic strategies can be found in the applied literature: Researchers (a) have attempted to remediate the choice biases of decision makers (e.g., through self-control training or similar strategies) or have provided incentives for better choices (e.g., through environmental restructuring; Bickel & Marsch, 2000) or (b) have accepted that biased choices are normative and have structured health messages, choices, interventions, and contexts in ways that exploit the biases in service of promoting good choices and health outcomes (Loewenstein et al., 2007; Ortendahl & Fries, 2005). Psychotherapeutic and behavior modification approaches tend to emphasize the former strategy, whereas behavioral economic and public health approaches are more opportunistic and make more use of the latter strategy (Marlatt, Tucker, Donovan, & Vuchinich, 1997).

Examples of the first strategy aimed at reducing biased choices include (a) teaching individuals to conceptualize the molar context of their personal cost–benefit situation to increase choice of health options that yield the best overall benefit (Logue, 2000); (b) providing incentives to individuals to receive self-control training, supports for prohealth behavior change attempts, and distribution of resources to increase stability in environments that promote the value of long-term rewards (Bickel & Marsch, 2000); and (c) offering incentives for abstinence from cigarettes or drugs of abuse (e.g., Higgins et al., 1994).

Examples of the second strategy that incorporate choice biases to promote health include (a) exploiting the sign effect and cost aversion bias through use of contingency contracting to make negative health consequences of unhealthy behaviors more immediate and certain (Logue, 2000); (b) linking pro-health behaviors in a concrete manner over time (e.g., by charting, self-monitoring) to exploit the sequencing effect in reducing discounting of longer term rewards (Logue, 2000; Simpson & Vuchinich 2000); (c) providing "treatment on demand" with minimal delays to increase utilization by substance abusers (Tucker & Davidson, 2000); and (d) framing health messages as a future loss rather than a future gain to lower the discount rate for health behaviors or outcomes and promote healthier choices (Bickel & Marsch, 2001; Ortendahl & Fries, 2005).

Loewenstein et al. (2007) systematized the second approach as part of their *asymmetrical paternalism* strategy for improving health behaviors. This strategy exploits choice biases to help those most susceptible to them make better choices without otherwise infringing on freedom of choice. As a prototypic example of discounting the long-term benefits of healthy food choices, they recommended changing the order of food presentation in a cafeteria line so that healthy foods, not desserts, are presented first. The overall availability of desserts is unchanged, but the switch helps overweight people with suboptimal self-control make better food choices. Obviously, the two approaches are not mutually exclusive, and what mix of options works best remains to be determined.

SOCIAL SYSTEMS AND TEMPORAL DISCOUNTING OF HEALTH AND RELATED COMMODITIES

We now consider some of these issues at the broader health system, public health, and health policy levels. Although research has shown that individuals can view their own health as a tradable commodity, at least in hypothetical situations, controversy exists about how to discount delayed health outcomes that involve large groups of people, both present and future, and what relationship, if any, such macro or social discounting rates should have to the discount rates and preferences of the individuals who make up the society (Cairns, 1992; Van Hout, 1998). Prevention programs, medical research, and other health and public health innovations depend on an exchange of current commodities, like time, effort, and primarily money, for future benefits that are delayed and often probabilistic (Belzer, 2000; Lynch & Zauberman, 2006; Ortendahl & Fries, 2006). There are also opportunity costs associated with funding one program and not others. Because most such decisions involve trade-offs of costs and benefits over time for groups and individuals, discount rates for program costs and benefits influence decision making either explicitly as in cost–benefit analysis or implicitly when individual policymakers allocate resources. As Chapman (2002) noted, "At a policy level, health is almost always traded for money, even if these trades cannot be made at an individual level" (p. 415).

The cost–benefit literature thoroughly discusses discounting the health benefits and monetary costs of programs with delayed and probabilistic outcomes (e.g., Gravelle & Smith, 2001; Keeler & Cretin, 1983; Ortendahl & Fries, 2006). Although beyond the scope of this chapter, in brief this work focuses on whether the same or different discount rates should be used for health outcomes (benefits) and monetary costs of programs and what rate should be applied to each domain. The simple course, often taken, is to use the same rate for costs and benefits, typically the current rate of market return for invested resources (Lazaro, 2002). This practice, however, has been questioned on theoretical, methodological, and ethical grounds (e.g., Gravelle & Smith, 2001; West, McNabb, Thompson, Sheldon, & Evans, 2003). When different rates are used, the discount rate for health is often set lower than that for money. However, if taken to an extreme (i.e., program costs are discounted, and the health discount rate equals zero), this practice equates the value of present and future lives (Ortendahl & Fries, 2006), and the cost effectiveness of a given program would theoretically always improve from delaying its implementation (Ganiats, 1994; Keeler & Cretin, 1983).

These debates notwithstanding, the choice and implementation of discount rates at the meso and macro levels often rest on the behavior of individuals, such as health system managers and health policymakers, and their decision making and discounting processes can be studied empirically (Lynch & Zauberman, 2006). In line with this approach, in the remainder of the chapter we review studies concerned with (a) discounting of private versus social health and money outcomes and (b) macro influences on health discounting and time preferences. We end with a consideration of behavioral economic studies of altruism because this issue is at the heart of health decision making at the macro level.

Discounting of Private Versus Social Future Health Outcomes

Most research on discounting of health effects, particularly in psychology, has focused on the choices of individuals for benefits or costs assumed to occur directly to them. Health system and health policies, however, often require individuals to make choices that affect others, sometimes far into the future (Chapman, 2001). This issue must typically be investigated hypothetically, with participants variously making choices that affect their own private or personal health versus the health of others ("public" or "social" preferences). The findings, described next, are somewhat mixed, but do not suggest a robust self-serving bias.

On the one hand, individuals apply discount rates to personal future health benefits that are much higher than the relatively low (3%) rates often used by health policy analysts (Chapman, 2002). However, when choosing between saving lives now or in the future, some people show extreme discounting, in that they are unwilling to choose any future benefits and instead choose only current lives saved under all scenarios (Cropper, Aydede, & Portney, 1991). Consistent with these findings from separate studies, a comparison of preferences for personal and social outcomes (Lazaro et al., 2001) found that personal health outcomes were discounted at a relatively higher rate over shorter intervals, but when choices were made over longer intervals, personal and social health outcomes were discounted similarly. Similar changes in rates of discounting have been reported with social health outcomes. Cropper, Aydede, and Portney (1994) found that participants discounted effects from a life-saving program at a 5-year delay at about 4 times the rate of a similar life-saving program at a 100-year delay.

When Chapman (2002) observed lower rates of discounting of social health outcomes in her study of hypothetical migraine headaches discussed earlier, she suggested that this increased "prudence" when making choices for others may undervalue the immediate pain or costs to the individual. Although discounting future health outcomes at a low rate is adaptive for the group, it requires that individuals experience pain until the future health benefits are realized. Similar results were obtained in a study of rates of discounting of private and public health outcomes in the United Kingdom. Representative samples of electoral registers ($n = 385$) and health professionals listed in national health registries ($n = 180$; West et al., 2003) discounted health and financial decisions made for the benefit of society at a significantly lower rate than those made on their own behalf. West et al. (2003) concluded that

> both the lay public and healthcare professionals consider that the discount rate appropriate for public decisions is lower than that for private decisions. . . . [suggesting] a general appreciation that society is more stable and has a more predictable future than does the individual. (p. iii)

Other studies, however, have failed to find differences between private and public health decisions. The previously described experiments by Chapman (2001) that examined inter- and intragenerational discount rates in different domains did not find differences in discount curves across domains, and rates in all conditions decreased with delay, consistent with a duration effect (hyperbolic discounting). Discounting did not vary by generational impact or the beneficiary's locale. Cairns and van der Pol (1999) assessed the length of hypothetical illness that participants would tolerate in the future to avoid illness now and found no significant differences in discounting one's own health and the health of unknown others. A Swedish study (Johannesson & Johannesson, 1996) also found no differences as a function of generational impact. Rather, annual discount rates for hypothetical life-saving programs in one's generation versus in 20, 50, or 100 years in the future showed a steady decline over time, consistent with a duration effect. Van der Pol and Cairns (2000) found wider variation in time preferences for self and others' health improvements that spanned positive, negative, and zero discounting of future health outcomes, and this heterogeneity was manifested for both self and other preferences.

Overall, the research has suggested that individuals are somewhat self-serving when their own health is at stake (i.e., they tend to prefer immediate relief from illness at the expense of future health), but in other choice contexts they tend to make choices on behalf of others that are not self-serving. These relationships tend to be adequately described by hyperbolic functions (Cairns & Van der Pol, 1997; Robberstad & Cairns, 2007), suggesting that a behavioral economic model has utility at the social or systems level of decision making as well as at the better researched microindividual level. The manner in which individuals discount social health compared with the public money necessary to fund programs appears to be influenced by many of the same biases that affect individual-level discounting, including framing, sign, duration, and magnitude effects and possibly demographic effects.

Macrolevel Influences on Health Decisions and Policies

Rates of discounting social health outcomes also vary as a function of broader economic conditions and general environmental stability. Robberstad (2005) found increased preferences for immediate but inferior health outcomes in developing countries in Africa than in developed countries. Choices for future health benefits from public programs reflected discount rates about twice those commonly recommended in policy analysis for discounting health benefits (0.03 to 0.05 range; Smith & Gravelle, 2001; Walker & Kumaranayake, 2002). Discounting did not differ significantly across choices framed at the personal or societal levels. A follow-up study using comparable methods and samples found similar results, and preferences were best described by a hyperbolic model of delay discounting (Robberstad & Cairns, 2007).

These findings tentatively suggest that the personal *income effect*, wherein lower incomes are associated with steeper discounting in individual choices (Green et al., 1994), generalizes to macroeconomic systems. Consequently, it may be appropriate to use different discount rates in making health program decisions in different countries or regions or in the same geographic area under different economic conditions (recession, inflation). Ostasewski, Green, and Myerson (1998) supported some of these ideas in a series of three experiments in Poland. Replicable, orderly effects suggesting increased discounting of hypothetical delayed and probabilistic rewards were found at the individual level in response to inflation and economic instability.

Altruism and Its Role in Health Decisions and Policies

Delaying resources into the future for the long-term benefit of others, particularly if those rewards are at the macro level and have little immediate or later benefit for the decision maker, represents a special type of choice that Takahashi (2007) has termed the *paradox of nonreciprocal altruism*. Reciprocal altruism has been well studied experimentally, most notably using the "prisoner's dilemma" design, which involves choices set up so that over time, cooperation results in the greatest overall value for both participants (prisoners), whereas selfish choices may have personal benefits or costs depending on the behavior of the other person (e.g., Jones & Rachlin, 2006; Rachlin, Brown, & Baker, 2001). Reciprocal altruism can be trained such that players use a mutually helpful tit-for-tat pattern, although this is often not the prevalent initial pattern. Moreover, higher discounters tend to be relatively less likely to engage in socially cooperative choices that produce greater molar good (Yi, Buchalter, Gatchalian, & Bickel, 2007; Yi, Johnson, & Bickel, 2005).

Although reciprocal altruism assumes some beneficial return for local cooperation and molecular-level sacrifices of goods, nonreciprocal altruism assumes no such future benefits for the giver or decision maker (Takahashi, 2007) and thus is more analogous to many long-term public policy decisions. Research on the extent to which individuals will forgo personal monetary rewards and share with others has found that greater willingness to share is associated with decreasing perceived social distance from the recipient (Jones & Rachlin, 2006; Rachlin, 2002, 2006). This relationship could be modeled using a variant of the hyperbolic discount equation after making an adjustment for increasing social distance.

A final thorny issue concerns whether all lives are equally valued when decision makers make choices on behalf of others. Although policy models often assume equal value for all lives, it is not clear that individual decision makers function this way. Some studies (e.g., Cropper et al., 1991; Johansson-Stenman & Martinsson, 2007) have found that decision makers tend to value social programs more when the intended recipients are younger. For example, a Swedish study (Johansson-Stenman & Martinsson, 2007) involving choices among road safety projects found that younger lives were valued more in all conditions, and respondents' personal characteristics influenced their choices; for example, those with children, especially young parents, valued saving children much more highly than did childless respondents in relation to saving 70-year-old drivers.

DISCUSSION AND CONCLUSIONS

Taken together, these studies paint a complex picture about decision-making patterns and influences when outcomes affect large groups of people, some as yet unborn. Decision makers can adopt a broad societal perspective under some conditions, but also appear susceptible to the same biases that affect individual choices with individual consequences. Altruistic choices tend to parallel individual patterns of self-controlled decision making and appear amenable to shaping through contingencies that promote cooperation. However, absent such influences, decision makers may make choices that favor themselves, their kin, or younger groups, and macroeconomic or environmental contexts with income and other resource constraints appear to promote steeper discounting and a more myopic view of health programs and outcomes.

Ortendahl and Fries (2006) suggested that because interindividual differences in discounting are large, society should use one low (3% to 5%) or even negative discount rate in formulating public health policies for the collective good. The challenge then is to devise health choice contexts across multiple market segments and stakeholder levels to promote decisions that maximize utility for the collection of stakeholders over some to-be-decided set of time horizons. Although macropolicy decisions affect aggregate national health, many pertinent choices are under individual control. As discussed earlier, the distribution and timing of rewards and costs for targeted and alternative competing behaviors influence individuals' valuation of health-related options and can be structured in ways that promote healthier choices, for example, by concurrently exploiting duration, domain, and magnitude biases and correcting for age biases in reward discounting (Lowenstein et al., 2007; Ortendahl & Fries, 2005).

To facilitate such actions at the individual level in the real-world health care environment, incorporation of clear information on the processes and biases with which individuals make intertemporal choices could be made a routine part of health education and practice. Although less often considered, modifiable, temporally driven reward and cost distributions also control micro-level health care provider behavior. For example, providers often avoid the immediate costs of unfilled appointment slots by overbooking or using waiting lists, but longer waiting times are a cost for treatment-seeking individuals that can discourage pro-health behaviors (Tucker & Davison, 2000). Innovative additions to systems of care, such as telehealth and computer-based approaches and greater use of paraprofessionals, may reduce costs, effort, and resources and better align cost–benefit distributions in ways that support health-promoting choices for consumers and providers alike (Tucker & Simpson, 2003).

At the meso level—which includes managed care organizations, health departments, hospitals, and treatment programs—timely reimbursement of, and easier access to, preventive services would improve the contingency distribution to promote individual prohealth behaviors through exploitation of the sign effect in decreasing upfront costs to health care consumers (Tucker & Davison, 2000). Similar effects could be achieved at state and local levels by providing positive contingencies such as vouchers for use of state-sponsored preventive programs like prenatal screenings, vaccinations, and HIV testing. However, prevention programs are notoriously difficult to market with funding agencies and the public because successful prevention typically results in averted costs and avoidance of negative outcomes that are fairly invisible compared with costly clinical treatments with positive health effects for select individuals.

It is important to appreciate that the contingencies controlling the choices of mesolevel systems are shaped in part by the contingencies controlling the choices of the microlevel entities that make up the larger unit. For example, managed care organizations are typically profit-seeking entities accountable to stakeholders for their financial progress, which is usually measured over much shorter intervals than the long-term health outcomes of the pool of patients served. Decision makers in managed care organizations are likely to respond to solid data that highlight ways of bringing financial realities in line with best practices for societal health rather than arguments based solely on health considerations. For example, including a behavioral health benefit in comprehensive health plans has repeatedly been shown to reduce the use of costly medical services, sometimes to the extent that they pay for themselves (Cummings, O'Donohue, & Ferguson, 2002; Fiedler & Wight, 1989). Framing presentation of data on such medical cost offsets to managed care organization decision makers in ways similar to those discussed earlier about delivery of targeted health messages to individuals may compensate for the status quo and risk aversion biases common in choices made under uncertainty and promote support for pro-health behaviors in a mutually beneficial manner.

Finally, macrolevel health entities such as the federal government have a pervasive role in health. The federal government defines what products, services, and working conditions are acceptable and how many billions of dollars will be spent annually to subsidize the demand for health (Fuchs, 1993). West (1985) noted that although the fortunes of individuals are transient, societies in most developed countries remain more constant over time. Thus, uncertainty regarding outcomes must be viewed differently at the societal than at the individual level (Sheldon, 1992; West et al., 2003). Society may benefit from reductions in morbidity and mortality (Sheldon, 1992), even if the effects for a given individual cannot be guaranteed.

In line with this view, Weinstein (1990) argued that health programs could be viewed as invested capital that should give a return, although costs may precede benefits by generations. For instance, are environmental changes designed to decrease neonatal lead exposure more important than funding dementia research? Is it a better legacy for future generations to leave better technologies or better health care systems? Will stronger financial systems produce better health systems downstream, so that commerce should be emphasized over health? Such societal questions should govern macrolevel choices (West et al., 2003), but "that life is priceless need not imply that [society] will spare no expense to save a life or cure a disease" (Fuchs, 1993, p. 49). Decisions must encompass immediate stakeholder issues and super-molar timeframes with layer on layer of complexities. Behavioral economics, with its emphasis on intertemporal choice and hyperbolic discounting, holds promise as a framework within which to research and debate the complex issues involved.

REFERENCES

Ainslie, G. (1975). Specious reward: A behavioral theory of impulsiveness. *Psychological Bulletin, 82*, 463–496.

Baker, F., Johnson, M. W., & Bickel, W. K. (2003). Delay discounting in current and never-before cigarette smokers: Similarities and differences across commodity, sign, and magnitude. *Journal of Abnormal Psychology, 112*, 382–392.

Belzer, R. B. (2000). Discounting across generations: Necessary, not suspect. *Risk Analysis, 20,* 779–792.

Berns, G. S., Laibson P., & Loewenstein, G. (2007). Intertemporal choice—Towards an integrative framework. *Trends in Cognitive Science, 11,* 482–488.

Bickel, W. K., & Marsch, L. A. (2000). The tyranny of small decisions: Origins, outcomes, and proposed solutions. In W. K. Bickel & R. E. Vuchinich (Eds.), *Reframing health behavior change with behavioral economics* (pp. 341–391). Mahwah, NJ: Erlbaum.

Bickel, W. K., & Marsch, L. A. (2001). Toward a behavioral economic understanding of drug dependence: Delay discounting processes. *Addiction, 96,* 73–86.

Bickel, W. K., & Vuchinich, R. E. (Eds.). (2000). *Reframing health behavior change with behavioral economics.* Mahwah, NJ: Erlbaum.

Cairns, J. (1992). Discounting and health benefits: Another perspective. *Health Economics, 1,* 76–79.

Cairns, J. A., & van der Pol, M. (1997). Saving future lives: A comparison of three discounting models. *Econometrics and Health Economics, 6,* 341–350.

Cairns, J., & van der Pol, M. (1999). Do people value their own future health differently from others' future health? *Medical Decision Making, 19,* 466–472.

Chapman, G. B. (1996). Temporal discounting and utility for health and money. *Journal of Experimental Psychology: Learning, Memory, and Cognition, 22,* 771–791.

Chapman, G. B. (1998). Sooner or later: The psychology of intertemporal choice. In D. L. Medin (Ed.), *The psychology of learning and motivation* (Vol. 38, pp. 83–113). San Diego, CA: Academic Press.

Chapman, G. B. (2001). Time preferences for the very long term. *Acta Psychologica, 108,* 95–116.

Chapman, G. B. (2002). Your money or your health: Time preferences and trading money for health. *Medical Decision Making, 22,* 410–416.

Chapman, G. B. (2005). Short-term cost for long-term benefit: Time preference and cancer control. *Health Psychology, 24*(Suppl. 4), S41–S48.

Chapman, G. B., Brewer, N. T., Coups, E. J., Brownlee, S., Leventhal, H., & Leventhal, E. A. (2001). Value for the future and preventive health behavior. *Journal of Experimental Psychology: Applied, 7,* 235–250.

Chapman, G. B., & Coups, E. J. (1999). Predictors of influenza vaccine acceptance among healthy adults. *Preventive Medicine, 29,* 249–262.

Chapman, G. B., & Elstein, A. S. (1995). Valuing the future: Temporal discounting of health and money. *Medical Decision Making, 15,* 373–386.

Chapman, G. B., & Johnson, E. J. (1995). Preference reversals in monetary and life-expectancy evaluations. *Organizational Behavior and Human Decision Processes, 62,* 300–317.

Critchfield, T. S., & Kollins, S. H. (2001). Temporal discounting: Basic research and the analysis of socially important behavior. *Journal of Applied Behavioral Analysis, 34,* 101–122.

Cropper, M. L., Aydede, S. K., & Portney, P. R. (1991). Discounting human lives. *American Journal of Agricultural Economics, 73,* 1411–1415.

Cropper, M. L., Aydede, S. K., & Portney, P. R. (1994). Preferences for life saving programs: How the public discounts time and age. *Journal of Risk and Uncertainty, 8,* 243–265.

Cummings, N. A., O'Donohue, W. T., & Ferguson, K. E. (2002). *The impact of medical cost offset on practice and research: Making it work for you.* Reno, NV: Context Press.

Drummond, M. F., Sculpher, M. J., Torrance, G. W., O'Brien, B., & Stoddart, G. L. (2005). *Methods for the economic evaluation of health care programmes* (3rd ed.). New York: Oxford University Press.

Epstein, L. H., Richards, J. B., Saad, F., Paluch, R., Roerman, J., & Lerman, C. (2003). Comparison of two measures of delay discounting in smokers. *Experimental and Clinical Psychopharmacology, 11,* 131–138.

Farr, C. A., Vuchinich, R. E., & Simpson, C. A. (1998, May). *Delayed reward discounting in sexual risk-takers and non-risk-takers.* Poster session presented at the Annual Meeting of the Association for Behavior Analysis, Orlando, FL.

Fiedler, J. L., & Wight, J. B. (1989). *The medical offset effect and public health policy.* New York: Praeger.

Fuchs, V. R. (1987). *The health economy.* Chicago: University of Chicago Press.

Fuchs, V. R. (1993). *The future of health policy.* Cambridge, MA: Harvard University Press.

Ganiats, T. G. (1994). Discounting in cost-effectiveness research. *Medical Decision Making, 14,* 298–300.

Gravelle, H., & Smith, D. (2001). Discounting for health effects in cost-benefit and cost effectiveness analysis. *Health Economics, 10,* 587–599.

Green, L., Fry, A., & Myerson, J. (1994). Discounting of delayed rewards: A lifespan comparison. *Psychological Science, 5,* 33–36.

Green, L., Myerson, J., Lichtman, D., Rosen, S., & Fry, A. (1996). Temporal discounting in choice between delayed rewards: The role of age and income. *Psychology of Aging, 11,* 79–84.

Grossman, M. (1972). *The demand for health: A theoretical and empirical investigation.* New York: Columbia University Press/National Bureau of Economic Research.

Higgins, S. T., Budney, A. J., Bickel, W. K., Foerg, F. E., Donham, R., & Badger, G. J. (1994). Outpatient behavioral treatment for cocaine dependence: One-year outcome. *Experimental and Clinical Psychopharmacology, 3,* 205–212.

Jaroni, J., Wright, S., Lerman, C., & Epstein, L. H. (2004). Relationship between education and delay discounting in smokers. *Addictive Behaviors, 29,* 1171–1176.

Johannesson, M., & Johannesson, P. (1996). The discounting of lives saved in future generations—Some empirical results. *Health Economics, 5,* 329–332.

Johansson-Stenman, O., & Martinsson, P. (2007). Are some lives more valuable? An ethical preferences approach. *Journal of Health Economics, 27,* 739–752. doi:10.1016/j.jhealeco.2007.10.001

Johnson, M. W., Bickel, W. K., & Baker, F. (2007). Moderate drug use and delay discounting: A comparison of heavy, light, and never smokers. *Experimental and Clinical Psychopharmacology, 15,* 187–194.

Jones, B., & Rachlin, H. (2006). Social discounting. *Psychological Science, 17,* 283–286.

Keeler, E. B., & Cretin, S. (1983). Discounting of life-saving and other non-monetary effects. *Management Science, 29,* 300–306.

Kirby, K., & Maracovic, N. (1996). Delay discounting of probabilistic rewards: Rates decrease as amounts increase. *Psychonomic Bulletin & Review, 3,* 100–104.

Lazaro, A. (2002). Theoretical arguments for the discounting of health consequences: Where do we go from here? *Pharmacoeconomics, 20,* 943–961.

Lazaro, A., Barberan, R., & Rubio, E. (2001). Private and social time preferences for health and money: An empirical estimation. *Health Economics, 10,* 351–356.

Locadia, M., van Grieken, R. A., Prins, J. M., de Vries, H. J., Sprangers, M. A., & Nieuwkerk, P. T. (2006). Patients' preferences regarding the timing of highly active antiretroviral therapy initiation for chronic asymptomatic HIV-1 infection. *Antiviral Therapy, 11,* 335–341.

Loewenstein, G. (2005a). Hot–cold empathy gaps and medical decision making. *Health Psychology, 24*(Suppl. 4), S49–S56.

Loewenstein G. (2005b). Projection bias in medical decision making. *Medical Decision Making, 25,* 96–104.

Loewenstein, G., Brennan, T., & Volpp, K. (2007, November 28). Asymmetric paternalism to improve health behaviors. *JAMA, 298,* 2415–2417.

Loewenstein, G., & Prelec, D. (1991). Negative time preference. *American Economic Review, 81,* 347–352.

Loewenstein, G., & Prelec, D. (1993). Preferences for sequences of outcomes. *Psychological Bulletin, 100,* 91–108.

Logue, A. W. (2000). Self-control and health behavior. In W. K. Bickel & R. E. Vuchinich (Eds.), *Reframing health behavior change with behavioral economics* (pp. 167–192). Mahwah, NJ: Erlbaum.

Lynch, J. G., & Zauberman, G. (2006). When do you want it? Time, decisions, and public policy. *Journal of Public Policy and Marketing, 25,* 67–78.

MacKeigan, L. D., Larson, L. N., Drugalis, J. R., Bootman, J. L., & Burns, L. R. (1993). Time preference for health gains versus health losses. *Pharmacoeconomics, 3,* 374–386.

Madden, G. J., Bickel, W. K., & Jacobs, E. A. (1999). Discounting of delayed rewards in opioid-dependent outpatients: Exponential or hyperbolic functions. *Experimental and Clinical Psychopharmacology, 7,* 284–293.

Marlatt, G. A., Tucker, J. A., Donovan, D. M., & Vuchinich, R. E. (1997). Help-seeking by substance abusers: The role of harm reduction and behavioral economic approaches to facilitate treatment entry and retention. In L. S. Onken, J. D. Blaine, & J. J. Boren (Eds.), *Beyond the therapeutic alliance: Keeping the drug dependent individual in treatment* (NIDA Research Monograph No. 165, pp. 44–84). Rockville, MD: National Institute on Drug Abuse.

Mazur, J. (1987). An adjusting procedure for studying delayed reinforcement. In M. Commons, J. Mazur, J. A. Nevin, & H. Rachlin. (Eds.), *Quantitative analysis of behavior: Vol. 5. The effect of delay and of intervening events on reinforcement value* (pp. 55–73). Hillsdale, NJ: Erlbaum.

Minott, J. (2007). Medicare advantage and the impact of Medicare HMOs on inpatient utilization. *Findings Brief: Health Care Financing & Organization, 10,* 1–3.

Morrisey, M. A. (1992). *Price sensitivity in health care: Implications for health care policy.* Washington, DC: National Federation of Independent Business Foundation.

Odum, A. L., & Baumann, A. A. (2007). Cigarette smokers show steeper discounting of both food and cigarettes than money. *Drug and Alcohol Dependence, 91,* 293–296.

Odum, A. L., Madden, G. J., Badger, G. J., & Bickel, W. K. (2000). Needle sharing in opioid-dependent outpatients: Psychological processes underlying risk. *Drug and Alcohol Dependence, 60,* 259–266.

Odum, A. L., & Rainaud, C. P. (2003). Discounting of delayed money, alcohol, and food. *Behavioural Processes, 64,* 305–313.

Ortendahl, M., & Fries, J. F. (2005). Framing health messages based on anomalies in time preference. *Medical Science Monitor, 11,* RA253–RA256.

Ortendahl, M., & Fries, J. H. (2006). A low tension between individual and societal aspects in health improved sequences. *Journal of Clinical Epidemiology, 59,* 1222–1227.

Ostasewski, P., Green, L., & Myerson, J. (1998). Effects of inflation on the subjective value of delayed and probabilistic rewards. *Psychonomic Bulletin & Review, 5,* 324–333.

Petry, N. M. (2001). Delay discounting of money and alcohol in actively using alcoholics, currently abstinent alcoholics, and controls. *Psychopharmacology (Berlin), 154,* 243–250.

Petry, N. M. (2003). Discounting of money, health, and freedom in substance abusers and controls. *Drug and Alcohol Dependence, 71,* 133–141.

Rachlin, H. (2002). Altruism and selfishness. *Brain and Behavioral Sciences, 25,* 239–250.

Rachlin, H. (2006). Notes on discounting. *Journal of the Experimental Analysis of Behavior, 85,* 425–435.

Rachlin, H., Brown, J., & Baker, F. (2001). Reinforcement and punishment in the prisoner's dilemma game. In D. L. Medin (Ed.), *The psychology of learning and motivation: Advances in research and theory* (pp. 327–364). San Diego, CA: Academic Press.

Rachlin, D., Raineri, A., & Cross, D. (1991). Subjective probability and delay. *Journal of the Experimental Analysis of Behavior, 55,* 233–244.

Raineri, A., & Rachlin, H. (1993). The effect of temporal constraints on the value of money and other commodities. *Journal of Behavioral Decision Making, 6,* 77–94.

Redelmeir, D. A., & Heller, D. N. (1993). Time preference in medical decision making and cost-effectiveness analysis. *Medical Decision Making, 13,* 212–217.

Robberstad, B. (2005). Estimation of private and social time preferences for health in northern Tanzania. *Social Science & Medicine, 61*, 1597–1607.

Robberstad, B., & Cairns, J. (2007). Time preferences for health in northern Tanzania: An empirical analysis of alternative discounting methods. *Pharmacoeconomics, 25*, 73–88.

Schleinitz, M. D., DePalo, D., Blume, J., & Stein, M. (2006). Can differences in breast cancer utilities explain disparities in breast cancer care? *Journal of General Internal Medicine, 21*, 1253–1260.

Sheldon, T. A. (1992). Discounting in healthcare decision-making: Time for a change? *Journal of Public Health Medicine, 14*, 250–256.

Shiv, B., Loewenstein, G., & Bechara, A. (2005). The dark side of emotion in decision-making: When individuals with decreased emotional reactions make more advantageous decisions. *Cognitive Brain Research, 23*, 85–92.

Simpson, C. A., & Vuchinich, R. E. (2000). Temporal discounting in the value of objects of choice: Discounting, behaviors patterns, and the value of health behavior. In W. K. Bickel & R. E. Vuchinich (Eds.), *Reframing health behavior change with behavioral economics* (pp. 193–218). Mahwah, NJ: Erlbaum.

Smith, D. H., & Gravelle, H. (2001). The practice of discounting in economic evaluations of healthcare interventions. *International Journal of Technological Assessment of Health Care, 17*, 236–243.

Sox, H. C, Blatt, M. A., Higgins, M. C., & Marton, K. I. (1988). *Medical decision making.* Newton, MA: Butterworth-Heinemann.

Swann, A. C., Bjork, J. M., Moeller, F. G., & Dougherty, E. M. (2002). Two models of impulsivity: Relationships to personality traits and psychopathology. *Biological Psychiatry, 15*, 988–994.

Takahashi, T. (2007). Non-reciprocal altruism may be attributable to hyperbolicity in social discounting function. *Medical Hypotheses, 68*, 194–187.

Torrance, G. W. (1997). Preferences for health outcomes and cost-utility analysis. *American Journal of Managed Care, 3*, 8–20.

Tucker, J. A., & Davison, J. W. (2000). Waiting to see the doctor: The role of time constraints in the utilization of health and behavioral health services. In W. K. Bickel & R. E. Vuchinich (Eds.), *Reframing health behavior change with behavioral economics* (pp. 219–264). Mahwah, NJ: Erlbaum.

Tucker, J. A., Klapow, J., & Simpson, C. A. (2003). Health psychology and public health. In L. M. Cohen, D. E. McChargue, & F. L. Collins (Eds.), *The health psychology handbook: Practical issues for the behavioral medicine specialist* (pp. 502–513). Thousand Oaks, CA: Sage.

Tucker, J. A., & Simpson, C. A. (2003). Merging behavioral economic and public health approaches to the delivery of services for substance abuse: Concepts and applications. In R. E. Vuchinich & N. Heather (Eds.), *Choice, behavioral economics, and addiction* (pp. 365–378). Oxford, England: Elsevier Science.

van der Pol, M. M., & Cairns, J. A. (2000). Negative and zero time preference for health. *Health Economics, 9*, 171–175.

van der Pol, M. M., & Cairns, J. A. (2001). Estimating time preferences for health using discrete choice experiments. *Social Science & Medicine, 52,* 1459–1470.

Van Hout, B. A. (1998). Discounting costs and effects: A reconsideration. *Health Economics, 7,* 581–594.

Vuchinich, R. E., & Simpson, C. A. (1998). Hyperbolic temporal discounting in social drinkers and problem drinkers. *Experimental and Clinical Psychopharmacology, 6,* 292–305.

Wagner, E. H., & Bledsoe, T. (1990). The Rand health insurance experiment and HMOs. *Medical Care, 28,* 191–200.

Walker, D., & Kumaranayake, L. (2002). Allowing for differential timing in cost analysis. *Health Policy and Planning, 17,* 112–118.

Weinstein, M. C. (1990). Economics of prevention. *Journal of General Internal Medicine, 5,* 89–92.

West, R. R. (1985). Valuation of human life in long run healthcare programmes. *British Medical Journal, 291,* 1139–1141.

West, R. R., McNabb, R., Thompson, A. G. H., Sheldon, T. A., & Evans, J. G. (2003). Estimating implied rates of discount in healthcare decision-making. *Health Technology Assessment, 7*(38). Retrieved January 14, 2008, from http:www.hta.ac.uk/fullmono/mon738.pdf

Yi, R., Buchalter, A., Gatchalian, K. M., & Bickel, W. K. (2007). The relationship between temporal discounting and the prisoners dilemma game in intranasal abusers of prescription opioids. *Drug and Alcohol Dependence, 87,* 94–97.

Yi, R., Johnson, M. W., & Bickel, W. K. (2005). Relationship between cooperation in an iterated prisoners dilemma game and the discounting of hypothetical outcomes. *Learning and Behavior, 33,* 324–336.

12

ATTENTION-DEFICIT/HYPERACTIVITY DISORDER AND DISCOUNTING: MULTIPLE MINOR TRAITS AND STATES

JONATHAN WILLIAMS

There has been considerable discussion of the relationship between delay discounting and attention-deficit/hyperactivity disorder (ADHD). Building on the idea that what is termed defective *behavioral inhibition* is at the core of ADHD, it was predicted that "a form of temporal myopia should exist in children with ADHD, in that behavior is more controlled by the temporal 'now' than by internally represented information pertaining to the past, the future, and the sense of time" (Barkley, 1997, p.77). Although this prediction was largely borne out (e.g., Tripp & Alsop, 1999), this chapter summarizes the evidence that these sequelae can be just as well attributed to other causes. More specifically, I argue that viewing discounting, impulsivity, and ADHD as high-level summaries of multiple lower level processes provides a good account of the commonalities between these concepts, as well as the clinical and experimental diversity. This chapter addresses the broad area of impulsivity, summarizing the evidence that most cases of ADHD result from the interacting effects of small or rare ("minor") aberrations in multiple traits and states. These traits and states differ in their relative importance across the population or in an individual. Given our current ignorance of the relative importance of these

I am grateful to Peter Dayan, the editors, and two anonymous reviewers for helpful comments.

323

factors, a full assessment of an individual with hyperactivity, impulsivity, or inattention requires consideration of numerous candidate traits and states.

IMPULSIVITY

The term *impulsivity* covers a wide range of "actions that are poorly conceived, prematurely expressed, unduly risky, or inappropriate to the situation and that often result in undesirable outcomes" (Daruna & Barnes, 1993, p. 23). Individuals' opinions of risk and appropriateness are personal and often unknown; therefore, the *Diagnostic and Statistical Manual of Mental Disorders* (4th ed.; *DSM–IV*; American Psychiatric Association, 1994) has operationalized impulsivity as such behaviors as blurting out the answer to a question before it is complete, difficulty waiting in line, and interrupting others. Impulsivity is elevated in ADHD, mania, personality disorders, substance abuse disorders, learning disability, and immaturity, and it has previously been hypothesized to be a core feature of ADHD (Johansen, Aase, Meyer, & Sagvolden, 2002; Sagvolden & Sergeant, 1998; Sonuga-Barke, Taylor, Sembi, & Smith, 1992). In the traditional view of ADHD illustrated in Figure 12.1, long-term traits (such as impulsivity) interact with environmental factors to produce the current behavior of the organism. A similar diagram might be drawn to illustrate variables affecting choices made in a delay-discounting paradigm.

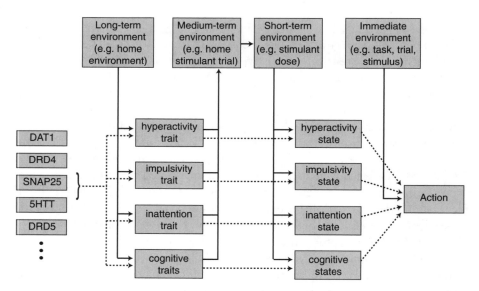

Figure 12.1. Traditional subdivision of traits and states contributing to a single action in attention deficit/hyperactivity disorder (ADHD). ADHD diagnoses, like discounting measures, are derived from behavior and so are better viewed as being downstream of the actions rather than upstream (see Figure 12.4).

Researchers studying impulsivity as a trait have attempted to identify independent tendencies, each of which might be described as a component of what it means to be impulsive. For example, Evenden (1999) suggested separate motivational (risk seeking, novelty seeking, frustratability), cognitive (ability to plan to obtain rewards, time estimation, and their integration), and motor (response inhibition, rate, accuracy) aspects of impulsivity. Each of these "varieties" of impulsivity may be independently assessed with experimental tasks such as an uncertain visual discrimination task; a paced, fixed consecutive-number task; or a delayed-reward task. Evidence of the independence of these varieties of impulsivity has come from studies demonstrating that alcohol, amphetamine, haloperidol (a dopamine antagonist), and serotonergic agents have quite distinct effects on performance in these tasks (Winstanley, Eagle, & Robbins, 2006). With respect to the delayed-reward task, there is some evidence that immediate and delayed rewards are coded in separate brain areas (Tanaka et al., 2004). Children with ADHD show a deficiency (or trend to deficiency) on every reported measure from the Maudsley Attention and Response Suppression task battery; variability of responding and premature responding were the characteristics most strongly associated with diagnosis (Rubia, Smith, & Taylor, 2007).

CONCEPTS OF ADHD

The most prevalent clinical view of ADHD maintains that the central deficits of the disorder are the inability to sustain attention and symptoms of hyperactivity and impulsivity. However, this view of ADHD is only a description of the most commonly observed characteristics. It is not a theory that could serve as a useful scientific tool for researchers, nor does it point us to the underlying neural pathways that might be involved. (Barkley, 2000, p. 1065)

Many clinicians see good reasons for ADHD to be defined broadly. First, many people, even groups not selected for ADHD symptoms, obtain cognitive and behavioral benefit from stimulants (e.g., d-amphetamine [Rapoport et al., 1978; Rapoport & Inoff-Germain, 2002], caffeine [Christopher, Sutherland, & Smith, 2005; Lieberman, Wurtman, Emde, Roberts, & Coviella, 1987]); further evidence of this can be found in any coffee shop. Second, in practice it is difficult to gauge the (usually multiple) underlying influences on children's impulsive–inattentive behavior, so it is very tempting for clinicians to interpret the subjective ADHD criteria broadly, allowing a trial of stimulants. This has caused great disquiet among people who prefer environmental remedies or who feel that children's individuality is being suppressed or that more serious problems are being missed (Timimi et al., 2004).

Researchers have struggled for decades to identify within ADHD a core physiological or psychological deficit, tests for which would presumably supersede the current behavioral approximation (Levy, 1991; Sagvolden, Johansen, Aase, & Russell, 2005). However, in the past few years it has become widely accepted that far from being monolithic, ADHD is multifactorial (Barkley, 2000; Coghill, Nigg, Rothenbarger, Sonuga-Barke, & Tannock, 2005; Faraone & Doyle, 2001; Hastings & Barkley, 1978; Nigg, 2005; Pennington, 2005; Sonuga-Barke, 2005; Taylor, 1998; Williams, 2008). Multifactoriality haunts most current psychiatric diagnoses. Hints of the number of factors that we will eventually have to understand in ADHD come from research domains in which measures are more precise: For example, there are 31 distinct learning processes in humans (Moore, 2004), at least 10 factors controlling activity rate in a single strain of rats (Williams, Taylor, Sagvolden, & Sagvolden, 2009b), at least five separately learned aspects of rewards (sensory, hedonic, motivational, temporal, and response based; Delamater & Oakeshott, 2007), and dozens of neurotransmitters, of which at least five are implicated in ADHD (Faraone et al., 2005). It is hard to imagine that assessment of behavior will ever achieve such precision.

Figure 12.2 depicts the way in which many factors are currently held under the "umbrella construct" that is ADHD (Sonuga-Barke & Castellanos, 2007). Under this umbrella are three layers, namely genes, traits and states,

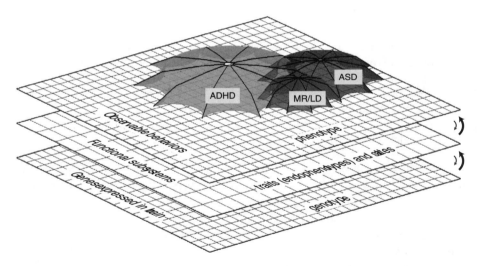

Figure 12.2. Relationship between neuroscience and the three common clinical groupings of developmental psychiatry. The genome (lowest layer) guides the development of interacting physiological systems (middle layer), which in turn produce behaviors (third layer). The construct of attention deficit/hyperactivity disorder (ADHD) is like an umbrella, overlapping similarly broad constructs of mental retardation–learning disability (MR/LD) and autistic spectrum disorders (ASDs). (For indications of the number and type of elements in each layer, see other figures and text.)

and behaviors. These three levels are not merely associated with one another, nor are they alternative views: They have a physical causative relationship, in that genes precede development of neural systems, and neural activity precedes behavior. There is no consensus on the issue of which variants, identifiable causes, and comorbid conditions should be under the ADHD umbrella and which should be regarded as ADHD mimics or part of a broader syndrome (Gillberg et al., 2004).

Causal relationships between genes, traits and states, and behaviors involve, in the simplest analysis, convergence and divergence of influences. Convergence is often detected when clearly separable causes (such as individual genes or genes and environment) are linked experimentally to a single outcome, as in Figure 12.3. Such convergence is a main theme of this

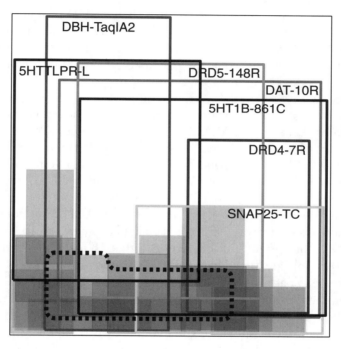

Figure 12.3. One possible population distribution of genes contributing to attention deficit/hyperactivity disorder (ADHD), amplifying the lowest layer of Figure 12.2. Individuals with ADHD are within the dotted outline. The size of named rectangles indicates actual frequency of alleles associated with ADHD in multiple studies (Faraone et al., 2005). Twenty unnamed alleles, each conferring 20% increased risk in 5% of the population, are hypothesized on the basis of nonreplications in genetic studies. Interactions of alleles are unknown, so arrangement is derived by optimizing individual and combined (additive) odds ratios, together with the normality of the resulting risk distribution. (For method, see Williams, 2006.) From "Problems With Models in Psychiatry," by J. Williams, in *Convergence: Interdisciplinary Communications, 2004/2005,* by W. Østreng (Ed.), 2005, p. 93. Copyright 2005 by Centre for Advanced Studies. Reprinted with permission.

chapter and is made explicit in the computational simulation at the end of the chapter. Divergence may be just as common, but it is usually less clear, given our current inability to rigorously tease apart behavioral measures (Caron & Rutter, 1991, and see Figure 12.4). Divergence only becomes obvious in rare conditions with multiple distinct outcomes (e.g., Lesch-Nyhan syndrome, in which a single rare mutation causes impulsivity, learning disability, and ego-dystonic behavior accompanied by kidney stones).

The core behavioral measures of ADHD are not qualitatively different in people with and without the disorder; instead, they are smoothly distributed throughout the population (C. S. Li, Chen, Lin, & Yang, 2005). Although ADHD is highly genetically determined, several of the risk alleles are found in more than half of the population, with each allele only slightly increasing the risk of ADHD, that is, the level of associated features (Faraone et al., 2005). The result is that ADHD is highly heterogeneous (as shown in Figure 12.3), with multiple risk alleles in most patients and major behavioral, pharmacological, and imaging differences between genetically identified subgroups (e.g., Durston et al., 2005; Swanson et al., 2000; Winsberg & Comings, 1999).

There are several reasons to think that the number of genes involved is far greater than is shown in Figure 12.3: the 20,000 genes expressed in mammalian brains (Lein et al., 2007); the 175 mutations per diploid genome per generation, of which 3 are expected to significantly affect function (Nachman & Crowell, 2000); and the paucity of diagnoses available for psychiatrists to describe most neurodevelopmental problems (Figure 12.2). However, the most convincing evidence that ADHD involves many more genes than depicted in Figure 12.3 comes not from research on ADHD but from research on addiction. Using data on 396 genes each implicated by at least two sources, C. Y. Li, Mao, and Wei (2008) determined that 18 metabolic pathways are significantly implicated in addiction to at least one of four types of addictive drugs; of these, 5 pathways are implicated for all types of drug. These are just the common pathways. Because ADHD is both more common and less circumscribed, it could well be more complicated.

Endophenotypes, shown as the middle layer in Figure 12.2, are traits intermediate between behavior and genes (Gottesman & Hanson, 2005). This chapter avoids using the term *endophenotype* not because it is wrong but because of its historical associations with specific disorders and genetic determinism. Even transient mental states are accompanied by changes in gene expression, and most traditionally "genetically determined" traits have turned out to have strong environmental influences (Gottesman & Hanson, 2005). Rather than using a word that groups together all the contributions to ADHD as essentially genetic, it is more useful to separate the long-term contributions (*traits*) from the more temporary *states* that complicate assessment and are more amenable to intervention. The importance of state regulation

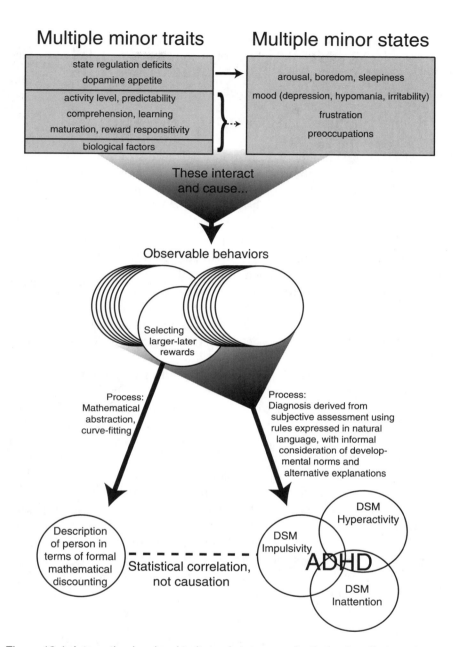

Figure 12.4. Interacting low-level traits and states causing behaviors that can be interpreted in terms of discounting or *Diagnostic and Statistical Manual of Mental Disorders* (4th ed., American Psychiatric Association, 1994) diagnosis (DSM). The figure amplifies elements of Figure 12.2 (traits and states, behaviors, and attention deficit/hyperactivity disorder [ADHD]) and relates them to discounting. Consideration of alternative explanations is an important part of clinical assessment (Williams & Hill, 2004), but it is not always included in research studies. Many influences are omitted for clarity.

in ADHD has been emphasized before (Kuntsi, Oosterlaan, & Stevenson, 2001; van der Meere, 1996), and no doubt contributes to its low test–retest validity (Applegate et al., 1997).

DELAY DISCOUNTING AND ADHD

ADHD has a natural relationship with delay discounting because of its definition, which incorporates impulsivity, and its temporary alleviation by rewards, which are the basis of intertemporal delay studies. There have been theoretical efforts to relate delay discounting to ADHD, treating both as fairly unitary concepts (e.g., Sagvolden et al., 2005; see also Killeen, 2005). However, the heterogeneity of ADHD and the subjective complexities of the diagnostic process make the relationship between ADHD and delay discounting far from straightforward. As shown in Figure 12.4, behavior can be summarized in different ways to produce measures of discounting or ADHD.

Delay discounting can be measured in behavioral tasks that involve choices between rewards of varying sizes, timing, and probability. Such methodology minimizes the use of language and so is fairly straightforward to relate to animal studies.

The literature on ADHD and delay discounting contains an interesting debate that attempted to identify the core cause of ADHD. Sonuga-Barke (1994) contrasted sensitivity to pre-reward delay (which he called *impulsiveness*) and sensitivity to the length of the experimental session (which he called delay aversion). Sonuga-Barke et al. (1992) reported that children diagnosed with ADHD were more delay averse than control children when given 20 opportunities to choose between a smaller–sooner and a larger–later reward. Because no postreward delays were programmed, the 20 trials could be completed sooner by choosing the smaller–sooner alternative. Thus, children with ADHD sacrificed half of their potential monetary earnings to complete the session more quickly and obtain their within-session earnings. A different condition of the same experiment suggested that this preference for smaller–sooner rewards was not the result of a preference for a higher local rate of earnings. When session duration was held constant at 10 minutes, both ADHD and control children strongly preferred the smaller–sooner reward, a choice pattern that maximized local and overall rates of earnings.

Other experiments were designed to determine whether children with ADHD are more sensitive than controls to pre-reward delays when selecting the smaller–sooner reward does not end the session more quickly. This was accomplished by imposing a postreward delay following the delivery of the smaller–sooner reward, a procedure that holds constant the duration of each trial regardless of the reward selected. Although Sonuga-Barke et al. (1992) reported no difference between children with ADHD and control children under this procedure, their finding may have been compromised by their paying participants the same amount of money at the end of the session regardless of the rewards selected during the session. In a later experiment in which variable postreward delays held the session duration constant and participants were paid on the basis of within-session earnings, children with ADHD were "undecided" about which choice to make (i.e., some consistently obtained one or the other reward, and others varied), whereas control children consistently chose the larger–later reward (Schweitzer & Sulzer-Azaroff, 1995). This higher percentage of impulsive choices in the children with ADHD was not due to a failure to discriminate the delay or reward amount because they were able to accurately describe these at the end of the experiment. Interestingly, the children with ADHD tended to choose the larger–later rewards less often as the experiment continued, a possible state-dependent finding like others discussed later. Unfortunately, these studies have not led to a consensus (e.g., Schweitzer, 1996), perhaps because they were based on an assumption of homogeneity within ADHD.

More recently, researchers have attempted to measure the derived construct of delay discounting instead of percentage choice of a smaller–sooner reward. The results have, like prior research on ADHD and this variety of impulsivity, been mixed. In the first of these studies, Barkley, Edwards, Laneri, Fletcher, and Metevia (2001) compared delay-discounting rates in controls to adolescents diagnosed with both ADHD and oppositional defiant disorder. For hypothetical $100 rewards, the dual-diagnosed group demonstrated significantly higher rates of discounting (20% to 50% more over delays from 1 month to 10 years compared with controls). This difference was not attributable to IQ, and it was also not observed when the delayed reward was increased to $1,000. Both groups performed time estimation (a perceptual skill) with similar accuracy. However, when they had to reproduce an observed interval without the use of a watch, reproduction errors were larger in the ADHD–oppositional defiant disorder group (whether the interval was systematically prolonged or shortened was not reported), perhaps because of a motor, working memory, or attentional problem, or a combination of these.

Two final studies conducted in the same laboratory once again produced mixed findings. Scheres, Lee, and Sumiya (2008) reported that college students' self-reported ADHD symptoms of hyperactivity and impulsivity were correlated with rates of delay discounting in a task that arranged real delays and rewards. However, Scheres et al. (2006) reported that when postreward delays were regulated to prevent session length from influencing responding, the ADHD and control participants were statistically indistinguishable.

These mixed findings may have more to do with procedural than participant variables. Nearly all of the studies mentioned here examined sensitivity to pre-reward delays when the rewards were conditioned reinforcers such as points that could be exchanged for money at the end of the session.

Previous studies conducted with adult humans (Hyten, Madden, & Field, 1994) and pigeons (Jackson & Hackenberg, 1996) have demonstrated that choice is not sensitive to delays to the delivery of a conditioned reinforcer; at least not in the range of delays investigated in the these experiments. In the Hyten et al. (1994) and Jackson and Hackenberg (1996) studies, humans and pigeons strongly preferred the larger–later number of points regardless of the delay to their delivery (an amazing finding given that pigeons discount delayed reinforcers at rate thousands-fold higher than humans). The reason for this finding is somewhat intuitive: Once points are received during the session, they cannot be used because they cannot be exchanged for a backup reinforcer until the session ends. As noted by several researchers (e.g., Schweitzer, 1996), procedural improvements are needed that arrange real delays to consumable rewards, that is, rewards with utility at the moment when they are obtained (for a first approximation of these procedures, see Lagorio & Madden, 2005).

Delay discounting can also be measured using tasks involving hypothetical long-term outcomes (e.g., asking whether the participant would prefer $1 after 6 months or $0.27 a year from now; Kable & Glimcher, 2007; McClure, Laibson, Loewenstein, & Cohen, 2004). Many cognitive functions are involved in making choices under these tasks. These tasks put demands on the participants' language comprehension, their ability to imagine rewards of different sizes, their ability to imagine themselves receiving these rewards in different situations in the future, working memory to compare these, and judgment of the likelihood that the experimenter will actually deliver the reward as promised. Because behavior and cognitive abilities are correlated (e.g., Rasmussen & Gillberg, 2000), it is not surprising that people with ADHD (a primarily behavioral concept) have difficulties with such cognitive tasks. However, this does not imply that highly cognitive tasks and the more behavioral tasks are measuring the same underlying functions.

Sonuga-Barke and colleagues (e.g., Solanto et al., 2001; Sonuga-Barke, Dalen, & Remington, 2003) have moved their emphasis from single-path to dual-path hypotheses; that is, from there being a single core cause of ADHD to there being two core causes and, more recently, to ADHD as an "umbrella concept" (as in Figure 12.2). This has rendered these old debates less relevant, but the progress in experimental designs remains instructive. Many older publications include rich experimental records more currently relevant than the hypotheses they were testing: for example, showing that children with ADHD greatly increased their activity as they completed more sessions in the same setting—that is, a change of state, not trait (Schweitzer & Sulzer-Azaroff, 1995). A small study that automatically manipulated reinforcer dimensions revealed that children with ADHD are most influenced in their allocation of effort by multiple factors of reinforcement: quality, immediacy, effort, and rate (in that order; Neef et al., 2005). Even more detailed information can be gleaned from the analysis of responding under variable-interval schedules of reinforcement. These demonstrate that response rates are affected simultaneously by short-term (seconds) and long-term (minutes to days) events. For example, response rates increase when recent interval lengths have been monotonous and decrease when they have been highly variable (Williams et al., 2009b). These results make it highly likely that many factors are interacting to determine animal and human responses in all situations, including discounting experiments and ADHD studies.

The Shape of Delay-Discounting Functions

Delay discounting is often assumed to be either exponential or hyperbolic. The former is simpler, specifying that a reinforcer loses a fixed proportion of its value at each time step. Hyperbolic curves generally fit the results better, but neither formula provides a precise fit. In a review of studies, exponential curves typically accounted for 70%–80% of variance and hyperbolic curves about 10% more (Green & Myerson, 2004).

Several lines of evidence have thrown hyperbolic discounting into doubt (Schweighofer et al., 2006), and to these need to be added difficulties relating specifically to ADHD. First, multiple brain areas cooperate to produce behavior (e.g., McClure et al., 2004), and many brain regions are implicated in ADHD (Seidman, Valera, & Makris, 2005). To emphasize this point, rats with upper mesencephalic transection can walk, grasp, and bite (Woods, 1964), demonstrating that in an intact animal, both forebrain and lower areas of the nervous system are contributing to behaviors used in studies of delay discounting. Using a simple equation to summarize behaviors produced by multiple cooperating regions may be useful for prediction but is likely to confound the search for underlying mechanisms. Second, brainstem and spinal responses are generally rapid, adding to longer term, cerebrally initiated activity. This applies to all tasks (including delay-discounting tasks) so that any curve will fit better than an exponential curve if, for delays under a few seconds, it exceeds the long-term trend. Therefore, the better fit of the hyperbolic curve in comparison with exponential curves is not a strong argument for the existence of an underlying hyperbolic process. This is relevant to ADHD because the basic drives involved are very likely to cause the preference reversals used as evidence for hyperbolic discounting (e.g., Loewenstein, 1996). The same argument applies to other delay-discounting functions such as sums of exponentials or higher order functions: If they are not risky predictions based on an underlying theory, then their better fit provides no evidence of underlying processes (Popper, 1959).

Evolution of Impulsivity and Diversity

The diversity of influences on discounting and ADHD (illustrated in Figures 12.2 to 12.6) becomes clearer when the reasons for that diversity are recognized. These are numerous influences on the evolutionary selection of behavioral characteristics, acting at both the individual and the group level. For example, in *group foraging*, a simple model of social interactions, both competitive and cooperative elements (Critchfield & Atteberry, 2003; Pietras, Cherek, Lane, & Tcheremissine, 2006; Williams & Taylor, 2005) affect reproductive success. In evolving social groups, the distribution of predictability within groups can adapt to rates of change in the environment (Williams & Taylor, 2005). A cooperating group can then have much lower collective discounting than the minority of impulsive individuals within it.

MINOR TRAITS AND STATES OF ADHD
AND DELAY DISCOUNTING

This section briefly summarizes the evidence for the multiple minor traits and states listed in Figure 12.4 (i.e., the factors contributing to ADHD and to delay discounting). Nondiagnostic behavioral and cognitive indicators are considered as well as those included in the *DSM–IV* because of their frequent co-occurrence with ADHD, which can be interpreted as their being part of the broad syndrome of ADHD. This broad interpretation is appropriate because some nonclinical tests are as good at predicting stimulant benefit as is formal clinical diagnosis (Denney & Rapport, 1999).

The list of traits and states shown in Figure 12.4 is similar to this one listing causes of *activation* (behavioral arousal, or vigor and frequency of behavior): food deprivation, stress, stimulant drugs, aversive stimuli, and conditioned stimuli predicting both appetitive and aversive events (Robbins & Everitt, 2007; for a related computational model, see Niv, Daw, Joel, & Dayan, 2007). The same list also describes the processes interacting to make an individual arousable (Hastings & Barkley, 1978), switching from a "baseline default mode to an active processing mode" (Sonuga-Barke & Castellanos, 2007, p. 978) or "toggling between introspective and extrospective modes of attention" (Sonuga-Barke & Castellanos, 2007, p. 980), although the list emphasizes the large number of ways of being disengaged.

Many previously suggested causes of ADHD are implicitly included in categories discussed in this section; others have been excluded because they are too theoretical or because they amalgamate as many traits as ADHD, thus providing at best a clarifying restatement of the problem. Therefore, the list presented in Figure 12.4 and discussed here represents a shift of emphasis in being (a) multifactorial, avoiding the assumption that the major task for such work is identifying the strongest, most consistent, or most independent developmental influences, and (b) lower level, emphasizing regulation and neuroscience and applicable to lower animals.

For each of these states and traits, I describe empirical links to ADHD and delay discounting. The relative importance of most of these factors is not well known but is sometimes demonstrated in individuals through clinical interventions, particularly when a child is mainly affected by one factor. How much of diagnosable ADHD is accounted for by the whole list is currently unknown, but in a rat model of ADHD that was produced by selectively breeding for hypertension, 10 similar factors accounted for the great majority of hyperactivity (Williams et al., 2009b).

States and the Traits Involved in Their Regulation

This section briefly summarizes the wide literature linking ADHD and discounting to identifiable states that an individual can be in and to the traits that more or less directly regulate these states (as listed in Figure 12.4).

Sensation Seeking and Dopamine Appetite

Sensation seeking has been hypothesized to satisfy a *dopamine appetite* (a satiable craving for stimuli that increase dopamine release in the brain) that is increased in ADHD (Williams & Taylor, 2004; Williams, Taylor, Sagvolden, & Sagvolden, 2008a). This hypothesis was suggested by the immediate, unlearned, and fully reversible reduction in activity levels that can be created in children with ADHD and control children by reward, novelty, or stimulants. These three are linked together by evidence that dopamine signals both reward and novelty. Such an appetite is able to account for the finding that children with ADHD are particularly impaired in tasks with long trials (Sonuga-Barke, 2002) and that auditory stimulation, perhaps by suppressing the appetite mechanism, improves the arithmetic performance of some boys with ADHD (Abikoff, Courtney, Szeibel, & Koplewicz, 1996; see also Schweitzer & Sulzer-Azaroff, 1995). Similarly, all children are more active when waiting than when watching a video, implying that the appetite is cross-saturable; this effect is increased in ADHD (Antrop, Roeyers, Van Oost, & Buysse, 2000).

Sleepiness and Underarousal

The relationship between sleepiness and ADHD is not yet clear (Owens, 2005). Some evidence suggests that delay discounting may be increased in normal adults by sleep deprivation (Reynolds & Schiffbauer, 2004). However, this finding must be interpreted cautiously because Reynolds and Schiffbauer

(2004) used an unusual procedure in which impulsive choices decreased session duration (which might be particularly valued by a sleep-deprived participant). Indeed, these authors pointed out that their results may be open to "other interpretations . . . such as irritability, motor impairments, and impairments in time/delay comprehension" (p. 353). Consistent with this caution, Acheson, Richards, and de Wit (2007) found no effect of sleep deprivation when delay discounting was assessed using hypothetical rewards and delays, although it should be noted that their assessment had limited statistical power. My view is that these "other interpretations" are actually minor traits and states and that the "construct of impulsive behavior" is a summary of them.

Children with ADHD are much more likely than controls to be sleepy in the daytime (44% vs. 17%; Holmberg & Hjern, 2006) and have a significantly reduced sleep latency in the multiple sleep latency test (Lecendreux, Konofal, Bouvard, Falissard, & Mouren-Simeoni, 2000). The number and duration of sleep episodes in this test are strongly correlated with severity of ADHD symptoms, particularly inattention. However, bedtime sleep interventions, even when effective for sleep, appear not to improve daytime ADHD symptoms (Mullane & Corkum, 2006; Weiss, Wasdell, Bomben, Rea, & Freeman, 2006). Daytime sleepiness therefore reflects not simply poor nighttime sleep, but a range of daytime problems such as fatigue caused by prolonged high cognitive demand (van der Linden, Frese, & Meijman, 2003) and, indeed, inadequate understanding of or engagement in required tasks.

Infections sometimes cause inattention. In a study of children referred for adenotonsillectomy, 50% of the children who also had ADHD no longer met diagnostic criteria 12 months after operation (Dillon et al., 2007). It is intriguing that the presence of obstructive sleep apnea did not alter the apparent ADHD response to adenotonsillectomy. This suggests that any benefits of surgery were mediated not by improvement in sleep, but by reduced daytime symptoms such as pharyngeal discomfort. Further work is needed to clarify issues such as referral bias, diagnostic methods, and reversion to the mean.

Overarousal

Many children with ADHD give the impression of being overaroused. Electroencephalography, skin conductance, and psychometric evidence have shown that this is generally not the case (e.g., Hermens et al., 2004), although extreme stress such as abuse occasionally causes all major symptoms of ADHD. About 25% of diagnosably anxious children have ADHD, and about 25% of ADHD children are diagnosably anxious (reviewed in March et al., 2000), but the increased discounting of delayed outcomes associated with ADHD is not affected by anxiety (Barkley et al., 2001).

Mood

The distinction between ADHD and hypomania continues to be debated. The most common view is that this is relevant to only a small proportion of ADHD diagnoses. Some evidence suggests that risk taking (in a driving simulation game) increases with briefly elevated mood (Gardner & Steinberg, 2005), but no studies have examined its effects on delay discounting. By contrast, depression is associated with greater delay discounting (Yoon et al., 2007), and clinically low mood often results from the social and academic effects of ADHD. Severe depression increases self-assessed impulsivity and suicide risk (Corruble, Benyamina, Bayle, Falissard, & Hardy, 2003).

High and low mood and sleepiness all increase irritability, "a feeling state characterized by reduced control over temper" (Snaith & Taylor, 1985, p. 128; see also Sims, 2003). This reduced control includes ready provocation and severity and duration of response. Irritability has been linked experimentally to both ADHD and discounting. For example, it may be that "explosive" irritability is characteristic of mood disorders, whereas a less severe "low frustration tolerance" is common in ADHD (Mick, Spencer, Wozniak, & Biederman, 2005, p. 580). Irritability is an important cause of violence, which is correlated with faster discounting of delayed rewards in adult parolees (Cherek, Moeller, Dougherty, & Rhoades, 1997).

Frustration

Frustration is an important cause of aggression that increases the speed and force of responding. Frustration is not just a subjective feeling; it has an operational definition (nonreward in the presence of anticipated reward; Amsel, 1992) that has allowed clear investigation in ADHD. Thus far, no research has examined the effects of experimenter-induced frustration on subsequent delay discounting. However, some evidence suggests that individuals diagnosed with ADHD display more frustration than controls (without necessarily actually being more frustrated), either because they do not learn cues signaling when their behavior is unlikely to be rewarded or because the resulting behavior is less controlled (Douglas & Parry, 1994; Sagvolden, Aase, Zeiner, & Berger, 1998). Children diagnosed with ADHD show stronger facial expressions of frustration during extinction and when exposed to partial reinforcement schedules (Wigal et al., 1998). Group means in the force used to press a lever showed only modest differences, but 20% of the participants with ADHD (vs. 3% of controls) found the experiment too frustrating to continue (Douglas & Parry, 1994).

Preoccupations

The presence of ADHD increases the risk that a child has preoccupations or intrusive thoughts that make it difficult for him or her to concentrate on tasks that adults view as salient. For example, children with tics, obsessive or depressive ruminations, or autistic interests and children who have suffered a bereavement or been abused (Glod & Teicher, 1996) can be distracted by these intrusions or by efforts to suppress them so that an independent observer would judge them to be insufficiently controlled by external events (i.e., to be impulsive or to have excessive discounting of delayed consequences). Because the majority of 9-year-olds with ADHD already have at least one other diagnosis (Gillberg et al., 2004; Jensen et al., 2001), and further diagnoses, present already in partial form, become clear years later (McNicholas & Baird, 2000), research samples of children with ADHD inevitably include such comorbidity.

Traits Not Primarily Concerned With State Regulation

This section very briefly summarizes the wide literature linking ADHD and discounting to long-term low-level traits of individuals.

Children with ADHD have a higher rate and range of movements than do controls, particularly during academic activities, and are increasingly active in repeated experimental sessions (reviewed by Teicher, Ito, Glod, & Barber, 1996). It might be argued that hyperactivity is a part of ADHD and so should not appear in a list of causes of ADHD. However, unlike impulsivity and inattention, it may have simple neural underpinnings. Short-term activity levels fluctuate along with other states (listed in Figure 12.4 and discussed earlier), but long-term levels of activity and impulsivity are highly genetically determined (e.g., Todd et al., 2001). Noncognitive factors cannot be ruled out, given intravenous catecholaminergic agents' ability to increase treadmill walking in spinal cats, suggesting a spinal action (reviewed in Smeets & Gonzalez, 2000).

Increased activity rates allow any organism to obtain the smaller–sooner reward more often. For example, although it does not necessarily indicate preference, the rate at which boys obtain the larger–later reward diminishes as their activity rate increases (Schweitzer & Sulzer-Azaroff, 1995). Spontaneously hypertensive rats, used as a model of ADHD, consistently obtain smaller–sooner rewards when compared with the control WKY strain (Fox, Hand, & Reilly, 2008, Figure 2). Similar results are shown in the simulation described later. Thus, measurements of discounting are only convincing when other possible causes such as activity level are measured and controlled (Williams et al., 2009b). (Other studies have found no relation between activity level and delay discounting; see chap. 9, this volume.)

Accuracy and Predictability Versus Pure Trait Indeterminacy

Inaccuracy and variability of responding are among ADHD's most characteristic features (Barkley et al., 2001; Leth-Steensen, Elbaz, & Douglas, 2000; Sagvolden et al., 2005). It is rarely clear whether unpredictability is absolute or simply the result of not finding the right predictor (Glimcher, 2005); either could in principle be state dependent. A trait of imprecision or unpredictability in executing tasks can prevent learned information from being demonstrated, and this can create the impression of increased discounting (Williams & Dayan, 2005). Conversely, in computational models and presumably in some humans, excess predictability of behavior reduces the exploration and experimentation that allows learning. Regulation of precision may be one role of dopamine, implicated in the genetics and treatment of ADHD (see the next section). Dopamine increases the signal-to-noise ratio in prefrontal cortex (Bandyopadhyay & Hablitz, 2007), as has long been hypothesized for the action of catecholamines in basal ganglia (Servan-Schreiber, Printz, & Cohen, 1990). 5HT is involved, too: Depletion reduces the tendency of people, especially impulsive people, to respond faster (and less accurately) for more reliable rewards in a cued-reinforcement reaction-time task (Cools et al., 2005).

Maturation

Objectively measured activity levels peak in the early school years (Eaton, McKeen, & Campbell, 2001), and subjective measures are mostly consistent with this. After this age, most measures of ADHD gradually decline. Similarly, Scheres et al. (2006) reported that children aged 6 to 11 were more delay averse (i.e., they chose to earn less and end the session more quickly) than children aged 12 to 17. Studies of delay discounting over the life span have shown similar trends toward lower rates of delay discounting with age (Green, Myerson, Lichtman, Rosen, & Fry, 1996), and some evidence suggests the same may be true of rodents when learning experiences are held constant (Simon et al., 2008).

Comprehension and Learning

In adults, IQ is inversely correlated with delay discounting (de Wit, Flory, Acheson, McCloskey, & Manuck, 2007). Similarly, children with ADHD have a mean IQ about 10 points lower than that of controls (Mill et al., 2006). In the Wechsler Intelligence Scale for Children (4th ed.), most of this discrepancy is confined to the Processing Speed and Working Memory subscales (Mayes & Calhoun, 2006). The Full Scale IQ deficit would almost certainly be greater if not for diagnostic boundaries: Children with severe learning problems as well as inattention or hyperactivity sufficient in principle to account for it are usually diagnosed with mental retardation rather than with ADHD.

Executive function deficits have been repeatedly demonstrated to be associated with ADHD, although some very large genetically defined subgroups are relatively spared (Swanson et al., 2000). Similarly, defects in working memory or in time and reward processing have been suggested as major causes of ADHD (Castellanos & Tannock, 2002). However, all of these high-level constructs may be statistically correlated merely because they all tap numerous mental functions, in which case they are alternate constructs at the bottom of Figure 12.4 rather than causes (see Rapport, Chung, Shore, Denney, & Isaacs, 2000). Sometimes they appear to be circumscribed problems simply because developmental assessment has not been comprehensive. A related practical problem is that in schools, clinics, and research, it is often difficult to work out whether children who do not seem to have a skill never learned it (because of motivation, environment, or ability) or learned it but are not performing it.

A separate approach focuses on the general learning mechanisms that permit acquisition of higher level functions. A specific deficit in operant learning has been proposed as the main cause of ADHD (Sagvolden et al., 2005), and a computational model has shown that very high or very low plasticity can impair learning to wait for delayed rewards (Williams & Dayan, 2005).

However, any substantial operant learning abnormality would seem to be contradicted by the effects of stimulants, which achieve considerable normalization that then spontaneously reverses in parallel with the reduction in blood concentration (Quinn et al., 2004), showing both that the prestimulant learning was more extensive than testing would have shown and that the stimulant-induced change in behavior was not learning based. Additionally, in ADHD there may be no memory deficit at all when interesting information is presented once (Kaplan, Dewey, Crawford, & Fisher, 1998). The relatively small deficit in occupational outcome found on long-term follow-up to adulthood (Mannuzza & Klein, 2000) is also consistent with learning being spared more than behavior. Thus, it appears likely that children diagnosed with ADHD have better executive functions and general skills than they show.

Hypo- and Hyperresponsivity to Rewards

The performance of children with ADHD on a *stop-signal task* (which measures how fast a participant can stop an already-begun action on the presentation of a "stop" stimulus) is deficient under conditions of low incentive but largely normalizes with higher incentives (Slusarek, Velling, Bunk, & Eggers, 2001). Learning by children with ADHD is particularly susceptible to disruption by noncontingent and partial reinforcement schedules (Douglas & Parry, 1983). Computational modeling supports the natural expectation that inadequate signaling of reward would reduce the likelihood of achieving larger–later rewards (Williams & Dayan, 2005), and there is empirical evidence for such inadequate signals in ADHD. For example, ventral striatal activity during a reward anticipation task is reduced in ADHD (Scheres, Milham, Knutson, & Castellanos, 2007). This may be why methylphenidate (MPH) is useful, amplifying weak dopamine signals in dorsal striatum (Volkow et al., 2002).

SOCIAL AND BIOLOGICAL INFLUENCES

Social and biological factors are sometimes important in hyperactivity, impulsivity, inattention, and presumably in delay discounting, too. Parents of a child with ADHD share strong genetic influences on behavior (such as unpredictability and inattention) that naturally shape the child's environment. Children with ADHD also influence their environment, making it less predictable. This is obviously difficult to study in human homes, but short-term predictability of the environment increases hyperactivity in the spontaneously hypertensive rat, an animal model of ADHD discussed earlier (Williams et al., 2009b). Theoretically, in more unpredictable environments it is optimal to discount delayed rewards more heavily (Williams & Dayan, 2005).

One of the most useful recommendations given to parents and teachers of children diagnosed with ADHD is to arrange consistent, small, frequent, rapid rewards for appropriate behavior. This advice is based on operant learning, but can also be interpreted as training the parents to minimize the probabilistic and temporal contributors to the child's discounting of the reward. Of course, to invest the considerable effort required to do this, parents need to be reminded of the larger–later improvements in the parent–child relationship, the child's mood, and specific target behaviors.

Individuals occasionally exhibit hyperactivity, impulsivity, or inattention because of physical factors such as toxins, sugar levels, hunger, pain, hyper- and hypothyroidism, chronic or acute infections, dehydration, heat and cold, or subclinical epilepsy (Masicampo & Baumeister, 2008; Taylor & Rogers, 2005; Williams & Hill, 2004). Usually, identifying these causes does not replace the broader psychological descriptions (as used in Figure 12.4). Awareness of the most common of these causes may be useful to researchers in monitoring the heterogeneity of their samples, ensuring the safety of their participants, and planning studies of discounting in biologically identifiable groups in whom the cause is often reversible.

STIMULANTS

Empirically, it is much more straightforward to study medication effects than the difference between children with and without ADHD. Medication studies reduce or avoid definitional problems, permit reversibility studies, and allow more obviously relevant animal research. The commonly prescribed medications for ADHD are MPH and dexamphetamine (often described as *stimulants*), which enhance dopamine and norepinephrine action in prefrontal cortex and basal ganglia. Atomoxetine has a similar effect, but only in prefrontal cortex (probably accounting for this medication's lack of the subcortically mediated increase in premature responding seen with MPH and dexamphetamine; Robinson et al., 2008).

These medications usually reduce clinically significant hyperactivity and impulsivity in humans (Jensen et al., 2001). The effects of MPH in children are dose dependent and somewhat task specific and differ between individuals (Rapport, Stoner, DuPaul, Birmingham, & Tucker, 1985). More precise behavioral assessments feasible in animals have clarified the effects of dose, task, and specific medication (e.g., Robinson et al., 2008). The literature is complicated by the nonlinear effects of drugs on behavior (discussed further with the simulation described in the section "Computational Simulation of Impulsive Choice as a Model of ADHD") and by the higher doses typically used in animal experiments (often more than 2 mg/kg d-amphetamine vs. a quarter of this in human studies; see Evenden & Robbins, 1983). In rats, low doses of amphetamine substantially reduce feeding, social activity, and sleep (Lyon & Robbins, 1975)—very similar to the effects of low-dose stimulant treatment in children (Barkley, McMurray, Edelbrock, & Robbins, 1990; Efron, Jarman, & Barker, 1997).

Relationship to ADHD

The relationship between stimulants and ADHD at first appeared simple, and this contributed enormously to clinical acceptance of the disorder. For a long time, stimulants were seen as essentially prodopaminergic agents. However, just as ADHD involves aberrations in multiple processes, ADHD medications affect multiple transmitter systems, including norepinephrine and serotonin (5-HT; cf. Figure 12.3). Indeed, the pro-5HT effect of amphetamine (which it does not share with MPH; Kuczenski & Segal, 1997) is important in its anti-impulsive effect (Winstanley, Dalley, Theobald, & Robbins, 2003).

Taking a broad view, it is hard to avoid the conclusion that the effectiveness of a stimulant in a particular individual depends on the fit between the processes altered by the drug and the processes that were abnormal (or had spare capacity to improve) in the patient. Unfortunately, even though a few of the genotypes that influence stimulant efficacy are known (e.g., Polanczyk et al., 2007), the effect size of stimulatins on a particular individual cannot yet be predicted.

Relationship to Discounting

Moderate doses of MPH appear to increase the likelihood that rats will select a lever delivering a larger–later reward rather than an adjacent lever delivering a smaller–sooner reward (Pitts & McKinney, 2005). Although this can be interpreted as a reduction in delay discounting, Pitts and McKinney (2005) pointed out that the effect may instead have arisen from the drug's perseverative action. That is, the Pitts and McKinney (and the van Gaalen, van Koten, Schoffelmeer, & Vanderschuren, 2006) experiments employed a commonly used procedure in which a large and a small food reward are both immediately available in an initial block of choice trials (which produces a strong preference for the lever associated with the larger reward) and then the delay to the larger reward is systematically increased within the session. If the perseverative effect of MPH, or more generally a reduction in exploration, prevented rats from switching to the lever with the smaller–sooner reward as the delay to the larger reward increased, then these findings may have little to do with delay discounting per se.

Thus far, only one study has examined the effects of MPH on delay discounting in humans. Pietras, Cherek, Lane, Tcheremissine, and Steinberg (2003) found that about half of their sample of adult healthy male criminals more strongly preferred larger–later monetary rewards when given presession MPH at doses of 0.3 and 0.6 mg/kg. This study excluded participants with a known history of ADHD, but 2 of the 11 participants screened positive for ADHD; these participants had drug responses consistent with those of the other participants. Numerous studies have examined the effects of other stimulants on human delay discounting, but the effects have been mixed (see chap. 8, this volume).

Other measures of impulsivity, such as the response-inhibition measures provided by the stop task and the go/no-go task, suggest that amphetamines decrease impulsivity. For example, in healthy adult humans, amphetamine decreased stop reaction time on the stop task and decreased false alarms on the go/no-go task (de Wit, Enggasser, & Richards, 2002). These results are all explicable in low-level terms such as improved accuracy, alertness, dopamine appetite, or strength of conditioned responses.

Lyon and Robbins (1975) outlined multiple effects of increasing doses of amphetamine on the likelihood of different classes of behavior. For example, d-amphetamine increased conditioned responding by a rat as the dose was progressively raised to 5 mg/kg, then decreased such responding at higher doses. More generally, if an experimental dose directly alters the probability of an external response, such responses cannot be used to measure the effect of medication on any of the internal influences on the response, such as a posited (internal, or "pure") discounting function.

COMPUTATIONAL SIMULATION OF IMPULSIVE CHOICE AS A MODEL OF ADHD

Bringing together results from diverse fields, and working out their interrelationships, is a complex task that can be made more rigorous and transparent through the formality of computer modeling. A model of brain parts interacting to simulate operant learning is shown in the left panel of Figure 12.5 (Williams, 2008; Williams & Dayan, 2005; Williams & Taylor, 2004). This model can be simulated on a computer. Because of space constraints, the following paragraphs give only a brief introduction to the model shown in Figure 12.5, which may motivate some readers to read the original publications.

During the simulation, information and rewards are fed into the model, and it decides what to do. If the information fed in creates a choice between responding now to obtain a smaller–sooner reward and waiting to respond so as to obtain a larger–later one, the model gradually learns to wait (right panel of Figure 12.5). The system learns by constantly predicting how much reward it will achieve if it responds at that moment. The system retrospectively corrects itself every time this prediction is wrong, a process called *temporal difference learning*. Because the task is learned from simple inputs, the model can master simple choice tasks without the need for language. The results are

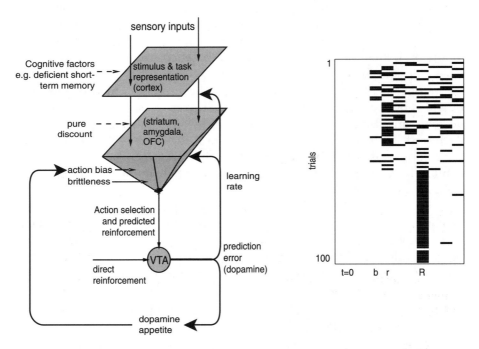

Figure 12.5. Left: A simple model of some of the brain subsystems interacting to produce impulsivity. This extended temporal difference model amplifies the middle layer of Figure 12.2 (after Williams & Taylor, 2004). Right: The record of the model learning to delay responding on the delayed response time task. Each horizontal sweep represents one trial, with the 1st at the top and the 100th at the bottom. Each trial starts with a buzzer (b), after which the model can wait or "decide to press a lever." If this happens first at time r, a small reward is received; if this happens first at time R, a large reward is received. The model learns to achieve r and later learns to reliably achieve R. OFC = orbitofrontal cortex; VTA = ventral tegmental area.

therefore more easily related to developmental disorders and evolutionarily conserved animal behavior than to complex cognitive tasks. Optimal settings of the model's parameters produce rapid learning, and the effects of other settings can be investigated.

The main parameters in this model are the learning rate and a "pure discounting" factor, both of which specify the information learned by the model, and the brittleness and action bias, which specify the way this information is used. Brittleness is a measure of predictability, that is, the extent to which the model's behavior is controlled by learned information. Action bias is the degree of preference for acting over not acting. The only regulatory factor implemented in this model is the dopamine appetite, which is specified by a setpoint and a decay rate. In turn, the dopamine appetite can regulate any of the other parameters, such as the action bias (as shown in Figure 12.5).

The pure numerical *discount factor* controls the propagation of reward predictions to earlier predictors. This factor was adjusted by Williams et al. (2005) according to the degree of unpredictability in an individual's environment. This approach is probably an oversimplification because empirical evidence has shown that such learning is highly context specific (Aloise & Miller, 1991). Indeed, many of the states listed in Figure 12.4 are influenced by the environment, implying that there will be different discounting rates in different situations, and this is indeed the case empirically (Schweighofer et al., 2006; Stevens, Rosati, Ross, & Hauser, 2005).

INTERACTION OF MINOR FACTORS

The "multiple minor causes" thesis implies that minor changes in distinct brain subsystems often interact in a cumulative way to reach pathological levels. The first piece of evidence for this came from the small effects of individual risk alleles targeting different neurotransmitters (Figure 12.3). The thesis also suggests that common minor psychological risks will interact to produce substantial problems diagnosable as ADHD. This is supported by Rapport et al.'s (2000) empirical demonstration that a clinical diagnosis of ADHD depends essentially on both the *number* and the *range* of distinct cognitive loads that can be managed together.

Computational simulations show the same (Figure 12.6). In preparing Figure 12.6, I first adjusted the parameters of the model shown in Figure 12.5 to produce optimal, almost perfect performance. This is shown as the leftmost point of Figure 12.6, Panel (a). Then, 100 times, one of the parameters was randomly selected for adjustment ("mutation"), and the curve in Figure 12.6, Panel (a), shows the gradual deterioration in performance this produces. Each mutation was arbitrarily in the range ±20%, but if a larger range had been chosen, the curve would have been steeper. The curve shown is the average

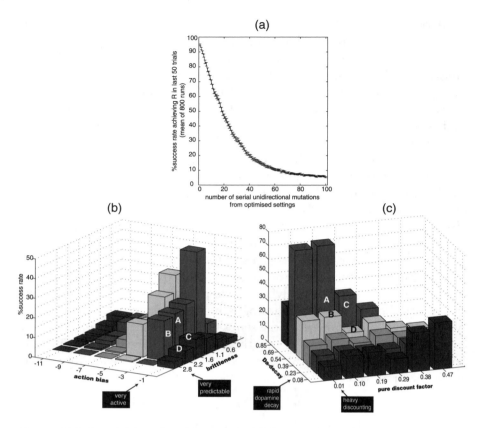

Figure 12.6. Impulsivity related to mutational distance from an optimal performer (simulation). Panels (a)–(c) are from the extended temporal difference model shown in Figure 12.5. This figure amplifies the relationship between one of the umbrella concepts depicted in Figure 12.2 (attention-deficit/hyperactivity disorder) and the lowest layer (a) or the middle layer (b)–(c). (a): At the left of the graph (number of mutations = 0), an optimized set of parameters allows the simulation to achieve the larger–later reward more than 90% of the time. Each increment on the *x*-axis indicates a single further mutation in one of seven parameters controlling the simulation. Mutations were uniformly distributed in the range ±20% and were for each parameter always in the same direction (randomized each run) to prevent them canceling each other, so the *x*-axis is mutational distance rather than mutational time. Error bars are standard errors of the mean. (b)–(c): Nonadditive interaction of traits. Vertical axes are as in Panel (a). Changes in action bias and brittleness each alter the effect on impulsivity of changes in the other (b). Individuals with a heavy temporal pure discounting function still achieve the larger–later reward if a slow dopamine decay rate prevents rapid responding (c). All 80,000 simulated individuals are included in all graphs, so each data point includes many heterogeneous individuals. See text for discussion of A, B, C, and D in Panels (b) and (c). Da = dopamine.

of 80 runs. Each run explored the space of possible disruptions like a random walk, sometimes reaching new places and sometimes reaching those previously reached via the same or different routes. The performance of the model (i.e., its success in achieving the large–late reward) was calculated at each point in this space; because of the difficulty of displaying seven dimensions, these were squashed into two dimensions for display as Panels (b) and (c) of Figure 12.6.

The landscapes of Panels (b) and (c) of Figure 12.6 are pale shadows of the real complexity of the brain, but they are sufficient to reinforce some of the key messages of this chapter. First, impulsivity, high rates of delay discounting, and ADHD exist in many forms and degrees of severity. Second, they have closely related causes (Figure 12.4). Third, the landscape is not a plateau of high idealized function in the general population, with occasional pits and gullies indicating dysfunction; rather, it is continuously variable, with perfect performance being quite unusual. Fourth, some parameters have values that can increase, alter, or disable other parameters (their relationships are much more complex than sums or logical algebra). The central point of the figure, and of this chapter, is that in moving down from a peak of idealized function, a step alteration in one or another parameter (from A to B or A to C in Figure 12.6, Panels (b)–(c)) will often produce minor, even clinically imperceptible, loss of function, whereas altering both parameters together (A to D) will produce substantial, even diagnosable, dysfunction.

SUMMARY

ADHD, impulsivity, and excessive delay discounting are attractively simple concepts that have considerable covariation in the general population. However, all three are high-level summaries of multiple lower level processes. As shown in this chapter, related lower level processes have been the subject of many previous studies, often under the assumption that they were core causes, unrelated comorbidities, or sequelae. However, evidence as summarized in this chapter suggests that the great majority of ADHD and discounting results can be accounted for by these multiple minor traits and states. Rather than attempting to devise subtle experiments to isolate a discounting function or a core principle of ADHD, we need to painstakingly study the size and interactions of all the causes we *can* identify.

REFERENCES

Abikoff, H., Courtney, M. E., Szeibel, P. J., & Koplewicz, H. S. (1996). The effects of auditory stimulation on the arithmetic performance of children with ADHD and nondisabled children. *Journal of Learning Disabilities, 29*, 238–246.

Acheson, A., Richards, J. B., & de Wit, H. (2007). Effects of sleep deprivation on impulsive behaviors in men and women. *Physiology & Behavior, 91*, 579–587.

Aloise, P. A., & Miller, P. H. (1991). Discounting in preschoolers: Effect of type of reward agent. *Journal of Experimental Child Psychology, 52*, 70–86.

American Psychiatric Association. (1994). *Diagnostic and statistical manual of mental disorders* (4th ed.). Washington, DC: Author.

Amsel, A. (1992). Frustration theory—Many years later. *Psychological Bulletin, 112*, 396–399.

Antrop, I., Roeyers, H., Van Oost, P., & Buysse, A. (2000). Stimulation seeking and hyperactivity in children with ADHD. *Journal of Child Psychology and Psychiatry and Allied Disciplines, 41*, 225–231.

Applegate, B., Lahey, B. B., Hart, E. L., Biederman, J., Hynd, G. W., Barkley, R. A., et al. (1997). Validity of the age-of-onset criterion for ADHD: A report from the *DSM-IV* field trials. *Journal of the American Academy of Child & Adolescent Psychiatry, 36*, 1211–1221.

Bandyopadhyay, S., & Hablitz, J. J. (2007). Dopaminergic modulation of local network activity in rat prefrontal cortex. *Journal of Neurophysiology, 97*, 4120–4128.

Barkley, R. A. (1997). Behavioral inhibition, sustained attention, and executive functions: Constructing a unifying theory of ADHD. *Psychological Bulletin, 121*, 65–94.

Barkley, R. A. (2000). Genetics of childhood disorders: XVII. ADHD, Part 1: The executive functions and ADHD. *Journal of the American Academy of Child & Adolescent Psychiatry, 39*, 1064–1068.

Barkley, R. A., Edwards, G., Laneri, M., Fletcher, K., & Metevia, L. (2001). Executive functioning, temporal discounting, and sense of time in adolescents with attention deficit hyperactivity disorder (ADHD) and oppositional defiant disorder (ODD). *Journal of Abnormal Child Psychology, 29*, 541–556.

Barkley, R. A., McMurray, M. B., Edelbrock, C. S., & Robbins, K. (1990). Side effects of methylphenidate in children with attention deficit hyperactivity disorder: A systemic, placebo-controlled evaluation. *Pediatrics, 86*, 184–192.

Caron, C., & Rutter, M. (1991). Comorbidity in child psychopathology: Concepts, issues and research strategies. *Journal of Child Psychology and Psychiatry and Allied Disciplines, 32*, 1063–1080.

Castellanos, F. X., & Tannock, R. (2002). Neuroscience of attention-deficit/hyperactivity disorder: The search for endophenotypes. *Nature Reviews Neuroscience, 3*, 617–628.

Cherek, D. R., Moeller, F. G., Dougherty, D. M., & Rhoades, H. (1997). Studies of violent and nonviolent male parolees: II. Laboratory and psychometric measurements of impulsivity. *Biological Psychiatry, 41*, 523–529.

Christopher, G., Sutherland, D., & Smith, A. (2005). Effects of caffeine in non-withdrawn volunteers. *Human Psychopharmacology, 20*, 47–53.

Coghill, D., Nigg, J., Rothenberger, A., Sonuga-Barke, E., & Tannock, R. (2005). Whither causal models in the neuroscience of ADHD? *Developmental Science, 8*, 105–114.

Cools, R., Blackwell, A., Clark, L., Menzies, L., Cox, S., & Robbins, T. W. (2005). Tryptophan depletion disrupts the motivational guidance of goal-directed behavior as a function of trait impulsivity. *Neuropsychopharmacology, 30,* 1362–1373.

Corruble, E., Benyamina, A., Bayle, F., Falissard, B., & Hardy, P. (2003). Understanding impulsivity in severe depression? A psychometrical contribution. *Progress in Neuro-Psychopharmacology and Biological Psychiatry, 27,* 829–833.

Critchfield, T. S., & Atteberry, T. (2003). Temporal discounting predicts individual competitive success in a human analogue of group foraging. *Behavioral Processes, 64,* 315–331.

Daruna, J. H., & Barnes, P. A. (1993). A neurodevelopmental view of impulsivity. In W. G. McCown, J. L. Johnson, & M. B. Shure (Eds.), *The impulsive client: Theory, research, and treatment* (pp. 23–37). Washington, DC: American Psychological Association.

Delamater, A. R., & Oakeshott, S. (2007). Learning about multiple attributes of reward in Pavlovian conditioning. In B. W. Balleine, K. Doya, J. O'Doherty, & M. Sakagami (Eds.), *Annals of the New York Academy of Sciences: Vol. 1104. Reward and decision making in corticobasal ganglia networks* (pp. 1–20). New York: New York Academy of Sciences.

Denney, C. B., & Rapport, M. D. (1999). Predicting methylphenidate response in children with ADHD: Theoretical, empirical, and conceptual models. *Journal of the American Academy of Child & Adolescent Psychiatry, 38,* 393–401.

de Wit, H., Enggasser, J. L., & Richards, J. B. (2002). Acute administration of d-amphetamine decreases impulsivity in healthy volunteers. *Neuropsychopharmacology, 27,* 813–825.

de Wit, H., Flory, J. D., Acheson, A., McClosky, M., & Manuck, S. B. (2007). IQ and nonplanning impulsivity are independently associated with delay discounting in middle-aged adults. *Personality and Individual Differences, 42,* 111–121.

Dillon, J. E., Blunden, S., Ruzicka, D. L., Guire, K. E., Champine, D., Weatherly, R. A., et al. (2007). DSM–IV diagnoses and obstructive sleep apnea in children before and 1 year after adenotonsillectomy. *Journal of the American Academy of Child & Adolescent Psychiatry, 46,* 1425–1436.

Douglas, V. I., & Parry, P. A. (1983). Effects of reward on delayed reaction time task performance of hyperactive children. *Journal of Abnormal Child Psychology, 11,* 313–326.

Douglas, V. I., & Parry, P. A. (1994). Effects of reward and nonreward on frustration and attention in attention deficit disorder. *Journal of Abnormal Child Psychology, 22,* 281–302.

Durston, S., Fossella, J. A., Casey, B. J., Hulshoff Pol, H. E., Galvan, A., Schnack, H. G., et al. (2005). Differential effects of DRD4 and DAT1 genotype on fronto-striatal gray matter volumes in a sample of subjects with attention deficit hyperactivity disorder, their unaffected siblings, and controls. *Molecular Psychiatry, 10,* 678–685.

Eaton, W. O., McKeen, N. A., & Campbell, D. W. (2001). The waxing and waning of movement: Implications for psychological development. *Developmental Review, 21,* 205–223.

Efron, D., Jarman, F., & Barker, M. (1997). Side effects of methylphenidate and dex-amphetamine in children with attention deficit hyperactivity disorder: A double-blind, crossover trial. *Pediatrics, 100,* 662–666.

Evenden, J. L. (1999). Varieties of impulsivity. *Psychopharmacology, 146,* 348–361.

Evenden, J. L., & Robbins, T. W. (1983). Increased response switching, perseveration and perseverative switching following d-amphetamine in the rat. *Psychopharmacology, 80,* 67–73.

Faraone, S. V., & Doyle, A. E. (2001). The nature and heritability of attention-deficit/hyperactivity disorder. *Child and Adolescent Psychiatric Clinics of North America, 10,* 299–316.

Faraone, S. V., Perlis, R. H., Doyle, A. E., Smoller, J. W., Goralnick, J. J., Holmgren, M. A., et al. (2005). Molecular genetics of attention-deficit/hyperactivity disorder. *Biological Psychiatry, 57,* 1313–1323.

Fox, A. T., Hand, D. J., & Reilly, M. P. (2008). Impulsive choice in a rodent model of ADHD. *Behavioural Brain Research, 187,* 146–152.

Gardner, M., & Steinberg, L. (2005). Peer influence on risk taking, risk preference, and risky decision making in adolescence and adulthood: An experimental study. *Developmental Psychology, 41,* 625–635.

Gillberg, C., Gillberg, I. C., Rasmussen, P., Kadesjo, B., Soderstrom, H., Rastam, M., et al. (2004). Co-existing disorders in ADHD —Implications for diagnosis and intervention. *European Child and Adolescent Psychiatry, 13*(Suppl. 1), I80–I92.

Glimcher, P. W. (2005). Indeterminacy in brain and behavior. *Annual Review of Psychology, 56,* 25–56.

Glod, C. A., & Teicher, M. H. (1996). Relationship between early abuse, post-traumatic stress disorder, and activity levels in prepubertal children. *Journal of the American Academy of Child & Adolescent Psychiatry, 35,* 1384–1393.

Gottesman, I. I., & Hanson, D. R. (2005). Human development: Biological and genetic processes. *Annual Review of Psychology, 56,* 263–286.

Green, L., & Myerson, J. (2004). A discounting framework for choice with delayed and probabilistic rewards. *Psychological Bulletin, 130,* 769–792.

Green, L., Myerson, J., Lichtman, D., Rosen, S., & Fry, A. (1996). Temporal discounting in choice between delayed rewards: The role of age and income. *Psychology and Aging, 11,* 79–84.

Hastings, J. E., & Barkley, R. A. (1978). A review of psychophysiological research with hyperkinetic children. *Journal of Abnormal Child Psychology, 6,* 413–447.

Hermens, D. F., Williams, L. M., Lazzaro, I., Whitmont, S., Melkonian, D., & Gordon, E. (2004). Sex differences in adult ADHD: A double dissociation in brain activity and autonomic arousal. *Biological Psychology, 66,* 221–233.

Holmberg, K., & Hjern, A. (2006). Health complaints in children with attention-deficit/hyperactivity disorder. *Acta Paediatrica, 95,* 664–670.

Hyten, C., Madden, G. J., & Field, D. P. (1994). Exchange delays and impulsive choice in adult humans. *Journal of the Experimental Analysis of Behavior, 62,* 225–233.

Jackson, K., & Hackenberg, T. D. (1996). Token reinforcement, choice, and self-control in pigeons. *Journal of the Experimental Analysis of Behavior, 66,* 29–49.

Jensen, P. S., Hinshaw, S. P., Swanson, J. M., Greenhill, L. L., Conners, C. K., Arnold, L. E., et al. (2001). Findings from the NIMH Multimodal Treatment Study of ADHD (MTA): Implications and applications for primary care providers. *Journal of Developmental and Behavioral Pediatrics, 22,* 60–73.

Johansen, E. B., Aase, H., Meyer, A., & Sagvolden, T. (2002). Attention-deficit/ hyperactivity disorder (ADHD) behaviour explained by dysfunctioning reinforcement and extinction processes. *Behavioural Brain Research, 130,* 37–45.

Kable, J. W., & Glimcher, P. W. (2007). The neural correlates of subjective value during intertemporal choice. *Nature Neuroscience, 10,* 1625–1633.

Kaplan, B. J., Dewey, D., Crawford, S. G., & Fisher, G. C. (1998). Deficits in long-term memory are not characteristic of ADHD. *Journal of Clinical and Experimental Neuropsychology, 20,* 518–528.

Killeen, P. R. (2005). Gradus ad parnassum: Ascending strength gradients or descending memory traces? *Behavioral and Brain Sciences, 28,* 432–434.

Kuczenski, R., & Segal, D. S. (1997). Effects of methylphenidate on extracellular dopamine, serotonin, and norepinephrine: Comparison with amphetamine. *Journal of Neurochemistry, 68,* 2032–2037.

Kuntsi, J., Oosterlaan, J., & Stevenson, J. (2001). Psychological mechanisms in hyperactivity: I. Response inhibition deficit, working memory impairment, delay aversion, or something else? *Journal of Child Psychology and Psychiatry and Allied Disciplines, 42,* 199–210.

Lagorio, C. H., & Madden, G. J. (2005). Delay discounting of real and hypothetical rewards III: Steady-state assessments, forced-choice trials, and all real rewards. *Behavioural Processes, 69,* 173–187.

Lecendreux, M., Konofal, E., Bouvard, M., Falissard, B., & Mouren-Simeoni, M. C. (2000). Sleep and alertness in children with ADHD. *Journal of Child Psychology and Psychiatry and Allied Disciplines, 41,* 803–812.

Lein, E. S., Hawrylycz, M. J., Ao, N., Ayres, M., Bensinger, A., Bernard, A., et al. (2007, January 11). Genome-wide atlas of gene expression in the adult mouse brain. *Nature, 445,* 168–176.

Leth-Steensen, C., Elbaz, Z. K., & Douglas, V. I. (2000). Mean response times, variability, and skew in the responding of ADHD children: A response time distributional approach. *Acta Psychologica, 104,* 167–190.

Levy, F. (1991). The dopamine theory of attention deficit hyperactivity disorder (ADHD). *Australian and New Zealand Journal of Psychiatry, 25,* 277–283.

Li, C. S., Chen, S. H., Lin, W. H., & Yang, Y. Y. (2005). Attentional blink in adolescents with varying levels of impulsivity. *Journal of Psychiatric Research, 39,* 197–205.

Li, C.-Y., Mao, X., & Wei, L. (2008). Genes and (common) pathways underlying drug addiction. *PLoS Computational Biology, 4,* e2.

Lieberman, H. R., Wurtman, R. J., Emde, G. G., Roberts, C., & Coviella, I. L. (1987). The effects of low doses of caffeine on human performance and mood. *Psychopharmacology (Berlin), 92,* 308–312.

Loewenstein, G. (1996). Out of control: Visceral influences on behavior. *Organizational Behavior and Human Decision Processes, 65,* 272–292.

Lyon, M., & Robbins, T. W. (1975). The action of CNS stimulant drugs: A general theory concerning amphetamine effects. *Current Developments in Psychopharmacology, 2*, 79–163.

Mannuzza, S., & Klein, R. G. (2000). Long-term prognosis in attention-deficit/hyperactivity disorder. *Child and Adolescent Psychiatric Clinics of North America, 9*, 711–726.

March, J. S., Swanson, J. M., Arnold, L. E., Hoza, B., Conners, C. K., Hinshaw, S. P., et al. (2000). Anxiety as a predictor and outcome variable in the multimodal treatment study of children with ADHD (MTA). *Journal of Abnormal Child Psychology, 28*, 527–541.

Masicampo, E. J., & Baumeister, R. F. (2008). Toward a physiology of dual-process reasoning and judgment: Lemonade, willpower, and expensive rule-based analysis. *Psychological Science, 19*, 255–260.

Mayes, S. D., & Calhoun, S. L. (2006). WISC–IV and WISC–III profiles in children with ADHD. *Journal of Attention Disorders, 9*, 486–493.

McClure, S. M., Laibson, D. I., Loewenstein, G., & Cohen, J. D. (2004, October 15). Separate neural systems value immediate and delayed monetary rewards. *Science, 306*, 503–507.

McNicholas, F., & Baird, G. (2000). Early-onset bipolar disorder and ADHD: Diagnostic confusion due to comorbidity. *Clinical Child Psychology and Psychiatry, 5*, 595–605.

Mick, E., Spencer, T., Wozniak, J., & Biederman, J. (2005). Heterogeneity of irritability in attention-deficit/hyperactivity disorder subjects with and without mood disorders. *Biological Psychiatry, 58*, 576–582.

Mill, J., Caspi, A., Williams, B. S., Craig, I., Taylor, A., Polo-Tomas, M., et al. (2006). Prediction of heterogeneity in intelligence and adult prognosis by genetic polymorphisms in the dopamine system among children with attention-deficit/hyperactivity disorder: Evidence from 2 birth cohorts. *Archives of General Psychiatry, 63*, 462–469.

Moore, B. R. (2004). The evolution of learning. *Biological Reviews of the Cambridge Philosophical Society, 79*, 301–335.

Mullane, J., & Corkum, P. (2006). Case series: Evaluation of a behavioral sleep intervention for three children with attention-deficit/hyperactivity disorder and dyssomnia. *Journal of Attention Disorders, 10*, 217–227.

Nachman, M. W., & Crowell, S. L. (2000). Estimate of the mutation rate per nucleotide in humans. *Genetics, 156*, 297–304.

Neef, N. A., Marckel, J., Ferreri, S. J., Bicard, D. F., Endo, S., Aman, M. G., et al. (2005). Behavioral assessment of impulsivity: A comparison of children with and without attention deficit hyperactivity disorder. *Journal of Applied Behavior Analysis, 38*, 23–37.

Nigg, J. T. (2005). Neuropsychologic theory and findings in attention-deficit/hyperactivity disorder: The state of the field and salient challenges for the coming decade. *Biological Psychiatry, 57*, 1424–1435.

Niv, Y., Daw, N. D., Joel, D., & Dayan, P. (2007). Tonic dopamine: Opportunity costs and the control of response vigor. *Psychopharmacology, 191*, 507–520.

Owens, J. A. (2005). The ADHD and sleep conundrum: A review. *Journal of Developmental and Behavioral Pediatrics, 26*, 312–322.

Pennington, B. F. (2005). Toward a new neuropsychological model of attention-deficit/hyperactivity disorder: Subtypes and multiple deficits. *Biological Psychiatry, 57*, 1221–1223.

Pietras, C. J., Cherek, D. R., Lane, S. D., & Tcheremissine, O. V. (2006). Risk reduction and resource pooling on a cooperation task. *Psychological Record, 56*, 387–410.

Pietras, C. J., Cherek, D. R., Lane, S. D., Tcheremissine, O. V., & Steinberg, J. L. (2003). Effects of methylphenidate on impulsive choice in adult humans. *Psychopharmacology, 170*, 390–398.

Pitts, R. C., & McKinney, A. P. (2005). Effects of methylphenidate and morphine on delay-discount functions obtained within sessions. *Journal of the Experimental Analysis of Behavior, 83*, 297–314.

Polanczyk, G., Zeni, C., Genro, J. P., Guimaraes, A. P., Roman, T., Hutz, M. H., et al. (2007). Association of the adrenergic alpha2A receptor gene with methylphenidate improvement of inattentive symptoms in children and adolescents with attention-deficit/hyperactivity disorder. *Archives of General Psychiatry, 64*, 218–224.

Popper, K. R. (1959). *Conjectures and refutations: The growth of scientific knowledge.* New York: Routledge.

Quinn, D., Wigal, S., Swanson, J., Hirsch, S., Ottolini, Y., Dariani, M., et al. (2004). Comparative pharmacodynamics and plasma concentrations of d-threo-methylphenidate hydrochloride after single doses of d-threo-methylphenidate hydrochloride and d,l-threo-methylphenidate hydrochloride in a double-blind, placebo-controlled, crossover laboratory school study in children with attention-deficit/hyperactivity disorder. *Journal of the American Academy of Child & Adolescent Psychiatry, 43*, 1422–1429.

Rapoport, J. L., Buchsbaum, M. S., Zahn, T. P., Weingartner, H., Ludlow, C., & Mikkelsen, E. J. (1978, February 3). Dextroamphetamine: Cognitive and behavioral effects in normal prepubertal boys. *Science, 199*, 560–563.

Rapoport, J. L., & Inoff-Germain, G. (2002). Responses to methylphenidate in attention-deficit/hyperactivity disorder and normal children: Update 2002. *Journal of Attention Disorders, 6*(Suppl. 1), S57–S60.

Rapport, M. D., Chung, K. M., Shore, G., Denney, C. B., & Isaacs, P. (2000). Upgrading the science and technology of assessment and diagnosis: Laboratory and clinic-based assessment of children with ADHD. *Journal of Clinical Child Psychology, 29*, 555–568.

Rapport, M. D., Stoner, G., DuPaul, G. J., Birmingham, B. K., & Tucker, S. (1985). Methylphenidate in hyperactive children: Differential effects of dose on academic, learning, and social behavior. *Journal of Abnormal Child Psychology, 13*, 227–243.

Rasmussen, P., & Gillberg, C. (2000). Natural outcome of ADHD with developmental coordination disorder at age 22 years: A controlled, longitudinal, community-based study. *Journal of the American Academy of Child & Adolescent Psychiatry, 39,* 1424–1431.

Reynolds, B., & Schiffbauer, R. (2004). Measuring state changes in human delay discounting: An experiential discounting task. *Behavioral Processes, 67,* 343–356.

Robbins, T. W., & Everitt, B. J. (2007). A role for mesencephalic dopamine in activation: Commentary on Berridge (2006). *Psychopharmacology, 191,* 433–437.

Robinson, E. S., Eagle, D. M., Mar, A. C., Bari, A., Banerjee, G., Jiang, X., et al. (2008). Similar effects of the selective noradrenaline reuptake inhibitor atomoxetine on three distinct forms of impulsivity in the rat. *Neuropsychopharmacology, 33,* 1028–1037.

Rubia, K., Smith, A., & Taylor, E. (2007). Performance of children with attention deficit hyperactivity disorder (ADHD) on a test battery of impulsiveness. *Child Neuropsychology, 13,* 276–304.

Sagvolden, T., Aase, H., Zeiner, P., & Berger, D. (1998). Altered reinforcement mechanisms in attention-deficit/hyperactivity disorder. *Behavioural Brain Research, 94,* 61–71.

Sagvolden, T., Johansen, E., Aase, H., & Russell, V. (2005). A dynamic developmental theory of attention-deficit hyperactivity disorder (ADHD) predominantly hyperactive impulsive and combined subtypes. *Behavioral and Brain Sciences, 28,* 397–419.

Sagvolden, T., & Sergeant, J. A. (1998). Attention deficit/hyperactivity disorder—From brain dysfunctions to behaviour. *Behavioural Brain Research, 94,* 1–10.

Scheres, A., Dijkstra, M., Ainslie, E., Balkan, J., Reynolds, B., Sonuga-Barke, E., et al. (2006). Temporal and probabilistic discounting of rewards in children and adolescents: Effects of age and ADHD symptoms. *Neuropsychologia, 44,* 2092–2103.

Scheres, A., Lee, A., & Sumiya, M. (2008). Temporal reward discounting and ADHD: Task and symptom specific effects. *Journal of Neural Transmission, 115,* 221–226.

Scheres, A., Milham, M. P., Knutson, B., & Castellanos, F. X. (2007). Ventral striatal hyporesponsiveness during reward anticipation in attention-deficit/hyperactivity disorder. *Biological Psychiatry, 61,* 720–724.

Schweighofer, N., Shishida, K., Han, C. E., Okamoto, Y., Tanaka, S. C., Yamawaki, S., et al. (2006). Humans can adopt optimal discounting strategy under real-time constraints. *PLoS Computational Biology, 2,* e152.

Schweitzer, J. B. (1996). Debate and argument: Delay aversion versus impulsivity: Testing for dysfunction in ADHD. *Journal of Child Psychology and Psychiatry and Allied Disciplines, 37,* 1027–1028.

Schweitzer, J. B., & Sulzer-Azaroff, B. (1995). Self-control in boys with attention deficit hyperactivity disorder: Effects of added stimulation and time. *Journal of Child Psychology and Psychiatry and Allied Disciplines, 36,* 671–686.

Seidman, L. J., Valera, E. M., & Makris, N. (2005). Structural brain imaging of attention-deficit/hyperactivity disorder. *Biological Psychiatry, 57,* 1263–1272.

Servan-Schreiber, D., Printz, H., & Cohen, J. D. (1990, August 24). A network model of catecholamine effects: Gain, signal-to-noise ratio, and behavior. *Science, 249,* 892–895.

Sims, A. (2003). *Symptoms in the mind*. Philadelphia: Elsevier.

Simon, N. W., LaSarge, C. L., Montgomery, K. S., Williams, M. T., Mendez, I. A., Setlow, B., & Bizon, J. L. (2008). Good things come to those who wait: Attenuated discounting of delayed rewards in aged Fischer 344 rats [corrected proof]. *Neurobiology of Aging*. doi: 10.1016/j.neurobiolaging.2008.06.004

Slusarek, M., Velling, S., Bunk, D., & Eggers, C. (2001). Motivational effects on inhibitory control in children with ADHD. *Journal of the American Academy of Child & Adolescent Psychiatry, 40*, 355–363.

Smeets, W. J. A. J., & Gonzalez, A. (2000). Catecholamine systems in the brain of vertebrates: New perspectives through a comparative approach. *Brain Research Reviews, 33*, 308–379.

Snaith, R. P., & Taylor, C. M. (1985). Irritability: Definition, assessment and associated factors. *British Journal of Psychiatry, 147*, 127–136.

Solanto, M. V., Abikoff, H., Sonuga-Barke, E., Schachar, R., Logan, G. D., Wigal, T., et al. (2001). The ecological validity of delay aversion and response inhibition as measures of impulsivity in AD/HD: A supplement to the NIMH multimodal treatment study of AD/HD. *Journal of Abnormal Child Psychology, 29*, 215–228.

Sonuga-Barke, E. J. (1994). On dysfunction and function in psychological theories of childhood disorder. *Journal of Child Psychology and Psychiatry and Allied Disciplines, 35*, 801–815.

Sonuga-Barke, E. J. (2002). Interval length and time-use by children with AD/HD: A comparison of four models. *Journal of Abnormal Child Psychology, 30*, 257–264.

Sonuga-Barke, E. J. (2005). Causal models of attention-deficit/hyperactivity disorder: From common simple deficits to multiple developmental pathways. *Biological Psychiatry, 57*, 1231–1238.

Sonuga-Barke, E. J., & Castellanos, F. X. (2007). Spontaneous attentional fluctuations in impaired states and pathological conditions: A neurobiological hypothesis. *Neuroscience and Biobehavioral Reviews, 31*, 977–986.

Sonuga-Barke, E. J., Dalen, L., & Remington, B. (2003). Do executive deficits and delay aversion make independent contributions to preschool attention-deficit/hyperactivity disorder symptoms? *Journal of the American Academy Child and Adolescent Psychiatry, 42*, 1335–1342.

Sonuga-Barke, E. J., Taylor, E., Sembi, S., & Smith, J. (1992). Hyperactivity and delay aversion—I. The effect of delay on choice. *Journal of Child Psychology and Psychiatry and Allied Disciplines, 33*, 387–398.

Stevens, J. R., Rosati, A. G., Ross, K. R., & Hauser, M. D. (2005). Will travel for food: Spatial discounting in two new world monkeys. *Current Biology, 15*, 1855–1860.

Swanson, J., Oosterlaan, J., Murias, M., Schuck, S., Flodman, P., Spence, M. A., et al. (2000). Attention deficit/hyperactivity disorder children with a 7-repeat allele of the dopamine receptor D4 gene have extreme behavior but normal performance on critical neuropsychological tests of attention. *Proceedings of the National Academy of Sciences, USA, 97*, 4754–4759.

Tanaka, S. C., Doya, K., Okada, G., Ueda, K., Okamoto, Y., & Yamawaki, S. (2004). Prediction of immediate and future rewards differentially recruits cortico-basal ganglia loops. *Nature Neuroscience, 7,* 887–893.

Taylor, E. (1998). Clinical foundations of hyperactivity research. *Behavioural Brain Research, 94,* 11–24.

Taylor, E., & Rogers, J. W. (2005). Practitioner review: Early adversity and developmental disorders. *Journal of Child Psychology and Psychiatry and Allied Disciplines, 46,* 451–467.

Teicher, M. H., Ito, Y., Glod, C. A., & Barber, N. I. (1996). Objective measurement of hyperactivity and attentional problems in ADHD. *Journal of the American Academy of Child & Adolescent Psychiatry, 35,* 334–342.

Timimi, S., Moncrieff, J., Jureidini, J., Leo, J., Cohen, D., Whitfield, C., et al. (2004). A critique of the international consensus statement on ADHD. *Clinical Child and Family Psychology Review, 7,* 59–63.

Todd, R. D., Rasmussen, E. R., Neuman, R. J., Reich, W., Hudziak, J. J., Bucholz, K. K., et al. (2001). Familiality and heritability of subtypes of attention deficit hyperactivity disorder in a population sample of adolescent female twins. *American Journal of Psychiatry, 158,* 1891–1898.

Tripp, G., & Alsop, B. (1999). Sensitivity to reward frequency in boys with attention deficit hyperactivity disorder. *Journal of Clinical Child Psychology, 28,* 366–375.

van der Linden, D., Frese, M., & Meijman, T. (2003). Mental fatigue and control of cognitive processes: Effects on perseveration and planning. *Acta Psychologica, 113,* 45–65.

van der Meere, J. (1996). The role of attention. In S. Sandberg (Ed.), *Hyperactivity disorders of childhood* (2nd ed., pp. 111–148). Cambridge, England: Cambridge University Press.

van Gaalen, M. M., van Koten, R., Schoffelmeer, A. N., & Vanderschuren, L. J. (2006). Critical involvement of dopaminergic neurotransmission in impulsive decision making. *Biological Psychiatry, 60,* 66–73.

Volkow, N. D., Wang, G. J., Fowler, J. S., Logan, J., Jayne, M., Franceschi, D., et al. (2002). "Nonhedonic" food motivation in humans involves dopamine in the dorsal striatum and methylphenidate amplifies this effect. *Synapse, 44,* 175–180.

Weiss, M. D., Wasdell, M. B., Bomben, M. M., Rea, K. J., & Freeman, R. D. (2006). Sleep hygiene and melatonin treatment for children and adolescents with ADHD and initial insomnia. *Journal of the American Academy of Child & Adolescent Psychiatry, 45,* 512–519.

Wigal, T., Swanson, J. M., Douglas, V. I., Wigal, S. B., Wippler, C. M., & Cavoto, K. F. (1998). Effect of reinforcement on facial responsivity and persistence in children with attention-deficit hyperactivity disorder. *Behavior Modification, 22,* 143–166.

Williams, J. (2005). Problems with models in psychiatry. In W. Østreng (Ed.), *Convergence: Interdisciplinary communications 2004/2005* (pp. 90–96). Oslo, Norway: Centre for Advanced Studies.

Williams, J. (2006). *Computational and animal models of ADHD.* Unpublished doctoral thesis, Institute of Psychiatry, Kings College London, England.

Williams, J. (2008). Working toward a neurobiological account of ADHD. *Journal of Child Psychology and Psychiatry and Allied Disciplines, 49*, 705–711.

Williams, J., & Dayan, P. (2005). Dopamine, learning and impulsivity: A biological account of attention-deficit/hyperactivity disorder. *Journal of Child and Adolescent Psychopharmacology, 15*, 160–179.

Williams, J. O. H., & Hill, P. (2004). ADHD: Overview of diagnosis and management. *Postgraduate Doctor, 20*.

Williams, J., & Taylor, E. (2004). Dopamine appetite and cognitive impairment in attention deficit/hyperactivity disorder. *Neural Plasticity, 11*, 115–132.

Williams, J., & Taylor, E. (2005). The evolution of hyperactivity, impulsivity, and behavioural diversity. *Journal of the Royal Society, Interface, 3*, 399–413.

Williams, J., Taylor, E., Sagvolden, G., & Sagvolden, T. (2009a). Dynamic behavioural changes in the spontaneously hyperactive rat: 2. Control by novelty. *Behavioural Brain Research, 198*, 283–290.

Williams, J., Taylor, E., Sagvolden, G., & Sagvolden, T. (2009b). Dynamic behavioural changes in the spontaneously hyperactive rat: 3. Control by reinforcer rate changes and predictability. *Behavioural Brain Research, 198*, 291–297.

Winsberg, B. G., & Comings, D. E. (1999). Association of the dopamine transporter gene (DAT1) with poor methylphenidate response. *Journal of the American Academy of Child & Adolescent Psychiatry, 38*, 1474–1477.

Winstanley, C. A., Dalley, J. W., Theobald, D. E., & Robbins, T. W. (2003). Global 5-HT depletion attenuates the ability of amphetamine to decrease impulsive choice on a delay-discounting task in rats. *Psychopharmacology (Berlin), 170*, 320–331.

Winstanley, C. A., Eagle, D. M., & Robbins, T. W. (2006). Behavioral models of impulsivity in relation to ADHD: Translation between clinical and preclinical studies. *Clinical Psychology Review, 26*, 379–395.

Woods, J. W. (1964). Behavior of chronic decerebrate rats. *Journal of Neurophysiology, 27*, 635–644.

Yoon, J. H., Higgins, S. T., Heil, S. H., Sugarbaker, R. J., Thomas, C. S., & Badger, G. J. (2007). Delay discounting predicts postpartum relapse to cigarette smoking among pregnant women. *Experimental and Clinical Psychopharmacology, 15*, 176–186.

V

EMPIRICAL AND THEORETICAL EXTENSIONS

13

THE ADAPTIVE NATURE
OF IMPULSIVITY

JEFFREY R. STEVENS AND DAVID W. STEPHENS

An old joke circulates among animal behavior instructors. One can, the joke goes, divide the topics of animal behavior into four Fs: fighting, fleeing, feeding, and reproduction. This somewhat tired joke carries considerable truth. Animals behaving in nature surely must make decisions about conflicts, predator avoidance, feeding, and mating. Male crickets, for example, are notoriously combative. Studies have shown, however, that they escalate fights in some situations and retreat to fight another day in others (Beaugrand, 1997; Parker, 1974; Parker & Rubenstein, 1981). Squirrels, like many small animals, respond to the presence or absence of protective cover; for example, they will carry large food items into the safety of the bushes to consume them but eat small items immediately (Lima, Valone, & Caraco, 1985). Female widow birds prefer males with long tails, and evolutionary theorists have argued that tail length correlates with male quality (Andersson, 1982, 1994). So a female confronted with a short-tailed male faces a dilemma: mate now or keep looking. Notice that in all of these choice situations, time complicates the animal's problem: Risk injury by fighting now or retreat to fight later; stay exposed to possible predation or invest time in moving to a safer place; settle for the short-tailed male or keep looking. Each of these situations, and indeed virtually any naturally occurring choice situation one can imagine, is an intertemporal choice problem. We define these as choice situations in which an animal's alternatives vary in the time at which the animal realizes consequences and in the quality of those consequences once the animal secures them.

Although intertemporal choice applies to many domains (and all four Fs), we need to focus on a specific situation to make scientific headway, and for virtually all behavioral ecologists interested in intertemporal choice that focal situation is foraging. We can observe animal foraging choices easily (e.g., animals eat more often than they reproduce), and we can manipulate the time and magnitude of foraging options much more easily than we can manipulate mate quality or predation risk. Moreover, we have a large base of theoretical and empirical results that help us frame the intertemporal choice problem in the context of animal foraging behavior. Foraging is not only a convenient topic but also a fundamentally important one; actively seeking food is a basic part of animal existence that deserves our attention. In the first part of this chapter, we focus on adaptive aspects of intertemporal choice in animal foraging behavior, and especially on the problem of impulsivity, which we see as a central problem in intertemporal choice. In the second part of this chapter, we take a broader perspective, including domains other than food and extending beyond impulsivity to a more encompassing view of intertemporal choice. Within this general view, we explore the adaptive nature of impulsivity.

FORAGING AND INTERTEMPORAL CHOICE

A pileated woodpecker (*Dryocopus pileatus*)—a crow-sized North American woodpecker—works its way through the trees along a suburban lake. It typically lands on a tree trunk and moves up the trunk, making distinctive hopping motions as it goes. The pileated woodpecker feeds on wood-boring insects, and it uses its beak to chisel its prey from their galleries below the bark. What sorts of choices must a foraging woodpecker make? It will surely make choices about where to search (along the lake shore or along a ridge), which behavioral ecologists call *habitat choice* decisions. It will also make choices about how to search (how fast to fly, where to land on a tree, which parts of the tree to focus on). It will make choices about what to eat; in lean periods, it will attack small prey that it might pass by in better times.

Although the woodpecker must make many decisions as it forages, we focus for the moment on the woodpecker's problem of deciding how thoroughly to exploit each tree before flying to the next one. Should it make a few quick probes and move on to the next tree, or should it exhaustively check every crevice and abnormality in the bark? The reader will immediately recognize costs and benefits of both strategies. The quick, "cream-skimming" visits will lead to much time spent traveling, and the departing woodpecker may leave many good food items behind, whereas the "bowl-licking" strategy will produce many prey per tree, but the woodpecker may waste time extracting the last dregs instead of moving to a fresh tree. This observation should lead the reader to think that foragers should be sensitive to environmental richness. In a rich environment, the next tree may offer a feast, so we would expect rich environments to favor cream skimming, whereas lean environments should favor thorough exploitation.

Behavioral ecologists call this the problem of *patch exploitation,* and it plays a central role in our thinking about animal foraging decisions. Moreover, we have both a well-developed body of theory about this problem and extensive experimental and observational data (Stephens, Brown, & Ydenberg, 2007; Stephens & Krebs, 1986). Formal models of how animals exploit patches of food begin by considering the relationship between the time spent exploiting a patch and the amount of food the animal extracts. We call this relationship the *gain function.* Although the gain function can take many forms, the most plausible and common form is a negatively accelerated shape, as Figure 13.1 shows. The amount of food in the patch sets an upper limit, so the gain function will asymptote to this maximum. The bending of the gain function captures an important property of natural resource exploitation: Resources deplete, and finding the next unit of food from a clump is typically harder and more time consuming than finding the previous unit of food. During a foraging bout, the animal spends its time doing two things: exploiting

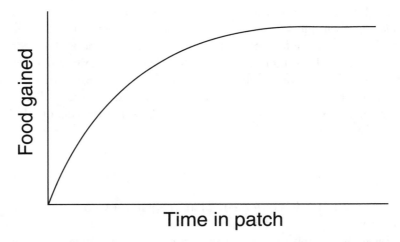

Figure 13.1. Hypothetical gain function. The gain function associated with extracting food from a patch is likely not linear. Instead, there are diminishing returns: As a patch depletes, it takes longer to find food.

patches or traveling to new patches. If τ represents the average time required to travel from one patch to the next, then the overall rate of food intake is

$$\frac{g(t)}{\tau + t},$$

where $g(t)$ is the patch gain function, and t is the time spent exploiting each patch. (Notice that for simplicity, we assume a situation with only one type of patch; we can easily generalize this approach to more types.) Mathematically, we can ask what value of t (the time spent exploiting patches, or patch-residence time) maximizes this intake rate, and we find that the best patch-residence time (t) is large when travel times between patches are large (i.e., in poor environments) and small when travel times are small (i.e., in rich environments; see Stephens & Krebs, 1986).

This model makes the qualitative prediction that animals should skim the cream (spend a short time, extracting relatively little) when the travel time is short (rich environments) but that they should adopt a thorough exploitation strategy (spend more time, extracting more) when travel time is long. Do the data support this claim? Yes, they do; we have very strong evidence from laboratory experiments, field experiments, and simple observations across many species and habitats that travel time affects patch-exploitation behavior, with increases in travel time leading to increases in patch-exploitation time (Stephens & Krebs, 1986). We develop a simple analysis of patch exploitation here to highlight an important naturally occurring problem in intertemporal choice and its basic structure. Two key features of the patch-exploitation problem stand out. First, the patch-exploitation problem is fundamentally sequential. Foragers make a sequence of patch visits such that the quality of the next patch influences the relative value of the present patch. Second, notice that although a forager exploiting a patch must choose between staying and leaving, choosing to stay does not prevent the animal from eventually leaving. This contrasts sharply with many experimental studies of choice behavior in which the investigators set up a situation in which subjects must make mutually exclusive choices: Choosing Option A irrevocably slams the door on Option B.

IMPULSIVITY AND SELF-CONTROL

Traditional models of foraging, like the patch-exploitation model, are derived from the premise of maximizing intake rate over a sequence of foraging choices, an assumption we call *long-term rate maximization*. Although one can raise many possible objections to this premise, it has served students of foraging quite well overall, as the success in predicting the relationship between travel time and patch-residence time shows. The long-term rate approach has, however, repeatedly failed to predict choice in laboratory studies using the self-control (or delay-discounting) paradigm. In self-control studies, the investigator trains subjects (typically pigeons [*Columba livia*], or rats [*Rattus norvegicus*]) to choose between a small reward it can obtain quickly (usually called smaller–sooner), and a larger reward it must wait a bit longer to obtain (larger–later; see Figure 13.2, Panel (a)). Using this scheme, the investigator can explore the effects of delay and amount on preference. The reader may notice that this procedure crudely resembles patch exploitation. The smaller–sooner option resembles a short patch stay yielding a smaller amount; conversely, the larger–later option is like staying longer and obtaining more. We might expect,

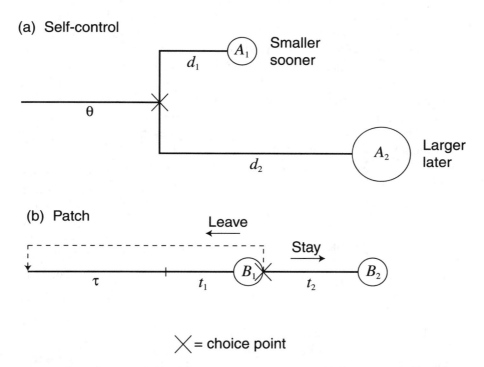

(a) Self-control

d_1 A_1 Smaller sooner

θ

d_2 A_2 Larger later

(b) Patch

Leave

Stay

τ t_1 B_1 t_2 B_2

$\times$ = choice point

Figure 13.2. Self-control and patch experimental designs. (a): In the self-control condition, subjects begin with an intertrial interval θ before facing a simultaneous choice between a smaller–sooner reward (A_1 = small amount, d_1 = short delay) and a larger–later reward (A_2 = large amount, d_2 = long delay). After experiencing the delay and consuming the reward, subjects begin another intertrial interval. (b): In the patch condition, subjects face a sequential choice between staying in the patch or leaving to find a new patch. Thus, all subjects wait for an intertrial interval τ, experience a short delay t_1 and receive a small reward B_1. Then, they choose between staying in the patch an additional delay t_2 and receiving the additional reward B_2 or leaving the patch to start another intertrial interval. Stephens and Anderson (2001) offered these conditions to blue jays and set the parameters such that choices in the self-control and patch treatments were economically equivalent.

therefore, some correspondence between observed choice in the two situations. Yet, results from the two approaches diverge dramatically. Animals in self-control situations commonly prefer the smaller–sooner option even when the larger–later option leads to a higher long-term rate of intake (Bateson & Kacelnik, 1996; Mazur, 1987; McDiarmid & Rilling, 1965). In addition, the time between choice presentations (intertrial interval—the experimental analogue of travel time) has virtually no effect on choice in the self-control preparation (Mazur & Romano, 1992), even though patch studies have nearly universally shown that travel time affects patch exploitation.

We describe this pattern of choice in self-control situations as impulsive. We define *impulsivity* as choosing a smaller–sooner option when a larger–later option produces a better outcome. In broad strokes, this definition agrees with the day-to-day meaning that impulsive decisions lead to error. "I bought the iPhone impulsively" means that had I stopped to think through the long-term consequences, I would not have made this purchase. Of course, to identify impulsivity in nonhumans, we need to say what we mean by a "better outcome." Motivated by foraging models and the tools they offer for calculating rate, here we operationally define impulsivity as choosing smaller–sooner alternatives when the larger–later option yields a higher long-term rate of intake. Clearly, observed behavior in the self-control situation satisfies this definition. In these experiments, subjects often obtain less food than they could, creating an evolutionary puzzle. Why should natural selection favor choice mechanisms that produce less food? It would seem to be relatively simple to "engineer" a decision-making system that does better. Why has natural selection not done this?

EVOLUTIONARY APPROACHES TO IMPULSIVITY

As we have outlined here, the data suggest that animals consistently favor immediate rewards even though it seems that they could achieve higher fitness gains by choosing more delayed options. For behavioral ecologists, the natural first response to this puzzle is to speculate that immediacy is valuable in some way that our traditional rate-based models fail to capture. Specifically, some have suggested that increasing delay reduces, or "discounts," the value of delayed benefits. We remark that the phrase *delay discounting* is closely linked to the study of impulsive choice, so much so that delay discounting and impulsivity are identical in the minds of some authors. From an evolutionary perspective, however, we see the puzzle of impulsivity as a description of the phenomenon of interest and delay discounting as an explanatory hypothesis derived from economic principles.

How can delay reduce value? There are two possibilities: costs due to collection risk and lost investment opportunity. According to the collection-risk hypothesis, the animal has a better chance of collecting (or realizing) more immediate options. Behavioral ecologists often call this the "discounting-by-interruptions" hypothesis. In this hypothesis, we suppose that interruptions prevent an animal from collecting any delayed benefit. The model requires that interruptions occur in some time-dependent way, so that they occur more frequently in long intervals, thereby enhancing the relative value of short delays. In nature, these interruptions could come from groupmates, from predators, from weather, or even from prey escaping, and we have clear evidence that interruptions occur. For example, groupmates often steal food from each other, so that a social forager who has located food surely experiences some risk of losing it, and presumably this risk increases with the time spent handling the food. Unfortunately, although we have many casual observations like this, we have virtually no rigorous information about the critical statistical properties of these interruption processes. To account for observed levels of impulsivity, we would need fairly high interruption rates, likely much higher than exist in nature.

For lost investment opportunities, consider a human investor who must choose between \$100 now and \$100 delayed for 1 year. Clearly, the \$100 now is more valuable because if the investor waits, she or he pays an opportunity cost by forgoing the benefits of investing the \$100 for 1 year. We can imagine situations in which this may be relevant to nonhuman animals. For example, if the next unit of food allows a forager to improve its breeding status or dominance, this could produce investment opportunity costs if benefits begin to accrue as soon as the animal gains its new status; so the sooner you obtain your new status, the better. Behavioral ecologists have not paid much attention to this possibility, perhaps because this sort of lost investment seems remote from the day-to-day world of animal behavior.

DELAY-DISCOUNTING MODELS OF IMPULSIVITY

We can explore more rigorously the delay-discounting idea that delay reduces value by using mathematical models. Students of choice have focused on two delay-discounting models, the exponential and hyperbolic models, which we discuss in the following sections (see also chaps. 1 and 3, this volume).

Exponential Model

Imagine that the value of a delayed resource decays at a constant rate as delay increases. This could happen because interruptions occur at constant rate or because investment opportunity costs accrue at a constant rate, or some combination of both. Restricting our attention to the interruptions idea simplifies our development. If interruptions occur at constant rate λ, then the expected value of a food reward of size A (for amount) delayed by d seconds is simply $V_d = Ae^{-\lambda d}$. If we knew or could estimate the interruption rate, λ, then we could, in theory, predict the outcome of a self-control experiment by comparing $A_S e^{-\lambda d_S}$ to $A_L e^{-\lambda d_L}$, where A_S, d_S, A_L, and d_L represent the amounts and delays associated with the smaller–sooner and larger–later alternatives. This otherwise appealing model fails to predict the phenomenon of preference reversal, which is a key observation in the self-control preparation (Ainslie, 1975; Ainslie & Herrnstein, 1981; Green, Fisher, Perlow, & Sherman, 1981). Preference reversal occurs when a subject's preference switches from smaller–sooner to larger–later as the delays associated with both options increase by the same amount. The exponential model cannot predict this because it predicts that adding a constant delay should modify the discounted value of both options by the same factor and therefore should not influence choice. Yet, animals are sensitive to this sort of general increase in delay; increasing both delays shifts preference toward the larger–later alternative.

Hyperbolic Model

At least partially in response to the failings of the exponential model, Mazur (1987) offered an algebraically simple delay-discounting model termed *hyperbolic discounting* (Ainslie, 1975), and Mazur's elegant empirical work has lead to broad acceptance of this approach. According the hyperbolic model, the expression

$$V_d = \frac{A}{1 + kd}$$

describes the decline of value with delay. The hyperbolic model can easily accommodate preference reversal. To predict the outcome of a self-control test we would compare $\dfrac{A_S}{1 + kd_S}$ and $\dfrac{A_L}{1 + kd_L}$. We call k the hyperbolic discount factor, and its meaning crudely parallels the meaning of λ in the exponential model: High k means that value declines more steeply with increasing delay— more discounting. Notice, however, that we can, in principle, calculate the exponential model's λ parameter a priori, for example, by observing or manipulating the interruption rate. In contrast, we must estimate the hyperbolic model's k parameter from observed preference. That is, k is a fitted parameter. From the perspective of our attempts to explain how natural selection influences patterns of intertemporal choice, the hyperbolic model offers a description of observed choice rather than an explanation.

Although these standard delay-discounting models play important roles in the fields of animal behavior and psychology, they inevitably leave those interested in the evolution of intertemporal choice unsatisfied. The exponential model offers the promise of explanation from first principles but ultimately fails empirically. The hyperbolic model describes many data but has little explanatory power. In addition, the models suffer from a seldom-recognized disconnect with naturally occurring decision making in foraging animals. Both focus on a single decision abstracted from the remainder of the animal's activities (Kacelnik, 2003). Although one can see that this "single-shot" approach may be an informative theoretical device—like a physicist's assumption of frictionless world—it is difficult to imagine animals facing single-shot decisions in the real world. Experiments with nonhumans require repeated trials for subjects to learn the payoffs and delays. Data from natural foraging (like patch exploitation) have suggested sensitivity to future consequences; indeed, even within the laboratory paradigm of self-control testing, we have evidence of sensitivity to consequences beyond the current choice (Mazur, 1994). In other words, it is clear that animal choice typically occurs in a sequential context, so that any model purporting to account for the economic consequences of choice needs to consider this basic reality. Yet, the empirical success of the single-shot hyperbolic model shows that we can often describe choice without references to this sequence. In our view, this is another perspective on the puzzle of impulsivity: Animals live in a world of sequential decision making, yet they often behave as if only the next choice matters to them.

Short-Term Rate Model

For some purposes, investigators prefer a simplified version of the hyperbolic model called the *short-term rate model*. Although not technically a discounting model, it can predict impulsive choice. To apply this model to the self-control situation, we would compare $\frac{A_S}{d_S}$ and $\frac{A_L}{d_L}$; that is, a rate comparison without the intertrial interval that we need to calculate the long-term rate over a sequence of trials. In effect, this model hypothesizes that the subject considers the rate from the choice point to the food delivery but nothing else. In practice, the hyperbolic and short-term rate models make similar predictions except when delays are very small, but the short-term rate model is convenient conceptually because we can compare it so easily to our standard of "economically sound" choice, the long-term rate model. Empirical studies that have tested a modified version of this model have shown that it can account for data in European starlings (*Sturnus vulgaris*) and cotton-top tamarins (*Saguinus oedipus*), even without the fitted k parameter of the hyperbolic model (Bateson & Kacelnik, 1996; Stevens, Hallinan, & Hauser, 2005).

Discounted-Sequence Model

Nothing about the concept of discounting necessitates single-shot decision making. We can, for example, build delay-discounting models that consider sequences of gains. Stephens (2002) offered a simple discounted-sequence model by considering a sequence of exponentially discounted gains, which he called the *exponentially discounted-sequence model*. This logically simple approach yields a hybrid of foraging theory's long-term rate model and the single-shot exponential model. Like the single-shot exponential model, it includes an a priori discount rate parameter—so, for example, we know how variations in interruption rate should affect the value of a sequence. It can, in principle, accommodate preference reversal (as any rate-based model can). Unfortunately, like most a priori models of discounted value, it fails to account for the self-control data quantitatively. For example, we need very high discount rates to explain the strength of observed preferences for immediacy, yet at these high discount rates the model loses its ability to predict preference reversal.

The failure of the exponentially discounted-sequence model illustrates the problems associated with finding a successful economic account of impulsive choice behavior. We can capture ratelike properties such as preference reversal easily enough, but the strength of preferences for immediacy suggests very high discount rates, and it is hard to imagine natural processes (interruption or opportunity cost) that could create such high discount rates. In addition, the discounting-by-interruption hypothesis that behavioral ecologists have long favored seems increasingly strained. Experiments on birds and humans (Henly et al., 2008; King & Logue, 1992) failed to find the predicted increase in preference for smaller–sooner options with experimentally created interruptions in a self-control situation. Suffice it to say, then, efforts to understand observed choice in terms of a priori models of discounted value leave something to be desired. Even though the economic forces that reduce the value of delayed benefits (opportunity costs and collection risk) are surely real, they seem too weak to explain the strong preferences for immediacy we see in the self-control situation.

Ecological Rationality of Impulsivity

As explained earlier, animals exploiting patches change their behavior when travel time increases, spending more time in patches and extracting more food; in contrast, animals tested in the self-control preparation seem insensitive to changes in the experimental analogue of travel time, the intertrial interval. Intrigued by this difference, Stephens and Anderson (2001) created an experimental comparison of the patch and self-control situations. To achieve this, Stephens and Anderson needed an experimentally tractable patch-choice situation that they could compare with self-control treatments. Figure 13.2 shows their approach. In the self-control situations (Figure 13.2, Panel A), the subject waits for a fixed intertrial interval θ and chooses between amount A_1 after delay d_1 and amount A_2 after delay d_2. In the patch situation (Figure 13.2, Panel B), the subject waits for a fixed intertrial interval–travel time, τ (note that $\theta = \tau$, but we use different notation to distinguish between self-control and patch variables). When this time expires, the apparatus presents a single stimulus; in the jargon of foraging theory, this single stimulus indicates a patch encounter. The subject "enters the patch" (in Stephens and Anderson's preparation, a blue jay [*Cyanocitta cristata*] hops forward to a perch just below the patch stimulus), and then the subject waits again: waiting time t_1 for a food delivery of B_1 (two pellets). After this initial food delivery, the subject must make a choice: look for a new patch (i.e., start a fresh cycle of wait–encounter–wait–get food), or stay in the patch, waiting a bit longer (additional waiting time t_2) for an additional two food pellets (amount B_2). Although natural patches can, in principle, contain many items, these experimental patches never produce more than two food deliveries, so the trial effectively ends after this second food delivery and the subject must start a new cycle of wait–encounter and so on.

By choosing the amounts and delays carefully, Stephens and Anderson (2001) created economically comparable patch and self-control situations, that is, situations in which the "leave and start over" choice produced the same amount of food ($B_1 = A_1 =$ two pellets) and took the same time ($\tau + t_1 = \theta + d_1$) as the smaller–sooner option and the "stay" choice produced the same amount of food and took the same time as the larger–later option ($B_1 + B_2 = A_2 =$ four pellets and $\tau + t_1 + t_2 = \theta + d_2$). Even if this experimental patch situation is hopelessly simple minded as compared with the complexity of naturally occurring patch exploitation, it frames the intertemporal choice problem in terms of leave versus stay rather than the more conventional A-versus-B–style choice.

Stephens and Anderson (2001) created a wide range of treatments systematically varying delays, amounts, and intertrial intervals but always ensuring comparable patch and self-control versions of each condition. Figure 13.3 shows conventional dose–response style plots that assess the subjects' sensitivity to long-term rate. As the figure shows, the jays followed an orderly sigmoid response in the patch situation, roughly following the predictions of long-term rate: choosing to stay when this gave the highest long-term rate and choosing to leave when the opposite was true. Moreover, with extreme differences in rate, the jays strongly preferred the "correct" option. In contrast, the self-control data show a very weak response to long-term rate; although they tend to increase their preference for larger–later when this gives the higher long-term rate, they still take the smaller–sooner option quite frequently. Indeed, one can readily see the notorious impulsiveness of self-control treatments by observing that subjects chose the smaller–sooner option more frequently under almost all conditions.

WHY BE IMPULSIVE?

Animals perform poorly in the self-control situation, achieving lower rates of intake and acquiring less food than a hypothetical "more patient" ani-

(a) Patch

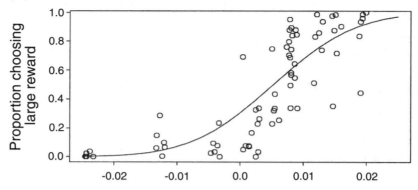

(b) Self-control

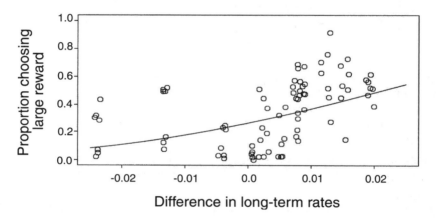

Difference in long-term rates

Figure 13.3. Influence of self-control and patch treatments on blue jay temporal preferences. The figure shows proportional choice of the option yielding the larger amount as a function of the difference in long-term rates associated with two options (Stephens & Anderson 2001). For example, zero means that large and small options produced the same long-term rate; a negative value means that the smaller option produced the higher long-term rate; and a positive value means the larger option yielded the higher long-term rate. Blue jays experienced treatments that varied in the intertrial interval, the delay to the smaller option, and the delay to the larger option. Each treatment pair created the same difference in long-term rates in the self-control and patch situations. The data points represent the performance of different individuals in each of the 12 treatments. The solid curves show the best least-square fit to a conventional dose–response relationship. As the data illustrate, the subject's behavior seems to track the difference in long-term rate in the patch situation but not in self-control. From "The Adaptive Value of Preference for Immediacy: When Shortsighted Rules Have Farsighted Consequences," by D. W. Stephens and D. Anderson, 2001, *Behavioral Ecology, 12*, p. 337. Copyright 2001 by Oxford University Press. Adapted with permission.

mal could. Yet, Stephens and Anderson's (2001) blue jays did quite well in the economically analogous patch situation. What explains this? There are two possibilities. Subjects could use different decision rules in the two situations; alternatively, the same mechanisms (e.g., decision rules such as "choose the option with the highest short-term rate") may simply work better in the patch situation.

Short-Term Rule, Long-Term Benefits

Stephens and Anderson (2001) argued for the second possibility. To see their argument, consider the long-term rates associated with the two options in patch choice. If the subject repeatedly leaves, it obtains a long-term rate of

$$\frac{B_1}{\tau + t_1}.$$

If the subject repeatedly stays, however, it obtains a long-term rate of

$$\frac{B_1 + B_2}{\tau + t_1 + t_2}.$$

Obviously, staying is better than leaving in the long run if

$$\frac{B_1 + B_2}{\tau + t_1 + t_2} > \frac{B_1}{\tau + t_1}.$$

This is a classical comparison in foraging theory that asks the following question: Will the forager benefit from adding an activity that yields amount B_2 in time t_2 to the things it is already doing (which, on average, yields amount B_1 every $\tau + t_1$ time units)? We can easily show that the answer is yes if and only if

$$\frac{B_2}{t_2} > \frac{B_1}{\tau + t_1}.$$

Although it may not be immediately obvious, this comparison is precisely the impulsive short-term rate rule we discussed earlier. In the patch situation, then, a subject who makes a short-term comparison (leaving, yielding B_1 in $\tau + t_1$ seconds, vs. staying, yielding B_2 in t_2 seconds) will coincidentally also be choosing the option that produces highest long-term rate. Yet, a subject who made the same short-term comparison in the self-control situation would compare B_1 in t_1 seconds and B_2 in t_2 seconds. By ignoring τ, subjects may be more likely to choose the smaller–sooner reward even though the larger–later reward offers a better long-term rate.

In light of this argument, the *ecological rationality* hypothesis holds that natural selection has favored short-sighted rules of choice because these rules fare well (achieve high long-term intake rates) in naturally occurring choice situations that have a structure similar to patch exploitation. However, these same rules fare poorly in tests of simultaneous, mutually exclusive choice, which are likely rare in nature. Notice that according to this hypothesis, selection could favor choice mechanisms that produce impulsive choice without discounting, even though the ecological rationality approach is not necessarily incompatible with discounting.

This application of the short-term rule to the patch situation hypothesizes that the subject views the intertrial interval (τ) and the first time to food (t_1) as a single combined delay. This is rather a bold claim given that self-control results suggest a strong asymmetry (delay has a powerful effect on choice, but the intertrial interval has little effect). To test this claim, Stephens and McLinn (2003) provided blue jays with a range of conditions using the same total delay (i.e., $\tau + t_1 =$ constant) but different mixes of intertrial interval (τ) and initial delay (t_1). They showed that increasing the total delay ($\tau + t_1$) shifted preference toward staying as predicted in the patch situation, but the jays did not respond to the different mixes of intertrial intervals and initial delay.

Foreground/Background

Our description of the ecological rationality hypothesis describes the choice structure that favors impulsiveness rather vaguely as "similar to patch exploitation." What does that mean? Stephens, Kerr, and Fernandez-Juricic (2004) have developed a more explicit description of situations that favor impulsive decision making that they call *foreground/background* structure. As a forager moves through its habitat, it encounters many types of resources and presumably makes many choices about how to exploit them. At any moment, we suppose that the forager follows what we call a background strategy that represents its default or standard behavior. Obviously, the background strategy yields a stream of gains, and we could characterize the benefits associated with this background strategy using any model we favor (e.g., long-term rate). Occasionally, the forager encounters a new resource that represents an opportunity to deviate from the background strategy (Figure 13.4). We refer to this as a "foreground" option, and the forager must now choose between continuing with the background strategy or deviating to exploit the foreground option and then returning to the background strategy. Notice that the critical feature of this form is that the background strategy is part of both options, and this fact greatly reduces the costs of short-sighted decision making. Many naturally occurring choices follow this pattern, including but by no means limited to patch exploitation. We can view diet choice, mate choice, and many other resource exploitation decisions in this way.

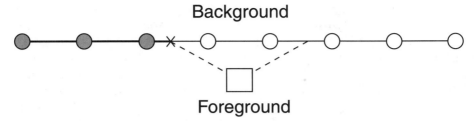

Figure 13.4. Foreground–background comparison. Animals often face choices between a "default" series of options (background) and the occasional chance to temporarily deviate from the default (foreground). In this example, a hypothetical forager has consumed three background options (filled circles) and must now choose between continuing with the background options (open circles) or opting for the foreground option (open square). It is important to note that choosing the foreground option forgoes the opportunity for some background options but eventually results in returning to the background strategy.

Discrimination Advantage

As we explained earlier, in the patch situation an animal using the short-term rule can achieve the same long-term intake rate as an animal that directly compares long-term rates. Some recent analyses have suggested an even stronger result (Stephens, 2002; Stephens et al., 2004). If judgments about differences in time follow Weber's law (Gibbon, 1977; Gibbon, Church, Fairhurst, & Kacelnik, 1988), then a short-term comparison can, in principle, be superior to a long-term comparison in the self-control situation. An animal that compares long-term differences will necessarily compare larger quantities because the intertrial interval is included, whereas an animal comparing short-term differences will compare smaller quantities. Because perceptual mechanisms usually generate more error when they compare larger quantities (e.g., 3 seconds vs. 5 seconds is easier to discriminate than 11 seconds vs. 13 seconds; Figure 13.5), an animal making long-term comparisons would discriminate between the two delays less accurately, resulting in occasional choices for a lower intake rate. This leads to the paradoxical conclusion that an animal making short-term comparisons could, in principle, achieve a higher long-term intake rate than an animal making long-term comparisons.

Although one can use discounting functions to describe animal impulsivity in the self-control paradigm, finding explanatory discounting models has proved quite challenging. Current evidence has suggested, for example, that interruptions do not create a bias favoring immediacy as delay-discounting models have long hypothesized (Henly et al., 2008; King & Logue, 1992). In addition, although we find explanatory models that predict the qualitative properties (e.g., preference reversal) correctly, the same models fail to capture the quantitative properties of observed choice. In the face of these challenges,

(a) Short-term rate

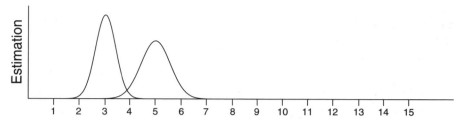

(b) Long-term rate

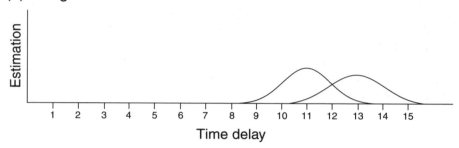

Figure 13.5. Discrimination advantage of short-term rates. Scalar expectancy theory states that the variance around estimates of temporal duration increases with the magnitude of the duration (Gibbon, 1977). Shorter durations, therefore, are easier to discriminate than longer durations. For instance, there may be little variance for estimations of 3- and 5-second durations, so discriminating between them is easy. When adding a constant time (e.g., the intertrial interval) of 8 seconds to these durations, however, the variance dramatically increases for 11 and 13 seconds, and estimates greatly overlap for these durations, making them difficult to distinguish.

the ecological rationality hypothesis offers an exciting and important alternative that can explain impulsive choice without discounting, although we could incorporate discounting into ecological rationality models if this proves to be important. We are just beginning to explore the ecological rationality idea; further experimentation and theorizing will undoubtedly refine this approach.

Adaptive Hypotheses for Intertemporal Choice

Up to now, our discussion has focused on the evolutionary puzzle of impulsivity, and we have argued that ecological rationality offers a new and compelling explanation of impulsivity in self-control experiments. In this final section, we take a larger view in two senses. First, we focus on the more general problem of intertemporal choice rather than the narrower topic of impulsivity. That is, we consider a broader view of intertemporal choice that includes the vast range of situations in which animals must choose between options that vary in both time and magnitude. Second, we consider how intertemporal choice problems arise in nature, and how natural selection, acting in real-world ecological situations, may have shaped animal mechanisms of intertemporal choice. Drawing from the models of impulsivity reviewed earlier, we recognize three explanatory principles. First, we can probably explain many aspects of naturally occurring intertemporal choice using simple rate models, as traditional models of foraging behavior advocate. Second, the economic forces associated with delay discounting (collection risk and the opportunity costs of investments) may be important for many species. Finally, approaches based on the premise of ecological rationality emphasize the mismatch between rules that work well in natural situations and the rules required to make economically perfect decisions. We recognize these as distinct approaches mostly because they have been handed down to us via different research traditions, yet the boundaries between them are often fuzzy. Nevertheless, we find it helpful to use these three approaches to organize this final section on the adaptive nature of intertemporal choice.

RATE EFFECTS ON INTERTEMPORAL CHOICE

Theoretical behavioral ecology offers an extensive menu of rate-based models, covering many different domains. We have rate models that deal with patch exploitation, diet choice, habitat choice, joining social groups, and so on (reviewed in Giraldeau & Caraco, 2000; Stephens et al., 2007; Stephens & Krebs, 1986). Yet, students of intertemporal choice often pass by rate-based explanations in the search for more elaborate approaches. Indeed, our discussion of impulsivity earlier in the chapter explicitly defined rate out of the problem. Although there certainly are situations in which we need to look beyond rate models to explain intertemporal choice, we should not throw the baby out with the bath water. Rate models describe the basic economics of repeated choice in a simple and powerful way. At worst, rate models provide baseline expectations (as in the study of impulsivity) and at best they make well-supported predictions (as in patch exploitation).

So what can rate models tell us about intertemporal choice in nature? Consider again the basic patch-exploitation problem described earlier. At one extreme, we can imagine an "impatient" cream-skimming tactic that grabs the good stuff in a patch and quickly moves on, and at the other extreme we might have a "patient" bowl-licking strategy extracting even the last dregs before moving to the next patch. Rate-based models tell us that an animal's options elsewhere should set the balance between these two approaches. In a rich environment, the animal has many good alternatives beyond the current patch, so we predict something like cream skimming; however, in a poor environment the current patch looks pretty good compared with the animal's options else-where, and we predict a strategy approximating bowl licking. Crudely speaking then, we expect that species adapted to rich environments should be less patient. Experimental data on chimpanzees (*Pan troglodytes*) and bonobos (*Pan paniscus*) in captivity support this prediction (Rosati, Stevens, Hare, & Hauser, 2007). In the wild, bonobos live in a richer environment, feeding more heav-ily on abundant herbaceous vegetation. Chimpanzees, in contrast, forage on fruit more than herbaceous vegetation, which is less abundant in their habitats (Malenky & Wrangham, 1994). When tested in repeated self-control tasks, bonobos seemed less patient, opting for the cream-skimming technique.

Our hypothetical cream skimmer leaves food patches early because stay-ing longer would reduce its chance to acquire food at a higher rate elsewhere. This, of course, follows from the assumption that an animal spending time in the current patch cannot simultaneously spend its time looking for new patches. This is the bedrock assumption of rate-based models. They owe their successes (and their limitations) to the simple way in which they caricature this basic trade-off. Yet, this is not always true. Some animals can search for new resources while they exploit others. A web-building spider can, for exam-ple, multitask in this way because it can extract nutrients from one prey item while its web works to capture a second. Some species, then, experience a sort of release from the conventional exploit versus search trade-off. Animals that experience no exploit–search trade-off should not really care about exploita-tion delays—after all, it costs them nothing.

Discounting Effects on Intertemporal Choice

Delay discounting refers to a reduction in a reward's value caused by delay. We are cautious with applying discounting as an explanation of choice in the self-control situation for two reasons. First, we now have several hypotheses that can, in principle, account for specific laboratory results with-out discounting (Bateson & Kacelnik, 1996; Kacelnik, 2003; Stephens & Anderson, 2001). Second, direct manipulation of delay-discounting variables did not have the predicted effect on choice (Henly et al., 2008; King & Logue, 1992). Despite these setbacks in the laboratory, we have good reasons to believe that delay-discounting effects—both collection risk and opportu-nity costs—have shaped animal temporal preferences in some important sit-uations. The laboratory tasks may not capture the ecologically relevant risks and opportunity costs that animals face in their natural environments.

Collection Risk

As we explained previously, animals may discount delayed rewards because the future is uncertain; some event—a so-called interruption—may prevent the animal from collecting a delayed reward. The discounting-by-interruptions hypothesis seems compelling to many students of animal behavior because natural interruptions can come in many forms, such as social interruptions, interruptions by predators, and so on. Indeed, some evidence has suggested that interruptions and cues predicting interruptions can influence intertemporal choice. This section reviews naturally occurring interruptions and the evidence that these interruptions affect intertemporal choice.

Life Expectancy

Death ultimately interrupts us all, humans and nonhumans alike. An evolutionary approach predicts differences in intertemporal choice for species that vary in life span. Mathematically, we can substitute the mortality rate (a classic parameter from demography) into the exponential discounting model to motivate a life-expectancy–based model of delay discounting. Clearly, adult insects with very short life spans would not do well to delay payoffs for long periods, when they are unlikely to survive long enough to reap the rewards. We intuitively expect, therefore, that intertemporal choice should scale with expected life span. To explore this, we can evaluate the comparative data shown in Figure 13.6. Here, we see that Old World monkeys and apes wait much longer than birds, rodents, and other primates. Although at first glance, life span appears to correlate with these comparative data, on closer inspection this is not the case. On the one hand, pigeons, cotton-top tamarins, common marmosets (*Callithrix jacchus*), and capuchin monkeys (*Cebus apella*) live much longer than rats but share similar temporal preferences. On the other hand, chimpanzees and bonobos have similar life spans but quite different temporal preferences. Life span and mortality-rate effects probably only influence intertemporal choice at the extremes—for example, explaining differences between very short-lived and very long-lived species.

Although the effect of life span on intertemporal choice may be swamped by other ecological factors at the species level, life expectancy may have a strong effect at the individual level. An adaptive approach predicts that temporal preferences should change over the life span of organisms (Daly & Wilson, 2005; Sozou & Seymour, 2003). In fact, as organisms age or perceive cues associated with a short life expectancy, they often prefer immediate payoffs rather than waiting for delayed payoffs. For instance, when parasitoid wasps (*Leptopilina heterotoma*) detect cues associated with a short life expectancy, they lay more eggs in lower quality hosts than in the absence of the cues (Roitberg et al., 1992). The wasps accept a lower reproductive output when the future appears uncertain. Thus, individuals can flexibly respond to a shortened temporal horizon, a finding also reported in older human adults (Carstensen, 2006).

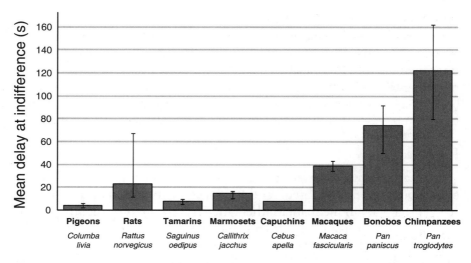

Figure 13.6. Comparison of animal species tested in self-control paradigm. Researchers have tested pigeons, rats, tamarins, marmosets, capuchin monkeys, macaques, bonobos, and chimpanzees in the self-control paradigm. In this comparison, individuals chose between two immediate rewards and six delayed rewards. In most cases, the bars represent the mean delay to receiving the large reward at which subjects were indifferent between the smaller–sooner and larger–later reward. Error bars represent the range of minimum and maximum indifference points for subjects. The capuchin data represent an interpolation of approximate indifference points with twofold and fourfold differences in food amounts. Data sources: pigeons and rats, Green, Myerson, Holt, Slevin, and Estle (2004); tamarins and marmosets, Stevens et al. (2005); capuchins, Ramseyer, Pele, Dufour, Chauvin, and Thierry (2006); macaques, Tobin, Logue, Chelonis, and Ackerman (1996); and bonobos and chimpanzees, Rosati et al. (2007).

Competition

For most species, competition with groupmates or other species poses an enormous interruption risk. Waiting to obtain a food item or mating opportunity gives others the chance to grab it in the meantime. For instance, bypassing a smaller, closer food item in favor of a larger, more distant one means that a social forager may well end up with nothing because groupmates have arrived first. We would expect, therefore, that species living in larger, competitive groups should exhibit stronger preferences for immediacy than solitary species. At the moment, we have not tested enough species to evaluate this comparative hypothesis.

At the individual level, however, we have clear evidence of competitive interference effects on intertemporal choice. In parallel with the wasp example mentioned previously, some species are quite sensitive to cues associated with social interruptions, especially caching species. *Caching* (or storing) food offers one of the most striking instances of delayed rewards for nonhuman animals because caching animals actively choose to delay consumption, often for months. This long-term storage makes cached food vulnerable to pilferage from competitors (Vander Wall, 1990). Both natural observations and laboratory experiments have shown that individuals adaptively respond to this social risk by eating rather than caching when in the presence of potential pilferers (Carrascal & Moreno, 1993; Emery, Dally, & Clayton, 2004). The threat of competitive interruption triggers a preference for immediate payoffs.

Opportunity Costs

In addition to increasing collection risk, waiting imposes opportunity costs because an animal must wait to put delayed rewards to use. In one of the first attempts to address species differences in intertemporal preference, Tobin and Logue (1994) argued that species with high metabolic rates simply cannot afford to wait long delays to receive food and will prefer immediate rewards more than will species with lower metabolic rates. Thus, for animals with high metabolic rates, waiting imposes high investment opportunity costs because they can put smaller–sooner rewards to use sooner to meet their high metabolic demands. Tobin and Logue used an analysis of previous experiments on pigeons, rats, and humans to support this hypothesis. Given their much smaller body size, pigeons and rats have higher specific metabolic rates than humans, and metabolic rates correlated with impulsive choice in self-control procedures. Although consistent with the differential metabolic rate hypothesis, these data do not demonstrate a definitive link between metabolic rate and intertemporal choice because these three species vary in many ways other than their metabolic rates. Nevertheless, metabolic costs—and investment opportunity costs more generally—may play a key role in determining temporal preferences, and an analysis with a wider range of species would certainly be illuminating.

Ecological Rationality of Intertemporal Choice

Todd and Gigerenzer (2000) defined ecological rationality as "adaptive behavior resulting from the fit between the mind's mechanisms and the structure of the environment in which it operates" (p. 728). That is, the appropriateness of a decision mechanism depends on the decision environment. In laboratory settings, ecological rationality may result in a mismatch between the domain of selection and the domain of testing. The Stephens and Anderson (2001) result clearly exemplifies this. According this hypothesis, natural selection has favored mechanisms that perform well in solving patch-exploitation problems (the domain of selection), yet these same mechanisms lead to errors in conventional laboratory tests of choice (the domain of testing).

The key point analytically is that identifying and understanding the domain of selection is critical to understanding the behavior revealed in a range of testing domains.

Clearly, this mismatch problem applies quite broadly, given that testing situations almost never match the domain of selection. For example, Stevens et al. (2005) tested temporal preferences in two closely related species of monkeys, cotton-top tamarins and common marmosets. Although similar in many ways, these two species differ in one crucial aspect: their diets. Tamarins eat primarily insects—which require quick action to capture—whereas marmosets feed primarily on sap and gum exuding from trees (Snowdon & Soini, 1988; Stevenson & Rylands, 1988). Marmosets chew on tree bark and wait for seconds, minutes, or hours for the sap to flow. Thus, the marmosets are adapted to waiting for food. In a self-control paradigm, marmosets waited almost twice as long as tamarins for the same amount of food (Stevens et al., 2005). Recall that the tamarins were one of the species whose preferences matched the predictions of the short-term rate model. Marmosets, therefore, exhibited more patience than this model predicts. The bonobo–chimpanzee difference we discussed previously also shows this pattern. The bonobo preferences matched predictions of the rate model (this time, the long-term rate model), whereas the chimpanzees were more patient than expected (Rosati et al., 2007). In both of these cases, the species that deals with longer delays in the natural foraging environment also waits longer than expected by a rate model. These may offer cases of the decision mechanisms being tuned to the delayed nature of their natural foraging environment. Under the artificial conditions of the self-control paradigm, the marmosets and chimpanzees seem overly patient when using ecologically rational decision mechanisms.

Uniquely Human Patience?

A glance at Figure 13.6 shows something striking. The animals tested so far in the self-control situation do not wait more than a few seconds or minutes for a threefold increase in food amount. Although we offer good explanations for why this is the case, these preferences, nevertheless, pale in comparison to the temporal preferences documented in humans. Economists and psychologists have repeatedly shown that humans are willing to wait months or years for delayed payoffs (reviewed in Frederick, Loewenstein, & O'Donoghue, 2002), leading some to propose patience as a unique capacity in humans (e.g., McClure, Laibson, Loewenstein, & Cohen, 2004).

Readers should evaluate these claims cautiously, however, because the methodologies used in human and nonhuman testing often differ dramatically. These different decision-making environments could tap different decision mechanisms, resulting in divergent but ecologically rational preferences. As we have already mentioned, in self-control experiments animals always experience repeated choices between food rewards with no other way to acquire food and few, if any, alternative activities available (for an alternative paradigm, see Beran, Savage-Rumbaugh, Pate, & Rumbaugh, 1999; Evans & Beran, 2007). In contrast, investigators usually ask humans about their temporal preferences for money (but for primary rewards such as food and juice, see Lagorio & Madden, 2005; McClure, Ericson, Laibson, Loewenstein, & Cohen, 2007). Often, both the monetary rewards and the delay periods are hypothetical, but even if real money is offered, participants can obviously leave the experiment and go about their daily lives while waiting for the payoffs. Thus, important differences exist in the reward types, number of exposures to options, sampling methods required (descriptions vs. experiences with options), and costs associated with waiting between human and nonhuman experiments.

Rosati et al. (2007) explored whether humans do indeed exhibit more patience than other animals by testing humans and chimpanzees in a comparable self-control experiment. Both species experienced repeated choices between a smaller food reward available immediately and a larger food reward available after 2 minutes. Humans rarely waited for the large rewards (even less than the chimpanzees did), demonstrating that (a) humans are not always patient and (b) comparing the existing human and animal data is not a valid comparison. When tested with similar rewards using similar procedures, humans look much more like other animals, showing a strong preference for immediate rewards. Thus, the intertemporal choice decision mechanisms are tuned to specific decision environments, supporting the ecological rationality hypothesis.

SUMMARY

The puzzle of impulsivity has been documented repeatedly in self-control experiments in pigeons, blue jays, and starlings. In each of these species, individuals prefer a smaller–sooner reward more often than expected by a long-term rate model. Much like the paradox of altruism, we believe that impulsivity is in the eye of the beholder—there are a number of reasonable explanations for it. The long-term rate-based approach of classic foraging theory fails to account for the data in this situation, although short-term models do quite well. The alternative, delay-discounting approach nicely captures quantitative aspects of the data, but offers no explanation of observed preferences, only a description. When viewed through the lens of an evolutionary approach, a preference for immediate rewards appears not impulsive but adaptive in a naturally occurring behavioral situation. A decision mechanism adapted to a common foraging problem may not work as well in an artificial situation contrived in the laboratory. This is a specific example of the more general phenomenon of ecological rationality—the adaptive match between decision mechanisms and the decision environment. We argue that this ecological rationality approach can be very informative to the study of impulsivity and to the study of intertemporal choice more broadly. In fact, the ecological rationality approach is broad enough to include both the rate and the delay-discounting approaches. It offers predictive models of intertemporal choice and emphasizes the general nature of trading off time delays and reward amounts, an important and ubiquitous class of decisions that all organisms face.

REFERENCES

Ainslie, G. (1975). Specious reward: A behavioral theory of impulsiveness and impulse control. *Psychological Bulletin, 82,* 463–496.

Ainslie, G., & Herrnstein, R. J. (1981). Preference reversal and delayed reinforcement. *Animal Learning & Behavior, 9,* 476–482.

Andersson, M. (1982, October 28). Female choice selects for extreme tail length in a widowbird. *Nature, 299,* 818–820.

Andersson, M. (1994). *Sexual selection.* Princeton, NJ: Princeton University Press.

Bateson, M., & Kacelnik, A. (1996). Rate currencies and the foraging starling: The fallacy of the averages revisited. *Behavioral Ecology, 7,* 341–352.

Beaugrand, J. P. (1997). Resolution of agonistic conflicts in dyads of acquainted green swordtails (*Xiphophorus helleri*): A game with perfect information. *Behavioural Processes, 41,* 79–96.

Beran, M. J., Savage-Rumbaugh, E., Pate, J. L., & Rumbaugh, D. M. (1999). Delay of gratification in chimpanzees (*Pan troglodytes*). *Developmental Psychobiology, 34,* 119–127.

Carrascal, L. M., & Moreno, E. (1993). Food caching versus immediate consumption in the nuthatch: The effect of social context. *Ardea, 81,* 135–141.

Carstensen, L. L. (2006, June 30). The influence of a sense of time on human development. *Science, 312,* 1913–1915.

Daly, M., & Wilson, M. (2005). Carpe diem: Adaptation and devaluing the future. *Quarterly Review of Biology, 80,* 55–60.

Emery, N. J., Dally, J. M., & Clayton, N. S. (2004). Western scrub-jays (*Aphelocoma californica*) use cognitive strategies to protect their caches from thieving conspecifics. *Animal Cognition, 7,* 37–43.

Evans, T. A., & Beran, M. J. (2007). Chimpanzees use self-distraction to cope with impulsivity. *Biology Letters, 3,* 599–602.

Frederick, S., Loewenstein, G., & O'Donoghue, T. (2002). Time discounting and time preference: A critical review. *Journal of Economic Literature, 40,* 351–401.

Gibbon, J. (1977). Scalar expectancy theory and Weber's law in animal timing. *Psychological Review, 84,* 279–325.

Gibbon, J., Church, R. M., Fairhurst, S., & Kacelnik, A. (1988). Scalar expectancy theory and choice between delayed rewards. *Psychological Review, 95*, 102–114.

Giraldeau, L.-A., & Caraco, T. (2000). *Social foraging theory.* Princeton, NJ: Princeton University Press.

Green, L., Fisher, E. B., Perlow, S., & Sherman, L. (1981). Preference reversal and self-control: Choice as a function of reward amount and delay. *Behaviour Analysis Letters, 1*, 43–51.

Green, L., Myerson, J., Holt, D. D., Slevin, J. R., & Estle, S. J. (2004). Discounting of delayed food rewards in pigeons and rats: Is there a magnitude effect? *Journal of the Experimental Analysis of Behavior, 81*, 39–50.

Henly, S., Ostdiek, A., Blackwell, E., Knutie, S., Dunlap, A. S., & Stephens, D. W. (2008). The discounting-by-interruptions hypothesis: Model and experiment. *Behavioral Ecology, 19*, 154–162.

Kacelnik, A. (2003). The evolution of patience. In G. Loewenstein, D. Read, & R. F. Baumeister (Eds.), *Time and decision: Economic and psychological perspectives on intertemporal choice* (pp. 115–138). New York: Russell Sage Foundation.

King, G. R., & Logue, A. W. (1992). Choice in a self-control paradigm: Effects of uncertainty. *Behavioural Processes, 26*, 143–153.

Lagorio, C. H., & Madden, G. J. (2005). Delay discounting of real and hypothetical rewards III: Steady-state assessments, forced-choice trials, and all real rewards. *Behavioural Processes, 69*, 173–187.

Lima, S. L., Valone, T. J., & Caraco, T. (1985). Foraging efficiency–predation risk trade-off in the grey squirrel. *Animal Behaviour, 33*, 155–165.

Malenky, R. K., & Wrangham, R. W. (1994). A quantitative comparison of terrestrial herbaceous food consumption by Pan paniscus in the Lomako Forest, Zaire, and Pan troglodytes in the Kibale Forest, Uganda. *American Journal of Primatology, 32*, 1–12.

Mazur, J. E. (1987). An adjusting procedure for studying delayed reinforcement. In M. L. Commons, J. E. Mazur, J. A. Nevin, & H. Rachlin (Eds.), *Quantitative analyses of behavior: The effect of delay and of intervening events on reinforcement value* (Vol. 5, pp. 55–73). Hillsdale, NJ: Erlbaum.

Mazur, J. E. (1994). Effects of intertrial reinforcers on self-control choice. *Journal of the Experimental Analysis of Behavior, 61*, 83–96.

Mazur, J. E., & Romano, A. (1992). Choice with delayed and probabilistic reinforcers: Effects of variability, time between trials, and conditioned reinforcers. *Journal of the Experimental Analysis of Behavior, 58*, 513–525.

McClure, S. M., Ericson, K. M., Laibson, D. I., Loewenstein, G., & Cohen, J. D. (2007). Time discounting for primary rewards. *Journal of Neuroscience, 27*, 5796–5804.

McClure, S. M., Laibson, D. I., Loewenstein, G., & Cohen, J. D. (2004, October 15). Separate neural systems value immediate and delayed monetary rewards. *Science, 306*, 503–507.

McDiarmid, C. G., & Rilling, M. E. (1965). Reinforcement delay and reinforcement rate as determinants of schedule preference. *Psychonomic Science, 2*, 195–196.

Parker, G. A. (1974). Assessment strategy and the evolution of fighting behaviour. *Journal of Theoretical Biology, 47,* 223–243.

Parker, G. A., & Rubenstein, D. I. (1981). Role assessment, reserve strategy, and acquisition of information in asymmetric animal conflicts. *Animal Behaviour, 29,* 221–240.

Ramseyer, A., Pele, M., Dufour, V., Chauvin, C., & Thierry, B. (2006). Accepting loss: The temporal limits of reciprocity in brown capuchin monkeys. *Proceedings of the Royal Society of London, Series B, 273,* 179–184.

Roitberg, B. D., Mangel, M., Lalonde, R. G., Roitberg, C. A., van Alphen, J. J. M., & Vet, L. (1992). Seasonal dynamic shifts in patch exploitation by parasitic wasps. *Behavioral Ecology, 3,* 156–165.

Rosati, A. G., Stevens, J. R., Hare, B., & Hauser, M. D. (2007). The evolutionary origins of human patience: Temporal preferences in chimpanzees, bonobos, and adult humans. *Current Biology, 17,* 1663–1668.

Snowdon, C. T., & Soini, P. (1988). The tamarins, genus *Saguinus.* In R. A. Mittermeier, A. B. Rylands, A. F. Coimbra-Filho, & G. A. B. Fonseca (Eds.), *Ecology and behavior of neotropical primates* (Vol. 2, pp. 223–298). Washington, DC: World Wildlife Fund.

Sozou, P. D., & Seymour, R. M. (2003). Augmented discounting: Interaction between ageing and time-preference behaviour. *Proceedings of the Royal Society of London, Series B, 270,* 147–153.

Stephens, D. W. (2002). Discrimination, discounting and impulsivity: A role for an informational constraint. *Philosophical Transactions of the Royal Society of London, Series B, 357,* 1527–1537.

Stephens, D. W., & Anderson, D. (2001). The adaptive value of preference for immediacy: When shortsighted rules have farsighted consequences. *Behavioral Ecology, 12,* 330–339.

Stephens, D. W., Brown, J. S., & Ydenberg, R. C. (2007). *Foraging: Behavior and ecology.* Chicago: University of Chicago Press.

Stephens, D. W., Kerr, B., & Fernandez-Juricic, E. (2004). Impulsiveness without discounting: The ecological rationality hypothesis. *Proceedings of the Royal Society of London, Series B, 271,* 2459–2465.

Stephens, D. W., & Krebs, J. R. (1986). *Foraging theory.* Princeton, NJ: Princeton University Press.

Stephens, D. W., & McLinn, C. M. (2003). Choice and context: Testing a simple short-term choice rule. *Animal Behaviour, 66,* 59–70.

Stevens, J. R., Hallinan, E. V., & Hauser, M. D. (2005). The ecology and evolution of patience in two New World monkeys. *Biology Letters, 1,* 223–226.

Stevenson, M. F., & Rylands, A. B. (1988). The marmosets, genus *Callithrix.* In R. A. Mittermeier, A. B. Rylands, A. F. Coimbra-Filho, & G. A. B. Fonseca (Eds.), *Ecology and behavior of neotropical primates* (Vol. 2, pp. 131–222). Washington, DC: World Wildlife Fund.

Tobin, H., & Logue, A. W. (1994). Self-control across species (*Columba livia, Homo sapiens*, and *Rattus norvegicus*). *Journal of Comparative Psychology, 108*, 126–133.

Tobin, H., Logue, A. W., Chelonis, J. J., & Ackerman, K. T. (1996). Self-control in the monkey *Macaca fascicularis*. *Animal Learning & Behavior, 24*, 168–174.

Todd, P. M., & Gigerenzer, G. (2000). Précis of *Simple heuristics that make us smart. Behavioral and Brain Sciences, 23*, 727–741.

Vander Wall, S. B. (1990). *Food hoarding in animals*. Chicago: University of Chicago Press.

14

RECURSIVE SELF-PREDICTION AS A PROXIMATE CAUSE OF IMPULSIVITY: THE VALUE OF A BOTTOM-UP MODEL

GEORGE AINSLIE

There seems to be a corollary of Murphy's Law that applies to human choice: Whenever there is a way to get a poorer deal to pay off faster than a better one, some people will fall for it, and some of those will become addicted to it. The grim awareness that "we have met the enemy, and he is us" has required motivational science to take a closer look than has been customary at the basic mechanisms of choice. This has provided an opportunity to rethink the elementary process of behavior selection and, in particular, to examine whether the reductionist approach, somewhat disused in the human literature since the cognitive revolution of the 1970s, might lead to explanations that more intuitively acceptable approaches have failed to find. That is, a mechanistic or *bottom-up* model of elementary reward-seeking processes that combine simple principles may describe the complexity of human behavior more parsimoniously than the extensions that holistic or *top-down* theories have had to make to accommodate addictive behavior. Meanwhile, brain imaging techniques are beginning to show a functional neuroanatomy of impulsiveness in general and addictions in particular that promises to make the basic units of choice visible (assembled recently in Redish, Jensen, & Johnson, 2008), but so far these studies have not revealed how the many processes located at various sites in the brain combine to determine choice. I do not try to anticipate those answers here; rather, I examine how much can be predicted from existing knowledge of the basic properties of choice.

I first discuss the differences in top-down and bottom-up approaches and the two leading theories of impulsiveness that have been associated with them. Then as an example, I compare these approaches in the case of a common experience that often precedes impulsive choice, sudden craving occasioned by noninformative reminders of consumption. I argue that the top-down solution, adding classical conditioning as an externality, is inadequate, whereas the seeming failure of the bottom-up approach in this example is repaired by the same interaction that builds higher order mental processes ("ego functions"), recursive self-prediction. Finally, I put this example in context by briefly summarizing implications of the basic hyperbolic evaluation function that I have described elsewhere, in particular intertemporal bargaining—another area of recursive self-prediction—and the reward dependence of involuntary mental processes, which frees motivational theory from any need to invoke classical conditioning beyond an informational role.

TOP-DOWN AND BOTTOM-UP THEORIES

There are two ways to model human choice systematically. You can start with familiar phenomena—addiction, financial investment, consumption, or emotion—and look for simplifying regularities, or you can start with the simplest elements of choice—binary alternatives, a selective factor, or a discount function—and look for combining properties by which you can fit the phenomena. Most of recent motivational science has favored the former, top-down approach, which has the advantage of allowing the theorist to stay close to her or his target. It also permits the theorist to avoid the question of reductionism—whether human choice can be accounted for entirely by the interaction of simpler mechanisms, a notion that many people find vaguely offensive.

The oldest theories have had to be top-down ones, for the obvious reason that these are closest to the observational level. Most philosophers and psychologists, and all economists, have generally taken the whole person as a given and studied her characteristics. In the area of choice, top-down theories start with norms for rational choice making, for instance in social settings and competitive markets, and make hypotheses about what factors disturb the execution of these norms in practice. Each might be called a modified *rational choice theory* (RCT). RCT depicts the self as an autonomous decision maker within—or above—whatever motivational mechanisms have been discovered. This self assigns value to alternative goals without being bound by these mechanisms. Valuation is said to be a matter of interpreting information according to principles that keep value both internally consistent—comprehensive and transitive—and consistent over time in the absence of new information (Boudon, 1996). The governing self assigns value to external events according to its irreduceable judgment, but to be rational these assignments must be transitive and consistent.

Thus, rationality demands that the self discount the value of future events according to the only function that will keep their relative values from shifting with changes in delay:

$$V_d = V_0 \delta^d, \tag{1}$$

where V_d is the discounted value of the future event, V_0 is the value of the event if immediate, $\delta = (1 - \text{discount rate})$, and d is delay. Any other function, if it does not generate a straight line, will generate curves from a given amount that sometimes crosses the curves from some other amounts at other moments, simply because of the passage of time; that is, it will describe inconsistent preference. Inconsistent preference is clearly irrational because it leaves people susceptible to being money pumps, that is, it opens them to exploitation by a competitor who repeatedly buys from them when their valuations fall below their exponentially discounted value and sells back to them when they rise (Arrow, 1959; Conlisk, 1996). Inconsistent preference implies in general that people can expect to make future choices that they do not currently want. To deal with instances in which people's choices have repeatedly deviated from rationality and in which explanations such as naiveté or a simple difference in discount rate do not apply, RCT has been modified to add an unmotivated principle that overrides rational choice: classical conditioning. Modified RCT is a top-down theory, in that it starts with a coherent executive faculty and seeks to explain its malfunctions.

Aside from errors in information processing (e.g., Kahneman, Slovic, & Tversky, 1982), the principal malfunction discussed has been impulsivity. *Impulses* are most usefully defined as temporary preferences for options that an individual usually values less than their alternatives. The problems raised by other senses of the word are trivial—spontaneous or whimsical choice, in one usage, or faulty motor control in another (Parker, Bagby, & Webster, 1993)—but the phenomenon of temporary preference is the central puzzle in drug addictions and the growing number of behaviors that are seen to have addictive patterns: overeating; credit abuse; habitually self-destructive relationships; absorption in electronic entertainments to the exclusion of personal relationships; and, archetypically, pathological gambling, to name just a few (Offer, 2006; Ross, Sharp, Vuchinich, & Spurrett, 2008). Substance abuse alone has been calculated to be the greatest cause of preventable death in young adults (Robins & Regier, 1990). Impulses are clearly motives.

Addicts engage in their behavior wholeheartedly and even shrewdly, despite being motivated at other times to limit or avoid it. The critical question is, then, how an ordinarily inferior motive is amplified enough to dominate the motives that had dominated it, in the absence of new information about it. In particular, why does this dominance last for comparatively short periods of time, to be followed repeatedly by either repudiation of or resignation to a consciously disliked behavior pattern?

The answer that has been most intuitively appealing is that there is an additional motivational factor, controlled by an unmotivated process such as association. This seeming invasion by a foreign process leaves RCT itself undisturbed. An association theory is especially credible because of the familiar experience of sudden craving for some specific pleasurable activity, occasioned by only a reminder of this activity. Appetites and emotions seem particularly susceptible to this kind of pattern, so it has been suggested that they form a special class of visceral rewards that when triggered by small reminders can produce the temporary amplification of reward that a theory of impulsivity needs (Laibson, 2001; Loewenstein, 1996).

> Visceral factors include drive states such as hunger, thirst, and sexual desire, moods and emotions, physical pain, and most importantly for addiction, craving for a drug. . . . At intermediate levels, most visceral factors, including drug craving, produce similar patterns of impulsivity, remorse, and self-binding. At high levels, drug craving and other visceral factors overwhelm decision making altogether, superseding volitional control of behavior. (Loewenstein, 1999, p. 235)

Ever since Plato made passion a distinct part of the soul, attribution of impulses to a separate motivational force has seemed necessary to preserve RCT as a descriptive—as opposed to a merely normative—theory of choice making. Triggering by reminders is the mechanism described by classical conditioning, a venerable theory of unwanted behavior of which visceral reward theory is just the latest restatement.

A bottom-up approach can do without this dualism. From the time Descartes realized that human physiology obeyed physical laws, theorists have speculated about how to build it from parts. The associationism of the empiricist philosophers, beginning with Hobbes, and La Mettrie's (1748/1999) first attempt to model choice making as mechanical, in *Man a Machine*, have been followed by many reductionist theories, most famously those of Freud, who developed an "economic" theory of what he imagined to be neural energy (Freud, 1895/1956b), later called *libido* (Freud, 1923/1956a), and Skinner (e.g., 1948), whose notoriety approached that of La Mettrie after he asserted that all choice can be traced to environmental reinforcement. A bottom-up approach such as Skinner's behaviorism takes the reductionist bull by the horns and tests how parsimoniously a higher order process can be predicted by the interaction of simpler elements. However, the behaviorists' models have been limited by a methodological norm that forbids the modeling of mental processes, leaving all complexity to be modeled in the external contingencies of reinforcement that the participant faces (Alston, 1974); this approach will be blind to any contingencies that lie within the participant. Ironically, only the methods developed by the behaviorists themselves have produced data precise enough to take the modeling of mental processes beyond the common sense level.

I argue that the extension of behavioral concepts to the conflict of motives within a participant can permit a model that fits familiar experience better than the behaviorists' own environmental contingency model and that the inadequacy of an RCT model, even when modified by conditioned appetite, makes the new model necessary. This model starts with a well-established observation (Green & Myerson, 2004; Kirby, 1997) that all reward-seeking organisms show a robust tendency to devalue expected reward according to a hyperbolic function (Mazur, 1987):

$$V_d = \frac{V_0}{1 + kd},\qquad(2)$$

where k is the discounting rate and the other variables are as defined earlier. Where smaller rewards precede larger alternatives, participants regularly prefer the larger reward when both are distant, but change to preferring the smaller reward as it becomes imminently available. Left uncompensated, spontaneous preference will make an individual impulsive by the elementary operation of this discount function, without the contribution of any other factor. Compensation for this phenomenon is a major task for the ego functions—perhaps the major task—but the same hyperbolic discount function that created the problem can be expected to motivate the learning of solutions. I have developed this argument elsewhere (Ainslie, 2001, pp. 73–140; Ainslie, 2005) and summarize relevant parts at the end of this chapter. However, my main object in this chapter is to examine a serious objection to the hyperbolic discount curve as the mechanism of impulsiveness: The hyperbolic discount curve itself does not predict the sudden craving elicited by stimuli associated with reward consumption when these stimuli do not predict increased availability or proximity of this consumption.

In craving induced by these uninformative cues, some amplifying factor beyond immediacy is clearly operating. Conditioned appetite is an obvious alternative: Perhaps even uninformative cues can amplify a participant's valuation of a good from having been associated with ("conditioned to") its consumption in the past. The conditioned appetite model meshes with the experience of sudden temptation that often precedes impulses. Many authors have continued to rely on conditioned appetite or emotion as an explanation for temporarily amplified valuations (Drummond, Tiffany, Glautier, & Remington, 1995; O'Brien, 1997). Problematic impulses usually involve visceral rewards—indeed, the occurrence of impulses has been used as a defining property of viscerality, as in the passage from Loewenstein (1999) presented earlier. An addict may suddenly get intense cravings while watching a show about drugs, for instance. Because such sudden cravings are sometimes implicated in relapses (e.g., Tiffany, 1995), the question naturally arises of whether conditioned appetite is responsible.

The discount function that became associated with visceral reward theory originally described the sudden amplification of value only in situations in which reward is imminently available:

$$V_d = V_0 \beta \delta^d, \tag{3}$$

where β (visceral excitatory factor) has one of only two values: If reward is not immediate, $0 < \beta < 1$; if reward is immediate, $\beta = 1$ (Laibson, 2001; McClure, Laibson, Loewenstein, & Cohen, 2004). The visceral effect was said to come from the immediacy of reward itself. This step function produces a curve that somewhat resembles a hyperbola, an effect that was intentional: Economist David Laibson (2001) originally adopted its dual, "hyperboloid" curve from an article on intergenerational transfers of wealth (Phelps & Pollack, 1968) because "the discount structure [of the curve] mimics the qualitative property of the hyperbolic discount function, while maintaining most of the analytical tractability of the exponential discount function" (Laibson, 1997, p. 450). However, this formula has the same limitation as the hyperbolic function that it approximates (Equation 2). Spikes of appetite often occur without any cue that predicts greater availability or proximity of the reward. Thus, it has been proposed that a sudden evocation of viscerality has the same effect as immediacy in sending β to 1.0 (McClure et al., 2004). This hypothesis converts Laibson's original proposal from a straightforward discounting theory to a two-factor, conditioning-and-exponential-discounting theory (Figure 14.1, Panel A).

The mechanism that evokes this viscerality obviously has to be classical conditioning. Research on conditioning has evolved considerably since Pavlov's (1927) first experiments. The initial observation was that some events (unconditioned stimuli, or UCSs) elicit reflexive responses (unconditioned responses, or UCRs). Initially, UCSs seemed to select for the transfer of UCRs to arbitrarily designated stimuli (conditioned stimuli, or CSs) that predicted their occurrence, regardless of whether the CSs predicted that the transferred responses (now called conditioned responses, or CRs) would be rewarded. However, experimenters' initial conclusion that UCSs were sufficient to select for the transfer of UCRs to new stimuli did not stand up. The site of selection by UCSs is stimuli, not behaviors; that is, the pairing of novel stimuli with UCSs produces only CSs, not true CRs (Mackintosh,

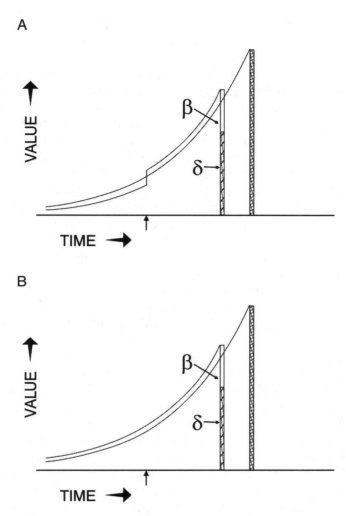

Figure 14.1. A: β–δ (exponential) curves drawn according to Equation 3, except that 0 < β < 1 before a conditioned stimulus (CS) occurs at the arrow on the *x*-axis and β = 1 afterward. The CS elicits a conditioned response (appetite, the unfilled β part of the bar) that raises the effective height of the smaller–sooner reward. B: β–δ curves at equilibrium drawn according to Equation 3, except that 0 < β < 1 before a CS occurs at the arrow on the *x*-axis and β = 1 afterward. Repeated elicitation of appetite by a CS should make the rise in smaller–sooner height expectable, eliminating the change of preference.

1983; Rescorla, 1988). Only information is learned by association; the occurrence and timing of CRs depends on what incentives are created by this information. Even the selection of the CR was recognized very early not to depend on what response is elicited by the UCS; only a few CRs happen to be the same, in detail or even in approximate kind, as those elicited by the UCS (Upton, 1929; Zener, 1937). However, many emotions and appetites lack external signs and are apt to be innately connected to particular kinds of expectation, making it unclear to what extent the disproof of conditioning as a mechanism of response selection applies to them. CRs might still exist in the form of appetites or emotions. This possibility has to be left open.

The assumption that appetites and thus amplification of reward can be transferred by association is consistent with the seemingly unmotivated appetites of visceral learning theory, but experiments on the timing of CRs—or operant responses to CSs—have been less supportive. These experiments have regularly shown that responses based on associated stimuli reflect the exact timing of when the original objects were available. In parametric experiments, CRs anticipate the occurrence of UCSs with great accuracy. If a CS occurs or begins well before a UCS is due, participants learn to estimate the delay and emit the CR just before the UCS (Gallistel & Gibbon, 2000; Kehoe, Graham-Clark, & Schreurs, 1989; Savastano, Hua, Barnet, & Miller, 1998). Appetites—specifically, cue-induced craving for cigarettes and skin conductance and salivation related to craving—are strongly dependent on whether puffing is available within the next minute (Carter & Tiffany, 2001; Field & Duka, 2001). Thus, in the laboratory involuntary responses closely track the prospect of reward. Furthermore, if the general process of learning behavioral contingencies in daily life counts as conditioning—the usual assumption—then nonanticipatory appetites are an anomalous variant here as well. Where the consumption of an addictive substance never happens in a given circumstance, humans do not crave it: People addicted to opiates and those with alcoholism in programs that allow consumption on only certain days report absence of craving on other days (Meyer, 1988), and observant Orthodox Jews, who never smoke on the Sabbath, are reported not to crave cigarettes then (Dar, Stronguin, Marouani, Krupsky, & Frenk, 2005; Schachter, Silverstein, & Perlick, 1977). Classical conditioning, which is just associative learning, does not explain appetites that are disproportionate to the prospect of consuming and that change without changes in this prospect. It is true that some cue-induced appetites and emotions have been reported to grow without further contact with UCSs (Eysenck, 1967), but such examples, if they are valid (Malloy & Levis, 1990), go beyond passive association and thus need explanation themselves. Furthermore, visceral reward theory does not make it clear why the associative process should not lead amplified visceral rewards to be anticipated and discounted like any other reward, so that they become preferred consistently, rather than temporarily, where the amplification is great enough to make them preferred at any point (Figure 14.1, Panel B). After all, rewards are usually remembered as being consumed in the presence of appetite; adjusting their value for current hunger or satiety is a distinct process (Balleine & Dickinson, 1998). Conditioning should not reduce the efficiency of the reward process but simply assign a true value to the prospect of a reward that has been consumed at the usual level of appetite.

Given the strictly informational role of conditioning, the premature occurrence of appetite is still a puzzle for visceral reward theory. Why does the addict develop craving when merely reminded of consumption? However, a straightforward application of hyperbolic discounting also fails to predict spikes of appetite in response to cues that do not convey new information. An extension of either conditioning or hyperbolic discounting theory can let these theories handle the occurrence of prematurely spiking appetites or emotions. However, I argue that this extension works well only for the hyperbolic theory.

RECURSIVE SELF-PREDICTION OF CONDITIONED RESPONSES

In laboratory experiments, consumption goods are necessarily outside of the participant's control. Appetite is studied as a function of when the experimenter signals the goods' availability. In daily life, by contrast, goods that might be consumed impulsively are available much of the time, and their consumption is limited by a person's decisions. CSs in life situations are very different than they are in the laboratory.

Conditioning theory has long departed from the notion that CSs have to be concrete stimuli. They can be just temporal patterns, interpreted stochastically by the participant (Gallistel, 2002), a finding that can be summarized by saying that the expectation of a UCS, in whatever form, functions as a CS. In humans, and possibly in other organisms to a limited extent, expectation includes predictions of the individual's own behavior. If a person's conscious intentions entirely committed him or her to future behavior, such prediction would be superfluous, of course; a person could predict his behavior directly by examining these intentions. But behavior in even the near future is increasingly recognized as beyond the scope of such examination (Wegner, 2002, especially pp. 63–144) and may depend on the dynamics of a population of motivated processes (Ainslie, 2001, pp. 39–44). This means that expectation is apt to be recursive, with an expectation of a UCS—say, taking cocaine—functioning as a CS and inducing the CR of appetite. But where availability is not a limiting factor, an increase in appetite will itself increase the likelihood of taking the cocaine. If this likelihood increases, the CS of expecting cocaine should increase, and in turn the CR of appetite again.

Wherever a person's consumption is limited mainly by her own choice, appetite can be a positive feedback system of the kind first described by Darwin, James, and Lange:

> The free expression by outward signs of an emotion intensifies it. On the other hand, the repression, as far as this is possible, of all outward signs softens our emotions. He who gives way to violent gestures will increase his rage; he who does not control the signs of fear will experience fear in greater degree. (Darwin, 1872/1979, p. 366)

As a mechanism for finding a response, Darwin's suggestion has been disproved by a number of experiments (concisely summarized by Rolls, 2005, pp. 26–28), but none of these findings touches on its possible role in the modulation of a given response once an individual has focused on it. Whenever an arbitrary stimulus has been associated with consumption in the past, the appearance of that stimulus might accurately predict an increased current likelihood of consumption, and accordingly function as a conventional CS. A sudden spike of appetite could thus come from the existence of positive feedback conditions. These conditions may obtain whenever the person's consumption is determined mainly by her choice about a readily available consumption good, but are apt to have the strongest effect when the person has weak to moderate resolve not to consume: When a person is not trying to restrain consumption, she will keep appetite relatively satisfied; when a person is confident of not consuming regardless of appetite (as in cases of opiates in scheduled addicts and smoking in Orthodox Jews), he or she will not expect appetite to lead to consumption. In both of these cases, a stimulus associated with consumption should be only a trivial CS and thus not lead to an exceptional CR. By contrast, cues predicting that a recovering addict or restrained eater might lapse could elicit significant CRs. Even in the numerous laboratory experiments in which drug cues have induced craving in addicts, the participants have known that they might be able to actually obtain drugs as soon as they leave.

However, conditioning theory itself limits the viability of this recursive model. CRs are supposed to be UCRs that have been passively transferred to CSs because CSs predict UCSs. If CRs are only such anticipatory responses, their amplitude should be limited to no more than that of their UCRs. If a person's expectation of consumption increases by $x\%$, his appetite (CR) should increase by no more than $x\%$ of the UCR, or at least what the CR would be when certainty is 100% and delay is zero. Because we are discussing delays that are significantly greater than zero—the cases in which hyperbolic curves per se do not explain the spiking—the increase in appetite should be markedly less than $x\%$. Conversely, if a person's appetite increases by $x\%$, the increase in estimated probability of consumption that this causes should also be fractional, reflecting the proportion of times when that much increase in appetite has been followed by actual consumption. If a recovering addict, for instance, has moderate resolve not to relapse, an initial confrontation with a drug stimulus should increase the addict's likelihood of relapsing by only a marginal amount. This increase should in turn have only a small effect on the addict's conditioned craving (CR), which would be expected to increase the expectation of relapse by an even smaller amount again. The positive feedback effect should be damped down unless the percentage of each increase is perfectly preserved, and even in that case the CR will be capped at the level of the UCR and discounted for whatever delay is unavoidable. The qualitative elements for explosive craving are there, but quantitatively the amplification that results from the recursive process will be limited.

RECURSIVE SELF-PREDICTION OF MOTIVATED APPETITE

If appetites themselves are operants—that is, if appetites are selected not by the simple transfer of a UCS but by reward for their activity, as I have proposed elsewhere (Ainslie, 2001, pp. 48–70, 161–174)—this limitation disappears. However, this is not a trivial change in the conventional view of appetite. I need to briefly review my argument that hyperbolic discount curves permit involuntary and even aversive processes to be incorporated into a unified motivational marketplace.

First, we must strip the selective factor, "reward," of its connotations of pleasure and reduce it to its defining function: that which selects for a process that it follows.[1] Then we can predict what pattern will be produced by recurring periods of reward, followed, if chosen, by obligatory periods of nonreward (or reduced reward). By changing the durations of the reward periods, we can variously describe the binge-followed-by-hangover pattern seen in many addictions (duration before negative consequences is maybe an hour for a person with bulimia, up to several days before a binge drinker gets sick); the repeated urges reported in psychogenic itches, tics, and unwanted mannerisms (duration before negative consequences is seconds); and, by extension, the attraction of attention that is fused experientially with behavioral aversion in negative emotions such as panic, the emotion-like aversive component of pain itself ("protopathic" pain; Melzack & Casey, 1970), and, variably, rage (duration before negative consequences is fractions of a second). Figure 14.2, Panel A depicts a level of background reward being replaced by a period of cyclic reward spikes that are each followed by reward inhibition. The figure can represent binges, tics, or negative emotions, depending on cycle length. Figure 14.2, Panel B shows hyperbolic discount curves drawn to the alternatives of a single cycle versus the same length of background reward. The spike that begins the cycle can

---

[1]Berridge (2003) has reported behavioral and neurophysiological evidence that seems to require a kind of reward that is not pleasurable, which he called *nonhedonic*.

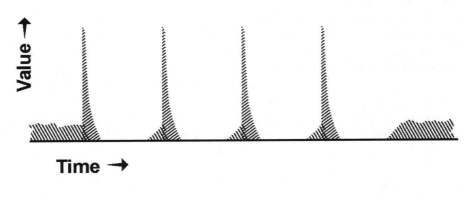

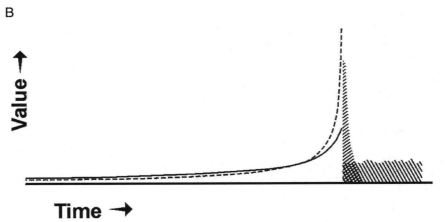

Figure 14.2. A: Motivated processes that are avoided at a distance range from behavioral impulses to painful emotions, depending on whether the time scale represents days or fractions of a second. Any such process can be accounted for as a cycle of brief, intense reward (rightward hatching) that interrupts an ongoing baseline reward (leftward hatching) for a relatively longer time (from Ainslie, 1992). B: Hyperbolic discount curves drawn from a single spike of reward (or urge) versus a lower but longer lasting alternative reward. Each curve is the sum of the curves from each moment of reward. The spike has less area than the baseline reward to which it is an alternative, but because it is taller it will be preferred just before it is available (from Ainslie, 1992).

be expected to make it preferred temporarily when it is close, even when the net effect on reward is strongly negative. At the short end of the spectrum of durations, the initial spikes characterize any option that is experienced as vivid; the subsequent troughs may vary in depth, with low troughs creating aversive experiences that individuals try to escape and shallow or absent troughs creating positive experiences (thrill, elation, some examples of rage) that are limited by satiation. In this model, conditions that make panic or rage possible can be viewed as enabling appetites for them just as nonsatiety enables appetites for the consumption of substances—offers of reward, even if they are frequently "offers you can't refuse." The value of this model is that both positive and negative appetites can be seen as luring organisms into participating in them, rather than springing up automatically like reflexes, outside of the marketplace of choice. As long as it is discounted hyperbolically, reward can then be the selective factor not only for enduring pleasures but for temporary, regretted pleasures and for urges that do not feel pleasurable at all.

Soon after the description of classical conditioning, experimenters noted that all stimuli that could induce CRs had motivating power as well (Hull, 1943; Miller, 1969). The possibility that reward and the selective principle in UCSs are identical has been proposed before (reviewed in Donahoe, Burgos, & Palmer, 1993, and Pear & Eldridge, 1984), but has not been pursued extensively, perhaps because a separate selective principle has seemed necessary to explain why aversive experiences can compete for attention and because no important hypotheses have hinged on this identity. But with hyperbolic discounting, seduction over various time courses accounts for attention to aversive experiences without any need for a separate selective principle, as I have just described. Of course, it may turn out that this attention can be better explained by other hypotheses that integrate reward and nonreward in close temporal proximity, or even simultaneity, as reported qualities such as "motivational salience" are analyzed (e.g., Berridge & Robinson, 1998, pp. 348–349), but so far no other hypothesis exists at the behavioral level about how an incentive can attract attention while repelling behavior in the marketplace of choice. As to whether any behavioral hypotheses depend on the question of one versus two basic selective factors, I argue that the sudden occurrence of appetite when its object is no nearer requires appetite to be reward dependent—that is, selected by the same factor as motor behavior.

If appetite is an operant, a recursive reward-seeking model is possible that can predict the same observations as a classical conditioning model but without the damping effect: A cue predicting availability will be a cue for generating appetite if the potential for consumption to be rewarding (nonsatiety) exists. When availability and nonsatiety exist and when consumption is limited by self-control—probably the case only in humans—appetite itself has the potential to obtain fast-paying reward by motivating the abandonment of (slow-paying) self-control. The most rewarding amount of appetite, then, may not be that which optimizes the experience of consumption, given its probability, but rather that which makes consumption most probable. The most productive timing of such appetite will take the form of concentrated attempts on discrete occasions; if appetite does not succeed in inducing consumption on a particular occasion, it would waste effort by prolonged activity. Occasions for appetites could be arbitrary, especially at higher levels of deprivation, but the occasions that are the most apt to promise successful attempts are limited ones—an external reminder, or a circumstance in which they have succeeded in the past. In this view, the force of symbols and other reminders in relapse comes not from their effect as CSs but from their providing reward-seeking appetites with focal occasions to try to overturn self-control.

This theory of appetite is part of a broader bottom-up model that depicts reward-dependent processes as competing for acceptance on the basis of the current, hyperbolically discounted value of the prospective reward for these processes. The fact that preferability among a set of processes can shift as a function of time alone puts these processes in a strategic competition with each other (Ainslie, 1992, pp. 154–179; 2001, pp. 90–100). They operate as somewhat independent agents that have some but not all interests in common, on the basis of what are common contingencies of reward but differently discounted valuations of them. An appetite in this model arises when an individual perceives the opportunity for consumption that can be made either more rewarding or more likely by this appetite. The contingencies that determine whether appetite as a quasi-independent agent asserts itself in a given situation will be roughly the same as those determining whether a pet begs its owner for food. Begging is a low-cost behavior and is apt to occur whenever the pet encounters food-related cues; again, continuous begging will not be worthwhile. But if the pet is never fed in a particular circumstance, the begging gradually extinguishes. Likewise, if food is so available that significant deprivation does not occur, begging adds no value. By analogy, the restrained eater or recovering addict has the potential to experience intense reward by indulging in immediate consumption. Insofar as appetite makes consumption look even a little more likely, it will pay for itself, and any signs of weakening will serve as cues that still more appetite may succeed in motivating consumption. The low cost of appetite may explain why it must go unrewarded consistently and over many trials in a given circumstance to extinguish—for instance, why the Orthodox Jews who do not get cravings on the Sabbath do get cravings at work, even though they know they must not smoke (Dar et al., 2005).

According to this theory, a person does not come to anticipate the higher value of the smaller–sooner reward, as in the progression from Figure 14.2, Panel A, to 14.2, Panel B, because the eruption of the positive feedback cycle is not a reliable occurrence. It may even be that people who are trying to prevent an impulse try not to anticipate the cycle for fear of triggering it.[2]

Thus, appetite as an operant can be subject to the same positive feedback mechanism as conditioned appetite, but there are two important differences between this and the recursive conditioning model. One is that the degree of appetite will not be limited to mere anticipation but can be what-

[2]Edward Tolman's (1939) original concept of vicarious trial and error, in which a participant estimates the reward for alternative choices by serially initiating them without committing to them, has recently been validated with single hippocampal neurons (Johnson & Redish, 2007).

ever increases the prospect of reward. The other is that appetite can occur without a stimulus or can be occasioned by a stimulus that has not been associated with consumption. Addicts commonly experience craving spontaneously and even invite it by daydreaming. Also, in a well-studied example of negative appetites, the phobias, conditioning events are not usually found (Lazarus, 1972; Wolpe, 1981). There will still be constraints on the generation of appetites—in modalities in which unsatisfied appetite brings hunger pangs or withdrawal symptoms, these will be deterrents, and appetite without a limited occasion will extinguish (see Ainslie, 2001, pp. 166–171)—but the explosive appetite that so often ends people's efforts at controlled consumption can be understood as a motivated process that has sought to do exactly that.

For completeness, I should mention a factor that is likely to increase the role of recursive self-prediction in appetite: the apparently intrinsic rewarding effect of some appetites (Herrnstein, 1977). Some people get pleasure from reading cookbooks without expecting to eat what they read about, and people who are prone to panic may have panic episodes without perceiving any danger. Some appetites at least must be intrinsically rewarding. This "rewardingness" will be limited not only by the aforementioned pangs or withdrawal symptoms that may follow it, but also by its own tendency to habituate, as is the case with emotions (Ainslie, 2001, pp. 164–174).

In summary, the model of appetite as an operant cued by recursive self-prediction is uniquely able to account for explosive appetite—that is, why a cue associated with consumption but not predictive of increased availability of a consumption good should lead to a great increase in appetite. In this model, the cue is needed only to give occasion, that is, to select one moment over another for a focused attempt at reversing the dominant preference. The model depends on the hyperbolic shape of the discount curve because an individual with consistent preferences over time would have no short-range motive to undermine her or his own resolutions, or indeed any long-range motive to make resolutions in the first place. Similar predictions are made by the hyperboloid (β–δ) step function of visceral reward theory (Equations 1 or 3), but this shape can be generated only by the explosive appetite that, according to the damping argument presented above, the theory's classical conditioning mechanism would be inadequate to produce. That is, the only viable mechanism for the β–δ discount curve is for discount curves to have an elementary hyperbolic or other hyperconcave shape to begin with.

A SELF-PREDICTION MODEL DESCRIBES WILL (AND ITS FAILURE) AS WELL AS SUDDEN APPETITE

Both modified RCT and hyperbolic discounting theory have come to include means of explaining most of the ways in which people make choices. I have selected a case in which the difference in their predictiveness is apparent:

the ways in which the models deal with the failure of one basic ego function, maintenance of consistent choice over time. This example should be seen in the context of larger models, which predict differences in how this ego function operates to begin with. These differences are in turn part of the fundamental difference in how these models depict the action and scope of motivation, which I have already described: RCT accounts for experientially unmotivated processes with the transferred reflexes of conditioning theory; hyperbolic discounting theory encompasses all processes that are not truly reflexes in a comprehensive marketplace of motivation. RCT assumes the maintenance of consistency to be implicit in the accurate gathering of information about goals because rationality itself dictates consistent long-range behavior; a faculty of will is sometimes recognized, but explicit hypotheses about willpower essentially restate common intuitions about it—for instance, that it resembles a muscle that can be exhausted by overuse but strengthened by exercise (Baumeister, Heartherton, & Tice, 1994). In the hyperbolic model, will is essential to consistent choice over time. Because of the innate tendency to form temporary preferences, hyperbolic discounting predicts not only inconsistency over time but recursive motivational processes, from which emerge both higher order mental functions and impulses that do not depend on temporal proximity.

The mechanism of willpower as intertemporal bargaining based on recursive self-prediction has been often presented over the past 30 years (Ainslie, 1975; 1992, pp. 144–173; 2001, pp. 78–116) and is only summarized here: Hyperbolically discounted reward will create what is in effect a population of reward-seeking processes that can be grouped loosely into interests on the basis of common goals, just as economic interests can be identified in market economies. The choice-making self will have many of the properties of an economic marketplace, with a scarce resource—access to the individual's limited channel of behavior—bid on with a common currency—reward. Maintenance and change of choice will be governed by intertemporal bargaining, the activity in which reward-seeking processes that share some goals (e.g., long-term sobriety) but not others (when to have drinks) maximize their individual expected rewards, discounted hyperbolically to the current moment. This limited warfare relationship is familiar in interpersonal situations, where it often gives rise to "self-enforcing contracts" such as nations' avoidance of using nuclear weapons lest nuclear warfare become general. In interpersonal bargaining, stability is achieved in the absence of an overarching government by the parties' recognition of repeated prisoner's dilemma incentives. In intertemporal bargaining, personal rules arise through a similar recognition among the successive motivational states of an individual, with the difference that a future state is not motivated to retaliate, as it were, against past states that have defected. The risk of future states' loss of confidence in the success of the personal rule, and consequent defection in their own short-term interests, will present the same threat as the risk of purposive retaliation. The reason that people recovering from alcoholism avoid taking a single drink is not that it will make them drunk but because it will impair the credibility of their sobriety, without which they do not have much current reason not to get drunk.

As with interpersonal negotiations, intertemporal cooperation is threatened by the availability of alternative truce lines. Under the pressure of current temptation, the person with alcoholism may reason that drinking on New Year's Eve would not reduce her expectation of staying sober the rest of the year. But then that might be true of her birthday, too, or your birthday, or Saturdays. At least with alcohol, there does exist a bright line between some drinking and none, whereas an overeater or spendthrift has much less defense against rationalizations: A person with these disorders still has to eat some food and spend some money, and it is hard to see one diet or budget as irreplaceable. This is a large topic, but the point for the present discussion is that the intertemporal bargaining situation that hyperbolic discount curves create for a self-aware person does not require any kind of overseer to reach a stable equilibrium. Repeated prisoner's dilemma contingencies can create a will without an organ, serving a self without a seat, just as the "will" of nations not to use nuclear weapons seems to be guided by an invisible hand.

Thus, the model that hyperbolic discounting makes possible does not postulate any preformed or overarching faculty that makes choice coherent. Its starting place is a sequence of preferences based on the shifting dominance of incentives, which strictly determine all choice but are not strictly controlled by external events. Higher order mental processes, which look beyond immediate advantage and make choice somewhat coherent, are formed from simpler reward-seeking processes that must compete on the basis of the leverage afforded by superior foresight. They therefore cannot stand outside of the reward process to evaluate it. This is a bottom-up theory, in that it starts with a population of processes that have been shaped by differential reward and seeks to explain the ways that this population creates an executive faculty.

The differences between this model and the muscle analogy are not only that the will's direction is implicit in the mechanism itself. This model also accounts for how the will can be simultaneously strong and weak in different areas, but also that this model predicts familiar pathologies of will—compulsiveness, denial, boredom, and circumscribed dyscontrol symptoms in which a person abandons attempts at will (Ainslie, 2001, pp. 143–197): The awareness of your choices as test cases for larger plans makes you lawyerly, perhaps at the expense of being able to live fully in the here and now; the loss of prospective reward that comes from recognizing a lapse moves you not to notice key aspects of your choice making; overly successful self-control reduces surprise, which is necessary to prevent the attenuation of emotional experience; and lapses in a particular circumstance often lead people to stop trying to use their will there, lest its general credibility be reduced.

The positive feedback system that I have just described for the sudden explosion of appetite follows the same pattern as the sudden wilting of a resolution following a lapse. The sudden appetite may indeed initiate the crash and form part of its motivational feedback loop, although it will probably not itself be experienced as a failure of will, but as the temptation that led to the failure. The difference between these two recursive processes—the collapse of will and the explosion of appetite—may be in the time it takes to review alternatives versus only registering new self-predictions about a single alternative. The process of reviewing predictions about the impact of alternative choices on future bargaining (sometimes called vicarious trial and error; Johnson & Redish, 2007; Tolman, 1939) must obviously take time, if only some fractions of a second; so "deliberate" choice making will govern only behaviors that do not kindle too rapidly once thought of. A shift of attention, for instance, occurs too rapidly to be tested against a personal rule, and the components of vicarious trial and error itself cannot be made contingent on a process that depends on vicarious trial and error—hence the famous impossibility of using will to not think about white bears (Wegner, 1989): Once you have tested whether you are thinking about white bears, you have already thought about them. People are strongly motivated to discriminate those recursive self-prediction processes that may support personal rules from the rapid ones that cannot support them, even when the difference is better described as a temporal continuum than as a dichotomy; you risk blaming yourself, and weakening your will, when you perceive personal rules as relevant to your action, but not when the action is "involuntary." This discrimination may have contributed to the intuition that appetites are reflexive, unmotivated processes.

CONCLUSIONS

People often deviate from their own plans after seeing or even thinking about poorer but faster paying alternatives. Because this experience often resembles laboratory observations of classical conditioning, both top-down (holistic) and bottom-up (mechanistic) theories of impulsiveness have borrowed this concept to explain irrational or seemingly less rewarded choices. However, analytic experiments have increasingly shown that conditioning is just the learning of information, and conditioned responses, including appetites, are timed precisely to make the most effective use of that information. Such learning does not account for the apparent elicitation of appetites by uninformative cues. The bottom-up approach offers a solution: Sudden appetite in this circumstance is best attributed to foraging by appetites as reward-seeking processes, becoming explosive (positively fed back) where consumption or not of the appetite's object is a matter of self-control. The theory that appetites and other involuntary mental processes are operants requires—and follows readily from—the hyperbolic discounting of reward and the definition of reward as whatever increases the frequency of a process that it follows. Amplification of prospective reward by recursive self-prediction, rather than by arbitrary association, lets the concept of conditioned responses finally return to the role that Pavlov originally described, responses simply "conditional" on new information (Dinsmoor, 2004).

REFERENCES

Ainslie, G. (1975) Specious reward: A behavioral theory of impulsiveness and impulse control. *Psychological Bulletin, 82*, 463–496.

Ainslie, G. (1992). *Picoeconomics: The strategic interaction of successive motivational states within the person.* Cambridge, England: Cambridge University Press.

Ainslie, G. (2001). *Breakdown of will.* New York: Cambridge University Press.

Alston, W. P. (1974). Can psychology do without private data? *Behaviorism, 1*, 71–102.

Arrow, K. J. (1959). Rational choice functions and orderings. *Economica, 26*, 121–127.

Balleine, B., & Dickinson, A. (1998). Goal-directed action: Contingency and incentive learning and their cortical substrates. *Neuropharmacology, 37*, 407–419.

Baumeister, R. F., Heatherton, T. F., & Tice, D. M. (1994). *Losing control: How and why people fail at self-regulation.* San Diego, CA: Academic Press.

Berridge, K. C. (2003). Pleasures of the brain. *Brain and Cognition, 52*, 106–128.

Berridge, K. C., & Robinson, T. (1998). What is the role of dopamine in reward? Hedonic impact, reward learning, or incentive salience. *Brain Research Reviews, 28*, 309–369.

Boudon, R. (1996). The "rational choice model": A particular case of the "cognitive model." *Rationality and Society, 8*, 123–150.

Carter, B. L., & Tiffany, S. T. (2001). The cue-availability paradigm: The effects of cigarette availability on cue reactivity in smokers. *Experimental and Clinical Psychopharmacology, 9*, 183–190.

Conlisk, J. (1996). Why bounded rationality? *Journal of Economic Literature, 34*, 669–700.

Dar, R., Stronguin, F., Marouani, R., Krupsky, M., & Frenk, H. (2005). Craving to smoke in orthodox Jewish smokers who abstain on the Sabbath: A comparison to a baseline and a forced abstinence workday. *Psychopharmacology, 183*, 294–299.

Darwin, C. (1979) *The expressions of emotions in man and animals.* London: Julian Friedman. (Original work published 1872)

Dinsmoor, J. A. (2004). The etymology of basic concepts in the experimental analysis of behavior. *Journal of the Experimental Analysis of Behavior, 82*, 311–316.

Donahoe, J. W., Burgos, J. E., & Palmer, D. C. (1993). A selectionist approach to reinforcement. *Journal of the Experimental Analysis of Behavior, 60,* 17–40.

Drummond, D. C., Tiffany, S. T., Glautier, S., & Remington, B. (1995). *Addictive behavior: Cue exposure theory and practice.* New York: Wiley.

Eysenck, H. J. (1967). Single trial conditioning, neurosis and the Napalkov phenomenon. *Behavior Research and Therapy, 5,* 63–65.

Field, M., & Duka, T. (2001). Smoking expectancy mediates the conditioned responses to arbitrary smoking cues. *Behavioural Pharmacology, 12,* 183–194.

Freud, S. (1956a). The ego and the id. In J. Strachey & A. Freud (Eds.), *The standard edition of the complete psychological works of Sigmund Freud* (Vol. 19, pp. 3–66). London: Hogarth Press. (Original work published 1923)

Freud, S. (1956b). Project for a scientific psychology. In J. Strachey & A. Freud (Eds.), *The standard edition of the complete psychological works of Sigmund Freud* (Vol. 1, pp. 283–397). London: Hogarth Press. (Original work published 1895)

Gallistel, C. R. (2002). Frequency, contingency and the information processing theory of conditioning. In P. Sedlmeier & T. Betsch (Eds.), *Frequency processing and cognition* (pp. 153–174). Oxford, England: Oxford University Press.

Gallistel, C. R., & Gibbon, J. (2000). Time, rate, and conditioning. *Psychological Review, 107,* 289–344.

Green, L., & Myerson, J. (2004). A discounting framework for choice with delayed and probabilistic rewards. *Psychological Bulletin, 130,* 769–792.

Herrnstein, R. J. (1977). The evolution of behaviorism. *American Psychologist, 32,* 593–603.

Hollander, E., & Stein, D. J. (2006). *Clinical manual of impulse-control disorders.* Washington, DC: American Psychiatric Publishing.

Hull, C. L. (1943). *Principles of behavior.* New York: Appleton-Century-Crofts.

Johnson, A., & Redish, A. D. (2007). Neural ensembles in CA3 transiently encode paths forward of the animal at a decision point. *Journal of Neuroscience, 12,* 483–488.

Kahneman, D., Slovic, P., & Tversky, A. (Eds.). (1982). *Judgment under uncertainty: Heuristics and biases.* New York: Cambridge University Press.

Kehoe, E. J., Graham-Clark, P., & Schreurs, B. G. (1989). Temporal patterns of the rabbit's nictitating membrane response to compound and component stimuli under mixed CS-US intervals. *Behavioral Neuroscience, 103,* 283–295.

Kirby, K. N. (1997). Bidding on the future: Evidence against normative discounting of delayed rewards. *Journal of Experimental Psychology: General, 126,* 54–70.

Laibson, D. (1997). Golden eggs and hyperbolic discounting. *Quarterly Journal of Economics, 62,* 443–479.

Laibson, D. (2001). A cue-theory of consumption. *Quarterly Journal of Economics, 66,* 81–120.

La Mettrie, J. (1999). *Man a machine.* Chicago: Open Court. (Original work published 1748)

Lazarus, A. (1972). Phobias: broad-spectrum behavioral views. *Seminars in Psychiatry*, *4*, 85–90.

Loewenstein, G. (1996). Out of control: Visceral influences on behavior. *Organizational Behavior and Human Decision Processes*, *35*, 272–292.

Loewenstein, G. (1999). A visceral account of addiction. In J. Elster & O.-J. Skog (Eds.), *Getting hooked: Rationality and addiction* (pp. 235–264). Cambridge, England: Cambridge University Press.

Mackintosh, N. J. (1983). *Conditioning and associative learning.* New York: Clarendon Press.

Malloy, P. F., & Levis, D. J. (1990). A human laboratory test of Eysenck's theory of incubation: A search for the resolution of the neurotic paradox. *Journal of Psychopathology and Behavioral Assessment*, *12*, 309–327.

Mazur, J. E. (1987). An adjusting procedure for studying delayed reinforcement. In M. L. Commons, J. E. Mazur, J. A. Nevin, & H. Rachlin (Eds.), *Quantitative analyses of behavior V: The effect of delay and of intervening events on reinforcement value* (pp. 55–73). Hillsdale, NJ: Erlbaum.

McClure, S. M., Laibson, D. I., Loewenstein, G., & Cohen, J. D. (2004, October 15). The grasshopper and the ant: Separate neural systems value immediate and delayed monetary rewards. *Science*, *306*, 503–507.

Melzack, R., & Casey, K. L. (1970). The affective dimension of pain. In M. B. Arnold (Ed.), *Feelings and emotions* (pp. 55–68). New York: Academic Press.

Meyer, R. E. (1988). Conditioning phenomena and the problem of relapse in opioid addicts and alcoholics. In B. Ray (Ed.), *Learning factors in substance abuse* (NIDA Research Monograph Series 84, pp. 161–179). Rockville, MD: National Institute on Drug Abuse.

Miller, N. (1969, January 31). Learning of visceral and glandular responses. *Science*, *163*, 434–445.

O'Brien, C. (1997, October 3). A range of research-based pharmacotherapies for addiction. *Science*, *278*, 66–70.

Offer, A. (2006). *The challenge of affluence: Self-control and well-being in the United States and Britain since 1950.* Oxford, England: Oxford University Press.

Parker, J. D. A., Bagby, R. M., & Webster, C. D. (1993). Domains of the impulsivity construct: A factor analytic investigation. *Personality and Individual Differences*, *15*, 267–274.

Pavlov, I. P. (1927). *Conditioned reflexes: An investigation of the physiological activity of the cerebral cortex* (G. V. Anrep, Trans.). Oxford, England: Oxford University Press.

Pear, J. J., & Eldridge, G. D. (1984). The operant–respondent distinction: Future directions. *Journal of the Experimental Analysis of Behavior*, *42*, 453–467.

Phelps, E. S., & Pollack, R. A. (1968). On second-best national saving and game-equilibrium growth. *Review of Economic Studies*, *35*, 185–199.

Redish, A. D., Jensen, S., & Johnson, A. (2008). A unified framework for addiction: Vulnerabilities in the decision process. *Behavioral and Brain Sciences*, *31*, 415–437.

Rescorla, R. A. (1988). Pavlovian conditioning: It's not what you think it is. *American Psychologist, 43,* 151–160.

Robins, L. N., & Regier, D. A. (1990). *Psychiatric disorders in America: The Epidemiologic Catchment Area Study.* New York: Free Press.

Rolls, E. T. (2005). *Emotion explained.* Oxford, England: Oxford University Press.

Ross, D., Sharp, C., Vuchinich, R., & Spurrett, D. (2008). *Midbrain mutiny: The picoeconomics and neuroeconomics of disordered gambling.* Cambridge, MA: MIT Press.

Savastano, H. I., Hua, U., Barnet, R. C., & Miller, R. R. (1998). Temporal coding in Pavlovian conditioning: Hall-Pearce negative transfer. *Quarterly Journal of Experimental Psychology: Journal of Comparative and Physiological Psychology, 51(B),* 139–153.

Schachter, S., Silverstein, B., & Perlick, D. (1977). Psychological and pharmacological explanations of smoking under stress. *Journal of Experimental Psychology: General, 106,* 31–40.

Skinner, B. F. (1948). Superstition in the pigeon. *Journal of Experimental Psychology, 38,* 168–172.

Tiffany, S. T. (1995). Potential functions of classical conditioning in drug addiction. In D. C. Drummond, S. T. Tiffany, S. Glautier, & B. Remington (Eds.), *Addictive behavior: Cue exposure theory and practice* (pp. 47–74). Chichester, England: Wiley.

Tolman, E. C. (1939). Prediction of vicarious trial and error by means of the schematic sowbug. *Psychological Review, 46,* 318–336.

Upton, M. (1929). The auditory sensitivity of guinea pigs. *American Journal of Psychology, 41,* 412–421.

Wegner, D. M. (1989). *White bears and other unwanted thoughts: Suppression, obsession, and the psychology of mental control.* New York: Penguin.

Wegner, D. M. (2002). *The illusion of conscious will.* Cambridge, MA: MIT Press.

Wolpe, J. (1981). The dichotomy between classical conditioned and cognitively learned anxiety. *Journal of Behavior Therapy and Experimental Psychiatry, 12,* 35–42.

Zener, K. (1937). The significance of behavior accompanying conditioned salivary secretion for theories of the conditioned response. *American Journal of Psychology, 50,* 384–403.

15

THE EXTENDED SELF

HOWARD RACHLIN AND BRYAN A. JONES

Gestalt psychologists have said that the whole is greater than the sum of its parts (Koffka, 1955). A behavioral–economic extension of that Gestalt dictum would be that the value of an activity may be greater than the sum of the values of its parts.

Suppose you are driving from New York to Chicago. Your car has a CD player, and you take along some CDs to play on the trip. You like both classical and popular music, so you take along several symphony CDs and several pop CDs. Suppose that your tastes are such that the following two inequalities apply:

1. You prefer listening to a 60-minute symphony to spending that 60 minutes listening to twenty 3-minute pop songs.
2. You prefer listening to a pop song for 3 minutes to spending that 3 minutes listening to a 3-minute section of a symphony.

Clearly, you have a self-control problem here. The problem is that to listen to the whole symphony (which you prefer to do), you must listen to the first

This article was prepared with the assistance of a grant from the National Institute of Mental Health.

3 minutes of it (which you prefer not to do). If you just do what you prefer at the moment (assuming your preferences remain constant throughout the trip), you would drive the whole way from New York to Chicago playing only popular songs, whereas (by assumption) you would have been happier if you had played only symphonies.

Similarly, a person with alcoholism prefers to be sober, healthy, and socially accepted and to perform well at his or her job than to be drunk all the time, unhealthy, and socially rejected and to perform poorly at his or her job. But at the same time, over the next few minutes, he or she prefers to have a drink than to not have one. If, over successive brief intervals, the person with alcoholism always does what he or she prefers, he or she will always be drinking.

The problem, for both the driver and the alcoholic, is how to make choices so as to maximize value over the longer time span and avoid making choices on a case-by-case basis. But this is self-control, and it is difficult to do; the value of the longer activity (listening to the symphony in the case of the driver; refusing drinks in the case of the person with alcoholism) is greater than the sum of the values of each of the components of that activity.

Of course, it would be better still if the driver could listen to a mixture of symphonies and pop music rather than just symphonies and if the person with alcoholism could be a social drinker rather than a teetotaler. These are both straightforward extensions of the argument. For example, if the driver listens to a mixture of symphonies and pop songs over the whole trip, the sum of the values of the symphonies plus the values of the pop songs over the whole trip would be less than the value of the mixture as a whole. Here, the time scale is expanded from an hour to a whole day of listening—and the self-control problem is even more difficult.

To return to the original self-control problem, each 3 minutes of symphony listening, each drink refusal, has virtually no value in itself. Moreover, to use familiar behavioristic language, these pieces of valuable behavioral patterns are never reinforced. They are not immediately reinforced, they are not conditionally reinforced, and they are not reinforced after a delay. It must be clear that a drink refusal is not immediately reinforced. It should also be clear that no single drink refusal is reinforced after a delay. If a person with alcoholism refuses a single drink, he or she does not wake up 3 weeks later suddenly a healthier and happier person. To realize the value of a drink refusal, you must put together a long string of them, just as to realize the value of a symphony, you must listen to the whole thing.

It is sometimes said that reinforcement can be internalized—that we can internally pat ourselves on the back, so to speak. But the concept of internal reinforcement is not a behavioral concept; we should be suspicious of it in the first place. Second, there is absolutely no evidence that internal reinforcement works. It is hard to imagine how you might obtain such evidence. The concept of internal reinforcement is no better than concepts such as willpower or ego strength as explanations of self-control. In fact, it is worse than those concepts. Why? Because it uses behavioral language to describe nonbehavioral events, thereby debasing behavioral language. Also, once you start using such terms as *internal reinforcement*, you lose the main advantages of behaviorism: the observability of its variables and methods, its emphasis on behavior of the organism as a whole. As Skinner (1938) concluded, "In spite of the conceptual nature of many of our terms we are still dealing with an existent subject matter, which is the behavior of the organism as a whole" (p. 441).

The fact that longer behavioral patterns may have a value greater than the sum of the values of their parts is not unique to these very broad patterns. Each broad pattern is nested in still broader patterns and contains narrower patterns within it. Listening to a symphony over an hour is nested within the pattern of listening to a mixture of symphonies and pop songs for a day. At the other extreme, listening to a single verse is nested within listening to a whole pop song. Even a seemingly unitary reinforcer such as a 3-second food delivery to a pigeon may be seen as a behavioral pattern.

Let us zoom in on a pigeon eating food in the laboratory. After the feeder comes up, the pigeon has to rebalance itself, orient its body and its head to the feeder, move its head into the feeder, open its beak, close its beak around the food, and swallow the food. Then it has to use the energy from the food to get more food, to groom itself, to hunt around its cage, and so forth. Where, in all this, does reinforcement actually occur? Is there really a brief period, as some neuroscientists tell us, when a "reward center" in the pigeon's brain is activated, before which the pigeon's peck was unreinforced and after which it was reinforced? There is no evidence for such a sudden transformation. A much more coherent description of the learning process is in terms of patterns of behavior evolving over the lifetimes of organisms.

In his early works, Skinner (e.g., 1938) argued that reinforcement effected sudden transformations in what he called *response strength*. On the basis of a model of behavior change based on individual reflexes, a single reinforcer was said to increase the "strength" of an operant such as a rat's lever press. The fundamental change was said to be in the operant's (internal) strength rather than in its (external) rate—a pattern of responses occurring over time. Later, Skinner abandoned this molecular conception for a Darwinian model in which the environment selects responses over the lifetimes of organisms just as it selects organisms over the lifetimes of species (Moxley, 2006).[1] However, to the end, Skinner's conception was that the object of change was the individual response rather than patterns of responses extended over time. We contend that even apparently simple, discrete molecular events such as a pigeon's

---

[1]See Baum (2005) for a detailed exposition of this Darwinian view of the action of reinforcement. See Staddon and Simmelhag (1971) for a cogent criticism of Skinner's early concept of superstition, based on simple contiguity of individual responses and reinforcers.

key pecks and a rat's lever presses are really complex patterns of choices. Still more, the value of complex patterns involved in self-control cannot be understood as the simple sum (or integration) of the values of individual responses.

A single 3-second reinforcer, in this close examination, is a complex sequence of subevents; the sum of the values of those events is less than the value of the sequence as a whole. So, even an apparently unitary high-valued reinforcer, such as a pigeon's eating of grain, has the same form as a problem in self-control. And eating would be a problem in self-control for pigeons were it not for inherited patterns. The pigeon is built to ignore individual microscopic values and behave as if the pattern of acts involved in eating were a single act. Humans too are built to ignore the values of the components of eating and choose according to the value of the pattern—or to quickly develop the ability to do so. As Teitelbaum (1977) pointed out, an adult mammal's eating pattern evolves (by a process of selection by reinforcement) from the innate sequence of turning to the breast and sucking; with brain damage, or under stress, the more complex eating pattern may regress to the simpler rooting behavior, just as the learned food-obtaining behavior of pigs may regress to innate rooting under the stress of extended ratios (Breland & Breland, 1961).

Unfortunately, people are not built to ignore the values of discrete acts and to choose according to values of more complex and temporally extended patterns. People have to learn to choose among long-term patterns and not make choices on a case-by-case basis. Fortunately, as we discuss later, these types of choices may be shaped by a process akin to group selection in biological evolution (Rachlin, 1995a, 1995b).

Corresponding relationships govern social behavior. In public goods situations such as contributing to public television, voting, contributing to charities, and not littering, very little or nothing is gained by contributing. Each member of the group benefits most as an individual by not contributing (receiving the benefits of contributions by others plus keeping their own potential contribution). Economic theory, based on maximization by each participant of his or her own utility, predicts that no one will contribute (the "free rider" problem). Yet many people do contribute. This, we argue, is because the unit of maximization is not always the individual self bounded by the skin but a group of individuals extended in social space—the extended self.

Figure 15.1 shows an example of contingencies in a two-person prisoner's dilemma game. If both players cooperate, each player earns a high reward (five units in the example of Figure 15.1), whereas if both players defect, each earns a low reward (two units). If one player cooperates and the other defects, the cooperator earns a very low reward (one unit) and the defector earns a very high reward (six units). On any given trial, each player would earn one more unit by defecting than by cooperating regardless of the other player's choice. (If the other player cooperates, defection earns six units rather than five; if the

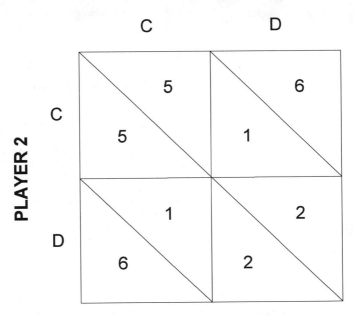

Figure 15.1. Contingencies in a prisoner's dilemma game. Two players (1 and 2) may each choose to cooperate (C) or defect (D). If both players cooperate, each earns a moderately high reward (five units in this example); if both defect, each earns a moderately low reward (two units). However, if one defects and one cooperates, the defector earns the highest reward (six units), whereas the cooperator earns the lowest reward (one unit). Regardless of the other player's choice, each player would earn more on a given trial by defecting than by cooperating. However, if both players defect, both earn less than they would have had they both cooperated.

other player defects, defection earns two units rather than one.) If this game is played repeatedly by two unrelated players, both usually end up defecting, earning two units each per game, whereas if both had cooperated, they would each have earned five units per game. What might engender cooperation? If instead of asking, "How can I maximize my own return?" the boundaries between the players are blurred and both ask, "How can I maximize our return?" both players would have earned more (five rather than two units).

To summarize, the concept that the value of a behavioral pattern may be greater than the sum of the values of its parts is not just an empty slogan borrowed from Gestalt psychology. It is the very basis of a consistent behavioral approach to problems of self-control and social cooperation.

Figure 15.2 illustrates the analogy between social cooperation and self-control. In the case of social cooperation, the dots in the diagram designate individuals distributed in social space. The large dot stands for the participant (P_0). The small dots ($P_{-N} \ldots P_N$) stand for other people; the closer a small dot

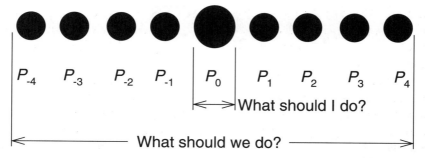

Figure 15.2. The point labeled P_0 stands for a person at a particular time and place. The points labeled P_{-4} to P_4 stand for the person extended in either time or social space. Some social choices, such as the prisoner's dilemma of Figure 15.1, place the interest of the individual (P_0) in conflict with the interests of the group (P_{-4} to P_4). Similarly, some temporal choices place the immediate interest of the person (P_0) in conflict with the person's long-term interests (P_{-4} to P_4). In either case, the answer to the question "What should I do?" is in conflict with that of the question "What should we do?" Self-control and social cooperation are both fostered by focusing on the latter question.

is to the large dot, the closer the social bond between that person and P_0. In the case of self-control, the dots in the diagram designate a single individual at different times. The large dot stands for P_0 now. The small dots stand for a single person at different times in the past and future; the closer a small dot is to the large dot, the nearer it is to the present time.

ALTRUISM AND SOCIAL COOPERATION

First, let us define some terms. *Altruism* and *social cooperation* both refer to acts of one person by which another person benefits. Socially cooperative acts benefit the actor him- or herself as well as the receiver of the benefit. Cooperation in building a house, sailing a boat, or economic trade are examples of social cooperation. Altruistic acts (in and of themselves) benefit only the receiver. Donating anonymously to charity would be classified as altruistic, even though it may make the giver feel good.

A *social dilemma* poses a choice between acting so as to maximize one's own reward and acting so as to maximize the reward to a group of people. Giving to charity, donating to public television or radio, recycling, and so forth are obvious examples, but virtually any social act requires a balancing between benefits to oneself alone and to the social group. Altruistic or socially cooperative people make choices so as to maximize reward over a wider range than do nonaltruistic or non–socially cooperative people. An important determinant of such balancing is the social distance between P_0 and the other person or group of people. The closer you feel to another person or group of people, the more likely you should be to cooperate with that person or group. Here we define a person's *extended self* not in terms of the space circumscribed by the person's skin but rather in terms of the social space over which that person maximizes reward.[2]

Different people may have wider or narrower extended selves. The sociopath may have an extended self circumscribed closely by his own skin, whereas the saint may have a self extended to all of nature. Jones and Rachlin (2006) and Rachlin and Jones (2008) attempted to measure such differences by means of social discount functions using a method akin to the usual procedure for obtaining delay-discount functions (Raineri & Rachlin, 1993). Rachlin and Jones (2008) gave participants a booklet with these paper-and-pencil instructions:

> The following experiment asks you to imagine that you have made a list of the 100 people closest to you in the world ranging from your dearest friend or relative at position #1 to a mere acquaintance at #100. The person at #1 would be someone you know well and is your closest friend or relative. The person at #100 might be someone you recognize and encounter but perhaps you may not even know their name.
>
> You do not have to physically create the list—just imagine that you have done so. (p. 33)

The next seven pages each summarized these instructions and then presented a list of questions as follows, with a different *N* value on each page:

> Now imagine the following choices between an amount of money for you and an amount for the #[N] person on the list. Circle A or B to indicate which you would choose in EACH line.
>
> A. $85 for you alone. B. $75 for the #[N] person on the list.
> A. $75 for you alone. B. $75 for the #[N] person on the list.
> A. $65 for you alone. B. $75 for the #[N] person on the list.
> . . . [continued down to] . . .
> A. $0 for you alone. B. $75 for the #[N] person on the list. (p. 33)

Column A listed nine amounts decrementing by $10 on each line between $85 and $5. For half of the participants, the money amounts decreased from $85 to $0 as earlier; for the other half, the order was reversed. Column B differed on each page by social distance (**N**). The social distances were 1, 2, 5, 10, 20, 50, and 100 in random order. On each line, participants were asked to choose between an amount of money for themselves and $75 for P_N.

---

[2]Skinner (1945) said that the skin was not necessarily the spatial boundary between a person and the world. However, Skinner also speculated that for some behavior, the crucial boundary might be within the skin rather than outside it (Skinner, 1945; Zuriff, 1985). This, we believe, was a mistake. By this conceptual move, Skinner abandoned the crucial advantage of behaviorism over other psychologies— the in-principle observability of its variables.

Figure 15.3 shows the group results. As with delay discounting, the medians (of 198 participants) were well described by a hyperbolic discount function ($R^2 = .997$):

$$V = \frac{A}{1 + kN} \qquad (1)$$

where A is the undiscounted value of the reward (amount); V is the value to P0 of the reward, A, given to PN; N is the social distance between P0 and PN, and k is a constant. The median k for the data of Figure 15.1 is 0.055. Equation 1 was fit to the data of individual participants (Stony Brook University undergraduates), and a k value was obtained for each of them. The bigger k, for a given person, the steeper that person's discount function and the less that person values rewards to other people. All participants had positive k values; all indicated that they would be more generous to people socially close to them than to people far away.

Jones (2007) obtained individual social discount functions by the method just described, obtained a k value for each participant, and also tested each (of 97) participants in a public goods game. For this game, participants (in a classroom) read the following instructions:

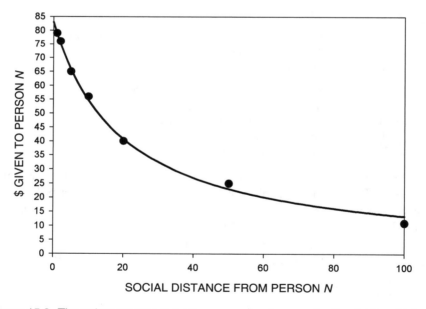

Figure 15.3. The points represent median amounts of money for themselves that participants indicated to be equivalent to $75 given to another person at various social distances from the participant. Amounts above each point were preferred to $75 for the other person; amounts below each point were dispreferred to $75 for the other person. The line is the best-fitting hyperbolic function (Equation 1).

Imagine the following situation (purely hypothetical we regret to say):

1. The experimenter gives you $100.
2. A box is passed around to each person in this room.
3. Each person may put all or any part or none of the $100 into the box. *No one else will know how much money anyone puts into the box.*
4. After the box goes around the room, the experimenter *doubles* whatever is in the box and distributes it equally to each person in the room regardless of how much money they put into the box.

Each person will then go home with whatever they kept plus what they received from the box.

Note that you will maximize the money you receive by not putting *any* money in the box. Then you will take home the original $100 you kept plus what the experimenter distributes after doubling whatever money was in the box.

HOWEVER: If everybody kept all $100, nothing would be in the box and each person would take home $100.

Whereas, if everybody put all $100 in the box, each person would take home $200 after the money in the box was doubled and distributed. (p. 33)

Donation amount in this "one-shot" public goods game is a measure of altruism. As the instructions emphasize, an individual participant gains nothing at all by contributing on the present occasion. Even if everyone else makes the full altruistic choice, any one person loses by contributing. Similarly, individuals gain virtually nothing by their individual $50 contribution to public television (the same programs would be programmed with or without any particular $50 contribution), but people do give money to public television. Jones found a significant negative correlation between the amount of money participants said they would put into the box and their k value, $r(90) = -.24$, $p = .02$. The more money a person donates to the public good, the shallower that person's discount function tends to be.

According to the economist Julian Simon (1995),

The conceptual framework employed here obviates the age-old question about whether an act of giving by one individual to another should properly be labeled "altruism," or whether instead one is "really" being "selfish" by making oneself feel good. An individual's discount weights vis-à-vis other individuals may be considered a full description of the individual in this connection, assuming that the individual's behavior corresponds to his or her discounts in relation to other individuals. . . . *Revealed preferences constitute the entire system* [italics added]. (pp. 375–376)

The concept of *revealed preferences* refers to an ability to derive utility functions (the discount function of Figure 15.3 is a form of utility function) from observations of behavior such as those we used to obtain the discount function (the function "reveals" the preferences), and then to use that function to predict behavior in some other situation (such as the public goods game described earlier). By implication, studies of the predictive power of delay-discount functions for various kinds of addiction, as reported in several chapters of this volume, constitute ontological definitions of self-control and addiction. Correspondingly, the finding reported earlier that behavior in a public goods game may be predicted by steepness of a social discount function is itself a defining property of altruism. The more such correspondences are found, the richer the behavioral and economic conception of altruism becomes. The other studies of social discounting reported here are further attempts to expand on that definition.

Moreover, the correspondences and parallels between social and delay discounting should serve to demystify altruism. Whereas it may seem self-evident that people will sacrifice some part of their present good for the benefit of their future selves and that delay-discount functions measure this tendency, it seems mysterious when people sacrifice some part of their own good for the benefit of another person. Yet, as Simon (1995) implied, the two forms of sacrifice are equally explicable in economic terms. A person has common interests with other people close to him or her just as he or she has common interests with him- or herself at other times. As Ainslie (2001) has explained, trade-offs, described in terms of hyperbolic delay discounting, may occur between P_0 and $P_1, P_2, \ldots P_N$ in temporal terms. Similarly, such trade-offs may be described in terms of social space. Both types of trade-off imply that our essential selves are not fixed by our skins but are extended beyond it both in time and in social space.

A RATIO SCALE FOR SOCIAL DISTANCE

Note that the scale used to determine social distance is an ordinal scale. In an ordinal scale, only order between whole numbers (the order of the 100 people closest to the participant) is known; distance between those numbers may vary. Ordinal numbers cannot be meaningfully added or subtracted (the 10th person on a list is not meaningfully the sum of the 3rd and the 7th) or multiplied or divided. In delay discounting, however, delay is measured by time—a ratio scale that starts at zero and is infinitely divisible (moreover, 3 minutes + 7 minutes = 10 minutes). Therefore, it may be argued, the hyperbolic function obtained in social discounting is only coincidentally comparable to that obtained in delay discounting. Jones (2007) performed an experiment to transform the ordinal scale of social distance to a ratio scale (physical distance) corresponding to the ratio scale (physical time) by which delay discounting is measured.

The method was magnitude estimation, first used by Stevens (1956) to determine the influence of physical magnitudes (such as sound intensity) on subjective judgments of those magnitudes (such as loudness). In Jones's (2007) experiment, the N value was the independent variable; equivalent physical distance was the dependent variable. Each participant was asked to imagine all 100 Ns standing with him or her on a large field with physical distance from the participant proportional to social distance. A questionnaire specified a set of N values. For each N, the participant responded with that person's distance from him or her on the field in terms of inches, feet, miles, football fields, and so forth, as the participant found convenient. That is, the modulus, or standard, was not fixed.

After reading instructions (as in prior social discounting experiments) to imagine a list of 100 of their closest friends or relatives, each of the 44 participants read the following:

> Now try to imagine yourself standing on a vast field with those 100 people. The actual closeness between you and each other person is proportional to how close you feel to that person. For example, if a given person were 10 feet away from you then another person to whom you felt twice as close would be 5 feet away from you and one to whom you felt half as close would be 20 feet away. We are going to ask you for distances corresponding to some selected individuals of the 100 on your hypothetical list.
>
> Remember that there are no limits to distance—either close or far; even a billionth of an inch is infinitely divisible and even a million miles can be infinitely exceeded. Therefore, do not say that a person is zero distance away (no matter how close) but instead put that person at a very small fraction of the distance of one who is further away; and do not say that a person is infinitely far away (no matter how far) but instead put that person at a very great distance compared to one who is closer.
>
> Of course there are no right or wrong answers. We just want you to express your closeness to and distance from these other people in terms of actual distance; the closer you feel to a person, the closer you should put them on the field; the further you feel from a person, the further they should be from you on the field. Just judge your own feelings of closeness and distance. (Jones, 2007, p. 30)

Each of the following seven pages differed in N value, randomly ordered, and stated the following question:

> How far away from you on the field is the [Nth] person on your list?
> Feel free to use any units you wish (inches, feet, miles, football fields, etc. Just indicate what the unit is).
> Please write a number and units of measurement for the [Nth] person on your list:
> (Jones, 2007, p. 30)

Participants found no difficulty in responding consistently to the rather odd instructions of this experiment. The judgments were converted to feet from whatever units the participants used and then averaged. Medians across participants are plotted in Figure 15.4 on a log-log scale. The best-fitting straight line ($r^2 = .988$) is

$$\log d = 2.2\ (\log N) - .72$$

$$d = .19N^{2.2}$$

$$N = 2.1d^{.45},$$

where d = distance in feet. As in psychophysical magnitude estimation experiments, a power function describes the median data well.

To obtain a discount function in terms of physical distance, we substitute physical distance (d) as given in the preceding equation for ordinal distance (N) in Equation 1:

$$V = \frac{A}{1 + k'(d)^{.45}}, \tag{2}$$

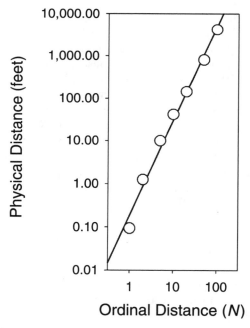

Figure 15.4. The physical distance (in feet) equivalent to the ordinal social distance. The straight line on this log-log scale is a power function. The positive, above-unity slope of the line equals the exponent of the power function.

where k' is a constant that, like the constant k of Equation 1, measures degree of social discounting.

Equation 2 provides a ratio measure of social distance that may be used in applications in which an ordinal scale is insufficient (i.e., where additive or multiplicative operations are required). It may seem strange that the discount function relating an ordinal scale of social distance (N) to value is simpler than the one relating a ratio scale of social distance (d) to value. But ordinal Ns may capture 1:1 social relationships with discrete people better than does a continuous, infinitely divisible ratio scale. We use the latter in the next several experiments discussed.

ULTIMATUM AND DICTATOR GAMES

In a two-player ultimatum game, a giver offers a portion of an initial endowment (usually money) to a receiver. For example, with a \$100 endowment, the giver may elect to keep \$60 and give \$40 to the receiver. The receiver may accept or reject the offer. If the receiver accepts the offer, each player receives the share assigned by the giver. In the earlier example, the giver gets \$60 and the receiver gets \$40. If the receiver rejects the offer, however, neither player receives anything. Dictator games differ from ultimatum games only in that the receiver cannot reject the giver's offer. Givers in ultimatum games typically offer about 40% of their initial endowment, and such offers are typically accepted. Offers below 40% are often rejected. Givers in dictator games, where rejection is not an option, typically offer considerably less than 40% (Camerer, 2003). These results have aroused interest because economic theory predicts that givers in both games will offer minimal amounts and receivers in ultimatum games will accept whatever amounts are offered—because otherwise they get nothing.

The refusal of an offer by the receiver in an ultimatum game effectively punishes the giver. However, in a one-shot game the beneficiary of the giver's presumed changed behavior would not be the receiver; it would be the other people who deal with the giver in similar games in the future. Thus, refusal by a receiver is generally considered altruistic (Camerer, 2003). We then need to ask what the receiver actually gains from his or her altruistic behavior when he or she refuses a greater-than-zero offer. The answer is that the receiver gains nothing from this particular act. It is not rewarded immediately or with a delay or internally (e.g., by an internal pat on the back). Rather, behavior of this kind is part of a generally valuable pattern of behavior. This particular sacrifice by the receiver may not be rewarded, but such behavior would in general be rewarded by the benefit to the receiver's extended self.

If we tried to calculate the net reward for each of our individual actions at each choice point encountered in life, we would suffer because we know, from hyperbolic discounting, that our prior preferences (our commitments) are often more consistent with our long-term goals than are our present choices (the ones made at the choice point). The latter are subject to spikes of temporary temptation. We may change our minds for the worse between a decision made in the past and one made at the present moment. For this reason, it is often better, contrary to economic theory, to take sunk costs (decisions made in the past) into account when choosing among future options. People often do so (Rachlin, 2000), and pigeons do so as well (De la Piedad, Field, & Rachlin, 2006). Instead of evaluating each alternative as it is offered, we obey a rule (which may be unconscious) that benefits our social group. The narrower the group, in terms of Figure 15.2, the greater the common interest among the members, the more altruism we should find.

We expect social distance to be the primary determinant of amount offered in both ultimatum and dictator games. The closer the receiver is to the giver, the more should be given. In most previous studies of these games, the giver and receiver have been strangers or anonymous classmates, so this issue could not be addressed. The pair of experiments we describe in the following paragraphs (Jones, 2007) varied social distance between giver and receiver. Moreover, because publication in the economic journals, where these experiments often appear, requires "real" rewards, amounts of money in the initial endowment have typically been small. These experiments, using hypothetical rewards, varied the endowment over a wide range and the social distance.

The first experiment, with 378 undergraduate participants, measured amount given in ultimatum and dictator games as a function of social distance between giver and receiver. All participants were givers. Three hypothetical endowment magnitudes ($10, $1,000, and $100,000) were tested in separate groups. Instructions for half the participants in each group included the statement that the receiver could reject the split, in which case neither player would get any of the endowment. The rest of the participants were given the same instructions but without the rejection clause. Without the rejection clause, the game becomes a dictator game rather than an ultimatum game.

Participants were given a five-page booklet. On the first page, as in the standard social-discounting procedure (Jones & Rachlin, 2006), they were asked to imagine that they had made a list of the 100 people closest to them. On subsequent pages, they chose how much money to share with a series of receivers at four social distances #[N]: 1, 10, 50, and 100. Each page looked similar to the next with #[N] replaced with a different social distance on each page. The endowment amount (C), remained the same across all pages:

The Game Show

Imagine that you are a contestant on a Game Show. With you is person **#N** from your list of 100 people closest to you.
The Game Show Host gives you a $[C] prize.

You can keep the entire amount of the money, or give any amount of it to person **#N.**

How much of the $[C] will you give to person **#N** _____.
(Jones, 2007, p. 34)

The participants in the ultimatum game received an additional line of instructions that differentiated between the ultimatum and dictator games:

However, **#[N]** may refuse his or her share of the money. If he or she rejects the money, neither of you will get any money at all. (Jones, 2007, p. 34)

Figure 15.5 shows best-fitting hyperbolic discount functions (Equation 1) for the ultimatum and dictator conditions. Note that the steepness increases with endowment amount. For the ultimatum game, normalized area under the curve (a function-independent inverse measure of steepness) was .354, .174, and .129 for the $10, $1,000, and $100,000 endowments, respectively. Note, too, that for all three endowments, the givers gave less in dictator games than they did in ultimatum games. However, the difference (what might be called the *premium* offered for the power to reject) decreased sharply (relative to the endowment) as the endowment increased.

The results show a reverse magnitude effect similar to that found in previous social discounting studies: the greater the endowment, the steeper the discounting (Rachlin & Jones, 2008). Givers were more generous with larger amounts of money in absolute terms, but they were less generous with larger amounts of money as a percentage of the initial endowment. Social distance had a strong impact on amount given in both ultimatum and dictator games. As social distance increased, amount offered decreased. The relatively small difference between ultimatum and dictator discount functions for the $100,000 endowment (top panel of Figure 15.5) may reflect givers' confidence that high absolute gift amounts would be accepted even though they were small proportions of the initial endowment.

Another experiment examined the behavior of the receiver under comparable conditions (Rachlin & Jones, 2008). We asked 119 participants to make a series of choices to determine the minimum amount of money they would accept from a giver. Three endowments were tested: $100,000, $1,000, and $100. Figure 15.6 shows median minimum amounts as a function of social distance between the participant and the giver.

Nearly half ($n = 56$) of the participants accepted all offers at every social distance, including the offer of $0. When the social distance of the receiver was less than $N = 50$, the median receiver accepted all offers at all tested endowments (behaving rationally according to economic game theory). As shown in Figure 15.6, the median minimum accepted offer for each social distance was zero except at the furthest social distances in the $1,000 and $100 conditions. Thus, the social distance between the giver and the receiver had a direct

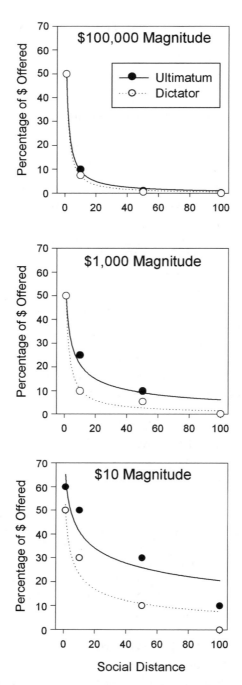

Figure 15.5. Median amount of money participants indicated that they would offer to other people at various social distances in ultimatum and dictator games as a percentage of a $100,000 initial endowment (top), a $1,000 initial endowment (middle), and a $10 initial endowment (bottom). The lines are best-fitting hyperbolic functions.

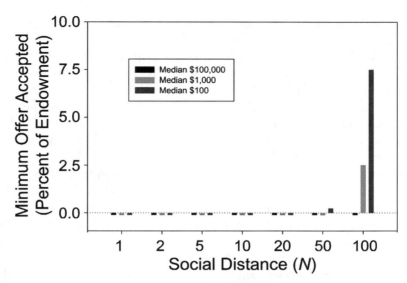

Figure 15.6. Minimum amount of money participants indicated they would accept from other people at various social distances as a percentage of initial endowments of $100,000, $1,000, and $100. The bars extend below the axis merely to indicate the data they represent. Their actual value is zero.

impact on the receiver's decision whether to accept an offer in an ultimatum game. For givers who were perceived to be close, the receiver was likely to accept all offers even when the offer was nothing. Only when social distance reached the maximum tested did the median minimum accepted offer begin to rise. (However, mean minimum accepted offers rose continuously as social distance increased, showing that the patterns of receiver behavior differed considerably from one participant to the other.) A receiver deciding whether to reject an offer from a person she or he knows essentially ignores the value of the offer and attends to the closeness of her or his relationship with the giver.

The results shown in Figure 15.6 combined with those of Figure 15.5 imply that expected rejection is only a minor factor in determining offers to receivers at close social distances. You would offer your mother or your best friend a very large portion of your endowment even though the probability of their rejecting even an offer of $0 is low. This indicates a blurring of the lines of the self at close social distances where common interest is a large fraction of all interests.

REINFORCING SELF-CONTROL AND SOCIAL COOPERATION

The question arises, how do we reinforce self-control or social cooperation? One way to effectively reinforce both self-control and social cooperation in the laboratory is to require choices to be made in patterns. In both repeated self-control and repeated social cooperation games, participants required to make a series of choices all at once tend to cooperate more and to show more self-control (Rachlin, 1995b). In everyday self-control situations, this relation is fundamental. Whether a person with alcoholism is sober or drunk, drinking is always better than not drinking. But the value of a year of no drinking (or moderate drinking) is greater than the value of a year of steady drinking.

Social cooperation situations have a similar structure. The good will and trust of other people are vague and abstract compared with the particular and immediate rewards of defection. A person may believe that it is always better to tell the truth (and would choose to tell the truth over the next 4 years rather than to lie over the next 4 years if such a choice could be made) but still be tempted to lie to get out of some particular ticklish situation. The problem is that in life, choices usually have to be made one at a time. How do we generate a valuable pattern of behavior when each component of that pattern is less valuable than its alternative?

The traditional neurocognitive answer to that question is that somewhere in our brains is a rational mechanism that evaluates the pattern, organizes it, and sends out commands to the motor system to emit the pattern's components— only to be opposed during periods of temptation by contrary commands rising from below (visceral impulses). From this viewpoint, each particular act— self-controlled or impulsive, cooperation or defection—is the product of a battle between our higher and lower nervous systems.

An alternative view, the behavioral view, is that valuable and complex patterns of behavior may evolve from simpler ones over a person's lifetime just as valuable and complex structures (like the eye) have evolved from simpler structures over generations. The environment (through reinforcement) selects individual acts in the same way in which the environment (through survival of the fittest) selects individual organisms. Patterns of behavior are selected in the same way as are groups of individual organisms.

Imagine a league of basketball teams in which points scored represents fitness. In this fictional league, new teams are continually being formed, with players varying in degree of general unselfishness. Unsuccessful teams lose their fans, periodically go bankrupt, and leave the league. Everything else being equal, teams whose players play nonselfishly tend to score more points than teams whose players play selfishly. Therefore, teams with a predominance of unselfish players will have more fitness (e.g., attract more fans and make more money) and survive, whereas teams with a predominance of selfish players will die out; more and more unselfish players will populate the league.

The problem with this scenario is that at the same time as group selection is progressing at the team level, another evolutionary process goes on at the individual level. Within a team, selfish players score more points than unselfish players. If the general manager of each team gets rid of the low-scoring players and acquires high-scoring players, the two evolutionary levels will compete. On the between-team level, unselfish players dominate; on the within-team level, selfish players dominate. Which level wins out depends on the relative speed of evolution at the two levels. If teams tend to be replaced in the league relatively quickly and players tend to be replaced on teams relatively slowly, then unselfishness will come to dominate the league; if players tend to be replaced on teams relatively quickly and teams tend to be replaced in the league relatively slowly, then in this fictional league, selfishness will come to dominate.

From a behavioral viewpoint, behavioral patterns within the lifetime of an individual person evolve by a Darwinian process just as do genetic and cultural patterns—by group selection. The crucial question for group selection is what is the relative speed of replacement. Which gets replaced faster, groups or individuals within groups? In the case of behavioral patterns within a person's lifetime, groups (i.e., larger, more complex patterns) are often replaced faster than their components (discrete acts). Thus, selection (by reinforcement) of patterns of acts in an individual's lifetime may overwhelm selection of components of those patterns.

Consider the habit of eating three meals a day and snacking a little between meals. Occasionally we vary it, but if we vary it too far, we gain or lose weight and lose social reinforcement, perhaps job performance, and even health. The unit of selection in this case is the wider (more molar) pattern. We vary the amount we eat by varying our pattern across days or weeks, whereas our rate of eating each meal remains fairly fixed. Similarly, a rat normally varies its rate of lever pressing (and eating and drinking) by adjusting the duration of bursts of behavior rather than the time between each lever press (or chew or lick). Reinforcement may thus shape the wider unit before it shapes the smaller unit. This is group selection, but the groups are groups of responses in the lifetime of an organism rather than groups of organisms in a society.

Individual acts that are part of valuable patterns may have little or no value relative to the pattern as a whole. The Gestalt dictum that the whole may be greater than the sum of its parts—or rather the value of the whole pattern (such as generally being sober, eating moderately, visiting sick friends, helping old ladies to cross the street, etc.)—may be greater than the sum of the values of its parts. Although the whole pattern may be reinforced or valuable in itself, the individual acts making up the patterns may be totally unreinforced and not valuable in themselves. When an observer sees just a piece of a pattern without its context, it may appear as if that piece is both of low value in itself and unreinforced externally. Thus, it would have to be caused by an unseen and mysterious internal mental event—willpower in the case of self-controlled acts, altruism in the case of social cooperation. So the person with alcoholism who refuses a drink must, it seems, be exerting willpower and the person who gives anonymously to charity must, it seems, be acting from a central altruistic mechanism. Similarly, the person who stops for a red light in the middle of the night on a deserted street with no other car in sight must, it seems, be obeying an inner rather than an outer law. But in all three cases, these acts occur as part of highly valuable and often reinforced patterns.

In general, it is not a good idea to make many sorts of decisions on a case-by-case basis. On a case-by-case basis, most of us would be having that second dessert, drinking that third martini at a party, throwing that candy wrapper into the gutter and that letter from public television into the wastebasket. There are often no rational justifications for doing the reverse (refusing the second dessert or the martini, holding the candy wrapper until you reach a wastebasket, sending a check to public television). Rational justifications appear only for the overall pattern that has evolved by a process akin to group selection and that we follow regardless of immediate contingencies to the contrary.

No part of this process need rely on a "deliberate, foresighted author." As wider and wider patterns are reinforced, the units selected evolve from simpler to more complex forms over our lifetimes, just as complex structures like the vertebrate eye evolve from simpler structures in the lifetime of a species. To explain self-control and social cooperation, we do not need to imagine a creator of behavior (a rational mechanism) lodged inside each person's head.

REFERENCES

Ainslie, G. (2001). *Breakdown of will.* Cambridge, England: Cambridge University Press.

Baum, W. M. (2005). *Understanding behaviorism: Behavior, culture, and evolution* (2nd ed.). Oxford, England: Blackwell.

Breland, K., & Breland, M. (1961). The misbehavior of organisms. *American Psychologist, 16,* 681–684.

Camerer, C. F. (2003). *Behavioral game theory: Experiments in strategic interaction.* Princeton, NJ: Princeton University Press.

De la Piedad, X., Field, D., & Rachlin, H. (2006). The influence of prior choices on current choice. *Journal of the Experimental Analysis of Behavior, 85,* 3–21.

Jones, B. (2007). *Social discounting: Social distance and altruistic choice.* Unpublished doctoral dissertation, Stony Brook University, Stony Brook, NY.

Jones, B., & Rachlin, H. (2006). Social discounting. *Psychological Science, 17,* 283–286.

Koffka, K. (1955). *Principles of gestalt psychology.* Oxford, England: Routledge & Kegan Paul.

Moxley, R. A. (2006). B. F. Skinner's other positivistic book: *Walden two. Behavior & Philosophy, 34,* 19–37.

Rachlin, H. (1995a). Self-control: Beyond commitment. *Behavioral and Brain Sciences, 18,* 109–159.

Rachlin, H. (1995b). The value of temporal patterns in behavior. *Current Directions, 4,* 188–191.

Rachlin, H. (2000). *The science of self-control*. Cambridge, MA: Harvard University Press.

Rachlin, H., & Jones, B. (2008). Social discounting and delay discounting. *Behavioral Decision Making, 21*, 29–43.

Raineri, A., & Rachlin, H. (1993). The effect of temporal constraints on the value of money and other commodities. *Behavioral Decision Making, 6*, 77–94.

Simon, J. (1995). Interpersonal allocation continuous with intertemporal allocation. *Rationality and Society, 7*, 367–392.

Skinner, B. F. (1938). *The behavior of organisms: An experimental analysis*. New York: Appleton-Century-Crofts.

Skinner, B. F. (1945). The operational analysis of psychological terms. *Psychological Review, 52*, 270–277.

Staddon, J. E. R., & Simmelhag, V. L. (1971). The superstition experiment: A reexamination of its implications for the study of adaptive behavior. *Psychological Review, 78*, 3–43.

Stevens, S. S. (1956). The direct estimation of sensory magnitudes: Loudness. *American Journal of Psychology, 69*, 1–25.

Teitelbaum, P. (1977). Levels of integration of the operant. In W. K. Honig & J. E. R. Staddon (Eds.), *Handbook of operant behavior* (pp. 7–27). Englewood Cliffs, NJ: Prentice-Hall.

Zuriff, G. E. (1985). *Behaviorism: A conceptual reconstruction*. New York: Columbia University Press.

INDEX

Neuroeconomics, *continued*
    and neural signatures of economic
        risk, 166–174
    of risk sensitivity, 160–166
Neurotransmitter effects, in vivo micro-
    dialysis, 111–114
Newman, J. L., 6, 259
Nicotine. *See also* Cigarettes
    delay discounting after abstinence
        from, 233–235
    delay discounting of, 193–194
    and discounting by rats, 53, 223,
        224, 228
    stable intake over time with, 248
Niv, Y., 141
Nomothetic theories, 80–81
Nonanticipatory appetites, 396
Nondrug incentives, in treatment of
    drug abuse, 255–256, 261
Nonexponential discounting functions,
    127–134
Nonhuman animals. *See also* Animal
    studies
    correlational analyses of research
        with, 82–85
    modeling delay discounting in,
        97–101
Nonhuman subjects, assessments of
    delay discounting for, 23–29
Nonlinear regression, of indifference
    points, 43
Nonreciprocal altruism, 313, 314
Norepinephrine (NE), 114, 341, 342
Norepinephrine system, 173
Normalization by estimates of average
    reward model, 134–135
Nosepoke response, 96
Nucleus accumbens (NAC), 101–103,
    168

Obesity, xii
Odum, A., 5, 44, 45, 52, 74, 193, 197,
    279, 306
OFC. *See* Orbitofrontal cortex
Ohmura, Y., 194, 199, 200
Olmstead, M. C., 231
Operant learning, ADHD and, 340
Operants, appetites as, 399, 401–403
Opioids
    delay discounting of, 196–197
    intake escalation over time with, 248

Opportunity costs, 367
    and delayed discount, 381
    in funding social programs, 310
Oppositional defiant disorder, 331
Orbitofrontal cortex (OFC), 53,
    105–107
    and ambiguity aversion, 174
    coding for gains and losses in, 168
    cooperation with BLA, 108
    in impulsivity, 140–141
    and in vivo microdialysis, 111–114
Organismic influences, 39. *See also* Trait
    variables
Ortner, C. N. M., 231
Ostaszewski, P., 74, 313
Overarousal, ADHD and, 336

Pan paniscus, 378, 380
Pan troglodytes, 378, 380
Paradox of nonreciprocal altruism, 313
Parasitoid wasps, 379
Parietal region, during delay-discounting
    tasks, 206
Past discounting, substance abuse-
    dependence and, 202–203
Patch exploitation, 363–366, 370
    rate-based models for, 377–378
    short-term vs. long-term rates of,
        373–374
Pathological gambling, 273–288
    comorbidity with substance use
        disorders, 275
    and context of choice, 45
    and delay discounting, 197–198,
        278–286
    diagnosis and prevalence of,
        274–275
    and Iowa gambling task, 277–278
    personality measures of impulsivity
        in, 276
    and probability discounting,
        285–286
Patterns of behavior, 427–430
Pavlov, I. P., 394
Pavlovian conditioning. *See* Classical
    conditioning
Payments, delayed, 69–70
PCP. *See* Phencyclidine
Pennicot, D. R., 102, 103
Perlow, S., 75
Perry, J. L., 6, 53, 84, 247, 252, 254

ABOUT THE EDITORS

Gregory J. Madden, PhD, is an associate professor in the Department of Applied Behavioral Science at the University of Kansas, Lawrence. He is the author or coauthor of a number of the seminal scientific papers in the field of delay discounting. His work in this area, and in the broader field of behavioral economics, has been supported by grants from the National Institute on Drug Abuse. Dr. Madden has served on the editorial boards of three prominent journals and is a past associate editor of the *Journal of the Experimental Analysis of Behavior*. His current research addresses biobehavioral links between delay discounting and gambling and techniques for teaching tolerance of delays.

Warren K. Bickel, PhD, is a professor of psychiatry; Wilbur D. Mills Chair of Alcoholism and Drug Abuse Prevention; director of the University of Arkansas for Medical Sciences (UAMS), Little Rock, Center for Addiction Research; and director of the interdisciplinary Tobacco Research Program at UAMS. He is the recipient of the Joseph Cochin Young Investigator Award from the College on Problems of Drug Dependence (CPDD), the Young Psychopharmacologist Award from the Division of Psychopharmacology and Substance Abuse of the American Psychological Association (APA), and a MERIT award from the National Institute on Drug Abuse. He has served as president of Division 28 (Psychopharmacology and Substance Abuse) of the APA and as president of CPDD. He was editor of the journal *Experimental and Clinical Psychopharmacology*, has coedited four books, and has published more than 230 papers. His research interests include the neurobehavioral mechanisms of addiction and therapeutic processes underlying recovery from addiction.